Tenth Edition

State and Local
Government

Ann O'M. Bowman
Texas A&M University

Richard C. Kearney
North Carolina State University

CENGAGE
Learning·

Australia • Brazil • Mexico • Singapore • United Kingdom • United States

CENGAGE
Learning®

State and Local Government,
Tenth Edition,
Ann O'M. Bowman, Richard C. Kearney

Product Director: Paul Banks

Product Team Manager: Carolyn Merrill

Content Developer:
Jessica Wang-Strykowski

Editorial Assistant: Michelle Forbes

Marketing Manager: Valerie Hartman

Manufacturing Planner: Fola Orekoya

IP Analyst: Alexandra Ricciardi

IP Project Manager: Farah Fard

Production Service:
Cenveo® Publisher Services

Cover Image: Danita Delimont/Getty
Images and Biddiboo/Getty Images

For product information and technology assistance, contact us at
Cengage Learning Customer & Sales Support, 1-800-354-9706

For permission to use material from this text or product,
submit all requests online at **www.cengage.com/permissions.**
Further permissions questions can be emailed to
permissionrequest@cengage.com.

Library of Congress Control Number: 2015947663

Student Edition:
ISBN: 978-1-305-38847-5

Cengage Learning
20 Channel Center Street
Boston, MA 02210
USA

Cengage Learning is a leading provider of customized learning solutions with employees residing in nearly 40 different countries and sales in more than 125 countries around the world. Find your local representative at **www.cengage.com.**

Cengage Learning products are represented in Canada by Nelson Education, Ltd.

To learn more about Cengage Learning Solutions, visit **www.cengage.com.**

Purchase any of our products at your local college store or at our preferred online store **www.cengagebrain.com.**

Printed in the United States of America
Print Number: 03   Print Year: 2017

Brief Contents

Contents

AP Images/Thom Bridge,
Independent Record

John Moore/Getty Images

Sacramento Bee/
ZUMAPRESS/Newscom

David R. Frazier Photolibrary, Inc./Alamy

AP Photo/Houston Chronicle/Eric Kayne

Matthew Cavanaugh/Getty Images

Bloomberg/Getty Images

*New York Daily News Archive/
Getty Images*

AP Images/Mel Evans

Mark & Audrey Gibson/Stock
Connection Blue/Alamy

Brandon Seidel/Shutterstock.com

AP Images/Doug McSchooler

*TennesseePhotographer/
iStockphoto.com*

AP Images/Jeffrey Collins

Glyn Jones/Corbis/Jupiter Images

ktsimage/iStockphoto.com

Tony Freeman/PhotoEdit

Jimmy Anderson/Getty Images

Preface

If someone had told us in 1990 that the first edition of *State and Local Government* would become what is now widely recognized as "the market leader" and followed eventually by a tenth edition, we would have been doubtful. That first edition broke the mold of traditional state and local government texts by offering a positive, thematic approach to introducing government at the grass roots. We were gratified and delighted when the book quickly built up adoptions in research universities, four-year colleges, and community colleges across the United States. There are quite a few rival texts today, but we like to think that the competition makes ours better. We heartily thank our colleagues in the State Politics and Policy section and the Urban Politics section of the American Political Science Association for their ideas and comments on various editions of this book. And we thank as well researchers, too numerous to mention individually, for their insightful analyses that are published in scholarly journals and inform our latest edition.

The tenth edition of this book was written as important public policy changes were underway in state legislatures throughout the country. The Great Recession was in the rear view mirror, but it had left behind residues of budget problems and policy issues that continue to call for attention. Painful as the Great Recession was, it did present opportunities to use the crisis to make improvements in the way the business of government is done.

Despite the drumbeat of criticism of government and public officials in the mass media and by anti-government talk-show hosts, we like politics and public service, particularly at the state and local levels. We believe that government can be—and often is—a force for good in society. We do acknowledge some of the concerns voiced by critics of government. Yes, there continue to be inefficiencies; and sure, there are some politicians who, once elected, seem to forget the interests of the people back home, not to mention what their parents taught them. But by and large, state and local governments work well. On a daily basis, they tackle some of the toughest issues imaginable, designing and implementing creative and successful solutions to problems ranging from crime and corrections to education and the environment. And they do so with a remarkable diversity of approaches.

In the tenth edition of our text, we again seek to capture the immediacy and vitality of state and local governments as they address the challenges facing the American people. A major goal is to foster continuing student interest and involvement in state and local politics, policy, and public service. Many of the students who read this text will work in state and local government. Some will run successfully for public office. All will deal with state and local governments throughout their lives. We want our readers to know that state and local governments are places where one person can still "do good," make a difference, and serve a cause. For students who go on to graduate study in political science, public administration, public policy, or related fields, states and localities are fertile fields for research. And for students taking this course because they "have to" and who purport to dislike politics and government, we invite them to keep an open mind as they explore the fascinating world of politics at the grass roots.

THE THEME OF *STATE AND LOCAL GOVERNMENT*

This book revolves around a central theme: the growing capacity and responsiveness of state and local government. Our theme was tested during the Great Recession, but not found to be wanting. Despite their many challenges, state and local governments continue to be proactive, expanding their capacity to address effectively the myriad problems confronting their citizens. From Alabama to Wyoming, they are responsive to their rapidly changing environment and to the demands of the citizens.

Our confidence in these governments does not blind us, however, to the varying capabilities of the fifty states and some 90,000 units of local government. Some are better equipped to operate effectively than others. Many state and local governments benefit from talented leadership, a problem-solving focus, and an engaged citizenry. Others do not fare so well, and their performance disappoints. Rank partisanship divides many states as they become increasingly "Red" or "Blue." Still, as a group, states and localities are the driving forces—the prime movers—in the U.S. federal system. Even those jurisdictions perennially clustered at the lower end of various ratings scales have made quantum leaps in their capability and responsiveness.

FEATURES OF THE TEXT

The themes of *State and Local Government* are supplemented by boxed features that provide compelling examples of nonnational governments in action. The boxes labeled "Controversies in States and Localities" highlight issues that may cause a jurisdiction to venture out on a limb, trying something new. The It's Your Turn boxes, which are new to this edition, present students with two sides to an issue and ask them to consider their own position.

The **Controversies in States and Localities** features are intended to generate debate and discussion among students. For example, state government responses to the Ebola crisis are featured in Chapter 2, participatory budgeting in Vallejo, California, is explored in Chapter 4, and the effort to get more third parties on state ballots is covered in Chapter 5. Utah's innovative website that engaged citizens in redrawing legislative districts is the focus in Chapter 6, governors with primarily private sector experience are examined in Chapter 7, and the proposal to split California into six states is the subject of Chapter 12's Controversies box. Chapter 16 looks at the issue of prison privatization, and mandatory drug testing for welfare applicants is considered in Chapter 17. Each of the Controversies in States and Localities now concludes with a series of critical thinking questions.

The **It's Your Turn** boxes engage students more directly, by asking them to take a side in a controversial issue. These issues include whether Washington

D.C., should become the 51st state, whether state legislatures should be more professionalized, and whether a state should bail out its financially-stressed local governments. Other It's Your Turn boxes ask students to consider the arguments for and against state governments providing tax incentives to the film industry for filming in their state, cities enacting plastic bag bans, states enforcing strict voter ID laws, and states legalizing marijuana.

Sincere effort has been invested in making this book accessible to the student. Each chapter opens with a series of **Learning Objectives** and closes with a **Chapter Recap** to help structure student learning. The Learning Objectives are now also called out within each chapter, to help students make the connection between each learning objective and chapter content. We have included updated photographs to provide visual images that bring the world of state and local government to life for the reader. Maps, tables, and figures offer an engaging format to assist in the identification of patterns and trends in the data. Many of these graphics are new to or updated for the tenth edition. As noted, boxes throughout the chapters showcase the innovative, the unusual, and the insightful in state and local politics. Lists of states appear in each chapter and facilitate comparisons across the states. **Key Terms** are bold-faced, defined in the margins, and listed at the end of each chapter. References to websites in the end-of-chapter list of **Internet Resources** encourage student curiosity, engagement, and individual research.

THE CONTENT OF THE TENTH EDITION

As in the first nine editions, this book provides thorough and completely updated coverage of state and local institutions, processes, and policies. The chapters blend the findings from the latest political science and public policy research with issues and events from the real world. It is intended to be a core text.

In Chapter 1, we introduce the functions of nonnational governments and explore the theme of capacity and responsiveness. The growing diversity in the United States and the contemporary controversy dubbed "culture wars" are featured in the chapter. Federalism's central importance is highlighted in Chapter 2, which traces the twists and turns of the federal system, from the scribblings of the Framers to the Supreme Court's latest pronouncements on the Tenth and Eleventh amendments. The fundamental legal underpinnings of state governments—their constitutions—are discussed in Chapter 3. Chapter 4 explores citizen participation and elections (including the 2014 elections), focusing on the increased access of citizens and the expectations they have for government. Chapter 5, "Political Parties, Interest Groups, and Campaigns," gets at subnational politics—the fascinating real world of candidates, lobbyists, organizations, and money.

Coverage of the three branches of government—legislative, executive, and judicial—is updated and reflects the institutional changes each branch has undergone recently. The intent of Chapter 6 is to show how legislatures actually work. In addition, responses of state legislatures to the institutional challenge posed by term limits are explored. Governors are featured in Chapter 7, including those who have misbehaved in various ways, and the issue of gubernatorial power is emphasized. Chapter 8, "Public Administration: Budgeting and Service Delivery," offers updated coverage of privatization as a strategy for improving government and the delivery of public services, as well as new material on e-government and budget transparency. In Chapter 9, the policy-making role of judges, judicial federalism, judicial accountability, and judicial selection mechanisms are emphasized.

Local governments are not treated as afterthoughts in this book. Two chapters focus solely on localities: Chapter 10 is devoted to the multiple types and structures of local government and Chapter 11 to leadership and governance, including new leadership approaches of mayors and city councils. Subsequent chapters consider localities within the context of the states: Chapter 12 focuses on the political and practical issues linking the two levels—and the resultant tensions between them—and Chapter 13 emphasizes the growing interdependence of state and local financial systems. Chapter 12 specifically tackles the issue of land use and urban sprawl, including New Urbanism approaches. Chapter 13 offers a comprehensive synthesis of the principles and political economy of taxation and spending and an overview of the strategies used by state and local governments to cope with the aforementioned economic crash.

Five policy chapters illustrate the diverse postures of state and local governments in responding to change and citizen demands. The roles of states and localities are different in each policy area. Chapter 14 examines economic development initiatives in the context of interstate and interregional competition for jobs and business. Chapter 15 focuses on the ever-important topic of public education; it includes examples of many of the most recent education reform efforts, including school choice plans, No Child Left Behind, homeschooling, and charter schools. Criminal justice policy is the subject of Chapter 16. Crime statistics have been updated, as have some of the newest initiatives for community policing, law enforcement technology, and criminal data applications. Social welfare and health care policy are featured in Chapter 17. Welfare traps are identified, state programs aimed at plugging the gaping holes in the national health system are examined, and the effects of the Affordable Care Act ("Obama-care") are explained. Finally, Chapter 18 covers a wide range of environmental topics such as sustainability, waste management, and hydraulic fracturing. Of special interest are some of the success stories in "greening" states and localities.

RESOURCES FOR INSTRUCTORS

Instructor Companion Web Site for *State and Local Government*, 10e

ISBN: 9781305643642

This Instructor Companion Website is an all-in-one multimedia online resource for class preparation, presentation, and testing. Accessible through Cengage.com/login with your faculty account, you will find available for download: book-specific Microsoft® PowerPoint® presentations; a Test Bank compatible with multiple learning management systems; and an Instructor Manual. The Test Bank, offered in Blackboard, Moodle, Desire2Learn, Canvas, and Angel formats, contains Learning Objective-specific multiple-choice, true/

false, and essay questions for each chapter. Import the test bank into your learning management system to edit and manage questions and to create tests.

The Instructor's Manual contains chapter-specific learning objectives, an outline, key terms with definitions, and a chapter summary. Additionally, the Instructor's Manual features a critical thinking question, a lecture launching suggestion, and an in-class activity for each learning objective.

The Microsoft PowerPoint presentations are ready-to-use, visual outlines of each chapter. These presentations are easily customized for your lectures. Access the Instructor Companion Website at www.cengage.com/login.

IAC Cognero for *State and Local Government, 10e*

ISBN: 9781305642829

Cengage Learning Testing Powered by Cognero® is a flexible online system that allows you to author, edit, and manage test bank content from multiple Cengage Learning solutions, create multiple test versions in an instant and deliver tests from your LMS, your classroom, or wherever you want. The test bank for *State and Local Government, 10e* contains Learning Objective-specific multiple-choice, true/false, and essay questions for each chapter.

ACKNOWLEDGMENTS

First, we thank the reviewers of the tenth edition, who provided us with many thoughtful observations and examples:

Justin DePlato, University of North Florida
Patricia Freeman, University of Tennessee
Fred R. Hertrich, Middlesex County College
Kevin Parsneau, Minnesota State University

We have incorporated their suggestions into this edition whenever possible.

We also extend our appreciation to our partners at Cengage. Jesse Rodriguez provided indispensable research assistance at Texas A&M University. Finally, Carson, Blease, Kathy, Joel, and Laura contributed in many special ways to the final product, as usual.

A. O'M. B.

R. C. K.

SOURCE: Photo courtesy of Ann O'M. Bowman

Ann O'M. Bowman (Ph.D., University of Florida) is professor and holder of the Hazel Davis and Robert Kennedy Endowed Chair in the Bush School of Government and Public Service at Texas A&M University. She teaches courses in state and local politics and policy, intergovernmental relations, environmental policy and management, and public policy process. Her research interests revolve around questions of institutional change, policy adoption and implementation, and intergovernmental dynamics. She has published numerous books and articles on these topics over the years.

SOURCE: Photo courtesy of Richard C. Kearney

Richard C. Kearney (Ph.D., University of Oklahoma) is retired as professor of political science and public administration at North Carolina State University. His career also included lengthy teaching, research, and administrative responsibilities at East Carolina University, the University of Connecticut, and the University of South Carolina. His research interests include comparative state politics and policy, labor relations, and human resource management policy. He has published prolifically on these and related topics.

1

State and Local Governments: New Directions

LEARNING OBJECTIVES

1.1 To understand the importance of state and local governments in contemporary America.

1.2 To identify ways in which states and localities have increased their capacity.

1.3 To appreciate the challenges that states and localities confront on a daily basis.

1.4 To recognize how changing public attitudes influence government behavior.

1.5 To understand the changing demographic landscape in the United States.

With appropriate oratorical flourishes, the governor of Montana, Steve Bullock, delivered his 2015 State of the State message to the people of the Treasure State. Although parts of the speech were specific to Montana—references to the Main Street Montana Project, for example—many of the themes resonated beyond the state's borders. Fiscal health, job creation, and educational improvement were topics in countless gubernatorial addresses throughout the country. Governor Bullock's tone was upbeat and determined: "My fellow Montanans, our state is strong. But I see us getting stronger. I see a Montana that remains fiscally responsible, with a balanced budget and some money socked away for a rainy day. I see a Montana where leaders of this State focus less on winning and losing, less on partisanship and political games, and more on the people we serve and the generation that will follow us."[1]

Spirited exhortations such as these were echoed in one state capitol after another in 2015. In Montana and elsewhere, state and local governments are indeed tackling difficult problems and seeking innovative solutions to contemporary issues.

LO 1.1

To understand the importance of state and local governments in contemporary America.

Studying State and Local Governments in the Twenty-First Century

The study of state and local governments has typically received short shrift in the survey of U.S. politics.[2] Scholars and journalists tend to focus on glamorous imperial presidents, a rancorous and gridlocked Congress, and an independent and powerful Supreme Court. National and international issues capture the lion's share of media attention. Yet, state and local politics are fascinating precisely because they are up close and personal. True, a governor seldom gets involved in an international peace conference, and state legislatures rarely debate the global narcotics trade. But the actors and institutions of states and localities are directly involved in our day-to-day lives. Education, job growth, health care, and crime are among the many concerns of state and local governments. And these issues affect all of us. Table 1.1 provides a sample of new state laws taking effect in 2015, laws that touch our daily lives.

TABLE 1.1   A Sample of New State Laws Taking Effect in 2015

STATE	DESCRIPTION OF THE LAW
Alaska	Legalizes the recreational use of marijuana for individuals over the age of 21.
Arizona	Allows terminally ill patients to try medications, treatments, and medical devices that have not yet been fully approved by the FDA.
California	Prohibits the dissemination of nude photos or videos of another individual without his or her consent.
Connecticut	Provides $250 payment to parents who invest in a college savings account for their children.
Florida	Makes the children of undocumented immigrants eligible for in-state tuition rates.
Georgia	Authorizes licensed firearm carriers to carry in checkpoint-free government buildings, and allows churches, bars, and restaurants to set their own firearm policies.
Hawaii	Bans talking on a cell phone, texting, or playing video games while driving a vehicle.
Idaho	Enables individuals with a concealed carry permit to carry guns on college campuses.
Illinois	Bars firms with more than 15 employees from asking job applicants about their criminal history until they have either interviewed the candidate or extended a conditional job offer.
Indiana	Permits cyclists (on bicycles or motorcycles) to cross through red lights if they have waited for at least two minutes.
New York	Outlaws the disposal of electronics, such as laptops and TVs, in curbside trash; they must now be recycled.
Pennsylvania	Increases the gasoline tax by 9.5 cents per gallon and the diesel tax by 13.2 cents per gallon.

SOURCES: Kelly Beaucar, "New 2015 Laws Tackle Wages and Weed, Pet Tattoos and Tiger Selfies," *Fox News* http://www.foxnews.com/politics/2014/12/31/new-laws-for-2015-ban-tiger-selfies-hike-minimum-wages/ (December 31, 2014); Reid Wilson, "Thousands of New Laws Take Effect Today, Part One," *Washington Post* http://www.washingtonpost.com/blogs/govbeat/wp/2014/07/01/thousands-of-new-state-laws-take-effect-today-part-one/ (July 1, 2014); and Greg Toppo, "New Year Brings Hundreds of New Laws," *USA Today* http://www.usatoday.com/story/news/nation/2015/01/01/new-laws-january-first/21055077/ (accessed January 1, 2015).

FROM SEWERS TO SCIENCE: THE FUNCTIONS OF STATE AND LOCAL GOVERNMENTS

State and local governments are busy. They exist, in large measure, to make policy for and provide services to the public. This is no easy task. Nonnational governments must perform efficiently, effectively, and fairly; and they must do so with limited financial resources. An efficient government is one that maximizes the output (services) from a given input (resources). A government operates effectively if it accomplishes what it sets out to do. Another expectation is that government function fairly—that its services be delivered in an equitable manner. It is no wonder, then, that state and local governments constantly experiment with new programs and new systems for producing services, all the while seeking efficiency, effectiveness, and fairness. For instance, the massive restructuring of Wyoming's state government several years ago was intended, according to the governor, to produce "a better method of delivering services from the state government to the citizens."[3] The quest for better functioning government never ends. A 2011 report found that, over a three-year period, nearly half of the states had eliminated or consolidated numerous state departments, agencies, boards, and commissions in an effort to increase the efficiency and effectiveness of government.[4]

To promote the exchange of innovative approaches developed by state governments, the Council of State Governments (CSG), a national nonpartisan nonprofit organization, created a website called "Capitol Ideas." The intent is to showcase the different ways states address the myriad contemporary problems they face.[5] For example, in 2015, issues garnering attention at the Capitol Ideas site included water resources, infrastructure investment, workforce development, cybersecurity, and international trade, among others. Although many of the innovations deal with public policies, some of the new ideas featured on the website are internal to government operations and are intended to make government function more effectively. These include the utilization of social media, the adoption of **evidence-based practices**, the analysis of data with geographic information system technology, and the use of logic models to achieve desired program results. The unifying characteristic among these innovations is governmental willingness to try something new. And good ideas travel; that is, they are often adopted by other states or localities. For example, after the city of Houston debuted a new web tool, "My Tax Dollars at Work," other cities followed suit. Using this tool, homeowners can quickly find out how much of their local property taxes go to various city departments such as public safety, trash and recycling pick up, parks and recreation services, land development, and city administration.

evidence-based practices
Making decisions based on the best research findings available.

OUR APPROACH

The argument of this book is that states and localities have the capacity to play central roles in the U.S. federal system. **Capacity** refers to a government's ability to respond effectively to change, make decisions efficiently and responsibly, and manage conflict.[6] Thus, capacity is tied to governmental capability and performance. In short, states and communities with more capacity work better than those with less capacity.

capacity
The ability of government to respond effectively to change, make decisions efficiently and responsibly, and manage conflict.

But what factors make one government more capable than another? Governmental institutions such as the bureaucracy matter. The fiscal resources of a **jurisdiction** and the quality of its leadership make a difference. Much of the research on capacity has focused on the administrative dimension of government performance, evaluating items such as financial management, information technology, human resources, and strategic planning. In a 2008 study of state government performance, the highest overall scores went to Utah, Virginia, and Washington (each state received an A–) and Delaware, Georgia, Michigan, Missouri, and Texas (with grades of B+).[7] Earlier evaluations of forty large counties showed that Fairfax, Virginia, and Maricopa, Arizona, had the best performance grades. Among thirty-five cities examined, Austin, Texas, and Phoenix, Arizona, were the leaders. Other factors being equal, we would expect high-scoring states, counties, and cities to produce "better" government than low-scoring jurisdictions.

A survey in Iowa showed another side to governance. When asked about the characteristics of good government, Iowans put trustworthiness, ethics, financial responsibility, and accountability at the top of the list.[8] Residents of the Hawkeye State are not unusual; all of us want our institutions and leaders to govern honestly and wisely. As political scientist David Hedge reminds us, better government is found in jurisdictions that are responsible and democratic.[9] But states and localities face significant challenges as they govern. Complex, often contradictory forces test the most capable of governments. As we have seen recently, trends in the national economy play out at the subnational level. Problems in one jurisdiction can spill over into nearby communities. State and local governments need all the capacity they can muster and maybe even a little bit of luck to meet those challenges. Sometimes states and localities fall short. For instance, in 2011, a budget imbroglio between the Democratic governor and the Republican legislature in Minnesota led to the partial shutdown of state government for nearly three weeks. Obviously, this was not one of the shining moments in the annals of state government. That the public often displays a little skepticism about governmental performance is not surprising.

Federalism, with its overlapping spheres of authority, provides the context for state and local action. (This topic is explored in depth in Chapter 2.) Intervention by the national government in the affairs of a state or local government is defensible, even desirable in some cases. For example, the environmental problems of the 1960s and 1970s exceeded state and local governments' ability to handle them (see Chapter 18), so corrective action by the national government was generally welcomed. However, some federal actions are greeted less enthusiastically. For instance, No Child Left Behind (NCLB), the education law promoted by President George W. Bush and enacted by the U.S. Congress in 2002, was considered too intrusive by many state leaders and school districts. Since its passage, state legislators throughout the country have debated resolutions challenging the authority of this federal act, and school districts have lamented the provisions related to student achievement and school accountability. In reaction, the U.S. Department of Education has granted a growing number of waivers to states so they can create their own programs to comply with the law.[10]

jurisdiction

The territorial range of government authority; "jurisdiction" is sometimes used as a synonym for "city" or "town."

federalism

A system of government in which powers are divided between a central (national) government and regional (state) governments.

Our approach takes into account intergovernmental relations (i.e., the relationships among the three levels of government)—particularly, the possibilities for cooperation and conflict. Jurisdictions (national, state, or local) possess policy-making authority over specific, but sometimes overlapping, territory. They confront innumerable situations in which boundaries blur and they must work together to accomplish an objective. However, cooperation in some cases is countered by conflict in other instances. Each level of government tends to see problems from its own perspective and design solutions accordingly. In sum, both cooperation and conflict define the U.S. federal system.

The Capacity of States and Localities

LO 1.2
To identify ways in which states and localities have increased their capacity.

To appreciate where state and local governments are today, it is important to understand where they were just fifty years ago. With notable exceptions, states and their local governments in the 1950s and 1960s were havens of traditionalism and inactivity. Many states were characterized by unrepresentative legislatures, glad-handing governors, and a hodgepodge court system. Public policy tended to reflect the interests of the elite; delivery of services was frequently inefficient and ineffective. According to former North Carolina governor Terry Sanford, the states "had lost their confidence, and people their faith in the states."[11] No wonder that, by comparison, the federal government appeared to be the answer, regardless of the question. In fact, political scientist Luther Gulick proclaimed, "It is a matter of brutal record. The American State is finished. I do not predict that the states will go, but affirm that they have gone."[12]

Those days are as outmoded as a 1950s-era black-and-white television. States and their local governments have proved themselves capable of designing and implementing "an explosion of innovations and initiatives."[13] As a result, even many national leaders have embraced the roles of states and localities as laboratories for policy experimentation. A *New York Times* story with the headline "As Congress Stalls, States Pursue Cloning Debate" is indicative of states pushing the policy envelope.[14]

The blossoming of state governments in the 1980s—their transformation from weak links in the federal chain to viable and progressive political units—resulted from several actions and circumstances, as discussed in the next section.[15] In turn, the resurgence of state governments has generated a host of positive outcomes. During the 1990s, states and localities honed their capacity and became **proactive** rather than reactive. They faced hard choices and creatively crafted new directions. A word of caution is necessary, however. The challenges of governance can be great, and not all states enjoy the same level of capacity. Furthermore, fiscal stresses such as those endured by state governments as the second decade of the twenty-first century sorely tested the ability of even the most capable states to function effectively.

HOW STATES AND LOCALITIES INCREASED THEIR CAPACITY

Several factors contributed to the resurgence of the states. U.S. Supreme Court decisions in the 1960s on legislative apportionment made for more equitable representation; the extension of two-party competition in the 1970s to states

proactive
An anticipatory condition, as opposed to a reactive one.

formerly dominated by one party gave voters more choices. At the same time, states and localities expanded their lobbying presence in the nation's capital, exerting influence on the design and funding of intergovernmental programs.

Most important, state governments quietly and methodically reformed themselves by modernizing their constitutions and restructuring their institutions. Since the 1970s, more than three-quarters of the states have ratified new constitutions or substantially amended existing ones. Formerly thought of as the "drag anchors of state programs" and as "protectors of special interests,"[16] these documents have been streamlined and made more workable. Even in states without wide-ranging constitutional reform, tinkering with constitutions is almost endless thanks to the amendment process. Nearly every state general election finds constitutional issues on the ballot. (State constitutions are discussed in Chapter 3.)

States have also undertaken various internal adjustments intended to improve the operations of state governments.[17] Modernized constitutions and statutory changes have strengthened the powers of governors by increasing appointment and removal powers and by allowing longer terms, consecutive succession, larger staffs, enhanced budget authority, and the power to reorganize the executive branch. Throughout the country, state agencies are staffed by skilled administrators, and the bureaucracy itself is more and more demographically representative of the public. Annual rather than biennial sessions, more efficient rules and procedures, additional staff, and higher salaries have helped make reapportioned state legislatures more professional, capable, and effective. State judicial systems have also been the targets of reform; examples include the establishment of unified court systems, the hiring of court administrators, and the creation of additional layers of courts. (State institutions—legislatures, governors, state agencies, and courts—are addressed in Chapters 6–9.)

INCREASED CAPACITY AND IMPROVED PERFORMANCE

The enhanced capacity enjoyed by state and local governments has generated a range of mostly positive results. The five factors discussed below reinforce the performance of states and localities.

Improved Revenue Systems Economic downturns and limits on taxing and spending have caused states to implement new revenue-raising strategies to maintain acceptable service levels. Some states also granted local governments more flexibility in their revenue systems. South Carolina, for example, now allows counties the option of providing property-tax relief to residents in exchange for increasing the local sales tax.

rainy day funds
Money set aside when a state's finances are healthy for use when state revenues decline. Formally called "budget stabilization funds."

As a rule, state governments prefer to increase user charges, gasoline taxes, and so-called sin taxes on alcohol and tobacco, and only reluctantly do they raise sales and income taxes. Over time, revenue structures have been redesigned to make them more diversified and more equitable. State **rainy day funds**, legalized gambling through state-run lotteries and pari-mutuels, and extension of the sales tax to services are examples of diversification strategies. Exemptions of food and medicine from consumer sales taxes and the enactment of property-tax breaks for poor and elderly people characterize efforts at tax equity. These revamped revenue structures helped states respond to the budget crises they confronted during the Great Recession of 2008–2011.

States continue to tinker with their revenue-raising schemes. One successful foray into creative revenue-raising has been the specialty license plate. Maryland, for example, has generated millions of dollars over the years with its "Treasure the Chesapeake" plate. Monies generated by the plates are earmarked for special programs—in this case, water quality monitoring and erosion control in the Chesapeake Bay. Nearly all states now offer specialty plates. In New York, for instance, owners can equip their cars, for an extra fee, with license plates honoring their favorite professional sports team or NASCAR driver. A brand new approach to generating cash for states comes from the world of retail stores: the marketing of official gift cards. For example, both Kentucky and Ohio sell gift cards that can be used at state park locations for various park services and merchandise.

Another effort of enterprising localities is to sell merchandise. Los Angeles County has marketed coroner toe tags as key chains; Tucson hosts online auctions of surplus property. New York City, which loses thousands of street signs (Wall Street is especially popular) to souvenir-stealing tourists, now sells replicas. But the revenue generated by those actions is dwarfed by Chicago, which has sold (actually, leased for 99 years) four city-owned parking garages to an investment bank for $563 million. As these examples show, states and localities are willing to experiment when it comes to revenue enhancement.

Expanding the Scope of State Operations State governments have taken on new roles and added new functions. In some instances, states are filling in the gap left by the national government's de-emphasis of an activity; in other cases, states are venturing into uncharted terrain. It was states that designed the first family leave legislation to give workers time off to care for newborn babies and ailing relatives, the first "Three Strikes" laws that mandated long prison sentences for habitual offenders, and the first Amber Alert systems to broadcast information about abducted children. The federal government eventually followed suit with a national family leave act, a federal Three Strikes law, and a national Amber Alert system. In addition, states have taken the initiative in ongoing intergovernmental programs by creatively using programmatic authority and resources. Prior to federal welfare reform in the mid-1990s, several states had established workfare programs and imposed time limits on the receipt of welfare benefits, provisions that were at the center of the subsequent federal legislation.

States persist in expanding their scope of operations, whether it is California's venture into stem-cell research or Florida's strides into bioterror readiness. Hawaii has begun development of an extensive network of plug-in spots where electric cars can be recharged; New Mexico is a partner in a new commercial spaceport facility that it hopes will become the center for space tourism. In 2012, Colorado and Washington became the first states to legalize marijuana for recreational, as opposed to medicinal, use. In short, states are embracing their role as policy innovators and experimenters in the U.S. federal system.

Local governments are also pushing the policy envelope. For instance, in 2012, San Francisco took a bold step when it launched its K2C program to provide college savings accounts to every kindergarten student in the city school district; Cuyahoga County, Ohio followed suit the next year. In an effort to offer more transit options to the public, Tulsa, Oklahoma, became the first city in the United States to establish an automated bike-share system, with two dozen bikes at three solar-powered stations; New York City took a slightly different approach by creating a public-private partnership for its Citi Bike system. Some cities have begun to address the problem of food deserts—the absence of grocery stores and fresh food in low-income neighborhoods—by incentivizing investment by food retailers and supporting urban agriculture. These examples make an important point: Local governments are not sitting idly by as problems emerge; instead they actively seek solutions.

Faster Diffusion of Innovations Among states, there have always been leaders and followers; the same is true for local governments. Now that states and localities have expanded their scope and are doing more policy making, they are looking more frequently to their neighbors and to similar places for advice, information, and models.[18] As a result, successful solutions spread from one jurisdiction to another. For example, Florida was the first state to create a way for consumers to stop telephone solicitations. By 1999, five more states had passed laws letting residents put their names on a "do-not-call" list for telemarketers. Seven additional states adopted similar legislation over the

It's Your Turn

Should Governments have Innovation Offices?

Businesses and corporations are often seen as engines of innovation, but to some folks, state and local governments seem slow-moving and reactive entities. In an effort to change that perception and to make government more proactive, city governments from Austin to Pittsburgh are creating innovation offices. These offices are tasked with discovering new and more efficient ways for government to do its job.

PROS	CONS
Having an innovation office could help cities become leaders in discovering new ideas and approaches rather than followers of others' innovations.	Creating a new office in city government means that money will need to be spent on that office. That money has to come from somewhere, whether it is from new revenue or diverted spending.
Internally-focused innovation offices can lead to cost savings and efficiency improvements in government.	There are no guarantees of cost savings. Generating cost savings depends on the capabilities of the people employed in the innovation office and their leadership . . . and maybe even some good luck.
Externally-focused innovation offices can lead to new government services or better ways to provide existing services. These offices may also identify new partnership opportunities.	

next two years before Congress enacted a national statute.[19] Another fast-moving innovation was a 2004 New York law that required cigarettes sold in the state to be self-extinguishing. Concerned over fire safety, California did the same and by 2009, forty other states had adopted the law.[20]

Local-level innovations spread rapidly, too. Education and environmental protection offer many examples of this phenomenon. When Miami-Dade County, Florida, hired a private company to run a public elementary school, other school districts hoping to improve quality and cut costs quickly did the same. Initial experiments with privatization spawned other innovations such as charter schools. The issue of climate change was addressed at the local level in 2005, when the mayor of Seattle became the first local official to commit his city to a plan to reduce the emission of greenhouse gases. Within five years, more than 1,050 mayors of other U.S. cities had joined the climate change bandwagon.[21] It is worth noting, of course, that the diffusion of new ideas depends in large part on their fit and effectiveness.

Obviously, state and local governments learn from one another. Communication links, including social media such as Facebook and Twitter, have become extensive. A state might turn to nearby states when searching for policy solutions. Regional consultation and emulation are logical: Similar problems often beset jurisdictions in the same region, a program used in a neighboring state may be politically more acceptable than one from a distant state, and organizational affiliations bring state and local administrators together with their colleagues from nearby areas. However, research has shown that states also borrow ideas from peer states, that is, states that are like them in important ways such as ideological leaning or economic base.[22] In the search for solutions, states and localities are increasingly inclusive.

Chip Somodevilla/Getty Images

A group of governors holds a press conference in Washington, D.C. after meeting with President Obama.

Interjurisdictional Cooperation Accompanying the accelerated flow of innovations has been an increase in interjurisdictional cooperation. States are choosing to confront and resolve their immediate problems jointly. A similar phenomenon has occurred at the local level with the creation of regional organizations to tackle area-wide problems collectively.

Interjurisdictional collaboration takes many forms, including informal consultations and agreements, interstate committees, legal contracts, reciprocal legislation, and interstate compacts. For example, all fifty states and the District of Columbia, Puerto Rico, and the U.S. Virgin Islands have a mutual agreement to aid one another when natural disasters such as hurricanes, earthquakes, and forest fires strike. Another illustration is the Streamlined Sales Tax Project, which led to an interstate agreement on the simplification of sales and use taxes. Twenty-four states were participating in the agreement as of 2015, the intent of which is to make it easier for states to collect taxes on items purchased online. In both the disaster-aid agreement and the tax project, the states worked together because they could see some benefit from cooperation.

States often cooperate when it comes to consumer protection litigation. Five states—Mississippi, Minnesota, West Virginia, Florida, and Massachusetts—were among the first to band together to share information and design tactics in their lawsuits against tobacco companies in the mid-1990s; by 1998, 37 other states had joined in the successful effort to recover the Medicaid costs of treating tobacco-related diseases.[23] In the same year, attorneys general in 20 states filed an antitrust lawsuit against Microsoft Corporation, claiming that the firm illegally stifled competition, harmed consumers, and undercut innovation in the computer software industry. In another illustration of interjurisdictional cooperation, two-thirds of the states joined together in a legal complaint against six computer chip manufacturers, alleging that they engaged in illegal price-fixing. The case was eventually settled out of court in 2010 for $173 million.[24]

Increased jurisdictional cooperation fosters a healthy climate for joint problem solving. In addition, when state and local governments solve their own problems, they protect their power and authority within the federal system. It appears that states are becoming more comfortable working with one another. The beginning of the twenty-first century was indeed historic: States were engaged in more cooperative interactions than ever before.[25]

Increased National-State Conflict An inevitable by-product of more capable state and local governments is intensified conflict with the national government. One source of this discord has been federal laws and grant requirements that supersede state policy; another is the movement of states onto the national government's turf. National-state conflict is primarily a cyclical phenomenon, but contention has increased in recent years. The issue of unfunded mandates—the costly requirements that federal legislation imposes on states and localities—has been particularly troublesome. In an effort to increase the visibility of the mandates issue, several national organizations of state and local officials sponsored a "National Unfunded Mandate Day" in the mid-1990s. Making a strong case against mandates, then-governor George Voinovich of Ohio stated, "Unfunded mandates devastate our budgets, inhibit flexibility and innovation in implementing new programs, pre-empt important state initiatives, and deprive states of their responsibility to set priorities."[26] Congress responded in 1995 by passing a mandate relief bill that requires cost-benefit analyses of proposed mandates; however, the law contains some loopholes that have weakened its impact.

Some of the disputes pit a single state against the national government, as in Nevada's fight to block the U.S. Energy Department's plan to build a nuclear fuel waste storage facility at Yucca Mountain, 100 miles northwest of Las Vegas. Another example is the effort by Texas to continue its use of a flexible permitting process to regulate industrial air pollution, a process that has been challenged repeatedly by the U.S. Environmental Protection Agency (EPA). In other conflicts, the national government finds itself besieged by a coordinated, multistate effort, for example, when twelve states sued the U.S. EPA in 2014 over the regulation of carbon emissions from existing coal plants or when twenty states challenged the federal Affordable Care Act in 2010.[27]

National-state conflicts are resolved (and sometimes intensified) by the federal judicial system. Cases dealing with alleged violations of the U.S. Constitution by state and local governments are heard in federal courts and decided by federal judges. Sometimes the rulings take the federal government into spheres long considered the purview of state and local governments. For instance, within the space of two days in 2009, Arizona both won and lost cases before the U.S. Supreme Court. The state was successful in its argument that state spending on language training for non-English-speaking students should not be subject to federal supervision, but it was unsuccessful in defending the actions of school officials who conducted a strip search of a middle-school student suspected of drug possession.

CHALLENGES FACING STATE AND LOCAL GOVERNMENTS

LO 1.3

To appreciate the challenges that states and localities confront on a daily basis.

Increased capacity does not mean that all state and local problems have been solved. A Gallup poll released in 2014 asked a sample of residents in each of the fifty states about their level of trust and confidence in their state government to handle problems facing the state.[28] On average, 60 percent of a state's residents said that they had a "great deal" or "fair amount" of trust and confidence in their state government. This level of trust and confidence is respectable but certainly not stellar. Moreover, the average masks substantial variation across the states ranging from North Dakota's 77 percent to Illinois' 28 percent. A look at Table 1.2 shows that trust and confidence in state government tend to be higher is less populated states and in states located in the upper plains region, but undoubtedly other factors contribute to these poll numbers. The percentages serve as a reminder that even though states (and localities) have made many strides forward, there is plenty of room for improvement. Three tough challenges for nonnational governments include fiscal stress, interjurisdictional conflict, and political corruption.

Fiscal Stress The most intractable problem for states and localities involves money. State and local finances are vulnerable to cyclical peaks and troughs in the national economy as well as to occasional changes in public finance.

The national economic recession of 2008–2011 hit states and localities hard—very hard—and the impact on governmental budgets was significant.

TABLE 1.2	Trust in State Government to Handle Problems		
STATE	PERCENTAGE WITH GREAT DEAL/FAIR AMOUNT OF TRUST	STATE	PERCENTAGE WITH GREAT DEAL/FAIR AMOUNT OF TRUST
Alabama	57	Montana	68
Alaska	71	Nebraska	73
Arizona	57	Nevada	52
Arkansas	65	New Hampshire	66
California	49	New Jersey	62
Colorado	59	New Mexico	55
Connecticut	52	New York	53
Delaware	61	North Carolina	51
Florida	52	North Dakota	77
Georgia	63	Ohio	54
Hawaii	57	Oklahoma	63
Idaho	65	Oregon	54
Illinois	28	Pennsylvania	46
Indiana	68	Rhode Island	40
Iowa	67	South Carolina	55
Kansas	56	South Dakota	74
Kentucky	53	Tennessee	59
Louisiana	48	Texas	72
Maine	40	Utah	75
Maryland	49	Vermont	57
Massachusetts	58	Virginia	62
Michigan	54	Washington	55
Minnesota	62	West Virginia	51
Mississippi	61	Wisconsin	57
Missouri	56	Wyoming	76

SOURCE: Jeffrey M. Jones, "Illinois Residents Least Trusting of their State Government," http://www.gallup.com/poll/168251/illinois-residents-least-trusting-state-government.aspx (accessed March 3, 2015).

Connecticut governor Jodi Rell did not mince words when she said, "These are the worst financial times any of us can remember . . . let's face it, it's scary."[29]

The fiscal impact of the Great Recession was deep and prolonged, with four consecutive years in which states faced significant mismatches between revenues and spending. During that time, state lawmakers scrambled to close budget gaps that, according to estimates by the National Conference of State

Legislatures, totaled $510.5 billion."[30] State rainy day funds grew precariously drier as legislators looked to them for short-term relief. In an effort to save money, some prisons were closed in Colorado, Kansas, Michigan, North Carolina, and Washington; in some states, funding for education was reduced, and cash assistance for low-income families was cut; in others, state agencies were **downsized** and employee wages were frozen. State leaders sought new revenues also: Income tax rates were increased in California, Hawaii, Illinois, and New York; sales tax increases were enacted in Arizona, California, and Massachusetts, among other states. Facing the largest deficit of any state, the governor of California battled with the legislature over several money-saving proposals including "selling the Los Angeles Memorial Coliseum, San Quentin State Prison and other state property, eliminating welfare benefits for 500,000 families, terminating health coverage for nearly 1 million low-income children and closing 220 of the state's parks."[31]

Local governments felt the recessionary heat as well; Dallas, one of the country's largest cities, provides an example. To close a $190.2 million deficit in its budget, the city of Dallas made cuts in numerous city services including street repairs, arts funding, library hours, and park maintenance; in addition, nearly 800 city employees lost their jobs.[32] The story was much the same in many other localities: reduce costs as painlessly as possible, and if necessary, increase fees. Some relief was forthcoming when Congress passed the $787 billion American Recovery and Reinvestment Act, informally known as the federal stimulus plan, but many states and communities felt the fiscal pinch well into 2012. Now, cash-strapped states and localities are confronting a **"new normal"** in which they are expected to provide public services with fewer dollars at their disposal.[33] If there were ever a time for innovation and fresh thinking, the aftermath of the Great Recession is it. (Chapter 13 takes up the issue of taxing and spending in states and localities in depth.)

Increased Interjurisdictional Conflict Tension is inherent in a federal system because each of the governmental entities has its own set of interests, as well as a share of the national interest. When one state's pursuit of its interests negatively affects another state, conflict occurs. Such conflict can become destructive, threatening the continuation of state resurgence. In essence, states end up wasting their energies and resources on counterproductive battles among themselves.

Interjurisdictional conflict is particularly common in two policy areas very dear to state and local governments: natural resources and economic development. States rich in natural resources want to use these resources in a manner that will yield the greatest return. Oil-producing states, for instance, levy severance taxes that raise the price of oil. And states with abundant water supplies resist efforts by arid states to tap into these supplies. The most serious disputes often occur among neighboring states. One illustration is the protracted dispute between California and six other western states over water allocations from the Colorado River, an issue made even more contentious due to California's multiyear drought. In short, the essential question revolves around a state's right to control a resource that occurs naturally and is highly desired by other states. Resource-poor states argue that resources are in fact national and should rightfully be shared among states.

downsize

To reduce the size and cost of something, especially government.

new normal

An environment characterized by stagnant revenues and budget cuts, leading to changes in the provision of public services.

In the area of economic development, conflict is extensive because all jurisdictions want healthy economies. Toward this end, states try to make themselves attractive to business and industry through tax breaks, regulatory relaxation, and even image creation. (The Controversies in States and Localities box explores how jurisdictions seek to reverse negative images and to **re-brand** themselves more positively.) Conflict arises when states get involved in bidding wars—that is, when an enterprise is so highly valued that actions taken by one state are matched and exceeded by another. Suppose, for example, that an automobile manufacturer is considering shutting down an existing facility and relocating. States hungry for manufacturing activity will assemble packages of incentives such as below-cost land, tax concessions, and subsidized job training in their efforts to attract the manufacturer. The state that wants to keep the manufacturer will try to match these inducements. In the long run, economic activity is simply relocated from one state to another. The big winner is the manufacturer. (Chapter 14 explores economic development issues much more extensively.)

A particularly fascinating interjurisdictional contest involves the recurring rounds of U.S. military base closures and consolidations. Military bases are economic plums that no jurisdiction wants to lose. Thus, states mount public relations efforts to protect local bases and to grab jobs that will be lost in other states. Politics and lobbying are supposed to play no role in the Pentagon's decisions about which bases will remain open and which ones will close, but states prefer to hedge their bets. In the most recent round of base closings, Texas devoted $250 million to defending its bases, and Massachusetts allocated $410 million for its own bases. As one observer put it, "It is a war of all against all."[34]

Political Corruption Corruption exists in government, which is no great surprise. Most political systems can tolerate the occasional corrupt official, but if corruption becomes commonplace, it undermines governmental capacity and destroys public trust. Public reaction ranges from cynicism and alienation (corruption as "politics as usual") to anger and action (corruption as a spur to reform). A survey found that the more extreme the corrupt act (a city clerk embezzling $100,000 versus a police officer accepting free food at a restaurant), the more harsh the public's judgment.[35] Even so, mitigating motives or circumstances tend to reduce the public's outrage (e.g., a public official taking a bribe but using the money to pay his sick child's hospital bills). But governmental scandals have been linked tentatively to another negative effect—a slowdown in economic growth. Research on states found that federal corruption convictions are associated with declines in job growth primarily because, from a business perspective, corruption creates uncertainty and inflates costs.[36]

States and localities have taken great precautions to reduce the amount of wrongdoing occurring in their midst. Government has much more **transparency** than it ever has before, with more openness and more rules. But the statutes and policies are only as good as the people whose behavior they regulate. Unfortunately, examples of corrupt behavior are not hard to find. For instance, in 2013, five former officials of Bell, California, a small, working-class city near Los Angeles, were convicted on corruption charges

re-brand

An effort to change how a state or city is perceived by the public, to create a new image of a place.

transparency

A characteristic of a government that is open and understandable, one in which officials are accountable to the public.

Controversies in States and Localities

Creating an Image, Re-Branding a Place

What image best captures a state's essential being? Ohio, for example, calls itself the Buckeye State, but most Americans do not know what a buckeye is. (It is a shrub or tree of the horse chestnut family and it produces buckeye nuts. There are a lot of these trees in Ohio.) Consider New Hampshire, which stamps the motto "Live Free or Die" on its license plates. A few years ago, some legislators advocated replacing the uncompromising phrase with the word *scenic*, arguing that the state needed to project a more caring image. In other words, New Hampshire wanted to re-brand itself.

The North Dakota legislature took the image issue to new heights when it seriously entertained a resolution that would have dropped the word *North* from the state's name. The name *North Dakota* was said to summon images of "snowstorms, howling winds, and frigid temperatures." Simply going with *Dakota*, a word that means "friend" or "ally" in the Sioux language, would project a warmer image of the state, supporters claimed. (The state senate ultimately defeated the name-changing resolution.) Image and reputation are serious business: West Virginia's governor protested an Abercrombie & Fitch T-shirt that featured a map of the state and the phrase "It's all relative in West Virginia." Not exactly the image the state wanted to project, to be sure. An aide to the governor said, "It really hinders our ability to market the state." In response, the company decided to pull the shirt from its shelves.

Images are not trivial. They matter because they project and reflect public perceptions, which can be both accurate and inaccurate. They offer a shorthand understanding of a place, a slice of the whole. States and communities have become much more conscious of their images in recent years, and many have launched promotional campaigns to re-brand themselves with more positive images. Jersey City, New Jersey, which has been termed "unfashionable" by some, "scruffy" by others, recently developed a campaign to change people's perception of the city, and ideally, encourage them to consider the city as a place to live, visit, and start businesses. The city's new slogan is "Make It Yours," which is incorporated into an inventive logo and even has a social media presence with a hashtag, #JCMakeItYours. The total budget for the city's rebranding effort? $1.2 million.

Critical Thinking Questions:

1. Every state has an image. Take a moment to think about your state, its culture, and its icons. What is your state's image? Has your state created a brand for itself? If it has, do you think that it is fitting, or can you think of a better brand for your state? If your state does not have a brand, what would it be?

2. Corporations such as Coca-Cola, Apple, and Disney spend millions of dollars each year maintaining their brand. Should public money go towards states creation and maintenance of a brand for themselves?

3. Do you think that brands are effective in changing the perceptions of a state?

SOURCES: Dale Wetzel, "Dakotans Consider Dropping 'North' to Thaw State's Image," *The Missoulian* (June 25, 2001), p. B4; Tony Dokoupil, "Hillbilly No More," *Newsweek*, www.newsweek.com/ (March 10, 2009); "A New Effort from a 'New' Jersey City Urges, 'Make it Yours," *New York Times*, http://www.nytimes.com/2014/10/06/business/media/a-new-effort-from-a-new-jersey-city-urges-make-it-yours.html?_r=0 (accessed October 6, 2014).

after overpaying themselves millions of dollars. In 2014, former Virginia governor Robert McDonnell was convicted of public corruption for using the governor's office to help advance the business interests of a benefactor who, in return, gave the governor and his wife money and expensive gifts. He was sentenced to two years in federal prison.

A pair of economists researching corruption in the states asked statehouse reporters—folks who are familiar with the goings-on in the capitol—to assess the overall level of corruption in their state compared with other states.[37]

At the top of the list was Rhode Island, followed by Louisiana and New Mexico. States at the bottom of the comparative corruption list included the Dakotas, Colorado, and Maine. Others have speculated that capital cities isolated from major population centers tend to breed more corruption. At the local level, data on the number of federal convictions for public corruption over a 35-year period showed the Chicago metropolitan area to be the most corrupt in the nation.[38] Clearly, states and localities are not corruption-free; however, the amount of corruption is relatively low, given the vast number of public officials serving in nonnational levels of government. Still, even a whiff of scandal can undermine public confidence in government and sap governmental capacity.

The People: Designers and Consumers of Government

LO 1.4

To recognize how changing public attitudes influence government behavior.

A book on state and local governments is not only about places and governments, it is also about people—the public and assorted officeholders—and the institutions they create, the processes in which they engage, and the policies they adopt. Thus, this volume contains chapters on institutions, such as legislatures, and on processes, such as elections; it also discusses policies, such as those pertaining to education. But in each case, *people* are the ultimate focus: A legislature is composed of lawmakers and staff members who deal with constituents; elections involve candidates, campaign workers, and voters (as well as nonvoters); and education essentially involves students, teachers, administrators, parents, and taxpayers. In short, the word *people* encompasses an array of individuals and roles in the political system.

ETHNIC-RACIAL COMPOSITION

LO 1.5

To understand the changing demographic landscape in the United States.

Nearly 320 million people live in the United States. Some can trace their heritage back to the *Mayflower*, whereas others look back only as far as a recent naturalization ceremony. Very few can claim indigenous (native) American ancestry. Instead, most Americans owe their nationality to some forebear who came here in search of a better life or—in the case of a significant minority, the descendants of slaves—to ancestors who made the journey to this country not out of choice but because of physical coercion. The appeal of the United States to economic and political refugees from other countries continues, with Mexicans, Central Americans, Asians, and eastern Africans among the most recent arrivals.

The United States is a nation of immigrants, and therefore ethnic richness and cultural diversity abound. Official U.S. Census figures for 2010 put the white population at 72 percent, the African American population at 13 percent, the Latino population at 16 percent, the Asian population at 5 percent, and the American Indian and Alaska Native population at 1 percent.[39] (The numbers total more than 100 percent because of double-counting.) Approximately 38 million, or 13 percent, of the nation's population was born in another country, with 53 percent of the foreign born from Latin America and another 28 percent from Asia.[40]

One aspect of immigration—illegal immigration—is putting the words from the sonnet inscribed on the Statue of Liberty ("Give me your tired, your poor, your huddled masses") to a severe test. Although accurate numbers are hard to come by, one recent estimate by the U.S. Department of Homeland Security placed the number of undocumented immigrants at approximately 11.5 million, of which approximately 59 percent were from Mexico.[41] The issue of illegal immigration has divided the American public into two camps. One camp argues that people who are in the United States illegally receive public benefits, take scarce jobs, and pay little in taxes. This group favors legislative proposals that clamp down on illegal immigration by requiring verification of workers' legal status and restricting the issuance of drivers' licenses to U.S. citizens and legal immigrants. The other camp contends that undocumented workers actually contribute more in taxes than they consume in public services; moreover, they take on jobs that others do not want and therefore contribute to economic growth. This group tends to support legislation such as the "path to citizenship," a federal proposal that sets up a procedure for becoming a legal resident, and the "DREAM Act," which makes high school graduates and those who have served honorably in the military eligible for citizenship, despite their parents' illegal immigration status. Emblematic of these differing perspectives, five states explicitly prohibit unauthorized immigrant students from receiving in-state tuition at state colleges or universities; twenty states offer these benefits to them.

Arizona's tough 2010 law required immigrants to carry documents proving they were in the United States legally, and it gave local police broad power to question and arrest anyone suspected of being in the country illegally. Critics claimed that the law was discriminatory and would lead to ethnic profiling. Upon enactment, the law unleashed a flurry of demonstrations, both supportive and oppositional, initially in Arizona and eventually around the country. Some jurisdictions such as Los Angeles threatened to boycott the Grand Canyon State in retaliation for the law, while several other states rallied around Arizona. Similarly tough laws were passed in 2011 in Alabama, Georgia, Indiana, South Carolina, and Utah. The federal government filed suit against the Arizona law, and in 2012 parts of the law were struck down by the U.S. Supreme Court, although the provision allowing policy to investigate the immigration status of individuals who were stopped or arrested was sustained. Further action on immigration occurred at the federal level when President Obama issued a series of executive orders in 2014 intended to protect some undocumented immigrants from deportation.

Clearly, ethnicity and culture still matter, despite the image of America as a melting pot. Researchers have found that a state's racial and ethnic diversity goes a long way in explaining its politics and policies.[42] Looking toward the future, census projections for the year 2050 estimate a nation of approximately 440 million people, with the Anglo population dropping to 50 percent of the total, the African American population increasing slightly to 15 percent, the Latino population reaching 25 percent, and an Asian population of 8 percent.[43] If these population trends hold, state politics and policy in the mid-twenty-first century will be affected.

POPULATION GROWTH AND MIGRATION

As a whole, the United States grew by an estimated 3.1 percent during the period 2010–2014. Disaggregating the data by state reveals several trends. Reflecting the pattern of the previous decade, high rates of growth occurred in the western states; substantially slower growth rates characterized the Northeast and to a lesser extent, the Midwest. (The map in Figure 1.1 displays the percentage change in each state's population from 2010 to 2014.) Among the states, North Dakota, Texas, Colorado, and Utah continued to outpace the growth in other states, with rates of 9.1 percent, 6.7 percent, 6.1 percent, and 6.1 percent, respectively. The District of Columbia was another high-growth jurisdiction with an 8.7 percent increase. Only one state (West Virginia) lost population (less than a one percent loss) during the four-year period. Several states experienced extremely low rates of growth: Maine and Vermont each grew by 0.14 percent, Rhode Island by 0.25 percent, Michigan by 0.26 percent, and Illinois by 0.39 percent. In terms of absolute increase from 2010 to 2014, the number of Texans rose by 1.8 million; California added 1.5 million new residents, and Florida replaced New York as the nation's third most populous state.[44]

For cities, the population trends for the four-year period are equally compelling. Higher rates of growth were much more prevalent in cities in the

FIGURE 1.1   Percent Change in State Population, 2000–2014

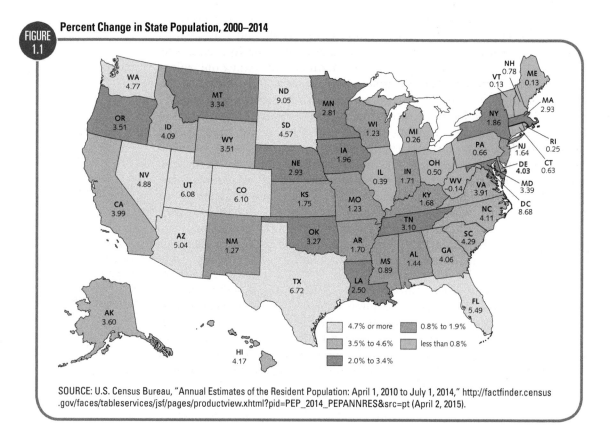

Legend:
- 4.7% or more
- 3.5% to 4.6%
- 2.0% to 3.4%
- 0.8% to 1.9%
- less than 0.8%

SOURCE: U.S. Census Bureau, "Annual Estimates of the Resident Population: April 1, 2010 to July 1, 2014," http://factfinder.census.gov/faces/tableservices/jsf/pages/productview.xhtml?pid=PEP_2014_PEPANNRES&src=pt (April 2, 2015).

Sunbelt region than in cities of the **Frostbelt**. The growth leaders among large cities (defined as cities of 200,000 population or more) between 2010 and 2014 were Irvine, California, and Gilbert, Arizona. Both of these Sunbelt cities experienced population increases of more than 14 percent. At the other end of the spectrum are large, older industrialized cities of the Frostbelt that lost more than two percent of their population during the same time frame: Detroit (−4.7 percent) and Toledo (−2.2 percent).[45]

Migration—moving from state to another—may be on the minds of many folks these days. A recent Gallup Poll showed that, on average, thirty-three percent of a state's residents want to move to another state.[46] The question was phrased like this: "Regardless of whether you *will* move, if you had the opportunity, would you *like* to move to another state, or would you rather remain in your current state?" Illinois had the dubious distinction of landing at the top of the out-migration list: half of the residents said they would leave the state if they had the opportunity; Connecticut and Nevada were close behind at 49 percent and 47 percent, respectively. At the other end of the spectrum were states like Montana, Hawaii, and Maine, where only 23 percent of the current residents would leave if they could.

Population changes carry economic and political consequences for state and local governments. As a general rule, power and influence follow population. A state's representation in the U.S. Congress and its votes in the Electoral College are at stake. As a result of the 2010 census, Texas picked up four seats in the U.S. House of Representatives, while Florida added two seats. Six other states (Arizona, Georgia, Nevada, South Carolina, Utah, and Washington) gained a single seat. This means, of course, that other states lost seats. New York and Ohio each lost two seats, with eight other states losing one apiece (Illinois, Iowa, Louisiana, Massachusetts, Michigan, Missouri, New Jersey, and Pennsylvania).[47] The number of congressional districts in the rest of the states did not change. Population projections suggest that the electoral influence of Sunbelt states will continue to grow into the foreseeable future. The stakes are high for local governments, too. As a central city's population size is eclipsed by its suburban population, a loss in the city's political clout typically occurs. Aware of the importance of "the count," many cities spent thousands of dollars on media advertisements, text messages, and social networking websites encouraging their residents to mail in their 2010 Census forms.

POLITICAL CULTURE

One of the phrases that a new arrival in town may hear from long-time residents is "We don't do things that way here." **Political culture**—the attitudes, values, and beliefs that people hold toward government—is the conceptual equivalent of simply saying "It's *our* thing."[48] As developed by political scientist Daniel Elazar in the 1960s, the term refers to the way people think about their government and how the political system operates. Political culture is a soft concept—one that is difficult to measure—yet it has remained quite useful in explaining state politics and policy.

According to Elazar, the United States is an amalgam of three major political cultures, each of which has distinctive characteristics. In an *individualistic*

Sunbelt
An unofficial region of the United States, generally consisting of the South and the West.

Frostbelt
An unofficial region of the United States, generally comprising the Northeast and the Midwest. The label *Rustbelt* is sometimes used as a synonym.

political culture
The attitudes, values, and beliefs that people hold toward government.

political culture, politics is a kind of open marketplace in which people participate because of essentially private motivations. In a *moralistic political culture,* politics is an effort to establish a good and just society. Citizens are expected to be active in public affairs. In a *traditionalistic political culture,* politics functions to maintain the existing order, and political participation is confined to social elites. These differing conceptions about the purpose of government and the role of politics lead to different behaviors. Confronted with similar conditions, officials in an individualistic community would resist initiating a program unless public opinion demanded it; leaders in moralistic areas would adopt the new program, even without pressure, if they believed it to be in the public interest; and traditionalistic rulers would initiate the program only if they thought it would serve the interests of the governing elite.

Political culture is a factor in the differences (and similarities) in state policy. Research has found that moralistic states demonstrate the greatest tendency toward policy innovation, whereas traditionalistic states exhibit the least.[49] In economic development policy, for example, political culture has been shown to influence a state's willingness to offer tax breaks to businesses.[50] Other research has linked political culture to state environmental policy and successful state implementation of welfare reform.[51]

Today, few states are characterized by pure forms of these cultures. The mass media have had a homogenizing effect on cultural differences; migration has diversified cultural enclaves. This process of cultural erosion and synthesis has produced hybrid political cultures. For example, Florida, once considered a traditionalistic state, now has many areas in which an individualistic culture prevails and even a moralistic community or two. In an effort to extend Elazar's pioneering work, researcher Joel Lieske has used race, ethnicity, and religion to identify contemporary subcultures.[52] With counties as the building blocks and statistical analysis as the method, he identified eleven distinctive regional subcultures. A state like Ohio, which Elazar characterized as individualistic, becomes a mix of Germanic, rural/urban, global, and "heartland" counties in Lieske's formulation. Very few states are dominated by a single subculture, except perhaps Utah, by a Mormon subculture, and New Hampshire, Rhode Island, and Vermont, by an Anglo-French subculture.

Political culture is not the only explanation for why states do what they do, of course. Socioeconomic characteristics (income and education levels, for example) and political structural factors (the amount of competition between political parties) also contribute to states' and communities' actions. In fact, sorting out the cause-and-effect relationships among these variables is a daunting job. For example, why do some states pass more laws to regulate handguns than other states do? Emily Van Dunk's study found that several factors were important, although the crime rate and partisanship, surprisingly, were not among them.[53] States with nontraditional political cultures adopt more handgun regulations, as do states with more women in the legislature and those with populations that are more urbanized and nonwhite. In general, political factors, socioeconomic characteristics, and the particulars of a specific problem combine to produce government action.

Protestors march to Indiana's state capitol after passage of the Religious Freedom Restoration Act in 2015.

CULTURE WARS

In 2004, when San Francisco's mayor ordered city clerks to remove all references to gender on local marriage license applications, it opened the door for same-sex marriages to take place in the city. As lesbian and gay activists and supporters celebrated, many politically conservative groups denounced the action and promised legal challenges and political repercussions for the mayor. This type of social conflict over morality issues is known informally as **culture wars**, or "morality politics." And these culture wars are defining the politics of many communities and states. Besides gay rights, battlegrounds in the culture wars include abortion, pornography, and prayer in schools.

These issues tend to involve deeply held values, sometimes connected to religion, and they are less about economics than are many political issues. According to political scientist Elaine Sharp, culture wars have several distinctive features.[54] Values are highly salient to people, eliciting passionate reactions; they mobilize people across different neighborhoods and racial and ethnic groups; and the ensuing political activism often takes unconventional forms, such as demonstrations. Recent research has confirmed the presence of wide disagreements in public opinion on fundamental values such as freedom, equality, individualism, and patriotism, among others.[55] Throughout the country, battle lines have been drawn over issues such as more restrictive abortion laws and displaying the Ten Commandments in public buildings. But the most volatile culture war during the past decade involved same-sex marriage.

As of 2010, more than thirty-five states had Defense of Marriage Acts (DOMA) in their statutes, defining marriage as between one man and one woman, but by 2015, same-sex marriage had been legalized in thirty-seven

culture wars
Political conflicts that emerge from deeply held moral values.

states. The explanation for the dramatic shift in public policy had a lot to do with pressure from gay and lesbian rights activists on state legislatures, and rulings by federal and state courts striking down DOMAs as a violation of the Fourteenth Amendment's equal-protection and due-process clauses.[56] In 2015, the U.S. Supreme Court ruled that states cannot ban same-sex marriage. Even as public attitudes became more supportive of same-sex marriage, many religious conservatives maintained their staunch opposition. The issue came to a head over states' adoption of the Religious Freedom Restoration Act (RFRA), which allows businesses to use their religious beliefs as a justification for refusing service to customers. Supporters claimed the law signaled a state's commitment to religious liberty; opponents contended that it undermined principles of nondiscrimination and could be used to deny services to same-sex couples. State officials found themselves buffeted in swirling political winds. The governor of Arizona vetoed RFRA when it reached her desk in 2014; in 2015, Indiana's governor signed RFRA into law, and Arkansas's governor convinced the legislature to modify RFRA before passing it. Storms of protest greeted all of these governors as RFRA became the latest skirmish in the culture wars.

Linking Capacity to Results

State and local governments have strengthened their position in the American federal system. On a regular basis, they tackle some of the most pressing problems facing the country.[57] The interaction of three unique characteristics of our fifty-state system—diversity, competitiveness, and resiliency—both facilitates and complicates their task.[58] Consider the *diversity* of the United States. States and their communities have different fiscal capacities and different voter preferences for public services and taxes. As a result, citizens and businesses are offered real choices in taxation and expenditure policies across different jurisdictions.

Diversity is tempered, however, by the natural *competitiveness* of a federal system. No state can afford to be too far out of line with the prevailing thinking on appropriate levels of taxes and expenditures because citizens and businesses may opt to relocate. In essence, each jurisdiction is competing with every other jurisdiction. Such competition over the price and performance of government stabilizes the federal system.

The third characteristic, *resiliency*, captures the ability of state governments to recover from adversity. This feature was certainly put to the test during the economic downturn of 2008–2011. The stresses of that period compelled states to retrench and rethink; the fresh policy ideas that resulted were successful in some instances, unsuccessful in others. But the larger point is that state governments squared their shoulders to meet the challenges head on. Resiliency is the key.

As one astute observer of the U.S. governmental scene has commented, "Over the past decade, without ever quite admitting it, we have ceased to rely on Congress (or the federal government, for that matter) to deal with our most serious public problems . . . [T]he states have been accepting the challenge of dealing with problems that no other level of government is handling."[59] Return to the first page of this chapter and reread Governor Bullock's inspirational words. The twenty-first century began full of challenges, but states and their local governments are taking charge. In the final analysis, that is what increased capacity is all about: results.

Chapter Recap

- State and local governments are directly involved in our daily lives.

- The story of states and localities over the past two decades has been one of transformation. They have shed their backward ways, reformed their institutions, and emerged as capable and proactive.

- State resurgence is exemplified in improved revenue systems, the expanded scope of state operations, faster diffusion of innovations, more interjurisdictional cooperation, and increased national-state conflict.

- Several persistent challenges confront states and localities: fiscal stress, interjurisdictional competition, and political corruption.

- The United States is becoming more racially and ethnically diverse. Sunbelt states tend to outpace the rest of the nation with their population growth.

- An outbreak of culture wars is redefining the politics of some communities and states.

- As a whole, the states are diverse, competitive, and resilient. Their increased capacity to govern effectively was sorely tested in the first decade of the twenty-first century.

KEY TERMS

evidence-based practices *(p. 3)*
capacity *(p. 3)*
jurisdiction *(p. 4)*
federalism *(p. 4)*

proactive *(p. 5)*
rainy day funds *(p. 6)*
downsize *(p. 13)*
new normal *(p. 13)*
re-brand *(p. 14)*

transparency *(p. 14)*
Sunbelt *(p. 19)*
Frostbelt *(p. 19)*
political culture *(p. 19)*
culture wars *(p. 21)*

INTERNET RESOURCES

Nearly all states use the URL suffix **gov** in their online addresses, such as **Ohio.gov** or **mt.gov**. Florida does something a little different with its URL: **www.myflorida.com**.

A website that offers a wealth of policy information about the states, along with links to multistate organizations, national organizations of state officials, and state-based think tanks is **www.stateline.org**, established by the Pew Center on the States. The Center's own website contains useful information on state policies and trends at **http://www.pewtrusts.org/en/topics/state-policy**.

Since 1933, the Council of State Governments has collected and disseminated information about state institutions, policies, and trends. Its website is **www.csg.org**.

The website of *Governing* magazine, **www.governing.com**, contains up-to-date, in-depth discussions of issues in states and localities.

At **www.census.gov**, the website of the U.S. Bureau of the Census, you can find historical, demographic data on states and localities.

The website for *State Politics and Policy Quarterly*, a scholarly journal that publishes research on important state-level questions, is **spa.sagepub.com**. Also, the journal *State and Local Government Review* contains the latest research on issues in the states and localities. Its URL is **slg.sagepub.com**.

Federalism and the States: Sorting Out Roles and Responsibilities

U.S. Border Patrol officer apprehends illegal child immigrant in Arizona. John Moore/Getty Images

LEARNING OBJECTIVES

2.1 To familiarize yourself with the history and evolution of American federalism from the writings of the Framers and the growth of national power to the contemporary time.

2.2 To understand the changing balance of formal and informal power and responsibility between the national government and the states.

2.3 To be able to describe the principal models of federalism that attempt to explain the nature of federal-state-local relationships.

2.4 To develop comprehension of the complex nature and tools of intergovernmental financial relations.

2.5 To understand finances as a source of friction and conflict between the three levels of government.

A single broad and enduring issue in American federalism transcends all others: What is the proper balance of power and responsibility between the national government and the states? The debate over this profound question was first joined by the Founders in pre-constitutional days and argued between the Federalists and Anti-Federalists. It continues today in the halls of Congress, the federal courts, and the state and local governments, over issues ranging from the mundane to the profound. For instance, which level of government is responsible for addressing illegal immigration? And what should the respective responsibilities of federal, state, and local governments be on immigration?

As illegal immigration has soared during the past few years, including an estimated 90,000 unaccompanied Central American children in 2014, Congress has been unable to act on the issue. As the burden of dealing with undocumented immigrants has grown on states and localities, particularly those on or near the Mexican border, they have taken to acting authoritatively on their own. Sometimes that means acting contrary to federal instructions, such as refusing to hold illegals for an extra forty-eight hours in jail to give federal authorities extra time to deport them.[1]

States are contesting the boundaries of federalism through varied approaches, some highly restrictive, and others much less so. Florida, Tennessee, and eighteen other states offer in-state college tuition to illegal immigrants; most states avert their eyes from evidence of local businesses employing undocumented workers; many issue them drivers' licenses, and Oregon and New York extend health care benefits to them. Other states, responding to Tea Party and other anti-immigrant views, come down hard on illegals. Arizona, for example, aggressively arrests unauthorized immigrants and denies then any services at all. At least seven states expressly prohibit in-state tuition assistance; others prohibit illegals from having drivers' licenses.[2]

In some cases, when Arizona, Alabama, and other states enacted laws that placed severe legal restrictions on illegal immigrants and their employers, the U.S. Justice Department has secured a court order blocking parts of the laws. A founding principle of our country is the right of the national government to keep states from enacting laws that usurp its powers. In these particular cases, the federal government asserted that "a state may not establish its own immigration policy or enforce state laws in a manner that interferes with the federal immigration laws."

Whereas traditionally the federal government has regulated immigration policy, in the absence of comprehensive national reform, immigration-restrictive states argue that they were simply stepping in where the federal government had failed to do so. The fault for immigration policy confusion, according to the states, resides primarily with a divided, do-little Congress and an uncooperative president that have not exercised their constitutional responsibilities. Until they do, a crazy-quilt pattern of state enforcement is certain, meaning differentiated treatment of illegal immigrants, as well as expenses and uncertainty in the business and law enforcement communities.

Complex and highly politicized issues like immigration control that Congress fears to act upon tend to expose the soft underbelly of federalism. Every response is intergovernmentally complex with respective roles and responsibilities needing to be sorted out, or ultimately resolved by the Supreme Court. Emotional issues like illegal immigration have spawned a critical analysis of American federalism that has significant implications for all levels of government. These types of events and conflicts help define U.S. federalism and exhibit both its strengths and weaknesses. As a system for organizing government, federalism has important consequences that often affect our political and personal lives in ways both direct and hidden.

The Concept of Federalism

In a nation—a large group of people organized under a single, sovereign government and sharing historical, cultural, and other values—powers and responsibilities can be divided among different levels of government in three ways: through a unitary government, a confederacy, or a federal system. To understand our federal system, we must know how it differs from the other forms of government.

UNITARY, CONFEDERATE, AND FEDERAL SYSTEMS

The large majority of countries (more than 90 percent) have a **unitary system**, in which most if not all legal power rests in the central government. The central government may create or abolish regional or local governments as it sees fit. These subgovernments can exercise only those powers and responsibilities granted to them by the central government. In France, the United Kingdom, Chile, Japan, and the many other countries with unitary systems, the central government is strong and the regional or local jurisdictions are weak. In the United States, the states themselves function as unitary systems.

A **confederacy** is the opposite of a unitary system. In a confederacy, the central government is weak and the regional governments are powerful. The regional jurisdictions establish a central government to deal with areas of mutual concern, such as national defense and a common currency, but they severely restrict the central government's authority in other areas. If they see fit, they may change or even abolish the central government. The United States began as a confederacy, and the southern states formed a new confederacy following secession in 1861.

A **federal system** falls somewhere between the unitary and confederate forms in the method by which it divides powers among levels of government. It has a minimum of two governmental levels, each of which derives its powers directly from the people and can act directly on the people within its jurisdiction without permission from any other authority. Each level of government is supreme in the powers assigned to it, and each is protected by a constitution from being destroyed by the other. Thus, federalism divides the power and functions of government between a central government and a specified number of geographically defined regional jurisdictions. In effect, people hold dual citizenship, in the national government and in their regional government.

In the U.S. federal system, the regional governments are called states. In others, such as Canada, they are known as provinces. Altogether, there are approximately twenty federal systems in the world.

THE ADVANTAGES AND DISADVANTAGES OF FEDERALISM

As it has evolved in the United States, federalism is a reasonably effective system of government. But, as immigration policy illustrates, it is not perfect, nor is it well suited to the circumstances of most other nations. Ironically, federalism's weaknesses are closely related to its strengths.

unitary system

One in which all government authority is derived from a central government.

confederacy

A league of sovereign states in which a limited central government exercises few independent powers.

federal system

A means of dividing the power and functions of government between a central government and a specified number of geographically defined regional jurisdictions.

STRENGTHS	WEAKNESSES
1. *A federal system helps manage social and political conflict.* It broadly disperses political power within and among governments, enabling national, as well as regional and local, concerns to reach the central government. Many venues, or "democratic safety valves," exist for resolving conflicts before they reach the crisis stage.	1. *If such conflicts are not addressed satisfactorily, they can eventually lead to regional or ethnic conflict on a fearsome scale.*
2. *Federalism promotes administrative efficiency.* The wide variety of services demanded by citizens is delivered more efficiently without a large central bureaucracy. From public elementary education to garbage collection, the government closest to the problem seems to work best in adapting public programs to local needs.	2. *Federalism presents problems in coordinating action across governments and boundaries.* Picture trying to get 90,000 squawking and flapping chickens to move in the same direction at once. Confusion and deadly delays in responding to the issues such as the Ebola crises and illegal immigration illustrate this point.
3. *Federalism encourages innovation.* States and localities can customize their policies to accommodate diverse demands and needs—and, indeed, such heterogeneity flourishes. New policies are constantly being tested by the more than 90,000 government "laboratories" that exist throughout the country, thus further encouraging experimentation and flexibility.	3. *Federalism's many points of involvement can encourage obstruction and delay and result in ineffective national government programs and priorities.* Duplication and confusion can be the result. Fifty sets of laws on banking and lending practices, firearms regulation, and medical marijuana can make crossing state lines an exercise in comparative public law.
4. *A federal system maximizes political participation in government.* Citizens have opportunities to participate at all three levels of government through elections, public hearings, and other means. The local and state governments fill almost 1 million offices in regular elections, serving as valuable political training camps for aspiring public leaders. The great majority of presidents and congressional representatives first wet their feet in state or local politics.	4. *Such broad participation encourages local biases inimical to national interests.* Problems in locating nuclear and hazardous waste disposal facilities readily illustrate this dilemma.

The History of U.S. Federalism

The men who met in Philadelphia during the hot summer of 1787 to draw up the U.S. Constitution were not wild-eyed optimists, nor were they revolutionaries. In fact, as we'll see in this section, they were consummate pragmatists whose beliefs shaped the new republic and created both the strengths and the weaknesses of our federal system.

EARLY HISTORY

The Framers of the Constitution held to the belief of English political philosopher Thomas Hobbes that human beings are contentious and selfish. Some of them openly disdained the masses. For example, Gouverneur Morris of

LO 2.1

To familiarize yourself with the history and evolution of American federalism from the writings of the Framers and the growth of national power to the contemporary time.

New York declared of the American people, "The mob begin to think and reason. Poor reptiles! . . . They bask in the sun, and ere noon they will bite, depend upon it."[3] Most of the Framers agreed that their goal in Philadelphia was to find a means of controlling lower forms of human behavior while still allowing citizens to have a voice in making the laws they were compelled to obey. The "philosopher of the Constitution," James Madison, formulated the problem in terms of factions, groups that pursue their own interests without concern for the interests of society as a whole. Political differences and self-interest, Madison felt, led to the formation of factions, and the Framers' duty was to identify "constitutional devices that would force various interests to check and control one another."[4]

Three practical devices to control factions were placed in the U.S. Constitution. The first was a system of representative government in which citizens would elect individuals who would filter and refine the views of the masses. The second was the division of government into three branches (executive, legislative, and judicial). The legislative body was divided into two houses, each with a check on the activities of the other. Equal in power would be a strong chief executive, with the authority to veto legislative acts, and an independent judiciary. Third, the government was structured as a federal system, in which the most dangerous faction of all—a national majority—would be constrained by the sovereign states. Alternatively, insurrection in one state would be put down by the others, acting through the national government. Madison's ultimate hope was that the new Constitution would "check interest with interest, class with class, faction with faction, and one branch of government with another in a harmonious system of mutual frustration."[5]

Sometimes today there appears to be more frustration, factionalism, and fragmentation than harmony, but Madison's dream did come true. The U.S. federal system is the longest-lived constitutional government on earth. Its dimensions and activities are vastly different from what the Framers envisioned, but it remains a dynamic, adaptable, responsive, and usually effective system for conducting the affairs of government.

THE MOVE TOWARD FEDERALISM

The drive for independence from the British Crown by the thirteen American colonies was in large measure a reaction to "a history of repeated injuries and usurpations" and "absolute tyranny" (according to the Declaration of Independence) under a British unitary system of government.

The immediate struggle for independence left little time to develop a consensus on the form of government best suited to the future needs of American society. Hence, the move toward federalism was gradual. The first independent government established in America was a confederacy; thus Americans tested two types of government—unitary and confederate—before deciding permanently on the third, federalism.

The Articles of Confederation During the War for Independence, the colonies, now called states, agreed to establish a confederation. A unicameral (one-house) Congress was created to exercise the authority of the new national government. Its powers were limited to the authority to wage war, make peace, enter into treaties and alliances, appoint and receive ambassadors, regulate Indian affairs, and create a postal system. The states held all powers not expressly granted to the Congress. The governing document was the Articles of Confederation (effective from 1776 to 1787).

The inherent weaknesses of the confederacy quickly became apparent. The states had significant authority within their own borders, but the federal government was unable to carry out its basic responsibilities or honor its financial obligations because it did not have the power to force the states to pay their share of the bill. The lack of national authority to regulate either domestic or international commerce led to discriminatory trade practices by the states. Anarchy and even warfare between the fractious states were a very real concern.[6] Indeed, the key event that brought together representatives of the states to draft a constitution for a new type of government was Shays' Rebellion. Daniel Shays, a Revolutionary War officer, led an armed revolt of New England farmers who were fighting mad about debt and taxes. The weak central government had difficulty putting down the rebellion.

The Constitutional Convention How did the Framers create a long-lasting and successful system of government that seems to have the best features of both unitary and confederate forms? They were familiar with developments in political and theological federalism in Europe and the ancient world. They were aware of tribal confederations among the Native Americans and, most important, the Framers were well informed by their own colonial experience.[7] Truly, the Framers were learned men, well schooled in the theories of politics, and most of them did believe in designing a government that would serve the people and ensure justice. But above all they were pragmatists; they developed a practical compromise on the key issues of the day, including the proper role of the national government and the states. The reconciliation of the interests and powers of the states with the need for a strong national government, what Madison called a "middle ground," was purely an American invention. Today, the United States stands as the prototypical federal system. It is our most distinctive political contribution.

Delegates representing each of the states assembled at the constitutional convention. Here, the self-interests of the large states and the small states diverged. The large states supported the Virginia Plan, which proposed a strong central government spearheaded by a powerful bicameral Congress. Because representation in both chambers was to be based on population, larger states would be favored. The smaller states countered with the New Jersey Plan, which put forward a one-house legislature composed of an equal number of representatives from each state. There were other differences between the two plans, but the issue of state representation was paramount.

The New Jersey Plan was defeated by a vote of 7 to 3, but the smaller states refused to give in. Finally, Connecticut moved that the lower house (the House of Representatives) be based on the population of each state and the

FIGURE 2.1

Constitutional Distribution of Powers

National Government Powers:
- Coin money
- Regulate interstate and foreign commerce
- Tax imports and exports
- Make treaties
- Make all laws "necessary and proper" to fulfill responsibilities
- Make war
- Regulate postal system

Powers Denied:
- Tax state exports
- Change state boundaries
- Impose religious tests
- Pass laws that conflict with the Bill of Rights

Concurrent Powers:
- Tax
- Borrow money
- Charter banks and corporations
- Seize property (eminent domain)
- Make and enforce laws
- Administer a judiciary

State Government Powers:
- Conduct elections
- Regulate intrastate commerce
- Establish republican forms of state and local government
- Protect public health, safety, and morals
- All powers not delegated to the national government or denied to the state by the Constitution

Powers Denied:
- Tax imports and exports
- Coin money
- Enter into treaties
- Impair a legal contract
- Enter compacts with other states without congressional consent

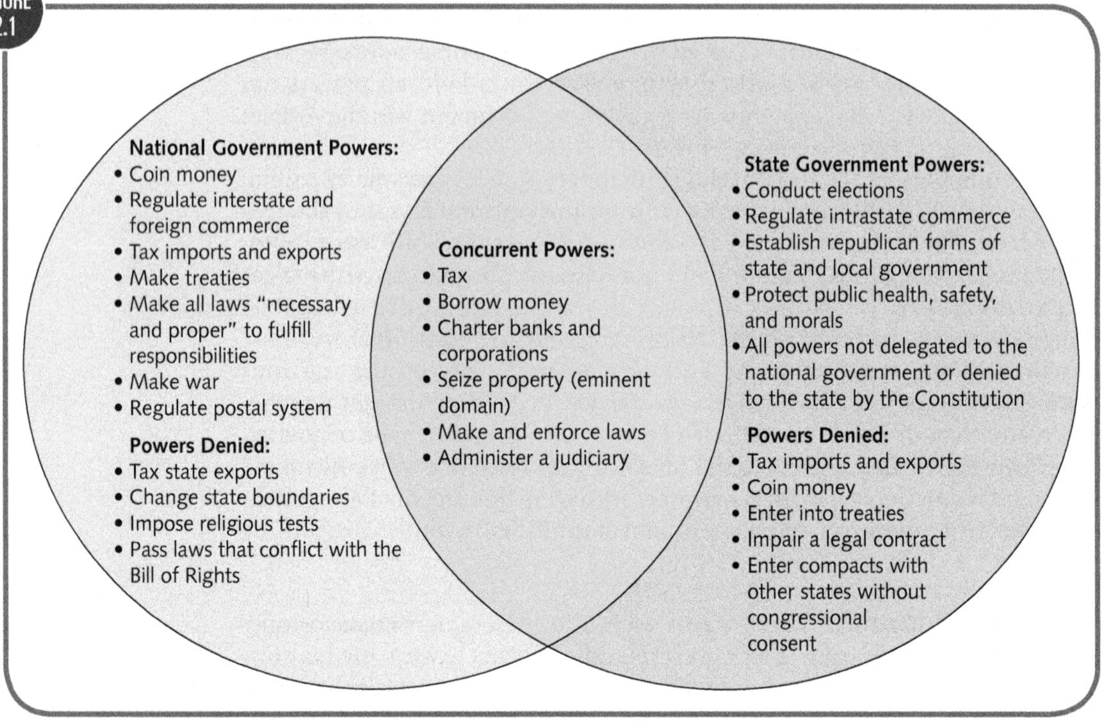

upper house (the Senate) be based on equal state membership. This Great Compromise was approved, ensuring that a faction of large states would not dominate the small ones.

The Framers reached another important set of compromises by specifying the powers of the new central government and the powers to be granted (and denied) to the states. The seventeen **enumerated (delegated) powers** were listed in the Constitution, along with state government powers and **concurrent powers** to be exercised by both the national and state governments. Figure 2.1 illustrates the constitutional distribution of powers.

LO 2.2

To understand the changing balance of formal and informal power and responsibility between the national government and the states.

STATE-CENTERED FEDERALISM

The first decades under the new Constitution witnessed a clash between profoundly different views on governing. George Washington, John Adams, Alexander Hamilton, and their fellow Federalists favored national supremacy, or **nation-centered federalism**. Opposed to their idea were Thomas Jefferson and the Republicans, who preferred **state-centered federalism**. Much of the debate then, as today, concerned the meaning of the **reserved powers** clause of the **Tenth Amendment** to the Constitution. Ratified in 1791, the Tenth Amendment gave support to the states by openly acknowledging that "the powers not delegated to the United States by the Constitution, nor prohibited by it to the States, are reserved to the states respectively, or to the people." But in fact, the Tenth Amendment was an early omen of the eventual triumph of nation-centered federalism. As pointed out by constitutional scholar Walter Berns, if the states were intended to be the dominant federal actors, they would not have needed the Tenth Amendment to remind them.[8]

Those who defended the power of the states under the Constitution—that is, state-centered federalism—saw the Constitution as a *compact*, an agreement, among the sovereign states, which maintained their sovereignty, or the right of self-governance. The powers of the national government enumerated in the Constitution were to be interpreted narrowly, and the states were obliged to resist any unconstitutional efforts by the national government to extend its authority.[9]

This **compact theory** of federalism became the foundation for states' rights arguments. In particular, it became central to the fight of the southern states against what they considered discrimination by the North. During the 1820s, a national tariff seriously damaged the economy of the southern states. The slave-based agricultural economy of the South had already begun a protracted period of decline while the North prospered. The tariff, which placed high taxes on imported manufactured goods from Europe, hit the South hard because it produced few manufactured goods. Rightly or wrongly, the southerners blamed the "tariff of abominations" for many of their economic problems. They also, of course, staunchly resisted calls for the abolition of slavery.

When in 2014 Missouri's legislature voted to nullify federal gun control laws and Arizona voters passed a ballot measure that gave voters or the legislature the power to refuse to enforce, administer, or cooperate with any federal law or program, the long-deceased political philosopher John C. Calhoun must have saluted in his musty grave. In 1828, the living Vice President John C. Calhoun of South Carolina had asserted that the United States was composed of sovereign states united in a national government through a compact. The powers of the national (central) government had been entrusted to it by the states, not permanently handed over. Calhoun claimed that a state thus had complete authority to reinterpret or even nullify (reject) a federal law or the compact itself, making it invalid within that state's borders. Most important, Calhoun declared that if a large majority of the states sided with the national government, the nullifying state had the right to *secede*, or withdraw from the Union. (Indeed, until the Civil War, when Americans referred to "my country," they usually meant their state—not the United States.)

In 1832, after an additional tariff was enacted by the national government, South Carolina nullified it. President Andrew Jackson and the Congress threatened military action to force the state to comply with the law, and Jackson even threatened to hang Calhoun, who by this time had resigned from the vice presidency.[10]

Ultimately, eleven southern states (led by South Carolina) did secede from the Union, at which point they formed the Confederate States of America. The long conflict between state sovereignty and national supremacy, and the question of slavery as well, was definitively resolved by five years of carnage in such places as Antietam, Shiloh, and Gettysburg, followed by the eventual readmittance of the renegade states to the Union. The Civil War, sometimes referred to in the South as The War Between the States, remains the single

---

enumerated (delegated) powers

Those expressly given to the national government, primarily in Article I, Section 8, of the Constitution.

concurrent powers

Those granted by the Constitution to both the national and the state governments.

nation-centered federalism

Theory holding that the national government is dominant over the states.

state-centered federalism

Theory holding that the national government represents a voluntary compact or agreement between the states, which retain a dominant position.

reserved powers

Those powers residing with the states by virtue of the Tenth Amendment.

Tenth Amendment

The amendment to the Constitution, ratified in 1791, reserving powers to the states.

compact theory

A theory of federalism that became the foundation for states' rights arguments.

most violent episode in American history, resulting in more than 620,000 deaths (more than in all our other wars combined) and countless civilian tragedies.

THE GROWTH OF NATIONAL POWER THROUGH THE CONSTITUTION AND THE JUDICIARY

After the Civil War, a *nation-centered* concept of federalism evolved. For the most part, the national government has become the primary governing force, with the states and localities generally following its lead. Recently, the states have been inclined to act more independently, but their power vis-à-vis the national government has been eroded by the Supreme Court's interpretations of key sections of the Constitution.

The National Supremacy Clause Article III of the Constitution established the U.S. Supreme Court. The supremacy of national law and the Constitution is constitutionally grounded in the **national supremacy clause** (Article VI), which provides that the national laws and the Constitution are the supreme laws of the land. Later decisions of the Supreme Court established its role as arbiter of any legal disputes between the national government and the states.

The Necessary and Proper Clause The fourth chief justice of the United States, John Marshall, was the architect of the federal judiciary during his thirty-four years on the bench. Almost single-handedly, he made the judiciary a coequal branch of government. Several of his rulings laid the groundwork for the expansion of national governmental power. In the landmark case of *McCulloch v. Maryland* (1819), two issues were before the bench: the right of the national government to establish a national bank and the right of the state of Maryland to tax that bank, once it was established.[11] The secretary of the treasury, Alexander Hamilton, had proposed a bill that would allow Congress to charter such a bank for depositing national revenues and facilitating the borrowing of funds. Those who wanted to limit the power of the national government, such as James Madison and Thomas Jefferson, argued that the Constitution did not provide the government with the specific authority to charter and operate a national bank.

The crux of the issue was how to interpret the **necessary and proper clause**. The final power delegated to Congress under Article I, Section 8, is the power "to make all laws which shall be *necessary and proper* for carrying into execution the foregoing powers, and all other powers vested by this Constitution in the Government of the United States" (emphasis added). Jefferson argued that *necessary* meant "indispensable," whereas Hamilton asserted that it merely meant "convenient." Hamilton argued that in addition to the enumerated powers, Congress possessed **implied powers**. In the case of the national bank, valid congressional action was implied through the powers of taxation, borrowing, and making currency found in Article I, Section 8.

Meanwhile, the state of Maryland had levied a tax on the new national bank, which was located within its borders, and the bank had refused to pay.

national supremacy clause
Article VI of the Constitution, which makes national laws superior to state laws.

necessary and proper clause
Portion of Article I, Section 8, of the Constitution that authorizes Congress to enact all laws "necessary and proper" to carry out its responsibilities.

implied powers
Those that are not expressly granted by the Constitution but that are inferred from the enumerated powers.

The bank dispute was eventually heard by Chief Justice Marshall. Marshall was persuaded by the Hamiltonian point of view. Marshall pointed out that nowhere in the Constitution does it stipulate that the only powers that may be carried out are those expressly described in Article I, Section 8. Thus, he ruled that Congress had the implied power to establish the bank and that Maryland had no right to tax it. Significantly, *McCulloch v. Maryland* meant that the national government had an almost unlimited right to decide how to exercise its delegated powers. Over the years, Congress has enacted a great many laws that are only vaguely, if at all, associated with the enumerated powers and that stretch the phrase *necessary and proper* beyond its logical limits.

The Commerce Clause Another important ruling of the Marshall Court extended national power through an expansive interpretation of the **commerce clause** (often referred to as the interstate commerce clause) of Article I, Section 8. The commerce clause gives Congress the power "to regulate commerce with foreign nations, and among the several states, and with the Indian tribes." In *Gibbons v. Ogden* (1824),[12] two important questions were addressed by Marshall: What *is* commerce? And how broadly should Congress's power to regulate commerce be interpreted?

The United States was just developing a national economy as the Industrial Revolution expanded. National oversight was needed, along with regulation of emerging transportation networks and of state activities related to the passage of goods across state lines (interstate commerce). The immediate question was whether New York could grant a monopoly to run a steamship service between New York and New Jersey. What was Marshall's answer? No, it could not. He defined commerce broadly and held that Congress's power to regulate commerce applied not only to traffic across state boundaries but, in some cases, also to traffic of goods, merchandise, and people *within* a state. The Court further expanded the meaning of "commerce" in later rulings.

The General Welfare Clause The **general welfare clause** of Article I, Section 8, states that "the Congress shall have power to lay and collect taxes, duties, imposts, and excises to pay the debts and provide for the common defense and *general welfare* of the United States" (emphasis added). Before the Great Depression of the 1930s, it was believed that it was up to private charity and state and local governments to provide limited assistance to the poor. The Great Depression brought massive unemployment and poverty throughout the country and made necessary a major change in the national government's attitude. The states and localities were staggered by the tremendous loss of tax revenues and the persistent pleas to help poor and displaced persons obtain food and shelter. Franklin D. Roosevelt, who won the presidency in 1932, set in motion numerous New Deal programs that completely redefined federal responsibility for the general welfare. These programs, such as Social Security, propelled the national government into a position of dominance within the federal system and extended it into fields previously within the province of the states, the localities, and the private sector.

commerce clause

Part of Article I, Section 8, of the U.S. Constitution, which gives Congress the power to regulate trade with foreign countries and among the states.

general welfare clause

The portion of Article I, Section 8, of the Constitution that provides for the general welfare of the United States.

Fourteenth Amendment

Enacted in 1868, this amendment contains citizenship rights, due process, and equal protection provisions that states must apply to all citizens.

The Fourteenth Amendment Ratified by the states in 1868, the **Fourteenth Amendment** had the effects of giving former slaves official status as citizens of the United States and of the state in which they lived, as well as setting a precondition for southern states to be readmitted to the Union. It included two other important principles as well: *due process* and *equal protection* under the law. The federal courts have used the Fourteenth Amendment to increase national power over the states in several critical fields, especially with regard to civil rights, criminal law, and election practices.

The judiciary's application of the Fourteenth Amendment to state and local governments is illustrated by many contemporary cases that have, for example, ordered local officials to hike property taxes to pay for school and required formal hearings for welfare recipients before benefits are terminated, and ruled in other cases involving civil rights, citizenship, and voting rights.

Controversies in States and Localities

What Level of Government Should Take the Lead for Ebola-Like Threats?

The Ebola virus causes severe, and often fatal, illness transmitted from person to person through bodily fluids such as saliva or blood. The Ebola virus disease was first identified in Africa in 1976. But in 2014, three central African countries experienced widespread outbreaks of the illness, with thousands of deaths recorded. Several Ebola cases were documented in the United States in health care workers returning from the fight against Ebola in Africa. It can only be spread by a symptomatic victim (fever, vomiting, diarrhea, etc.); the latency period is twenty-one days.

Preparations for dealing with the sickness in the states were uncertain and disjointed. New Jersey Governor Chris Christie imposed mandatory quarantines on returning travelers exposed to Ebola. A nurse, Kaci Hickox, who worked with Doctors Without Borders in one of the infected countries, was placed in a quarantine tent outside a New Jersey hospital even though she tested negative for the virus. She complained loudly and publicly and after four days was permitted to leave for her house in Maine. In turn, Maine imposed a twenty-one day in-home quarantine, which Hickox promptly refused to obey. (She was eventually pronounced free of the virus.)

The Tenth Amendment of the U.S. Constitution recognizes the powers of the state governments. Traditionally, these included the "police powers" of health, education, and welfare. The Tenth Amendment states: "The powers not delegated to the United States

by the Constitution, nor prohibited by it to the states, are reserved to the states respectively, or to the people." The seventeen "express powers" of the national government in the Constitution do not list anything about protecting the health and safety of the Citizens; this resides with the states though their "police powers." The U.S. Constitution contains two references to "the General Welfare," one occurring in the Preamble and the other in the Taxing and Spending Clause. The U.S. Supreme Court has held that these clauses are not a general grant of legislative power to the federal government.

The Obama administration and the Centers for Disease Control and Prevention issued national guidelines for voluntary isolation and monitoring of people exposed to Ebola, but the national government lacks authority to do much more. States and their health departments can reject the federal guidelines and substitute their own.

Critical Thinking Questions:

1. Which level of government should exercise primary responsibility for addressing the Ebola crisis or any other serious health-related epidemic? Why?

2. Should the fifty states be permitted to determine such policy as they see fit, or should there—indeed can there—be a single, comprehensive national policy to handle such problems?

THE GROWTH OF NATIONAL POWER THROUGH CONGRESS

The U.S. Supreme Court has not been the only force behind nation-centered federalism; Congress has worked hand in hand with the judiciary. The commerce clause represents a good example. Given the simple authority to control or eliminate state barriers to trade across state lines, Congress now regulates commercial activities within a state's boundaries as well, as long as these activities purportedly have substantial national consequences (examples include banking, insurance, and the movement of goods). Congress has also used the authority of the commerce clause to expand national power into fields only vaguely related to commerce, such as protecting endangered species. The states have made literally hundreds of legal challenges to such exercise of the commerce power. Until recently, almost all of these were resolved by the U.S. Supreme Court in favor of the national government. But the court dramatically changed direction on June 28, 2012, when a 5-to-4 majority held that the Patient Protection and Affordable Care Act ("Obamacare") overstepped Congress's constitutional authority under the commerce clause by mandating that states extend Medicaid to hundreds of thousands of new recipients. Fourteen states had filed litigation challenging the constitutionality of the federal health care law. (The court revisited the law in 2015, ruling that the federal government could legally subsidize the federal government legally subsidize federally-run health insurance exchanges (see Chapter 17 for a fuller treatment of the Affordable Care Act)).

Taxing and Spending Power Probably the most controversial source of the rise in national power in recent years has been the use of the *taxing and spending power* by Congress to extend its influence over the state and local governments. Under Article I, Section 8, Congress holds the power to tax and spend to provide for the common defense and general welfare. But the **Sixteenth Amendment**, which grants Congress the power to tax the income of individuals and corporations, moved the center of financial power from the states to Washington, D.C. Through the income tax, the national government raises huge amounts of money. A portion of this money is sent to the states and localities through grants-in-aid. Congress insists on some sort of accountability in the way these funds are spent, and as a consequence, attaches various conditions to which the recipients must adhere if they are to receive the money. These conditions include requirements for recipient governments to match national grant dollars with some portion of state contributions. (The interstate highway program requires one state dollar for every ten federal dollars, for example.) Congress also imposes mandates and regulations directly related to the purposes of the individual grant, such as effectively forcing the states to adopt national policies on driver's licenses (noncomplying states face the loss of federal transportation dollars).

Federal Pre-emption The national government has also seized power through the process known as **federal pre-emption**. The legal basis for pre-emption is Article VI of the Constitution, the national supremacy clause. Whenever a state law conflicts with a national law, the national law is dominant.

Sixteenth Amendment
Enacted in 1913, this amendment grants the national government the power to levy income taxes.

federal pre-emption
The principle that national laws take precedence over state laws.

Congressional passage of a national law that supersedes existing state legislation is directly pre-emptive. An example is the Real ID Act of 2005, which imposed forty-three requirements on how states must validate personal identification when issuing driver's licenses. Designed to fight terrorism by imposing more strenuous requirements for obtaining a driver's license, Real ID was so unpopular that Washington, Montana, and twenty-three other states passed statutes or resolutions to go on record as refusing to cooperate with the law. A game of intergovernmental "chicken" ensued when the Department of Homeland Security (DHS) threatened to refuse to accept those states' driver's licenses to board airplanes or enter federal buildings. For their part, states objected that this unfunded mandate posed a threat to personal privacy and would require states to issue new, more costly licenses to all drivers to the tune of some $14.6 billion.[13] Finally, DHS blinked and granted all fifty states extensions to 2013, then to 2016, for compliance. Yet by 2015, thirteen states still did not meet the federal standards.[14] Meanwhile, state officials sought and gained approval to adopt their own "Enhanced Driver's License" program at significantly lower cost.

Smothering (Then Resuscitating) the Tenth (and Eleventh) Amendments
Actions by Congress and the federal courts have gradually undermined the Tenth Amendment, which reserves to the states all powers not specifically granted to the national government or prohibited to the states. In fact, it is very difficult to identify any field of state activity not intruded on by the national government today. Although the Tenth Amendment is a declaration of the original division of powers between nation and states under the Constitution, the configuration is hardly descriptive of American federalism today.

The Supreme Court has sent mixed messages on the relevance of the Tenth Amendment. A good example of the Court's fickle federalism involves the Fair Labor Standards Act (FLSA). Following forty years of case law that essentially relegated the Tenth Amendment to the basement of federalism, the Court surprisingly ruled in favor of state and local governments in the 1976 case of *National League of Cities v. Usery*. At issue was the constitutionality under the commerce clause of the 1974 amendments to the FLSA, which extended federal minimum wage and maximum hour requirements to state and local employees. In this case, the Court said that Congress did not have the constitutional right to impose wage and hour requirements on employees carrying out basic—or integral—functions, such as law enforcement or firefighting.[15]

But just nine years later, the Court reversed that decision in *Garcia v. San Antonio Metropolitan Transit Authority*. A spate of litigation had not been able to resolve the issue of just which state and local activities are "integral." So the Court overturned its findings in *Usery* and once again applied federal wage and hour laws to nonnational governments—in this specific instance, to a mass transit system run by the city of San Antonio.[16] What really offended the states was the written opinion of the Court, in which it excused itself from such future controversies involving state claims against congressional and executive branch power exercised under the commerce clause. Now Congress alone, with little or no judicial oversight, would be allowed to determine, through the political process, how extensively it would intrude on what had previously been state and local prerogatives. One dissenting Supreme Court justice wrote that "all that stands between the remaining essentials of state sovereignty and Congress is the latter's underdeveloped capacity for self-restraint."[17] In the view of some critics, the states were relegated to the status of any other special-interest group and the Tenth Amendment was irrelevant. Other critics more optimistically observed that the narrow 5-to-4 decision could be revisited by a more conservative Supreme Court at a later date.[18]

Sure enough, in 1995, the Court reaffirmed the Tenth Amendment in *U.S. v. Lopez* by recognizing a limit to Congress's power over interstate commerce. Ironically, this case also involved San Antonio, where a high-school student, Alfonso Lopez, was arrested for bringing a handgun to school. He was charged with violating the Gun Free School Zones Act of 1990, which banned the possession of a firearm within 1,000 feet of a school. Here, the Court ruled that in this instance Congress had unconstitutionally extended its power to regulate commerce because there was no connection between the gun law and interstate commerce.[19]

The Court continued to recalibrate the scales of power in favor of the states in a series of rulings beginning in 1997. First, the Court upheld states' authority to incarcerate sexual predators in mental institutions after their criminal sentences had been served.[20] Next, the Court ruled that Congress offended "the very principle of separate state sovereignty" by requiring local police to conduct background checks on people who want to purchase handguns.[21] More recently, the Court affirmed the right of state and local governments to seize private land for commercial development[22] and the authority of states to grant tax breaks and other financial inducements to attract and keep businesses.[23] And as noted above, the Court overturned the power of Congress to mandate that states extend Medicaid benefits to a new—and large—segment of their citizenry.

Recent rulings based on the *Eleventh* Amendment have revived the notion of the sovereign immunity of the states. According to this doctrine, which dates back to the Middle Ages, a king (the state) cannot be sued without his (its) consent (the Eleventh Amendment protects states from lawsuits by citizens of other states or foreign nations). Supreme Court decisions have upheld the sovereign immunity of the states from being sued in federal courts in cases involving lawsuits by Indian tribes[24] and discrimination against older or disabled employees.[25] The Court also protected the states against private complaints taken before federal agencies.[26] But in another case, the Court restricted the states' Eleventh Amendment immunity under the Americans with Disabilities Act.[27]

Federalism and the Courts Today The Supreme Court under Chief Justice William Rehnquist (1986–2005) clearly and decisively positioned itself on the side of the states in most conflicts with the national government. However, the Supreme Court does not decide unilaterally in favor of the states in all cases, notwithstanding one justice's complaint that the majority has become "[a] mindless dragon that indiscriminately chews gaping holes in federal statutes." In many cases that involve federalism, there are other, sometimes more compelling issues that the Court chooses to prioritize. For example, the Court limited the authority of the states to regulate tobacco advertising,[28] ruled that federal laws trump state laws with respect to product liability claims and certain restrictions on voting,[29] and held that states cannot under federal law compel coal-burning power plants to reduce their greenhouse emissions.[30] In these and many other cases, business interests, ideology, and partisanship sometimes trump federalism.

During the Rehnquist Court, a large majority of the Court's decisions in federalism cases were by a fragile 5-to-4 margin. Two pro-state justices, William Rehnquist and Sandra Day O'Connor, left the bench in 2005. The federalism feelings of today's Chief Justice John Roberts and other recently appointed justices Samuel Alito, Sonia Sotomayor, and Elena Kagan are not clearly defined.[31] For instance, in deciding that corporations—like individuals—have free political speech rights, the Roberts Court effectively abrogated states' authority to limit corporate and nonprofit campaign contributions directly to or in the interests of candidates in state and local elections; struck down Arizona's and other states' voter registration laws;[32] and held unanimously that Massachusetts' 35-foot abortion clinic protest buffer zone violated the First Amendment by limiting free speech.[33]

Pivoting in a 2012 ruling on the Affordable Care Act ("Obamacare"), the Roberts Court held that the federal government cannot force the states to expand Medicaid funding or penalize them for not doing so. American federalism, by its nature, is ambiguous: It "was born in ambiguity, it institutionalizes ambiguity in our form of government, and changes in it tend to be ambiguous, too."[34] Judicial intervention in the affairs of state and local governments has not rendered them mere administrative appendages or relics of the past. But federal intrusions into the affairs of state and local governments continue to be burdensome and unwelcome, and the states are pushing back through resisting intrusive federal laws and regulations.[35] The Tenth and Eleventh Amendments have been useful weapons for fending off federal encroachments on the power of state and local officials, but those weapons can be shattered by a single justice's change of heart or a new appointment to the bench.

Models of Federalism

LO 2.3

To be able to describe the principal models of federalism that attempt to explain the nature of federal-state-local relationships.

Perceptions of the role of the states in the federal system have shifted from time to time throughout our history. Those who study the federal system have generally described these perceptions through various models or metaphors which attempt to present federalism's complexity in a form that is intuitively understandable. Such models have been used both to enhance understanding and, when opportunities arise, to pursue ideological and partisan objectives. One complete inventory uncovered 326 models of federalism,[36] but only the best-known ones are reviewed here to demonstrate that the U.S. federal system and people's perceptions of it change over time.

DUAL FEDERALISM (1787–1932)

dual federalism

Model in which the responsibilities and activities of the national and state governments are separate and distinct.

The model of **dual federalism** holds that the national and state governments are sovereign and equal within their respective spheres of authority as set forth in the Constitution. The national government exercises those powers specifically designated to it, and the remainder are reserved for the states. The nation and the states are viewed as primarily competitive, not cooperative, in their relationships with one another. The metaphor is that of a layer cake, with two separate colored layers, one on top of the other.

Dual federalism, which has its roots in the compact theory, was dominant for the first 145 years of U.S. federalism, although the Civil War and other events led to substantial modifications of the model.[37] Until 1860, the functions of the national government remained largely restricted to the delegated powers. Federal financial assistance to the states was extremely limited. The states had the dominant influence on the everyday lives of their citizens, acting almost unilaterally in areas such as elections, education, economic development, labor relations, and criminal and family law.[38] After the Civil War shattered secession and dealt the compact theory of state-centered federalism a death blow, the nation-centered view became paramount.

COOPERATIVE FEDERALISM (1933–1964)

The selection of a specific date for the demise of dual federalism is rather subjective, but 1933, when Franklin D. Roosevelt became president, is a reasonable estimate. Roosevelt's New Deal buried dual federalism by expanding national authority over commerce, taxation, and the economy.

Cooperative federalism recognizes the sharing of responsibilities and financing by all levels of government. Beginning with the Great Depression, the national government increasingly worked with states and localities to provide jobs and social welfare, develop the nation's infrastructure, and promote economic development.

The cooperative aspects of this era were measured in governmental finances. The national government spent huge amounts of money to alleviate the ravages of the Great Depression and to get the U.S. economic machinery back into gear. Total federal expenditures rose from 2.5 percent of the gross national product (GNP) in 1929 to 18.7 percent just thirty years later, far surpassing the growth in state and local spending during the same period. The number of federal grants-in-aid rose from twelve in 1932, with a value of $193 million, to twenty-six five years later, with a value of $2.66 billion. A substantial amount of the federal aid was sent directly to local governments, particularly counties and school districts. The variety of grant programs also exploded, with grants for maternal and child health, old-age assistance, fire control, treatment of venereal disease, public housing, road and bridge construction, and wildlife conservation.

CONTEMPORARY VARIATIONS ON COOPERATIVE FEDERALISM (SINCE 1964)

The broad theme of cooperative federalism has many variations. All of them stress intergovernmental sharing. Among these variations are creative federalism and new federalism.

Creative federalism was devised by President Lyndon B. Johnson to promote his dream of a Great Society. Johnson sought to build the Great Society through a massive national government attack on the most serious problems facing the nation: poverty, crime, poor health care, and inadequate education,

cooperative federalism
A model of federalism that stresses the linkages and joint arrangements among the three levels of government.

creative federalism
A model of cooperative federalism in which many new grants-in-aid, including direct national-local financial arrangements, were made.

among others. The weapon for the attack was the federal grant-in-aid. More than 200 new grants were put into place during the five years of Johnson's presidency. Johnson's policy of vast government spending bypassed the states in distributing funds directly to cities and counties for many of the new programs, a major change. Understandably, the states did not appreciate losing influence over how localities could spend their national dollars.

New federalism is a model that has been employed with separate but related meanings during different presidencies. The new federalism initiated by President Richard Nixon was intended to restore power to the states and localities and to improve intergovernmental arrangements for delivering services. Among the major policy changes brought about by the Nixon administration were establishment of ten regional councils to coordinate national program administration across the country and granting to states and localities greater flexibility in program spending and decision making.

Ronald Reagan's brand of new federalism, like Nixon's version, sought to give more power and program authority to states and localities, at least in theory. However, Reagan's main goal—to shrink the size of the national government—soon became obvious. Reagan's new federalism initiative won congressional approval to merge fifty-seven categorical grants into nine new block grants and to eliminate another sixty categorical grants. The states got more authority, but the funding for the new block grants decreased almost 25 percent from the previous year's allocation for the separate categorical grants.[39]

Reagan and his congressional allies chipped away steadily at other grant programs in an effort to shrink the size of government and also terminated revenue sharing. Called *general revenue sharing* (GRS) when enacted during the Nixon administration, this program provided funds, with no strings attached, to state and general-purpose local governments (cities, counties, towns, and townships). It was discontinued largely because of the mounting national budget deficit and Congress's desire to exert greater control over, and take more credit for, the way federal monies were spent. A new form of GRS, popularly known as the "stimulus plan," was adopted by Congress in 2009 to help bail out the states from the Great Recession. When these funds expired in 2011, most states' budgets suffered significantly.

In 1994, with the election of Republican majorities in the U.S. House and Senate and also the election of many new Republican governors, new federalism came back in style with impressive force. The new federalists, whose ranks included many Democrats, sought once again to sort out intergovernmental responsibilities. For the first time in recent memory, the states and localities were basically united and working together through a coalition of government interest groups, including the National Governors' Association and the National League of Cities, to design smaller, more efficient government with greater program and policy flexibility for the states and localities.

This planned delegating of power from the federal to state and local governments is termed **devolution**. The constellation of supporters for devolution is impressive. The governors, acting as individuals and through the National Governors' Association, found a sympathetic President Bill Clinton and congressional majority, and a Supreme Court inclined to rule in favor of state authority. Public opinion is generally in favor of greater state and local

new federalism

A model that represents a return of powers and responsibilities to the states.

devolution

The delegating of power and programs from the federal government to state and local governments.

government authority, though it varies over time.[40] Public opinion polls consistently show that citizens believe the state and local governments do a better job than the national government in spending money and delivering services. Together, these powerful forces for devolution reversed more than a century of centralizing tendencies in U.S. federalism. This trend was so striking that it earned the moniker "devolution revolution."

Coercive federalism characterized the actions of the presidency of George W. Bush (2000–2008) and of Republican supporters in Congress, who pre-empted state authority over school testing systems and other aspects of public education, driver's license procedures, and right-to-die decisions; obstructed state laws that permit the medical use of marijuana; and imposed burdensome new homeland security requirements on the states; among other pre-emptive acts. The predominance of business interests in Washington, D.C., appeared to have deterred devolution through what one writer calls "the law of political physics—that for every flurry of state and local business regulations, there is an equal and opposite" effort by business to counter it in the nation's capital.[41] The centralizing tendencies of the "War on Terror" served as a convenient justification for other coercive actions by President Bush and congressional supporters,[42] including citizen surveillance, nationalization of the state national guards, and various mandates that pulled power into the White House. By 2008, state dissatisfaction had reached such a peak that governors from both political parties denounced the coercive federalism of Washington, D.C., and increasingly pushed back by roundly criticizing some actions, ignoring others, and litigating still others.[43]

With the economic crisis of 2008–2011, a mild version of coercive federalism lived on in the administration of President Barack Obama, on terms somewhat more acceptable to state and local governments. Obama's federalism tendencies were to mix coercion with collaboration, depending on the issue at hand.[44] This hybrid approach "mixed money, mandates and flexibility in new and distinctive ways."[45] For example, the American Recovery and Reinvestment Act, designed to inject money and jobs to stimulate the struggling economy, permitted flexibility to the states in how they spent the money, while mandating strong spending and accountability provisions. Yet the Obama approach to health care reform and climate change policy was highly centralized and unpalatable to many of the states. Thus, Obama federalism was more opportunistic than theory- or principle-driven.

Perhaps the most appropriate metaphor today is "fragmented federalism."[46] Political polarization at all levels of government is producing highly diverse approaches to policy making, as witnessed in same-sex marriage, immigration, abortion, and drug policy. With the national government tied up in partisan and ideological knots since at least 2012, the states have enjoyed greater latitude in pursuing their own policy interests and inclinations.

Intergovernmental Relations

Whatever the current trend in federal-state-local relations, both cooperative and coercive activities are always in evidence. Relationships between the states and the American Indian tribes present an interesting example of the presence of both.

Coercive federalism
A form of federalism in which the national government uses regulations, mandates, conditions, preemptions, and other actions to impose national priorities on the states.

TRIBAL GOVERNMENTS

With the arrival of the Europeans, the estimated 7–10 million people who lived in what is now the United States soon were severely depleted by warfare, disease, and famine. Hundreds of treaties, statutes, and other agreements notwithstanding, the Native Americans were eventually deprived of their traditional lands and isolated on reservations. Today, some 5.1 million people identify themselves as Native American, belonging to 566 recognized tribes. About one-third of them continue to live on tribal reservations, mostly in the western portion of the United States. The Navajo Nation, for instance, has a population of more than 250,000 and covers some 17 million acres extending from northwest New Mexico to northeast Arizona and southeast Utah. At the other extreme of the tribal spectrum are the Mashantucket Pequots. Registering just thirty-five to forty members with "only the barest trace of Indian descent"[47] when officially recognized by the federal government in the 1990s, the Pequots today occupy about 1,250 acres in Connecticut, where they operate Foxwoods Resort Casino— once the largest and most profitable such establishment in North America, though today threatened by nearby tribal competition. On average, however, Native Americans are the poorest and least healthy group in the United States.

Tribes are semisovereign nations exercising self-government on their reservations. They are under the general authority and supervision of Congress and are subject to the federal courts and the U.S. Bill of Rights, but their legal relationship with the states is complex. Tribal governments are permitted to regulate their internal affairs, hold elections, and enforce their own laws, codes, and constitutions under congressional supervision. States are generally prevented from taxing or regulating tribes or extending judicial power over them. Off the reservation, however, Native Americans are, with some exceptions such as local hunting and fishing rights, subject to the same laws as any other state residents. They have the right to vote in tribal, federal, and state elections.

Recently, the tribes and the states have adopted a cooperative relationship[48] to pursue certain interests, such as fishing and hunting rights and regulation of reservation gaming. The highly lucrative gaming enterprises of some tribes have advanced tribal political interests and clout by providing financial resources to politicians and others. Many tribal governments have developed policy and lobbying expertise to advance gaming and other enterprise activities.[49]

Occasionally, however, interactions among tribal governments, the state, and nearby local governments are testy. Some tribes seek to recover ancestral lands from present occupants. Actions concerning tribal land use may conflict with local zoning or state environmental policy. The tax-free sale of gasoline, alcohol, and tobacco products on the reservation diminishes state sales tax revenues. And tribes sometimes offer casino games that are prohibited under state law. When conflicts arise, states and tribal governments may sort out their differences through compacts. Otherwise, Congress may be asked to enter the fray.

INTERSTATE COOPERATION

Cooperation under the Constitution
Four formal provisions exist for cooperation among the states:

1. *The full faith and credit clause* of the Constitution binds every citizen of every state to the laws and policies of other states. This means, among many other things, that a person who has a legitimate debt in North Dakota will be made to pay even if he moves to Montana. Crossing a state boundary does not alter a legal obligation. The courts have interpreted full faith and credit to apply to contracts, wills, divorces, and many other legalities.

   An interesting test of full faith and credit arises from civil union and gay marriage laws. Must Alabama honor Vermont's gay marriage law when a gay couple moves from Montpelier to Birmingham? Can a gay couple obtain a divorce in another state? The courts continue to ponder these questions. *The interstate rendition clause* begins where full faith and credit leave off, covering persons convicted of criminal violations. Governors are required to extradite (return) fugitives to the state in which they were found guilty or are under indictment (although in certain cases they refuse).

2. *The privileges and immunities clause* states that "the citizens of each state shall be entitled to all privileges and immunities of citizens in the several states." This clause was intended by the Framers to prevent any state from discriminating against citizens of another state who happen to be traveling or temporarily dwelling outside their own state's borders. Of course, states do discriminate against nonresidents in matters such as out-of-state tuition, hunting and fishing license fees, and residency requirements for voting. The Supreme Court has upheld these and other minor discrepancies, as long as the "fundamental rights" of nonresidents are not violated. The issue of same-sex marriage raised questions before a 2015 U.S. Supreme Court decision upheld the right of gay couples to wed.

3. Finally, the *interstate compact clause* authorizes the states to negotiate compacts, which are binding agreements between two or more states that address important cross-boundary issues. Early interstate compacts were used to settle boundary disputes. About 175 of them are in effect today in various areas, including rights to interstate water resources, pest control, riverboat gambling, and education.[50]

Informal Cooperation among the States
Interstate cooperation can be facilitated through several informal methods. One example is the establishment of regional interstate commissions such as the Appalachian Regional Commission (ARC), which was created by federal law in 1965 to attack poverty in the states of Appalachia. Another example is found in the Mississippi Delta region, where several states adopted a ten-year economic development plan to help pull the area out of its own cycle of poverty.

In addition, states have developed uniform laws to help manage common problems ranging from child support to Medicaid cheating.[51] Interstate cooperation also occurs through information sharing among elected and appointed officials and the organizations to which they belong, such as the National

Governors' Association and the National Conference of State Legislatures. It may take place in legal actions, as demonstrated by state attorneys general who unite to file class action lawsuits against various corporate malefactors and even federal agencies. Or one state may contract with another for a service, as Hawaii does with Arizona for health care. States have also marshaled their resources in cooperative efforts to reduce greenhouse emissions, establish common core curriculum education standards in their schools, and protect interstate fisheries.

But just as states may cooperate, they also compete for firms, tax revenues, tourists, and gamblers. Some of their fiercest conflicts are joined over water. Vital for human and farm animal consumption, fishing and shell fishing, fracking for oil and gas, industry, electric power generation, transportation, and many other critical uses, water has elicited interstate disputes since the earliest days of the Republic. Such conflicts have been settled in a variety of ways including memoranda of understanding, enactment of identical or similar laws, voluntary associations, and litigation before the U.S. Supreme Court.

But water wars continue to rage as population increases and drought appears more frequently and persistently in some parts of the United States. Usually, states can resolve their concerns and differences rather informally. In more complex cases involving more than two disputants, the interstate compact is the method of choice.[52] Twenty-seven interstate compacts have been ratified by states and Congress to address water issues.[53] Recent examples include the Great Lakes Compact (eight states and two Canadian provinces) and the Colorado River Compact (seven states). But what if the states cannot reach an acceptable solution to water problems?

When the states cannot settle their own differences, the federal government becomes the final and binding arbitrator. Although Congress has the power to act through statute, the most likely venue is the federal courts. For instance, Georgia is at loggerheads with Tennessee over a water-related issue. The Georgia–Tennessee border was originally drawn in 1818 using primitive measuring devices later found to have placed the border 1.1 miles northward from where it should have been. The border should have been delineated up to the middle of the Tennessee River, thereby permitting the thirsty Peach State to extract water supplies from the river. Tennessee asserted that the "law of adverse possession" meant that the original boundary should remain the de facto border. Georgia disagreed. The issue remained unresolved in 2015 as it proceeded through the federal courts. In Oklahoma and Texas, the "Red River Showdown" raged over the Red River water basin for years until the Supreme Court settled the issue in 2013.[54]

Such water wars are illustrative of intergovernmental conflict that ignites local passions, and in some instances may provoke head scratching or ruffle feathers, such as in the case of California's ban of the sale of eggs from hens kept in tiny cages. Six egg-exporting states have challenged the "egg law" in federal courts. As Alabama's attorney general crowed , "It is preposterous and quite simply wrong for California to tell Alabama how we must produce eggs."[55] Importantly, such conflicts demonstrate that federalism "lives" and indeed will always be a work in progress—a journey, not a destination.

INTERGOVERNMENTAL FINANCIAL RELATIONS

LO 2.4

To develop comprehension of the complex nature and tools of intergovernmental financial relations.

Revenues are the funds that governments have at their disposal. They are derived from taxes, fees and charges, and transfers from other levels of government. Expenditures are the ways in which governmental revenues are disbursed. Governments spend money to operate programs, build public facilities, and pay off debts.

The **grant-in-aid** is the primary mechanism for transferring money from the national to the state and local governments. The national government makes grants available for several reasons: to redistribute resources, to encourage policy experimentation, to establish minimum policy standards, and to achieve national goals. But grants (they number more than 1,100) are primarily designed to help meet the needs of state and local governments, including environmental protection, transportation, education, health care, and security. Federal grant outlays totaled about $643 billion in 2014.

Discretion of Recipients There are two major variations in grants: the amount of discretion (independence) the recipient has in determining how to spend the money and the conditions under which the grant is awarded. A **categorical grant** can be used by the recipient government only for a narrowly defined purpose, such as food stamps or Medicaid supplements.

Block grants are *broad-based grants*; that is, they can be used anywhere within a functional area such as transportation, energy efficiency, or health care. The difference between categorical and block grants is that the recipient government decides how block grants will be spent. For instance, a local school system can decide whether the purchase of distance education technology is more important than buying microscopes for the science laboratory. Today there are some 625 grants in existence, including 21 block grants. By giving nonnational governments considerable flexibility in responding to pressing needs and preferred goals, the grant mechanisms assume that state and local governments can make fair and rational choices among competing claims.

Conditions for Grants Grants also vary in the manner in which they are allocated. A **formula grant** makes funding available automatically, based on state and local conditions such as poverty level or unemployment rate. A **project grant** is awarded to selected applicants based on the granting agency's assessment of the strength of competing proposals. Block grants are distributed on a formula basis; categorical grants can be either formula- or project-based.

Another factor also affects intergovernmental financial relations: the existence of *matching requirements*. Most federal grants require that the recipient government use its own resources to pay a certain percentage of program costs. This arrangement is designed to stimulate state and local spending on programs deemed to be in the national interest and to discourage participation in a program simply because money is available. For example, if a state government wants funding through the Boating Safety Financial Assistance program administered by the U.S. Department of Transportation, it must contribute 50 percent itself. And for a state government to participate in a wind

grant-in-aid
An intergovernmental transfer of funds or other assets, subject to conditions.

categorical grant
A form of financial aid from one level of government to another to be used for a narrowly defined purpose.

block grant
A form of financial aid from one level of government to another for use in a broad, functional area.

formula grant
A funding mechanism that automatically allocates monies based on conditions in the recipient government.

project grant
A competitive funding mechanism that awards monies based on the strength of an applicant government's proposal.

energy demonstration project, a 50 percent match is required. In each case, the recipient government's commitment to boating safety or renewable energy is likely to be high because of the joint funding.

LO 2.5

To understand finances as a source of friction and conflict between the three levels of government.

Federal Purse Strings

Federalism today turns less on theory and more on money. The distribution of intergovernmental monies and the conditions attached to them define the distribution of governmental power and authority. Federalism is a matter not only of which level of government will do what, but also of which level will pay for it. Some have called this "fend-for-yourself" federalism, with each jurisdiction essentially on its own in a Darwinian struggle for financial survival.

THE IMPORTANCE OF FEDERAL FUNDS

Figure 2.2 provides a historical look at national grant-in-aid expenditures. The growing proportion of national dollars in the total expenditures of states and localities should be placed in the context of the fact that aid to states and localities consumes a relatively small share of the federal government's budget

FIGURE 2.2

Historical Trends in Federal Grant-in-Aid Outlays

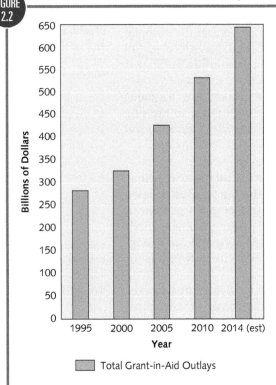

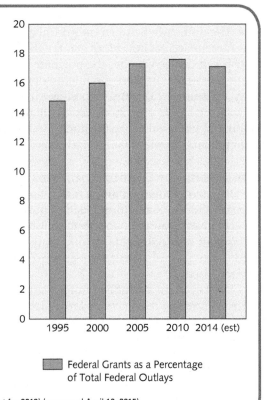

Total Grant-in-Aid Outlays

Federal Grants as a Percentage of Total Federal Outlays

SOURCE: U.S. Census Bureau, http://www.whitehouse.gov (OMB budget for 2013) (accessed April 12, 2015).

Federal Aid to State and Local Governments: Amounts and Percentages by Major Function, 2014 (in billions of dollars)

FIGURE 2.3

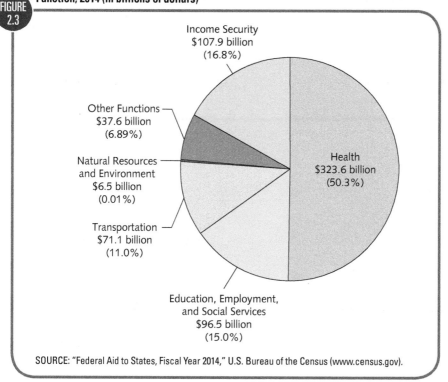

SOURCE: "Federal Aid to States, Fiscal Year 2014," U.S. Bureau of the Census (www.census.gov).

(only 4 percent of GDP). In 2009, for the first time in history, federal aid became the single largest source of total state and local revenues, as the national government pumped billions of dollars into state and local treasuries to stimulate the economy out of its prolonged slide.

The Washington-funded portion of state and local government expenditures has been around 31 percent recently, representing a critical source of financial support for major functions of nonnational governments (see Figure 2.3). However, the funds are not spread evenly across the country (see Figure 2.4). Federal financial support represents 45.8 percent of Mississippi's general fund revenue, but only 20 percent of Alaska's. (On a per-capita basis, Alaska actually receives more in federal support than any other state.) These amounts shot up in 2009–2010 as a federal stimulus package injected additional billions into state and local coffers for quick pass-through for job creation, but then plummeted in 2011 when the spigot was turned down. Then in 2013, federal budget "sequestrations" imposed even further cuts, causing serious hardships for recipients of some state and local services.[56]

In competition with forty-nine others, each state battles in Congress over its share of grant allocations, which are affected by factors such as military installations and other federal offices and installations in the state. The states attempt to influence competitive project grant awards, and they lobby Congress to adjust the weighting of certain factors in formula grants in their

FIGURE
2.4

Federal Aid to State Governments in 2012

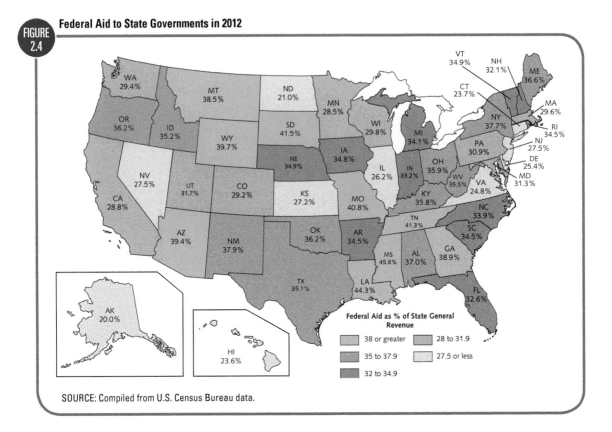

Federal Aid as % of State General Revenue

- 38 or greater
- 35 to 37.9
- 32 to 34.9
- 28 to 31.9
- 27.5 or less

SOURCE: Compiled from U.S. Census Bureau data.

favor. State and local influence is wielded by their representatives sitting in Congress and through various actions by elected state and local officials and their Washington lobbyists.

National expenditures in nongrant forms also affect state and local economies substantially. In the nongrant category are payments to individuals (representing about 65 percent of total federal grants today, up from 36 percent in 1980), notably through the Social Security system; Medicaid payments; purchases by the national government; and wages and salaries of federal employees, most of whom work outside of Washington, D.C. In this sense, federal expenditures emphasize people more than places, at the expense of other types of federal aid to states and localities.

HERE'S THE MONEY AND HERE'S WHAT YOU MUST DO WITH IT: MANDATES AND PRE-EMPTIONS

Although many voices cry, "Let the states and localities do it," Congress continues to impose mandates and pre-empt the states' actions. In addition, Congress includes set-asides and cost ceilings in block grants. Old habits die hard, and one of Congress's oldest habits is to place requirements and conditions on the states. Washington-based politicians may claim to support state power in principle, but when it conflicts with other priorities, devolution takes a back seat. States, of course, have the option to turn down a federal grant, and occasionally they do just that. Governors of Florida, Ohio, and Wisconsin recently left on the table billions of dollars in federal grants for high-speed rail.[57] And some twenty-seven states have refused 100 percent federal funding for Medicaid expansion under the Affordable Care Act, forgoing tens of billions of dollars. But more typically, the money is accepted, along with the conditions attached to it.

Federal mandates are especially burdensome when they are entirely or partially unfunded—that is, when the national government requires the states and localities to take action but does not fully pay for it, and the states and localities must foot the bill. The Affordable Care Act imposed approximately $20 billion in new Medicaid costs on the states by requiring them to expand coverage and eligibility levels and to set up health insurance exchanges. More than half the states sued the federal government to block the law. Oppositional states heaved a sigh of relief when the 2012 Supreme Court decision freed them from the expansion of coverage, thus permitting to forgo federal Medicaid dollars.

The total cost of these mandate millstones hanging round the necks of states and localities has been estimated to be $34 billion.[58] Mounting opposition to mandates without money finally convinced Congress to enact the Unfunded Mandate Reform Act of 1995 (UMRA), which provides that any bill imposing a mandate of more than $50 million (adjusted in 2013 to $75 million) on a state or local government must include a cost estimate. If passed, the legislation is supposed to include sufficient funds to pay for the mandate. Indications are that proposed laws containing unfunded mandates are facing tougher scrutiny in Congress than before and that Congress is taking a more consultative approach with state and local elected officials. However, UMRA is riddled with loopholes and members of Congress still seize opportunities to revert to their mandating ways. Since UMRA was adopted, eighteen mandates have exceeded the dollar threshold by billions of dollars.[59]

As noted earlier, *pre-emption* represents another intrusion of the national government into the state sphere. It takes two forms: *total* pre-emption, whereby the national government seizes all regulatory authority for a given function from states and localities; and *partial* pre-emption, whereby the national government establishes minimum national standards for state-implemented programs. Both forms prevent states from doing what they want. One example of a totally pre-emptive action is the Americans with Disabilities Act, which requires states and localities to make physical and occupational accommodation for disabled persons. A more current example is federal litigation to strike down highly restrictive immigration laws in Arizona, Alabama, and other states. Many partial pre-emptions involve environmental protection, whereby states may regulate pollution emissions as long as state standards are at least as stringent as those of the federal government.

Thus, when mandates and pre-emptions are taken into consideration, a less positive picture of intergovernmental relations emerges. To the states and localities, it seems that the country has shifted from cooperative federalism to coercive federalism, or, in the words of former Governor Ben Nelson of Nebraska, demoted states from significant policy makers to branch managers "of a behemoth central government."[60] The result has been an escalation of federal-state conflict that is probably at the highest level since the Civil War.

federal mandate

A requirement that a state or local government undertake a specific activity or provide a particular service as a condition of funding.

The Future of Federalism

For the states and localities, national political gridlock has meant a golden opportunity to reverse more than a century of centralizing forces. They have taken up the slack in the federal system, busily innovating, developing, and implementing policies in a great variety of fields. Public opinion polls consistently show that there is greater trust in state and local governments than in the federal government.[61] As laboratories of democracy, state and local governments have designed and experimented with numerous policies that later have served as models for other states and for Congress. Research shows that the states actively learn from one another in a targeted and systematic way. For instance, states have recently pioneered policy initiatives on prescription drug costs, immigration control, stem-cell research, nanotechnology, and global climate change, among many other fields. Lobbyists who once focused their attentions on Washington, D.C., are now spending hundreds of millions of dollars to woo state legislators. Hordes of lobbyists representing the health care, insurance, and banking and finance industries and other special interests have been attracted to state capitals like fleas to a dog.

States are definitively not all on the same page. Political party polarization, one-party control of state governments, and basic policy beliefs have led to markedly diverse policy approaches. Groups of states have both legalized or banned medical marijuana, the death penalty, gun control, and abortion rights. It is as if politics abhors the policy vacuum that has been Congress and therefore flows into the states and localities.

Journalists and many citizen routinely refer "to 'the government' as if there were only one—the Big One."[62] But the United States is a nation of many governments, and Washington is not the best location for addressing all the nation's complex policy problems. Whereas centrally designing and implementing policies and programs can sometimes be the best approach, it can also result in wasteful and ineffective one-size-fits-all government. The trend in government, as well as in business, is to decentralize decision making to the lowest feasible level of the organization. For the U.S. federal system, that means shifting decision making to the states and localities and even, in some instances, to nonprofit organizations and citizens' groups.

At the very time that the state and local governments are most needed as policy leaders and problem solvers, powerful social and economic forces seriously threaten state and local governments' capability. The collapse of the financial and housing markets and the ensuing free-fall in the U.S. economy in 2008–2011 produced frightening revenue declines in nearly all the states, putting at risk children, the poor, and the infirm. Ranks of Medicaid recipients climbed, as did the homeless. Following expiration of the federal stimulus funds, record budget deficits and budget sequestration severely depressed federal funding for state and local grants-in-aid. Yet the problems of the poor, the long-term jobless, the homeless, and undocumented immigrants are great. And the growing disparity of wealth and income threatens our great reservoir of political and social stability: the middle class.

For its part, the federal government provokes criticism for tying the hands of the states and localities with mandates, pre-emptions, and confused and

It's Your Turn

Should the States Legalize Marijuana?

The possession, cultivation, and use of marijuana for any purpose are prohibited under the federal Controlled Substances Act. An estimated 20 million Americans have been arrested, and many of them jailed for long periods of time for marijuana offenses over the past fifty years. Millions of law enforcement, court, and prison dollars have gone into marijuana offenses. Yet the herb is relatively easy to acquire and is widely available throughout the United States. Despite federal law, twenty-three states have legalized prescription-based medical consumption of marijuana and four-teen states have decriminalized possession. Recently, Colorado, Washington, Alaska, Oregon, and the District of Columbia have legalized the recreational sale and use of marijuana.

PROS	CONS
The money now spent on enforcement and justice could be diverted to treatment and prevention programs.	Legalization could lead to higher use by teens and serve as a stepping stone to more harmful drugs.
Marijuana arrests and prosecutions disproportionately target minorities.	Citizens in some localities vehemently oppose legalization in their communities.
A sales tax on marijuana is expected to bring in tens of millions of dollars in those states that have legalized it.	Medical studies have indicated that heavy marijuana use affects the young brain, and causes memory problems.
Marijuana has been shown to ease symptoms of nausea from chemotherapy and other invasive treatments, control seizures, and to have other medical benefits.	Wider use of marijuana would lead to more impaired driving and endanger the public.
Marijuana is much less dangerous to health than alcohol, which is legal and regulated.	Traffickers could purchase marijuana in a legal state and sell it in a neighboring state that prohibits its sale and possession.
A majority of Americans (around 58 percent) now favor legalization, according to recent polls.	Marijuana remains illegal under federal law; a shift in congressional, presidential, or Justice Department sentiment could result in aggressive enforcement, throwing state policies into disarray.
Marijuana is widely available anyway on the street, much of it controlled by drug gangs. Legalization would take it out of the hands of criminals.	There are cases in which children have eaten marijuana cookies and other edibles mistakenly left within their grasp, and become very ill.
	Colorado prices 1/8 ounce at $50–60, more than black market marijuana. A black market will continue to thrive even with legalization.

conflicting policy directives. Most state and local governments *want* to become more creative, but they are also being *forced* to, so that they can figure out how to implement and pay for increasingly onerous federally mandated require-ments. The result is an increasingly state and local policy world. But should it be? See the It's Your Turn feature above.

Nigel Spicer arranges the bakery of marijuana brownies and treats at "Green Oasis" medical marijuana dispensary in Los Angeles.

Even homeland security, usually considered to be primarily a national government responsibility, actually calls for more—not less—intergovernmental cooperation. State and local governments play critical roles in all four key functions of homeland security: prevention, preparedness, response, and recovery. Local governments are first responders to any sort of domestic disaster, natural or human-caused, whereas states provide crisis management and emergency services while coordinating and steering recovery efforts.

In homeland security, disaster response, and almost all other fields, what the states and localities are demanding is cooperative, consultative relationships and flexible or facilitative federalism, in which the national government helps them through selective funding for technical assistance—a federalism in which they are treated as partners in governance, not as just another self-absorbed interest group. It is something of a paradox that even as state and local governments have assumed the primary policymaking duties in the federal system, their influence with the national government has diminished. Many of their calls for national action, such as permitting state online sales taxes and adopting a coherent national immigration policy, have fallen on the deaf ears of a navel-gazing, unresponsive Congress and president.[63] As Andrew Romanoff, Colorado's speaker of the house, put it, "We want the federal government to recognize that there are problems that are best solved at the state level. Either give us the tools or remove the barriers so we can solve the problem. The worst thing the feds can do is say it's your problem and we're going to make it harder for you to solve it."[64]

In fairness to the national government, remember that much federal intervention has been in response to state failures to govern effectively and fairly. Corruption, racial prejudice and exclusion, and rampant parochialism, among other shortcomings, have prompted presidential, congressional, and judicial interventions that have, on the whole, helped the states move to the much higher plane they inhabit today.

The question of the balance of power and responsibility in U.S. federalism is no less important now than it was when the representatives of the colonies met in Philadelphia's Independence Hall, first to draft the Articles of Confederation and later to design the Constitution. The focus of the debate has shifted, however, to a pragmatic interest in how the responsibility of governing should be sorted out among the three levels of government. As pointed out by an insightful observer of U.S. government, "[the] American federal system has never been static. It has changed radically over the years, as tides of centralization and decentralization have altered the balance of power and the allocation of functions among the different levels of government."[65]

Centripetal forces steadily pull things to the federal center. The fiscal crisis, continuing fears of terrorist attacks, foreign wars, the Ebola threat, among other issues, encourage a centralizing direction, yet for many years, Congress has been deadlocked along partisan and ideological lines. American federalism tends to oscillate with national government policy activism—when Washington, D.C., wanes, the states wax. When national government policy activism is at a low level, the states step in to fill the gap.[66] The hope, then, is for a new era of cooperative federalism to supplant the coercive and fragmented federalism of previous years.

Chapter Recap

- U.S. federalism is an ongoing experiment in governance.

- A fundamental question is: What is the proper balance of power and responsibility between the national government and the states?

- Actions of the courts, Congress, and the executive branch have expanded powers of the national government.

- Over time, the trend has generally been in the direction of a stronger national government. Beginning in the early 1980s, however, there was a resurgence of the state and local governments as political and policy actors. States and localities continue to lead today.

- The power relationships among the three levels of government are described by various models, including dual and cooperative federalism. The operative model is cooperative federalism, under the variant known as new federalism, but intergovernmental relations have become increasingly coercive and fragmented.

- A key concept in federalism is intergovernmental relations, particularly financial relationships among the three levels of government.

- The national government imposes certain controversial requirements on grants-in-aid, including mandates and pre-emptions.

KEY TERMS

unitary system *(p. 26)*
confederacy *(p. 26)*
federal system *(p. 26)*
enumerated (delegated) powers *(p. 30)*
concurrent powers *(p. 30)*
nation-centered federalism *(p. 30)*
state-centered federalism *(p. 30)*
reserved powers *(p. 30)*
Tenth Amendment *(p. 30)*

compact theory *(p. 31)*
national supremacy clause *(p. 32)*
necessary and proper clause *(p. 32)*
implied powers *(p. 32)*
commerce clause *(p. 33)*
general welfare clause *(p. 33)*
Fourteenth Amendment *(p. 34)*
Sixteenth Amendment *(p. 35)*
federal pre-emption *(p. 35)*

dual federalism *(p. 38)*
cooperative federalism *(p. 39)*
creative federalism *(p. 39)*
new federalism *(p. 40)*
devolution *(p. 40)*
coercive federalism *(p. 41)*
grant-in-aid *(p. 45)*
categorical grant *(p. 45)*
block grant *(p. 45)*
formula grant *(p. 45)*
project grant *(p. 45)*
federal mandate *(p. 49)*

INTERNET RESOURCES

Examples of unfunded mandates are found on a Heritage Foundation webpage at **www. regulation .org/states.html**.

Federalism decisions by the U.S. Supreme Court may be reviewed at the Council of State Governments' website at **www.statenews.org or www .csg.org**. For other sites with federalism content, see **www.governing.com** and **www.stateline.org**.

For current information on relationships among the three levels of government, see **www.governing.com**. The leading scholarly journal on federalism is *Publius: The Journal of Federalism.*

The website **www.census.gov** has comparative data on the states and localities, particularly state and local finances. It is not particularly user-friendly—you'll have to dig around for what you seek.

Information on tribal governments and politics may be acquired at **www.tribal-institute.org and www.narf.org**.

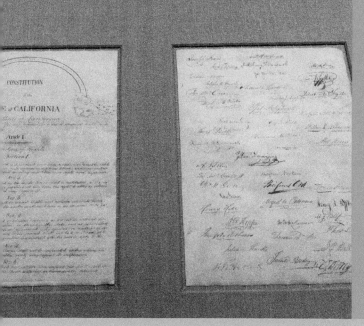

State Constitutions: The Fundamental Rules of State Government

S tate constitutions are alike in many important respects, but they are decidedly different in others. Consider recent public votes on state constitutional changes. Mississippi finally outlawed slavery by passing the Thirteenth Amendment to the U.S. Constitution. A "Right to Farm" amendment was approved in Missouri. Alabama voters, finding that Sharia (Islamic) law was a threat to legal processes in the Yellowhammer State, joined those of six other states in banning its use. Vermont became the third state to legalize assisted suicide for the terminally ill. These actions demonstrate that constitutions are, in their essence, political documents—products of state history, culture, events, economics, and above all, the clash of interests.

LEARNING OBJECTIVES

3.1 To understand the origins, evolution, and purposes of state constitutions.

3.2 To explain how state constitutions have evolved to meet the challenges of modern governance and how they have not.

3.3 To comprehend the basic content of state constitutions and how they compare with the U.S. Constitution.

3.4 To be able to describe the formal and informal methods for changing state constitutions.

LO 3.1

To understand the origins, evolution, and purposes of state constitutions.

The History and Development of the Fundamental Documents

All state constitutions both distribute and constrain political power among groups and regions. They set forth the basic framework and operating rules for government, allocate power to the three branches, establish the scope of state and local governmental authority, protect individual rights, and address various public policy concerns.[1] Constitutions represent the **fundamental law** of a state, superior to statutory law. They provide a set of rules for running state government, and those who master the regulations and procedures have a distinct advantage over novices. Everything that a state government does and represents is rooted in its constitution. Constitutions do not describe the full reality of a political system, but they do provide a window through which to perceive its reality. Only the federal Constitution and federal statutes take priority over state constitutions.

To most people, however, constitutional law still means the federal document. State constitutions are often neglected in secondary school and college history and even American Government courses. Astonishingly, one national survey discovered that 51 percent of Americans were not aware that their state had its own constitution.[2] Yet state constitutions are distinctly different from the federal constitution in their length, inclusion of policy concerns, and relative ease of amendment or revision.

In the U.S. system of *dual constitutionalism*, in which there are both national and state constitutions, the national government is supreme within the spheres of authority specifically delegated to it in the U.S. Constitution. Powers granted exclusively to the national government are denied to the states. But the national Constitution is incomplete. It leaves many key constitutional issues to the states, including local finance, public education, and the organization of state and local governments.[3] In theory, state constitutions are supreme for all matters not expressly within the national government's jurisdiction or pre-empted by federal constitutional or statutory law. In practice, however, congressional actions and federal court interpretations have expanded the powers of the national government and, in some cases, eroded the powers of the states. And in reality, many concurrent (shared) powers, such as taxing, spending, and protecting citizens' health and safety, are shared by all levels of government.

The earliest state constitutions were simple documents reflecting an agrarian economy, single-owner businesses, and horse-and-buggy transportation. As American society and the economy changed, the rules of state government also required transformation. Constitutional reform is a regular theme throughout the U.S. experiment in federalism. As a result, state constitutions "are a mine of instruction for the national history of democratic communities. They are distinctive in history, design, and underlying premises."[4]

Some reforms have reflected changing political fortunes. Newly powerful groups have pressed to revise the state constitution to reflect their interests, or one or another political party has gained control of state government and

fundamental law

The basic legal and political document of a state; it prescribes the rules through which government operates.

sought to solidify its power. Constitutional reforms have promoted widely different views of politics and the public interest. In more recent years, some state constitutional revisions have sought to make state government more effective and responsive to shifting social and economic forces. Other revisions have established individual rights such as same-sex marriage and the right to hunt and fish. The fact that constitutions are subject to change also recognizes that human judgment is fallible and human understanding imperfect.[5] Through constitutional reform, states can elevate their role as democratic laboratories and respond to the changing needs and opinions of citizens. This capacity for change is in sharp contrast to the seldom-amended federal Constitution.

The Evolution of State Constitutions

LO 3.2

To explain how state constitutions have evolved to meet the challenges of modern governance and how they have not.

When the states won their independence from Great Britain almost 240 years ago, there was no precedent for writing constitutions. A constitution for the Five Nations of the Iroquois called the Great Binding Law existed, but it was oral and not particularly appropriate for consideration by the people in the colonies.[6] The thirteen colonial charters provided the foundation for the new state constitutions. These were brief documents (around five pages each) that the British Crown had granted to trading companies and individuals to govern settlements in the new territories. As the settlements became full colonies, the charters were expanded to incorporate the "rights of Englishmen"—political and civil rights first enumerated by the Magna Carta in 1215. For territories too remote from their native country to be governed by its laws, these charters also laid down some basic principles of colonial government.[7]

In a sense, the existence of these documents helped fuel the fires of independence. In what was to become Connecticut, early settlers escaping the oppressive rule of the Massachusetts Bay Colony took matters of governance into their own hands. Under the leadership of Thomas Hooker, these ambitious farmers established an independent government free from references to the Crown. The Fundamental Orders of 1639 contended that "the choice of the public magistrates belongs unto the people by God's own allowance. The privilege of election belongs to the people . . . it is in their power, also, to set and limit the bounds and limitations of the power [of elected officials]."[8] Elements of the Fundamental Orders were later incorporated into Connecticut's Royal Charter. Years later, a representative of King James II was sent to take possession of the Royal Charter and unite the New England colonies under the Crown. In a night meeting, as the Charter was laid out on a table before the king's men, the candles suddenly were extinguished. When they were relighted, the document had disappeared. According to legend, a patriot had hidden the Charter in a nearby hollow tree, later to be known as the Charter Oak. Infuriated, the king's men dissolved the colony's government and imposed autocratic rule that lasted many years. But they never found the Royal Charter, which essentially governed Connecticut until the Constitution of 1818 was adopted.[9]

THE FIRST STATE CONSTITUTIONS

In a May 1776 resolution, the Continental Congress instructed the thirteen colonies "to reorganize their governments solely on the basis of 'the authority of the people.'" This task, of critical importance, had never been achieved in human history. How would "the people" write the laws of their states?[10] Following the War of Independence, the former colonies turned their attention to this task, drafting their first constitutions in special revolutionary conventions or in legislative assemblies. Apparently without a sense of irony, the new states put their constitutions into effect immediately, without popular ratification (Massachusetts was an exception).

Making the first state constitutions was not a simple affair. Issues of political philosophy were debated. How would citizens' "natural rights" be defined and protected? How would the principle of popular sovereignty be addressed in words and in practice? Many practical questions had to be answered in constitutional conventions, including the structure of the new government, how and when elections would be held, and how land once owned by the Crown would be distributed.

Territorial integrity was not well defined. For example, in what is now known as Kentucky, people frustrated with Virginia's rule met in 1784 and petitioned the Congress for statehood. It took six years and nine constitutional conventions before Kentucky became a state. Complicating factors causing delay involved the "necessity of communicating across the mountains, the change from the Articles of Confederation to the Constitution of the United States, Indian attacks, [and] the revelation of a plot to have Kentucky secure independence and join Spain."[11]

Other Western territories were constituted as states under terms of the Northwest Ordinance of 1787, which established the principle that the United States would expand westward by drawing boundaries for and admitting new states, rather than simply extending the boundaries of existing states to the West. Each new state had to write its own constitution.

In content, most of these documents simply extended the colonial charters, removing references to the king and inserting a bill of rights. All the documents incorporated the principles of limited government: a weak executive branch, the separation of powers, checks and balances, a bill of rights to protect the people and their property from arbitrary government actions, and (except for Pennsylvania) a bicameral legislature.[12] The earliest constitutions were not truly democratic. Essentially, they called for government by an aristocracy. Office holding and voting, for instance, were restricted to white males of wealth and property.[13]

Only one of the thirteen original state constitutions, that of Massachusetts, survives (although it has been amended 120 times). It is the oldest functioning constitution in the world. Its longevity can be attributed in large part to the foresight of its drafter, John Adams, who grounded the document in extensive research of governments that took him all the way back to the ancients and the Magna Carta. Even after many amendments, the Massachusetts constitution reflects a composite of the wisdom of the foremost political philosophers of the eighteenth century: John Locke, Jean-Jacques Rousseau, and the Baron de Montesquieu.[14] In this enduring document, Massachusetts establishes itself as a commonwealth (from the words *common weal*, meaning "general well-being"), on the principle that its citizens have a right to protect and manage their collective interests. (Kentucky, Pennsylvania, and Virginia are also commonwealths.)[15] Rhode Island was established as "The State of Rhode Island and Providence Plantations."

LEGISLATIVE SUPREMACY

The first state constitutions reflected the Framers' fear and distrust of the executive—a result of their experiences with the colonial governors. The governors were not all tyrants, but because they represented the British Crown and Parliament, they became a symbol of oppression to the colonists. As a result, the guiding principle of the new constitutional governments was **legislative supremacy**, and the legislatures were given overwhelming power at the expense of governors. Most governors were to be elected by the legislature, not the people, and were restricted to a single term of office. State judiciaries also were limited in authorized powers; judges, like governors, were to be elected by the legislature. The preeminence of legislative power was so great that an English observer, Lord James Bryce, was moved to remark: "The legislature . . . is so much the strongest force in the several states that we may almost call it the government and ignore all other authorities."[16]

THE GROWTH OF EXECUTIVE POWER

Disillusionment with the legislatures soon developed, spreading rapidly through the states during the early 1800s. There were many reasons for disenchantment, including the legislatures' failure to address problems caused by rapid population growth and the Industrial Revolution; the growing amount of legislation that favored private interests; and a mounting load of state indebtedness, which led nine states to default on their bonds in a single two-year period.

Gradually, the executive branch began to accumulate more power and stature through constitutional amendments that provided for popular election of governors, who were also given longer terms and the authority to veto legislative bills. The constitutions of those states admitted to the Union during the early 1800s established stronger executive powers at the outset.

As executive power grew, public confidence in state legislatures continued to erode. This trend was reflected in the process of constitutional revision. One delegate at Kentucky's 1890 constitutional convention proclaimed that "the principal, if not the sole purpose of this constitution which we are here to frame, is to restrain the legislature's will and restrict its authority."[17] Also affecting constitutional change were broader social and economic forces in the United States, such as the extension of suffrage and popular participation in government, the rise of a corporate economy, the Civil War and Reconstruction, the growth of industry and commerce, the process of urbanization, and a growing movement for government reform. States rapidly replaced and amended their constitutions from the early 1800s to 1920s in response to

legislative supremacy
The legislature's dominance of the other two branches of government.

these forces and others. The decade immediately after the Civil War saw the highest level of constitutional activity in U.S. history, much of it in the southern states; between 1860 and 1870, twenty-seven constitutions were replaced or thoroughly revised as Confederate states ratified new documents after secession, then redrew the documents after Union victory to incorporate certain conditions of readmission to the United States.

Constitutional change after Reconstruction was driven by the Populist and Progressive reform movements. During the late 1800s, the Populists championed the causes of the "little man," including farmers and laborers. They sought to open the political process to the people through constitutional devices such as the initiative, the referendum, and the recall (see Chapter 4). The Progressives, who made their mark during 1890–1920, were kindred spirits whose favorite targets were concentrated wealth, inefficiencies in government, machine politics, corruption, and boss rule in the cities. Reformers in both groups successfully promoted constitutional reforms such as regulation of campaign spending and party activities, replacement of party conventions with direct primary elections, and selection of judges through nonpartisan elections.

Weaknesses of Constitutions

Despite the numerous constitutional amendments and replacements enacted during the nineteenth and twentieth centuries, by 1950, the states were buffeted by a rising chorus criticizing their fundamental laws. Ironically, many states were victims of past constitutional change, which left them with documents that were extravagantly long, frustratingly inflexible, and distressingly detailed. In general, state constitutions now provided for a feeble executive branch because they limited the governor's administrative authority, permitted the popular election of numerous other executive branch officials, and organized the executive into a hodgepodge of semiautonomous agencies, boards, and commissions. State judiciaries remained uncoordinated and overly complex, whereas legislatures suffered from archaic structures and procedures. Statutory detail, outdated language, local amendments (those that apply only to designated local governments), and other problems contaminated the documents and strait-jacketed state government.

EXCESSIVE LENGTH

From the first constitutions, which averaged 5,000 words, state documents expanded into enormous tracts averaging 27,000 words by 1967. (The U.S. Constitution contains 8,700 words.) Some of this increase resulted from growing social and economic complexity and from a perceived need to be very specific about what the legislatures, and local governments, could and could not do.

Some constitutions became positively verbose. Georgia's contained around 583,500 words, surpassing Tolstoy's *War and Peace* in length. (The Peach State's constitution was replaced with a much briefer version in 1982.) Even today, the constitution of South Carolina limits local government indebtedness but lists seventeen pages of exceptions. Oklahoma's sets the flash point for kerosene at 115 degrees for purposes of illumination, and California's addresses a compelling issue of our time—the length of wrestling matches. A constitutional initiative in Florida prohibits "cruel and unusual confinement of pigs during pregnancy." The dubious prize for the most verbose constitution in the world today goes to Alabama's 367,000-word document. An estimated 70 percent of the amendments apply to only one county, and provisions regulate garbage fees and the disposal of dead farm animals.[18] Table 3.1 provides an overview of the fifty state constitutions, including each one's length.

TABLE 3.1	State Constitutions, 2014				
				NUMBER OF AMENDMENTS	
STATE	NUMBER OF CONSTITUTIONS	EFFECTIVE DATE OF PRESENT CONSTITUTION	NUMBER OF WORDS	SUBMITTED TO VOTERS	ADOPTED
Alabama	6	Nov. 28, 1901	367,006	1,209	880
Alaska	1	Jan. 3, 1959	13,479	42	29
Arizona	1	Feb. 14, 1912	47,306	274	151
Arkansas	5	Oct. 30, 1874	59,120	198	99
California	2	July 4, 1879	67,048	894	527
Colorado	1	Aug. 1, 1876	66,140	340	158
Connecticut	4	Dec. 30, 1965	16,401	31	30
Delaware	4	June 10, 1897	25,445	not submitted to voters	145
Florida	6	Jan. 7, 1969	56,705	165	121
Georgia	10	July 1, 1983	41,684	96	73
Hawaii	1	Aug. 21, 1959	21,498	133	110
Idaho	1	July 3, 1890	24,626	212	125
Illinois	4	July 1, 1971	16,401	19	12
Indiana	2	Nov. 1, 1851	11,476	79	47
Iowa	2	Sept. 3, 1857	11,089	59	54
Kansas	1	Jan. 29, 1861	14,097	126	96
Kentucky	4	Sept. 28, 1891	27,234	76	42
Louisiana	11	Jan. 1, 1975	69,876	248	176
Maine	1	March 15, 1820	16,313	205	172
Maryland	4	Oct. 5, 1867	43,198	264	228
Massachusetts	1	Oct. 25, 1780	45,283	148	120

(continued)

TABLE 3.1   **State Constitutions, 2014 (continued)**

STATE	NUMBER OF CONSTITUTIONS	EFFECTIVE DATE OF PRESENT CONSTITUTION	NUMBER OF AMENDMENTS		
			NUMBER OF WORDS	SUBMITTED TO VOTERS	ADOPTED
Michigan	4	Jan. 1, 1964	31,164	73	30
Minnesota	1	May 11, 1858	11,734	217	120
Mississippi	4	Nov. 1, 1890	26,229	161	125
Missouri	4	March 30, 1945	69,394	177	115
Montana	2	July 1, 1973	12,790	56	31
Nebraska	2	Oct. 12, 1875	34,934	354	230
Nevada	1	Oct. 31, 1864	37,418	233	137
New Hampshire	2	June 2, 1784	13,060	289	145
New Jersey	3	Jan. 1, 1948	26,360	83	48
New Mexico	1	Jan. 6, 1912	33,198	298	165
New York	4	Jan. 1, 1895	44,397	301	225
North Carolina	3	July 1, 1971	17,177	38	31
North Dakota	1	Nov. 2, 1889	18,746	271	154
Ohio	2	Sept. 1, 1851	53,239	287	172
Oklahoma	1	Nov. 16, 1907	81,666	360	193
Oregon	1	Feb. 14, 1859	49,016	495	253
Pennsylvania	5	April 23, 1968	26,078	36	30
Rhode Island	2	Dec. 4, 1986	11,407	14	12
South Carolina	7	Jan. 1, 1896	27,421	687	498
South Dakota	1	Nov. 2, 1889	27,774	233	217
Tennessee	3	Feb. 23, 1870	13,960	62	39
Texas	5	Feb. 15, 1876	86,936	661	483
Utah	1	Jan. 4, 1896	17,849	169	117
Vermont	3	July 9, 1793	8,565	212	54
Virginia	6	July 1, 1971	21,899	56	48
Washington	1	Nov. 11, 1889	32,578	180	106
West Virginia	2	April 9, 1872	33,324	122	71
Wisconsin	1	May 29, 1848	15,102	194	145
Wyoming	1	July 10, 1890	26,349	128	100

SOURCE: *Book of the States*, 2014, http://knowledgecenter.csg.org/kc/system/files/1.1%202014.pdf, Table 1.1/John Dinan and The Council of State Governments, (accessed March 17, 2015).

Not surprisingly, lengthy state constitutions tend to be plagued by contradictions and meaningless clauses, legal jargon, and redundancy. Some address problems that are no longer with us, such as the regulation of steamboats[19] or the need to teach livestock feeding in Oklahoma public schools. Some, such as Alabama's, are burdened by embarrassingly discriminating and illegal provisions (under U.S. Constitutional law) including passages calling for segregated schools for black and white students and poll taxes. New Jersey's archaic wording uses terms like "bastardly" and provides that a woman forfeits her property rights to her husband if she has been "ravished" by another man *with* her consent.

Long-winded constitutions, such as those of Alabama, Oklahoma, and Colorado, fail to distinguish between the fundamental law and particularistic issues that properly should be decided by the state legislature.[20] Excessive detail invites litigation and then the courts must rule on conflicting provisions and challenges to constitutionality; hence, the courts are often burdened unnecessarily with decisions that should be made more appropriately by the legislature. Colorado's constitutional contradictions, for instance, led the speaker of the Colorado House to observe in 2008 that "We're one of the only states where the constitution requires simultaneous revenue reductions and spending increases."[21]

Once incorporated into a constitution, a decision becomes as close to permanent as anything can be in politics (though congressional or federal court review can overturn state constitutional provisions). In contrast to a statute, which can be changed by a simple legislative majority, constitutional change requires an extraordinary majority, usually two-thirds or three-fourths of the legislature, or a majority of the voting public. This requirement hampers the legislature's ability to confront problems quickly and makes policy change more difficult. Of course, enshrining a principle in the constitution can be a deliberate strategy to protect special interests. Too many amendments may also deprive local governments of needed flexibility to cope with their own problems. Indeed, excessive detail generates confusion, not only for legislatures and court, but also for the general public. It encourages political subterfuge to get around archaic or irrelevant provisions and breeds disrespect or even contempt for government.

State constitutions are political documents and, contrary to the admonitions of reformers, may sometimes be used to address some of the most controversial issues in politics, such as abortion rights, gun rights, same-sex marriage, and immigration policy. Many detailed provisions favor or protect special interests, including public utilities, farmers, timber and mining companies, oil and gas drillers, designated businesses, and many others.

There is enormous variance in the length of state constitutions (see Table 3.1). What accounts for such disparity? Studies by political scientists find, not surprisingly, that interest groups play an important role. In states with a single dominant political party, where legislative outcomes tend to be unpredictable because of dissension among members of the majority party, interest groups try to insulate their favorite agencies and programs from uncertainty by seeking protective provisions for them in the constitution.[22] Also, research indicates that long, detailed documents tend to become even longer because their very complexity encourages further amendment, until they finally become so cumbersome that political support develops for a simpler version. Finally, the easier it is to amend a constitution, the higher the amendment rate.[23]

PROBLEMS OF SUBSTANCE

In addition to the contradictions, anachronisms, wordiness, and grants of special privilege found in state constitutions, their *substance* has drawn criticism. Specific concerns voiced by reformers include the following:

- *The long ballot.* Because elected executive branch officials are not accountable to the governor for their jobs, the governor has little or no formal influence on their decisions and activities. Reformers who seek to maximize the governor's powers would restrict the executive branch ballot to only two elected leaders: the governor and the lieutenant governor.
- *A glut of executive boards and commissions.* Such entities were originally intended to expand opportunities for public participation in state government and to limit the powers of the governor. Today, they lead to fragmentation and a lack of policy coordination in the executive branch.
- *A swamp of local governments.* There are some 90,000 municipalities, counties, school districts, and special-purpose districts in the states. Sometimes they work at cross-purposes, and nearly always they suffer from overlapping responsibilities and an absence of coordination.
- *Restrictions on local government authority.* Localities in some states have to obtain explicit permission from the state legislature before providing a new service, tapping a new source of revenue, or exercising any other authority not specifically granted to them by the state.
- *Discriminatory Treatment* Constitutional language sometimes discriminates against African Americans, Latinos, immigrants, or gay people by denying them certain rights guaranteed to straight white males. (Although a few holdouts remain, most states have now adopted race- and gender-neutral language.)

LO 3.3

To comprehend the basic content of state constitutions and how they compare with the U.S. Constitution.

Model State Constitution

An ideal of the structure and contents of a state constitution that emphasizes brevity and broad functions and responsibilities of government.

Constitutional Reform

Shortly after World War II, problems of constitutional substance began to generate increasing commentary on the sorry condition of state constitutions. An important voice for constitutional reform was the National Municipal League, which developed a **Model State Constitution** in 1921, which is now in its sixth version.[24]

Another influential voice came in 1955 from the U.S. Advisory Commission on Intergovernmental Relations, popularly known as the Kestnbaum Commission. In its final report to the president, the commission stated that:

the Constitution prepared by the Founding Fathers, with its broad grants of authority and avoidance of legislative detail, has withstood the test of time far better than the constitutions later adopted by the States . . . The Commission believes that most states would benefit from a fundamental review of their constitutions to make sure that they provide for vigorous and responsible government, not forbid it.[25]

Thomas Jefferson believed that each generation has the right to choose for itself its own form of government. He suggested that a new constitution every nineteen or twenty years would be appropriate. Between 1960 and 1980, it seems that the states took his remarks to heart. Every state altered its fundamental law in some respect during this period, and new or substantially revised constitutions were put into operation in more than half the states. During the 1970s alone, ten states held conventions to consider changing or replacing their constitution. One such state was Louisiana, which set a record by adopting its eleventh constitution; Georgia is in second place with ten.

Two state constitutional traditions are evident today.[26] The newer **positive-law tradition** is represented by the detailed and lengthy documents of states such as Alabama, New York, and Texas. Detailed provisions tend to usurp the law-making powers of state legislatures by locking in rigid procedures and policies that typically favor strong political or economic interests. The original **higher-law tradition** is represented by the U.S. Constitution and the National Municipal League's Model State Constitution. It is embodied in brief documents that put forward basic and enduring framework principles and processes of government, recognizing that public policy choices are the proper responsibility of legislatures. Of course, no constitutional formula can be suitable for all the states because they differ too much in so many respects. The best constitutions strike a balance between the need for stability and the requirement for enough flexibility to deal with emerging problems. Today the higher-law tradition is in favor in those states whose constitutions have become briefer, more readable, and simple enough for the average citizen to understand. In others, however, conflicts between special interests are often resolved through constitutional change, particularly through citizen initiatives (see pages 74–75).

THE ESSENTIAL STATE CONSTITUTION

The Model State Constitution has twelve basic articles, which are embodied to a greater or lesser extent in the various state constitutions today. A brief description of each article and the ways in which its contents are changing follows.

Bill of Rights Individual rights and liberties were first protected in state constitutions. They closely resemble, and in some cases are identical to, those later delineated in the first eight amendments to the U.S. Constitution. Originally, the national Bill of Rights protected citizens only from actions by the U.S. government. State constitutions and courts were the principal guardians of civil liberties until the Supreme Court's interpretation of the Fourteenth Amendment extended the protective umbrella of the national courts over the states in 1925.[27] U.S. Supreme Court rulings also applied the U.S. Bill of Rights to the states, especially during the Warren Court beginning in 1953. Some states had failed to uphold their trust, particularly those that perpetuated the unequal treatment of women and minorities.

In the 1980s, however, activist states began to reassert guarantees of individual rights under state constitutions. At a minimum, all state constitutions must protect and guarantee those rights found in the U.S. Bill of Rights. But state constitutional provisions may guarantee additional or more extensive

positive-law tradition
A state constitutional tradition based on detailed provisions and procedure.

higher-law tradition
A state constitutional tradition based on basic and enduring principles that reach beyond statutory law.

rights to citizens. Twenty-two states now have equal rights amendments that guarantee sexual equality and prohibit sex-based discrimination. (But more than half the states once banned same-sex marriages.) The U.S. Constitution does not guarantee a right of privacy, but ten states do guarantee it. And thirteen states give constitutional rights to crime victims. Some constitutional provisions border on the exotic. Residents of New Hampshire hold the right to revolution, and all Massachusetts citizens enjoy freedom from excessive noise. Constitutions of Missouri and North Dakota guarantee the right to farm. To counter animal rights activists, eighteen states have inserted the rights to hunt and fish into their constitutions. As observed above, constitutions are political documents reflecting state interests and culture; they bear the marks of the state's people, embodied in the fundamental law in response to a serious concern or issue of the time. (See Table 3.2 for other rights provisions.)

The major reason for the rebirth of state activism in protecting civil liberties and individual rights has been the conservatism of the U.S. Supreme Court. One commentator accused the Supreme Court of having abdicated its role as "keeper of the nation's conscience."[28] The states' power to write and interpret their constitutions differently from the U.S. Constitution's provisions in the area of protecting civil rights and liberties has been upheld by the Supreme Court, as long as the state provisions have "adequate and independent" grounds.[29] Increasingly, civil rights and liberties cases are being filed by plaintiffs in state rather than federal courts, based on state bill of rights protections.

As we observed above, constitutions are "living" documents that evolve over time and bear the temporal imprints of the people of a state. Table 3.2 illustrates this point with a selection of constitutional quirks and oddities, many of them anachronisms.

TABLE 3.2	Excerpts from States Bills of Rights
Alabama	"The legislature may hereafter, by general law, provide for an indemnification program to peanut farmers for losses incurred as a result of *Aspergillus flavus* and freeze damage in peanuts."
Alaska	"Public schooling shall always be conducted in English."
Illinois	"The equal protection of the laws shall not be denied or abridged on account of sex by the State or its units of local government."
Montana	"Human dignity is inviolable."
New York	"Every citizen may freely speak, write, and publish his sentiments on all subjects. . . ."
North Carolina	"Secret political societies shall not be tolerated."
Pennsylvania	"The people have a right to clean air, pure water, and to the preservation of the natural, scenic, historic and esthetic values of the environment. Pennsylvania's public natural resources are the common history of all the people, including generations yet to come. . . ."
Rhode Island	"The power of the state and its municipalities to regulate and control the use of land and waters in the furtherance of the preservation, regeneration, and restoration of the natural environment, and . . . of the rights of the people to enjoy and freely exercise the rights of fishery and the privileges of the shore . . . shall be liberally construed, and shall not be deemed a public use of private property."

Controversies in States and Localities

New States' Rights?

Lately, a revolt of the states has been witnessed. This "New States' Rights" is perhaps less a movement than an angry backlash against perceived overreaching by the federal government into state affairs at a time when economic problems have been building up. Its principals include Tea Party activists, political conservatives, and other "new states' righters."

Examples of the new revolt abound:

- South Dakota and Wyoming declared federal firearms regulation invalid for weapons made and used in their states.
- Utah enacted a law prohibiting the federal government from carrying out its Affordable Care Act ("Obamacare") without explicit legislative approval, asserted Utah's authority to seize federal land, and declared that the state can restrict federal law enforcement authority on federal lands within the state.
- Alaska filed suit against the federal government to overturn federal laws protecting polar bears and other endangered species so that oil and gas drilling could proceed more expeditiously.
- Twenty-three states have legalized medical marijuana, despite federal policy prohibiting it; four have legalized recreational possession, use, and sales of the substance.
- Several states, including Utah, introduced Repeal Amendments to the U.S. Constitution that would grant states the power to veto any act of Congress they disagreed with if two-thirds of the states opposed the act.
- Following President Obama's executive order deferring deportation for some five million illegal immigrants in late 2014, seventeen states sued in an attempt to derail the order.

Article VI of the U.S. Constitution, as interpreted by the courts, establishes the supremacy of federal law when it conflicts with state law. Yet the Tenth Amendment states that "powers not delegated to the United States by the Constitution . . . are reserved to the states respectively, or to the people." In instances of conflict or confusion, the U.S. Supreme Court has the final say.

Critical Thinking Questions:

1. How genuine is the New States' Rights? Is it a legitimate response of states to federal inactions or intrusions? Or, is it simply political grandstanding by elected state officials?

2. How, if at all, *should* the states be able to act when the federal government refuses to move forward on a pressing problem or, alternatively, when the federal government acts in such a way that one or more states feel they must resist?

Power of the State This very brief article states simply that the powers enumerated in the constitution are not the only ones held by the state—that, indeed, the state has all powers not denied to it by the state or national constitutions.

Suffrage and Elections Voter registration and election procedures are provided for here. Extensions—and retractions—of voting rights and changes in election procedures have been made in response to U.S. Supreme Court decisions and to federal law. Some states have improved election administration; liberalized registration, voting, and office-holding requirements; and enhanced election technology and security. Other (Republican controlled) states have shortened early voting periods, imposed restrictive voter identification requirements, and taken other measures that supporters claim help to prevent voter fraud. Opponents assert that these restrictions are intended to discourage traditional Democratic voters (minorities and the young) from participating in elections.

The Legislative Branch This article sets forth the powers, procedures, and organizing principles of the legislature, including apportionment of state legislatures on the basis of one person, one vote. District lines must be redrawn every ten years after the national census has revealed population changes (most recently in 2011–2012). Nineteen states have placed term limits on their elected officials in this article.

Interestingly, the Model State Constitution originally recommended a unicameral (one house) legislature as a means to overcome complexity, delay, and confusion. In its most recent revision, the National Municipal League tacitly recognized the refusal of the states to follow this suggestion by providing recommendations appropriate only for a bicameral body. Only Nebraska has a single-house general assembly today. The bold—even radical—constitutional amendment for unicameralism was adopted by the voters of Nebraska in 1934 in a popular initiative. Why Nebraska? Apparently several events were at least partly responsible for what Nebraskans have come to call "Unicam." For one thing, it was on the same statewide ballot with two other popular initiatives: repeal of Prohibition and approval of pari-mutuel horse racing. In addition, the bicameral body had been suffering increasing criticism for its apparent inability to conduct the state's business efficiently and effectively. But the key factor was the unrelenting preaching of the evils of bicameralism and the virtues of unicameralism by influential and popular U.S. Senator George W. Norris. Norris "wore out two sets of tires and two windshields" driving around on Nebraska's dusty back roads to make the case for Unicam.

Unicameralism has several virtues. It eliminates conference committees, which speeds up the legislative process and prevents the two houses from passing the buck to one another, each hoping the other will deal with the tough or complicated issues. The unicameral legislature can be small (it numbers forty-nine representatives in Nebraska, the smallest legislature among the states). And if because the single body is nonpartisan, as in Nebraska, representatives may be more likely to focus on the important business of the state than on national issues of partisan significance.

Nebraska's Unicam gets high marks for efficiency, simplicity, and effectiveness. And it remains popular except for its nonpartisan feature. The major complaint is that nonpartisanship depresses voter interest and turnout in elections because voters do not have party identification as a voting cue.

The Executive Branch The powers and organization of the executive branch, which are outlined in this article, have seen many notable modifications. Governors have won line item vetoes, the authority to make appointments within the executive branch, and the ability to reorganize the state bureaucracy (see Chapter 7). A number of states have opted for team election of the governor and lieutenant governor.

The Judicial Branch Court organization and procedures are outlined here, along with the selection method for judges. Most states have unified their court systems under a single authority, usually the state Supreme Court. Many states now select judges through a merit plan rather than by gubernatorial appointment, legislative election, or popular election (see Chapter 10). The states have also established means to investigate charges against judges and to recommend discipline or removal from the bench when necessary.

Finance Taxation, debt, and expenditures for state and local governments are the subjects of this article. In many states, tax relief has been granted to senior citizens, veterans, and disabled people. In others, taxation and expenditure limitations have been added (see Chapter 13).

Local Government Here, the authority of municipalities, counties, and other local governments is recognized. Most states have increased local authority through home-rule provisions, which give localities more discretion in providing services; some have extended local taxing authority. In addition, mechanisms for improved intergovernmental cooperation, such as consolidated city and county governments and regional districts to provide services, have been created.

Public Education On the basis of this article, the states establish and maintain free public schools for all children. Higher education institutions, including technical schools, colleges, and universities, are commonly established in this section.

Civil Service The Model State Constitution sets forth a *merit system* of personnel administration for state government, under which civil servants are to be hired, promoted, paid, evaluated, and retained on the basis of competence, fitness, and performance instead of political party affiliation or other such criteria (see Chapter 8).

Intergovernmental Relations Some states stipulate specific devices for cooperation among various state entities, among local jurisdictions, or between a state and its localities. They may detail methods for sharing in the provision of certain services, or they may list cost-sharing mechanisms such as local option sales taxes.

Constitutional Revision The methods for revising, amending, and replacing the constitution are described.

Constitutions Today In general, state constitutions today conform more closely to the higher-law tradition and the Model State Constitution than did those of the past. They are shorter, more concise, and simpler, and they contain fewer errors, anachronisms, and contradictions. The latest states to enter the Union, Alaska and Hawaii, have constitutional documents that follow the Model State Constitution quite closely.

However, work always remains to be done. Some state constitutions are still riddled with unnecessary details because new amendments have continually been added to the old documents, and obsolete provisions and other relics can still be found. But more important deficiencies exist in states whose constitutions inhibit the administrative and financial operations of state government and obstruct the ability to adapt to change. In some jurisdictions, the governor's formal powers remain weak; a plethora of boards and commissions makes any thought of executive management and coordination a pipe dream; local governments chafe under the tight leash of state authority; and many other problems persist. Constitutional revision must be an ongoing process if the states are to cope with the changing contours of American society and stay in the vanguard of innovation and change.

Methods for Constitutional Change

LO 3.4

To be able to describe the formal and informal methods for changing state constitutions.

There are only two methods for altering the U.S. Constitution. The first is the constitutional convention, wherein delegates representing the states assemble to consider modifying or replacing the Constitution. Despite periodic calls for a national constitutional convention, only one has taken place—in Philadelphia, more than two and a quarter centuries ago. Two-thirds of the states must agree to call a convention; three-fourths are required to ratify any changes in the Constitution.

The second means of amending the U.S. Constitution is through congressional initiative, wherein Congress, by a two-thirds vote of both houses, agrees to send one or more proposed changes to the states. Again, three-fourths of the states must ratify the proposals.

Since 1787, more than 1,000 amendments have been submitted to the states by Congress. Only twenty-seven have been approved (the most recent one, in 1992, limits the ability of members of Congress to increase their pay), and the first ten of these were appended to the Constitution as a condition by several states for ratification. Note that neither method for amending the U.S. Constitution requires popular participation by voters, in sharp contrast to the citizen participation requirements for state constitutional change, as we shall see in the next section.

INFORMAL CONSTITUTIONAL CHANGE

interpretation

An informal means of revising constitutions whereby members of the executive, legislative, or judicial branch apply constitutional principles and law to the everyday affairs of governing.

In a letter to James Madison, Thomas Jefferson wrote the following: "The earth belongs to the living, and not to the dead . . . Every constitution, then, and every law, naturally expires at the end of 19 years. If it be enforced longer, it is an act of force and not of right."[30] Though Jefferson's admonitions are not followed literally, the states do frequently alter their constitutions.

One informal and four formal methods for amending state constitutions exist. The informal route is **interpretation** of constitutional meaning by the state legislature, executive branch, courts, or attorneys general, or through usage and custom.[31] Governors issue executive orders; courts and attorneys general produce advisory opinions on meanings of specific provisions; state agencies make decisions and implement policy. The force of habit can be a

? It's Your Turn

Should Washington, DC, Become the 51st State?

The residents of the District of Columbia demand the right to statehood. They make some compelling points and arguments. The District has its own license plates, prison system, and income tax. It has three electoral votes. But it has no U.S. Senator and only a single, nonvoting member of the U.S. House of Representatives.

Though it granted the District some self-governing authority under a 1974 home rule charter, Congress retains full veto power over the District's legislative and financial affairs, including its budget. Congress has been known to overturn laws enacted by the District.

The U.S. Constitution (Article I, section 8) designates D.C. as the seat of the national government. The Framers believed that a separate district would not only prevent the state, whose territory included the national capital, from exerting powerful pressures on Congress

but also prevent the national government from being dependent on any single state for services and security. It did not help that Congress, concerned about a near mutiny of General Washington's army in 1783, had to flee the early capital of Philadelphia after Pennsylvania refused to protect it.

Several attempts have been made to gain D.C. statehood for the sixty-eight square-mile District, including a proposed constitutional amendment that received approval by only sixteen of the necessary thirty-eight states. Congressional hearings on the issue have been held, the most recent one in October, 2014. President Obama stated that he favored D.C. statehood, but he decided not to risk political capital promoting it in Congress. Some have suggested sending the District back to its original home, the state of Maryland.

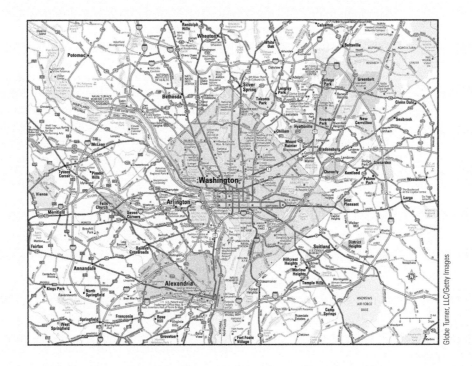

Globe Turner, LLC/Getty Images

(*continued*)

(continued)

PROS	CONS
The district's 646,000 population outnumbers that of Vermont and Wyoming.	Constitutional problems weigh heavily.
Residents pay billions in federal taxes each year; they serve on juries and in the armed forces.	The District has no meaningful agriculture or industry, except for tourism and, of course, government.
Residents say they are disrespected and treated like second-class citizens who are taxed without meaningful representation.	Its population is majority African-American, two-thirds minority, and decidedly Democratic in its voting. Republicans are adamantly against statehood for the District.
	The District has been rocked by numerous high-level corruption scandals during recent decades, tarnishing the reputation of the District's elected officials.

powerful influence, specific constitutional provisions notwithstanding. It is a good bet that one or more antiquated or unrealistic constitutional provisions are ignored in every state. A common example is the requirement that all bills be read, in their entirety, three times in each house for enactment. Another is the list of requirements for holding political office, such as a belief in God.

State supreme courts play the most direct role in changing constitutions through interpretation. In large measure, a constitution is what the judges say it is in their decisions from the bench. Judicial interpretation of constitutions may be based on various standards, including strict attention to the express language of the document and to the original intent of the Framers or authors of amendments, deference to legislative enactments or executive actions, precedent, policy considerations, and individual rights. The power of the state supreme courts to review executive actions, legislative actions, and decisions of lower courts is known as **judicial review**. This power evolved in the states much as it did on the national level—through the courts' own insistence that they hold this authority. During recent years, as the U.S. Supreme Court has become more conservative and less activist in its interpretations of the law, some state courts have moved in the opposite direction and earned reputations as judicial activists. On occasion, federal courts strike down state constitutional law. For instance, federal courts have recently overturned constitutional amendments banning same-sex marriage and voting procedures.

We have already noted that state supreme courts have the authority to interpret and apply state guarantees of civil rights and liberties more broadly than the U.S. Supreme Court's interpretation of the Bill of Rights in the U.S. Constitution. For instance, the New Hampshire Supreme Court extended the right to privacy to household garbage, even when it is placed at the curb for

judicial review

The power of the U.S. Supreme Court or state supreme courts to declare unconstitutional actions of the executive and legislative branches, as well as decisions of lower courts.

collection. The U.S. Supreme Court does not review state court decisions that are clearly and properly based on state constitutional provisions.[32] In practice, however, state supreme courts are often guided by constitutional rulings of the U.S. Supreme Court and high courts in other states. Because courts apply similar constitutional language to many common issues, it is natural for them to share their experiences in legal problem solving.[33] Of course, the national courts are paramount under the U.S. Constitution and will strike down any serious constitutional contradictions between the nation and the states, but for more than two decades now, the U.S. Supreme Court has shown "a studied deference to the work of the state judiciaries."[34]

FORMAL CONSTITUTIONAL CHANGE

The four formal procedures for constitutional change are legislative proposal, initiative, constitutional convention, and constitutional commission. All involve two basic steps: initiation and **ratification**. The state legislature, or in some cases the voters, propose (initiate) a constitutional change. Then the proposed amendment is submitted to the voters for approval (ratification).

Legislative Proposal Legislative proposal is the most common road to revision. More than 90 percent of all changes in state constitutions have come through this method, which is permitted in all fifty states.

The specifics of legislative proposal techniques vary, but most states require either two-thirds or three-fifths of the members of each house to approve a proposal before it is sent to the voters for ratification. Twelve states require two consecutive legislative sessions to consider and pass a proposed amendment. The procedure can become quite complicated. For instance, South Carolina's legislative proposal must be passed by two-thirds of the members of each house; then it is sent to the people during the next general election. If a majority of voters approve, the proposal returns to the next legislative session, in which a majority of legislators have to concur.

Almost all states accept a simple majority for voter ratification of a proposed revision. In New Hampshire, however, two-thirds of the voters must approve the proposal. And Tennessee requires approval by a majority of the number of citizens who cast a vote for governor.

Legislative proposal is probably best suited to a limited number of revisions that are relatively narrow in scope. The disadvantage to presenting a far-reaching amendment is that voters may not understand it, or distrust it. And a multitude of individual proposals threatens to overwhelm and confuse voters. This was demonstrated in 2012 when Florida voters, presented with twelve constitutional revision proposals, resoundingly rejected all of them as "too conservative, too controversial, too long, and too confusing."[35] Moreover, a patchwork of amendments can conflict with or overlap other constitutional provisions. This circumstance spawns additional revisions, which in turn lead to increased litigation in the state supreme court. Either strategy—a far-reaching proposal or a plentitude of amendments—is likely to go down in defeat at the polls.

ratification

The formal approval of a constitution or constitutional amendment by a majority of the voters of a state.

legislative proposal

The most common means of amending a state constitution, wherein the legislature proposes a revision, usually by a two-thirds majority.

Initiative Eighteen states permit their citizens to initiate and ratify changes in the constitution and thus bypass the legislature (see Table 3.3). Only five of these initiative states are east of the Mississippi River, thus reflecting the fact that the initiative was a product of the Progressive reform movement of the early 1900s. Most of the territories admitted as states during this period chose to permit the **initiative** (known as "constitutional initiative" in some states). Twenty-three states also authorize the initiative for enacting statutory change (see Chapter 4).

The initiative is used much less often than legislative proposal in amending constitutions, although recently proposed initiatives have won more frequently on state ballots. The initiative is less successful than legislative proposal in terms of the percentage of amendments that are adopted by the voters. Less than half of all initiatives have been written into state constitutions in recent years.

The number of signatures needed for the initiative petition to be valid varies widely: Arizona requires 15 percent of total votes cast in the last gubernatorial election, whereas Massachusetts requires 3 percent (see Table 3.3). Eight states specify that the petition signatures must be collected widely throughout the state as a means of ensuring that an initiative that favors one specific region does not become embodied in the constitution.

In general, a petition for constitutional amendment is sent to the office of the secretary of state for verification that the required number of registered voters have signed their names. Then the question is placed on a statewide ballot in the next general election. Ratification requires a majority vote of the people in most states.

It is usually easy enough to collect the required number of signatures to place a proposed amendment on a statewide ballot (for a fee, a firm will be happy to perform this service, and a surprising number of people will sign almost anything). But actual passage of the initiative is much more difficult once it receives a close public examination and opposing interests proclaim their objections. If the legislature is circumvented altogether and propositions are placed directly on the general-election ballot by citizens, the procedure is called a **direct initiative**. If a legislature participates by voting on the citizen proposal, as in Massachusetts and Mississippi, the procedure is known as an **indirect initiative**.

The initiative is useful in making limited changes to the state constitution and, in recent years, has addressed some controversial issues that state legislatures are hesitant to confront. Voters in several states have recently addressed abortion rights, same-sex marriage, immigration policy, property rights, school vouchers, the right to carry firearms, and bans on foreign (Sharia) law. A major advantage of the initiative is that the people's will can counter a despotic or inertia-ridden legislature. Another advantage is that this method appears to enhance citizen interest and participation in government.

However, the initiative can also be abused through signature fraud or by well-heeled special interests with selfish motives or social agendas who seek to gain privileges, and under crisis conditions it can result in ill-conceived, radical changes to the constitution. Indeed, the initiative can result in just the

initiative

A proposed law or constitutional amendment that is placed on the ballot by citizen petition.

direct initiative

A procedure by which the voters of a jurisdiction propose the passage of constitutional amendments, state laws, or local ordinances, bypassing the legislative body.

indirect initiative

Similar to the direct initiative, except that the voter-initiated proposal must be submitted to the legislature before going on the ballot for voter approval.

TABLE 3.3	States Authorizing Constitutional Amendment by Citizen Initiative	
STATE	**YEAR ADOPTED**	**NUMBER OF SIGNATURES REQUIRED ON INITIATIVE PETITION**
Arizona	1910	15 percent of total votes cast for all candidates for governor at last election.
Arkansas	1909	10 percent of voters for governor at last election.
California	1911	8 percent of total voters for all candidates for governor at last election.
Colorado	1910	5 percent of total legal votes for all candidates for secretary of state at last general election.
Florida	1972	8 percent of total votes cast in the state in the last presidential election.
Illinois*	1970	8 percent of total votes cast for candidates for governor at last election.
Massachusetts†	1918	3 percent of total votes cast in the last gubernatorial election.
Michigan	1908	10 percent of total votes for all candidates at the gubernatorial election.
Mississippi	1992	12 percent of total votes for all candidates for governor at last election.
Missouri	1906	8 percent of legal voters for all candidates for governor at last election.
Montana	1904	10 percent of qualified electors, the number of qualified electors to be determined by the number of votes cast for governor in the preceding general election.
Nebraska	1912	10 percent of registered voters.
Nevada	1904	10 percent of voters who voted in entire state in last general election.
North Dakota	1914	4 percent of population of the state.
Ohio	1912	10 percent of total number of electors who voted for governor in last election.
Oklahoma	1907	15 percent of legal voters for state office receiving the highest number of voters at last general state election.
Oregon	1902	8 percent of total votes for all candidates at last election, at which the governor was elected for a four-year term.
South Dakota	1898	10 percent of total votes for governor in last election.

*Only Article IV, the Legislature, may be amended by initiative petition.

†Before being submitted to the electorate for ratification, initiative measures must be approved at two sessions of a successively elected legislature by not less than one-fourth of all members elected, sitting in joint session.

SOURCE: Copyright 2014 The Council of State Governments. Adapted with permission from *The Book of the States*. Reprinted by permission of The Council of State Governments.

kind of excessive detail and poorly drafted verbiage that is so widely condemned by constitutional scholars and reformers. It can also make doing routine business extremely difficult. In Colorado, for example, an initiative appears to require simultaneous tax cuts and spending increases.

The perceived excesses of the initiative have recently spawned efforts to raise the threshold for voter approval. Ironically, in a constitutional referendum, Florida voters agreed to raise the bar for initiative approval from a simple majority to 60 percent. Montana banned paid signature gatherers and restricted the time for signature acquisition to one year.[36]

Constitutional Convention Legislative proposals and initiatives are quite specific about the type of constitutional change that is sought. Only those questions that actually appear on the ballot are considered. By contrast, a **constitutional convention** assembles delegates who suggest revisions or even an entirely new document, then submit the proposed changes to the voters for ratification. The convention is especially well suited to consider far-reaching constitutional changes or a new fundamental law.

The convention is the oldest method for constitutional change in the states and is available in all fifty of them. The process begins when the electorate or the legislature decides to call for a constitutional convention. In fourteen states, the question of calling a convention must be regularly voted on by the electorate, but all convention calls have been routinely rejected since Rhode Island's won approval in 1986. Alaskans and Iowans hold an automatic convention call every ten years; in New York and Maryland, the convention issue is submitted to the voters every twenty years. Except in Delaware, where the legislature can take direct action, proposals emerging from the convention must be ratified by the voters before they become part of the constitution. Delegates to a convention are usually elected on a nonpartisan ballot by the voters from state house or senate districts.

Voter approval of convention proposals is problematic. If partisan, racial, regional, or other disagreements dominate media reports on the convention, voter approval is difficult to obtain. Greater likelihood of voter approval occurs when specific changes are considered.[37] As with the case of legislative proposals, people naturally tend to be skeptical of suggestions for sweeping, unsettling changes in the basic structures and procedures of government. Once a convention is approved and convened, delegates usually understand these dynamics and are sensitive to how their proposed changes may affect the general public.

Constitutional Commission Often called a *study commission*, the **constitutional commission** is usually established to examine the existing document and to recommend changes to the legislature or to the voters. Depending on the mandate, the constitutional commission may study the entire constitution with a view toward replacement or change, focus on one or more specific articles or provisions, or be given the freedom to decide its own scope of activity. Commission recommendations are only advisory, thus helping to account for this method's popularity with elected officials, who sometimes prefer to study a problem to death rather than engage it head on. Some or all of the recommendations may be submitted to the voters; others may be completely ignored. Only in Florida can a commission send its proposals directly to the voters.

Constitutional commissions operated in 2013 in Alabama and Ohio, and Utah's revision commission functions permanently. Service on a constitutional commission can be a thankless task because legislators sometimes ignore the commission's recommendations or employ them as a symbolic device for relieving political pressure. For example, Kentucky's 1987–1988 Revision Commission recommended seventy-seven changes to the constitution, but only one

constitutional convention

An assembly of delegates chosen by popular election or appointed by the legislature or the governor to revise an existing constitution or to create a new one.

constitutional commission

A meeting of appointed delegates established to study an existing constitution, or specific provisions, and to recommend proposed changes.

was referred by the legislature to the voters as a proposed amendment.[38] When used properly, however, commissions can furnish high-quality research both inexpensively and relatively quickly.

State Responsiveness and Constitutional Reform

Each state's constitution is designed specifically to meet the needs of that state. The rich history, economics, values, ideals, and political culture of the state are reflected in its constitutional language. Through their constitutions, the states experiment with different governmental institutions and processes. As Thomas Paine observed in 1791 in his essay entitled "The Rights of Man," "It is in the interest of all the states, that the constitution of each should be somewhat diversified from each other. We are a people founded upon experiments, and . . . have the happy opportunity of trying variety in order to discover the best."[39]

State constitutions were the original guardians of individual rights and liberties, with their own bills of rights preceding those of the U.S. Constitution by many years. They have generally resumed that responsibility during the past several decades. Yet, few tasks in government are more difficult than modernizing a constitution. As one writer on constitutional change observed, the process requires "sustained, dedicated, organized effort; vigorous, aggressive and imaginative leadership; bipartisan political support; education of the electorate on the issues; judicious selection of the means; and seemingly endless patience."[40] In the words of another constitutional scholar, "The advocate of constitutional reform in an American state should be endowed with the patience of Job and the sense of time of a geologist."[41] The solemn duty of framing the original state constitutions, which was so effectively discharged by our predecessors, is now vested in the continuous oversight of present and future generations.

The constitutional changes enacted in the states since the Kestnbaum Commission report have generally resulted in documents in the higher-law tradition, documents that "are shorter, more clearly written, modernized, less encumbered with restrictions, more basic in content and have more reasonable amending processes. They also establish improved governmental structures and contain substantive provisions assuring greater openness, accountability, and equity."[42] The states have made a great deal of progress in modernizing their governments. As state constitutional scholar Richard Leach has put it, "There are not many constitutional horrors left."[43]

Old-style constitutions were "the drag anchors of state programs, and permanent cloaks for the protection of special interests and points of view."[44] These constitutions held back progress and delayed the states' resurgence as lead players in the drama of U.S. federalism. Recent constitutional amendments have responded to, and indeed caused, profound changes in state government and politics. Problems persist, and future constitutional tinkering and replacements will be necessary—indeed, inevitable.

Chapter Recap

- The constitution is the fundamental law of a state, superior to statutory law.

- State constitutions evolved from the original colonial charters. Shifting from an original basis of legislative supremacy, they have gradually increased executive power.

- Some constitutions continue to suffer from excessive length and substantive problems.

- Constitutional reform has modernized the documents and made them conform more closely to present challenges of governance.

- Methods for changing constitutions include interpretation and judicial review, legislative proposal, initiative, constitutional convention, and constitutional commission.

KEY TERMS

fundamental law *(p. 56)*
legislative supremacy *(p. 59)*
Model State Constitution *(p. 64)*
positive-law tradition *(p. 65)*
higher-law tradition *(p. 65)*

interpretation *(p. 70)*
judicial review *(p. 72)*
ratification *(p. 73)*
legislative proposal *(p. 73)*
initiative *(p. 74)*

direct initiative *(p. 74)*
indirect initiative *(p. 74)*
constitutional convention *(p. 76)*
constitutional commission *(p. 76)*

INTERNET RESOURCES

For full texts of state statutes and constitutions, see individual state websites (e.g., **www.state.fl.us**).

State constitutions can also be accessed through Findlaw at **www.findlaw.com/11stategov/indexconst.html or www.constitution.org**.

The Alaska constitution draws heavily on the Model State Constitution. It is located in the State of Alaska Documents Library at **www.law.state.ak.us**.

For everything you want to know about Nebraska's Unicam, go to **www. nebraskalegislature**

.gov. Live webcasts of Unicam may be viewed at **www.netnebraska.org/publicmedia/capitol.html**.

Another helpful site is the Center for State Constitutional Studies at **www.camlaw.rutgers.edu/statecon/**

The most recent data on state constitutional change can be accessed at the Council of State Governments website: **www.csg.org**.

Citizen Participation and Elections: Engaging the Public in Government

The city of Takoma Park, Maryland, a suburb of Washington, D.C., made history in 2013 when it granted 16- and 17-year-olds the right to vote in city elections. Why take such an unprecedented step? Simple: City leaders believed that lowering the voting age would help local residents develop a lifelong habit of participation in government. Sure, there were naysayers who claimed that teenagers are too immature to handle the responsibility. But in the end, the desire to engage local teens in the most basic right of citizenship prevailed. After all, as one of the newly enfranchised high school students said, "We cultivate interest in democracy by giving people opportunities to participate."[1] In 2015, Hyattsville, Maryland, located just four miles from Takoma Park, followed suit and lowered the voting age in its city elections. It remains to be seen whether larger cities will emulate Takoma Park's bold action and grant their 16- and 17-year-old residents the right to vote in municipal elections.

LO 4.1

To recognize the various ways in which citizens can participate in government.

Participation

Democracy assumes citizen **participation**—acting to influence government. In contemporary America, there is persistent evidence that citizens are not much interested in participation. We have grown accustomed to reports of low voter turnout and public hearings that few attend. In his influential book *Bowling Alone*, political scientist Robert Putnam documented this gradual disengagement of people from all sorts of community activities and organizations.[2]

On the surface, government works just fine with limited participation: The interests of the active become translated into public policy, and those who are inactive can be safely ignored because they do not vote.[3] If, however, some traditional nonvoters such as low-income, less-educated citizens went to the polls or engaged in other forms of political participation, then vote-seeking candidates would be forced to pay more attention to their interests, and public policy might be nudged in a different direction.[4] In this light, it is important to understand both why many people do participate and why others do not. This chapter addresses individual citizen involvement in government; Chapter 5 takes up collective participation (i.e., participation by political parties and interest groups).

WHY AND HOW PEOPLE PARTICIPATE

In a representative democracy, voting is the most common form of participation. For many citizens, it is a matter of civic responsibility. It is a fundamental facet of citizenship—after all, it is called "the right to vote." Citizens go to the polls to elect the officials who will govern them. But there are other methods of participation. Consider the citizen who is unhappy because the property taxes on her home have increased substantially from one year to the next. What options are available to her besides voting against incumbent office-holders at the next election? As shown in Figure 4.1, she can be either active or passive; her actions can be either constructive or destructive. Basically, she has four potential responses: loyalty, voice, exit, and neglect.[5]

According to this formulation, voting is an example of *loyalty*, a passive but constructive response to government action. Specifically, this response reflects the irate taxpayer's underlying support for her community despite her displeasure with specific tax policies. An active constructive response is *voice*: The aggrieved property owner could contact officials, work in the campaign of a candidate who promises to lower tax assessments, or, assuming that others in the community share her sentiments, participate in anti-tax groups and organize demonstrations. Research has shown that emotions, especially anger, can be a powerful stimulant to participation.[6] The Occupy Movement of 2011 and 2012, in which protestors camped out in tents near city halls to protest the growing economic inequality in the United States, is an example of exercising the voice option. The use of social media by Occupy protestors gave rise to the phrase "**hashtag activism**."

Destructive responses (those that undermine the citizen-government relationship) are similarly passive or active. If the citizen simply shrugs and concludes that she can't fight city hall, she is exhibiting a response termed *neglect*.

participation

Actions through which ordinary members of a political system attempt to influence decisions.

hashtag activism

Using social media, especially Twitter to raise public awareness of an issue.

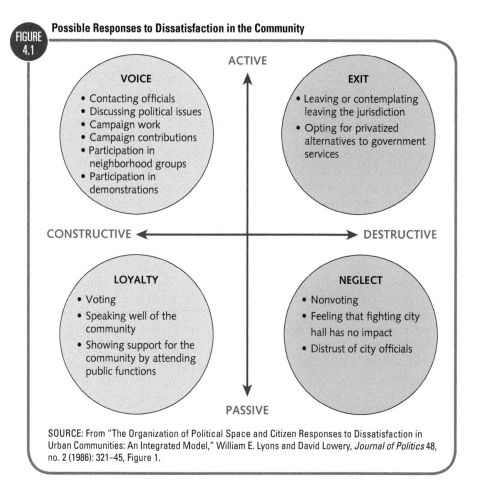

FIGURE 4.1

Possible Responses to Dissatisfaction in the Community

ACTIVE

VOICE
- Contacting officials
- Discussing political issues
- Campaign work
- Campaign contributions
- Participation in neighborhood groups
- Participation in demonstrations

EXIT
- Leaving or contemplating leaving the jurisdiction
- Opting for privatized alternatives to government services

CONSTRUCTIVE ←—————————————→ DESTRUCTIVE

LOYALTY
- Voting
- Speaking well of the community
- Showing support for the community by attending public functions

NEGLECT
- Nonvoting
- Feeling that fighting city hall has no impact
- Distrust of city officials

PASSIVE

SOURCE: From "The Organization of Political Space and Citizen Responses to Dissatisfaction in Urban Communities: An Integrated Model," William E. Lyons and David Lowery, *Journal of Politics* 48, no. 2 (1986): 321–45, Figure 1.

She has nearly given up on the community and does not participate. A more active version of giving up on a community is to *exit*—that is, to leave the community altogether (a response often referred to as "voting with your feet"). The unhappy citizen will relocate to a community that is more in line with her tax preferences.

Every citizen confronts these participatory options. Local residents' satisfaction with their city government tends to be a direct result of their experiences with city services and their perception of governmental responsiveness.[7] It is much healthier for the political system if citizens engage in the constructive responses, but some individuals are likely to conclude that constructive participation is of little value to them and opt for neglect or, in more extreme cases, exit.[8]

NONPARTICIPATION

What motivates the citizens who choose neglect as their best option? One explanation for nonparticipation in politics is socioeconomic status. Individuals with lower levels of income and education tend to participate less than wealthier, more educated individuals do.[9] Tied closely to income and education levels is occupational status. Unskilled workers and hourly wage earners do not participate in politics to the same degree as white-collar workers and professionals. Individuals of lower socioeconomic status may not have the time, resources, or civic skills required to become actively involved in politics.

Other explanations for nonparticipation have included age (younger people have participated less than middle-aged individuals have), race (blacks have participated less than whites have), and gender (women have participated less than men have). Of these factors, however, only age continues to affect political activity levels. African American political participation actually surpasses that of whites when socioeconomic status is taken into consideration,[10] and the gender gap in the types and levels of political participation has disappeared.[11] America's youth, however, remain less likely to frequent polling places. The upsurge in voting among 18- to 24-year-olds in the 2008 presidential election was thought by many to signal a new trend in youthful participation, but turnout in that age group dropped in the 2012 elections. Only 41.2 percent of eligible 18- to 24-year-olds voted in 2012 compared to 71.9 percent of those aged 65 or older. Groups such as Kids Voting USA have developed programs to socialize children about political affairs, surmising that children who get into the habit of citizen participation at an early age will be more politically active as adults.[12] For older youth, websites such as the MTV-sponsored "Rock the Vote" encourage active participation in politics and government.

Another factor that exerts an independent effect on participation is where one lives. Big-city dwellers (those who live in places with a population of 1 million or more) are less likely than people in small communities (with fewer than 5,000 inhabitants) to participate in various civic activities, including contacting local officials, attending community meetings, and voting in local elections.[13]

When nonvoters are asked why they failed to participate in an election, the responses show that events in the potential voter's own life often play a major role. Also, a lack of enthusiasm for the candidates or the campaign issues contributes to nonvoting. Table 4.1 provides data from a survey conducted by the U.S Census Bureau into the reasons why people don't vote. Also on the list of reasons are factors related to the voting process such as ballots and polling places.

The explanation for nonparticipation does not rest solely with the individual. Institutional features—the way the political system is designed—may suppress participation. For example, local governments that have instituted nonpartisan elections, in which candidates run without political party affiliation, have removed an important mobilizing factor for voters. Voter turnout tends to be lower in these elections than in partisan contests. City council meetings scheduled at 10 a.m. put a tremendous strain on workers who must take time off from their jobs if they want to attend; consequently, attendance is low. And local governments in which it is difficult for citizens to contact the appropriate official with a service request or complaint are not doing much to facilitate participation. Features like these play an often unrecognized role

TABLE 4.1   Reasons for Not Voting

PERCENTAGE SAYING[a] ...	
Too busy, conflicting schedule	18.9
Not interested	15.7
Illness or disability	14.0
Did not like candidates or campaign issues	12.7
Other reason (e.g., did not receive absentee ballot, did not know where to vote, lines too long at polling place)	11.1
Out of town on Election Day	8.6
Registration problems	5.5
Forgot to vote	3.9
Transportation problems	3.3
Inconvenient polling place	2.7
Bad weather conditions	0.8

[a] Three percent of nonvoters surveyed declined to give a reason for not voting.

SOURCE: U.S. Census Bureau, Current Population Survey, Table 10; Reasons For Not Voting, By Selected Characteristics: November 2012.

in dampening participation. Although participation in politics and government is often considered a civic duty, it is not a costless act, a point that economist Anthony Downs argued more than fifty years ago.[14] It is no wonder that some folks who are reasonably content with the actions of government decide that nonparticipation is a rational use of their time. These **free riders** receive the benefits of government, although they do not participate.

Nonparticipants typically have lower levels of interest in politics and tend to be weakly connected to their communities.[15] In many communities, the media have launched efforts to boost participation in civic life. Television stations convene forums and town meetings on the issues of the day, and local newspapers report the views of ordinary citizens on current events. Called public or civic journalism, the idea is to reconnect people with the democratic process and, in doing so, to make them active participants in public life. This is just one effort at restoring some of the **social capital** that Putnam found lacking in contemporary communities. In the language of Figure 4.1, greater social capital leads to more constructive forms of citizen participation.

THE STRUGGLE FOR THE RIGHT TO VOTE

State constitutions in the eighteenth and early nineteenth centuries entrusted only propertied white males with the vote. They did not encourage public involvement in government, and the eventual softening of restrictions on suffrage did not occur without a struggle. Restrictions based on property

free rider

A person who enjoys the benefit of a public good without bearing the cost.

social capital

A dense network of reciprocal social relations that promotes greater civic engagement.

Voting Rights Act of 1965

The law that effectively enfranchised racial minorities by giving the national government the power to decide whether individuals are qualified to vote and to intercede in state and local electoral operations when necessary.

voting-age population

Adults eighteen years of age and older.

ownership and wealth were eventually dropped, but women, blacks, and Native Americans were still denied the right to vote.

In an effort to attract women to its rugged territory, Wyoming enfranchised women in 1869. The suffragists—women who were actively fighting for the right to vote—scored a victory when Colorado extended the vote to women in 1893. Gradually, other states began enfranchising women, and in 1920 the Nineteenth Amendment to the U.S. Constitution, forbidding states to deny the right to vote "on account of sex," was ratified.

Even after the Fifteenth Amendment (1870) extended the vote to blacks, some southern states clung defiantly to traditional ways that denied blacks and poor people their rights. Poll taxes, literacy tests, and white primaries were among the barriers erected by the segregationists. U.S. Supreme Court decisions such as *Smith v. Allwright* (1944), which outlawed white primaries, and federal actions such as the Civil Rights Act of 1964 and the Twenty-Fourth Amendment (1964), which made poll taxes unconstitutional, helped blacks gain access to the polls. But in some jurisdictions, informal methods designed to discourage participation by African Americans continued.

The **Voting Rights Act of 1965** (VRA) finally broke the back of the segregationists' efforts. Under its provisions, federal poll watchers and registrars were dispatched to particular counties to investigate voter discrimination. Counties covered under the Voting Rights Act (all of nine southern states and parts of seven other states) had to submit to the U.S. Department of Justice any changes in election laws, such as new precinct lines or new polling places, well in advance of the election. This is known as the *preclearance* provision. During the ensuing decades, the VRA has been revised and extended several times by Congress. One of the most important modifications of the law has been to substitute an effects test for the original intent test. In other words, if a governmental action has the effect of discouraging minority voting, whether intentionally or not, the action must be rejected. Civil rights activists welcomed this change because proving the intent of an action is much more difficult than demonstrating its effect. A dramatic change occurred in 2013 when the U.S. Supreme Court, arguing that times had changed, ruled that the formula used to determine which jurisdictions were covered under the VRA was flawed, thereby eliminating the preclearance requirement.

LO 4.2

To compare state differences in election administration, voter turnout, and election results.

VOTING PATTERNS

Voter turnout is affected by several things. First, it varies according to the type of election. A presidential race usually attracts a higher proportion of eligible voters than a state or local election does. In 2012, with a presidential race under way, turnout was approximately 55 percent of the **voting-age population**; in 2014, when there was no presidential election on the ballot—but many governors' races—turnout was only 33 percent, the lowest turnout rate in seven decades. Second, popular candidates running a close race seem to increase voter interest. When each candidate has a chance to win, voters sense that their vote will matter more than in a race with a sure winner. Third, not only partisan competition, but also party ideology affects voter turnout.[16] When candidates take distinctive ideological stances in competitive elections, the incentive for party-identifiers to vote increases. Finally, based on new research, it appears that media handwringing about low-voter turnout may have a quite unintended effect: rather than stimulating turnout, it may actually depress it.[17]

Nationally, voter registration stands at approximately 76 percent of the voting-age population. Not everyone who is of voting age is actually eligible to vote, however. Noncitizens cannot vote (although they can in school board elections in a few localities), and most states have laws barring convicted felons and the mentally incompetent from participating. When you remove the ineligible population from consideration, registration among the **voting-eligible population** stood at approximately 88 percent in 2012. Registration matters because people who are registered tend to vote, and votes translate into political power. Thus, groups anxious to increase their electoral clout will launch registration drives among their membership.

Registering to vote has gotten easier. Passage of the National Voter Registration Act in 1993 means that individuals can register to vote when they apply for a driver's license, welfare benefits, or unemployment compensation or when they register their automobile. Oregon has taken it a step further by automatically registering people using drivers' license data collected at the Department of Motor Vehicles. (There is an opt-out option.) States allow voters to register by mail, and more than twenty-five states, such as Indiana and Nevada, have taken another step by allowing online voter registration; any computer terminal with an Internet connection can be a registration site. Washington has pioneered registration via Facebook in a bid to attract younger voters. And many states have moved the closing date for registration nearer to the actual date of the election, giving potential voters more time to register. This factor is important because campaigns tend to heighten the public's interest in the election.[18] Most states now close their registration books fewer than thirty days before an election, and ten states allow registration on Election Day, with Illinois and Hawaii set to implement same-day registration in 2015 and 2018, respectively.[19] Allowing voters to register on Election Day has been shown to be an important way to increase turnout.[20] North Dakota is the only state in the nation that does not require voter registration.

States can be differentiated according to voter turnout rates (see Figure 4.2 for voter turnout levels in 2014). In 2014, the states recording turnout rates of more than 50 percent of those eligible were Maine (58 percent), Wisconsin, (56.5 percent), Alaska (53.8 percent), Colorado (53.4 percent), Oregon (51 percent), and Minnesota (50.5 percent). Garnering the dubious distinction of being the states with the lowest voter turnout in 2014 were Indiana, with 27.8 percent voting, New York, where 28.2 percent of the eligible voters participated, and Texas, with a 28.3 percent turnout.[21] States with moralistic political cultures typically experience higher voter turnout than do states with traditionalistic political cultures. States with competitive political parties (as opposed to states where one party dominates) tend to have elections with a higher proportion of voters participating; each party needs to mobilize individuals who identify with it in order to win. When parties and other political organizations reach out to the public, participation in state politics increases.[22] Studies have shown that sending "remember to vote tomorrow" text messages can boost turnout; so can thanking voters for having voted in a previous election.[23]

voting-eligible population

The voting-age population excluding those who are noncitizens, and depending on a state's law, convicted felons or mentally incompetent.

It's Your Turn

Voter ID Laws: Good or Bad Idea?

Voter ID laws, enacted in several states in 2012, require voters to show a government-issued photo ID card at the polling place before voting. These laws have caused much debate. What do you think?

PROS	CONS
Every fraudulent vote cast dilutes the integrity of all the other votes cast.	The occurrence of voter fraud is very low. Few instances of voter fraud that a voter ID law could have prevented have been reported since 2000.
Elections are the bedrock of democracy. Therefore, they deserve the highest protections that we can achieve.	Voter ID laws disproportionately affect older, poorer, and minority populations, and are therefore discriminatory.
Many other activities require providing identification, such as owning a firearm or driving a car. Voting should be no different.	Voting is one of the core rights that we have as citizens, and therefore, the burden should be on the government to prove fraud rather than on the citizen to prove innocence.
Many states offer free state identification cards so there is no cost to the person who gets the card.	

States can affect turnout by the way in which they administer the registration and election processes. Is voting a convenient exercise, or is it an arduous task marked by long lines at the polling places, a requirement to show photo identification, and confusing ballots inside the voting booth? For instance, when Los Angeles County consolidated voting precincts and changed polling locations in an effort to cut administrative costs, turnout dropped by 3 percent.[24] Voter ID laws, enacted in several states in 2012, require voters to show a government-issued photo ID card at the polling place. This has caused much debate: supporters contend the laws will reduce fraud, while opponents expect the laws to reduce turnout, especially among poor voters.[25] The pros and cons of voter ID laws are considered in the It's Your Turn box.

The voting experience is changing too, with many states giving their citizens the choice to cast their votes before the day of the election. The list below outlines the options:

- Thirty-three states and the District of Columbia allow "no-excuse" in-person early voting at a county courthouse or satellite voting locations, on average, nineteen days before Election Day (e.g., California and Texas).
- Forty-seven states have procedures for regular absentee voting by mail; twenty states require an excuse (e.g., out of town on Election Day, disabled), and twenty seven do not require an excuse.

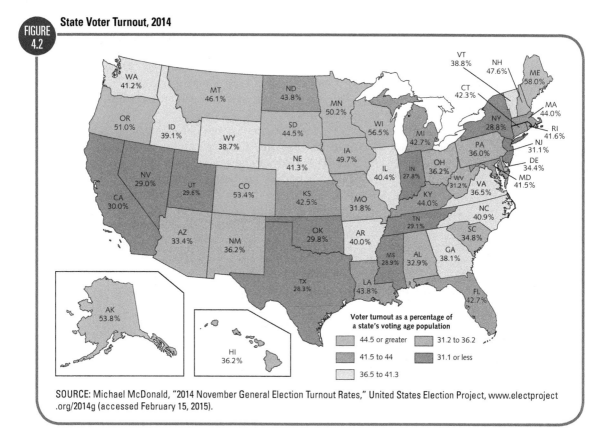

FIGURE 4.2

State Voter Turnout, 2014

Voter turnout as a percentage of a state's voting age population

- 44.5 or greater
- 41.5 to 44
- 36.5 to 41.3
- 31.2 to 36.2
- 31.1 or less

SOURCE: Michael McDonald, "2014 November General Election Turnout Rates," United States Election Project, www.electproject .org/2014g (accessed February 15, 2015).

- Two states have set up a vote-by-mail system for their elections (a ballot is automatically mailed to every eligible voter) and do not operate traditional polling places (Colorado, Oregon, and Washington).[26]

Does making voting easier really matter? The findings of research on conveniently located Election Day vote centers—alternatives to precinct-based polling places—suggest that it does, especially among people who tend to be infrequent voters.[27] Moreover, analysis of Oregon's vote-by-mail system showed that the turnout rate increased in some types of elections.[28] More voters are choosing to cast their ballots early, upwards of 60 percent in some states. As more states loosen the restrictions on early voting, the notion of Election *Day* is gradually giving way.

Elections

Elections are central to a representative democracy. Voters choose governors and legislators, and in most states, lieutenant governors, attorneys general, secretaries of state, and state treasurers. In some states, they also choose the heads of the agriculture and education departments, judges, and the public utility commissioners. At the local level, the list of elected officials includes

LO 4.3

To differentiate primary election types, general elections, and nonpartisan elections.

mayors and council members, county commissioners, county judges, sheriffs, tax assessors, and school board members. If state and local governments are to function effectively, elections must provide talented, capable leaders. But elections are not just about outcomes; they are also about the process itself. Florida's troubles with ballot design, voting machines, and recount rules in the 2000 presidential election underscored the need for elections to be administered fairly and transparently.

Significant changes in election management and especially in voting technology have occurred during the past few years. Lever-operated voting machines and punch card devices have lost favor, while electronic voting machines and optical scan ballots are being used more widely. This is an important trend because improvements in voting technology have been shown to lead to a significant decline in the number of "lost" or uncounted votes, which are referred to as **residual votes**.[29] Although electronic voting machines (akin to automatic teller machines) are becoming more popular, concerns over their accuracy and security remain. At issue is whether these systems should provide a VVPAT, or voter-verified paper audit trail, to supplement the record of the count in the electronic machine's memory.

PRIMARIES

For a party to choose a nominee for the general-election ballot, potential candidates must be winnowed. In the pre-Jacksonian era, party nominees were chosen by a legislative caucus—that is, a conference of the party's legislators. Caucuses gave way to the mechanism of state party conventions, which were similar to national presidential nomination conventions but without most of the spectacle; popularly elected delegates from across a state convened to select the party's nominees. Then the Progressive movement made an effort to open up the nomination process and make it more democratic. Political parties adopted the **primary system**, whereby voters directly choose from among several candidates to select the party's nominees for the general election. The use of primaries has effectively diminished the organizational power of political parties.

Thirteen states still allow for party conventions in particular instances, such as nominations for secretary of state and attorney general (Michigan) and selection of a slate of nominees by third parties (Kansas). Connecticut, the last state to adopt primaries, operates a unique challenge system whereby party nominees for various state offices are selected at a convention; but if a contest develops at the convention and a second candidate receives as much as 15 percent of the votes, the convention's nominee and the challenger square off in a primary.[30]

Primary Types Primaries can be divided into two types: closed and open. The only voters who can participate in a **closed primary** for a particular party are those who are registered in that party; an **open primary** does not require party membership. Even this basic distinction, however, lends itself to some variation. States differ, for example, in the ease with which voters can change party

residual votes

The number of uncounted, unmarked, or spoiled ballots in an election.

primary system

The electoral mechanism for selecting party nominees to compete in the general election.

closed primary

A primary in which only voters registered in the party are allowed to participate.

open primary

Voters decide which party's primary they will participate in.

affiliation and participate in the closed primary of the other party. In eleven closed primary states, a voter is an enrolled member of one party (or is an independent and may or may not be eligible to vote in either party's primary, depending on state law) and can change that affiliation only well in advance of the primary election. Democrats vote in the Democratic Party primary, Republicans vote in the GOP primary. Eleven states operate open primaries in which a voter secretly selects the ballot of the party in which she wishes to participate. Voters unaffiliated with either of the major parties may vote in open primaries. Obviously this system allows people who consider themselves Republicans to vote in a Democratic primary if they wish, and vice versa. The other twenty-eight states have primary systems that are neither completely closed nor open.[31] Table 4.2 groups the states by the types of primaries they operate.

The "hybrid" category in Table 4.2 reflects significant variation across states, not only in whether they lean toward closed or open primaries, but also in how much leeway they give political parties to alter their rules. Some of the twenty-four hybrid states hold "semi-closed" primaries in which voters register as members of a party but are allowed to change that affiliation on the day of the primary election. Still other hybrid states operate "semi-open" primaries in which voters can select either party's ballot but must do so publicly at the polling place.

Louisiana and three other states do something completely different: the Pelican State uses a single primary for its state and congressional races. Candidates, regardless of party affiliation, appear on the same ballot, and voters are free to choose from among them. If a candidate receives a majority of votes in the first round of voting, he is elected to office; if he does not, the top two vote-getters face each other in a **runoff election**. In 2010, California voters, dissatisfied with the level of partisan rancor in the Golden State, approved a constitutional amendment that provided a similar top-two primary system there, starting with the 2012 elections. Washington, which historically had allowed voters to cross over from one party to another in a single election, adopted its own variation on the top-two primary scheme. Finally, Nebraska uses a top-two primary for its nonpartisan legislative races.

Primary Runoff Elections A runoff election is held in some states if none of the candidates for an office receives a majority of votes in the primary. Primary runoff elections are used by parties in eight states: Alabama, Arkansas, Georgia, Mississippi, North Carolina, Oklahoma, South Carolina, and Texas. (South Dakota uses primary runoffs but only in certain instances; Florida abolished primary runoffs in 2005, Kentucky in 2008.) In the past, most of these states were one-party (Democratic) states, so the greatest amount of competition for an office occurred in the Democratic Party's primaries, in which as many as ten candidates might enter the race. When many candidates compete, it is quite probable that no one will receive a majority of the votes, so the top two vote-getters face each other in a runoff election. This process ensures that the party's nominee is preferred by a majority of the primary voters.

Theoretically, the rationale for the runoff primary is majority rule. But political circumstances have changed since several southern states adopted the

runoff election

A second election pitting the top two vote-getters from a first election in which no candidate received a majority of the votes cast.

TABLE 4.2   State Use of Different Types of Primary Elections

CLOSED	OPEN	HYBRID	TOP-TWO
Delaware	Alabama	Alaska	California
Florida	Arkansas	Arizona	Louisiana
Kansas	Georgia	Colorado	Nebraska*
Kentucky	Hawaii	Connecticut	Washington
Maine	Michigan	Idaho	
Nevada	Minnesota	Illinois	
New Jersey	Missouri	Indiana	
New Mexico	Montana	Iowa	
New York	North Dakota	Maryland	
Pennsylvania	Vermont	Massachusetts	
Wyoming	Wisconsin	Mississippi	
		New Hampshire	
		North Carolina	
		Ohio	
		Oklahoma	
		Oregon	
		Rhode Island	
		South Carolina	
		South Dakota	
		Tennessee	
		Texas	
		Utah	
		Virginia	
		West Virginia	
(11)	(11)	(24)	(4)

*In Nebraska, the top-two primary is used for the state's nonpartisan legislative races and for some statewide elections.

SOURCE: "State Primary Elections Types," National Conference of State Legislatures, http://www.ncsl.org/research/elections-and-campaigns/primary-types.aspx (June 24, 2014).

runoff primary system in the 1920s, and the Democratic Party no longer dominates the region. In fact, the two parties are competitive in some southern states, and in others the Republican Party has overtaken the Democrats. This raises an important question: Has the runoff primary outlived its usefulness? It is often difficult for a party to mobilize its voters for the second election, and voter participation in the runoff drops, on average, by one-third.[32] And they are costly to operate: Kentucky estimated the administrative cost of holding a statewide gubernatorial runoff primary to be approximately $5.4 million.[33] And, of course, a primary runoff campaign can be expensive for candidates themselves. One solution to this problem for parties might be the "ranked choice" or **"instant runoff"** that San Francisco, California, Minneapolis, Minnesota, and Burlington, Vermont, and a few other cities have begun using in their municipal elections. In an instant runoff, voters rank the primary candidates in their order of preference. If no candidate receives a majority of first choices, the candidate with the fewest of them is eliminated and voters who ranked the eliminated candidate first now have their ballots counted for their second choice. The process continues until one candidate has a majority; a runoff election is avoided.

GENERAL ELECTIONS

Primaries culminate in the general election, through which winning candidates become officeholders. When the general election pits candidates of the two major parties against one another, the winner is the candidate who receives a majority of the votes cast. In a race in which more than two candidates compete (which occurs when an Independent or a third-party candidate enters a race), the winner may not receive a majority but instead receives a **plurality**. Seven states allow candidates to run under the label of more than one party, which is called **fusion**. In New York, in 2014, for instance, Andrew Cuomo was the candidate for governor of the Democratic. Working Families, Women's Equality, and Independence parties.

Political parties have traditionally been active in general elections, mobilizing voters in support of their candidates. Their role has diminished over time, however, because general-election campaigns have become more candidate-centered and geared to the candidate's own organization. One new twist in the past two decades has been the emergence of legislative party caucuses as major factors in general elections. In large states with professionalized legislatures, the funds distributed to their party's nominees by legislative party caucuses run into the millions of dollars. In addition to funding, legislative party caucuses provide other types of election assistance, such as seminars on issues and campaign management, making these organizations powerful players in some states' politics.

Most states schedule their gubernatorial elections in off-years, that is, in years in which no presidential election is held. Only eleven states elected governors during the presidential election year of 2012; forty-one held their statewide races in other years. (The number sums to fifty-two because New Hampshire and Vermont limit their governors to two-year terms, thereby holding gubernatorial elections in both off- and on-years.) Among those forty-one off-year states, five—Kentucky, Louisiana, Mississippi, New Jersey, and Virginia—have elections that take place in odd-numbered years. Off-year elections prevent the presidential race from diverting attention from state races and also minimize the possible **coattail effect**, by which a presidential candidate can affect the fortunes of state candidates of the same party. By holding elections in off-years, races for governor may serve instead as referenda on the sitting president's performance in office. Generally, however, the health of a state's economy tends to be a critical issue in gubernatorial elections.[34]

instant runoff
Voters use preference rankings to select candidates at a single election.

plurality
The number of votes (though not necessarily a majority) cast for the winning candidate in an election with more than two candidates.

fusion
A state election provision that allows candidates to run on more than one party ticket.

coattail effect
The tendency of a winning (or losing) presidential candidate to carry state candidates of the same party into (or out of) office.

RECENT STATE ELECTIONS

State elections in 2013 were limited to gubernatorial and legislative races in New Jersey and Virginia. Republican Governor Chris Christie won reelection in New Jersey, but in Virginia where there was no incumbent running, the Democratic candidate, Terry McAuliffe, beat the state's Republican attorney general in a hotly contested race. Only 220 state legislative seats were at stake in 2013. In New Jersey, the elections produced no change in party control: Democrats continued to hold 60 percent of the seats in both chambers. In Virginia, Republicans added two seats, bringing their total in the House of Delegates to 67 out of 100 seats.

The stakes were high in 2014, with thirty-six governors' seats, 6,057 state legislative seats in forty-six states, and 225 statewide executive branch offices up for election. In the governors' races, Republicans had a net gain of two seats, winning in Arkansas, Illinois, Maryland, and Massachusetts, but losing seats the party previously held in Pennsylvania (to a Democrat) and Alaska (to an independent). In Vermont, none of the six gubernatorial candidates received a majority of the votes cast, so, as required by the state constitution, it fell to the state legislature to select the governor. The legislature chose the top vote-getter, the Democratic incumbent, who had received 46.4 percent of the vote and held a 1.3 percentage point edge over the Republican candidate. (This marked the twenty-third time that the Vermont legislature had selected the state's governor, with most of these actions occurring in the nineteenth century.)[35] As of 2015, the partisan composition of America's governors was thirty-one Republicans, eighteen Democrats, and one Independent.

In state legislatures, the 2014 elections were favorable to the GOP, with a net increase of nearly 350 seats. Of course, what really matters is how the number of seats gained or lost plays out at the state level. Republicans gained control of thirty-five state senates and thirty-three state house chambers; the Democrats held a majority in fourteen state senates and sixteen lower houses. When the dust settled, the GOP had control of both houses in thirty states; Democrats controlled both houses in eleven states, and in eight states control was split.[36] (The total is forty-nine states because Nebraska's unicameral legislature is officially nonpartisan.)

NONPARTISAN ELECTIONS

A **nonpartisan election** removes the political party identification from the candidate in an effort to make campaigns and elections less partisan. Elections that have been made nonpartisan include those for many judicial offices and for many local-level positions. The special task of judges—adjudicating guilt or innocence, determining right and wrong—does not lend itself to partisan interpretation. The job of local governments—delivering public services—has also traditionally been considered nonideological. Nonpartisan local elections are likely to be found in municipalities and in school districts and special districts (see Chapters 10 and 11).

Under a nonpartisan election system, all candidates for an office compete in a first election, and if there's no majority winner, the top two vote-getters

nonpartisan election
An election without party labels.

run in a second election (runoff). Although approximately three-quarters of cities use nonpartisan elections, some regional variation exists in their usage. The prevalence of nonpartisanship is somewhat lower in the Northeast and Midwest than it is in western cities.[37]

Most studies have concluded that nonpartisanship depresses turnout in municipal elections that are held independent of state and national elections. The figures are not dramatic, but in what are already low-turnout elections, the difference can run as high as 10 percent of municipal voters.[38] Studies have shown that lower turnout results in lessened representation of Latinos and Asian Americans on city councils and in the mayor's office.[39] Nonpartisan elections seem to produce a city council that is somewhat well-to-do by socioeconomic standards and a greater number of officeholders who consider themselves Republicans.

What does it take to get elected? In the absence of political parties, candidates are forced to create their own organizations to run for office. They raise and spend money (much of it their own), and they seek the support of business and citizen groups. Money matters, and according to studies of city elections in Atlanta and St. Louis, so do incumbency and newspaper endorsements.[40] In some communities, **slating groups** function as unofficial parties by recruiting candidates and financing their campaigns; citizens' groups can also be an important factor in local elections.[41]

Direct Democracy

What happens when the government does not respond to the messages that the people are sending? More and more frequently, the answer is to transform the messages into ballot propositions and let the citizens make their own laws. As explained in Chapter 3, *initiatives* are proposed laws or constitutional amendments that are placed on the ballot by citizen petition to be approved or rejected by popular vote. An initiative lets citizens enact their own laws, bypassing the state legislature. This mechanism for legislation by popular vote was one of several reforms of the Progressive era, which lasted roughly from 1890 to 1920.

Other Progressive reforms included the popular referendum and the recall. The **popular referendum** allows citizens to petition to vote on actions taken by legislative bodies. It provides a means by which the public can overturn a legislative enactment. (A popular referendum is different from a general **referendum**—a proposition put on the ballot by the legislature that requires voter approval before it can take effect. Constitutional amendments and bond issues are examples of general referenda.) The **recall** election, another citizen-initiated process, requires elected officials to stand for a vote on their removal before their term has expired. Recall provides the public with an opportunity to force an official out of office.

The key characteristic shared by initiative, popular referendum, and recall is that they are actions begun by citizens. The Progressives advocated these mechanisms to expand the role of citizens and to restrict the power of intermediary institutions such as legislatures, political parties, and elected officials. Their efforts were particularly successful in the western part of the United States, probably due to the difficulty of amending existing state constitutions in the East and to an elitist fear of the working class (namely, the industrialized immigrants in

LO 4.4

To understand the pros and cons of the mechanisms of direct democracy.

slating groups

Nonpartisan political organizations that endorse and promote a slate of candidates.

popular referendum

A special type of referendum whereby citizens can petition to vote on actions taken by legislative bodies.

referendum

A procedure whereby a governing body submits proposed laws, constitutional amendments, or bond issues to the voters for ratification.

recall

A procedure that allows citizens to vote elected officials out of office before their terms have expired.

the Northeast and the rural black sharecroppers in the South). The newer western states, by contrast, were quite open, both procedurally and socially. In 1898, South Dakota became the first state to adopt the initiative process; the initiative was actually used for the first time in Oregon in 1902 when citizens successfully petitioned for ballot questions on mandatory political party primaries and local option liquor sales. Both of the initiatives were approved.

Today, twenty-four states allow the initiative for constitutional amendments, statutes, or both; Mississippi is the most recent addition, having adopted it in 1992. A few of the twenty-four states use the indirect initiative, which gives the legislature an opportunity to consider the proposed measure. If the legislature fails to act or if it rejects the measure, the proposal is put before the voters at the next election. Popular referendum is provided in twenty-three states, and recall of state officials is provided in nineteen, with Illinois voters the most recent to approve a recall provision in 2010. Table 4.3 compares the states on their direct democracy provisions.

TABLE 4.3	Direct Democracy Provisions		
STATE	INITIATIVE	POPULAR REFERENDUM	RECALL*
Alabama	no	no	local
Alaska	yes	yes	yes
Arizona	yes	yes	yes
Arkansas	yes	yes	local
California	yes	yes	yes
Colorado	yes	yes	yes
Connecticut	no	no	no
Delaware	no	no	no
Florida	yes	no	local
Georgia	no	no	yes
Hawaii	no	no	no
Idaho	yes	yes	yes
Illinois	yes	no	yes
Indiana	no	no	no
Iowa	no	no	no
Kansas	no	no	yes
Kentucky	no	no	no
Louisiana	no	no	yes
Maine	yes	yes	no
Maryland	no	yes	no

(continued)

TABLE 4.3 **Direct Democracy Provisions (*continued*)**

Massachusetts	yes	yes	no
Michigan	yes	yes	yes
Minnesota	no	no	yes
Mississippi	yes	no	no
Missouri	yes	yes	local
Montana	yes	yes	yes
Nebraska	yes	yes	local
Nevada	yes	yes	yes
New Hampshire	no	no	local
New Jersey	no	no	yes
New Mexico	no	yes	local
New York	no	no	no
North Carolina	no	no	no
North Dakota	yes	yes	yes
Ohio	yes	yes	local
Oklahoma	yes	yes	no
Oregon	yes	yes	yes
Pennsylvania	no	no	no
Rhode Island	no	no	yes
South Carolina	no	no	no
South Dakota	yes	yes	local
Tennessee	no	no	local
Texas	no	no	no
Utah	yes	yes	no
Vermont	no	no	no
Virginia	no	no	no
Washington	yes	yes	yes
West Virginia	no	no	local
Wisconsin	no	no	yes
Wyoming	yes	yes	local

* "yes" means recall of state and local officials is allowed; "local" means that only certain types of local officials are subject to recall; "no" signifies that no recall provisions exist.

SOURCES: "State by State List of Initiative and Referendum Provisions," Initiative & Referendum Institute, http://www.iandrinstitute.org/statewide_i%26r.htm (accessed March 1, 2015); "Recall of State Officials," National Conference of State Legislatures, www.ncsl.org/legislatures-elections/elections/recall-of-state-officials.aspx (accessed September 11, 2013); "Recall of Local Officials," National Conference of State Legislatures, www.ncsl.org/legislatures-elections/elections/recall-of-local-officials.aspx (accessed February 28, 2011).

THE INITIATIVE

The first step in the initiative process is the petition. A draft of the proposed law (or constitutional amendment) is circulated along with a petition for citizens to sign. The petition signature requirement varies by state but usually falls between 5 and 10 percent of the number of votes cast in the preceding statewide election. To ensure that a matter is of statewide concern and that signatures have been gathered beyond a single area, some states set geographic distributional requirements. In Montana, for example, signature requirements must be met in at least one-third of the legislative districts and in Nebraska in two-fifths of the counties. Signatures can be gathered by door-to-door canvassing, buttonholing people at shopping malls and sporting events, posting downloadable petition forms on the Internet, and sending forms to a pre-selected list of likely signers.

The Popularity of Initiatives One of the most influential modern initiatives was California's Proposition 13 (1978), which rolled back property taxes in the state and spawned an immediate wave of tax-reduction propositions across the land. The increased popularity of initiatives has at least two explanations: (1) Some observers believe that wavering public confidence in government has led citizens to take matters into their own hands. The attitude seems to be that "if government can't be trusted to do the right thing, we'll do it ourselves." (2) New methods of signature collection have brought the initiative process within the reach of almost any well-financed group with a grievance or concern. An example from Massachusetts makes the point. When then-governor Paul Cellucci could not get the legislature to pass his tax-cut proposals, he took the issue straight to the voters. Using donations from supporters, he paid a company to collect sufficient signatures on petitions, and he got his issue on the ballot.[42] Massachusetts voters approved it.

Recent Initiatives If ballot questions are any indication of the public's mood, then the public has had quite an attitude lately. There were thirty-five initiatives on the ballot in 2014 (compared to fifty initiatives in the 2012 elections); 49 percent of them passed, a slightly better passage rate than the average 41 percent.[43] Listed below is a sampling of the initiatives (including one popular referendum) in particular states and the outcomes.

- Alaska: A proposal to allow individuals 21 years of age and older to possess up to one ounce of marijuana and up to six plants; also legalizes the manufacture, sale, and possession of marijuana paraphernalia (passed).
- Massachusetts: A proposal to expand the state's beverage container deposit law to cover all nonalcoholic, noncarbonated drinks in liquid form (failed).
- Missouri: A proposal to implement teacher performance evaluations in public schools to be used to determine a teacher's retention, promotion, or dismissal (failed).
- North Dakota: A proposal requiring that public school classes begin after Labor Day, thereby removing the power of local school districts to set earlier start dates (failed).
- Oregon: A proposal to amend the state constitution to guarantee equal rights for women (passed).

Questions about the Initiative By resorting to initiatives, citizens can bypass (or, in the case of indirect initiatives, prod) an obstructive legislature. And initiatives can be positive or negative—that is, they can be used in the absence of legislative action or they can be used to repudiate actions taken by the legislature. But is the initiative process appropriate for resolving tough public problems? Seldom are issues so simple that a yes-or-no ballot question can adequately reflect appropriate options and alternatives. A legislative setting, by contrast, fosters the negotiation and compromise that are likely to produce workable solutions.

Is the public sufficiently informed to make intelligent choices or to avoid susceptibility to emotional appeals? Ballot questions are considered low-information elections: Facing little information or conflicting claims, voters respond to readily available cues that may be misleading or erroneous. One interesting experiment showed that putting different titles on the same ballot question—but keeping the wording of the proposal exactly the same—produced very different outcomes in terms of voting "yes" or "no" on that question.[44] Initiatives seem to have positive effects on the electoral process by stimulating more participation but do ballot initiatives place citizens in an adversarial relationship with their government? Research has found that voters with frequent exposure to ballot questions are more likely to vote, donate money to political campaigns, and feel more politically efficacious.[45] However, amid these salutary effects, ballot initiatives seem to place citizens at loggerheads with government and spur distrust of public officials.[46]

Legislators are of two minds when it comes to direct citizen involvement in policy making. On the one hand, having the public decide a controversial issue such as abortion or school prayer helps legislators out of tight spots. On the other hand, increased citizen lawmaking intrudes on the central function of the legislature and usurps legislative power. Given the popularity of initiatives, legislators must proceed cautiously with actions that would alter the initiative process. In 2014, California revised its initiative law to increase the transparency of initiative campaign contributions, provide more voter-friendly explanations of propositions, allow for legislative review modifications, and pre-identify flaws or errors in proposed initiative language. These changes were aimed at making the initiative process in California work better.[47] After all, citizens in states that have an initiative process value it. A survey of Oregon citizens found 81 percent agreeing with this statement: "Ballot initiatives enhance the democratic process in Oregon by allowing voters to decide important policy issues."[48]

Once an initiative is passed, the new law has to be implemented and, as research has shown, "under normal conditions, legislatures, bureaucrats, or other government officials will work to alter a winning initiative's impact on public policy."[49] Direct democracy enthusiasts should heed the words of political scientist Valentina Bali, who studied local compliance with a California initiative intended to dismantle bilingual education programs: ". . . the large number of constraints suggests that the final policy outcome of an initiative can be quite limited after the initiative's implementation."[50] Initiative sponsors have learned that if they want their initiative to have the desired impact, they have to keep the pressure on, even after the measure has been approved.

THE RECALL

Recalls were once a little-used mechanism in state and local governments. Only nineteen states provide for recall of state officials, and in seven of them, judicial officers are exempt. City and county government charters, even in states without recall provisions, often include a process for recalling local elected officials. In fact, the first known recall was aimed at a Los Angeles city council member in 1904. Recalls have a much higher petition signature requirement than initiatives do; it is common to require a signature minimum of 25 percent of the votes cast in the last election for the office of the official sought to be recalled. Kansas, for example, requires a 40 percent minimum.

Recall efforts usually involve a public perception of official misconduct. On occasion, however, simply running afoul of citizen preferences is enough to trigger a recall, as former California governor Gray Davis discovered in 2003. Californians unhappy with Davis's leadership in resolving the state's budget crunch and its problems with energy deregulation, collected sufficient signatures (a total of 986,874) to force a recall election. Governor Davis was recalled from office by a 55-to-45 percent margin. What can only be described as "recall fever" hit Wisconsin as nine state senators (six Republicans and three Democrats) faced recall elections in 2011 as a result of controversy surrounding Governor Scott Walker's efforts to eliminate most collective bargaining for public employees. Two Republican senators who had supported the governor's proposal in the legislature were recalled from office. And in 2012, as public discontent continued, recall elections were held for governor, lieutenant governor, and four Republican state senators in the Badger State. Except for one state senator, these officials survived their recall elections and continued in office.

The rationale for the recall process is straightforward: Public officials should be subject to continuous voter control. The power to recall elected officials is valued by the public. But it can be a costly process, not only for the groups organizing the recall petition process and for the candidates, but for state and local government. Wisconsin estimated the price tag for the nine state Senate recall elections it held in 2011 at about $2.1 million, with the statewide gubernatorial recall election in 2012 costing taxpayers an estimated $13 million.[51] Initiatives and recalls have helped open up state and local governments to the public. Yet ironically, increased citizen participation can also jam the machinery of government, thus making its operation more cumbersome. Advocates of greater citizen activism, however, would gladly trade a little efficiency to achieve their goal.

Citizen Access to Government

As we saw in Figure 4.1, citizens have opportunities to participate in government in many nonelectoral ways. Because state and local governments have undertaken extensive measures to open themselves to public scrutiny and stimulate public input, citizen access to government has been increased. Many of these measures are directly connected with the policy-making process.

Controversies in States and Localities

Participatory Budgeting: Letting the Public Decide How to Spend Public Money

Vallejo, California, a city of 117,000 people near San Francisco, got serious about citizen participation when it adopted a participatory budgeting process for the 2013 budget cycle. Participatory budgeting (PB) directly involves residents in deciding how public funds should be spent. The process is far more participatory than simply showing up at a meeting or two and making the case for building a new library or hiring more firefighters. In participatory budgeting, citizens decide the rules for the process and identify an array of spending ideas through a series of budget assemblies; a steering committee then winnows the ideas into a set of viable options and places them on a ballot for a vote.

In Vallejo, $3.2 million was made available for PB, which was a portion of the revenue generated by an increase in the sales tax. Of the 800 ideas initially generated, thirty-three of them made it to the ballot and of them, twelve were funded. Any resident who was 16 or older could vote for as many as six projects; about 3,600 residents voted. The three projects receiving the most votes were: pothole and street repair ($550,000), street light installation ($170,000), and park improvements ($621,500). Voters also approved funding the purchase of science, art, and math equipment for the schools, the development of community gardens, a series of grants to small businesses, installation of security cameras around the city, and renovations at a local Boys & Girls Club facility, among others.

In 2015, Vallejo was in its third year of PB. It has experienced a few bumps along the way. Some of the folks who have been involved in PB have found the process time-consuming and frustrating. And it can be difficult to draw other residents into the process, so participation has remained relatively low. Some members of the city council have become a bit skeptical of PB, contending that as the elected representatives of the public, they are ones who should be making spending decisions. Moreover, the amount of revenue to be allocated via the PB process has been reduced, thereby limiting its impact. Still, to PB's avid proponents in the city and beyond, it holds tremendous promise as a tool to spur civic engagement and restore public trust in government.

Critical Thinking Questions

1. Budget experts spend years in school to learn how to prepare a budget. Do citizens have adequate information to make budgeting decisions?

2. Vallejo committed $3.2 million to PB the first year that it was implemented, but has since dropped that figure to $1 million. How much of the budget should be subject to this process?

3. The city of Vallejo estimates that it costs $300,000 to administer the program. Do the administrative costs justify the increased citizen participation?

4. Cities like New York City, Chicago, San Francisco, and St. Louis have experimented with PB as a way to determine public spending preferences in some of their city council districts. Would PB work better on a less-than-citywide basis?

SOURCES: Alana Semuels, "The City that Gave Its Residents $3 Million," *The Atlantic*, http://www.theatlantic.com/business/archive/2014/11/the-city-that-gave-its-residents-3-million/382348/?single_page=true (accessed November 2014); John M. Kamensky, "When Citizens Decide How Public Money is Spent," http://www.governing.com/blogs/bfc/col-neighborhood-participatory-budgeting-ibm-center-business-government-report.html (accessed September 15, 2014).

ROBERT GALBRAITH/Reuters/Corbis

At a minimum, they enable government and the citizenry to exchange information, and thus they contribute to the growing capacity of state and local governments. At most, they may alter political power patterns and resource allocations. Participatory budgeting, the subject of the Controversies in States and Localities box, describes the efforts of one California city to engage its residents in determining which projects and activities should receive city funds.

OPENING UP GOVERNMENT

Many of the accessibility measures adopted by state and local governments are the direct result of public demands that government be more accountable. Others have resulted from an official effort to involve the public in the ongoing work of government.

Open Meeting Laws Florida's 1967 Sunshine Law is credited with sparking a surge of interest in openness in government, and today **open meeting laws** are on the books in all fifty states. These laws do just what the name implies: they open meetings of government bodies to the public, or, in Florida's parlance, they bring government "into the sunshine." Open meeting laws apply to both the state and local levels and affect the executive branch as well as the legislative branch. Basic open meeting laws have been supplemented by additional requirements in many states. Advance public notice of meetings is required in all states; most insist that minutes be kept, levy penalties against officials who violate the law, and void actions taken in meetings held contrary to sunshine provisions.

Although some states might prefer to resist the sun's rays, the trend is toward more openness. But this is complicated by the fact that most states' sunshine laws were written for a world of paper-based records stored in metal filing cabinets. Colorado was one of the first states to make the archived e-mail files of the state's politicians open to the public. Now, forty states make governmental e-mails subject to their open-records laws, and twelve states treat text messages the same way.[52] Table 4.4 groups states according to their transparency grades from a study done by U.S. Public Interest Research Group.[53] The scores reflect how well states do in providing online access to government spending data. The states earning "A's" are performing substantially better at opening up government to public scrutiny than the states with "D's" and "F's."

Administrative Procedure Acts After state legislation is passed or a local ordinance is adopted, an administrative agency typically is responsible for implementation. This process involves the establishment of rules and regulations and hence constitutes powerful responsibility. In practice, agencies often have wide latitude in translating legislative intent into action. For example, if a new state law creates annual automobile safety inspections, it is the responsibility of the state's Department of Motor Vehicles to make it work. Unless the law specifies the details, bureaucrats will determine the items to be covered in the safety inspection, the location of inspection stations, and the fee to be charged. These details are just as important as the original enactment.

open meeting laws
Statutes that open the meetings of government bodies to the public.

TABLE 4.4	State Transparency in Spending Data	
STATE	**GRADE**	**2015 SCORE**
Alabama	D	55
Alaska	F	43
Arizona	B	84
Arkansas	B−	82
California	F	34
Colorado	B+	89
Connecticut	A	96
Delaware	C	71
Florida	A	95
Georgia	C	74
Hawaii	C	71
Idaho	F	45
Illinois	A−	93
Indiana	A	97
Iowa	A−	94
Kansas	B	84
Kentucky	B	86
Louisiana	A	96
Maine	C+	76
Maryland	B+	87
Massachusetts	A	95.5
Michigan	B+	87
Minnesota	B	85
Mississippi	C+	79
Missouri	C+	77
Montana	A−	92
Nebraska	B+	87
Nevada	C	74
New Hampshire	C+	75
New Jersey	B	84
New Mexico	C+	77
New York	A−	91

(*continued*)

TABLE 4.4	State Transparency in Spending Data (*continued*)	
STATE	**GRADE**	**2015 SCORE**
North Carolina	B+	89.5
North Dakota	D+	64
Ohio	A+	100
Oklahoma	B+	88
Oregon	A	96.5
Pennsylvania	B	83
Rhode Island	C+	76
South Carolina	C+	78
South Dakota	A−	90
Tennessee	B−	82
Texas	A−	91
Utah	B	86
Vermont	B+	89
Virginia	B−	82
Washington	B	86
West Virginia	C	73
Wisconsin	A	96.5
Wyoming	C−	67

SOURCE: U.S. PIRG, "Report: Transparent and Accountable Budgets," http://www.uspirg.org/news/usp/new-report-ranks-all-fifty-states-government-spending-transparency (March 18, 2015).

administrative procedure acts

Acts that standardize administrative agency operations as a means of safeguarding clients and the general public.

advisory committee

An organization created by government to involve members of the public in studying and recommending solutions to public problems.

focus group

A small group of individuals assembled to provide opinion and feedback about specific issues in government. Participants are often paid for their time.

To ensure public access to this critical rule-making process, states have adopted **administrative procedure acts**, which require public notice of the proposed rule and an opportunity for citizen comment. All states provide for this "notification and comment" process, as it is known. These provisions offer the public and various political actors a way to influence the content of agency rules.[54] In addition, some states give citizens the right to petition an administrative agency for an adjustment in the rules.

Advisory Committees Another arena for citizen participation that is popular in states and especially local governments is the **advisory committee**, in the form of citizen task forces, commissions, and panels. Regardless of name, these organizations are designed to study a problem and to offer advice, usually in the form of recommendations. People chosen to serve on an advisory committee tend to have expertise, as well as interest, in the issue and, in most cases, political connections. These days, the **focus group** plays a similar role by providing a small group setting for intense discussion and debate of public issues.[55]

Citizen advisory committees provide a formal structure for citizen input. Many cities have created community boards to provide a channel for communication between neighborhoods and city government. If officials heed public preferences, citizen advice can become the basis for public policy. Citizen advisory organizations also provide elected officials with a "safe" course of action. In a politically explosive situation, a governor can say, "I've appointed a citizen task force to study the issue and report back to me with recommendations for action." The governor thus buys time, with the hope that the issue will gradually cool down. Another benefit of these organizations is that they ease citizen acceptance of subsequent policy decisions since the governor can note that an action "was recommended by an impartial panel of citizens." This is not to suggest that citizen advisory committees are merely tools for manipulation by politicians, but they do have uses beyond citizen participation.

E-GOVERNMENT

The Internet has brought state and local governments into citizens' homes in a way earlier technology could not. States and localities of all sizes have incorporated electronic communications into their daily operations. Websites abound and e-mails proliferate. State governments have created elaborate websites that link the user to vast databases and information resources. People can click on a city's homepage and find an array of useful information, such as the agenda for the next city council meeting, the minutes of previous council sessions, the city budget, the comprehensive plan, crime statistics, and the like. Some elected officials use blogs as a way to stay in touch with their constituents—and to bypass conventional media. Facebook, Twitter, and You-Tube offer more ways for politicians to connect with the public.

Now states and localities are expanding their use of the Internet and social media in dealing with the public. It started with the downloading of public reports and generic forms and has moved into more highly individualized interaction such as filing taxes, applying for licenses and permits, and making service requests. Although some have touted the use of the Internet in voting, worries over security and accuracy have slowed the move to the Internet as a virtual polling place.

An example of a local jurisdiction that has embraced citizen participation through e-government is Tacoma, Washington, a city of 200,000 people and with a territorial range of 63 square miles. On the city's official website, the first page features a box titled "Connect with Us," which features several connection options that can be clicked on and opened from the webpage. The city posts on Facebook, sends out tweets via Twitter, and uploads videos to You-Tube. TV Tacoma lets people watch livestreamed and archived city council meetings, while the Newsroom option provides access to news releases and the city's media office. By clicking on "Contact Us," citizens can make service requests online, and even upload an attachment such as a photo of a pothole on a neighborhood street or a broken bench at a city park. At Tacoma Today, people can sign up for e-mail updates about the latest events and alerts in the city. The intent of these "Connect with Us" options is to make it easier for Tacoma residents and businesses to interact with the city. The expectation is

LO 4.5

To appreciate the importance of the Internet and social media in connecting the public with government.

that this interaction will produces a more effective city government and a more engaged and satisfied public.

The Internet also offers an efficient way for government to gauge public opinion and preferences. This aspect of e-government was put to good use recently when many states and localities were struggling to balance their budgets. Several jurisdictions developed online simulations to engage the public in budget-balancing exercises. For instance, in Colorado's "backseat budgeter," players have the option to expand or shrink state programs, as well as to increase or decrease various revenue sources, all in an effort to keep the budget in balance. As players quickly learn, balancing budgets is a task more easily said than done, especially because constitutional provisions limit the range of options. But the engaging online format acquaints the public with the budget process and policymakers with the public's preferences.

One of the major concerns as the push toward e-government grows is that the so-called "technology have-nots" will be left behind. Low-income Americans lag far behind middle- and upper-income groups in their access to the Internet. This digital divide has led many communities to install personal computers in libraries, as well as in government information kiosks located in shopping malls and transit stations. Some rural areas have found it difficult to attract start-up businesses and related investment because high-speed Internet is not available. To combat this, New York has created a $25 million fund to expand broadband Internet access to rural and underserved urban areas of the Empire State. Other e-government concerns involve security and privacy. Fear that hackers might break into government computers (as they did in 2012 in South Carolina's Department of Revenue) or that personal information might be misused tempers some public enthusiasm for e-government.

VOLUNTEERISM AS PARTICIPATION

LO 4.6

To articulate the impact of volunteerism in states and localities.

Voluntary action is another constructive participatory activity unrelated to the ballot box. People and organizations donate their time and talents to supplement or even replace government activity. **Volunteerism** is a means of bringing fresh ideas and energy, whether physical or financial, into government while relieving some of the service burden. Washington created the first statewide volunteerism office in 1969, and within twenty years, all states had volunteer programs in place.

One highly visible example of volunteerism is the Adopt a Highway program, which is active in forty-nine states and Puerto Rico. The program grew out of a successful anti-littering effort in Texas, dubbed "Don't Mess with Texas." Over the past twenty years, the number of local businesses and civic clubs willing to pick up litter along designated stretches of state highways has skyrocketed. You have probably noticed the Adopt-a-Highway signs, with the names of volunteering groups listed underneath. The state saves money, the roadsides stay cleaner, and the volunteering groups have good feelings and free advertising to go along with their sore backs.

Successful volunteer programs like Adopt a Highway are emblematic of the concept of social capital, as mentioned earlier in this chapter. Stephen Knack's study showed a positive relationship between several indicators of social

volunteerism

A form of participation in which individuals or groups donate time or money to a public purpose.

capital, especially the percentage of the public engaged in volunteerism, and state governmental quality.[56] States with a greater propensity toward volunteerism scored higher on several government performance measures, including financial management, capital management, and information technology.

Local governments use volunteers in various ways. Generally, volunteerism is most successful when citizens can develop the required job skills quickly or participate in activities they enjoy, such as library work, recreation programs, or fire protection. In addition to providing services to others, volunteers can be utilized for self-help; that is, they can engage in activities in which they are the primary beneficiaries. For example, some New York City neighborhoods take responsibility for the security and maintenance of nearby parks. Residential crime-watch programs are another variety of self-help. In both these instances, the volunteers and their neighborhoods benefit. Overall, studies show that volunteerism is especially successful in rural areas and small towns.[57]

Important supplements to government volunteer programs are those of the nonprofit sector. Members of local faith-based groups and civic organizations, for example, often volunteer their time in support of community improvement projects such as Habitat for Humanity, Meals on Wheels, and Sistercare. Sometimes volunteerism has a political agenda, as does the Minutemen Civil Defense Corps, a group of volunteers who in 2005 launched a border watch program that remained active until 2010. Periodically, they massed along stretches of the border with Mexico to monitor illegal entry into the United States. Their actions have added fuel to the firestorm of debate over illegal immigration.

The Effects of Citizen Participation

Consider again the four quadrants of Figure 4.1. Constructive participatory behaviors, whether active or passive, invigorate government. The capacity of state and local governments depends on several factors, one of which is citizen participation. Underlying this argument is the implicit but strongly held belief shared by most observers of democracies that an accessible, responsive government is a legitimate government. Some commentators held out hope that new media technologies such as cable television and the Internet would stimulate interest in politics and move more people into the constructive quadrants. However, research indicates that this has not happened. Instead, politically interested individuals use these technologies to become better informed, whereas the politically uninterested opt for entertainment programming.[58]

An active public, one that chooses the *voice* option in Figure 4.1, has the potential to generate widespread change in a community. Public policy tends to reflect the interests of active citizens. The mobilization of lower-class voters, for instance, is linked to more generous state welfare policies.[59] The challenge for government is to incorporate citizen participation into ongoing operations. Some places are trying to do just that. One is Durham, North Carolina, which has posted a clever one-minute YouTube video inviting its residents to join the city council for coffee and conversation about the city's budget priorities.[60] Citizen involvement may not always be easy or efficient, but in a democracy, it is the ultimate test of the legitimacy of that government.

Chapter Recap

- Citizen participation in the community can be active or passive and constructive or destructive. Local governments have devoted much time and energy to encouraging active, constructive participation among the citizenry.

- Voter turnout rates vary dramatically from one state to another, and the reasons have to do with the political culture of the state, the competitiveness of the political parties, and the way elections are administered.

- After the 2014 elections, thirty-one gubernatorial offices were in Republican hands; eighteen were held by Democrats; and there was one Independent.

- Almost half of the states have an initiative process, and in those that do, it has become an important tool for policy making.

- The use of recall has increased, led by efforts in Wisconsin to oust the governor, lieutenant governor, and thirteen state senators.

- e-government is on the rise, with states and localities adopting more and more high-tech ways of interacting with citizens. This trend holds tremendous potential for increasing citizen participation in government.

- Volunteerism is a way of bringing fresh ideas and energy into government and helps connect citizens to their community.

- State and local governments continue to encourage their citizens in meaningful participation.

KEY TERMS

participation *(p. 80)*
hashtag activism *(p. 80)*
free rider *(p. 83)*
social capital *(p. 83)*
Voting Rights Act of 1965 *(p. 84)*
voting-age population *(p. 84)*
voting-eligible population *(p. 85)*
residual votes *(p. 88)*
primary system *(p. 88)*

closed primary *(p. 88)*
open primary *(p. 88)*
runoff election *(p. 89)*
instant runoff *(p. 91)*
plurality *(p.91)*
fusion *(p. 91)*
coattail effect *(p. 91)*
nonpartisan election *(p. 92)*
slating groups *(p.93)*

popular referendum *(p. 93)*
referendum *(p. 93)*
recall *(p. 93)*
open meeting laws *(p. 100)*
administrative procedure acts *(p. 102)*
advisory committee *(p. 102)*
focus group *(p. 102)*
volunteerism *(p. 104)*

INTERNET RESOURCES

The website of the Federal Election Commission, **www.fec.gov**, contains information about U.S. elections, including laws, campaign financing, and results. To learn more about various state laws on elections, visit each state's home page or see the website of the National Association of Secretaries of State at **www.nass.org**.

The League of Women Voters, a well-respected organization that encourages informed and active participation of citizens in government, maintains a website at **www.lwv.org**.

MTV's Rock the Vote, an effort to boost political participation among young voters, is at **www.rockthevote.com**.

You can find just about anything you want to know about ballot measures at **www.iandrinstitute.org** and election results at **www.ballotpedia.org**.

A candidate for the state senate in Texas talks with potential voters at a restaurant in Houston. AP Photo/Houston Chronicle/Eric Kayne

Political Parties, Interest Groups, and Campaigns: Influencing Public Policy

Research tells us that, on average, Americans prefer to live near people whose political beliefs and ideology are similar to their own. But how can someone determine which area is most closely aligned with her ideology? Finding out how a neighborhood voted in a presidential election is a logical starting point, but then what? That's where consulting firms such as Clarity Campaign Labs come in. Clarity, which provides an array of services to political campaigns, has developed an algorithm that uses big data and your responses to a series of agree/disagree questions to identify the area (defined by postal zip code) that most fits your ideological profile. Answer seven questions on Clarity's "What Town Matches My Politics?" website about your partisanship, positions on abortion, climate change, taxes, and gun control, and preferences for urban living and religious practice, select the state you live in, and voila, your ideological "best place" is identified.[1]

An interesting exercise to be sure, but the larger point is that big data, advanced analytics, and technology are changing the way political campaigns operate. Campaign strategists can design specifically targeted messages that resonate with potential voters in an area. Research on state legislative campaigns has shown that these approaches can be successful in increasing both candidate name recognition and voter turnout.[2] And it just goes to show that political campaigns aren't what they used to be.

Political Parties

LO 5.1

To understand the functions of political parties in state government.

The two major **political parties**, the Democratic Party and the Republican Party, offer slates of candidates to lead us. Candidates campaign hard for the high-profile jobs of governor, state legislator, mayor, and various other state and local positions. In some states, even candidates for judicial positions compete in partisan races. But party involvement in our system of government does not end on Election Day—the institutions of government themselves have a partisan tone. Legislatures are organized along party lines; governors offer Republican or Democratic agendas for their states; county commissioners of different ideological stripes fight over the package of services provided to local residents. Through the actions of their elected officials, political parties play a major role in the operation of government.

THE CONDITION OF POLITICAL PARTIES

The condition of contemporary American political parties has been described with words such as *decline*, *decay*, and *demise*. In some ways, the description is accurate, but in other ways, it is overstated. True, fewer people consider themselves members of either of the two major political parties these days, whereas the number of people calling themselves independents is often as much as 40 percent of the electorate.[3] Furthermore, campaigns are increasingly candidate-centered rather than party-centered, and they rely on personal organizations and political consultants. But at the same time, the party organization has become more professionalized, taking on new tasks and playing new roles in politics and governance. Parties have more financial and technological resources at their disposal. Thus, to some observers, political parties are enjoying a period of revitalization and rejuvenation. While the debate over the condition of political parties continues, it seems clear that they have undergone a transformation during the past thirty years and that they have proven to be quite adaptable.

political parties

Organizations that nominate candidates to compete in elections, and promote policy ideas.

ideology

Core beliefs about the nature and role of the political system.

American political parties are composed of three interacting parts: the party organization (party committees, party leaders, and activists), the party in government (candidates and officeholders), and the party in the electorate (citizens who identify with the party).[4] These parts interact to do many things, but among their central tasks are nominating and electing candidates, educating (some might say propagandizing) citizens, and, once in office, governing.

Parties in the United States function as umbrella organizations that shelter loose coalitions of relatively like-minded individuals. In terms of **ideology**,

Republicans tend to be more conservative, favoring a limited role for government; Democrats tend to be more liberal, preferring a more activist government. A general image for each party is discernible: The Republicans typically have been considered the party of big business; the Democrats, the party of workers. In foreign affairs, Republicans favor a more assertive U.S. policy than Democrats typically do. On many of the social issues of the day—gay rights, abortion, pornography, and prayer in schools—the two parties tend to take different positions. By 2015, approximately 28 percent of the voting-age public considered themselves Democrats, while Republican identifiers numbered about 27 percent and the independent segment had climbed to 44 percent.[5] Note, however, that typically about one-third to one-half of the independents lean toward one of the two major parties. (See Figure 5.1, which tracks party identification during the recent past.) These national percentages mask tremendous variation across jurisdictions: Washington, D.C., Hawaii, Rhode Island, and Massachusetts have substantially higher percentages of voters favoring the Democratic Party; Utah, Wyoming, and Idaho have significantly more Republicans.

The geographical distribution of partisan loyalties has produced some interesting patterns. The South, where conservative political attitudes predominate, has become a region of so-called red states—that is, states that vote Republican in presidential elections. Other red states are found in the plains region and the Rocky Mountain west. States that are more reliably Democratic in presidential elections—usually the Northeastern region, the Pacific Coast, and the upper Midwest—are designated "blue" states. (The labels "red" and "blue" have become the norm, originating from the color-coded maps used by television broadcasters to show election returns.) States with greater partisan diversity have been called "purple" by some pollsters.[6] It is important not

Party Identification in the United States, 2005–2015
NOTE: Poll data for 2005–2014 as of November each year, poll data for 2015 as of March 2015.

FIGURE 5.1

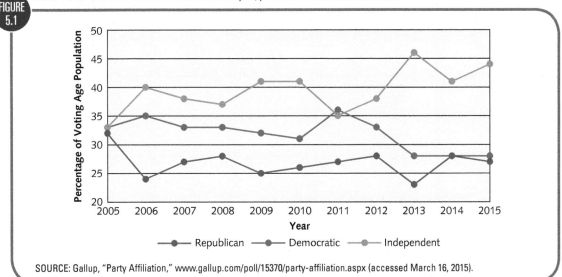

SOURCE: Gallup, "Party Affiliation," www.gallup.com/poll/15370/party-affiliation.aspx (accessed March 16, 2015).

to overgeneralize from these colorful, but simple, descriptors of state-level partisanship. Within an individual state, various partisan configurations exist from one place to another, as research on presidential voting at the county level has shown.[7] Voters display a remarkable penchant for **ticket splitting**— that is, voting for a Democrat for one office and a Republican for another in the same election. In fact, many voters are fond of saying that they "vote for the person, not the party."

LO 5.2

To analyze the evolution of political parties over time.

PARTY ORGANIZATION

Political parties are decentralized organizations, with fifty state Republican parties and fifty state Democratic parties. Each state also has local party organizations, most typically at the county level. Although they interact, each of these units is autonomous, a situation that promotes independence but is not so helpful to party discipline. Specialized partisan groups, including the College Democrats, the Young Republicans, Democratic Women's Clubs, Black Republican Councils, and so on, have been accorded official recognition. Party organizations are further decentralized into precinct-level clusters, which bear the ultimate responsibility for turning out the party's voters on Election Day.[8] Figure 5.2 shows a typical state party organization.

Typical State Party Organization
Most political party organizations look something like this.

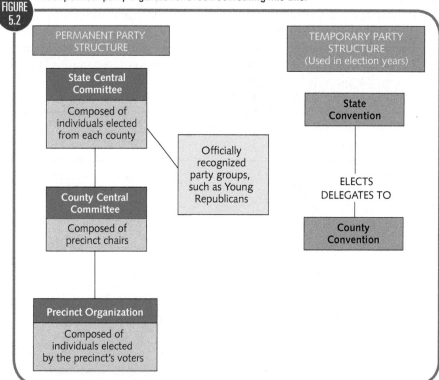

FIGURE 5.2

ticket splitting

Voting for candidates of different political parties in a general election.

State Parties State governments vary in how closely and vigorously they regulate political parties. In states with few laws, parties have more discretion in their organization and functions.[9] Regardless, each state party has a charter or bylaws to govern its operation. The decision-making body is the state committee, sometimes called a "central committee," which is headed by a chairperson and is composed of members elected in party primaries or at state party conventions. State party organizations differ in their organizational vitality and resources. In nonelection years, the parties operate with limited staff and revenue; in election years, however, their employment and their funds increase dramatically. Republican organizations generally outstrip Democratic ones in these measures of organizational strength.

State parties, officially at least, lead their party's push to capture statewide elected offices. Although they may formulate platforms and launch party-centered fund-raising appeals, their value to candidates is in the services they provide.[10] In many states, parties host seminars for party nominees about campaigning effectively, they conduct research into the public's mood, and they advertise on behalf of their candidates. To a candidate, one of the most valuable services the state party can provide is access to its database of party voters.[11] Although partisan volunteers still canvass neighborhoods, knocking on doors and talking to would-be voters, these activities are increasingly supplemented by web-based and e-mail appeals for funds and votes.

Local Parties County party organizations are composed of committee members chosen at the precinct level. Local parties are less professionally organized than state parties. Although many local organizations maintain campaign headquarters during an election period, few operate year-round offices. County chairpersons report devoting a lot of time to the party in the months before an election, but otherwise the post does not take much of their time. Most chairpersons lead organizations without any full-time staff, and vacancies in precinct offices are common.

Local party workers are volunteers whose primary reward is the satisfaction of being involved in politics. But the work is rarely glamorous. Party workers are the people who conduct voter registration drives, drop off the lawn signs for residents' front yards, and organize candidate forums. On behalf of the party's candidates, they distribute campaign literature, organize fund-raising events, contact voters, and run newspaper advertisements. But what impact do these activities have on the campaign? State legislative candidates report that local parties are most beneficial when providing traditional grassroots services such as rounding up volunteer workers and getting voters to the polls on Election Day.[12]

Factions Political parties frequently develop factions—that is, identifiable subsets. These may be ideologically based, such as the struggle between moderates and liberals for control of state Democratic parties. They may be organized around particular political leaders, or they may reflect sectional divisions within a state. When factions endure, they make it difficult for a party to come together on behalf of candidates and in support of policy.[13] Persistent intraparty factions create electoral opportunities for the opposing party.

A challenge facing the GOP in many states has come from the **Tea Party**, a loosely-organized, conservative/libertarian grassroots movement that emerged in 2009. Favoring budget cuts and less government, Tea Party candidates took on establishment Republican candidates in gubernatorial primaries in several states in 2010 and 2012 and experienced some success. By the 2014 elections, the Tea Party's influence at the gubernatorial level appeared to have waned, with only two GOP incumbents drawing (and ultimately, defeating) Tea Party challengers in primary elections.[14] However, in Texas, a state senator who had created a Tea Party caucus in the legislature was elected lieutenant governor, a powerful position in the Lone Star state.

THE TWO-PARTY SYSTEM

General elections in the United States are typically contests between candidates representing the two major political parties. Such has been the case for the past century and a half. The Democratic Party has been in existence since the 1830s, when it emerged from the Jacksonian wing of the Jeffersonian Party. The Republican Party, despite its label as the Grand Old Party, is newer; it developed out of the sectional conflict over slavery in the 1850s.

Why Just Two? There are numerous reasons for the persistence of two-party politics. Explanations that emphasize sectional dualism, such as East versus West or North versus South, have given way to those focusing on the structure of the electoral system. Parties compete in elections in which there can be only one winner. Most legislative races, for example, take place in single-member districts in which only the candidate with the most votes wins; there is no reward for finishing second or third. Hence, the development of radical or noncentrist parties that appeal to a small subset of the electorate is discouraged. In addition, laws regulating access to the ballot and receipt of public funds contribute to two-partyism by creating high start-up costs for third parties. Another plausible explanation has to do with tradition. Americans are accustomed to a political system composed of two parties, and that is how we understand politics. The institutionalization of the two-party system is reflected in these numbers: In 2015, of the nation's 7,333 state legislators (this number excludes Nebraska where legislators are elected in nonpartisan races), only 35 were not Democrats or Republicans—and 12 of the 35 were in the Vermont House of Representatives.[15]

Third Parties The assessment of former Alabama governor George Wallace that "there ain't a dime's worth of difference between Democrats and Republicans," although exaggerated, raises questions about the need for alternative parties. Third parties (also called nonmajor or minor parties) are a mostly unsuccessful but constant phenomenon in U.S. politics. The Greens, Libertarians, Progressives, and the Constitution Party are some examples of third parties currently active in some states. The two major parties may not differ substantially, but for the most part their positions reflect the public mood. Third parties suffer because the two established parties have vast reserves of money and resources at their disposal; new parties can rarely amass the finances or

Tea Party

A conservative/ libertarian grassroots political movement whose supporters favor smaller government.

Controversies in States and Localities

Opening up the Ballot to More Parties

Tired of Pennsylvania's restrictive ballot access laws, a group of individuals and organizations, including several third parties (Libertarian, Green, Constitution, and Reform, among others) formed an interest group called the Pennsylvania Ballot Access Coalition (PABAC). The goal of the group was simple: to change the state's laws to make it easier for minor parties to get on the ballot. They argued that it would create more political competition and give voters more choices. PABAC got the ball rolling in 2009, when a Pennsylvania state senator introduced the Voters' Choice Act. The bill relaxes the definition of a minor party and allows these parties to create their own rules for nominating candidates since they would be unlikely to hold primaries. "No state makes it tougher to get on the ballot than Pennsylvania, as independent and minor party candidates face significantly more difficult barriers than Republicans and Democrats," the senator said. "My bill would enhance our democratic process by leveling the playing field." His legislative colleagues weren't persuaded, however, and the bill died, only to be reintroduced in subsequent sessions.

Pennsylvania is not the only state in which the issue of ballot access for third parties has been on the agenda. Arkansas recently amended its law not only lowering the petition signature requirement for minor parties to 10,000, but also increasing the time frame in which to collect the signatures from sixty to ninety days. Some states have moved in the opposite direction, however. In Arizona, a change in state law in 2015 made it more difficult for minor party candidates to get on the ballot, by redefining the signature requirements. Under the new law, a minor party candidate would need signatures of one-quarter of one

percent of the party's registered voters <u>and</u> registered independents in the district in which he is competing. That may not sound like a lot, but because many places in Arizona have a large number of independents, the change had the effect of substantially increasing the signature requirements.

Although ballot access for minor parties is on the agenda, the resolution of this issue is not necessarily automatic or uniform across the states. The issue certainly raises a series of interesting questions.

Critical Thinking Questions

1. Are there any representatives in your state's legislature who are neither Republican nor Democrat? If so, what party are they affiliated with? If not, do you think there should be?

2. Would having more parties on the ballot would expand voter choice or make elections more difficult to navigate?

3. Opening the ballot to more parties could force more compromise and cooperation and perhaps more coalition-building among various parties in the legislature. But this would likely make it harder to get bills that are more ideologically pure passed. Why would this be a good or a bad thing?

SOURCES: "Voter's Choice Act," Pennsylvania Ballot Access Coalition, www.paballotaccess.org/ (accessed March 10, 2015); Conor M. Dowling and Steve B. Lern, "Explaining Major and Third Party Candidate Entry in U.S. Gubernatorial Elections, 1980–2005," *State Politics and Policy Quarterly* 9 (Spring 2009): 1–23; "Gov. Doug Ducey Signs Elections-Related Measures," http://azcapitoltimes.com/news/2015/04/14/gov-doug-ducey-signs-elections-related-measures/ (accessed April 14, 2015).

assemble the organization necessary to make significant inroads into the system. Moreover, as noted above, most states have erected barriers making it difficult for minor parties to get on the ballot; lawsuits challenging these barriers typically have been dismissed by the courts. (The Controversies in States and Localities box discusses efforts in some states to ease minor party access to the ballot.) Further, third parties typically receive scant attention from the news media, and, without it, their credibility wanes. Still, even with the odds stacked against them, many third parties contest elections because a campaign provides an opportunity to promote the party's policy positions.

Public interest in partisan alternatives may be increasing. One national survey reported that 53 percent of the electorate believed that there should be a third major political party; scholarly research has found among self-described independents support for the creation of more parties.[16] Many indicated that their estrangement from the Democratic and Republican parties had reached the point that they would willingly affiliate with a third party that reflected their interests. Two third parties that have enjoyed some success in local races in recent times are the Libertarian Party, which celebrates individual rights, and the Green Party, which grew out of the environmental movement. By 2015, Libertarians held 147 elective offices in local jurisdictions in 33 states, with their numbers highest in California and Pennsylvania. That same year, a similar number of Greens held local offices in 25 states, including city council positions in cities such as Cleveland and Minneapolis.[17]

INTERPARTY COMPETITION

These days, most states exhibit meaningful two-party electoral competition. In other words, when you look at a general-election ballot, you will find both the Democrats and the Republicans offering credible candidates for state offices. The extension of interparty competition to states that had lacked it in the past is a healthy development in American politics. Citizens who are dissatisfied with the performance of the party in power have another choice. And there is an interesting twist to increased party competition and more choices for voters. Research has found that the amount of competition for legislative seats appears to be related to the policy outputs of the legislatures. States with higher levels of electoral competition tend to adopt more progressive policies than do states with less competitive legislative elections.[18] To be sure, the relative strength of the two parties helps explain partisan competition and legislative actions.

Patterns of Competition Another way of thinking about interparty competition is to examine which party controls the major policy-making institutions in the state: the governor's office and the state legislature. In the past, some states experienced long periods of institutional dominance by one party, but that trend has been on the decline for years. These days, party strength is fairly balanced. Based on gubernatorial vote margins and legislative seats held, as many as thirty-two states can be classified as two-party competitive, and no states fall into the "one-party" category.[19] Of the remaining states, five are considered modified Democratic states (i.e., Democrats control more institutions more often); thirteen are modified Republican states. During the period 2007–2011, Massachusetts was the closest to a one-party Democratic state; Idaho was the closest to a one-party Republican state. However, even in these two states, candidates of the other party can be successful. For instance, in 2014, Massachusetts voters elected a Republican governor even as its legislature remained heavily Democratic.

Generally, there is a link between the partisan composition of the electorate and partisan control of a state's institutions. For instance, in Utah in 2014,

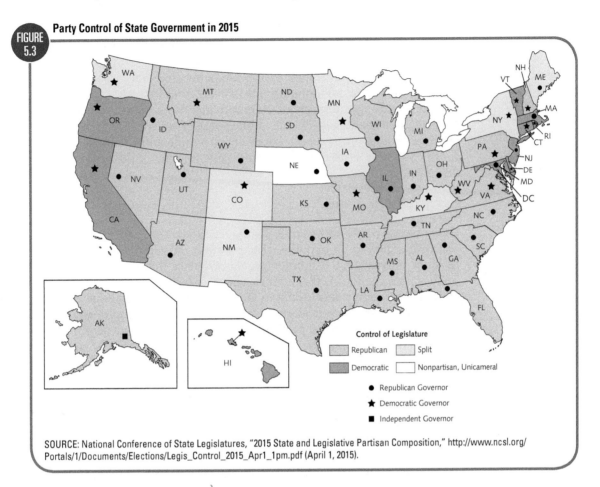

FIGURE 5.3

Party Control of State Government in 2015

Control of Legislature

Republican · Split · Democratic · Nonpartisan, Unicameral

● Republican Governor
★ Democratic Governor
■ Independent Governor

SOURCE: National Conference of State Legislatures, "2015 State and Legislative Partisan Composition," http://www.ncsl.org/Portals/1/Documents/Elections/Legis_Control_2015_Apr1_1pm.pdf (April 1, 2015).

the Republican Party had a voter registration advantage over the Democratic Party of more than 2 to 1. Not surprisingly, in the Utah legislature, Republicans outnumbered Democrats by a substantial margin, and a Republican occupied the governor's office. When the governorship and both legislative chambers are controlled by the same party, the result is **unified government**. But the electorate-institution relationship is not a simple one. Sometimes control of policy-making institutions is split between the two parties, and the result is called **divided government**. The patterns of partisan control in the states in 2015 are displayed in Figure 5.3. Thirty states were characterized by unified government (twenty-three states in Republican hands, seven states controlled by the Democratic Party); nineteen states experienced divided government.

Consequences of Competition Two-party competition has spread at a time when states are becoming the battleground for the resolution of difficult policy issues. Undoubtedly, as governors set their agendas and legislatures outline their preferences, cries of partisan politics will be heard. But in a

unified government

Both houses of the legislature and the governor's office are controlled by the same party.

divided government

One party controls the governor's office and the other party controls the legislature or each party controls one legislative chamber.

dealignment

The weakening of an individual's attachment to political parties.

interest groups

Organizations of like-minded individuals who desire to influence government.

positive sense, such cries symbolize the maturation of state institutions. Partisan politics will probably encourage a wider search for policy alternatives and result in innovative solutions.

In the view of many, two parties are better than one. Heated partisan competition turns a dull campaign into a lively contest, sparking citizen interest and increasing voter turnout. In governance, however, many believe that unified government is preferable to divided government. When competitive elections produce unified party control of government institutions, it is easier for the public to hold the party accountable for what it does—or does not do—while in office.

IS THE PARTY OVER?

Have political parties as we know them outlived their usefulness? Will they be cast aside as new forms of political organization and communication emerge? As some have argued, a more educated populace that can readily acquire political information via the Internet is likely to be less reliant on party cues.[20] Today's generation is less loyal to political parties than its grandparents were and is not so likely to vote along party lines. The trend toward **dealignment**, or weakening of individual partisan attachments, slowed for a period but has begun to pick up again. According to one political consultant, "A large group of the electorate tends to be socially tolerant and more receptive to fiscally conservative methods. They don't have a home in either party."[21] This trend is not good news for the two major parties. Neither are the conclusions of a recent study showing that in states with an initiative process, political parties find it difficult to shape public policy.[22]

The two major political parties are not sitting idly by as their role in the political system is challenged. Party organizations are making their operations more professional and have more money to spend and more staff to spend it. They are actively seeking to make their organizations more meaningful to younger voters, using various new technologies to engage the millennial generation. The past several years have seen the development of party-centered advertising campaigns, the embrace of new campaign technology, and a renewed commitment to get-out-the-vote drives.[23] Moreover, both parties are developing networks that connect party leaders across state boundaries. All in all, parties are doing their best to adapt to the changing environment.

LO 5.3

To summarize the roles of interest groups in states and localities.

Interest Groups

Interest groups have become powerful players in our democratic system. Joining a group is a way for individuals to communicate their preferences—their interests—to government. Interest groups attempt to influence governmental decisions and actions by pressuring decision-making bodies to, for example, put more guidance counselors in public schools, restrict coastal development, keep a proposed new prison out of a neighborhood, or strengthen state licensing of family therapists. Success is defined in terms of getting the group's preferences enacted—or blocking actions that are detrimental to the group's interests.

In considering the role of groups in the political system, we must remember that people join groups for reasons other than politics. For instance, a teacher may be a member of a politically active state education association because the group offers a tangible benefit such as low-cost life insurance, but he may not be interested in or may even disagree with some of the political positions taken by the organization. In general, then, motivations for group membership are individually determined.

TYPES OF INTEREST GROUPS

LO 5.4

To categorize interest groups according to their influence.

Interest groups come in all types and sizes. If you were to visit the lobby of the state capitol when the legislature was in session, you might find the director of the state school boards association conversing with the chairperson of the education committee, or the lobbyist hired by the state hotel-motel association exchanging notes with the lobbyist for the state's restaurateurs. If a legislator were to venture into the lobby, she would probably receive at least a friendly greeting from the lobbyists and at most a serious heart-to-heart talk about the merits of a bill. You would be witnessing efforts to influence public policy. Interest groups want state government to enact policies that are in their interest or, conversely, not to enact policies at odds with their preferences.

The interests represented in the capitol lobby are as varied as the states themselves. One interest that is well represented and powerful is business. Whether a lobbyist represents a single large corporation or a consortium of businesses, when he talks, state legislators tend to listen. From the perspective of business groups (and other economically oriented groups), legislative actions can cost or save their members money. Therefore, the chamber of commerce, industry groups, trade associations, financial institutions, and regulated utilities maintain a visible presence in the state capitol during the legislative session. Table 5.1 documents the influential nature of business interests at the state level. It is important to remember, however, that business interests are not monolithic; occasionally they may find themselves on opposite sides of a bill.

Other interests converge on the capitol. Representatives of labor, both established AFL-CIO unions and professional associations such as the state optometrists' group or sheriffs' association, frequent the hallways and committee meeting rooms to see that the legislature makes the "right" decision on the bills before it. For example, if a legislature were considering a bill to change the licensing procedures for optometrists, you could expect to find the optometrists' interest group immersed in the debate. Another employees' group, schoolteachers, has banded together to form one of the most effective state-level groups. In fact, as Table 5.1 indicates, schoolteachers' organizations are ranked among the most influential interest groups in thirty-one states.

Many other interest groups are active (but not necessarily influential) in state government, and a large number are ideological in nature. For some, their political activity is oriented toward some higher good, such as clean air or fairer tax systems or consumer protection. Members of these groups do not

TABLE 5.1   The Twenty Most Influential Interests in the States

RANK	INTEREST	NUMBER OF STATES IN WHICH THE INTEREST WAS SEEN AS VERY EFFECTIVE
1	General business organizations (chambers of commerce, etc.)	39
2	Schoolteachers' organizations (NEA and AFT)	31
3	Utility companies and associations (electric, gas, water, telephone/telecommunications)	28
4	Manufacturers (companies and associations)	25
5	Hospital/nursing home associations	24
6	Insurance: general and medical (companies and associations)	22
7	Physicians/state medical associations	21
8	Contractors/builders/developers	21
9	General local government organizations (municipal leagues, county organizations, elected officials)	18
10	Lawyers (predominately trial attorneys and state bar associations)	20
11	Realtors' associations	20
12	General farm organizations (state farm bureaus, etc.)	14
13	Bankers' associations	15
14	Universities and colleges (institutions and employees)	14
15	Traditional labor associations (predominantly the AFL-CIO)	15
16	Individual labor unions (Teamsters, UAW, etc.)	13
17	Gaming interests (race tracks, casinos, lotteries)	13
18	Individual banks and financial institutions	11
19	State agencies	10
20	Environmentalists	8

NOTE: The influence ranking is determined by more than the "very effective" score.

SOURCE: Adapted from Anthony J. Nownes, Clive S. Thomas, and Ronald J. Hrebenar, "Interest Groups in the States," in Virginia Gray and Russell L. Hanson, eds., *Politics in the American States: A Comparative Approach* (Washington, D.C.: Congressional Quarterly Press, 2008), pp. 117–18.

have a direct economic or professional interest in the outcome of a legislative decision. Instead, their lobbyists argue that the public as a whole benefits from their involvement in the legislative process. Consider PennPIRG, which describes itself as a nonprofit, nonpartisan watchdog group working on behalf of consumers, the environment, and responsive government in Pennsylvania. The group's motto, and that of other PIRGs (public interest research groups), is "Standing Up to Powerful Interests."

INTEREST GROUPS IN THE STATES

For the most part, interest group politics is defined by its state context. First of all, interest groups and political parties have evolving, multidimensional relationships. Typically, in states where political parties are weak, interest groups are stronger; where political parties are strong, interest groups tend to be weaker.[24] Strong parties provide leadership in the policy-making process, and interest groups function through them. In the absence of party leadership and organization, interest groups fill the void, becoming important recruiters of candidates and financiers of campaigns; accordingly, they exert tremendous influence in policy making.

A second, related truth adds a developmental angle to interest group politics. As states diversify economically, their politics are less likely to be dominated by a single interest. Studies of state interest systems show that the number of groups has increased over time and the power of once-dominant economic interests has decreased.[25] As states increasingly become the arena in which important social and economic policy decisions are made, more and more groups go to statehouses hoping to find a receptive audience.

TECHNIQUES USED BY INTEREST GROUPS

Interest groups want to have a good public image. It helps a group when its preferences can be equated with what is good for the state (or the community). Organizations use slogans like "What's good for the timber industry is good for Oregon" or "Schoolteachers have the interests of New York City at heart." Groups, then, invest resources in creating a positive image.

Being successful in the state capitol or at city hall involves more than a good public image, however. For example, interest groups have become effective at organizing networks that exert pressure on legislators. If a teacher pay-raise bill is in jeopardy in the senate, for instance, schoolteachers throughout the state may be asked by the education association to contact their senators to urge them to vote favorably on the legislation. To maximize their strength, groups with common interests often establish coalitions.

Sometimes related groups carve out their own niches to avoid direct competition for members and support.[26] For example, when gay and lesbian groups first became active in state politics, they tended to focus on narrow issues such as ending prohibitions on same-sex marriages rather than on broader concerns.[27] This type of targeting strategy allows more groups to flourish. To ensure that legislators will be receptive to their pressures, groups try to influence the outcome of elections by supporting candidates who reflect their interests. Interest groups also hire lobbyists who can effectively promote their causes.

Several factors affect the relative power of an interest group. In their work, Thomas, Hrebenar, and Nownes identify twelve characteristics that give some groups more political clout than others:

- The degree of necessity of group services and resources to public officials.
- Whether the group's lobbying focus is primarily defensive or offensive.
- The extent and strength of group opposition.

- Potential for the group to enter into coalitions.
- Group financial resources.
- Size and geographical distribution of group membership.
- Political cohesiveness of the membership.
- Political, organizational, and managerial skill of group leaders.
- Timing and the political climate.
- Lobbyist–policymaker relations.
- Legitimacy of the group and its demands—how these are perceived by the public and public officials.
- Extent of group autonomy in political strategizing.[28]

No single interest group is at the high end of all twelve of these characteristics all of the time. Many of the effective groups listed in Table 5.1, for example, possess quite a few of these factors. An indispensable group armed with ample resources, a cohesive membership, and skilled leaders, when the timing is right, can wield enormous influence in the state capitol. This is especially true when the group has taken a defensive posture—that is, when it wants to block proposed legislation. On the other hand, victory comes less easily to a group lacking these characteristics.

LO 5.5

To debate the impact of lobbying in state politics.

LOBBYING

Lobbying is the attempt to influence government decision makers. States have developed official definitions to determine who is a lobbyist and who is not. A common definition is "anyone receiving compensation to influence legislative action." A few states, such as Nevada, North Dakota, and Washington, require everyone who attempts to influence legislation to register as a lobbyist (even those who are not being paid), but most states exclude from this definition public officials, members of the media, and people who speak only before committees or boards. Because of definitional differences, comparing the number of lobbyists across states creates the proverbial apples-and-oranges problem. But with that in mind, some cautious comparisons can be made. As of 2011, the number of clients represented by lobbyists exceeded 3,300 in four states: Florida, New York, Texas, and California. At the other end of the spectrum, smaller interest group universes existed in Hawaii and Wyoming, with fewer than 300 lobbyist clients.[29]

As state government has expanded and taken on more functions, the number of interests represented in statehouses has exploded.[30] The increase in the number of lobbyists has a very simple but important cause: Interests that are affected by state government cannot afford to be without representation. An anecdote from Florida makes the point. Several years ago, legislators supported a new urban development program that Florida cities had lobbied for but about which they could not agree on a funding source. After much debate, they found one: a sales tax on dry cleaning. Because the dry-cleaning industry did not have a lobbyist in Tallahassee, there was no one to speak out on its behalf. Indeed, because their views were not represented in the debate over funding sources, dry cleaners were an easy target. (The dry-cleaning industry learned its lesson and hired a lobbyist a few days after the tax was enacted.)[31]

lobbying

The process by which groups and individuals attempt to influence policy makers.

To win over legislators in their decision making, lobbyists need access, so they cultivate good relationships with lawmakers. In other words, they want connections; they want an "in." There are many ways of establishing connections, such as contributing to campaigns, gift giving (if allowed), and entertaining. For example, during the 2012 legislative session in Georgia, the Savannah Chamber of Commerce spent $88,000 to host a seafood festival for lawmakers.[32] The relaxed venue offered Chamber members an opportunity to build goodwill with legislators who would be taking up bills of particular interest to the Chamber and the Savannah area.

Social lobbying—wining and dining legislators—still goes on, but it is being supplemented by another technique: the provision of information. Lawmakers want to know how a proposed bill might affect the different interests throughout the state and especially in their legislative districts and what it is expected to achieve. And lobbyists are only too happy to provide that information. A new breed of lobbyists has emerged, trained as attorneys and public relations specialists, skilled in media presentation and information packaging.

An analysis of the lobbying environment in three states—Colorado, Ohio, and West Virginia—identified the kinds of techniques that lobbyists rely on.[33] Table 5.2 lists the techniques that more than 75 percent of the 376 lobbyists surveyed said they used. Making contacts with key actors in the policy-making process—legislators, legislative and gubernatorial staff, and agency officials—is at the top of a lobbyist's "to-do" list. Moreover, a substantial 92 percent of the lobbyists indicated that they helped draft legislation, which makes them key actors as well. Notice that lobbying is not confined to the legislative process. Lobbyists regularly attempt to shape the implementation of policies after they are enacted.

TABLE 5.2	The Most Popular Techniques Used by Lobbyists
1	Meeting personally with state legislators
2	Meeting personally with state legislative staff
3	Entering into coalitions with other organizations
4	Helping to draft legislation
5	Meeting personally with executive agency personnel
6	Testifying at legislative committee hearings
7	Meeting personally with members of the governor's staff
8	Talking with people from the media
9	Inspiring letter-writing, telephone, or e-mail campaigns to state legislators
10	Submitting written testimony to legislative committees
11	Submitting written comments on proposed rules/regulations
12	Helping to draft regulations, rules, or guidelines

SOURCE: Anthony J. Nownes and Krissy Walker DeAlejandro, "Lobbying in the New Millennium: Evidence of Continuity and Change in Three States," *State Politics and Policy Quarterly* 9 (Winter 2009): 429–55.

The influence of lobbyists specifically and of interest groups generally is a subject of much debate. The popular image is one of a wheeler-dealer lobbyist whose very presence in a committee hearing room can spell the fate of a bill. But, in fact, his will is done because the interests he represents are considered vital to the state, because he has assiduously laid the groundwork, and because legislators respect the forces he can mobilize if necessary. Few lobbyists cast this long a shadow, but in many states, some of the most effective lobbyists are former legislators themselves. They know how the policy-making system works, thus making them valuable to myriad interests.

A not-so-new tactic that is enjoying a resurgence is **grassroots lobbying**, in which groups use their members to communicate with legislators (translation: bombard with mail, e-mail, faxes, and telephone calls) on behalf of the group's issue. Grassroots lobbying is not just a technique for outsiders. Citizen groups, unions, religious/charitable groups, corporations, and trade and professional associations all use grassroots techniques.[34] Are they effective? A recent study reached this unequivocal conclusion: "Grassroots lobbying by e-mail has a substantial influence on legislative voting behavior."[35]

In most states, lobbyists are required to file reports indicating how and on whom they spent money. Concern that lobbyists would exert undue influence on the legislative process spurred states to beef up reporting requirements and to impose tougher penalties for their violation. Maine and New Jersey, for instance, require lobbyists to report their sources of income, total and categorized expenditures, the names of the individual officials who received their monies or gifts, and the legislation they supported or opposed.

Disclosure requirements offer one way of dealing with the problem of undue influence; another approach is to limit gifts from lobbyists to public officials. In Arizona, lobbyists may not give a public official a gift with a total value of more than ten dollars, unless the official donates the higher-value gift to charity within fifteen days. In Minnesota, a lobbyist is prohibited from giving a legislator any gift except trinkets or mementos of insignificant value.[36] There is evidence that these laws produce the desired effect. In a fifty-state study, political scientist Joshua Ozymy found that when states increase the number of formal lobbying regulations, the influence of interest groups in the legislative process declines.[37] In a similar vein, recent research has shown that citizens' opinions receive greater consideration in states that regulate lobbyists more strictly.[38] In other words, in states with strict lobbying regulations, state policy conforms more closely to public opinion.

Political Action Committees

Political action committees (PACs) have been a regular feature of state politics since the 1980s. Narrowly focused subsets of interest groups, PACs are political organizations that collect funds and distribute them to candidates. PACs serve as the campaign-financing arm of corporations, labor unions, trade associations, and even political parties. They grew out of long-standing federal laws that made it illegal for corporations and labor unions to contribute directly to a candidate. Barred from direct contributions, these organizations set up "political action" subsidiaries to allow them legal entry into campaign finance.

LO 5.6

To critique the role of money in state political systems.

---

grassroots lobbying

Group mobilization of citizens to contact public officials on behalf of shared public policy views.

political action committees (PACs)

Organizations that raise and distribute campaign funds to candidates for elective office.

The impact of PACs on state politics is potentially far-reaching. Some Michigan legislators, for example, consider PACs a potentially dangerous influence on state politics because their money "buys a lot of access that others can't get."[39] And access usually means influence. Analysis of tobacco industry PACs suggests that their campaign contributions affect legislative behavior: "As legislators [in California, Colorado, Massachusetts, Pennsylvania, and Washington] received more tobacco industry campaign contributions . . . legislators were more likely to be pro-tobacco industry."[40] Similarly, in Florida, campaign contributions from teacher union PACs were shown to have influenced legislators' votes on a school vouchers bill.[41]

States have responded to the proliferation of PACs by increasing their regulation. In New Jersey, for instance, PACs are required to register and to provide information regarding their controlling interests. One likely possibility is that an independent interstate network of groups with money to spend could emerge as a real threat to political parties as a recruiter of candidates and a financier of campaigns. As a harbinger of tighter regulation of PACs, Alaska and Washington enacted a law that restricts contributions from out-of-state PACs. Most states have acted to limit PAC contributions, although the content of the laws varies. For example, Tennessee restricts the proportion of PAC contributions to fifty percent of a candidate's total contribution amount; Colorado allows "small donor" PACs to contribute more than "regular" PACs.[42] Some states such as Nevada and New Mexico have set absolute dollar amount ceilings on PAC contributions ($5,000 per candidate per election campaign); others differentiate by office and set lower amounts for legislative races than for statewide campaigns. States with extremely low-allowable contribution levels include Florida ($500 per candidate per election) and Rhode Island ($1,000 per candidate per election year). Thirteen states (Alabama, Indiana, Iowa, Mississippi, Missouri, North Dakota, Oregon, Pennsylvania, South Dakota, Texas, Utah, Virginia, and Wyoming) have taken a completely different approach and allow unlimited contributions from PACs to candidates.

Table 5.3 lists the five highest-spending interest groups and political action committees in Alabama, Iowa, and Texas during the 2014 election cycle. It is important to remember that these figures are just a snapshot but even so, they show the variation across the three states in the types of big-spending interests and their spending patterns.

In addition to PACs, another type of political organization has sprung up: **527 groups**. These groups are not connected to candidates but spend money to influence the outcome of elections. For instance, in West Virginia in 2004, a 527 group called "For the Sake of the Kids" spent $3.6 million in a massive advertising campaign to defeat an incumbent state Supreme Court justice. West Virginia's limits on campaign contributions did not apply because it was a 527 group that was spending the money on an issue (ostensibly, the future for the Mountain State's children), not a candidate. That same year in Washington, a 527 group called the Voters Education Committee spent nearly $1.5 million to defeat a candidate for state attorney general. As it turned out, in both West Virginia and Washington, the 527 groups were funded by the U.S. Chamber of Commerce, which disagreed with the candidates' positions

527 groups
Nonprofit, tax-exempt political organizations set up to accept contributions and make expenditures in campaigns, although not explicitly connected to candidates.

TABLE 5.3 Big Spending Interest Groups and Political Action Committees in Three States, 2014 Elections					
ALABAMA		**IOWA**		**TEXAS**	
FIVE HIGHEST SPENDING GROUPS	**AMOUNT**	**FIVE HIGHEST SPENDING GROUPS**	**AMOUNT**	**FIVE HIGHEST SPENDING GROUPS**	**AMOUNT**
Alabama Education Association	$2,934,864	Iowa Republican Party	$4,553,945	Texans for Lawsuit Reform	$5,446,505
Business Council of Alabama	$1,543,500	Iowa Democratic Party	$4,039,964	Texas Association of Realtors	$2,238,553
Alabama 2014	$1,220,282	Republican Governors Association	$1,113,756	Empower Texas	$2,177,842
Alabama Farmers Federation	$1,114,604	Associated General Contractors of Iowa	$319,500	Border Health PAC	$1,202,519
Alabama Power Company	$974,800	Iowa Association of Realtors	$284,100	AT&T	$1,076,263

SOURCE: National Institute on Money in State Politics, "State Overviews," http://www.followthemoney.org/our-data/state-overviews/ (accessed April 25, 2015).

on issues related to the regulation of business.[43] The spending of 527 groups has not diminished. In the 2012 election cycle, 527 groups spent $290 million in support of (or opposition to) state and local candidates and ballot issues.[44] Expenditures by 527 groups weaken a state's campaign finance laws. They skew spending upward, and circumvent disclosure provisions.

LOCAL-LEVEL INTEREST GROUPS

Interest groups also function at the local level. Because so much of local government involves the delivery of services, local interest groups devote a great deal of their attention to administrative agencies and departments. Groups are involved in local elections and in community issues, to be sure, but much of their major focus is on the *actions* of government: policy implementation and service delivery. According to surveys of local officials in small cities, the two functional areas in which interest groups have the greatest influence are economic development and parks and recreation.[45]

As in states, business groups are influential in local government. Business-related interests, such as the local chamber of commerce, a downtown merchants' association, and land developers, usually wield power in the community. These groups speak with a loud voice because business contributes both to the local tax base and to candidates for local offices. An increasingly important group at the local level is the neighborhood-based organization, which in some communities rivals business interests in influence. Other groups active at the local level include faith-based organizations, public employee unions, and ethnic minority groups.[46] Thus far, these groups have not achieved the degree of influence accorded business and neighborhood groups.

Neighborhood organizations deserve a closer look. Some have arisen out of issues that directly affect neighborhood residents—a nearby school that is scheduled to close, a wave of violent crime, a proposed freeway route that will destroy homes and businesses. Members of these groups devote much of their time to networking, to building relationships with policy makers, and to recruiting more individuals to their cause.[47] Others have been formed by government itself as a way of channeling citizen participation. In Los Angeles, for instance, the city established neighborhood councils in an effort to increase governmental responsiveness to local needs. In practice, these councils have been most active in opposing the city's land use and taxation decisions.[48]

Neighborhood groups, as well as others lacking a bankroll but possessing enthusiasm and dedication, may resort to tactics such as **direct action**, which might involve protest marches at the county courthouse or standing in front of bulldozers clearing land for a new highway. Direct action is usually designed to attract attention to a cause, and it tends to be a last resort, a tactic employed when other efforts at influencing government policy have failed. A study of citizen groups in seven large cities found that 34 percent of the groups engaged in protests or demonstrations at least occasionally.[49]

Political Campaigns

Political parties and interest groups bump into each other all the time, especially in political campaigns. Like so many things these days, political campaigns aren't what they used to be. But despite changes in campaign styles and technologies, the goal remains the same: attracting enough voters to win the election. Figure 5.4 diagrams the voting configuration in a hypothetical election district. This district typically splits its vote evenly between Democrats and Republicans. Thus, in any given election, each party can count on about 25 percent of the vote (labeled the "base" in the diagram), with another 17 percent that is fairly likely to vote for the party's candidate (the "soft" partisan vote). That leaves about 16 percent of the vote up for grabs (the toss-up vote).[50] The toss-up vote and the soft partisan vote comprise what is typically referred to as the *swing vote*. Candidates target their energies on the swing vote, the size of which varies with the distribution of the partisan base vote. Keep in mind that most districts are not so evenly divided in their partisan loyalties.

A NEW ERA OF CAMPAIGNS

Campaigns of the past conjure images of fiery oratory and county fairs. But campaigns orchestrated by rural courthouse gangs and urban ward bosses have given way to stylized video and electronic campaigning that relies on the mass media and political consultants. In the new era of campaigns, direct contact with potential voters still matters, of course. Candidates for state legislative seats, for example, devote time to door-to-door canvassing, neighborhood drop-ins, and public forums. New studies confirm the value of these types of contacts in mobilizing voter turnout, especially among folks who are considered "occasional voters."[51] Yet more and more, candidates rely on direct mail and electronic media to deliver their messages and on political

LO 5.7

To propose the use of new campaign technologies.

direct action

A form of participation designed to draw attention to a cause.

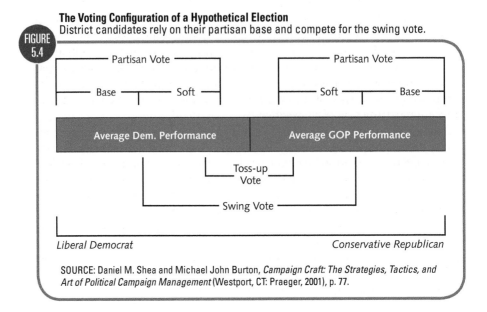

The Voting Configuration of a Hypothetical Election

FIGURE 5.4

District candidates rely on their partisan base and compete for the swing vote.

SOURCE: Daniel M. Shea and Michael John Burton, *Campaign Craft: The Strategies, Tactics, and Art of Political Campaign Management* (Westport, CT: Praeger, 2001), p. 77.

consultants to help them craft their messages to targeted subsets of potential voters. The paragraph that opened this chapter makes precisely this point.

Using Old and New Media The mass media, especially television, are intrinsic aspects of modern statewide campaigns. Even candidates for legislative and local offices are increasingly using the mass media to transmit their messages. Campaigns can either buy their air time and newspaper space for advertising or get it free by arranging events that reporters are likely to cover. These events range from serious (a candidate's major policy statement) to gimmicky (a candidate climbing into the ring with a professional wrestler to demonstrate his "toughness"); either way, they are cleverly planned to capture media attention. A candidate seeking free media attention needs to create visual events, be quotable, and relentlessly attack opponents or targeted problems. Televised debates, common in campaigns for statewide office, offer another opportunity for free media time.

Free media time is seldom sufficient. Candidates, particularly those running for higher-level state offices and for positions in large cities, rely on paid advertisements to reach the public. Paid media advertisements seem to be of two distinct varieties: generic and negative. Generic advertisements include the following:

1. *The sainthood spot*, which glorifies the candidate and her accomplishments.
2. *The testimonial*, in which other people (celebrities, average citizens) attest to the candidate's abilities.
3. *The bumper-sticker policy spot*, which emphasizes the campaign's popular and noncontroversial themes (good schools, lower taxes, more jobs).
4. *The feel-good spot*, which identifies and capitalizes on the spirit of a place and its people (e.g., "Vermont's a special place" or "Nobody can do it better than Pennsylvania").[52]

Media advertising is important because it is frequently the only contact a potential voter has with a candidate. A candidate's personal characteristics and style—important considerations to an evaluating public—are easily transmitted via the airwaves. Experimental research on gubernatorial campaigns has shown that television advertising has a statistically significant effect on voter preferences.[53] Notably, however, the effects of these advertisements dissipate rapidly—sometimes within a week or two.

The Internet has become a powerful campaign tool that can disseminate the candidate's message to far-flung audiences, mobilize potential supporters, and serve as a vehicle for attracting contributions. Nearly all major candidates for state and local offices routinely maintain campaign websites, some rudimentary, others much more elaborate. The current challenge is to design campaign websites that effectively scale down in size for smartphones and tablets, which are estimated to account for more than 60 percent of Americans' digital media time.[54] Several statewide candidates pioneered the use of campaign e-cards (the electronic equivalent of chain letters) so that supporters could contact people in their e-mail address books about the candidate. The advent of YouTube provided opportunities for candidates and for their opponents as videos of campaign high points—and low moments—made their way to the website. YouTube is easy to use, cost-effective for campaigns, and increasingly popular.

Social networking sites such as Facebook and Twitter hold tremendous potential for generating a fan base for candidates and for raising money. As might be expected, the increased popularity of social media has led to some abuses and, in reaction, to efforts by government to address them. In 2010, Maryland was one of the first states to act, and in 2013, California followed suit. The Golden State's Fair Political Practices Commission now requires anyone paid $500 or more by a campaign to provide social media content to

Empty lots along a busy road become crowded with campaign signs as the election nears.

report that activity to the state.[55] As with other media, campaign tweets, texts, and blogs must include an attribution such as "The author was paid by the Committee to Re-Elect Mayor Jane Doe in connection with this posting."

Negative Campaigning Negative campaign advertising comes in three flavors: fair, false, and deceptive. A fair ad might emphasize some embarrassing aspect of an opponent's voting record or some long-forgotten indiscretion. A false ad, as the label implies, contains untrue statements. More problematic are deceptive advertisements, which distort the truth about an opponent. The task for states is to regulate negative campaign advertising without violating free-speech guarantees of the U.S. Constitution. False advertising that is done with actual malice can be prohibited by a state, but deceptive ads, replete with accusation and innuendo, are more difficult to regulate.[56]

Most states have enacted laws prohibiting false campaign statements; candidates who use false ads against their opponents can be fined. One of the problems with these laws is that the damage is done long before the remedy can be applied. Fining a candidate after the election is akin to latching the barn door after the horse has fled. Some states, such as California and Nevada, have adopted a fair campaign practices code. These codes typically contain broad guidelines such as "do not misrepresent the facts" or "do not make appeals to prejudice based on race or sex." The limitation of the codes is that compliance is voluntary rather than mandatory.

In addition to government action, many newspapers and websites report regularly on the content, presentation, and relative accuracy of campaign advertising. Ad watches or truth boxes, as they are often called, occasionally have led to the retraction or redesign of ads. Despite the efforts of government and the media, however, negative campaign advertising persists because many candidates believe that, if done cleverly, it can benefit their campaigns. Research by political scientist Ted Braden has confirmed that negative messages, accompanied by fear-evoking music and images, trigger strong reactions in viewers.[57] People may not like negative ads, but they certainly seem to remember them.

Political Consultants An occupational specialty that sprang up during the 1970s and 1980s is clearly here to stay: political consulting. Individuals with expertise in polling, direct mail, fund-raising, advertising, and campaign management put their talents to work in political campaigns. These consultants form the core of the professional campaign management team assembled by candidates for state offices. They identify and target likely voters, both those who are already in the candidate's camp and need to be reminded to vote *and* those who can be persuaded to vote for the candidate. Consultants use survey research and focus groups to find out what the public is thinking. They carefully craft messages to appeal to specific voters, such as the elderly, homeowners, or environmentalists. Advertising on cable television, radio, and through direct mail are three popular means of getting a candidate's message to targeted segments of the voting public. In fact, research has found that much of the public actually prefers narrowcast messages, tailored to their interests.[58]

Any number of factors can influence the result of an election, such as the presence of an incumbent in a race and the amount of funds that a challenger has accumulated, but one significant factor is the ability to frame or define the issues during the campaign. Even in a quietly contested state legislative race, district residents are likely to receive mailings that state the candidates' issue positions, solicit funds, and perhaps comment unfavorably on the opposition. The candidate who has an effective political consultant to help set the campaign agenda and thereby put her opponent on the defensive is that much closer to victory. A study of legislative elections indicates that the use of campaign professionals is especially valuable to challengers who are hoping to unseat incumbents.[59]

CAMPAIGN FINANCE

To campaign for public office is to spend money—frequently a lot of money. For instance, in 2014, running for reelection in New York, Governor Andrew Cuomo spent nearly $21 million on his campaign, with half of that amount going to television advertising. The New York governor's race was not unique: Gubernatorial elections are multi-million dollar affairs these days. Table 5.4 lists the contributions received by gubernatorial candidates in ten states across the country in 2014. Variation across the states both in the total amounts and in the partisan shares is substantial.

Big spending is not confined to gubernatorial contests. Spending in legislative races is climbing, and fast. Consider 2010 data from two large states, New York and Texas, each with 150 seats in their lower legislative chamber. In New York, 304 candidates competed for the Assembly seats, spending a total of $23 million, or an average $76,000 per candidate. In Texas, the 332 candidates for House seats spent a total of $78.5 million, which averages to

LO 5.8

To compare state differences in the regulation of campaign finance.

TABLE 5.4	Contribution Totals for Gubernatorial Races by Party and State, 2014, Selected States			
STATE	**CONTRIBUTION TOTAL (ALL GUBERNATORIAL CANDIDATES) ($)**	**CONTRIBUTIONS TO DEMOCRATS ($)**	**CONTRIBUTIONS TO REPUBLICANS ($)**	**CONTRIBUTIONS TO THIRD PARTIES/ NONPARTISAN ($)**
Arkansas	$ 11,477,145.62	$ 6,387,319.33	$ 5,082,197.87	$ 7,628.42
Colorado	$ 10,758,513.35	$ 5,625,853.42	$ 5,074,945.62	$ 57,714.31
Florida	$ 33,864,325.20	$ 16,551,436.92	$ 17,151,446.04	$ 161,442.24
Illinois	$ 127,090,487.61	$ 33,412,378.20	$ 93,648,109.41	$ 30,000.00
Kansas	$ 9,426,063.78	$ 4,611,363.60	$ 4,734,235.38	$ 80,464.80
Massachusetts	$ 29,882,052.66	$ 15,095,426.11	$ 10,531,249.77	$ 4,255,376.78
Maryland	$ 28,332,451.15	$ 21,107,698.12	$ 7,220,002.03	$ 4,751.00
Pennsylvania	$ 85,351,075.73	$ 53,611,394.35	$ 31,739,681.38	$ —
South Carolina	$ 16,362,113.32	$ 3,634,380.69	$ 8,411,693.25	$ 4,316,039.38
Wisconsin	$ 51,263,051.84	$ 17,426,656.01	$ 33,828,933.86	$ 7,461.97

SOURCE: National Institute on Money in State Politics, "State Overviews," http://www.followthemoney.org/our-data/state-overviews/ (accessed April 27, 2015).

approximately $236,400 per candidate.[60] It should be noted, however, that spending in some states is substantially less. For instance, in Arkansas, the average expenditure total for lower House seats was $29,000 in 2010; in Kansas, it was $22,000; and in Idaho, it was $15,000.

Political science research has confirmed several long-standing truths about the costs of campaigning.[61] For instance, close elections cost more than elections in which one candidate is sure to win because uncertainty regarding the outcome is a spur to spending. A candidate quickly learns that it is easier to get money from potential contributors when the polls show that she has a chance of winning. Also, elections that produce change—that is, in which an incumbent is unseated or the out-of-office party gains the office—typically cost more. Taking on an existing officeholder is a risky strategy that drives up election costs. And an open race in which there is no incumbent represents an opportunity for the party out of office to capture the seat, thus triggering similar spending by the in-office party in an effort to protect the seat. It is no wonder that campaign costs are exploding. But there may be a side benefit to more campaign spending: an increase in voter turnout. Studies of state legislative elections revealed a link between expenditure levels and voter turnout.[62]

State Efforts at Campaign Reform Concerns over escalating costs and the influence of deep-pocketed special interests in campaigns have led reform groups such as Common Cause to call for changes including: (1) Improve state laws to provide comprehensive and timely disclosure of campaign finances, (2) impose limitations on contributions by individuals and groups, (3) create a combined public-private financing mechanism for primaries and general elections, and (4) establish an independent commission to enforce tough sanctions on violators of campaign finance laws.

States have performed impressively on the first of these recommendations; in fact, all states have some sort of campaign financing reporting procedure. Most states make information on campaign contributions available online in a searchable database; many states provide similar access to campaign expenditure data. In response to the fourth recommendation, more than half of the states have established independent commissions, such as California's Fair Political Practices Commission, to oversee the conduct of campaigns, although these organizations have found it somewhat difficult to enforce the law and punish violators.

The other recommendations have proved more troublesome. States have grappled with the issue of costly campaigns but have made only modest progress in controlling costs. A 1976 decision by the U.S. Supreme Court in *Buckley v. Valeo* made these efforts more difficult; the Court ruled that governments cannot limit a person's right to spend money in order to spread his views about particular issues and candidates. In essence, then, candidates have unlimited power to spend their own money on their own behalf, and other individuals may spend to their hearts' content to promote their own opinions on election-related issues. The U.S. Supreme Court extended this logic to corporations and labor unions, ruling in 2010 in *Citizens United v. Federal Election Commission* that these entities have a constitutional right to advertise on issues and influence elections. A 2014 case, *McCutcheon v. Federal Election*

Commission, pushed the logic even further by striking down limits on the total amount of money an individual can donate in a two-year period to candidates for federal offices and to political committees. In an earlier case involving a lawsuit from Colorado, the Court had decided that independent spending by political parties, so-called **soft money**, could not be limited, either. What the Court let stand, however, were state limits on an individual's contributions to candidates and parties; it also ruled that if a candidate accepts public funds, then he is bound by whatever limitations the state may impose. The 2002 Federal Bipartisan Campaign Reform Act, typically referred to as the McCain-Feingold law, aims at controlling the flow of soft money, but reports from recent election cycles suggest that loopholes remain.[63]

Amid the evolving web of federal court rulings, the states have tried to address campaign finance. Some states established specific limits on the amount of money that organizations and individuals can contribute to a political race. In New York, for example, corporations are limited to a contribution maximum of $5,000 per calendar year, and individuals (other than official candidates) are restricted to $50,000 in a gubernatorial election and to $10,300 and $4,100 in general elections for senate and house seats, respectively. Florida's approach is straightforward: Individuals (other than the candidate herself), corporations, labor unions, and PACs are allowed to contribute a maximum of $500 per candidate per election. Some states, such as Arizona, Iowa, Kentucky, Massachusetts, Minnesota, Rhode Island, South Dakota, Wisconsin, and Wyoming, have gone even further by prohibiting direct contributions from corporations and labor unions.[64] But a totally different philosophy pervades the politics of several states that continue to operate their election systems without any limitations on contributions. In Missouri, Oregon, Utah, and Virginia, organizations and individuals can contribute as much as they wish.

States have also considered the other side of the campaign financing equation: expenditures. All states require candidates and political committees to file reports documenting the expenditure of campaign funds. A few states tried to impose limits on a candidate's total expenditures, but a 2006 U.S. Supreme Court ruling that Vermont's spending limits were too low to allow candidates to compete effectively has complicated that approach. Many have followed Hawaii's lead and set voluntary spending limits. Colorado, for example, adopted a nonbinding $2.5 million spending cap for gubernatorial candidates. Michigan takes a different approach: Publicly funded candidates (governor and lieutenant governor) are restricted to $2 million per election, with additional spending allowable in certain circumstances. Florida has a similar system in place for candidates receiving public funds.

PUBLIC FUNDING AS A SOLUTION

One-third of the states have adopted some sort of public funding of some campaigns, although in most of these states, public financing supplements the private contributions candidates receive. As a condition of accepting public money, whether it is a matching grant (as in Florida and Hawaii) or a fixed subsidy (as in Minnesota), candidates must abide by state-imposed spending limits. In states that have adopted a fully funded "clean elections" system of

soft money
Unregulated funds contributed to national political parties and nonparty political groups.

It's Your Turn

Should Political Spending in Campaigns Be Unrestricted by Government?

Money plays a significant role in today's political campaigns. States have struggled to reform and control the influence of money in campaigns.

PROS	CONS
Money is an essential part of campaigns. It allows candidates to convey their views to potential voters, thereby making candidates' positions more clear. Therefore, people should be able to spend as much as they like on candidates and on political issues.	Allowing money to flow unrestricted in political campaigns means that the wealthiest interests have the greatest opportunity to influence public policy.
Interest groups are aggregations of people who share similar views on certain issues. People have the right to express their opinions (the U.S. constitutional guarantee of freedom of speech), and expressing opinions often costs money. Consequently, interest group spending should be unrestricted, just so long as it is disclosed.	The government must protect both freedom and equality. However, to the vast majority of Americans, the "freedom" to contribute unlimited funds to a campaign is purely theoretical, as they often cannot spare *any* money to give to candidates. The government could, however, give some protection to their equality of input by limiting the amount of money in politics. In other words, contribution limits help level the playing field.
The current system of regulations is so complicated that it requires a fleet of accountants and lawyers to navigate it and a host of bureaucrats to administer it. Abolishing campaign finance laws would simplify the process and save the government money.	Allowing the unrestricted flow of private money into campaigns increases the likelihood of corruption and bribery.
Placing limits on campaign spending encourages the proliferation of PACs and 527s as a way to circumvent the limits. And these organizations are much more difficult for the public to monitor.	Limiting contributions lessens the likelihood of government capture by private economic interests.

campaign finance (Arizona, Connecticut, Maine, New Mexico, North Carolina, and Vermont), a candidate who wishes to participate must first demonstrate her viability by getting signatures on a petition and/or collecting a certain number of small dollar contributions. Once in the program, she may spend only public funds.[65] Not all elective offices are covered by public funding, however. For instance, Arizona's and Connecticut's programs cover statewide offices and the legislature, Maine's applies to the governor and the legislature, New Mexico's affects the Public Regulation Commission and statewide judicial offices, North Carolina's program covers several statewide offices and judges, while Vermont's applies to the governor and lieutenant governor. It is worth noting that in 2012, West Virginia launched a pilot program for public funding of Supreme Court races—the same state where expenditures by 527 groups shook up a state Supreme Court campaign eight years earlier.

The public financing system is fairly easy to administer and is relatively transparent for citizens. In most of the public funding states, citizens can use their state income tax form to earmark a portion (a dollar or two) of their tax liability for the fund. A check-off system of this sort does not directly increase taxpayers' tax burden. (Iowa, Kentucky, and Utah are among the eight states in which a taxpayer can specify that a political party be the recipient of the check-off amount.) In a few states, the public fund is amassed through a voluntary surcharge, or additional tax (usually $1.00 or $5.00). In addition to check-offs and surcharges, some of the public-funding states, including Arkansas and Virginia offer taxpayers a tax credit (usually a percentage of the contribution, up to a specific maximum) when they contribute to political campaigns. Another option is a state tax deduction for campaign contributions, an approach used in Oklahoma. In addition to taxpayer contributions, some states also allocate money from specific sources such as Arizona's traffic and criminal fine surcharges.

Public campaign financing is supposed to rid the election process of some of its evils. Proponents argue that it will democratize the contribution process by freeing candidates from excessive reliance on special-interest money. Other possible advantages include expanding the pool of potential candidates, allowing candidates to compete on a more equal basis, and reducing the cost of campaigning. Not everyone has embraced public funding, however. Obviously, it represents a cost to taxpayers, and some contend that incumbents will benefit from limits on campaign spending and that nonserious candidates will be able to use public funds as their own personal treasury. In Arizona, in 2002, Janet Napolitano became the first governor to be elected with full public financing of her campaign. In the next election cycle, 60 percent of state legislative candidates ran with public money, and 93 percent of them were elected. Research on Arizona and Maine shows that clean elections programs deliver on the promise of increased competition.[66] A U.S. Supreme Court ruling in 2011, however, weakened some aspects of Arizona's law.

By contributing to the fund, average citizens may feel that they have a greater stake in state elections. Although more research needs to be done, studies suggest that public financing produces at least some of the benefits its supporters claim. For instance, an analysis of gubernatorial campaigns indicated that the use of public funds by incumbents and challengers holds down overall spending. It also narrows the expenditure gap between them.[67] In 2007, North Carolina adopted its version of clean elections, the "Voter-Owned Elections Act," amid high expectations. This following excerpt from the language of the act sets out the lofty purpose of the law:

> The purpose of this Article is to ensure the vitality and fairness of democratic elections in North Carolina to the end that any eligible citizen of this State can realistically choose to seek and run for public office. It is also the purpose of this Article to protect the constitutional rights of voters and candidates from the detrimental effects of increasingly large amounts of money being raised and spent in North Carolina to influence the outcome of elections.[68]

It should be noted that North Carolina repealed the Voter-Owned Elections Act in 2013 law as part of an overhaul of its election laws. Clearly, states continue to struggle in their efforts to reform and control the influence of money in campaigns.

Chapter Recap

- Even though voter loyalties have weakened, political parties have proved remarkably resilient and have taken on new roles in politics and governance.

- The Democratic Party can claim about 28 percent of the voting-age public for itself and the Republican Party around 27 percent. The rest of the electorate is considered independents (although they might lean toward one of the major parties), with a small fraction affiliated with third parties.

- Interparty competition has increased over time. One result has been a rise in divided government in the states.

- Interest groups exert a powerful force in state government, with business lobbyists and teachers' groups the most influential in the majority of states.

- The state interest group system is changing: A more diverse set of interests lobbies at the statehouse; meanwhile, state governments have tightened their regulation of lobbyists.

- Groups are involved in local elections and in community issues, but their major focus is on the *actions* of government: policy implementation and service delivery.

- Campaigns for state office still involve door-to-door canvassing, neighborhood drop-ins, and public forums, but they increasingly use direct mail, various electronic media, and political consultants.

- Running for public office can be an expensive proposition. To try to level the playing field and diminish the role of private money, most states limit contributions and some states provide public financing.

KEY TERMS

political parties *(p. 108)*
ideology *(p. 108)*
ticket splitting *(p. 110)*
Tea Party *(p. 112)*
unified government *(p. 115)*

divided government *(p. 115)*
dealignment *(p. 116)*
interest groups *(p. 116)*
direct action *(p. 125)*
lobbying *(p. 120)*

grassroots lobbying *(p. 122)*
political action committees (PACs) *(p. 122)*
527 groups *(p. 123)*
soft money *(p. 131)*

INTERNET RESOURCES

The major political parties have official websites: the Democratic Party is at **www.democrats.org**, and the Republican Party is at **www.gop.com**. At the state level, illustrative websites are Hawaii's at **www.hawaiidemocrats.org** and Virginia's at **www.rpv.org**. An interesting state-level, third-party website, **www.cagreens.org**, is the site for the Green Party of California.

Common Cause has a website, **www.commoncause.org/states**, that tracks the activities of its thirty-five state offices and the progress of campaign finance reform.

A group devoted to cleaning up elections is Public Campaign. Its website is **www. publicampaign.org**. Another group with a reform focus is the Center for Public Integrity at **www.public-integrity.org**.

The National Institute on Money in State Politics provides an abundance of information on the subject at **www.followthemoney.org**.

To learn more about 527 groups, see **www.opensecrets.org/527s**.

Different perspectives are reflected in the websites of the American Civil Liberties Union, **www.aclu.org**, and the Christian Coalition, **www.cc.org**.

www.flchamber.com and **ilchamber.org** are the websites for the chambers of commerce for Florida and Illinois, respectively. Other state chambers use similar URLs.

The Texas State Teachers' Association at **www.tsta.org** is an example of a state school teachers' organization. A different but related perspective is provided by the Oregon PTA at **www.oregonpta.org**.

Other examples of state-level interest groups include the Mississippi Association of Realtors at **msrealtors.org** and the Arizona Hospital and Healthcare Association at **www.azhha.org**.

State Legislatures: The People's Representatives

6

The New York Senate in session in its historic chamber.
Matthew Cavanaugh/Getty Images

The start of a new legislative session is a time of celebration in state capitols around the country. Bouquets of flowers decorate the chamber as family members join legislators on the floor for the swearing-in ceremony. In West Virginia, opening day 2015 was even more special than usual. There, the nation's youngest state legislator, 18-year-old college freshman Saira Blair was sworn in as a member of the state's House of Delegates. Delegate Blair had defeated a 67-year-old incumbent representative to win the seat, and she did so quite handily, receiving 63 percent of the vote. Once elected, she was quoted as saying "I like to multitask and keep myself busy."[1] Those are good traits for a state legislator to have because once the swearing in ceremony draws to a close, the serious work begins.

The Essence of Legislatures

LO 6.1

To differentiate the three functions of legislatures.

The new year dawns quietly in Boise, Idaho, in Jefferson City, Missouri, and in Harrisburg, Pennsylvania, but it does not remain quiet for long: State legislators are set to converge on state capitols. Every January (or February or March in a few states; every other January in a few others), state legislatures reconvene in session to do the public's business. More than 7,000 legislators hammer out solutions to intricate and often intransigent public problems. They do so in an institution that is steeped in tradition and governed by layers of formal rules and informal norms.

Legislatures engage in three principal functions: *policymaking, representation,* and *oversight.* The first, policymaking, includes enacting laws and allocating funds. The second decade of the twenty-first century found legislators debating issues such as health care, public education, criminal justice, and immigration. These deliberations resulted in the revision of old laws, the passage of new laws, and changes in spending, which is what policymaking is all about. Legislatures do not have sole control of the state policymaking function; governors, courts, and agencies also determine policy through executive orders, judicial decisions, and administrative regulations, respectively. But legislatures are the dominant policymaking institutions in state government. Table 6.1 lists the issues that attracted legislative attention in 2015.

TABLE 6.1	Popular Legislative Issues in 2015
ISSUE	**WHAT IT'S ALL ABOUT**
Health Insurance Exchanges	Creating, adopting, or regulating the health insurance exchanges mandated in the federal Affordable Care Act
Marijuana	Legalizing, de-criminalizing, regulating, and taxing marijuana
Student Assessments	Implementing tests for students that measure communication, reasoning, analytical, and synthesization skills as well as student knowledge
Police Authority	Deciding if/when officers can search phone records, use no-knock search warrants, or perform asset seizure
Pretrial Release	Releasing low risk inmates before trial to reduce prison populations
Pension Investments	Investing appropriate amounts of funding in pension funds in order to protect bond ratings and future budget liquidity
Sex Trafficking	Tightening sex trafficking laws in order to come into compliance with the federal Preventing Sex Trafficking and Strengthening Families Act in 2014
Social Impact Financing	Government contracts with an outside organization to provide a government service. The organization is repaid with interest by the governmental agency if it is successful.
Immigration	Addressing various immigration related topics, including in-state tuition and driver's licenses for immigrants, as well as creating rules for E-Verify
Net-Metering	Reconciling the need to increase renewable energy use with the need for utility companies to cover fixed infrastructure costs

SOURCE: Julie Lays, "What's Hot for 2015?" *State Legislatures,* http://www.ncsl.org/bookstore/state-legislatures-magazine/what-s-hot-for-2015.aspx (accessed February 2, 2015).

In their second function, legislators are expected to represent their constituents—the people who live in their districts—in two ways. At least in theory, they are expected to speak for their constituents in the legislative chamber—to do the will of the public in designing policy solutions. This is not easy. On quiet issues, a legislator seldom has much of a clue about public opinion. However on noisy issues, constituents' will is rarely unanimous. Individuals and organized groups with different perspectives may write to or visit their legislator to urge her to vote a certain way on a pending bill. In another representative function, legislators act as their constituents' facilitators in state government. For example, they may help a citizen deal with an unresponsive state agency. This kind of constituency service (or **casework**, as it is often called) can be time-consuming, but it pays dividends at re-election time because voters tend to look favorably on a legislator who has helped them.[2]

The third function, oversight, is different from the policymaking and representation functions. Concerned that the laws they passed and the funds they allocated frequently did not produce the intended effect, lawmakers began to pay more attention to the performance of the state bureaucracy. Legislatures have adopted several methods for checking on agency implementation and spending. The oversight role takes legislatures into the administrative realm of state government. Not surprisingly, agencies rarely welcome this scrutiny, although legislatures see it as a logical extension of their policymaking role.

Legislative Dynamics

State legislative bodies are typically referred to as the legislature, but their formal titles vary. In Colorado, it is the General Assembly that meets every year; in Massachusetts, the General Court; and in Oregon, the Legislative Assembly. The legislatures of forty-six states meet annually; in only four states (Montana, Nevada, North Dakota, and Texas) do they meet every other year. (Arkansas and Oregon had been among the biennial sessions group until 2008 and 2010, respectively, when voters approved a switch to annual legislative sessions.) The length of the legislative session varies widely. For example, the Utah General Assembly convened in Salt Lake City on January 26, 2015, and left town on March 12, 2015, for a total of forty-five calendar days in session. By contrast, in states like Michigan and New Jersey, legislative sessions run nearly year-round.

The length of a state's legislative session can be a sensitive issue. In 1997, the Nevada legislature met for 169 days—the longest, most expensive session in its history.[3] Nevadans showed their displeasure the following year when they passed a measure limiting future legislative sessions to 120 days. Voters in the Silver State apparently believed that it should not take more than four months—every two years—to conduct their state's business.

casework

Legislative assistance on behalf of constituents who have a problem or grievance with a state agency.

THE SENATE AND THE HOUSE

Forty-nine state legislatures are bicameral, that is, they have two houses or chambers, similar to those of the U.S. Congress. (As noted in Chapter 3, the exception is Nebraska, which in 1934 established a nonpartisan unicameral legislature.) Bicameralism is a legacy of the postcolonial era, in which an upper house, represented the interests of the propertied class, and a lower house represented everyone else. Even after this distinction was eliminated, states stuck with the bicameral structure, ostensibly because of its contribution to the concept of checks and balances. It is much tougher to pass bills when they have to survive the scrutiny of two legislative houses. Having a bicameral structure, then, reinforces the status quo. Unicameralism might improve the efficiency of the legislature, but efficiency has never been a primary goal of the consensus-building deliberative process.

In the forty-nine bicameral states, the upper house is called the Senate; the lower house is usually called the House of Representatives. The average size of a state senate is forty members; houses typically average about 100 members. As with many aspects of state legislatures, chamber size varies substantially—from the Alaska senate, with twenty members, to the New Hampshire house, with 400 representatives. Chamber size seldom changes, but in 2003, a voter mandate forced Rhode Island to reduce the size of its 150-member legislature by one-fourth. Size matters in a legislature. Research has found that large and small chambers produce different patterns of interaction among their members.[4]

For senators, the term of office is usually four years; approximately one-quarter of the states use a two-year senate term. In many states, the election of senators is staggered. House members serve two-year terms, except in Alabama, Louisiana, Maryland, Mississippi, and North Dakota, where four-year terms prevail. The 2015 state legislative sessions found Republicans in control of both chambers in thirty states, the Democratic Party controlling both houses in eleven states, and split control in the remaining eight states.

There are 7,383 state legislators in this country: 1,972 senators and 5,411 representatives. As of 2015, Democrats held 43 percent of the seats, Republicans held 56 percent; men outnumbered women 75.7 to 24.3 percent. (The legislatures of Colorado and Vermont had the highest percentage of female legislators at 41 percent.) Legislatures are becoming more racially and ethnically diverse. African Americans occupied 9 percent of all legislative seats; Latinos, 3 percent; Asian Americans, 1 percent; and Native Americans, 1 percent. Yet even these small proportions of women and racial-ethnic minorities represent a substantial increase, relative to their near absence from most pre-1970s legislatures. Increased diversity is important with respect to the representation function of a legislature. A recent study found that constituents are less likely to communicate with legislators of a different race than they are with legislators of their same race.[5]

The average age of legislators is 56, but as the example that opened this chapter showed, an occasional "millennial" can be found amid the lawmakers. In terms of occupations, full-time legislators are the single largest category (16.4 percent), overtaking attorneys (15.2 percent), which historically had been the dominant occupation. These two groups are followed by retirees (11.7 percent), business owners (9.2 percent), and business executives/managers (8.7 percent).[6]

LO 6.2

To examine the
redistricting process
and its consequences.

LEGISLATIVE DISTRICTS

Legislators are elected from geographically based districts, with each district in a state containing approximately the same number of inhabitants. Most legislative districts are single-member districts (SMDs), that is, one legislator represents the district. In Nebraska, for instance, each member of the unicameral legislature represents 37,272 people, more or less. Dividing or apportioning a state into districts is an intensely political process that affects the balance of power in a state. In the 1960s, for example, Florida's legislative districts were drawn such that the less-populated panhandle area was overrepresented in the legislature at the expense of the heavily populated southern areas of the state. Therefore, despite Florida's rapid urbanization during that period, public policy continued to reflect the interests of a rurally based minority of the population.

Eight states, including Minnesota and the Dakotas, continue to use **multimember districts (MMDs)** containing more than one lower house seat. (Usually, it is a two-member district, and the number of people residing in the MMD is approximately double that of an SMD.) There are two main types of MMDs. In the first type, all candidates compete against one another, and the two candidates with the most votes are elected. In the other type, candidates have to declare which of the district's two seats they are seeking. In both types, voters in the district vote in as many races as there are seats in the district. Once elected, the two legislators represent the entire MMD area. Is there any difference between legislators in MMDs and those in SMDs? The answer is a cautious yes, if research on the Arizona legislature can be extended to other states. Researchers found that lawmakers in the MMD House of Representatives tended to be more ideologically extreme than lawmakers in the SMD senate.[7]

Malapportionment Unequal representation, or **malapportionment**, has characterized many legislative bodies. In the past, for example, some states allocated an equal number of senators to each county. (This system calls to mind the U.S. Senate, which has two senators per state.) Because counties vary in population size, some senators were representing ten or twenty times as many constituents as their colleagues were. New Jersey offered one of the most extreme cases. In 1962, one county contained 49,000 residents and another had 924,000, yet each county was allotted one senator, and each senator had one vote in the senate. This kind of imbalance meant that a small group of people had the same institutional power as a group that was nineteen times larger. Such disproportionate power is inherently at odds with representative democracy in which each person's vote carries the same weight.

Until the 1960s, federal courts ignored the legislative malapportionment issue. It was not until 1962, in a Tennessee case in which the malapportionment was especially egregious (house district populations ranged from 2,340 to 42,298), that the courts stepped in. In *Baker v. Carr*, the U.S. Supreme Court ruled that the Fourteenth Amendment guarantee of equal protection applies to state legislative apportionment. With this decision as a wedge, the Court ruled that state houses should be apportioned on the basis of population. Two years later, in *Reynolds v. Sims* (1964), which extended the principle of

**multimember
districts (MMDs)**
Legislative districts
containing more than
one seat.

malapportionment
Skewed legislative
districts that violate
the "one person,
one vote" ideal.

equal representation to state senates, Chief Justice Earl Warren summed up the apportionment ideal by saying, "Legislators represent people, not trees or acres."[8] Accordingly, districts should reflect population equality: one person, one vote. In the aftermath of this decision, which overturned the apportionment practices of six states, a **reapportionment** fever swept the country, and district lines were redrawn in every state.

Reapportionment provided an immediate benefit to previously underrepresented urban areas, and increased urban representation led to a growing responsiveness in state legislatures to the problems and interests of cities and suburbs. Where reapportionment had a partisan effect, it generally benefited Republicans in the South and Democrats in the North. Other impacts of reapportionment have included the election of younger, better-educated legislators and, especially in southern states, better representation of African Americans. All in all, reapportionment is widely credited with improving the representativeness of American state legislatures.

Redrawing District Lines State legislatures are redistricted following the U.S. Census, which is taken every ten years. Redistricting allows population fluctuations—growth in some areas, decline in others—to be reflected in redrawn district lines. Twenty-six legislatures **redistrict** themselves; by contrast, thirteen states attempt to depoliticize the process by using impartial commissions to develop their redistricting plans.[9] In the remaining states, the redistricting task involves the legislature and either a commission or another political institution such as the governor (Maryland) or the state Supreme Court (Florida). A state's decision to use a less politicized approach such as a commission often comes about after a well-publicized redistricting controversy that creates a climate for reform of the process.[10]

In states where the legislature redistricts itself (and the state's congressional districts), the party controlling the legislature controls the redistricting process. Therefore, district lines have traditionally been redrawn to protect incumbent legislators and to maximize the strength of the party in power. The art of drawing district lines creatively was popularized in Massachusetts in 1812, when a political cartoonist for the *Boston Gazette* dubbed one of Governor Elbridge Gerry's district creations a **gerrymander** because the district, carefully configured to reflect partisan objectives, was shaped like a salamander. Two hundred years later, gerrymandering has not disappeared and neither has the partisan politics surrounding the process. Republicans claim that the district lines drawn by Democrats disadvantage the GOP; when Republicans create the maps, it is the Democrats who cry "foul." Litigation often ensues. Clearly, the practice of redrawing district lines in response to population shifts is highly politicized, as a study of the Kansas legislature demonstrated.[11] The goal, of course, is to maintain and grow the partisan majority. Not surprisingly, gerrymandering makes it more difficult for true two-party competition—as discussed in Chapter 5—to develop.

Amid the politics, redistricting has become a sophisticated operation in which statisticians and geographers use computer mapping to assist the legislature in designing an optimal districting scheme. (Check out Utah's efforts to engage the public in redistricting in the Controversies in States and Localities

reapportionment
The reallocation of seats in a legislative assembly.

redistrict
The redrawing of legislative district lines to conform as closely as possible to the "one person, one vote" ideal.

gerrymander
The process of creatively designing a legislative district, usually to enhance the electoral fortunes of the party in power.

box.) Although "one person, one vote" is the official standard, some unofficial guidelines are also taken into consideration. Ideally, districts should be geographically compact and unbroken. Those who draw the lines pay close attention to traditional political boundaries such as counties and, as noted, to the fortunes of political parties and incumbents. As long as districts adhere fairly closely to the population-equality standard (if a multimember district contains three seats, it must have three times the population of an SMD), federal courts tolerate the achievement of unofficial objectives. But redistricting does occasionally produce some oddly shaped districts resembling lobsters, spiders, and earmuffs. Dividing Montgomery County, Maryland, into legislative districts after the 2010 Census produced the shapes displayed in Figure 6.1.

Legislatures have to pay attention to the effects of their redistricting schemes on the voting strength of racial minorities. In fact, amendments to the Voting Rights Act and subsequent court rulings instructed affected states

FIGURE 6.1

State Legislative Districts in Montgomery County, Maryland, 2012

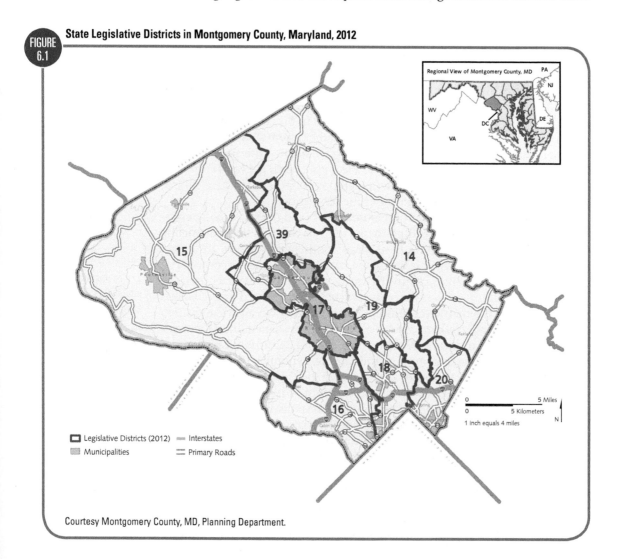

Courtesy Montgomery County, MD, Planning Department.

Controversies in States and Localities

Do-It-Yourself e-Redistricting

Redistricting is a controversial process, as the discussion in this chapter indicates. It is contentious and often becomes litigious. To the general public, it seems mysterious and opaque. Cognizant of this, the Utah legislature tried something different in 2011, when residents were encouraged to access map-drawing software on their home computer and try their hand at redistricting. More than 1,000 Utahans took a crack at carving the state's 82,170 square miles into four congressional districts, 29 state senate districts, 75 state house districts, and 15 state board of education districts. In each category, districts had to have substantial equality of population based on the 2010 census ($+/-$ 1 percent for congressional districts, $+/-$ 3.5 percent for the others), and be contiguous and reasonably compact. (Note that party considerations did not factor explicitly into the public's process. The legislative redistricting committee, made up of 14 Republicans and 5 Democrats, paid more attention to the partisan impact when they drew their own maps.) Eventually, more than 400 plans were submitted by the citizenry to the redistricting committee for its review.

The reason for the state's outreach to the public was twofold: to engage the citizenry in the process to increase their understanding of it, and importantly, to increase their influence in it. Anyone who submitted a plan and attended a redistricting hearing could present arguments in favor of his or her plan. According to the chair of the redistricting committee, legislators actually moved district lines based on the logic offered by some of the map drawers. Once the process ended and official maps were adopted by the legislature, comments from participants were generally positive. One thing for certain, the online do-it-yourself map drawing experience generated a lively public conversation on redistricting. By the next round of redistricting after the 2020 census, expect to see most states following Utah's example.

Critical Thinking Questions

1. Are average citizens qualified to draw district boundaries? How can they gain the information that is required to make these decisions?

2. What components would be included in a computer program to produce unbiased district lines?

3. Should there be a political component to the districting process? Do politics serve a valid social function here?

SOURCE: Mary Branham, "Technology Opens Redistricting Process," *Capitol Ideas* (Jan./Feb. 2012): 40–41; Redistrict Utah, www.redistrictutah.com/category/basics (accessed April 17, 2012).

to create districts in which racial minorities would have majority status. The intentional creation of majority minority districts more favorable to the election of African Americans had a partisan consequence. African Americans are more likely to be Democrats than Republicans; therefore, clustering black voters into specific districts diluted the potential Democratic vote of adjacent districts. This increased the likelihood that Republican candidates would win in those nearby districts. For instance, Florida drew thirteen heavily African American house districts, leaving the other 107 districts with fewer black voters. Some observers contended that this situation made it easier for Republicans to win sixty-five of those seats and thus control the house.[12]

The courts have not spoken with crystal clarity on the question of reapportionment. Yes, the racial composition of districts should be taken into account, but no, racial considerations should not be the sole criterion. In *Vieth v. Jubelirer* (2004), the U.S. Supreme Court ruled that reliance on partisan considerations remains an appropriate redistricting option. As one expert, political scientist Ronald Weber, put it, the strategy for line-drawers is "to determine the best way to waste the vote of the partisans of the other party."[13] Deals are made, interests are protected, and coalitions are built, all in an effort to craft an acceptable map, one that the legislature will adopt and the courts will uphold.

COMPENSATION

Legislative compensation has increased handsomely in the past three decades, again with some notable exceptions. Before the modernization of legislatures, salary and *per diem* (a daily amount to cover legislators' expenses while staying in the state capital during the session) levels were set in the state constitution and thus were impossible to adjust without a constitutional amendment. The lifting of these limits in most states puts legislatures, as the policymaking branch of state government, in the curious position of setting their own compensation levels. Recognizing that this power is a double-edged sword (legislators can vote themselves pay raises, and the public can turn around and vote them out of office for doing so), almost half the states have established compensation commissions or advisory groups to make recommendations on legislative remuneration. Arizona carries it a step further, requiring that a commission-recommended pay raise for legislators be submitted to the voters for approval—or rejection.

As of 2015, annual salaries of legislators ranged from a low of $100 in New Hampshire to a high of $97,197 in California.[14] (California legislators had topped the $115,000 mark just a few years ago, but a state commission reduced legislative salaries by 18 percent in 2009 and another 5 percent in 2012 before granting an increase in 2015.) Other states at the top of the compensation list include Pennsylvania ($85,339), New York ($79,500), Michigan ($71,685), Illinois ($67,836), Massachusetts ($60,033), and Ohio ($60,584). Eleven states pay their lawmakers between $30,000 and $50,000 annually. Compare these figures with the more modest pay levels of legislators in Georgia ($17,342), Idaho ($16,684), Nebraska ($12,000), Texas ($7,200), and South Dakota ($6,000). (These figures do not include *per diem*, which can increase overall compensation, depending on the state's rules for documenting expenses.)

As a general rule, states paying a more generous compensation typically demand more of a legislator's time than do low-paying states. And in most states, legislative leadership positions such as speaker of the house come with additional pay; in a few states, the chairs of major committees get a salary supplement. New Mexico legislators cannot be accused of seeking elective office for the money. There, legislators receive no salary. What is their financial reward for legislative service? One hundred sixty-five dollars per day for living expenses while in Santa Fe during the session, plus a travel allowance.

Legislative pay is but a fraction of the cost of operating a legislature. Legislative staff salaries—all totaled, state legislatures employ around 33,000 professional staffers–consume a large chunk of institutional expenditures, as do building maintenance and technological improvements.

LEADERSHIP

Legislatures need leaders, both formal and informal. Each chamber usually has four formal leadership positions. In the senate, a president and a president pro tempore (who presides in the absence of the president) are in charge of the chamber; in the house, the comparable leaders are the speaker and the speaker pro tempore. These legislative officials are chosen by the members, who almost always vote along party lines. (In twenty-six states, the post of senate president is occupied by the lieutenant governor, but the role is ceremonial in most of these states.[15]) Both houses have two political party leadership positions: a majority leader and a minority leader.

The leaders are responsible for making the legislature, which is a relatively decentralized system, run smoothly and for seeing that it accomplishes its tasks. In a typical chamber, the presiding officer appoints committee members, names committee chairs, controls the activity on the floor, allocates office space and committee budgets, and (in some states) selects the majority leader and the holders of other majority-party posts. The actual influence of the leadership varies from one chamber to another. One study found that House speakers in West Virginia, Indiana, New Hampshire, and New York enjoy the greatest power; while the North Dakota and Wyoming speakers possess the least power.[16] One factor that affects leaders' power is whether the positions are rotated or retained. Leaders who have the option of retaining their position can build power bases. In the case of rotation, however, one set of leaders is replaced with another on a regular basis, so the leaders are **lame ducks** when they assume the posts.

On average, today's leaders are different from the caricatured wheeler dealers of the past. For one thing, in 2014, eight women were senate presidents; six women served as speakers of the house.[17] New Hampshire scored two historic firsts in 2009: the first state with a female majority in a legislative chamber (the senate: 54 percent women) and the first state to have women occupy both the house speakership and the senate presidency. More evidence that legislative leadership has changed comes from Colorado, where, in 2009, it became the first state in which African Americans led both chambers of the legislature at the same time. Another indicator of change has less to do with diversity and more to do with process: Rank-and-file members of the legislature are not as reluctant as they used to be to challenge their leaders on both procedural and policy matters.

Leadership in legislatures is linked to political parties. As noted, voting to fill leadership posts follows party lines. In chambers with even numbers of members, the possibility exists that election results might produce a tie (assuming the absence of independents and third-party members in the chamber). For example, in 2012, the Oregon House of Representatives had 30 Democrats and 30 Republicans. Realizing that neither party could marshal a majority and hoping to avoid a deadlock, the two parties negotiated a power-sharing arrangement. Lawmakers elected co-speakers (one Democrat, one Republican) and each committee was led by co-chairs of each party. A sufficient level of bipartisan goodwill was generated so that the work of the chamber could proceed.[18]

lame duck
An elected official who cannot serve beyond the current term of office.

Lobbyists cluster in the Florida Capitol rotunda that connects (and separates) the house and senate sides of the building.

As political parties become more competitive in the states, legislative behavior and decisions take on a more partisan cast, that is, the legislature becomes more "procedurally partisan."[19] There are Democratic and Republican sides of the chamber and Democratic and Republican positions on bills. Each party meets in a caucus to design its legislative strategy and generate camaraderie. In states where one political party continues to dominate, partisanship is less important; moreover, in one-party settings, the dominant party typically develops splits or factions at the expense of party unity. But when the outnumbered minority party begins to gain strength, the majority party usually becomes more cohesive.

In many states, legislative leaders have embraced a new function: fundraising. Leaders tap interest groups and lobbyists for money and divide it among their party's candidates for legislative seats. California has led the way, with multimillion-dollar **war chests**. In other states, the amount of money thus raised is not as great, of course, but it has become a significant source of campaign funding. Lobbyists find it difficult to say no to a request for funds from the leadership. The leaders allocate the funds to the neediest candidates—those in close races. If these candidates are victorious, their loyalty to party leaders pays legislative dividends.

THE COMMITTEE SYSTEM

The workhorse of the legislature is the committee. Under normal circumstances, a committee's primary function is to consider bills—that is, to hear testimony, perhaps amend the bills, and ultimately approve or reject them. A committee's action on a bill precedes debate in the house or senate. Along with the leadership, committees provide a structure for organizing the process of making laws.

All legislative chambers are divided into committees, and most committees have created subcommittees. Committees can be of several types. A *standing*

war chest

A stash of funds accumulated in advance of a campaign.

committee regularly considers legislation during the session. A *joint committee* is made up of members of both houses. Some joint committees are standing; others are temporary (sometimes called ad hoc or select committees) and are convened for a specific purpose, such as investigating a troubled agency or solving a particularly vexing public policy problem. A *conference committee* is a special type of joint committee that is assembled to iron out differences between house- and senate-passed versions of a bill. Most states use *interim committees* during the period when the legislature is not in session to get a head start on an upcoming session. The number of committees varies, but most senates and houses have standing committees on the issues listed in Table 6.2. Most of these committees, in turn, have professional staffs assigned to them.

A substantive standing committee tends to be made up of legislators who have expertise and interest in that committee's subject matter.[20] Thus, farmers would be assigned to the agriculture committee, teachers to the education committee, small-business owners to the commerce committee, lawyers to the judiciary committee, and so on. These legislators bring knowledge and commitment to their committee assignments; they also may bring a certain bias because they tend to function as advocates for their career interests. Note, too, that every chamber has at least one undesirable committee (usually defined as one whose substance is boring) to which few legislators want to be assigned.[21]

The central concern of a standing committee is its floor success—getting the full chamber to accede to its recommendations on a bill. Several plausible explanations exist for a committee's floor success. A committee whose ideological composition similar to that of the whole chamber is likely to be more successful than one whose members' views are at odds with the chamber.

TABLE 6.2   Standing Committees of the Legislature

Both houses of state legislatures typically have standing committees dealing with these substantive issues:

Agriculture	Government operations
Banking/financial institutions	Health
Business and commerce	Insurance
Communications	Judiciary and criminal justice
Education	Local affairs
Elections	Public employees
Energy	Rules
Environment and natural resources	Social/human services
Ethics	Transportation

In addition, both houses have standing committees that address the raising and allocating of state funds. These committees may have different names in different chambers:

Appropriations	Finance and taxation
Ways and means	

The leadership takes this situation into account when it makes committee assignments; thus, very few committees are ideological outliers.[22] Also, committees full of legislatively experienced members generally have more floor success than committees composed of legislative novices. And committees that have a reputation for being tough have more floor success with their bills than committees that pass everything that comes before them.

LO 6.3

To appreciate the importance of informal norms amid formal rules in the legislative institution.

Legislative Behavior

Legislatures have their own dynamics, their own way of doing things. Senate and house rule books spell out what can and cannot be done in the same way that an organization's bylaws do. Studies show that these rules matter, that is, they account for much of what happens in a given legislative chamber.[23] Legislatures are self-regulating institutions for the most part; it is especially important, therefore, that participants know what is expected of them. To make certain that the chamber's rules are understood, most legislatures conduct orientation sessions for new members.

NORMS OF THE INSTITUTION

An understanding of the legislature involves not only knowledge of formal structures and written rules, but also awareness of informal norms and unwritten policies. For example, nowhere in a state's legislative rules does it say that a freshman legislator is prohibited from playing a leadership role, but the unwritten rules of most legislatures place a premium on seniority. A primary rule of legislative bodies is that you must "go along to get along," a phrase that emphasizes teamwork and paying your dues. Legislators who are on opposite sides of a bill to regulate horse racing might find themselves on the same side of a bill outlawing the use of cell phones while operating a motor vehicle. Yesterday's opponent is today's partner. For this reason, no one can afford to make bitter enemies in the legislature and expect to flourish.

Those who aspire to rise from rank-and-file legislator to committee chairperson and perhaps to party leader or presiding officer find consensus-building skills quite useful. These skills come in handy because many norms are intended to reduce the potential for conflict in what is inherently a setting full of conflict. For instance, a freshman legislator is expected to defer to a senior colleague. Although an energetic new legislator might chafe under such a restriction, one day he will have gained seniority and will take comfort in the rule. Moreover, legislators are expected to honor commitments made to each other, thus encouraging reciprocity: "If you support me on my favorite bill, I will be with you on yours." A legislator cannot be too unyielding. Compromises, which are sometimes principled but more often political, are the backbone of the legislative process. Few bills are passed by both houses and sent to the governor in exactly the same form as when they were introduced.

Informal rules are designed to make the legislative process flow more smoothly. Legislators who cannot abide by the rules find it difficult to get along. They are subjected to not-so-subtle efforts at behavior modification,

such as powerful social sanctions (ostracism and ridicule) and legislative punishment (the bottling up of their bill in committee or their assignment to an
unpopular committee), actions that promote adherence to norms.

LEGISLATIVE CUE TAKING AND DECISION MAKING

Much has been written about how legislators make public policy decisions,
and a number of explanations are plausible. Legislators may adopt the policy
positions espoused by their political party. They may follow the dictates of
their conscience—that is, do what they think is right. They may yield to the
pressures of organized interest groups. They may be persuaded by the arguments of other legislators, such as a committee chairperson who is knowledgeable about the policy area or a trusted colleague who is considered to be
savvy; or they may succumb to the entreaties of the governor, who has made
a particular piece of legislation the focus of her administration. Of course,
legislators may also attempt to respond to the wishes of their constituents. On
a significant issue—one that has received substantial media attention—they
are likely to be subjected to tremendous cross-pressures.

A legislator reflecting on his years in the Massachusetts house tells this
revealing story. During one session, he voted yes on corporate tax break legislation that he was opposed to because the speaker of the house favored the
bill and wanted him to vote yes. Why was the speaker's position so compelling? Because the legislator's favorite bill was due to be voted on later and he
wanted the speaker's support on it.[24] Another remarkably candid assessment
of how legislators make public policy decisions was offered by a freshman in
the Tennessee House of Representatives. He identified two often unspoken
but always present considerations: "Will it cost me votes back home?" and
"Can an opponent use it against me [in the] next election?"[25] These pragmatic
concerns intrude on the more idealistic notions of decision making. They also
suggest a fairly cautious approach to bold policy initiatives.

Assuming that legislators are concerned about how a vote will be received
back home, it seems logical that they would be particularly solicitous of public opinion. In actuality, state legislators frequently hold opinions at odds
with those of their constituents. They occasionally misperceive what the public is thinking; at such times, it is difficult for them to act as mere **delegates**
and simply fulfill the public's will. To improve the communications link,
some lawmakers use mail questionnaires and interactive websites to poll constituents about their views; others hold town meetings at various places in the
district to assess the public's mood.

It is quite probable that first-term legislators feel more vulnerable to the
wishes of the public than legislative veterans do. Hence, the new legislator
devotes more time to determining what the people want, whereas the experienced legislator "knows" what they want (or perhaps knows what they need)
and thus functions as a **trustee**—someone who follows his or her own best
judgment. Because the vast majority of legislators are returned to office election after election, it appears that there is some validity to this argument. In
fact, a study of lawmakers in eight states found that the members' personal
opinions were consistently important in their decision choices.[26]

delegate
A legislator who
functions as a conduit
for constituency
opinion.

trustee
A legislator who votes
according to his or her
conscience and best
judgment.

In the final analysis, the determining factor in how legislators make decisions depends on the issue itself. On one hand, "when legislators are deeply involved with an issue, they appear to be more concerned with policy consequences" than with constituency preferences.[27] In this situation, the legislators are focused on a goal other than re-election. On the other hand, if lawmakers are not particularly engaged in an issue that is important to their constituents, they will follow their constituents' preference. In that sense, they act as **politicos**, adjusting as the issues and cues change.

LO 6.4

To understand the intricacies of the lawmaking process.

How a Bill Becomes Law (or Not)

A legislative bill starts as an idea and travels a long, complex path before it emerges as law. It is no wonder that of the 1,501 bills introduced in the Missouri legislature in 2013, only 145 had become law by the end of the regular session.[28] A legislative session has a rhythm to it. Minor bills and symbolic issues tend to be resolved early, whereas major, potentially divisive issues take a much longer time to wend their way through the legislative labyrinth. With the clock ticking at the end of the session, legislators try to broker compromises and build coalitions to get key bills passed.[29] The budget or appropriations bill typically generates several rounds of contentious debate among legislators. And if legislatures cannot get their work completed, they may end up back in the state capitol at a later date in a special session. In 2013, for example, twenty-two special legislative sessions were called; some states held more than one extra session.

The lawmaking process has been described in many ways: a zoo, a circus, a marketplace. Perhaps the most apt description is a casino because there are winners and losers, the outcome is never final, and there is always a new game ahead.[30] Lawmaking is a dynamic and exciting process; it can be an arduous process as well. Ideas for bills are everywhere: with constituents, interest groups, and state agencies. Legislators may turn to other states for ideas or to their staffs. **Policy entrepreneurs**, people who are knowledgeable about certain issues and are willing to promote them, abound. Introducing a bill—"putting it in the hopper," in legislative parlance—is just the beginning. A bill can get sidetracked at many points, and even derailed altogether. Subcommittee and committee hearings may pose a challenge, and even if the committee does approve the bill, getting it scheduled for floor debate can be another hurdle. Assuming successful passage in the first chamber, a bill goes through the same steps in the second chamber. Even if it is successful there, a conference committee may be needed to resolve any differences between the two passed versions. And most legislatures impose deadlines for the completion of the various steps.

Clearly, a bill does not make it through the legislative process without a lot of effort and even a little luck. A bill's chances of passage rise as more legislators sign on as co-sponsors, and if the co-sponsors are legislative leaders, even better. Assignment of the bill to a favorable committee improves the likelihood that the bill will be scheduled for a hearing in a timely manner. Many bills get bottled up in committee and never receive a hearing. Strong support from key interest groups is a powerful advantage as is the emergence of only weak

politico

A legislator who functions as either a delegate or a trustee, as circumstances dictate.

policy entrepreneurs

People who bring new ideas to a policy-making body.

opposition to the bill. Sometimes bill passage is a matter of fortuitous timing. For example, a spectacular prison break from an overcrowded state penitentiary would help garner support for passage of a prison construction bill.

Controversial issues such as abortion raise the stakes. The former speaker of the Wisconsin Assembly, Tom Loftus, described abortion politics in his state as trench warfare in which compromise was almost impossible. Leadership on the issue came from legislators who felt strongly about the matter and who held safe seats. (In this instance, "safe" meant that taking a position was not likely to cost them too many votes or generate too many serious challengers when they ran for re-election.) As anti-abortion bills were introduced, battle lines were drawn. According to the speaker:

> The pro-choice side, which included the Democratic leadership, tried to keep the bill bottled up in committee, and the pro-life side, through political pressure on the Republicans and conservative Democrats, tried to pull it out so the whole assembly could vote on it on the floor of the chamber. If the pro-life people could get the bill to the floor for a vote, they would win. To accomplish this end, they needed to gain supporters from the pivotal middle group of legislators, usually moderates of both parties from marginal districts.[31]

The powerful anti-abortion group, Wisconsin Citizens Concerned for Life, pressured vulnerable legislators. These legislators were in a tough position because they knew "regardless of how you voted, you were going to make a slew of single-issue voters mad."[32] Their strategy became one of parliamentary maneuvering.

Even if a bill is successful in one chamber, potential hurdles await in the other chamber. Representatives and senators may see the same issue in very different terms. In Ohio, a few years back, everyone agreed that the state's system for funding public education needed reform. (The Ohio Supreme Court had found the state's school-funding system unconstitutional and had given the legislature one year to devise a new system.) But initial efforts derailed when the house and senate could not agree on a plan. The senate approved a funding package that would have increased the sales tax, provided debt financing, and allowed local school boards to propose property tax increases.[33] The house, dominated by Republicans who had signed an anti-tax pledge the preceding year, approved a bill that did not include tax hikes. Each chamber rejected the other's plan. Hammering out a compromise agreeable to both chambers took a long time, even with the court's order as a spur to action.

Once conference or concurrence committees resolve differences and agreement is secured in both chambers, then the bill is enrolled (certified and signed) and sent to the governor. The governor may do one of three things: (1) sign the act (once passed, a bill is called an *act*) into law, (2) veto it (in which case the legislature has a chance to have the last word by overriding the veto), or (3) take no action. If the governor does not take action and the session has ended, then in most states the act will become law without the governor's signature. Why not simply sign it if the act will become law anyway? Sometimes it is a matter of political symbolism for the governor. In approximately one-third of the states, if the governor does not sign or veto the act and the legislature has adjourned, the act dies (a circumstance called a *pocket veto*).

During its 2013 regular session, the Missouri General Assembly passed less than 10 percent of the bills that were introduced. Is this a sign of success or failure? Missouri's figures are lower than those of most states—20 to 25 percent is a common passage rate—but not necessarily a cause for alarm. Not all bills are good ones, and the inability to generate sufficient consensus among legislators may reflect that condition.

LO 6.5

To assess the efforts to reform state legislatures.

Legislative Reform and Capacity

During the 1970s, fundamental reforms occurred throughout the country as legislatures sought to increase their capacity and become more professional. And, even though these reforms have had a substantial impact, the institutional modernization process never really ends.

THE IDEAL LEGISLATURE

In the late 1960s, the Citizens' Conference on State Legislatures (CCSL) studied legislative performance and identified five characteristics critical to legislative improvement.[34] Ideally, a legislature should be functional, accountable, informed, independent, and representative (FAIIR).

The *functional* legislature has almost unrestricted time to conduct its business. It is assisted by adequate staff and facilities and has effective rules and procedures that facilitate the flow of legislation. The *accountable* legislature's operations are open and comprehensible to the public. The *informed* legislature manages its workload through an effective committee structure, legislative activities between sessions, and a professional staff; it also conducts regular budgetary review of executive branch activities. The *independent* legislature runs its own affairs independently of the executive branch. It exercises oversight of agencies, regulates lobbyists, manages conflicts of interest, and provides adequate compensation for its members. Finally, the *representative* legislature has a diverse membership that effectively represents the social, economic, ethnic, and other characteristics of the state.

The fifty state legislatures were evaluated and scored by CCSL according to the FAIIR criteria. For the first time ever, the rankings offered a relatively scientific means of comparing one state legislature with another. Overall, the "best" state legislatures were found in California, New York, Illinois, Florida, and Wisconsin. The "worst," in the assessment of CCSL, were those in Alabama, Wyoming, Delaware, North Carolina, and Arkansas.

The CCSL report triggered extensive self-evaluation by legislatures around the country. Most states launched ambitious efforts to reform their legislatures. The results are readily apparent. In terms of the CCSL criteria, states have made tremendous strides in legislative institution building. The evidence of increased professionalism includes more staff support, higher legislative compensation, longer sessions, and better facilities. Many legislatures revamped their committee systems, altered their rules and procedures, and tightened their ethics regulations. The consequences of these actions are state legislatures that are far more FAIIR now than they were found to be in the late

1960s. The National Conference of State Legislatures sums it up this way: "Legislatures became more muscular, agile, intelligent, and independent than at any other time in American history."[35]

THE EFFECTS OF REFORM

Today's legislative institutions are different, but are they better? Although many observers would answer in the affirmative, the legislative reform picture is not unequivocally rosy. Political scientist Alan Rosenthal, who has closely observed legislative reform, warns that "the legislature's recent success in enhancing its capacity and improving its performance may place it in greater jeopardy than before."[36] Rosenthal's argument is that a constellation of demands pulls legislators away from the legislative core. That is, the new breed of legislators gets caught up in the demands of re-election, constituent service, interest groups, and political careerism and thus neglects institutional matters such as structure, procedure, staff, image, and community. The legislature as an institution suffers because it is not receiving the necessary care and attention from its members. For example, California's highly reformed legislature performed poorly in the early 2000s, mired in a period of bitter partisanship and gridlock. Some observers blame reform for some of the Golden State's legislative troubles.

Consider the idea of a citizen-legislator, one for whom service in the legislature is a part-time endeavor. Since the onset of reform, the proportion of legislators who are lawyers, business owners, or insurance or real estate executives has dropped, and the number of full-time legislators has risen. In states such as California and Pennsylvania, roughly three-quarters of lawmakers identify themselves as legislators with no other occupation. The critical issue is whether the decline of the citizen-legislator is a desirable aspect of modernization. Should a state legislature represent a broad spectrum of vocations, or should it be composed of career politicians? One perspective is this: "If I'm sick, I want professional help. I feel the same way about public affairs. I want legislators who are knowledgeable and professional."[37] Another view is represented by a Michigan legislator who believes that his careerist colleagues have lost touch with their constituents: "When you spend all your time in Lansing, you're more influenced by the lobbyists than by your constituents."[38]

In effect, state legislatures are becoming more like the U.S. Congress.[39] In many states, legislators are staying in the legislature in record numbers. Modernization has made the institution more attractive to its members, so turnover rates are declining. But do we really want fifty mini-Congresses scattered across the land? Today's legislatures are more FAIIR than in the past, but reform has also brought greater professionalization of the legislative career, increased polarization of the legislative process, and more fragmentation of the legislative institution.[40] Figure 6.2 shows the pattern of "citizen" (16 states), "professional" (10 states), and "hybrid" (24 states) state legislatures throughout the land. The categories are derived from an index developed by the National Conference of State Legislatures that reflects legislator salary and benefits, the time demands of legislative service, and the staff resources available to the legislature.[41] Lawmakers in the most professionalized legislatures

It's Your Turn

Should State Legislatures Be More Professionalized?

PROS	CONS
Employing more staff improves a legislature's ability to analyze legislation. This should result in more thoughtful, effective laws.	Legislators in professional legislatures spend more time in the state capitol and risk becoming "part of the system" and perhaps disconnecting from their constituents. In less-professional legislatures, lawmakers likely have regular jobs back home, and likely remain more connected to their communities.
By meeting more often and in longer sessions, legislatures have more time to tackle the state's problems. The pressure of a ticking time clock is lessened.	Professional legislatures are more expensive to operate due to larger staffs, longer terms, and higher salaries, and that's money that comes out of taxpayers' pockets.
Paying legislators a higher salary would likely make legislative races more competitive thereby giving voters more choices.	Thomas Jefferson was an advocate of a citizen legislature. If it was good enough for Thomas Jefferson, it should be good enough for us today. It is important to keep legislators grounded in the communities they represent.
A professional legislature can work more effectively with the state's full-time governor.	

are paid more, devote more time to the job, and have far greater staff resources at their disposal than their counterparts in citizen legislatures. States categorized as hybrids fall between professional and citizen on these characteristics. The It's Your Turn box takes up the issue of legislative professionalization.

Change continues in state legislatures, but much of it is cloaked in an anti-reform guise. Term limits (discussed below) are, of course, a major component in the effort to limit the legislature. Other attempts to chip away at reform include Louisiana's approval of a constitutional amendment that, in even-numbered years, limits the legislature to a thirty-day session that addresses only fiscal issues. Also, as noted earlier, Nevada has trimmed the length of legislative sessions, whereas Illinois and Rhode Island have reduced the size of their legislatures. And California legislators have endured pay cuts.

To some analysts, the reforms of the past decades have produced a legislative monster. Richard Nathan, a veteran observer of the states, argues that the key to increased government productivity is the empowerment of the governor.[42] Nathan advocates term limits, unicameral legislative bodies, rotation of committee memberships, and reduction of legislative staff and sessions as a means of reining in the legislature vis-à-vis the governor. If adopted, Nathan's recommendations would undo thirty-five years of legislative reform. And the

Legislative Professionalism

FIGURE
6.2

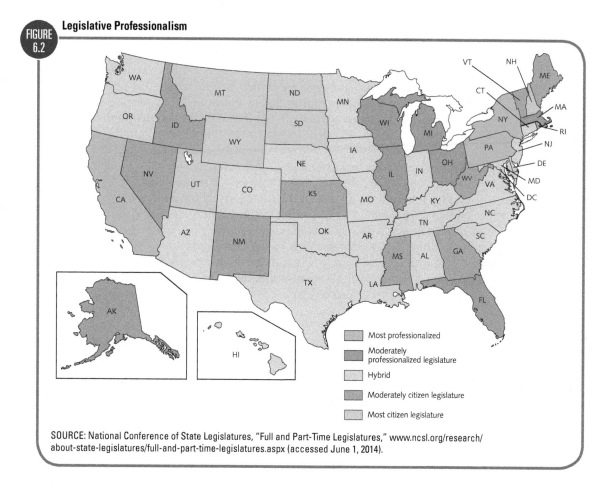

Most professionalized

Moderately
professionalized legislature

Hybrid

Moderately citizen legislature

Most citizen legislature

SOURCE: National Conference of State Legislatures, "Full and Part-Time Legislatures," www.ncsl.org/research/about-state-legislatures/full-and-part-time-legislatures.aspx (accessed June 1, 2014).

governor's political power would be significantly strengthened. This helps explain why, in 2007, Pennsylvania's governor Ed Rendell proposed a far-reaching plan to trim the size of the Keystone State's General Assembly, limit legislative terms, and change the redistricting process. As you might imagine, Governor Rendell's plan fell on deaf ears in the legislative branch.[43] The legislative-gubernatorial nexus is the subject of a later section of this chapter.

TERM LIMITS

In September 1990, Oklahoma voters took an action that has sent state legislatures reeling. Oklahomans overwhelmingly approved a ballot measure limiting the tenure of state legislators and statewide officers. As it turned out, limiting terms was not just a Sooner thing. Within two months, voters in California and Colorado had followed suit. With a close defeat in Washington State slowing it only slightly, the term-limits movement swept the country. In Oregon, a group called LIMITS (Let Incumbents Mosey into the Sunset) grew out of a tax limitation organization. In Wisconsin, a coalition known as Badgers Back in Charge took up the cause of term limitation. And political activists of many stripes—

LO 6.6

To debate the impact of legislative term limits.

populists, conservatives, and libertarians—found a home in the term limitation movements in Florida, Michigan, and Texas.[44] In time, twenty-one states slapped limits on state legislative terms, although in six of these states, term limits were repealed by state courts or the legislature itself. All told, approximately one-fourth of state legislative seats are subject to term limits. The term-limits laws gradually bore the intended fruit: In any even-numbered election year, at least 100 state legislators are termed out of office. Table 6.3 compares the term-limit provisions of the states where legislative term limits remain in force. Note that Nebraska voters had approved term limits three times prior to the 2000 initiative, but the courts had invalidated the measures.

In most states, the measures limit service in each chamber separately. In Maine, for example, a legislator is limited to eight years in the house and eight years in the senate. It is quite possible, then, that an individual could serve a total of sixteen years in the legislature under this plan. In a few states, the restriction is on total legislative service. In California and Oklahoma, for instance, the limitation is twelve years, whether in the house, the senate, or a combination of the two. Some term limits are for a lifetime (as in Arkansas and Nevada); others simply limit the number of consecutive terms (as in Ohio and South Dakota).

TABLE 6.3   Term Limits in the States

STATE	YEAR ADOPTED	SENATE	HOUSE	YEAR LAW TOOK EFFECT	REFERENDUM VOTE	BALLOT STATUS
Arizona	1992	8	8	2000	74 to 26	Initiative
Arkansas	1992	16	16	2000/1998	60 to 40	Initiative
California	1990	12	12	1998/1996	52 to 48	Initiative
Colorado	1990	8	8	1998	71 to 29	Initiative
Florida	1992	8	8	2000	77 to 23	Initiative
Louisiana	1995	12	12	2007	76 to 24	Referendum
Maine	1993	8	8	1996	67 to 33	Indirect Initiative
Michigan	1992	8	6	2002/1998	59 to 41	Initiative
Missouri	1992	8	8	2002	74 to 26	Initiative
Montana	1992	8	8	2000	67 to 33	Initiative
Nebraska	2000	8	—	2006	56 to 44	Initiative
Nevada	1994	12	12	2010	70 to 30	Initiative
Ohio	1992	8	8	2000	66 to 34	Initiative
Oklahoma	1990	12	12	2004	67 to 33	Initiative
South Dakota	1992	8	8	2000	63 to 37	Initiative

NOTE: In California and Oklahoma, a legislator may serve a total of twelve years in the legislature during his or her lifetime. The total time may be split between the two chambers or spent in its entirely in a single chamber. In Arkansas, a 2014 change extended the amount of time a legislator can serve to a total of sixteen years.

SOURCES: State Term Limits (2015), www.termlimits.org, and the National Conference of State Legislatures, "The Term-Limited States," www.ncsl.org/research/about-state-legislatures/chart-of-term-limits-states.aspx (accessed March 13, 2015).

Limiting legislative terms captured the fancy of a public angry with entrenched politicians. The measure offers voters a chance to strike back at an institution that they perceive as self-serving and out of touch. But not everyone favors limiting legislative terms. Opponents offer several arguments against them. On a theoretical level, they argue that term limits rob voters of their fundamental right to choose their representatives. In a related vein, they contend that these measures unfairly disqualify a subset of the population—legislators—from seeking office. And, finally, they claim that term limits are unnecessary, that sufficient legislative turnover occurs without them.

Term limits were expected to produce several consequences:

- Ending the domination of a chamber by powerful, entrenched veteran legislators.
- Increasing the proportion of first-term legislators in any given session.
- Increasing representation by groups underrepresented in the legislature, especially women and minorities, because of the guarantee of open seats.[45]
- Shifting power from the legislature to the governor and to lobbyists.

Three of the four expected consequences have indeed come to pass. The exodus of veteran legislators and the influx of inexperienced members have some observers shaking their heads in dismay. For instance, twenty-nine of Michigan's thirty-eight senators (76 percent) could not seek re-election in 2010 due to term limits. Not surprisingly, data from term-limit states reflect procedural difficulties, a slower-working institution, less deliberation in committees, and less complex legislation.[46] As for shifting power to other actors, consensus seems to exist among researchers that governors, agency heads, legislative staff, and interest groups have benefited at the expense of the term-limited legislature.[47]

The expectation that term limits would produce greater representation of underrepresented groups has not been borne out, at least not yet. The number of women in term-limited legislatures has actually decreased slightly, and the increase in racial and ethnic minorities may be due more to their increased voting strength rather than to term limits.[48] Term-limit devotees who wanted to strike back at an out-of-touch institution would be surprised to learn that term-limited legislators actually become less beholden to their constituents.[49] Moreover, a recent study found that term-limited legislatures appear to be less able to develop effective fiscal policy for their states.[50] Furthermore, term limits have had partisan effects by removing more senior Democrats from office than Republicans.[51] In sum, limiting the terms of legislators has consequences beyond simply forcing incumbents out of office.

Despite these effects, term limits remain popular with the public.[52] In 2008, South Dakota legislators asked voters if they wanted to repeal legislative term limits; the answer was a resounding "no"—76 percent to 22 percent. But the term-limit movement has lost steam. As Table 6.3 indicates, citizen initiatives are the primary vehicle through which the term-limit question has been placed before the voters. And the issue has just about run the gamut of states that allow initiatives. (The Utah legislature imposed term limits on itself in 1994, but it had a change of heart and repealed the law in 2003.) Court challenges have undone legislative term limits in Massachusetts, Oregon,

TABLE 6.4	Repeals of Legislative Term Limits			
STATE	**YEAR ADOPTED**	**YEAR REPEALED**	**REPEALED BY**	
Idaho	1994	2002	Legislature	
Massachusetts	1994	1997	State Supreme Court	
Oregon	1992	2002	State Supreme Court	
Utah	1994	2003	Legislature	
Washington	1992	1998	State Supreme Court	
Wyoming	1992	2004	State Supreme Court	

Washington, and Wyoming (see Table 6.4). And in a surprising move, the Idaho legislature, bowing to an array of political pressures, repealed the term-limits law that was adopted via the initiative process in 1994.[53] Angry Idahoans gathered a sufficient number of signatures to place a question on the 2002 ballot asking whether the legislature's action should be upheld. After a heated campaign, the "Repeal the Repeal" question was defeated, thus ending term limits in Idaho before they took effect.

Support for legislative term limits comes from other quarters as well. Not surprisingly, governors often look fondly at legislative term limits. For instance, when campaigning for the governorship in 2014, Republican Bruce Rauner proposed an initiative that would have imposed an eight-year term limit on Illinois lawmakers. Despite getting substantially more signatures than required on initiative petitions, Illinois courts ruled the measure violated the state's constitution, thus the term limits question was not put before the voters.

LO 6.7

To explore the interaction of the legislative branch with the executive branch.

Relationship with the Executive Branch

In Chapter 7, you will read about strong governors leading American states boldly in the twenty-first century. In this chapter, you have read about strong legislatures charting a course for that same century. Do these institutions ever collide in their policymaking? You bet they do. Conflict between the legislature and the governor is inevitable, but it is not necessarily destructive. It is inevitable because both governors and legislators think that they know what is best for the state. It is not necessarily destructive because, during the posturing, bargaining, and negotiating that produces a consensus, governors and legislators may actually arrive at an optimal solution.

DEALING WITH THE GOVERNOR

The increased institutional strength of the legislature and its accompanying assertiveness have made for strained relations with a governor accustomed to being the political star. Institutional conflict is exacerbated under conditions of divided government, that is, when a legislature is controlled by one party and the governor is of the other party. The result of divided government is often gridlock, accompanied by finger pointing and blame-gaming. As the former Republican governor of Mississippi, Haley Barbour, said to the Democratic-controlled legislature in his first "State of the State" address, "As Governor of Mississippi you have two choices . . . you can work with the Legislature, or you can fail. Well, I'm not into failure, so I look forward to working with each of you to make sure we all succeed."[54] As Governor Barbour quickly learned, that is much easier said than done.

A governor and a legislature controlled by the same party do not necessarily make for easy interbranch relations either. Especially in states where the two parties are competitive, legislators are expected to support the policy initiatives of their party's governor. Yet the governor's proposals may not mesh with individual legislators' attitudes, ambitions, and agendas. South Carolina offers an illustration. In 2012, the Republican governor and the overwhelmingly Republican legislature battled long and hard over issues as diverse as comprehensive tax reform and dredging at a state port. Despite their partisan affinity, they saw these and many other issues very differently.

Sometimes governors who have previously served as legislators seem to have an easier time dealing with the lawmaking institution. For example, former governor Madeleine Kunin of Vermont assumed the office after three terms in the legislature and one term as lieutenant governor, "knowing the needs of legislators, the workings of the legislative process, the sensitivities of that process."[55] Usually about two-thirds of the governors have had legislative experience, although the proportion has recently declined.

Governors have a media advantage over deliberative bodies such as a legislature. The governor is the visible symbol of state government and, as a single individual, fits into a media world of thirty-second sound bites. By contrast, media images of the legislature often portray deal making, pork barrel politics, and general silliness. To be sure, those images can be quite accurate at times. "Gotcha" journalism, the term for media efforts to catch public officials in seemingly questionable situations, certainly complicates legislative life.

The legislature is not without its weapons. If the legislature can muster the votes, it can override a gubernatorial veto. In fact, new research shows that in states with term limited legislatures, the incidence of veto overrides is actually higher than it is in states that do not limit legislative terms.[56] Legislatures have also enacted other measures designed to enhance their control and to reduce the governor's flexibility in budgetary matters. For example, some states now require the governor to obtain legislative approval of budget cutbacks in the event of a revenue shortfall. Professional legislatures with their longer sessions and higher-paid members can hold their own in budget battles with the governor.[57] Other states have limited the governor's power to initiate transfers of funds among executive branch agencies. These actions reflect the continuing evolution of legislative-executive relations.

OVERSEEING THE BUREAUCRACY

Legislative involvement with the executive branch does not end with the governor. State legislatures are increasingly venturing into the world of state agencies and bureaucrats, with the attitude that after authorizing a program and allocating funds for it, they should check on what has happened to it. Legislative oversight involves four activities: policy and program evaluation, legislative review of administrative rules and regulations, sunset legislation, and review and control of federal funds received by the state.

Policy and Program Evaluation Legislatures select auditors to keep an eye on state agencies and departments. (In a few states, auditors are independently elected officials.) Auditors are more than super-accountants; their job is to evaluate the performance of state programs as to their efficiency and effectiveness, a task sometimes known as the *postaudit function*. Specifically, they conduct periodic performance audits to measure goal achievement and other indicators of progress in satisfying legislative intent, a process that has been credited with both saving money and improving program performance. Virginia's Joint Legislative Audit and Review Commission (JLARC), is regarded as a model for the rest of the country. Throughout its forty-year history, JLARC has conducted hundreds of evaluations of state programs and saved the state millions of dollars. The key to a useful auditing function is strong legislative support (even in the face of audits that turn up controversial findings) and, at the same time, a guarantee of a certain degree of independence from legislative interference.

Legislative Review of Administrative Rules Forty-seven state legislatures conduct reviews of administrative rules and regulations, but they vary in their methods. They may assign the review function to a special committee (such as a rule review committee) or to a specific legislative agency, or they may incorporate the review function in the budgetary process. In this role, the legislature acts as a gatekeeper, striving to keep agency rules in line with legislative preferences.[58]

Legislative review is a mechanism through which administrative abuses of discretion can be corrected. Legislative bills frequently contain language to the effect that "the Department of Youth Services shall develop the necessary rules and regulations to implement the provisions of this act." Such language gives the agency wide latitude in establishing procedures and policies. The legislature wants to be certain that, in the process, the agency does not overstep its bounds or violate legislative intent. If it is found to have done so, then the legislature can overturn the offending rules and regulations through modification, suspension, or veto—depending on the state.

This issue is a true gray area of legislative-executive relations, and court rulings at both the national and state levels have found the most powerful of these actions, the **legislative veto**, to be an unconstitutional violation of the separation of powers. For example, in 1997, the Missouri Supreme Court ruled that the legislature's rule-review process was an unconstitutional intrusion into the functions of the executive branch.[59] Legislatures continue to use the budgetary process to review (and sanction) agency behavior. Increasingly, legislatures are requiring state agencies to furnish extensive data to justify their budget requests, and they can use their appropriations power to indicate their displeasure with agency rules and regulations.

legislative veto

An action whereby the legislature overturns a state agency's rules or regulations.

Sunset Legislation Half the states have established **sunset laws** that set automatic expiration dates for specified agencies and other organizational structures in the executive branch. An agency can be saved from termination only through an overt renewal action in the legislature. Review occurs anywhere from every four years to every twelve years, depending on individual state statute, and is conducted by the standing committee that authorized the agency or by a committee established for sunset review purposes (such as a government operations committee). The reviews evaluate the agency's performance and its progress toward achieving its goals.

During the 1970s, sunset legislation was widely hailed as an effective tool for asserting legislative dominion over the executive branch, but more than thirty years' experience with the technique has produced mixed results, and some states have repealed their sunset laws. Agency reviews tend to be time-consuming and costly. And the process has become highly politicized in many states, involving not only agencies and legislators, but lobbyists as well. On the positive side, sunset reviews are said to increase agency compliance with legislative intent. Statistics show that, nationwide, only about 13 percent of the agencies reviewed are eventually terminated, thus making termination more of a threat than an objective reality.[60]

Review and Control of Federal Funds Since the early 1980s, legislatures have played a more active role in directing the flow of federal funds once they have reached the state. Before this time, the sheer magnitude of federal funds and their potential to upset legislatively established priorities caused great consternation among legislators. The executive branch controlled the disposition of these grant funds almost completely by designating the recipient agency and program. In some cases, federal money was used to fund programs that the state legislature did not support. Federal dollars were simply absorbed into the budget without debate and discussion, and legislators were cut out of the loop. By making federal fund disbursement part of the formal appropriations process, however, legislators have redesigned the loop.

If legislatures are to do a decent job in forecasting state priorities, some control of federal funds is necessary. In the face of reduced federal aid to states, it is critical for legislators to understand the role that federal dollars have played in program operation. When funding for a specific program dries up, it is the legislature's responsibility to decide whether to replace it with state money.

How effectively are legislatures overseeing state bureaucracies? As with so many questions, the answer depends on who is asked. From the perspective of legislators, their controls increase administrative accountability. A survey of legislators in eight states found legislative oversight committees, the postaudit function, and sunset laws to be among the most effective bureaucratic controls available.[61] Another effective device, and one that legislatures use in special circumstances, is legislative investigation of an agency, an administrator, or a program. But from the perspective of the governor, many forms of legislative oversight are simply meddling and, as such, they undermine the separation of powers.

sunset laws

Statutes that set automatic expiration dates for specified agencies and other organizations.

LO 6.8

To reflect on the link
between legislatures
and the public.

Legislatures and Capacity

State legislatures are fascinating institutions. Although they share numerous traits, each maintains some unique characteristics. Houses and senates have different traditions and styles, even in the same state. And across states, the variation in legislative systems is notable. As Alan Rosenthal writes, "Legislatures are interwoven in the fabric of their states."[62] As institutions, legislatures are dynamic; amid the layers of traditions and rules, they change and evolve.

The demands placed on state legislatures are unrelenting. Challenges abound. The ability of a legislature to function effectively depends on institutional adaptation. The extensive modernization that almost all legislatures underwent in the 1970s is evidence of institutional renewal. Structural reforms and a new breed of legislator have altered state legislatures and made them more capable. How ironic then, with all their institutional improvement, legislatures continue to struggle with their public image. Figure 6.3 arrays the states on two dimensions: public approval of the institution and the degree of legislative professionalism. As is evident, in the vast majority of states, public approval falls below the 50 percent mark. This is especially the case with the more professional legislatures. Research has found that it is among ideological conservatives that the negative relationship between professionalism and approval is greatest.[63]

FIGURE 6.3   **Legislative Approval across the States**

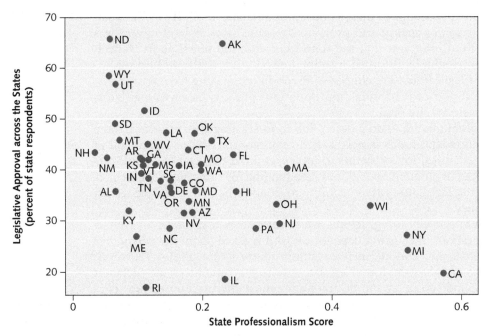

SOURCE: Legislative Approval across the States Lilliard E. Richardson, Jr., David M. Konisky, and Jeffrey Milyo, "Public Approval of U.S. State Legislatures," *Legislative Studies Quarterly* 37 (February 2012): 99–116.

Other stressors remain. Another real concern is that the legislatures of some states are being marginalized through a citizen-empowering mechanism, the initiative, and an institution-weakening provision, term limits. No wonder then that the National Conference of State Legislatures has encouraged its members to develop "a process that clarifies the current problems, what changes are needed, and how to put those remedies into place."[64] Perhaps a new and different era of legislative reform is upon us.

Chapter Recap

- The three principal functions of legislatures are policymaking, representation, and oversight.

- Redistricting is a battleground for state legislatures because drawing district lines is a partisan process.

- Legislatures operate with their own formal and informal rules. Violations of institutional norms result in sanctions.

- The lawmaking process is a complex one, with multiple opportunities for delay and obstruction. Most bills never make it through; those that do seldom look like they did when they were introduced.

- Although legislatures perform more effectively than they used to, in 2015, fifteen states had term limits in effect. Term limits create open seats and thus increase competition for legislative seats. But when legislative terms are limited, other institutional actors such as the governor gain power.

- Legislators vie with governors in the policymaking process. Governors have the power to veto, but legislators have the power to override a gubernatorial veto. In addition, the legislature plays several oversight roles with regard to the bureaucracy.

- Legislative capacity has increased but at the same time, legislatures risk becoming marginalized in states with the initiative process and term limits.

KEY TERMS

casework *(p. 138)*

multimember districts (MMDs) *(p. 140)*

malapportionment *(p. 140)*

reapportionment *(p. 141)*

redistrict *(p. 141)*

gerrymander *(p. 141)*

lame duck *(p. 145)*

war chest *(p. 146)*

delegate *(p. 149)*

trustee *(p. 149)*

politico *(p. 150)*

policy entrepreneurs *(p. 150)*

legislative veto *(p. 160)*

sunset laws *(p. 161)*

INTERNET RESOURCES

To find out what's up in state legislatures, visit the website of the National Conference of State Legislatures at **www.ncsl.org**.

Most states have websites that allow citizens to follow the progress of legislation during the session. See, for example, the legislative sites for Iowa and West Virginia at **www.legis.iowa.gov** and **www.legis.state.wv.us**, respectively.

The scholarly journal *Legislative Studies Quarterly* is a good source for research on legislatures at

**http://onlinelibrary.wiley.com/journal/
10.1002/%28ISSN%291939-9162.**

The website **votesmart.org** tracks the performance of political leaders, including state legislators.

To learn about model state laws, see the National Conference of Commissioners on Uniform State Laws at **http://uniformlaws.org**.

An advocacy website, **www.termlimits.org,** provides up-to-date coverage of the term-limits issue.

An avowedly conservative organization that drafts model legislation on various topics and reviews legislative activities across the states maintains a website at **www.alec.org**.

California Governor Jerry Brown. Bloomberg/Getty Images

Governors: Power, Politics, and Executive Leadership

7

Today's governors speak as voices of authority on important national policy issues. Although they do not always agree on what they want, the governors assert themselves as a righteous third force in U.S. politics and speaking through the National Governors' Association (NGA), other organizations, and the media, they have helped shape federal reform of welfare, education, and health care policies, and even led the response to combating global warming. And while Congress feuds along partisan and ideological lines over virtually all issues of significance and many issues of no significance at all, the governors preach—and often practice—partisan peacemaking to reach common policy ground with their own legislatures to advance positive policy changes. The challenges of conciliation are complicated by a voting public with no stomach for raising taxes and tight state budgets, in which some three-quarters of expenditures are earmarked to education, Medicaid, and local government. Governors are further challenged by the divisive partisan politics that infect the national government and that are threatening to sicken the states.

LEARNING OBJECTIVES

7.1 To understand the evolution in powers of the governor from postcolonial days to the present.

7.2 To be able to discuss the diverse roles of the governor.

7.3 To evaluate the dynamics of working with the legislature to enact policy.

7.4 To be able to explain the formal powers of the office today and how they are used.

7.5 To analyze the informal powers of the office, their importance, and how they can enhance the formal powers.

7.6 To explain the responsibilities of the other elective statewide executive branch offices.

The governors must make tough choices. Some bravely advance tax hikes despite the possible electoral consequences. Others impose brutal spending cuts on prisons, aid to the poor and helpless, and higher education. Their responsibilities are prodigious. But the governors' enhanced visibility and contributions in national politics and policy are a tribute to their policy-making capacity and responsiveness to common—and uncommon—problems affecting the citizens of their respective states. It also reflects the policy leadership of the states in the U.S. federal system.

LO 7.1

To understand the evolution in powers of the governor from postcolonial days to the present.

The Office of Governor

It has been said that the American governorship was conceived in mistrust and born in a straitjacket. Indeed, because the excesses of some colonial governors appointed by the English Crown resulted in strong dislike and distrust of executive power by the early American settlers, the first state constitutions concentrated political power in the legislative branch.

HISTORY OF THE OFFICE

Early governors were typically elected by the legislature rather than by the voters, were restricted to a single one-year term of office, and had little authority. Two states, Pennsylvania and Georgia, even established a plural (multimember) executive. Slowly the governorships became stronger through longer terms, popular election, and the power to veto legislation, but power did not come easily. The movement for popular democracy during the Jacksonian era led to the election of other executive branch officials, and reaction to the excesses of Jacksonian democracy resulted in numerous independent boards and commissions in the executive branch. Although governors did gain some power, they were not able to exercise independent authority over these executive boards and commissions.

In the early 1900s, along with their efforts to democratize national politics and clean up the corrupt city political machines, Progressive reformers launched a campaign to reform state government. Their principal target was the weak executive branch. Efforts to improve the state executive branch continue throughout in the twenty-first century. The essential goal has been to increase the governor's powers to make them more commensurate with the increased duties and responsibilities of the office. As a result, constitutional and statutory changes have fortified the office of the chief executive, reorganized the executive branch, and streamlined the structure and processes of the bureaucracy. The capacity of governors and the executive branch to apply state resources to the solution of emerging problems has thus been greatly enhanced.[1] And, as observed at the beginning of this chapter, the governors have become prominent players in national policy making.

TODAY'S GOVERNORS

Today, being governor is a high-pressure, physically demanding, and emotionally draining job. As one political scientist states, "Governors must possess many skills to be successful. They are expected to be adroit administrators, dexterous executives, expert judges of people, combative yet sensitive and inspiring politicians, decorous chiefs of state, shrewd party tacticians, and polished public relations managers."[2] The job is also hard on the governor's private life. It consumes an enormous number of waking hours at the expense of family activities; hobbies; and, in some cases, more significant moneymaking opportunities in law, consulting, or business.

Fortunately, governorships are attracting well-qualified chief executives, most of whom are a far cry from the figureheads of the eighteenth and nineteenth centuries and the stereotypical backslapping, cigar-smoking wheeler dealers of the early twentieth century. Today's governors are better educated and better prepared for the job than their predecessors were. Many recent governors hold law or other advanced degrees. Most of today's governors paid their political dues in state legislatures, gaining an understanding of important issues confronting the state, a working familiarity with influential figures in government and the private sector, and a practical knowledge of the legislative process and other inner workings of state government (see Table 7.1). About 40 percent of governors have served previously as elected state executive branch officials, including lieutenant governor and attorney

TABLE 7.1	Separately Elected State Officials	
OFFICE	**NUMBER OF ELECTED OFFICIALS**
Governor	50
Lieutenant governor	42
Attorney general	44
Treasurer	39
Secretary of state	37
Education (superintendent or board)	14
Auditor	24
Secretary of agriculture	13
Controller	14
Public utilities commissioner	6
Insurance commissioner	12
Land commissioner	5
Labor commissioner	4
Mines commissioner	1
Adjutant General (National Guard)	1

SOURCE: Adapted from *The Book of the States* 2014, Table 4.10.

general (AG). Several are former mayors. Although previous elected experience is a tremendous advantage in winning a governorship, a number have come straight from the private sector, touting their business credentials. (See the Controversies in States and Localities Box.) The attractiveness of the governorship is evident in the fact that several of the current chief executives left a congressional seat to take statewide office. Why would someone desert the glamour of the nation's capital for the statehouse in Baton Rouge, Topeka, or Providence? For political power and the opportunity to make a difference in one's own state. Simply put, being a state chief executive is just more rewarding and more fun. It is, according to current and former governors, "the best job in politics."[3] As Rhode Island governor Gina Raimondo has said, "It's incomparable to any other job ... On any given day, you deal with public health, public safety, labor and training, schools, the economy. The breadth is huge."[4]

Although still predominantly white males, today's governors are more representative of population characteristics than former chief executives were. Two Latinos serve as governors: Susana Martinez of New Mexico (2011–2015) and Brian Sandoval of Nevada (2011–2015). Three African Americans have served as governor: L. Douglas Wilder, Virginia (1990–1994), Deval Patrick, Massachusetts (2006–2015), and David Paterson (2009–2014) of New York. Gary Locke, the first Asian-American governor not from Hawaii, was elected governor of Washington in 1996. Bobby Jindal (2007–present) was elected as the first Indian-American (Asian) governor in 2007 in Louisiana, followed by Nikki Haley (2011–present) in South Carolina. A substantial number of women have been elected to their state's top office. The first to be popularly elected was Mirium "Ma" Ferguson of Texas in 1924. She served two terms. Five women were serving in their state's top office in 2015.

Maine Governor Paul LePage is a rags-to-riches story. Born the oldest of eighteen children, he suffered a rough childhood, running away from home at 11 after enduring beatings from his father. For a time, he shined shoes on the street to support himself. Following adoption at age 13, he later graduated from college, earned an MBA, worked as manager of a discount store, and eventually became mayor of Waterville, Maine. In 2011, he was elected governor.

GETTING THERE: GUBERNATORIAL CAMPAIGNS

Without question, the governorship is an alluring office. Occasionally its luster attracts true wackos as candidates. One such case was Jonathan "The Impaler" Sharkey. A self-proclaimed PhD and "Satanic Dark Priest, Sanguinarian Vampyre and . . . Hecate Witch," Sharkey announced his candidacy for the 2006 governorship of Minnesota. A former pro-wrestler and co-owner of "Kat's Underworld Coven," the gubernatorial wannabe announced a unique plan for dealing with terrorists who might be tempted to infiltrate the Gopher State. Any such terrorist caught in Minnesota would "find out what the true meaning of my nickname 'The Impaler' means." Literally, the unfortunate suspect would be impaled on a stake on the capitol grounds.[5] Georgia's 2010 gubernatorial candidate Neal Horsley, running on the Creator's Rights party

Controversies in States and Localities

Is Private Sector Experience the Best Preparation for the Governorship?

Rhode Island Governor Gina Raimondo addresses a crowd on a cold day in the Ocean State.

Historically, governors have previously served their state in the legislature or in other executive branch positions. Hands-on government experience is conventionally considered to be an important advantage for governors, as they presumably enter office with an understanding of the workings of the three branches of government and the state bureaucracy, and knowledge of key political actors. Such experience should help the new governor to successfully achieve his goals and exercise effective leadership.

But the 2014 elections ushered into office eleven new governors, most of whom had relatively little state government experience. Instead, they have invested most of their professional life in the private sector. Gina Raimondo, governor of Rhode Island, rose to the governorship following four years as state treasurer, but before that she made her mark by heading up a venture capital business. Arizona governor Doug Ducey also served a term as state treasurer, but before that was CEO of an ice cream parlor chain. Maryland governor Larry Hogan had been a real estate developer; he had held no state or local office. As candidates, all appealed to voters by presenting themselves as political outsiders who would draw from their business experience to run the state efficiently and effectively.

Critical Thinking Questions:

1. What advantages does significant private sector experience bring to the office of governor? Should a business background produce better results than a political background?

2. What disadvantages might relative unfamiliarity with state government likely bring to the governorship in terms of attaining legislative priorities, working with state agencies (including some headed up by other elected officials), and avoiding legal problems with the courts?

ticket, revealed in an interview that "When you grow up on a farm in Georgia, your first girlfriend is a mule."[6]

Another colorful candidate has been Texas mystery writer, songwriter, and performer Kinky Friedman. His progressive country band in the 1970s called "Kinky Friedman and the Texas Jewboys" recorded various alternative hits, including "They Ain't Makin' Jews Like Jesus Anymore," "Asshole from El Paso," and "The Mail Don't Move Too Fast in Rapid City, South Dakota." While cracking jokes and one-liners, he has also campaigned on serious issues, including election reform, education improvement, and legalization of marijuana. Friedman has placed his name in the Democratic primary on three occasions, most recently in 2014 when he campaigned for agriculture commissioner.

The lure of the governorship must be weighed against the financial costs. Campaigning for the office has become hugely expensive. Because candidates no longer rely on their political party to support them, they must continuously solicit great sums of money from donors to pay for campaign costs—political consultants, opinion polls, air travel, media advertisements, telephone banks, direct mailings, websites, and interactive video links.

Until 2010, the most expensive governor's race was the 2002 election in New York, in which $146.8 million was spent by three candidates. Loser Thomas Golisano spent $76.3 million; the winner, George Pataki, spent "only" $44.2 million. But in 2010 candidate Meg Whitman spent $141.5 million of her own money, and $160 million in total, only to lose in the California election! Official figures do not include in-kind donations, such as free transportation, door-to-door canvassing, telephones, and other contributions from supporters. On a cost-per-vote basis, races in the 2010–2013 period ranged from $32.77 in Hawaii to $3.00 in Nebraska.[7]

Money has a profound influence on gubernatorial elections, but it isn't the only important factor. As one veteran of political campaigns has reflected, "Everyone knows that half the money spent in a political campaign is wasted. The trouble is that nobody knows which half."[8] Other factors are also important in candidate success, such as incumbency, the strength of the candidate's political party in the electorate, and prevailing levels of unemployment and other economic conditions[9] because party identification usually translates into votes for a party's candidate. High-profile candidates stand a solid chance of being elected because they possess campaign skills, political experience, and other characteristics that help them raise the campaign funds needed to get their message and persona across to the electorate.

Incumbency is a particularly important aspect of a candidate's profile. An incumbent governor running for re-election stands an excellent chance of victory; about three-quarters of incumbents have retained their seats since 1970. Incumbents enjoy a number of important advantages, including the opportunity while in office to cultivate popularity with the voters and collect campaign donations from interest groups. However, re-election is no sure thing. Budget and tax woes can lead voters to toss chief executives out of office, particularly those who, as candidates, pledged not to raise taxes but then do so after election.[10]

LO 7.2

To be able to discuss the diverse roles of the governor.

Being Governor: Duties and Responsibilities

In performing the duties of the office, the governor wears the hats of top policy maker, chief legislator, chief administrator, ceremonial leader, intergovernmental coordinator, economic development promoter, and political party leader. Sometimes several of these hats must be balanced atop the governor's head at once. All things considered, these roles make the governorship one of the most difficult and challenging, yet potentially most rewarding, jobs in the world.

DEVELOPING AND MAKING POLICY

Transforming good ideas from concept to practice is an exciting but extraordinarily difficult challenge for governors. A governor is the leading formulator and initiator of public policy in his state, from his first pronouncements as a gubernatorial candidate until his final days in office. The governor's role as chief policy maker involves many other players, including those in the legislature, bureaucracy, courts, interest groups, and the voting public. Most major policies are initiated by the governor, and success or failure depends largely on how competently the governor designs and frames policy proposals and develops public support for them. The governor must also follow through to see that adopted policies are put into effect as originally intended.

Some issues are by nature transitory, appearing on the agenda of state government and disappearing after appropriate actions are taken. These issues are often created by external events, such as a federal court decision that mandates a reduction in prison overcrowding; a new national law requiring a state response; or an act of nature such as a hurricane, tornado, forest fire, or flood.

Most policy issues, however, do not emerge suddenly out of the mists. Perennial concerns face the governor each year: education, corrections, social welfare, health care, the environment, and economic development. Cyclical issues also appear, increase in intensity, and slowly fade away. Examples of the latter type are consumer protection, ethics in government, reapportionment, and budget shortfalls. Of course, national policy issues sometimes absorb the governor's time as well, such as preparing for and addressing an influx of illegal immigrants, economic downturns, and proposals to drill or "frack" for oil and gas in the state or near state shorelines.

Several factors have contributed to stronger policy leadership from the chief executives in recent years, including larger and more capable staffs who are knowledgeable in important policy fields; a more integrated executive branch with department heads appointed by the governor; strengthened formal powers of the office, such as longer terms and the veto and budget powers; and the assistance of the National Governors Association (NGA) along with regional associations, which offer ideas for policy and program development.

MARSHALING LEGISLATIVE ACTION

LO 7.3

To evaluate the dynamics of working with the legislature to enact policy.

The gubernatorial role of marshaling legislative action is closely related to that of policy maker because legislative action is required for most of the chief executive's policies to be put into effect. In fact, the governor cannot directly introduce bills; party leaders and policy supporters in the statehouse and senate must put the bills in the hopper. Dealing with legislators is a demanding role for a governor, consuming more time than any other role and representing for many the single most difficult aspect of the job.

Relationship with the Legislature Developing a positive and productive relationship with the legislature requires great expenditures of a governor's time, energy, and resources. Several factors hinder smooth relations between the chief executive and the legislature, including partisanship and personality clashes. Even the different natures of the two branches can cause conflict. Governors are elected by a statewide constituency and therefore tend to take a broad, comprehensive, long-range view of issues, whereas legislators, representing relatively small geographical areas and groups of voters, are more likely to take a piecemeal, parochial approach to policy making. Conflicts inevitably erupt during budget time, when critical spending decisions are at hand.[11]

According to one study, the amount of strife between the two branches is influenced by three factors: the size of the majority and the minority parties, the personalities of the governor and legislative leaders, and the nearness of an election year.[12] Following the 2014 elections, there were twenty-one Democratic governors, twenty-eight Republicans, and one Independent (Bill Walker of Alaska). Today, the governor has to deal with a one- or two-house majority from the opposing political party. When the opposition party is strong, the governor must seek bipartisan support to get favored legislation passed. Often a governor facing a large legislative majority from the opposing party has only the veto and the possibility of mobilizing public support as weapons against the legislature. Yet minority governors like Kathleen Sebelius of Kansas and Jodi Rell of Connecticut earned reputations for being nonpartisan, while still getting their way on legislation important to them.

Independent governors don't even have a minority party to count on, but this situation doesn't preclude success. Former Independent governor Angus King of Maine asserted that not having a party affiliation brought some advantages. For instance, he says, "I have no automatic friends in the legislature, but I have no automatic enemies. I have 186 skeptics."[13]

A governor who ignores or alienates members of the opposing political party can quickly find himself in the desert without a drink of water. Former New York governor David Paterson compared legislators in Albany to "a bunch of bloodsuckers" who cater to special interests during the day and go home without taking action on bills.[14] New Jersey's Chris Christie entered the governorship as a Republican with tough talk and a brusque manner. He "never found a battle he didn't want to pick or a position he was willing to compromise."[15] He fought with the Democratic legislature over judicial appointments, taxes, employee pensions, education funding, and many other issues. Soon, however, even he learned the value of the occasional legislative compromise.

The approach of elections can also bring gubernatorial-legislative deadlock because incumbents in both branches of government may become extremely cautious or overtly partisan in their efforts to please (or at least not to offend) the voters while discrediting their opponents. Gridlock may result. These three conflict-producing factors of partisanship, personalities, and proximity of an election are intensified during debates on the budget, when the principal policy and financial decisions are made. In some instances, including in Minnesota in 2010, executive-legislative stalemates have produced a state government shutdown, with negative outcomes for many, if not most, state residents.

Even in states in which the governor's own party enjoys a large majority in both houses of the legislature, factions are certain to develop along ideological, rural-urban, geographical, institutional (house versus senate), or other divisions. Ironically, a large legislative majority can create the greatest problems with factionalism primarily because a sizable opposition doesn't exist to unite the majority party. The stronger the numbers of the majority party, the more likely it is to degenerate into intraparty rivalries beyond the governor's control. As one Democratic governor lamented in the face of a 4-to-1 majority of his own party in the legislature, "You've got Democrats, you've got moderate Democrats, you've got suburban Democrats, you've got urban Democrats, you've got rural Democrats."[16]

Executive Influence on the Legislative Agenda Despite the difficulties in dealing with the legislature, most governors dominate the policy agenda, usually by working hand in hand with legislative leaders. The governor's influence begins with the "State of the State" address, which kicks off each new legislative session and continues in most states with the annual budget message. In 2014, governors stressed economic development, health care, public safety, and tax and revenue issues.[17] During the legislative session itself, the governor might publicly (or privately) threaten to veto a proposed bill or appeal directly to a particular legislator's constituency. Governors may also take their fight to the people, as Missouri Governor Jay Nixon did to overcome legislative opposition to bills involving tax cuts and gun control in 2013.[18]

Most of the drama, however, takes place behind the scenes. The governor might promise high-level executive branch jobs or judgeships (either for certain legislators or for their friends) to influence legislative votes. Kentucky Governor Steve Beshear, a Democrat, appointed two Republican legislators to posts in the executive branch to gain the legislative majority needed to pass a bill expanding betting on horse races.[19] Or a governor might offer some sort of **pork barrel** reward, such as funding a highway project in a legislator's district or approving a special appropriation for the local Strawberry Festival. Private meetings or breakfasts in the governor's mansion flatter and enlist support from individuals or small groups of legislators. Virginia Governor Terry McAuliffe governed by happy hour, stocking the executive mansion with top-shelf spirits and craft beer, and inviting legislators over for nightly receptions. For teetotalers, McAuliffe served daily breakfasts.[20] Successful governors can usually relate to representatives and senators on a personal level. Many are former members of the state legislature, so they can rely on personal connections and experiences to win over key members. One of the most successful governors recently, for example, was Governor Mike Beebe (2011–2014) of Arkansas, who labored in the state senate for twenty years and as attorney general for four, before winning the state's top office.

In addition, all governors have legislative liaisons who are assigned to lobby for the administration's program. Members of the governor's staff testify at legislative hearings, consult with committees and individuals on proposed bills, and even write floor speeches for friends in the legislature. Some governors designate a floor leader to steer their priorities through the legislature.

Most governors, however, are careful not to be perceived as unduly interfering in the internal affairs of the legislature. Too much meddling in

pork barrel
Favoritism by a governor or other elected official in distributing government monies or other resources to a particular program, jurisdiction, or individual.

legislative affairs can bring a political backlash that undermines a governor's policy program. The role of chief legislator, then, requires a balancing act that ultimately determines the success or failure of the governor's agenda.

GOVERNORS AND THE COURTS

Sometimes the best laid plans of governors are squelched by the courts, either state or federal. Florida Governor Rick Scott's aggressive and controversial actions to compel drug testing on all state employees and job applicants, restrict the right of physicians to ask patients about guns in their houses, retract 3 percent of state employee salaries, and censor K-12 textbooks spawned a tornado of lawsuits aimed at overturning his actions.[21] Nevada Governor Brian Sandoval's "No-Tax Pledge" resulted in a proposed state budget that, among other things, raided local government funds to balance the state accounts. With less than two weeks left in the legislative session, the Nevada Supreme Court ruled that such local funds transfers were unconstitutional. Sandoval was forced to release a revised budget that included an increase in the personal income tax.[22] And in New Mexico, the state Supreme Court ruled against Governor Susana Martinez's freeze on publication of new pollution control measures by the state environmental agency. Such court actions demonstrate the need for governors and their legal staffs to be attentive to the legality of their actions and decisions.

ADMINISTERING THE EXECUTIVE BRANCH

As chief executive of the state, the governor is (in name, at least) in charge of the operations of numerous agencies, departments, boards, and commissions. In the view of many voters, the governor is directly responsible not only for pivotal matters such as the condition of the state's economy, but also for more mundane concerns such as clearing the snow off state highways in a timely manner. Most governors are sensitive to their chief administrative responsibilities and spend a great amount of time and energy attending to them. Constitutional and statutory reforms, including the concentration of executive power in the office of the governor and the consolidation of numerous state agencies, have considerably strengthened the governor's capacity to manage the state. (See Chapter 8 for further discussion of public administration.) If governors are diligent and expeditious in appointing talented and responsive people to policy-making posts, they should feel no compulsion to micromanage the state's day-to-day affairs. Instead, they can focus their energies on leadership activities such as identifying goals, marshaling resources, and achieving results.

In many respects, the governor's job is comparable to that of the chief executive officer (CEO) of a very large corporation. Governors must manage tens of thousands of workers, staggering sums of money, and complex organizational systems. They must establish priorities, handle crises, and balance contending interests. But there are important differences as well. For one, governors are not paid comparably for their responsibilities. In terms of expenditures and employees, most states are as big or bigger than Fortune

500 companies, whose CEOs typically earn tens of millions of dollars a year in salary, stock options, and other forms of remuneration. Yet the fifty governors average only about $134,390 in annual salary. (The highest paid is the governor of Pennsylvania, at $187,818; the lowest is Maine's, at $70,000.)[23]

In addition to being woefully underpaid, today's governors experience high levels of stress from interest group criticism, legislative sniping, extraordinarily long hours on the job, and constant media attention to every possible misstep.

Restraints on Management Reforms of the executive branch have allowed far more active and influential gubernatorial management, but significant restraints remain. For example, the separation-of-powers principle dictates that the governor share his or her authority with the legislature and the courts, either or both of which may be politically or philosophically opposed to any given action. Changes in state agency programs, priorities, or organization typically require legislative approval, and the legality of such changes may be tested in the courts.

The governor's ability to hire, fire, motivate, and punish is severely restricted by the courts; merit-system rules and regulations; collective bargaining contracts; independent boards and commissions with their own personnel systems; and other elected executive branch officials pursuing their own administrative and political agendas. Thus, most employees in the executive branch are outside the governor's formal sphere of authority and may challenge that authority almost at will. Career bureaucrats, who have established their own policy direction and momentum over many years of seeing governors come and go, usually march to their own tune. In sum, governors must lead and manage through third parties and networks in the three branches of government, as well as in the private and nonprofit sectors. They have little unilateral authority.

Governors as Managers Some governors minimize their managerial responsibilities, preferring to delegate them to trusted staff and agency heads. Others provide strong administrative and policy leadership in state government. The honor of "Best Managed State" went to Governor Jack Dalrymple of North Dakota in 2014. The fact that the "Peace Garden State" enjoyed the proceeds of a huge oil and gas boom surely played a part. Perhaps an award of "In the Bureaucratic Weeds" should go to Maryland's Walter O'Malley, who reveled in the notion of "data-driven performance management."[24] But there are substantial constraints on the governor's managerial activities, along with associated political liabilities. The governors who courageously wade into the bureaucratic fray must invest a great deal of time and scarce political resources, yet they risk embarrassing defeats that can drag their administrations into debilitation and disrepute. After all, "Reorganized the State Bureaucracy" hardly resonates as a campaign slogan. Meanwhile, in the face of social, political, and economic change, the management of state government has become increasingly complex, yet the need for strong administrative leadership more critical than ever before.

MASTER OF CEREMONIES

Some governors thrive on ceremony and others detest it, but all spend a large portion of their time on it because it helps garner re-election votes. Former governors remember ceremonial duties as the second most demanding of the gubernatorial roles, just behind working with the legislature.[25] Cutting the ribbon for a new highway, celebrating the arrival of a new business, welcoming potential foreign investors, receiving the queen of the Collard Green Festival, announcing "Respect Your Parents Week," opening the state fair, and handing out diplomas are the kind of ceremonial duties that take a governor all over the state and often consume a larger portion of the workweek than does any other role.[26] Even a seemingly pleasant task can have its personal horrors. George A. Aiken, the late governor of Vermont, dreaded having to pin the ribbon on the winner of the Miss Vermont contest because he couldn't figure out how to put the pin in without getting his hand under the bathing suit.

COORDINATING INTERGOVERNMENTAL RELATIONS

Governors serve as the major points of contact between their states and the president, Congress, and federal agencies. Everything from emergency response to settling disputes over cross-border water pollution issues are carried out through the governor's office. At the local level, governors are involved in allocating grants-in-aid, promoting cooperation and coordination in economic development activities, and various other matters. Governors also provide leadership in resolving disputes with Native American tribes involving casino gambling and related issues.

The role of intergovernmental coordinator is most visible at the national level, where governors are aided by the NGA and the state's Washington office. The NGA meets twice a year in full session to adopt policy positions and to discuss governors' problems and "best practice" policy solutions. The governors also meet in separate regional organizations. (C-SPAN covers national meetings of the governors.) The NGA's staff analyzes important issues, distributes its analyses to the states, offers practical and technical assistance to the governors, and holds a valuable seminar for new governors. The NGA, however, has recently come under fire from conservative Republicans, who object to the organization's perceived "tax-and-spend" agenda, even when it benefits their own states. In fact, Republican governors of Texas, Idaho, Maine, and Ohio have withdrawn from the NGA over this and related concerns, preferring to work with the Republican Governors Association instead.

Most states have established Washington offices to fight for their interests in Congress, the White House, and, perhaps most important, the many federal agencies that interact with states on a daily basis. A governor's official inquiry can help speed up the progress of federal grant-in-aid funds or gain special consideration for a new federal facility. Washington offices are commonly assisted by major law and lobbying firms under contract to individual states.

The governor's role as intergovernmental coordinator is of great importance. It reflects the elevated position of the states in the scheme of American federalism and the increasing state importance in national and international affairs. It is also a reaction to provocations and intrusions from the national government, such as unfunded mandates, poorly framed laws, and unwelcome blundering into state affairs. Acting together and as individuals, the governors have exercised national policy leadership on critical issues such as environmental protection, climate change, taxation of Internet sales, public education, and health care reform. Frequently, when the national government confronts a policy problem, it turns to the states for solutions. Yet political polarization in Congress, and increasingly in the states, discourages compromise and lessens state influence in Washington, D.C.[27]

PROMOTING ECONOMIC DEVELOPMENT

Unfairly or not, governors may be held responsible by the voters for their state's economic health. As promoter of economic development, a governor works to recruit businesses and tourists from out of state and to encourage economic growth from sources within the state (see Chapter 14). Governors attend trade fairs; visit the headquarters of firms interested in locating in the state; telephone and e-mail promising business contacts; and welcome business leaders. The role may take the governor and the state economic development team to Mexico, China, Germany, and other countries, as well as to other states. Governors also work hard to promote tourism. But mostly, economic development entails making the state's climate "good for business" by improving infrastructure, arranging generous tax and service incentives, and engaging in other strategies designed to entice out-of-state firms to relocate and encourage in-state businesses to expand or at least stay put.

When a state enjoys success in economic development, the governor usually claims a major portion of the credit. Sometimes the personal touch of a governor can mean the difference between an industrial plum and economic stagnation. Success stories are heralded proudly. Are incumbent governors punished in a re-election effort when promised economic growth falls short? Research findings on this question are mixed.[28]

LEADING THE POLITICAL PARTY

By claiming the top elected post in the state, the governor becomes the highest-ranking member of her political party. This role is not as significant as it was several decades ago, when the governor controlled the state's party apparatus and legislative leadership and had strong influence over party nominations for seats in the state legislature and executive branch offices. Primaries have replaced party conventions and put nominations largely in the hands of the voters. And legislative leaders are a much more independent breed than they were, for example, in Illinois, when Governor Richard Ogilvie (1969–1973) brought up the need for income tax legislation during a breakfast meeting at the mansion. Senate president Russ Arrington angrily asked, "Who is the crazy son of a bitch who is going to sponsor this thing?" The governor calmly replied, "Russ, you are." And he did.[29] Such an order is unlikely these days. Still, some governors get involved in legislative elections through campaign aid, endorsements, or other actions. If the governor's choice wins, she may feel a special debt to the governor and support him on important legislation.

The political party remains useful to the governor for three principal reasons.[30] Legislators from the governor's own party are more likely to support the chief executive's programs. Communication lines to the president and national cabinet members are more likely to be open when the president and the governor are members of the same party. And finally, the party remains the most convenient means through which to win nomination to the governor's office.

As most states have highly competitive political parties, governors find that they must work with the opposition if their legislative programs are to pass. For Independent governors, a special challenge exists: how to govern without a party behind you to organize votes and otherwise push proposed laws through the convoluted legislative process. The recent record has been mixed. Maine's Independent governor, Angus King, demonstrated a talent for working with shifting legislative coalitions on various major issues, as did Rhode Island Governor Lincoln Chaffee.

Formal Powers of the Governor

LO 7.4

To be able to explain the formal powers of the office today and how they are used.

A variety of powers are attached to the governor's office. A governor's **formal powers** include the tenure of the office, power of appointment, power to veto legislation, responsibility for preparing the budget, authority to reorganize the executive branch, and the right to hire professional staff in the governor's office. These institutional powers give governors the *potential* to carry out the duties of office as they see fit. However, the formal powers vary considerably from state to state. Some governors' offices (Illinois, New York) are considered strong and others (Alabama, Georgia) weak. Also, the fact that these powers are available does not mean that they are used effectively. Equally important are the **informal powers** that governors have at their disposal. These are potentially empowering features of the job or the person that are not expressly provided for in the law. Many of the informal powers are associated with personal traits on which the chief executive relies to carry out the duties and responsibilities of the office. They are especially helpful in relations with the legislature.

formal powers

Powers of the governor derived from the state constitution or statute.

informal powers

Powers of the governor not derived from constitutional or statutory law.

Both sets of powers have increased over the past several decades. And governors are more influential than ever before, primarily because of their enhanced formal powers; charisma, however, remains as important as ever. The most successful governors are those who employ their informal powers to maximize the formal powers. The term for this concept is *synergism*, a condition in which the total effect of two distinct sets of attributes working together is greater than the sum of their effects when acting independently. An influential governor, then, is one who can skillfully combine formal and informal powers to maximum effectiveness. Counted among the most effective governors today are those who do so: Daniel Malloy (Democrat, Connecticut), Jerry Brown (Democrat, California), and Bill Haslam (Republican, Tennessee).

TENURE

The governor's tenure power has two characteristics: the duration (number of years) of a term of office and the number of terms that an individual may serve as governor. From the onerous restriction of a single one-year term of office placed on ten of the first thirteen governors, the duration has evolved to today's standard of two or more four-year terms (only New Hampshire and Vermont restrict their governors to two-year terms). In addition, gubernatorial elections have become distinct from national elections because thirty-nine states hold them in nonpresidential election years. This system encourages the voters to focus their attention on issues important to the state rather than allowing national politics to dominate state election outcomes.

The importance of longer consecutive terms of office is readily apparent. A two-year governorship condemns the incumbent to a perpetual re-election campaign. As soon as the winner takes office, planning and fund-raising must begin for the next election. For any new governor, the initial year in office is typically spent settling into the job. In addition, the first-term, first-year chief executive must live with the budget priorities adopted by his or her predecessor. A two-year governorship, therefore, does not encourage success in matters of legislation or policy. Nor does it enable the governor to have much effect on the bureaucracy, whose old hands are likely to treat the governor as a mere bird of passage, making him almost a lame duck when his term begins. As Governor Alfred E. Smith of New York observed after serving four two-year terms during the 1920s, "One hardly has time to locate the knob on the State-house door."[31]

By contrast, Virginia's governor, the only one who is restricted to a single four-year term, is a bit less confined in carrying out his responsibilities. But he really has only two years to put his programs and priorities in place, sandwiched on one side by the initial learning year and on the other by the lame-duck period. The incumbent needs another four-year term to design new programs, acquire the necessary legislative support to put them into place, and get a handle on the bureaucracy by appointing loyal, competent people to top posts. Eight years in office also enhances the governor's intergovernmental role, particularly by giving him sufficient time to develop and nurture key relationships and win leadership positions in organizations such as the NGA. The record of an eight-year chief executive stands on its own, untainted by the successes or failures of the office's previous inhabitant.

The average time actually served by governors has grown with fewer restrictions on tenure. The first gubernatorial graybeard was Illinois governor Jim Thompson, who stepped down after serving his fourth consecutive term in 1990—a twentieth-century record.[32] Recent "comeback governors" have been elected in California (Jerry Brown, 1975–1983, 2011–2019), Iowa (Terry Branstad, 1983–1999, 2011–2019), and Oregon (John Kitzhaber, 1995–2003, 2011–2015). Long periods in office strengthen the governor's position as policy leader, chief legislator, chief administrator, and intergovernmental coordinator, and leave strong policy legacies.

APPOINTMENT POWER

Surveys of past governors indicate that they consider appointment power to be the most important weapon in their arsenal when it comes to managing the state bureaucracy. The ability to appoint one's supporters to top positions in the executive branch also enhances the policy management role. When individuals who share the governor's basic philosophy and feel loyal to the chief executive and her programs direct the operations of state government, the governor's policies are more likely to be successful. Strong appointment authority can even help the governor's legislative role. The actual or implicit promise of important administrative and especially judicial positions can generate a surprising amount of support from ambitious lawmakers.

Unfortunately for today's governors, the long ballot lives on in the **plural executive**. Most states continue to provide for popular election of numerous officials in the executive branch, including insurance commissioners, public utility commissioners, and secretaries of agriculture. Proponents of popular election claim that these officials make political decisions and therefore should be directly responsible to the electorate. Opponents contend that governors and legislators can make appointment decisions more properly, because they are not beholden to special interests that offer up generous campaign contributions.

Perhaps appointment authority should depend on the office under consideration. Table 7.1 shows the number of states that popularly elect various executive branch officials.

The It's Your Turn box gives you a chance to offer your opinion.

Professional Jobs in State Government The vast majority of jobs in the states are filled through objective civil service (merit-system) rules and processes. Governors are generally quite content to avoid meddling with civil service positions. Gubernatorial sacrifice of **patronage** power is understandable in view of the time and headaches associated with naming political supporters to jobs in the bureaucracy. There is always the possibility of embarrassment or scandal if the governor accidentally appoints a person with a criminal record, a clear conflict of interest, or a propensity for sexual harassment or other inappropriate behavior, or someone who causes harm through simple incompetence. Moreover, those who are denied coveted appointments may become angry. One governor is quoted as stating, as he was about to name a new member of a state commission, "I now have twenty-three good friends who want [to be] on the Racing Commission. [Soon] I'll have twenty-two enemies and one ingrate."[33] Governors who abuse the merit hiring system can be prosecuted, as were Kentucky governor Ernie Fletcher and fifteen members of his administration, who were indicted in a hiring scandal in 2006. A governor benefits from a stable, competent civil service that hires, pays, and promotes on the basis of knowledge, job-related skills, and abilities rather than party affiliation, friendship with a legislator, or campaign donations.

The Power to Fire The power of the governor to hire is not necessarily accompanied by the power to fire. Except in cases of extreme misbehavior or

plural executive

A system in which more than one member of the executive branch is popularly elected on a statewide ballot.

patronage

The informal power of a governor (or other officeholder) to make appointments on the basis of party membership and to dispense contracts or other favors to political supporters.

It's Your Turn

Should Executive Branch Officers Be Elected?

As seen in Table 7.1, fourteen officials are popularly elected in at least one state, including mines commissioner and adjutant general of the National Guard. There are arguments to be made both pro and con for offering voters a "long ballot."

What do you think? Are long ballots preferable to short ballots?

PROS	CONS
It makes sense to elect an auditor and an AG, because they require some independence in carrying out their responsibilities. (The auditor oversees the management and spending of state monies; the AG is concerned with the legality of executive and legislative branch activities.)	Some of these offices tend to cater to special interests, such as agriculture, insurance, and education. These special interests can be expected to contribute generously to their preferred candidates.
The number of elected branch officials has remained virtually the same for decades. Why change it now?	Governors are weakened by their inability to directly appoint the heads of major state agencies, boards, and commissions. These high-ranking officials make policy decisions in the executive branch, but if they owe their jobs in whole or in part to popular election, the governor's authority as chief executive is significantly diminished. Although nominally in charge of these executive branch agencies, the governor is severely constrained in his ability to manage them.
Incumbent education superintendents, agricultural commissioners, and others have strong supporters in the electorate.	It would be unthinkable in a corporation to preclude the CEO from appointing her own top staff members.
Interest groups will fiercely resist proposals to make certain offices appointive.	The fragmented nature of power in the executive branch diminishes accountability and frustrates governors.
Most citizens simply like having an opportunity to vote on a large number of executive branch officials. Surveys show that they want the long ballot.	Most reformers interested in "good government" agree on the need to consolidate power in the governor's office by reducing the number of statewide elected officials and expanding the power of appointment to more policy-related, or "unclassified," posts in the executive branch.

corruption, it is very difficult to remove an appointed subordinate from office. For instance, if a governor attempts to dismiss the secretary of agriculture, he can anticipate an orchestrated roar of outrage from legislators, bureaucrats, and farm groups. The upshot is that the political costs of dismissing an appointee can be greater than the pain of simply living with the problem.

A good appointment to a top agency post is the best way for a governor to influence the bureaucracy. By carefully choosing a competent and loyal agency head, the governor can more readily bring about significant changes in the programs and operations of that agency. Where appointment powers are circumscribed, the chief executive must muster his or her informal powers to influence activities of the state bureaucracy or rely on the seasoned judgment of professional civil servants.

VETO POWER

As we noted in Chapter 6, the power to veto bills passed by the legislature bolsters the governor as chief policy maker and chief administrator. A bill may be vetoed because its contents are contrary to a governor's principles or preferences, or for many other reasons. A veto accompanied by an explanation makes a powerful symbolic statement or can instruct the legislature about how the bill might be amended for the governor's signature. A veto can also punish an offending legislator or state agency by eliminating a favored program or severely cutting its budget. Often the mere threat of a veto is enough to persuade a recalcitrant legislature to see the governor's point of view and compromise on the language of a bill. Vetoes are not easy to override. Most states require a majority of three-fifths or two-thirds of the legislature.

package veto

The governor's formal power to veto a bill in its entirety.

line item veto

The governor's formal power to veto separate items in a bill instead of the entire piece of proposed legislation.

pocket veto

The governor's power to withhold approval or disapproval of a bill after the legislature has adjourned for the session, in effect vetoing the measure.

executive amendment

A type of veto used by the governor to reject a bill and also to recommend changes that would cause the governor to consider the bill's approval.

Types of Vetoes The veto can take several forms. The **package veto** is the governor's rejection of a bill in its entirety. All governors hold package veto authority. The **line item veto** allows the governor to strike out one or more objectionable sections of a bill, permitting the remaining provisions to become law. Only Nevada, Maine, and six other states forbid this gubernatorial power. Several states permit a hybrid form of line item veto in which the governor may choose to reduce the dollar amount of a proposed item to hold down state expenditures or cut back support for a particular program. In some states, the line item veto is permitted only in appropriations bills.

The **pocket veto**, which is available in fourteen states, allows the governor to reject a bill by refusing to sign it after the legislature has adjourned. In two states (Hawaii and Utah), the legislature can reconvene to vote to override a pocket veto; otherwise, the bill dies. A governor might use the pocket veto to avoid giving the legislature a chance to override a formal veto or to abstain from going on record against a proposed piece of controversial legislation.

A fourth type of veto is the **executive amendment**, formally provided in fifteen states and informally used in several others. With this amendatory power, a governor may veto a bill, recommend changes that would make the bill acceptable, and then send it back to the legislature for reconsideration. If the legislature concurs with the suggestions, the governor signs the bill into law.

Use of the Veto The actual use of the veto varies by time, state, and issue. Some states, such as California and New York, often record high numbers of vetoes, whereas others, like Virginia, report few. On average, governors veto around 4 percent of the bills that reach their desks.[34] The variation among states reflects the tensions and conflicts that exist between the governor and the legislature. The largest number of vetoes typically occurs in states with divided party control of the executive and legislative branches. Occasionally, the governor stands as the last line of defense against a flawed bill backed by the legislature because of powerful interest groups or a bill passed just to score political points. It is not unknown for legislators to secretly ask the governor to veto a questionable bill they have just passed because the bill's contents, although problematic, are politically popular.[35]

Differences in party affiliation between the governor and the legislative majority probably provoke more vetoes than any other factor, especially when party ideology and platforms openly clash. In 2015, Maine Governor Paul LePage followed through on a threat to veto all bills sponsored by Democrats unless the legislature approved his call for a constitutional amendment to abandon the income tax, vetoing ten bills in a single day. The legislature rebuked LePage two days later by overriding nine of his vetoes.[36] New York Governor David Patterson vetoed some 6,700 budget items during a single week in 2010. But when mutual respect and cooperation prevail between the two branches, the governor rarely needs to threaten or actually use the veto.[37]

Most governors interact with the legislature throughout the bill-adoption process. Before rejecting a bill, the governor will request comments from key legislators, affected state agencies, and concerned interest groups. He may ask the AG for a legal opinion. And before actually vetoing proposed legislation, the governor usually provides advance notification to legislative leaders, along with a final opportunity to make amendments.

The veto can be a powerful offensive weapon that may be used to obtain a legislator's support for a different bill dear to the governor's heart, particularly near the end of the legislative session. The governor may, for instance, hold one bill hostage to a veto until the legislature enacts another bill that he favors, as did Maine's governor LePage. Former California governor Arnold Schwarzenegger also did so also in 2008, when he began vetoing all bills sent to his desk until the legislature approved a budget bill; all told, he vetoed 35 percent of the bills sent to him that session. Wisconsin's storied history includes the "Vanna White Veto" and the "Frankenstein Veto." The first, abolished in 1990, permitted the governor to delete individual letters and numbers to change a bill's content. The second, killed by a 2008 voter referendum, allowed the governor to strike out some words and piece together others to alter a bill's content. For instance, Governor Jim Doyle (2003–2011) used the Frankenstein Veto to delete 752 words from a bill, which effectively shifted $427 million from transportation to education.[38]

BUDGETARY POWER

The governor's budget effectively sets the legislative agenda at the beginning of each session. By framing the important policy issues and attaching price tags to them, the governor can determine the scope and direction of budgetary debates in the legislature and ensure that they reflect her overall philosophy on taxing and spending. All but a handful of governors have the authority to appoint (and remove) the budget director and to formulate and submit the executive budget to the legislature. In Mississippi and Texas, budget authority is shared with the legislature or with other elected executive branch officials. And in these two states, two budgets are prepared each year, one by the governor and one by a legislative budget board.

Because budgetary authority is normally housed in the office of the chief executive, the governor can not only drive the budgetary process in the legislature, but also enjoys a source of important leverage in the bureaucracy. The executive budget can be used to influence programs, spending, and other activities of state agencies. For example, uncooperative administrators may discover that their agency's slice of the budget pie is smaller than expected, whereas those who are attentive to the concerns of the governor may receive strong financial support. Rational, objective criteria usually determine departmental budget allocations, but a subtle threat from the governor's office does wonders to instill a cooperative agency attitude.

The governor's budget requests are rarely, if ever, enacted exactly as put forward. Rather, they are argued and debated thoroughly in both houses of the legislature. A legislature dominated by the opposing political party is nearly certain to scorn and disparage the governor's budget as "dead on arrival." Governors, who are elected statewide, must appeal to a large and diversified electorate. Legislatures must please localized geographic constituencies. Ultimately, "the governor proposes, but the legislature disposes." In fact, no monies may be appropriated without formal action by the legislature. Which branch of government is most powerful in a budgetary sense? Research is inconclusive—it depends.[39] (The budget process is discussed further in Chapter 8.)

During state budget crises, governors find themselves in an extremely vulnerable political position, particularly if they signed a "no new taxes" pledge when running for office. Legislatures struggle with the governor over the question of who will assume primary responsibility for reducing state expenditures or hiking taxes. Usually, governors take the heat, and even light the match, by cutting spending, introducing tax increases, or both.[40] Such bold actions, though fully appropriate, are not taken without due caution by the governor because the electoral consequences can be direct and negative.

REORGANIZATION POWER

Reorganization power refers to the governor's ability to create and abolish state agencies, departments, and other offices and to reallocate administrative responsibilities among them. Reorganizations are usually aimed at the upper levels of the bureaucracy in an effort to streamline the executive branch and thereby make it work more efficiently and effectively. The basic premise is that the governor, as chief manager of the bureaucracy, needs the authority to arrange administrative structures and processes to meet changing demands. For instance, serious and recurring problems in coordinating the delivery of social services among several existing state agencies may call for a consolidated human services department with expanded powers. A governor with strong reorganization power can bring about such a department without approval of the legislature.

Traditionally, legislatures have been responsible for the organization of state government, and in the absence of a constitutional amendment to the contrary or a statutory grant of reorganization power to the governor, they still are. But today, thirty-five states specifically authorize their chief executive to reorganize some or all elements of the bureaucracy through **executive order**, through which the governor can make needed administrative changes when she deems it necessary.

Administrative reorganization today takes place under the assumption that streamlined government improves bureaucratic performance and saves money by cutting down on duplication, waste, and inefficiency. Achieving a more efficient and user-friendly government is a top priority of most governors. Initiatives to reinvent or reinvigorate government aim to make the bureaucracy more flexible and responsive by changing incentive systems for state employees; privatizing certain operations; reducing layers of bureaucracy; implementing e-government; and consolidating information technology, purchasing and payroll, and human resource management activities.

Executive branch reorganization is widely practiced, but its actual benefits are often ephemeral. Reorganization typically achieves modest financial savings, if any at all, and it can produce bureaucratic infighting, delays, unanticipated financial costs, and widespread confusion. Reorganization is not a panacea for state fiscal ills. However, executive branch reorganization may help to provide a clearer focus on a particular problem, such as the needs of children; or help to contain administrative costs, such as by eliminating superfluous or unnecessary boards, commissions, and task forces, and it may serve various political purposes, such as rationalizing the pain of employee layoffs.[41]

The Politics of Reorganization Reorganization is a politically charged process. Mere talk of it sounds alarms in the halls of the legislature, in the honeycombs of state office buildings, and in the offices of interest groups. Reorganization attempts usually spawn bitter controversy and conflict both inside and outside state government as assorted vested interests fight for favorite programs and organizational turf. Accordingly, comprehensive reorganization proposals are frequently defeated or amended by the legislature, or abandoned by discouraged chief executives. One study of proposed state reorganizations discovered that almost 70 percent resulted in rejection of the plan either in part or in its entirety.[42] Even when implemented, reorganizations may generate fierce opposition from entrenched interests in the bureaucracy and, in the final analysis, be judged a failure. In the memorable words of former Kansas governor Robert F. Bennett:

> In the abstract, [reorganization] is, without a doubt, one of the finest and one of the most palatable theories ever espoused by a modern-day politician. But in practice . . . it becomes the loss of a job for your brother or your sister, your uncle or your aunt. It becomes the closing of an office on which you have learned to depend. . . . So there in many instances may be more agony than anything else in this reorganization process.[43]

Most governors who have fought the battle for reorganization would concur. Perhaps such predictable opposition helps explain the rarity of

executive order
A rule, regulation, or policy issued unilaterally by the governor to change executive branch operations or activities.

far-reaching state agency restructuring and the preference for small, incremental steps to reorganize and streamline state agencies.[44]

STAFFING POWER

The governor relies on staff to provide policy analysis and advice, serve as liaisons with the legislature, assist in managing the bureaucracy, and provide constituent services. Professional staff members are a significant component of the governor's team, composing a corps of political loyalists who help the governor cope with the multiple roles of the office. From the handful of political cronies and secretaries of several decades ago, the staff of the governor's office has grown in number, quality, and diversity[45] Today, the average number of professional and clerical staff members is approximately sixty-five.[46] In some larger, more highly populated states, staff members number well over 100: Texas reports 277 staffers. The principal staff positions of the governor's office includes those of chief of staff, legislative liaison, budget director, policy director, legal counsel, scheduler, press secretary, and intergovernmental coordinator.

Perhaps the most important to the governor is her chief of staff. Among the wide range of duties discharged by the chief of staff are gatekeeping access to the governor, representing the governor's views, protecting the governor's time and good name, recruiting and filling appointive executive branch positions, coordinating emergency planning and response, and acting as personal confidant to the governor.[47]

A question of serious concern, especially in the states whose governors have large staffs, is whether these nonelected officials have too much power and influence. Clearly, professional staff members have been highly influential in developing and promoting policies for the governor in some states, particularly in states where the governor lacks a coherent set of priorities and lets the staff have free rein to advance their own agenda. In other states, the chief executive is very much in charge, relying on staff primarily for drafting bills and providing technical information. Given their physical and intellectual proximity to the governor, staff members are in a highly advantageous position to influence their boss. In their role as the major funnel for policy information and advice, they can affect the governor's decisions by controlling the flow of information and individuals into his office.

THE RELEVANCE OF THE FORMAL POWERS

In Table 7.2, the states are scored according to the strength of the governor's formal powers of office. As noted, governors have won stronger powers over time. But how helpful are the formal powers? Despite the major transformation of the governor's office, governors remain relatively weak because of the setting of state government. They must function within a highly complex and politically charged environment with formal authority that is quite circumscribed by the legislature, the courts, and constitutional and statutory law. Owing to the nature of our federal system, the national government effectively

TABLE 7.2 **Relative Power of the Governors' Offices**

2.5	2.6	2.7	2.8	2.9	3	3.1	3.2	3.3	3.4	3.5	3.6	3.7	3.8	3.9	4	4.1	4.2	4.3
VT	RI		AL	IN	NV	WY	CA	ID	AZ	DE	AR	NM	IL	CO	UT	AK		MA
			OK	MS	SC		GA	KS	HI	MT	CT		IA	ND		MD		
				NC	SD		NH	KY	LA	OR	FL		NE			NJ		
							TX			WI	ME		PA			NY		
							VA				MI		TN			WV		
											MN							
U.S. Average: 3.5											MC							

SOURCE: Adapted from Thad Beyle, http://www.unc.edu/~beyle/gubnewpwr.html. Reprinted by permission of the author.

strips them of control over many policy and administrative concerns. Moreover, the business of state government is carried out in a fishbowl, open to regular scrutiny by the media, interest groups, talk-show hosts, bloggers, Tweeters, and other interested parties. Notwithstanding the continued constraints on the exercise of their authority, however, today's governors as a group are probably more effective than their predecessors were in carrying out their varied responsibilities.

In theory, governors with strong formal powers, such as the governors in Alaska, New Jersey, and Massachusetts, should be more effective than their counterparts in Vermont and Rhode Island. In practice, that tends to be true—but not always. The potential for power and influence must not be confused with action. A governor with strong formal powers enjoys the capacity to serve effectively, but he may choose not to do so or, for various reasons, be unable to utilize the formal powers properly. This point is indirectly confirmed by a study that finds that formal gubernatorial power does not translate into greater success for incumbent governors seeking re-election.[48] Alternatively, a governor with weak formal powers can nonetheless be an effective, strong chief executive if she actively and skillfully applies the levers of power available in the constitution and in statutes.

Informal Powers

No doubt a governor with strong formal powers has an advantage over one without them. But at least equally important for a successful governor is the exploitation of the informal powers of the office. These powers carry authority and influence that are not directly attached to the governorship through statute or constitution, but rather are associated with the human being who happens to occupy the governor's mansion. Governors who can master these powers can be highly effective, even in the absence of strong formal powers.

LO 7.5

To analyze the informal powers of the office, their importance, and how they can enhance the formal powers.

The informal powers help transform the capacity for action into effective action. They react in synergy with the formal powers to create a successful governorship. An incumbent chief executive in the strong-governor state of Massachusetts will be hopelessly weak unless he also uses his personal assets in performing the multiple roles of the office. Alternatively, a chief executive in a weak-governor state such as Oklahoma can be remarkably successful if she fully employs her informal powers to excel in persuading the legislature and the people in the state to adopt new ideas. The informal powers are not as easy to specify as the formal powers are. However, they generally include such tools of persuasion and leadership as popular support; prestige of the office; previous elected experience; public relations and media skills; negotiating and bargaining skills; pork barrel and patronage; and personal characteristics such as ambition, experience, and energy.

TOOLS OF PERSUASION AND LEADERSHIP

Popular support refers to public identification with and support for the governor and his priorities. It may be measured in terms of the margin of victory in the primary and general elections or in terms of the results of public opinion polls. Governors with large victory margins and high levels of public support can lay claim to a popular mandate. They can parlay popular support into legislative acceptance of a policy proposal, channeling the pressures of public opinion to their advantage.

Popular support can quickly vanish when a governor's words or actions alienate voters and/or powerful interest groups, as demonstrated by the cases of two recent governors. Pennsylvania Governor Tom Corbett was reported to be a member of a club that traded pornographic photos and videos on safe e-mail accounts during the work day.[49] In a televised appearance, Corbett also equated same-sex marriage to incest. Neither helped him with voters. Governor Paul LePage of Maine "told the state chapter of the NAACP to kiss his butt, likened the Internal Revenue Service to the Nazi Gestapo, issued blanket gag orders to the state's largest newspaper chain (whose headquarters he also joked about bombing), and denounced—on camera—a Democratic state legislator for always wanting to 'give it to the people without Vaseline'."[50] Remarkably, LePage was returned to office by the voters in 2014 for a second term.

The *prestige of the office* helps the governor open doors all over the world that would be closed to an ordinary citizen. National officials, big-city mayors, corporate executives, foreign officials, and even the president of the United States recognize that the governor sits at the pinnacle of political power in the state, and they treat her accordingly. Governors of California, New York, and Texas—the largest states—almost automatically assume roles of national and even international prominence. Within the state, the governor typically makes use of the prestige of the office by inviting important individuals for an official audience or perhaps to a special meal or celebration at the mansion. Previous electoral experience is a valuable asset. Those who have made their way up the state's political ambition ladder by serving in the state legislature or serving as attorney general (AG) or lieutenant governor have learned how to find their way through political briar patches and avoid tar pits.[51] They can also take advantage of political friends and allies they cultivated along the way. Arkansas Governor Mike Beebe (2007–2011) leveraged the experience of twenty years in the state senate and four years as attorney general to get just about everything he asked for from the legislature.[52]

Public relations and media skills help the governor command the "big mike": the captive attention of the press, radio, and television. Any governor can call a press conference at a moment's notice and get a substantial turnout of the state's major media representatives, an advantage enjoyed by precious few legislators. Some chief executives appear regularly on television to explain their policy positions and initiatives to the people. Others write regular news-paper columns. Nearly all use blogs, Tweets, or Facebook messages for the same purpose. Frequent public appearances, staged events, telephone calls, YouTube videos, and even state-funded "public interest" advertisements deliv-ered through the mass media are also tools in the governor's media kit. Governors have used such techniques to attain statewide voter approval rat-ings of up to 90 percent. The ability to improvise in unpredictable, chaotic situations doesn't hurt. Former New York governor David Paterson illustrated that point effectively. When the wife of Jonathan Lippman, whom Paterson had just nominated as a judge, fainted at a press conference during Lippen's remarks, the governor quipped to the audience, "It's the usual reaction when Jonathan is speaking."[53] Spontaneity may serve the governor well, but one must also weigh his words carefully before speaking.

Effective governors know instinctively that the media can be a strong ally in carrying out their programs and responsibilities, and they cultivate the press like a flower garden. But media relations are a two-way street. The media expect the governor to be honest, forthright, and available. If he instills respect and cooperation, the governor's media relations can be "of incalculable value in his contest for the public eye and ear."[54] After all, most or even all of what the public knows about the governor comes from the media.

Negotiating and bargaining skills are leadership tools that help the governor to convince legislators, administrators, interest groups, and national and local officials to accept his point of view on whatever issue is at hand. These skills are of tremendous assistance in building voting blocs in the legislature, par-ticularly in divided-power settings. They also help persuade new businesses to locate in the state and help the governor effectively represent a state's interests before the national government.

Pork barrel and patronage are aspects of the seamier side of state politics. Although they are utilized much less frequently now than they were before the civil service reforms of the first half of the twentieth century, governors are still known to promise jobs, contracts, new roads, special policy consider-ation, electoral assistance, and other favors to influential citizens, legislators, donors, and others in return for their support. All governors have discretion-ary funds with which to help out a special friend who has constituents in need. And although patronage appointments are now severely limited in most jurisdictions, a personal telephone call from the governor can open the door to an employment opportunity in state government.

CHARACTERISTICS OF A SUCCESSFUL GOVERNOR

The *personal characteristics* of an effective governor are nearly impossible to measure. However, leadership is generally agreed to be a very important quality. Leadership traits are difficult to define, but former Utah governor Scott Matheson identified the best governors as "men and women who have the right combination of values for quality public service—the courage to stick to their convictions, even when in the minority; integrity by instinct, compassion by nature, leadership by perception; and the character to admit wrong and when necessary, to accept defeat."[55]

A successful governor achieves her objectives by blending these qualities with the formal and informal powers of office. For example, following the political campaign to win the election, the governor must conduct a "never-ending campaign" to win the loyalty and support of her cabinet, state employees, the legislature, and the people if she is to be effective.[56] Sixteen-hour days and one hundred-hour workweeks are not uncommon. Some governors demonstrate amazing determination and commitment to the job. On an African vacation, Virginia Governor Terry McAuliffe fell from a horse and broke seven ribs. Yet he returned to Virginia and immediately resumed his obligations (though he was later briefly hospitalized after complications developed).

At the outset, successful governors are careful not to allow eloquent and elevated campaign promises to greatly exceed practical political possibilities. Realizing that to try to do everything is to accomplish nothing, they focus on a few critical issues at a time and marshal their formal and informal resources behind them. Eventually, the determined governor can wear down opponents. But more important, the successful governor exercises leadership by convincing the public that he is the person to pursue their vision and their interests. He prevails in the legislature by applying the pressure of public opinion and by building winning blocs of votes, and leads the bureaucracy by personal example. Above all else, the successful governor must be persuasive.

In short, the formal powers of the office are important to any governor, but even strong formal powers do not guarantee success. As noted earlier, they must be combined with the informal powers to be effective. Whatever approach the governor chooses as chief executive, her individual skills are probably more important than formal powers. Evidence of this conclusion is provided by governors who have won and held their state's top job and successfully pursued their policy agendas in the face of significant opposition. Of course, how a governor proceeds to govern is in part situational.

Leaving Office

Upon leaving office, the vast majority of governors simply continue their public service in another venue. Four out of the last five presidents were ex-governors. President Obama raided the ranks of sitting governors to fill several key federal cabinet positions. California governor Jerry Brown was elected mayor of Oakland following his first years as governor, then as state attorney general, and in 2010 and 2014, as governor again; Colorado's Roy Romer became superintendent of Los Angeles, California's public schools; former Indiana

Governor Mitch Daniels was named president of Purdue University; and former governor of Hawaii, Linda Lingle, became chief operating officer for new Illinois Governor Bruce Rauner. Ten former governors were serving in the U.S. Senate in 2015.

A handful of former governors, however, have served time in prison for illegal actions or gross conflicts of interest. All states but one provide in their constitutions for the impeachment of the governor and other elected officials (in Oregon, they are tried as regular criminal offenders). Impeachment proceedings are usually initiated in the state house of representatives, and the impeachment trial is held in the senate. A two-thirds vote is necessary for conviction and removal of the governor in most states. Of the more than 2,100 governors who have held office, only twenty-three have been either impeached and removed from office or resigned under a cloud of legal problems. Besieged governors are much more likely to resign than face a lengthy public scourging through impeachment and legislative trial, or to be prosecuted upon expiration of their term.

The most recent governors to leave office in disgrace were John Kitzhaber of Oregon, Robert McDonnell of Virginia, Eliot Spitzer of New York, and Rod Blagojevich of Illinois. Kitzhaber resigned in 2015 over ethical questions about his live-in fiancée's dealings as a consultant while also advising the governor. McDonnell and his wife were prosecuted in 2015 for illegally accepting gifts, vacations, and large loans from a Richmond businessman. Spitzer resigned after getting snared in a federal prostitution sting operation. The Blogojevich saga involved a host of federal criminal charges, including trying to sell the U.S. Senate seat that was vacated when Barack Obama assumed the presidency. It ended with the former governor convicted on eighteen corruption accounts and sentenced to fourteen years in prison.

But these fallen unfortunates are the gubernatorial black sheep—the political throwbacks of state government who spawn media feeding frenzies. They deflect proper attention from the vast majority of hard-working, capable, and honest chief executives who typify the American state governorship today.

Other Executive Branch Officials

LO 7.6

To explain the responsibilities of the other elective statewide executive branch offices.

The states elect more than 300 officials to their executive branches, not counting the fifty governors, ranging from attorneys general (AGs) and treasurers to railroad commissioners. The four most important statewide offices are described here.

LIEUTENANT GOVERNOR

This office was originally created by the states for two major reasons: to provide for orderly succession to a governor who is unable to fulfill a term because of death or other reasons, and to provide for an official to assume the responsibilities of the governor when the incumbent is temporarily incapacitated or out of the state. Five states do not see a need for the office: Arizona, Maine, New Hampshire, Oregon, and Wyoming. Others attach little importance to it, as indicated by an extremely low salary or the absence of official responsibilities.

The historical reputation of the lieutenant governor was that of a corpse at a funeral; you are needed for the ceremony but no one is expecting much from you; or, as one wag suggested, "dismissed as a ribbon-cutting version of the appendix—prominently situated but without any discernible function."[57] The absence of significant responsibilities gets some lieutenant governors into mischief. Three resigned in 2013 amid scandals.

But several recent lieutenant governors have risen to occupy the executive office because of a death, impeachment, or resignation. Even when a governor's unplanned exit is not the cause of a vacancy in the executive mansion, the lieutenant governorship can be a springboard to the state's top elected office.[58] Twelve governors in 2015 had paid their dues as lieutenant governor.

The lieutenant governorship in the majority of states has become a more visible and responsible position. Many lieutenant governors hold important powers in the state senate, including serving as presiding officer, making bill assignments to committees, and casting tie-breaking votes in the senate. They are official members of the cabinet or of the governor's top advisory body in twenty-one states.[59] Indiana's lieutenant governor serves as secretary of agriculture and runs six state agencies; Colorado's directs the department of higher education. And virtually all lieutenant governors accept special assignments from the chief executive, some of which are quite visible and important. For example, Utah's heads up that state's homeland security efforts. Several lieutenant governors act as agency heads. In general, lieutenant governors' salaries, budget allocations, and staff have grown markedly.

A lingering problem is that twenty states continue to elect the governor and lieutenant governor independently. This system can result in conflict when, for example, the chief executive is out of state and the two officeholders are political rivals or members of opposing political parties. On several recent occasions, a lieutenant governor, assuming command, has proceeded to make judicial appointments, veto legislation, convene special sessions of the legislature, and take other actions at odds with the governor's wishes.

To avoid partisan bickering and politicking in the top two executive branch offices, twenty-six states require team election. In addition to avoiding embarrassing factionalism, team election has the advantages of promoting party accountability in the executive branch, making continuity of policy more likely in the event of gubernatorial death or disability and ensuring a measure of compatibility and trust between the two state leaders.

ATTORNEY GENERAL

The AG is the state's chief legal counsel. The AG renders formal written opinions on legal issues, such as the constitutionality of a statute, administrative rule, or regulation, when requested to do so by the governor, agency heads, legislators, or other public officials. The AG can also independently question the constitutionality of actions by the governor and even the federal government. In most states, the AG's opinions have the force of law unless they are successfully challenged in the courtroom. Many high profile AGs have successfully positioned themselves for the governorship, including eight sitting governors in 2015.

The AG represents the state in litigation in which the state government is a legal party, represents the state in federal and state courts, and can initiate civil and criminal proceedings in most states. More active today than ever before, AGs regularly contest national government statutes and administrative rulings in controversial fields such as consumer rights, environmental protection, education reform, and business regulation. AGs today are bringing litigation against the national government that argues against portions of the national health care law (the ACA), air pollution regulations, and immigration policy. Activist AGs have initiated actions to protect consumers against mail fraud, mortgage fraud, cybercrime, Medicaid fraud, misleading advertisements by pharmaceutical companies, mortgage fraud and illegal foreclosure actions by banks, and other white-collar crimes.

Some of their collective actions have helped to reform corrupt corporate behavior and to push the national government to regulate business more aggressively. Conservative AGs have taken quite a different tack, litigating for looser environmental, financial, and other regulations. Their litigation and arguments often push issues onto the policy agenda of Congress and to the U.S. Supreme Court. Predictably, the AGs' activism has spawned intense interest and participation in AG elections. A 2014 *New York Times* investigation uncovered numerous cozy relationships between certain AGs and corporate lobbyists in the energy, pharmaceutical, food, and financial industries,[60] raising important questions about the AG's integrity and independence.

What should be done when an AG is told by the governor or legislature to defend a law that she herself is convinced is unconstitutional? Some AGs mount a defense as best they can, but others refuse to do so. For example, Virginia AG Mark Herring and Pennsylvania AG Kathleen Kane refused in 2014 to defend their states' same-sex marriage bans.

TREASURER

The treasurer is the official trustee and manager of state funds and the state's chief financial officer. He collects revenues and makes disbursements of state monies. (The treasurer's signature is on the paycheck of all state employees and on citizens' state tax refunds.) Another important duty is the investment of more than $3.2 trillion in state funds, including state employee pension monies and college savings plans. The failure to make profitable investments can cost the treasurer his job. West Virginia treasurer A. James Manchin was impeached for losing $279 million in state funds through bad investments. Other treasurers have been criticized for taking lucrative private-sector jobs in the middle of their terms (Connecticut, New Jersey), accepting gifts from financial firms (Massachusetts), or using their post to raise large sums of campaign money from investment companies. Arkansas treasurer Martha Shoffner was arrested and briefly jailed in 2013 on charges of taking kickbacks and directing state bond transactions to a single, favored broker.[61]

SECRETARY OF STATE

In the past, the duties of the secretary of state were rather perfunctory, entailing record keeping and election responsibilities. But voting system reforms, e-government, and other changes in how states run elections have substantially elevated the responsibilities of the position. Secretaries of state typically register corporations, securities, and trademarks, and commission people to be notaries public. The typical secretary of state also maintains state archives, files agency rules and regulations, publishes statutes and copies of the state constitution, and registers lobbyists.

In their election-related responsibilities, they determine the ballot eligibility of political parties and candidates, receive and verify initiative and referendum petitions, supply election ballots to local officials, file the expense papers and other campaign reports of candidates, maintain voter registration rolls, and to deter voter fraud. A function of growing importance in the secretary of state's offices is to protect citizens' Social Security numbers and other private identification data placed in public databases that put citizens at risk of identity theft.[62]

The Capability of U.S. Governors

The governor, as chief executive, enjoys extensive powers, both formal and informal. Today's governors are capable, active, and, in general, impressive political actors. However, severe national political divisions over such issues as same-sex marriage, gun control, health care, and immigration threaten to conscript governors into the bitter, dysfunctional partisanship that characterizes the nation's capital. This is a development that raises concern, and bears close attention.

In addition, today's governors are better educated, more experienced in state government, and more competent than their predecessors. Unfortunate exceptions notwithstanding, their strength and policy influence impresses. They are better able to employ the informal powers of their office in meeting multiple and complex responsibilities. In sum, the governorships display both capability and vigor.

Chapter Recap

- The American governorship historically was institutionally weak, with limited formal powers.

- Today's governors are generally well qualified for the office, but some recent governors have disappointed. Winning the office is increasingly expensive.

- Duties of the governors include making policy, marshaling legislative action, administering the executive branch, serving as master of ceremonies, coordinating intergovernmental relations, promoting economic development, and leading their political party.

- Formal powers of the office, which have strengthened over time, are tenure, appointment, veto, budgeting, reorganizing the executive branch, and staffing.

- To be successful, a governor must master the informal powers of the office and integrate them with the formal powers. Among the informal sources of power are tools of leadership and persuasion, such as public relations skills and negotiating and bargaining skills.

- Governors who violate the law may be removed from office through impeachment, while unpopular governors may be recalled.

- Other key executive branch officials are the attorney general, lieutenant governor, treasurer, and secretary of state. Like the governors, they too have been expanding their importance in state government.

KEY TERMS

pork barrel *(p. 173)*
formal powers *(p. 178)*
informal powers *(p. 178)*
plural executive *(p. 180)*

patronage *(p. 180)*
package veto *(p. 182)*
line item veto *(p. 182)*
pocket veto *(p. 182)*

executive amendment *(p. 182)*
executive order *(p. 185)*

INTERNET RESOURCES

Each state's governor has his or her own website, which can be located through the state homepage or from links at **www.nga.org**, the NGA's website. It features, among other items, governors' biographies, the latest "State of the State" addresses, and a subject index on various state and local issues.

For information about the attorneys general, see **www.naag.org.** State treasurers can be audited at **www.nast.org,** and lieutenant governors at **www.nlga.us.** Even secretaries of state have a national organization: see **www.nass.org**/.

Public Administration: Budgeting and Service Delivery

A firefighter rescues a boy after an auto accident.
New York Daily News Archive/Getty Images

LEARNING OBJECTIVES

8.1 To appreciate the size, scope, and characteristics of state and local government employment.

8.2 To understand the state government budgetary process, including key actors and critical processes.

8.3 To be familiar with the components of merit systems.

8.4 To be able to explain the challenges of representative bureaucracy and affirmative action, sexual harassment, and public employee unionization and collective bargaining.

8.5 To explain the clash of politics and bureaucracy.

8.6 To describe new public management, its strategies, and its pros and cons.

Bureaucracy is a paradox. On one hand, bureaucracy is portrayed as "the problem" with U.S. government at all levels. From the ponderous department of social services, to the dilatory department of motor vehicles, to the extractive county tax assessor's office, it is depicted as all-powerful, out of control, inefficient, wasteful, and drowning in red tape. Public employees ("bureaucrats") are often portrayed as insensitive and uncaring, yet they stay in their jobs forever. Nearly everyone, from elected officials—presidents, governors, mayors, and legislators at all levels—to talk-show commentators, television and film script writers, bloggers, and even product advertisers have stridently bashed the bureaucrats, blaming them for all imaginable sins of omission and commission (and all too often for their own personal shortcomings). The answer to the problem is no less than bureaucratic liposuction to "get the fat out" and surgery to "get the government off our backs."

On the other hand, bureaucracy can be beautiful.[1] Bureaucratic organization is indispensable to public administration. Legislative bodies and chief executives enact public policies through vague laws and then must depend on various state and local agencies to deal with the specifics, such as operationally defining key components of the policies and putting the policies into effect. Some bureaucracies make our lives more difficult, but others improve the quality of our existence by enforcing the laws and punishing the criminals, putting out the fires, repairing and maintaining the roads, and helping the poor and disadvantaged among us. Heroic, life-saving actions by police and firefighters are commonplace but seldom recognized publically.

A theme of this chapter is that state agencies and local departments (the public administration) should not be treated as scapegoats for all the social, economic, and political maladies that befall society, and that they should be respected—not rebuked. The quality and capacity of public administration have improved markedly in the vast majority of the country's states, municipalities, and counties in terms of the characteristics of employees and the efficiency, effectiveness, and professionalism with which they perform their duties. In fact, studies comparing public employees with cohort groups in the private sector find few important differences between them. Government workers are just as motivated, competent, and ethical as private-sector workers. Moreover, public employees tend to be more sensitive to other human beings and more highly educated than their counterparts in business and industry, and most are imbued with a "public service" ethos that motivates them (see Table 8.1).[2]

State and local employees are responding to citizen demands by providing a wider range of services, in greater quantities, to more people than ever before, and publicly provided services are perceived to be just as good as the same services provided by private firms. Public employees are much more accountable and responsive to political actors and to the public than they are popularly perceived to be. And contrary to popular opinion, government work does not consist of pay without labor. Public employees perform some of the most unpleasant (but necessary) tasks imaginable, from saving abused or threatened children from their parents to caring for the mentally ill and guarding prisoners who hurl feces at them. Many jobs are dangerous, as public employees must contend daily with clients who are criminals, deadbeats, emotionally disturbed, drug abusers, and worse,[3] and expend considerable quantities of "emotional labor."[4] They serve as our first—and continuing—response to disasters and terrorist events.

bureaucracy
The administrative branch of government, consisting of all executive offices and their workers.

TABLE 8.1	Comparing Public- and Private-Sector Employees	
CHARACTERISTIC	**ADVANTAGE**	
Motivation	Equal (though public workers favor intrinsic rewards and private workers prefer extrinsic rewards)	
Work habits	Equal	
Competence	Equal	
Personal achievement	Private employees	
Educational achievement	Public employees	
Values of civic duty and public service	Public employees	
Ambition	Private employees	
Compassion and self-sacrifice	Public employees	
Ethics	Public employees	
Helping other people	Public employees	
Making a difference	Public employees	
Concern for compensation	Private employees	

SOURCES: Adapted from Mary K. Feeney, "Sector Perceptions Among State-Level Public Managers," *Journal of Public Administration Research and Theory* 18(3) (2008): 465–94; Richard W. Stackman, Patrick E. Connor, and Boris W. Becker, "Sectoral Ethos: An Investigation of the Personal Values Systems of Female and Male Managers in the Public and Private Sectors," *Journal of Public Administration Research and Theory* 16 (October 2006): 577–97; Alice Munnel, et al., "Comparing Compensation: State-Local Versus Private Sector Workers," *Issue Brief*, Center for State and Local Government Excellence (September 2011).

It is only on those rare occasions when someone fouls up that a public outcry is raised and a media investigation is noisily launched; praise for consistency and excellence in public-service delivery is seldom heard. When government fails to perform effectively, blame can occasionally be laid at the feet of public employees. But more often than not, good government workers are the scapegoats for vague and poorly designed statutes and policies, failed political and corporate leadership, insufficient resources, and other factors beyond the control of civil servants. It must also be pointed out that occasional lapses in government administrative ethics often pale in comparison to corporate scandals such as recent ones involving defense contractors, pharmaceutical firms, and banking and finance companies.

LO 8.1

To appreciate the size, scope, and characteristics of state and local government employment.

Public Employees in State and Local Governments: Who They Are, What They Do

More than 19.1 million employees work for states and localities. Their numbers have grown fairly steadily since accurate counts were first compiled in 1929, though have tailed off since the Great Recession. The distribution of

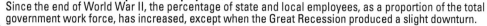

Distribution of Full-Time Equivalent Employment, 1929–2015
Since the end of World War II, the percentage of state and local employees, as a proportion of the total government work force, has increased, except when the Great Recession produced a slight downturn.

FIGURE 8.1

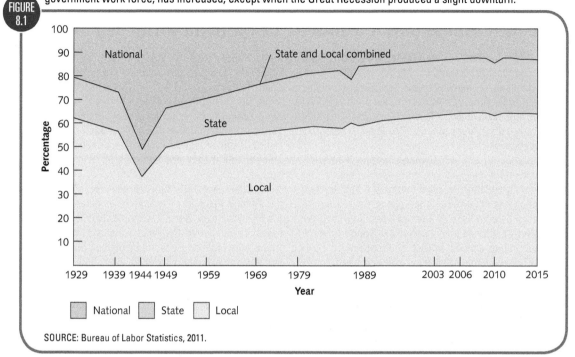

SOURCE: Bureau of Labor Statistics, 2011.

government employees is of interest (see Figure 8.1). Government work tends to be labor-intensive. As a result of this fact and because of inflation, personnel expenditures for states and localities have risen even faster than the number of workers. Total payroll costs for state and local governments exceed $65 billion per month.[5]

Of course, the number of employees varies greatly among jurisdictions. Generally, states and localities with large populations and high levels of per capita income provide more services and thus employ larger numbers of workers than do smaller, less affluent jurisdictions. California, for instance, has some 21 million state and local employees on its payroll, compared with only 49,922 in Vermont. Employment figures are further influenced by the distribution of functions and service responsibilities between states and their local jurisdictions. Such figures do not adequately represent the real people who work for states, cities, counties, towns, townships, and school districts. These workers include the police officer on patrol, the eleventh-grade English teacher, the state trooper, and even your professor of state and local government (if you attend a public institution).[6] Their tasks are as diverse as their titles: sanitation engineer, animal-control officer, heavy-equipment operator, planner, case worker, and so on. Many of these jobs are quite difficult (See the It's Your Turn feature). The diversity of state and local government work rivals that of the private sector,

It's Your Turn

Take the Children into Custody or Leave Them with Their Mom?

Welfare caseworkers are staffing the frontlines of the states' and localities' efforts to change the welfare system and its culture. Many of these individuals are highly educated and trained, with Master of Social Work (MSW) degrees and casework certificates. But sometimes they are called on to intervene or provide counseling in terribly difficult situations.

Put yourself in the following situation. You are a county welfare caseworker who specializes in the well-being of children who live in troubled households. Your office has received two telephone calls from the neighbors of a welfare mother complaining that her two young children (ages two and four) appear to have suffered bruises on their bodies, and that they are frequently heard crying when their mother's boyfriend is in their apartment. You visit the welfare mother's apartment, and the children look fine, except for a couple of minor bruises. The mother assures you that they are not

in any danger from the boyfriend or from anyone else. Obviously, however, the children are not in an entirely healthy environment. Trash is strewn around the apartment, the children are not well clothed, and the older child seems to be a bit slow or mentally challenged. You tell the mother that you will be back next week to check on the situation and that she should let you know immediately if they are endangered in any way. She agrees.

Three days later, you receive a call from your department head. The boyfriend has disappeared, and the four-year-old is dead. The mother claims he fell down the stairs, but a neighbor reports that she heard the boyfriend, who often appeared to be high on drugs, screaming at and then beating the child.

Media reaction is immediate and highly critical. In hindsight, was the right decision made? Should you have acted differently?

PROS	CONS
Department policy did not require you to remove the children from home based on neighbors' allegations of concern	Your office had been called twice by neighbors worried about the children
Case workers are encouraged to give the benefit of the doubt to the family so that the children can remain with their relatives	You saw that the children were poorly clothed and living in a potentially unsafe environment
You had no clearly convincing evidence that the children were in immediate danger	You should have erred on the side of caution and recommended that the children be removed immediately and placed in a foster home until their well-being could be assured

although important distinctions are made in the nature of the work. As Table 8.2 shows, public- and private-sector management differ in terms of constraints, clients, accountability, and purpose. From the sewer maintenance worker to the director of human resources, all are public servants—often known as bureaucrats. Almost one of every six working Americans is employed by government at some level. If bureaucrats are the enemy, we have met them and they are us.

TABLE 8.2	Public Management and Private Management: What Are the Distinctions?	
	PUBLIC MANAGEMENT	**PRIVATE MANAGEMENT**
CONSTRAINTS	Politics, public opinion, resources	Markets, competitors, resources
CLIENTS	Citizens, legislatures, chief executives, interest groups	Customers who purchase products or services
ACCOUNTABILITY	To citizens and elected and appointed officials	To customers, boards of directors, and shareholders
PURPOSE	To serve the public interest and the common good	To make profits and grow the organization

Budgeting in State and Local Governments

LO 8.2

To understand the state government budgetary process, including key actors and critical processes.

The budget is the very lifeblood of public administration. Without a budgetary appropriation, state and local organizations would cease to exist. The monies are allocated (usually on an annual basis) by legislative bodies, but the politics of the budgetary process involves all the familiar political and bureaucratic players: chief executives, interest groups, other government employees, the general public, firms and industries, and, of course, the recipients of legislative appropriations—the state highway department, the municipal police department, the county sanitation office, and so on. In a phrase, budget making is a highly charged political poker game with enormous stakes. To understand public administration, one must have a grasp of budgetary politics.

An often-quoted definition of politics is Harold Lasswell's famous line: "Politics is who gets what, when, where, and how."[7] The budget document provides hard dollars-and-cents data in answer to this question. It is a political manifesto—the most important one you will find in state and local governments. It is a policy statement of what government intends to do (or not do), detailing the amount of the taxpayers' resources that it will dedicate to each program and activity. The outcomes of the budgetary process represent the results of a zero-sum game—for every winner there is a loser—because public resources are limited. An extra million dollars for corrections can mean that much less for higher education; an expensive new fleet of sanitation trucks may require higher trash collection fees from residents.

THE BUDGET CYCLE

The process of governmental budgeting is best understood as a cycle with overlapping stages, five of which can be identified: preparation, formulation, adoption, execution, and audit (see Figure 8.2). Several stages are simultaneously taking place at any single time. For example, while the 2016 budget is

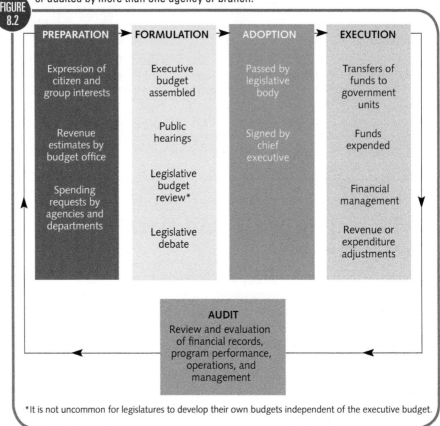

The Budget Process
The budget process has built-in checks and balances because all spending is approved or audited by more than one agency or branch.

FIGURE 8.2

PREPARATION	FORMULATION	ADOPTION	EXECUTION
Expression of citizen and group interests	Executive budget assembled	Passed by legislative body	Transfers of funds to government units
Revenue estimates by budget office	Public hearings	Signed by chief executive	Funds expended
Spending requests by agencies and departments	Legislative budget review*		Financial management
	Legislative debate		Revenue or expenditure adjustments

AUDIT
Review and evaluation of financial records, program performance, operations, and management

*It is not uncommon for legislatures to develop their own budgets independent of the executive budget.

being executed and revenues and expenditures are being monitored to guard against an operating deficit, the governor and the legislature are developing the 2017 budget. Meanwhile, the 2015 budget is being audited to ensure that monies were properly spent and otherwise accounted for.

Budgets are normally based on a *fiscal* (financial) *year* rather than on the calendar year. Fiscal years for all but four states run from July 1 through June 30 (the exceptions are Alabama, Michigan, New York, and Texas). Nineteen states, including Montana, Nevada, and Texas, have biennial (two-year) budget cycles. Most local governments' fiscal years also extend from July 1 to June 30.

The initial phase of the budget cycle involves demands for slices of the budget pie and estimates of available revenues for the next fiscal year. State and local agency heads join the chorus of interest groups and program beneficiaries seeking additional funding. (With no concern for "profits," agencies have little incentive to ask for less funding instead of more.) Large state agencies are typically represented by their own lobbyists, or "public information specialists." State and local finance administrators and analysts develop estimates of revenues based on past tax receipts and expected economic conditions, and they communicate them to their respective state agencies or municipal departments, which then develop their individual spending requests for the fiscal year. Such spending requests may be constrained by legislative and executive guidance, such as agency or program dollar ceilings, program priorities, or performance-based budgeting considerations.

Formulation, or initial development, of the budget document is the formal responsibility of the chief executive in most states and localities. Exceptions include states in which the balance of power rests with the legislature (such as Arkansas, Mississippi, and South Carolina) and local governments in which budgeting is dominated by a council or commission. Legislatures sometimes develop their own budget, essentially ignoring that of the governor. Once finalized, the executive budget is then presented to the appropriate legislative body for debate, review, and modification. The lengthy review process that follows allows agencies, departments, interest groups, lobbyists, and citizens to express their points of view. Finally, the legislative body enacts the amended budget. Usually the budget moves forward in accordance with mandated deadlines. Sometimes fiscal crises or political disputes delay budget passage, forcing legislators into all-nighters and casting state and local operations into a sea of uncertainty over what they can and cannot afford to do. For various reasons, New York state is famously tardy in adopting its annual budget, chronically missing its April 1 deadline.

The state legislature or city council ensures that the final document balances revenues with expenditures. Balanced-budget requirements are contained in the constitutions or statutes of forty-eight states and operate through precedent and custom in Vermont and Indiana. These requirements usually apply to local governments as well and are also enforced through municipal ordinances in many localities. Balanced-budget requirements force state and local governments to balance projected expenditures with revenues, but they may be circumvented to some extent (See Figure 8.3). Big-ticket items, for instance, may be funded in a capital budget with payments scheduled over several years.

Before the budget bill becomes law, the chief executive must sign it. Last-minute executive-legislative interactions may be needed to stave off executive vetoes or to override them. Once the chief executive's signature is on the document, the budget goes into effect as law, and the execution phase begins. During budget execution, monies from the state or local general fund are periodically allocated to agencies and departments to meet payrolls, purchase goods and materials, help average citizens solve problems ranging from a rabid raccoon in the neighborhood to a car-swallowing sinkhole in the front yard, and generally achieve program goals.

Accounting procedures and reporting systems continually track revenues and outlays within the agencies. If revenues have been overestimated, the chief executive or legislative body must "rebudget" by making adjustments to keep the budget in the black. They may draw on a rainy day fund to meet a shortfall (see Chapter 13) or, if the deficit is a large one, order such actions as shown in Figure 8.3. In a crisis, the governor may call the legislature into special session, or the mayor may request a tax increase from the city council. Governments are forced into a series of Hobson's Choices to raise taxes, reduce expenditures, cut services, delay or cancel needed capital expenditures, or use some combination thereof to balance the budgets—unpopular

FIGURE 8.3

Coping Strategies to Balance an Unbalanced Budget

REVENUE ENHANCEMENT STRATEGIES	SPENDING REDUCTIONS
• Hike taxes or fees • Borrow from employee pension funds • Borrow from next year's anticipated revenues • Assume extra new revenues from a prosperous tax year • Sell excess land, buildings, or other assets • Aggressively collect delinquent tax payments	• Postpone infrastructure and equipment maintenance • Exempt certain costs or projects from the operating budget by creating an "off-budget" • Reduce spending across-the board • Reduce services • Impose a hiring freeze, unpaid furlough, or travel restrictions • Refuse to transfer promised funds to local governments (a version of "shift-and shaft federalism" that imposes new and unforeseen costs of local governments) • Use volunteers to perform appropriate jobs • Reduce contributions to employee health care or pensions • Shift state expenditures to local governments • Privatize a public service

SOURCES: Jonathan Walters, "Richard Ravitch: How Budgets Really Work," www.governing.com (accessed April 28, 2014); Kimberly L. Nelson, "Municipal Choice during a Recession: Bounded Rationality and Innovation," *State and Local Government Review* 44 (July 2012): 44–63; John Goodman, "Budget Gimmicks Explained: Five Ways States Hide Deficits," www.stateline.org (accessed June 23, 2011).

choices all. Rainy day funds are tapped as well. Eventually, real pain is experienced by many different organizations and individuals.

The final portion of the budget cycle involves several types of audits, or financial reviews—each with a different objective. Fiscal audits seek to verify that expenditure records are accurate and that financial transactions have been made in accordance with the law. Performance audits examine agency or department activities in relation to goals, objectives, and outcomes, and ensure that the government is serving its citizens efficiently and effectively. Operational and management audits review how specific programs are carried out and assess administrators' performance.

A performance measurement and management trend has firm traction in state and local governments today, reflecting these jurisdictions' genuine determination to improve service provision to citizens.[8] Washington State, a leader in outcomes-based budgeting, solicits public and agency input to help prioritize statewide goals and thereby develops a set of priorities to guide and inform agency spending. Those programs that accomplish their goals and objectives are funded; those that fail are not.[9]

THE ACTORS IN BUDGETING

Four main institutional actors participate in the budget process: interest groups, agencies, the chief executive, and the legislative body. Interest groups organize testimony at budget hearings and pressure the other three actors to pursue favored policies and programs. The role of the agency or department is to defend the base—the amount of the last fiscal year's appropriation—and to advocate spending for new or expanded programs. Agency and department heads are professionals who believe in the value of their organization and its programs, but they often find themselves playing Byzantine games to get the appropriations they want, as set forth in Table 8.3, which lists tactics used by state and local officials to maximize their share of the budget during negotiations and hearings with governors, local chief executives, and the legislative body.

TABLE 8.3	The Games Spenders Play	
MASSAGE THE CONSTITUENCY	Locate, cultivate, and utilize clientele groups to further the organization's objectives. Encourage them to offer committee testimony and contact legislative members on your behalf.
ALWAYS ASK FOR MORE	If your agency or department doesn't claim its share of new revenues, someone else will. The more you seek, the more you will receive.
WHINING FOR DOLLARS	Keep whining to your boss until his annoyance level is so high that he coughs it up to shut you up.
SPEND ALL APPROPRIATED FUNDS BEFORE THE FISCAL YEAR EXPIRES	An end-of-year surplus indicates that the elected officials were too generous with you this year; they will cut your appropriation next time.
CONCEAL NEW PROGRAMS BEHIND EXISTING ONES	Incrementalism means that existing program commitments are likely to receive cursory review, even if an expansion in the margin is substantial. An announced new program will undergo comprehensive examination. Related to this game is *camel's nose under the tent*, in which low-program startup costs are followed by ballooning expenses down the road.
"HERE'S A KNIFE; CUT OUT MY HEART WHILE YOU'RE AT IT"	When told that you must cut your budget, place the most popular programs on the chopping block. Rely on your constituency to organize vigorous opposition. Alternatively, state that all your activities are critically important so the elected officials will have to decide what to cut (and answer for it to voters).
A ROSE BY ANY OTHER NAME	Conceal unpopular or controversial programs within other program activities. And give them appealing names (for instance, call a sex education class "Teaching Family Values").
"LET'S STUDY IT FIRST" (AND MAYBE YOU WON'T BE RE-ELECTED)	When told to cut or eliminate a program, argue that the consequences would be devastating and should be carefully studied before action is taken.
SMOKE AND MIRRORS	Support your requests for budget increases with voluminous data and testimony. The data need not be especially persuasive or even factual, just overwhelming. Management writer James H. Boren calls this "bloatating" and "trashifying."
A PIG IN A POKE	Place an unneeded item in your budget request so you can gracefully give it up while protecting more important items.
END RUN	If the chief executive initiates a budget cut, scurry quickly to friends in the legislature.
EVERY VEIN IS AN ARTERY	Claim that any program cut would so completely undermine effectiveness that the entire program would have to be abandoned.

Political scientist Aaron Wildavsky described the basic quandary of agency and departmental representatives as follows:

> Life would be simple if they could just estimate the costs of their ever-expanding needs and submit the total as their request. But if they ask for amounts much larger than the appropriating bodies believe is reasonable, their credibility will suffer a drastic decline. . . . So the first decision rule for agencies is: do not come in too high. Yet the agencies must also not come in too low, for the assumption is that if the agency advocates do not ask for funds they do not need them.[10]

What agency heads usually do is carefully evaluate the fiscal-political environment. They take into consideration the previous year's events, current and estimated agency expenditures, the composition of the legislature, the economic climate, policy statements by the chief executive, the strength of clientele groups, and other factors. Then they put forward a figure somewhat larger than they expect to get.

The chief executive has a much different role in the budget process. In addition to tailoring the budget to his preferred program priorities as closely as possible, he acts as an economizer. Individual departmental requests must be reconciled, which means that they must be cut because the sum of the requests will greatly exceed estimated revenues. Of course, an experienced governor or mayor recognizes the games played by administrators; she knows that budget requests are likely to be inflated in anticipation of cuts. In fact, various studies on state and local budgeting indicate that the single most influential participant is the chief executive.[11] Not surprisingly, astute public administrators devote time and other resources to cultivating the chief executive's support for their agency's or department's activities.

Unless it develops its own budget independently, the role of the legislative body in the initial stage of the budget cycle is essentially to respond to and modify the initiatives of the chief executive. The governor, mayor, or city manager proposes, and the legislature or council reacts. Later in the budget cycle, the legislative body performs other important functions through its review of agency and department spending and its response to constituents' complaints. Occasionally, a state court will find a budget to violate constitutional or statutory law, and invalidate it.[12]

What about the taxpayers whose salaries, homes, and vehicles will be taxed to fund the budget? The traditional approach is essentially to exclude them from the process. But more and more state and local governments offer budget transparency by encouraging citizens to attend and speak in budget hearings, focus groups, coffees, or to participate through Web-based applications. Web access to government revenues and expenditures is increasingly being made available by state and local governments. Unfortunately, few taxpayers avail themselves of the opportunity. Boston, St. Louis, Hampton, Virginia, and several other cities are experimenting with "participatory budgeting, "in which citizens decide how public funds should be spent in their neighborhoods.[13]

PERVASIVE INCREMENTALISM

In a perfect world, budgeting would be a purely rational enterprise. Objectives would be identified, stated clearly, and prioritized; alternative means for accomplishing them would be considered; resulting revenue and expenditure decisions would be coordinated within the context of a balanced budget.

That is how budgeting *should* be done. But state and local officials have to allocate huge sums of money in a budgetary environment where objectives are unclear or controversial and often conflict with one another. It is nearly impossible to prioritize the hundreds or thousands of policy items on the agenda. Financial resources, time, and the capacity of the human brain are severely stretched.

To cope with such complexity and minimize political conflict over scarce resources, decision makers "muddle through."[14] They simplify budget decision making by adopting decision rules. For example, instead of searching for the optimal way to address a public policy problem, they search only until they find a feasible solution. As a result, they sacrifice comprehensive analysis and rationality for **incrementalism**, in which small adjustments (usually an increase if times are good) are made to the nature and funding base of existing programs. Thus, the policy commitments and spending levels of ongoing programs are accepted as a given—they become the base for next year's funding. Decisions are made on a very small proportion of the total budget: the increments from one fiscal year to the next. If the budget has to be cut, it is done decrementally—small adjustments are subtracted from the base. In this way, political conflict over values and objectives is held to a minimum.

The hallmarks of incremental budgeting are consistency and continuity: The future becomes an extension of the present, which is itself a continuation of the past. Long-range commitments tend to be made, then honored indefinitely. This is not to say that state and local budgeting is a pedestrian affair. On the contrary, it is as tangled and intricate as the webs of a thousand spiders on methamphetimines. (If in doubt, the reader is urged to access his or her state or local budget online and see for him- or herself.)

TYPES OF BUDGETS

A budget document can be laid out in various ways, depending on the purposes one has in mind: control, management, or planning. Historically, *control*, or fiscal accountability, has been the primary purpose of budgeting, incrementalism the dominant process, and the line item budget the standard document.

Control through Line Item Budgets The **line item budget** facilitates control by specifying the amount of funds each agency or department receives and monitoring how those funds are spent. Each dollar can be accounted for with the line item budget—which lists every object of expenditure, from police uniforms to toilet paper—on individual lines in the budget document. Line item budgets show where the money goes, but they do not tell how effectively the money is spent.

incrementalism

A decision-making approach in the budgetary process in which the previous year's expenditures are used as a base for the current year's budget figures.

line item budget

A budget that lists detailed expenditure items such as personal computers and paper, with no attention to the goals or objectives of spending.

performance budgeting

Budgeting that takes into account the outcomes of government programs.

capital budget

A budget that plans large expenditures for long-term investments, such as buildings and bridges.

Budgeting for Performance Budget formats that are intended to help budget makers move beyond the narrow constraints of line items and incrementalism toward more rational and flexible decision-making techniques that help attain program results are known as performance budgets. Chief executives and agency officials seek to ensure that priorities set out in the budget are properly carried out. Formal program and policy evaluations are necessary to ensure program performance and public accountability.

In **performance budgeting**, the major emphasis is on services provided and program outcomes. The idea is to focus attention on how effectively goals are attained rather than on what is acquired or spent. Whereas line item budgets are input oriented, performance budgets are output and outcome oriented. Governments and their managers decide what they want to accomplish and then measure these accomplishments versus expenditures. For example, the performance of a fire department can be evaluated by response times to emergency calls and by how quickly a fire is contained once the firefighters arrive on the scene. Police departments can track arrests, clearance rates, crime rates, and citizen satisfaction surveys. Results can be compared to those of similar jurisdictions. By focusing on program objectives and work performance, performance budgets can assist managers, elected officials, and citizens in improving the quality of government operations.[15]

Capital Budgets The budget formats described above apply to operating budgets, whose funds are depleted within a year. Capital outlays are made over a longer period of time and are composed of big-ticket purchases such as hospitals, university buildings, rapid transit systems, and bridges. They represent one-time, nonrecurring expenditures that call for special funding procedures, or a **capital budget**. Because such items cannot be paid for within a single fiscal year, governments borrow the required funds, just as most individuals borrow when buying a house or an automobile. The debt, with interest, is paid back in accordance with a predetermined schedule.

Capital projects are funded through the sale of general obligation or revenue bonds. *Bonds* are certificates of debt sold by a government to a purchaser, who eventually recovers the initial price of the bond plus interest (see Chapter 13). *General obligation bonds* are paid off with a jurisdiction's regular revenues (from taxes and other sources). In this instance, the "full faith and credit" of the government is pledged as security. *Revenue bonds* are usually paid off with user fees collected from use of the new facility (e.g., a parking garage, auditorium, or toll road). Payments for both types of bonds are scheduled over a period of time that usually ranges from five to twenty years. The costs of operating a new facility, such as a school or a sports arena, are met through the regular operating budget and/or user fees.

LO 8.3

To be familiar with the components of merit systems.

Human Resource Policy in State and Local Governments: Patronage vs. Merit

Whether the tasks of state and local governments are popular (fighting crime, educating children), unpopular (imposing and collecting taxes and fees), serious (saving a helpless infant from an abusive parent), or mundane (maintaining the grass on municipal sports fields), they are usually performed by public employees. The 5.1 million state workers and 14.1 million city, county, and town employees are the critical links between public policy decisions and how those policies are implemented. Agencies and departments must be organized to solve problems and deliver services effectively and reliably. Human resource (personnel) rules and procedures determine how public employees are recruited, hired, paid, and fired.

In the nation's first decades, public employees came mainly from the educated and wealthy upper class and, in theory, were hired on the basis of fitness for office. During the presidency of Andrew Jackson (1829–1837), who wanted to open national government jobs to all segments of white, male society, the *patronage* system was adopted to fill many positions. Hiring could depend on party affiliation and other political alliances rather than on job-related qualifications.

Patronage became entrenched in many states and localities, where jobs were awarded almost entirely on grounds of partisan politics, personal friendships, family ties, or financial contributions. This system made appointees accountable to the governor, mayor, or whoever appointed them, but it did nothing to ensure honesty and basic competence. By the beginning of the Civil War, the spoils system permeated government at all levels, and the quality of public service plummeted.

THE MERIT SYSTEM

The concept of the **merit system** is usually associated with the national campaign to pass the federal Pendleton Act of 1883. Two key factors led to its realization. First, Anglo-Saxon Protestants were losing political power to urban political machines dominated by new Americans of Catholic faith and Irish, Italian, and Polish descent. Second, scandals rocked the administration of President Ulysses S. Grant and spawned a public backlash that peaked with the assassination of President James Garfield by an insane attorney seeking a political appointment. The Pendleton Act set up an independent, bipartisan civil service commission to make objective, merit-based selections for federal job openings.

merit system

The organization of government personnel to provide for hiring and promotion on the basis of knowledge, skills, and abilities rather than patronage or other influences.

The *merit principle* was to determine all personnel-related decisions. Those individuals best qualified would receive a job or a promotion based on their knowledge, skill, and abilities. Far from perfect, the federal merit system was thoroughly overhauled by the Civil Service Reform Act of 1978, and strong calls for further changes are being made today. But as a result of the Pendleton Act, the negative effects of patronage politics in national selection practices were mostly eliminated. **Neutral competence** became the primary criterion for obtaining a government job, and public servants are expected to perform their work competently and in a politically neutral manner.

neutral competence

The concept that public employees should perform their duties competently and without regard for political considerations.

During the period of national merit system reform, the state and local governments were also busy. New York was the first state to enact a merit system, in 1883, and Massachusetts followed its example in 1884. The first municipal merit system was established in Albany, New York, in 1884; Cook County (Chicago), Illinois, became the first county with a merit system, in 1895. (Ironically, both Albany and Cook County, Chicago, were later consumed once again by machine politics and spoils-ridden urban governance, a condition not entirely eradicated even today.)[16]

Most states and numerous local governments enacted merit-based civil service systems on their own. Congressional passage of the 1939 amendments to the Social Security Act of 1935 gave additional impetus to such systems. This legislation obligated the states to set up merit systems for employees in social service and employment security agencies, and departments that were at least partly funded by national grants-in-aid under the Social Security Act. Thus, all states were required to establish a merit system for a sizable segment (around 20 percent) of their workforce; most of them have in fact developed comprehensive systems that encompass almost all state employees. Common elements of these merit-based personnel systems include recruitment, selection, and promotion according to knowledge, skills, and ability; regular performance appraisals; and employee incentive systems.

Some merit systems work better than others. In a handful of states and localities, they are mere formalities around which a shadowy world of patronage, spoils, favoritism, and incompetence flourishes.[17] Such conditions came to public attention when terrorists at Boston's Logan airport boarded, hijacked, and ultimately crashed two commercial aircraft on 9/11. For years, gubernatorial patronage appointees with little or no experience in security or law enforcement had run Logan's security operations.[18]

Rigid personnel rules, a lack of training programs, and inadequate salaries continue to plague some jurisdictions. Political control over merit-system employees is limited because most cannot be fired without great difficulty, and many are rigidly protected by union contracts. However, there is a movement in some states to increase political control of public employees by hiring new employees on fixed-term contracts, with no guarantee of tenure in the job, and by expanding the number of positions "exempt" from merit system procedures.

STATE AND LOCAL ADVANCES

State and local governments are experimenting with recruitment and testing innovations, pay-for-performance plans and other incentive systems, participative management innovations, new performance-appraisal methods, and many other concepts. Virtually every state has reformed its civil service in some way.[19] General public dissatisfaction with government at all levels, combined with increasing needs for government to become more sophisticated and responsive to its clients, means that efforts to "reinvent" human resource management are certain to continue.

These reforms are designed to make the executive branch leaner and more responsive to the chief executive; to improve service efficiency and effectiveness; to shift the overarching focus to outputs and outcomes from inputs and processes; and, through decentralization of authority, to enhance flexibility for chief executives, agency heads, city managers, and other officials.[20] Old-style reformers have expressed grave concerns that political blows to the merit system in Georgia, Florida, and other states herald a return of patronage and favoritism in hiring, leading inevitably to a less qualified, politicized public service.[21]

These reformers remain dedicated to the principle of protecting the civil service from unnecessary and gratuitous interference by politicians with patronage considerations in mind. But new-wave reformers want to increase the capacity of government executives and political appointees to manage programs and people in their organizations and to achieve desired results.

MERIT SYSTEM CONTROVERSIES

As we shall see, state and local governments have been leaders in addressing controversial questions that involve merit-system principles and practices, including **representative bureaucracy** and **affirmative action**, sexual harassment, and public employee collective bargaining.

Representative Bureaucracy The concept of representative bureaucracy— which is related to another key concept, affirmative action—suggests that the structure of government employment should reflect major gender, racial, socioeconomic, religious, geographic, and related components in society. The assumptions behind this idea are that (1) bureaucrats have discretion; (2) a workforce representative of the values, points of view, and interests of the people it governs will be responsive to their special problems and concerns; and (3) a representative bureaucracy provides strong symbolic evidence of a government "of the people, by the people, and for the people." In some situations, representative bureaucracy has "active" dimensions through decisions that may favor a class of people, such as women and minorities.[22]

Women and minority public workers sometimes use their discretion to improve the treatment of, and outcomes for, minority clients. For instance, female employees tend to be more active in representing female child support recipients than male recipients.[23] Elected officials tend to advance the interests of those who most resemble them in gender and race.[24] Blacks are more likely to perceive police interactions as legitimate when African-American officers are present.[25] Black and white police officers tend to treat victims and suspects differently, according to their race.[26] And African-American local government administrators tend to be more supportive of governmental decisions that specifically serve the interests of the black community.[27] The symbolic, or "passive," aspects of representative bureaucracy are also important. A government that demonstrates the possibility of social and occupational mobility for all sorts of people gains legitimacy in the eyes of its citizens and expands the diversity of views taken into account in bureaucratic decisions.

A controversial question is how to *achieve* a representative workforce, particularly at the upper levels of government organizations, without sacrificing the merit principle. *Equal employment opportunity (EEO)*—the policy of prohibiting employment practices that discriminate for reasons of race, sex, color, religion, age, disability, or other factors not related to the job—is mandated by federal law. This policy has been the law for well over a century, yet progress was slow until affirmative action policies were adopted throughout government.

Affirmative action recognizes that equal opportunity has not been sufficient because employment discrimination against women, minorities, and the disabled persists. Governments must take proactive steps to hire and retain

LO 8.4

To be able to explain the challenges of representative bureaucracy and affirmative action, sexual harassment, and public employee unionization and collective bargaining.

representative bureaucracy

The concept that all major groups in society should participate proportionately in government work.

affirmative action

Special efforts to recruit, hire, and promote members of disadvantaged groups to eliminate the effects of past discrimination.

those categories of workers legally defined as "protected classes" who have suffered discrimination in the past. These measures may be adopted voluntarily, but they are required under certain conditions (such as a history of deliberate discrimination) specified by the U.S. Equal Employment Opportunity Commission (EEOC), the regulatory body created to enforce EEO and, in some instances, by the courts. The measures include goals, timetables, and other preferential selection and promotion devices intended to make the workforces of public and private organizations more representative of the racial, gender, and other characteristics of the available labor pool.

Under affirmative action, the absence of overt or intentional discrimination in employment may not be sufficient; organizations can implement preferential recruitment, hiring, and promotion schemes to redress existing imbalances. However, the legitimacy of affirmative action policies imposed on employers by the EEOC has been seriously questioned in a series of U.S. Supreme Court decisions and by state legislative actions and referendums.[28]

Obviously, affirmative action is highly controversial. Establishing specific numerical goals and timetables for hiring and promoting minorities does not necessarily correspond with selection or promotion of the best person for the job. In other words, affirmative action appears to conflict with the merit principle. It has also alienated many white males, who feel that they have become victims of "reverse discrimination."

Legal clashes among the federal courts, Congress, and the states and localities continue but have not produced an entirely coherent interpretation of affirmative action's legal standing. Two examples illustrate the complexity of the issues surrounding affirmative action policy. The first concerns the 1996 passage of Proposition 209 in California, which amended the state constitution by prohibiting race and gender consideration in contracting decisions and in hiring for state and local jobs. The initiative was approved by nearly 55 percent of the voters. However, a federal judge blocked enforcement on grounds that Proposition 209 was discriminatory and therefore unconstitutional. Judges for the Ninth Circuit Court of Appeals reinstated Proposition 209, an action that was affirmed by the Supreme Court in a 2014 decision upholding an identical Michigan law adopted through referendum. The Court's reasoning was that voters have the right and capability to decide such issues.[29] Seven other states have banned preferential treatment on the basis of race through similar actions. The second example of confusion and complexity involves a U.S. Supreme Court ruling concerning admissions procedures at the University of Michigan and the University of Texas. In a 2008 decision involving the University of Michigan law school, the Supreme Court held that higher education institutions have a "compelling interest" in enrolling a diverse student body.[30] The court stated that consideration of race to meet diversity goals was permissible only if improper admissions criteria were not employed, such as a numerical quota of African-American or Latino students.

After the court disallowed the University of Texas' use of race in the admissions process, Texas adopted a rule such that 10 percent of the top graduating high school seniors would be admitted automatically. This passed the Court's "strict scrutiny" test. But then the University went a step further by implementing a policy in which race was included as one factor in the admissions process for individuals not graduating in the top ten percent. The Court held that this was a step too far because it made race a 'defining factor . . . of his or her application, and sent the case back to the lower court for more careful consideration of the strict scrutiny standard.'[31]

Despite such confusion, substantial progress toward representative bureaucracy has been made, especially in recruiting and hiring protected-class individuals for entry-level positions. Indeed, African Americans are *over*-represented relative to their presence in the overall civilian labor force in most state governments. Latinos, however, have had much less success in gaining public jobs at all levels.[32] Granted, some minorities and women continue to bump against a "glass ceiling" as they try to penetrate the upper levels of state and local agencies,[33] as well as "glass walls" that restrict their access to certain agencies, departments, or occupations.[34] And women in public service, as in the private sector, continue to face barriers that most men do not, including work–life conflicts and biased perceptions by men.[35] But progress is being recorded even with respect to these barriers to representative bureaucracy; the number of female, African-American, and Latino professionals in state and local governments has grown dramatically in recent years.[36]

Indeed, state and local governments today widely recognize the need to recruit, motivate, and manage a workforce that reflects an increasingly diverse general population. EEO and affirmative action approaches have been recast as "diversity" policies.[37] Of course, when employees working together differ in terms of gender, color, religion, customs, and other key characteristics, misunderstandings and miscommunications are inevitable. The astute public manager helps employees recognize and accept such differences while leveraging the different experiences, perspectives, and knowledge of a diverse workforce to maintain and even raise levels of organizational productivity and effectiveness.[38]

Sexual Harassment Sexual harassment has long been a problem in public and private employment. Sexual harassment can consist of various behaviors: unwanted touching or other physical contact of a sexual nature, implicit or overt sexual propositions, or (in one of its worst forms) extortion of a subordinate by a supervisor who demands sexual favors in return for a promotion or a raise. A "hostile working environment" that pervasively discriminates on the basis of gender also constitutes sexual harassment.[39] Examples in this category include repeated—and unwelcome—leering, sexual joking or teasing, sexually inappropriate remarks, or lewd calendars or electronic communications at the workplace. Isolated incidents of sexual teasing or innuendo do not constitute sexual harassment; a pattern must be present. For instance, three female sheriff's detectives in King County, Washington, settled outside court for $1 million after showing that they had been subjected to repeated acts of sexual harassment and verbal abuse for years. One sergeant regularly boasted about his sexual prowess and exploits. Others ridiculed the detectives about their buttocks and breasts.[40]

Sexual harassment is illegal according to federal and state laws, and a form of punishable employee misconduct under civil service rules. It is also prosecuted in the courts. Surveys of women consistently find that at least half of the respondents report being a victim. Approximately 15 percent of men have experienced sexual harassment. Such behavior subverts the merit principle when personnel decisions such as hiring or promotion are influenced by illegal or discriminatory considerations of a sexual nature, or when an employee cannot perform his or her assigned duties effectively because of sexual harassment. Sexual harassment can exact a high price on organizational productivity, not to mention the cost of monetary settlements with victims. Unfortunately for the recipient of unwanted sexual attention, there are seldom any witnesses. The matter becomes one person's word against another's. And when one of the parties is the supervisor of the second party, a formal complaint may be decided in favor of the boss.

Much of the official activity aimed at stopping sexual harassment has been concentrated in the states, with local governments following suit. Michigan was the first to adopt a sexual harassment policy, in 1979; since then nearly every state has adopted a statewide policy through legislation or executive order. State and local governments offer employee-training programs that help workers and supervisors identify acts of sexual harassment, establish procedures for effectively addressing it, and enforce prompt, appropriate disciplinary action against offenders.

The consequences of sexual harassment go far beyond the personal discomfort, stress, or injury suffered by victims. The problem also results in significant financial costs to organizations whose employees lose productive work time. Such misconduct is unacceptable today in a national workforce that is almost 50 percent female.

Unions Nearly always controversial in government, *public-employee unions* present a potentially serious threat to the merit principle. They usually insist on seniority as the primary criterion in personnel decisions, often seek to effect changes in merit-system rules and procedures that benefit their membership, and regularly challenge management authority. Moreover, unions aggressively seek higher pay and benefits, threatening to drive up the costs of government and, in some instances, prompting tax increases.

Until the 1960s, unionization was largely a private-sector phenomenon. Federal legislation protected the rights of workers in industry to organize and engage in **collective bargaining** with their employers over wages, benefits, and working conditions. Workers then organized in record numbers. Unionization in state and local governments developed and flourished in the 1960s and 1970s, some thirty years after the heyday of private-sector unionism. Why the sudden growth? Several reasons are apparent.

First, the rise of unionism in government was spurred by the realization by state and local employees that they were underpaid and otherwise poorly treated in comparison with their counterparts in the private sector, who had progressed so well with unionization and collective bargaining. Second, the bureaucratic and impersonal nature of work in large government organizations encouraged unionization to preserve the dignity of the workers. A third reason for the rise of state and local unionism was the employees' lack of confidence in many civil service systems. Not only were pay and benefits inadequate, but grievance processes were controlled by management; employees had little or no say in setting personnel policies; and merit selection, promotion, and pay were often fraught with management favoritism.

collective bargaining

A formal arrangement in which representatives of labor and management negotiate wages, benefits, and working conditions.

Perhaps most important, the growth of unions in government was facilitated by a significant change in the legal environment. The rights of public employees to join unions and bargain collectively with management were guaranteed by several U.S. Supreme Court rulings, state legislation, local ordinances, and various informal arrangements that became operative during the 1960s and 1970s. Wisconsin was the first state, in 1959, to permit collective bargaining for state workers. Today, forty-one states specifically allow at least one category of state or local government employees to engage in collective bargaining.

The extent of unionization and collective bargaining is greatest in the states of the Midwest and Northeast—the same areas so fertile for the growth of private-sector unions. Traditionalistic states, including Mississippi, Arizona, Virginia, and the Carolinas, continue to resist the incursion of state and local unions (see Figure 8.4). Public employees in these jurisdictions have the legal and constitutional right to join a union, but their government employers do not have a corresponding duty to bargain with them over wages, benefits, or conditions of work.

Approximately 33 percent of state and 42 percent of local government workers are represented by unions, compared with only 6.6 percent of workers in private industry. The highest proportions of union workers are found in education, highway departments, public welfare, police and fire protection, and sanitation.[41]

The surge in the fortunes of state and local unions was partially arrested by the taxpayer revolt of the late 1970s and by President Ronald Reagan's successful effort to "bust" a federal air traffic controllers' union. Additional resistance to

FIGURE 8.4   **Public Employee Collective Bargaining Rights in the States**

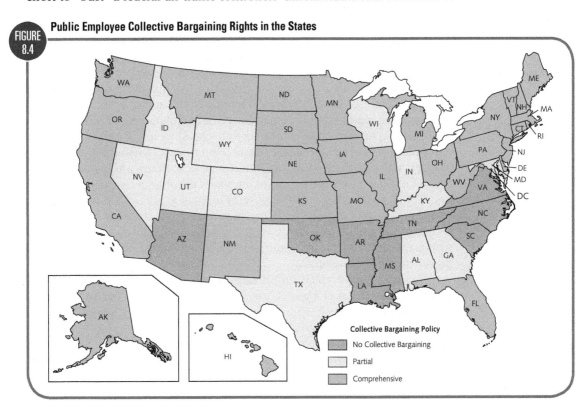

Collective Bargaining Policy
- No Collective Bargaining
- Partial
- Comprehensive

unions developed in the 1990s and has stiffened today as a determined crop of Republican governors and legislatures has taken control of traditionally union-friendly states such as Michigan and Wisconsin. In these and other states, unions have been stripped of collective bargaining rights and suffered cuts in pension, health care, and other benefits. Wisconsin governor Scott Walker declared that "we can no longer live in a society where the public employees are the haves and the taxpayers who foot the bill are the have nots."[42] In many states, budget balancing means extensive public employee layoffs which, in conjunction with voter anger, has weakened the unions both economically and politically. Despite these recent attacks, unions remain an important and highly visible component of many state and local governments.

What is the impact of collective bargaining in state and local governments? Market forces, such as profit levels and the supply and demand for labor, largely determine the outcomes of bargaining between a union and a firm in the private sector. In government, political factors are much more important. The technical process of negotiating over wages and other issues is very similar to that in business. But the setting makes government labor relations much more complex, mostly because the negotiating process culminates in the *political* allocation of *public* resources.

Four factors make government labor relations highly political. First, public officials are under greater pressure than private employers to settle labor disputes. Public services are highly visible and often monopolistic in nature; for example, there are no other convenient suppliers of police and fire protection. Accordingly, elected officials who confront a controversial labor dispute in an "essential service" may fear that negative developments will derail their opportunity for re-election.

Second, despite recent setbacks, public-employee unions continue to wield political clout. Their members can influence election outcomes, particularly at the local level. A recalcitrant mayor or city council member who opposes a generous union wage or benefit increase may suffer defeat at the polls in the next election if the municipal union members vote as a bloc. Unions actively engage in politics by raising money, writing letters to the editor about candidates, knocking on doors to get out the vote, endorsing candidates, or using any of the other electoral techniques employed by interest groups. Many unions have professional lobbyists to represent them at the state capitol or in city hall.

A third politicizing factor in government labor relations is the symbiotic relationship that can develop between unions and elected officials. In exchange for special consideration at the bargaining table and perhaps elsewhere, the unions can offer public officials two valued commodities: labor peace and electoral support.

Finally, a hard-pressed union can use the strike or a related job action (such as a slowdown or a picket line) as a political weapon. In the private sector, a strike is not likely to have widespread public repercussions unless it involves goods or services that the nation relies on for its economic well-being (such as air transportation, coal mining, or communications). In government, however, a strike can directly involve the health and safety of all the citizens of a jurisdiction. Striking workers shut down Minnesota state government for twenty days in 2011. A general strike involving police officers, firefighters, and sanitation workers has the potential to turn a city into filthy, life-threatening anarchy. At a minimum, any strike leaves the public inconvenienced.

Strikes and other job actions by public employees are illegal in most jurisdictions, although twelve states permit work stoppages by certain "nonessential" workers under strictly regulated conditions. Even where strikes are forbidden, teachers, health care workers, firefighters, and others sometimes walk off the job anyway. It is extremely rare for police or firefighters to strike today, and it is illegal everywhere. But parents angry about a teacher strike or commuters paralyzed by a transportation walkout have convinced many an elected official to seek prompt settlement of an impasse.

Given these politicizing factors, one might expect unions in government to be extravagantly successful at the bargaining table. Public-employee unions have raised wages and salaries an average of 4–8 percent, depending on the service, place, and time period under consideration (e.g., teachers earn around 5 percent more and firefighters around 8 percent more if represented by a union). These figures are much lower than the union-associated wage effects identified in the private sector, and the union advantage dissipated during and after the Great Recession. Greater success has come in the form of better benefits, particularly pensions and health care insurance, though these, too, have experienced significant reductions as a consequence of budget shortfalls and political assaults. It should be noted that union-driven wage and benefit hikes in the private sector are absorbed through profits, layoffs, or higher product prices. In government, by contrast, the choices are to raise taxes or fees, cut services, increase productivity, or contract out.[43]

Certain personnel impacts have also been associated with collective bargaining in government. Clearly, unions have gained a stronger employee voice in management decision making. All personnel-related issues are potentially negotiable, from employee selection and promotion procedures to retention in the event of a reduction in force. As a result of collective bargaining, many government employers have altered civil service rules, regulations, and procedures. In heavily unionized jurisdictions, two personnel systems coexist uncomfortably—the traditional merit-based civil service system and the collective bargaining system.[44] Certainly, the rights of public employees have been strengthened by unions, but in the view of critics, it damages the merit principle.

Generally speaking, governments and collective bargaining have reached an uneasy accommodation. The principle of merit in making personnel decisions is still largely in place, and it is usually supported by the unions as long as seniority is fully respected as an employment decision rule. However, political attacks on collective bargaining are likely to continue and even sharpen in the near future.

Garbage strike in Chicago produces ugly (and smelly) results.

LO 8.5

To explain the clash
of politics and
bureaucracy.

The Politics of Bureaucracy

In an ideal representative democracy, political officials popularly elected by the people would make all decisions regarding public policy. They would delegate to public administrators in the executive branch the duty of carrying out these decisions through the agencies of state and local governments. In the real world of bureaucratic politics, however, the line dividing politics (policy) and administration is anything but clear. Politicians frequently interfere in administrative matters, as when a legislator calls an agency head to task for not treating a constituent favorably. Administrators practice politics at the state capitol and in city hall by participating in and influencing policy formulation decisions.

JOINING ADMINISTRATION AND POLITICS

Bureaucrats are intimately involved in making public policy, from the design of legislation to its implementation. Government workers often plant and tend the seed bed for policy ideas that grow to become law, in large part because they are more familiar with agency, departmental, and clientele problems and prospective solutions than anyone else in government. It is not unusual, for instance, for law enforcement policy to originate with police administrators or highways policy to be the brainchild of transportation officials.

Passage of a bill usually "signal(s) not the end of the policy story, only the start of a new chapter."[45] State and local employees must interpret the language of the legislation to put it into effect. Because most legislation is written in general terms, civil servants must apply a great deal of **bureaucratic discretion** in planning and delivering services, making rules for service delivery, adjudicating cases and complaints, and otherwise managing the affairs of government. All states have legal systems for hearing and acting on disputes over agency rules and regulations, such as environmental permitting and determination of social service eligibility. These administrative procedures allow individuals, firms, and local governments to challenge agency rules and regulations before an administrative law judge, who issues an order settling the dispute.

In a very real sense, the ultimate success or failure of a public policy depends on the administrators and "street-level bureaucrats" who are responsible for its implementation.[46] Experienced legislators and chief executives understand this, and they bring relevant administrators into the legislative process at an early stage. The knowledge and expertise of these administrators are invaluable in developing an appropriate policy approach to a specific problem, and their cooperation is essential if a policy enacted into law is to be carried out as the lawmakers intend.

Thus, bureaucratic power derives from knowledge, expertise, information, and discretionary authority. It also comes from external sources of support for agency activities—that is, from the chief executive, legislators, and interest groups. Those who receive the benefits of government programs—the clientele, stakeholders, or customers—are also frequently organized into pressure groups. All government programs benefit some interest—agriculture policy for the farm community; tourism policy for the hotel and restaurant community;

bureaucratic
discretion

The ability of public
employees to make
decisions interpreting
law and administrative
regulations.

public assistance policy for the poor; education policy for parents, students, teachers, and administrators—and these **clientele groups** are often capable of exerting considerable influence in support of policies that benefit them. Their support is crucial for securing the resources necessary to develop and operate a successful government program. They serve as significant political assets to state agencies and municipal and county departments that are seeking new programs or additional funding from legislative and executive bodies and they can become fearsome political in-fighters when their program interests are threatened. Often, clientele and other concerned interest groups form ad hoc coalitions with relevant government agencies and legislative committees to dominate policy making and implementation in a particular policy field.

The problem of politics and administration, then, has two dimensions. First, elected officials have the duty of holding administrators responsible for their decisions and accountable to the public interest, as defined by the constitution and by statute. Second, political oversight and intrusion into administrative activities should be minimized so that administrative decisions and actions are grounded in objective rules and procedures—not in the politics of favoritism. For example, legislators have the duty of ensuring that decisions by a state department of environmental protection guard the public from the harmful effects of pollution while treating polluting companies fairly. Nevertheless, state representatives should not instruct agency employees to go easy on a favored business constituent. Most government agencies discharge their tasks competently and professionally, and therefore require little direct oversight. Occasionally, however, a rogue agency or department head may strike out in the wrong direction.

An example of the proper balance of politics and administration is in the attempt by legislators to influence public administrators. This typically occurs when elected officials or their staff members perform casework for constituents. Although the legislator may occasionally seek favorable treatment that borders on illegality, the bulk of legislative casework comprises responses to citizens' inquiries or complaints, or requests for clarification of administrative regulations or decisions. Such legislative casework is useful because it promotes both feedback on the delivery of services and helpful exchanges of information between elected officials and administrators. If inquiries determine bias or error in the means by which services are delivered, corrective actions can be taken.

In sum, state and local politics are intricately joined with administration. Public policy is made and implemented through the interaction of elected officials, interest groups, and public administrators. Nonetheless, the vast majority of administrative decisions are based on the neutral competence and professionalism of public employees. When the municipal transportation department must decide which streets to repave, for example, a formula is applied that takes into account factors such as the date of the last repaving, intensity of public usage, and the condition of the road.

This is not to say that such decisions are never made on the basis of political favoritism. Sometimes political pressures influence bureaucratic discretion. For example, a telephone inquiry from the mayor or city council member can advance the road-paving schedule in front of the house of a powerful constituent. On the whole, however, state and local services are provided in an unbiased fashion through applying professional norms and standards.

clientele groups
Groups that benefit from a specific government program, such as contractors and construction firms in state highway department spending programs.

LO 8.6

To describe new public management, its strategies, and its pros and cons

New Public Management

State and local government employment has burgeoned at a rate much faster than that of population growth. In Texas, for instance, the number of state workers jumped from 223,000 in 1990 to 347,601 in 2011. The total state and local payroll today in the Lone Star state exceeds $5.3 billion.[47] Explanations for this huge expansion in the size and costs of state governments are numerous, including federal mandates, expanding levels of services, partisan politics, and the power of incremental budgeting. The Great Recession (2008–2011), however, wreaked havoc on state budgets and resulted in significant reductions in state jobs through attrition and layoffs. Some of the larger jurisdictions experienced reductions of tens of thousands of workers.

Fueled by economic fires over the states and burning conservative criticism, taxpayer ire and criticism of government are high at all levels. Moreover, state and local employees find little public sympathy for their plight. New strategies are being tried in an effort to solve this perplexing puzzle for public administrators, particularly those intended to make government more productive, responsive, and efficient. But many agencies and departments suffer personnel and resource shortages that have produced service delivery backlogs in everything from restaurant inspections to crime lab testing.

A far-reaching approach to performance enhancement is called **New Public Management (NPM)**. It is a global movement, but in the United States, it is often associated with the widely read book *Reinventing Government*, by David Osborne and Ted Gaebler.[48] According to NPM proponents, governments today are preoccupied with rules, regulations, and hierarchy; their bureaucracies are bloated, inefficient, and altogether poorly suited for meeting the demands made on them. The solution is for governments to free up managers to tap their powers of entrepreneurship and market competition to design and provide efficient and effective services to state and local "customers." In short, governments should "steer, not row," by stressing a facilitative or cooperative approach to getting services to citizens rather than delivering all services directly. Governments should act as collaborators, catalysts, and partners with the objective of creating public value.[49] Among the alternative service-delivery systems are public-private partnerships, intergovernmental cooperation, volunteerism, and voucher plans. Once transformed, the governments would be enterprising, mission-driven, outcome oriented, focused on the needs of their customers, and prepared to "do more with less."

Among the formidable obstacles to such profound change in government activities and behavior are labor-intensive tasks such as teaching and policing that do not readily lend themselves to labor-saving technology; rule-bound civil service systems, which tend to discourage management and entrepreneurial risk taking; the inevitable inertia that plagues public organizations having no bottom line and few market-driven incentives; the difficulties of innovating in organizations created essentially to regulate; the need for politicians to buy into and support the movement, which implies greater autonomy and discretion for administrative agencies but more risks and more mistakes as well; and the certain opposition by powerful vested interests, such as public-employee unions, that feel threatened by change.

New Public Management

An administrative reform movement that argues government should manage for results, through entrepreneurial activity, privatization, and improvements in efficiency and effectiveness.

Undeterred by the carping critics and maligning malcontents, many state and local governments have adopted a reinventing attitude in tackling various problems. Principally, they have placed their bets on (1) alternative service delivery mechanisms and (2) e-government.

ALTERNATIVE SERVICE DELIVERY MECHANISMS

Three popular alternatives to traditional service delivery arrangements are intergovernmental cooperation, **coproduction**, and privatization.

Intergovernmental Cooperation Governments can compete, or they can cooperate. One common means of achieving efficiencies in service provision is coordination of services with neighboring jurisdictions.[50] Though intergovernmental cooperation in such areas as law enforcement, fire protection, and water and sewer service have long histories as shared services, cooperation is today being extended into new service functions.

A recent study found that 24 percent of local governments share some services with another jurisdiction. Common examples include ambulance and emergency management services, libraries, tax assessment, workforce development, and transit systems.[51]

Coproduction Traditionally, states and local governments have produced and delivered public services to citizens. But citizens themselves as well as other entities may also become partners in service delivery. In a traditional arrangement, for example, garbage is collected from residential containers by municipal government and taken to the landfill. When residents sort recyclables and cart them to a central municipal location, they are partnering—or coproducing—to reduce waste.[52] Both residents and public employees are involved. But if the recycling center is operated by a business under contract with the city, then a third party is involved in coproduction. As government has become more complicated and costly, coproduction of services has expanded at both the state and local levels. When a partnership entails a government contracting with a business to deliver a public service, such as building and operating a prison or toll bridge, for instance, coproduction has moved into the realm of privatization.

Privatization Privatization is service delivery through such arrangements as vouchers, franchises, public-private partnerships, and contracting out. It is an alternative that garners much support today, especially among conservatives, Republicans, and others who want to see a "businesslike" approach to government. Virtually any government service is a candidate for contracting out (outsourcing), from jails to janitorial work, from teaching to trash collection. Sandy Springs, Georgia, a wealthy suburb of Atlanta with 94,000 residents, contracts out everything except police, fire protection, and seven staff positions.[53] (In theory, most government facilities can even be sold to private interests and operated as businesses; airports and bridges are examples.) The purported benefits of privatization include cost savings, higher-quality services, the acquisition of highly specialized skills, and more efficient service

coproduction
Coproduction involves service delivery through combined efforts of government, citizens, nonprofits, and/or businesses.

delivery. It is a popular strategy for reducing service costs. To date, privatization has been used most frequently to outsource vehicle towing, solid waste collection, building maintenance and security, street repair, ambulance services, printing, information technology, human resource management tasks, and social welfare services.[54]

In choosing the privatization route to reinventing government, Massachusetts has contracted out mental health care, prison health care, various highway maintenance functions, and operations of interstate highway rest stops, among many other functions. Chicago outsources window washing, sewer cleaning, compost processing, and parking garages. Privately built and operated toll roads and bridges operate in a growing number of states. Indiana leased a toll road to a foreign consortium, raising $3.85 billion but when tolls were set at much higher levels, a sharp political backlash ensued.[55]

Privatization isn't as easy as it sounds, and it doesn't always generate savings.[56] It usually elicits virulent opposition from public-employee unions, who fear the loss of their jobs or reductions in pay and benefits. Unless governments carefully negotiate and then monitor the quality and effectiveness of privatized services, performance may decline and costs may actually rise. Contracts that are vaguely worded or filled with loopholes, and insufficient contract oversight on the part of some jurisdictions, have resulted in cost overruns, shoddy services, and fraud or corruption by the contractors. For instance, Indiana's $1.3 billion contract with IBM to administer state welfare services met with so many complaints and delays that Governor Mitch Daniel was forced to cancel the contract, but at a cost of $10 million in legal bills and a $52 million court judgment.[57]

Successful outsourcing requires not only careful government planning, design, and analysis of what the jurisdiction and its citizens need and want to have done, but also a recognition that government accountability cannot be negotiated. The state, county, or city must remember that ultimately *it* will be held accountable for long-term successful, reliable delivery of a service. If anything goes wrong, government officials—not the private provider—will be blamed and held responsible. Successful contract monitoring requires careful inspections; comprehensive "on-time" performance reports; and assiduous investigations of citizen complaints. In some instances, dissatisfaction with outsourcing arrangements has led jurisdictions to "insource" the service by returning it to government control.[58]

To keep contractors honest, some governments use multiple, competing firms, government agencies, or nonprofit organizations to deliver the same service to different state or local activities. In Phoenix, Arizona, for example, garbage workers compete head-to-head with private trash collection firms. Such collaboration among governments, nonprofit organizations, and private firms saved Indianapolis some $100 million in four years through negotiated arrangements in waste-water treatment, recycling, sewer billing, street sweeping, and many other services.[59]

Is privatization worthwhile? Local officials believe that outsourcing improves service delivery in most cases, and some research indicates that it saves cities and states up to about 20 percent for some service categories, but little or nothing for others. After all, firms must figure a profit margin into their costs, whereas government providers do not. And there are many notable failures of privatization, particularly those involving sweetheart deals, no-bid contracts, or inept contract administrators. Businesses are known to underestimate costs to win a contract, then submit "change orders" for "unanticipated costs," adding to the total price tag.[60] Privatization is not a cure-all for the problems besetting states and local governments, but it does represent one potentially useful alternative for delivering services.

E-GOVERNMENT AND SOCIAL MEDIA

E-government involves re-engineering the way various government activities are conducted and making the face of government more user-friendly. Some improvements are rather mundane and commonsensical, such as permitting online tax filing and renewal of licenses and registrations. To both improve government-citizen communications and to relieve pressure on overburdened 911 calls, Chicago, Denver, Charlotte, and many other cities have launched 311 apps, web chats, and Twitter for citizens to report service problems and communicate directly with city hall.

Other improvements run the gamut. Arizonians can vote in primary elections on the web and view live proceedings of the state legislature through their state's "digital democracy." Cities mount computer-coordinated attacks on crime that electronically track incidents and suspects, detect emerging crime patterns, and coordinate crime-fighting activities with other state and local jurisdictions. Many jurisdictions send mass alerts to their citizens on their smartphones, PCs, and cell phones. Facebook, LinkedIn, and other social media enable citizens to connect and interact with their governments in new, convenient, and timely ways. New York City tracks citizen posts on reported food-borne illnesses acquired from restaurants.

"Virtual offices" operating through the Internet are establishing convenient, 24/7 connections among citizens, businesses, nonprofit organizations, and their governments. Beyond e-government, which is mostly a one-way (asynchronous) flow of information, comes social media, which essentially features a two-way (synchronous) conversation between government and citizens. Despite great enthusiasm, various hurdles must be cleared for e-government and social media to function fully as intended: the substantial investments required to pay for the computer hardware, software, and trained personnel; staff expertise may be lacking; sticky, unresolved legal questions of liability, privacy, and security are troublesome; like all users, governments and their sensitive data are vulnerable to cyber attacks; it is difficult to integrate software across multiple agencies and departments; and, there exists a "data paradox": the explosion of data and information sometimes overwhelms public officials, rendering them unable to decide or act. Other problems have also appeared: the Controversies in States and Localities box presents some of them for your consideration. Nevertheless, the potential of e-government and social media to make government more accessible, understandable, and efficient is enormous.[61]

e-government
The use of information technology to simplify and improve interactions between governments and citizens, firms, public employees, and other entities.

The Quality of Public Administration

Despite the cascade of criticism and virulent vitriol hurled at government agencies, departments, and workers by the media, elected officials, and others, the quality of public administration in state and local governments has improved markedly. Of course, there is considerable variance among jurisdictions; that capacity generally is of a higher quality in affluent, highly educated, and urban jurisdictions.

Administrative quality is a critical factor in support of revitalization and responsiveness of states and localities. State and local governments, particularly through partnership with other governments and private and nonprofit organizations, have the capacity to accomplish more on a grander scale than ever before. The basics of providing services, from disposing of dead animals to delivering healthy human babies, will continue to depend on government employees with high standards of performance and professionalism. But adequate financial and human resources are required to make and keep state and local government what it should be: efficient, effective, responsive, and transparent.

Controversies in States and Localities

Social Media: Problematic or Panacea?

The advantages of social media for citizens and government are numerous and impressive. Problems, from potholes to crime, can be identified and resolved more quickly; the pulse of the people can be gauged through posts, tweets, chats, and other devices. Residents can be informed immediately about anything from traffic pileups to dangerous weather events. Perhaps most importantly, citizens can become directly engaged with their state or local government and feel more a part of it.

But problems with social media are legion. A balance between free speech rights and prohibited content must be maintained. Some postings are obscene, vulgar, inflammatory or personally insulting. Sometimes government officials and politicians shoot from the hip. When Washington state representative Joe Fitzgibbon tweeted after his Seattle Seahawks lost to the Arizona Cardinals, "Losing a football game sucks. Losing to a desert racist wasteland sucks a lot," he stirred up a "twit storm."[1]

Unintended consequences of social media sometimes appear. After the New York City police department created the hashtag #myNYPD, citizen critics began tweeting photos and videos of cops clubbing, tear gassing, and tackling citizens.[2]

The Wild West world of social media offers plenty of advantages for state and local governments, to be sure, but at a price some officials might not be willing to pay.

Critical Thinking Questions:

1. Where should a line be drawn between free speech and messages that should be censored or deleted? Who should decide—a committee? A single individual?

2. What social media policies might states and localities adopt to discourage or prevent unintended consequences, confusing messages, and unwise or potentially embarrassing messages from public officials?

References:

1. Jonathan Walters, "Governments Struggling to Get Social Media Right," www.governing.com (July 2014).

2. Jonathan Walters, "Lost in Translation," Governing (July 2014): 46–49.

Chapter Recap

- The quality and capacity of public administration have greatly improved in the majority of the states and local governments.

- State and local government employment has grown rapidly but declined during the Great Recession and its aftermath.

- State and local operating budgets must be balanced each year.

- Interest groups, agencies, the chief executive, and the legislative body are the four principal actors in the budgetary process.

- Budgets tend to expand (or contract) incrementally.

- The trend in accounting for revenues and expenditures is performance-based budgeting.

- Most state and local jobs are part of a merit system and are filled based on knowledge, skills, and experience, but there are challenges to traditional merit systems.

- Affirmative action led to gains in the advancement of minorities and women in state and local employment, but it is very controversial.

- Unions and collective bargaining present special challenges to many state and local governments.

- Bureaucratic discretion makes public employees important decision makers.

- New Public Management is aimed at reinventing government through privatization, e-government, coproduction, intergovernmental cooperation, and other steps.

KEY TERMS

bureaucracy *(p. 196)*
incrementalism *(p. 207)*
line item budget *(p. 207)*
performance budgeting
(p. 208)
capital budget *(p. 208)*

merit system *(p. 209)*
neutral competence *(p. 209)*
representative bureaucracy
(p. 211)
affirmative action *(p. 211)*
collective bargaining *(p. 214)*

bureaucratic discretion *(p. 218)*
clientele groups *(p. 219)*
New Public Management
(p. 220)
coproduction *(p. 221)*
e-government *(p. 223)*

INTERNET RESOURCES

All major municipalities and states have webpages. Many provide links to jobs, NPM, initiatives, service-provision information, and other data. Innovative, award-winning websites include Indianapolis's "Electronic City Hall" at **www.indygov.org**, Service Arizona at **http://servicearizona.com**, NC@YourService at **www.ncgov.com**, and AccessWashington at **www.access.wa.gov**.

An informative public-employee union website is AFSCME's at **www.afscme.org**.

An interesting site on technology, e-government, and social media is **www.govtech.net**.

To view streaming video of public meetings in Indiana, see **www.hoosier.net/cats**.

The Judiciary: Independence vs Accountability

A state trial court judge questions the prosecuting attorney
AP Images/Mel Evans

In the case of *Barnes v. Glen Theatre Inc.* (1991), a prudish U.S. Supreme Court ruled that nude dancing, being dangerous to "order and morality," is not protected as free expression under the First Amendment of the U.S. Constitution. This case, which arose in Indiana, was tried in the federal courts under national constitutional law. But in Ohio, strippers may freely cavort in their full birthday suits; patrons, however, are barred from touching the "naughty bits" at risk of six months in jail and a $1,000 fine.[1]

And in Boston, Massachusetts, a city once known for banning all manner of objects and activities deemed to be immoral, totally naked women grind, bump, and pirouette at tacky cabarets, fully confident that their activity is legal. In Massachusetts, the voluntary display of a naked body has been protected under the *state* constitution as a form of free expression since the state supreme court ruled it so in 1984.[2] In Texas, strip clubs are also permitted under the state constitution, but must pay a $5 "pole tax" to the state for each patron.[3]

State courts have become more open to individuals and groups advocating causes such as civil rights, free speech, and freedom of expression. All sorts of conflicts and problems find their way to state and local courts, from the profound (abortion rights) to the profane (nude dancing). Decisions of state courts have a weighty "impact on the overall distribution of wealth and power in the United States and on the daily well-being of the citizens."[4] Courts at this level are busy; 99 percent of the nation's cases are filed in state courts—approximately 100 million cases a year! New York State's cases alone outnumber those filed in all federal courts by a factor of 9 to 1. Many of the state courts are innovative in their decision making and administration; in addition, all are far more accessible to the people and responsive to their concerns than are the federal courts. Surveys show that Americans have greater confidence in their state courts than in the legislature or governor.[5]

As the third branch of government, the judiciary is the final authority on the meaning of laws and constitutions and the ultimate arbiter of disputes between the executive and legislative branches. It also makes public policy through rulings on questions of political, social, and economic significance and may serve as the last chance for minority interests to defend themselves from the decisions of the majority. As noted in Chapter 3, state courts have become more active policy makers in recent years and have increasingly based important decisions on state constitutions rather than on the national constitution. As with the other branches of state government, their structures and processes have been reformed and modernized. In our lifetimes, nearly all of us will personally experience the judicial branch as direct participants (juror, plaintiff, defendant, or witness). At times, the courts are more accessible to us than are the other branches of government. Disputes that cannot be resolved through ordinary legislative, executive, and political processes frequently wind up before a judge, as litigation.

The work of the fifty state court systems is divided into three major areas: civil, criminal, and administrative. In **civil cases**, one individual or corporation sues another over an alleged wrong. Occasionally, a governmental body is party to a civil action. Typical civil actions are divorces, property disputes, and suits for damages arising from automobile or other accidents. **Criminal cases** involve the breaking of a law by an individual or a corporation. The state is usually the plaintiff; the accused is the defendant. Murder, assault, embezzlement, disorderly conduct, and tax fraud are common examples. **Administrative cases** concern court actions such as probating wills, revoking driver's licenses, or determining custody of a child. Some administrative cases involve administrative law judges and quasi-judicial (less formal) proceedings. A government entity is usually a party to an administrative case.

LO 9.1

To understand what state courts do, their position within the federal system, and the types of law they address

civil case
A case that concerns a dispute involving individuals or organizations.

criminal case
A case brought by the state against persons accused of violating a law.

administrative case
Usually, a case in which a government agency applies rules to settle a legal dispute.

State courts adjudicate (resolve disputes and administer justice) by interpreting state statutes, the state and federal constitutions, and **common law**. In developing and deciphering the common law, courts are concerned with the legal rules and expectations that have developed historically through the citizens' custom, culture, and habits, and that have been given standing through the courts' decisions rather than from statutes. The most important applications of common law today concern enforcing contracts (contract law), owning and selling property (property law), and establishing liability for death or injuries to people, as well as damage to property (tort law).

The Structure of State Court Systems

State courts have evolved in response to changes in their environment. In colonial days, they developed distinctively, influenced by local customs and beliefs. Because of a shortage of trained lawyers and an abiding distrust of English law, the first judges were laymen who served on a part-time basis. It did not take long for the courts to become overwhelmed with cases: case overloads were reported as long ago as 1685.[6] More than three centuries later, case backlogs still plague our state judiciaries.

We are a litigious people. As the population and the economy grew, so did the amount of litigation. Courts expanded in number and in degree of specialization. However, their development was not carefully planned. Rather, new courts were added to existing structures. The results were predictably complex and confusing, with overlapping, independent jurisdictions and responsibilities. For instance, Chicago offered an astounding array of jurisdictions, estimated at one time to number 556.[7] State court systems were beset as well by a host of other serious problems, including underfunding, administrative inefficiency, congestion, and excessive delays. In short, the American system of justice left much to be desired.

The organization of the state courts is important because it affects the quality and pace of judicial decisions and the access of individuals and groups to the legal system. It also influences how legal decisions are made. An efficiently organized system, properly staffed and administered, can do a better job of deciding a larger number of cases than a poorly organized system can. Court structure is of great interest to those who make their living in the halls of justice—lawyers, judges, and court staff. It is also an issue of concern to citizens who find themselves in court.

LO 9.2

To understand that state courts are organized into two tiers.

THE TWO TIERS OF COURTS

Most states today have a two-tiered court structure: trial courts and appellate courts. There are two types of trial courts: those of limited jurisdiction and major trial courts. Each tier, or level, has a different *jurisdiction*, or range of authority. *Original* jurisdiction gives courts the power to hear certain types of cases first, in contrast to *appellate* jurisdiction, which grants the courts the power to review cases on appeal after they have been tried elsewhere. Trial courts, which comprise the lower tier, include (1) minor courts of limited jurisdiction and (2) major trial courts of general jurisdiction.

common law

Unwritten law based on tradition, custom, or court decisions.

Limited jurisdiction trial courts, also known as special trial courts, handle minor, specialized cases, such as those involving juveniles, traffic offenses, and small claims. Most states have several courts of limited jurisdiction, with names that reflect the type of specialized case: traffic court, police court, probate court, municipal court, and so on. Criminal cases here are usually restricted by law to misdemeanor violations of municipal or county ordinances that are punishable by a small fine, a short jail term, or both. Additional courts of limited jurisdiction, sometimes called "boutique" or "problem-solving" courts, have been created to deal with special types of cases or circumstances. For example, all states have created drug courts, with the dual aims of processing drug-related offenses more efficiently and reducing the recidivism rates of drug offenders on probation or parole. Domestic violence and mental health courts are common as well. "Water courts" in Colorado and Montana hear disputes over water rights. Illinois, Texas, Colorado, and other states have created special "veterans courts" to hear minor offenses charged against Iraq and Afghanistan war vets who have had scrapes with the law. In San Francisco, "neighborhood courts" grant individuals charged with minor offenses the option of accepting "restorative justice" in exchange for having their record expunged. For instance, a graffiti "artist" might be required to clean up his artwork and apologize at a neighborhood meeting.[8]

Present in almost all states are *small claims courts*, which offer a relatively simple and inexpensive way to settle minor civil disputes without either party having to incur the financial and temporal burdens of lawyers and legal procedures. Small claims courts are usually divisions of county, city, or district trial courts. In cases they hear, the plaintiff (the person bringing the suit) asks for monetary recompense from the defendant (the individual or firm being sued) for some harm or damage. Claims are limited to varying amounts, usually around $1,000. The proceedings are informal. Each party presents to a judge the relevant facts and arguments to support his side. The party with the preponderance of evidence on his or her side wins. Most disputes involve tenant-landlord conflicts, property damage, or the purchase of goods (e.g., shoddy merchandise or the failure of a customer to pay a bill).

The plaintiff usually wins in small claims court. About half the time, defendants do not show up to plead their case and thereby lose by default. In contested cases, plaintiffs win around 80 percent of the time. Unfortunately for the plaintiff, winning a case is often easier than collecting from the defendant. It's the plaintiff's responsibility to get written court permission to extract the amount due from the debtor's wages, bank account, or other assets, and to retain the local sheriff or constable to deliver and enforce the court order.

The second type of trial court is the **major trial court**, which exercises general authority over civil and criminal cases. Most cases are filed initially under a major trial court's original jurisdiction. However, trial courts also hear cases on appeal from courts of limited jurisdiction. Major trial courts are often organized along county or district lines. Their names (circuit courts, superior courts, district courts, courts of common pleas) vary by state.

limited jurisdiction trial courts
Those courts with original jurisdiction over specialized cases such as juvenile offenses or traffic violations.

major trial court
Court of general jurisdiction that handles major criminal and civil cases.

The upper tier of the two-tiered state court system consists of appellate courts: **supreme courts** (sometimes called "courts of last resort") and, in most states, **intermediate appellate courts**. Oklahoma and Texas have two supreme courts: one for criminal cases and the other for civil disputes. Forty states have intermediate appellate courts. Alabama, Oklahoma, Oregon, Texas, Pennsylvania, and Tennessee have two, typically one each for criminal and civil cases. Most intermediate appellate courts are known as courts of appeals. Their work generally involves cases on appeal from lower courts. Thus, these courts exercise appellate jurisdiction by reviewing a trial court's interpretation and application of the law. By contrast, state supreme courts have original jurisdiction in certain types of cases, such as those dealing with constitutional issues, as well as appellate jurisdiction.

Intermediate appellate courts represent an important element in the landscape of state courts. They are intended to increase the capability of supreme courts by reducing their caseload burden, speeding up the appellate process, and improving the quality of judicial decision making. The weight of the evidence points to moderate success in achieving each of these objectives. Appellate case backlogs and delays have been somewhat reduced, and supreme court justices are better able to spend an appropriate amount of time on significant cases. Counteracting this positive trend, however, is the growing number of mandatory appeals, such as for death penalty cases, which can make up more than 60 percent of the caseload.

If a state supreme court so chooses, it can have the final word on any state or local case except one involving a federal constitutional question. Some cases can be filed in either federal or state court. For example, a person who assaults and abducts a victim and then transports her across a state line can be charged in state court with assault and in federal court with kidnapping. Some acts violate nearly identical federal and state laws; possession or sale of certain illegal drugs is a common example. Other cases fall entirely under federal court jurisdiction, such as those involving treason, mail theft, or currency law violation.

Thus, there exists a *dual system* of courts that is sometimes referred to as *judicial federalism*. Generally, state courts adjudicate, or decide, matters of state law, whereas federal courts deal with federal law. The systems are separate and distinct. In some instances, however, there is jurisdictional overlap and even competition for a case. Following the April 15, 2013 Boston Marathon bombings, one of the suspects, Tamerlan Tsarnaev, was killed, and his brother Dzhokhar was arrested. The State of Massachusetts first sought jurisdiction over the case, but because this was an act of terrorism, the U.S. Department of Justice brought the multiple murder case to trial first (three victims were killed in the bombings). A much more complicated case involved the "Beltway Snipers," who killed people in Virginia, Maryland, and the District of Columbia. All sought to bring the case to trial first. (Virginia was given the honor of first prosecution.)

Although state courts cannot overturn federal law, they can base certain rulings on the federal constitution. Recently, state courts have decided cases governed by both state and federal laws in hate crimes, freedom of speech,

supreme court
The highest state court, beyond which there is no appeal except in cases involving federal law.

intermediate appellate court
A state appellate court that relieves the case burden on the supreme court by hearing certain types of appeals.

the right to die, and gay rights. It is very unusual for a case decided by a state supreme court to be heard by the U.S. Supreme Court or any other federal court. Even if such a review is done, the U.S. Supreme Court usually upholds the state high court decision. Exceptions do occur. Though Alabama's and other states' supreme courts upheld bans on gay marriage, federal courts have overridden them.

STRUCTURAL REFORMS

LO 9.3

To describe how structural reforms have been implemented to to make the courts more effective.

Although the two tiers of state courts appear to represent a hierarchy, in fact they do not. Courts in most states operate with a certain degree of autonomy. They have their own budgets, hire their own staff, and use their own procedures. The decisions of major and specialized trial courts usually stand unchallenged. Only a fraction of lower-court cases are appealed, mainly because great expense and years of waiting are certain to be involved.

Unified court systems consolidate the various trial courts with overlapping jurisdictions into a single administrative unit and clearly specify each court's purpose and jurisdiction. The aim of this arrangement, which includes centralized management and rulemaking, is to make the work of the courts more efficient, saving time and money and avoiding confusion. Instead of a system whereby each judge runs his or her own fiefdom, such responsibilities as rulemaking, recordkeeping, budgeting, and personnel management are standardized and centralized, usually under the authority of the state supreme court or the chief justice.

Centralization relieves judges from some of the mundane tasks of day-to-day court management so that they can concentrate on adjudication. Additional efficiencies are gained from *offices of court administration*. Court administration involves actively managing, monitoring, and planning the courts' resources and operations. Information technology is enabling tremendous improvements in the way the courts manage criminal cases. Courts are moving to paperless systems in which documents are submitted, disseminated, and stored electronically. Judges and attorneys download case information on their laptops.[9]

Responsiveness to the public is also growing. An increasing number of state courts are electronically disseminating court documents to reporters and the public; judicial rulings; speed and efficiency measures; and general information such as instructions for jury duty, maps showing directions to the courthouse, and answers to commonly asked questions about the courts. Some display photographs and biographies of judges, many permit interested citizens to ask questions via e-mail, and others even provide performance evaluations of judges and broadcast cases live over the Internet. (See Internet Resources at the end of this chapter.)

Despite consolidation and centralization, court structures and processes continue to vary widely among the states, as shown in Figure 9.1. Generally, the most modern systems are found in the "newer" states, including Alaska and Hawaii, whereas some of the most antiquated are situated in southern states, among them Arkansas and Georgia.

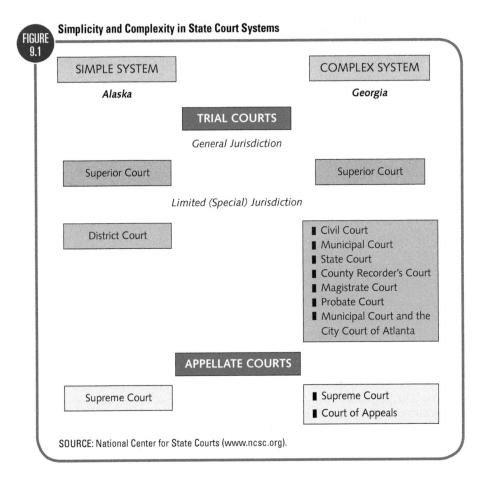

FIGURE 9.1

Simplicity and Complexity in State Court Systems

SOURCE: National Center for State Courts (www.ncsc.org).

How Judges Are Selected

LO 9.4

To compare and contrast the five methods for selecting judges.

The quality of a state court system depends heavily on the selection of competent, well-trained, impartial judges. According to the American Bar Association (ABA), the leading professional organization for lawyers, judges should be chosen on the basis of solid professional and personal qualifications, regardless of their political views and party identification. Judges should have "superior self-discipline, moral courage, and sound judgment."[10] They should be good listeners. They should be broadly educated and professionally qualified as lawyers (though Arizona, New Mexico, New York, Texas, and Utah have a large number of non–law-degreed judges[11]). An appellate or general trial court judge should also have relevant experience in a lower court or as a courtroom attorney.

Since the founding of the nation itself, controversy has swirled around the selection of state judges. Should they be elected by popular vote? Should they be appointed by the governor? By the legislature? Some critics insist that judicial selection be free from politics and interest group influences, so that judges act independently. Others claim that judges should regularly be held accountable to a majority of the voters or to elected officials for their decisions.[12]

The historic conflict between judicial independence and accountability is manifest in the five types of selection systems used in the states: legislative election, partisan popular election, nonpartisan popular election, the merit plan, and gubernatorial appointment. Most states use a single selection system for all appellate and major trial court judges. The others take separate approaches to selecting judges, depending on the tier. Figure 9.2 shows the presence of these selection techniques for appellate and major trial courts. Some states have rather elaborate systems that defy simple categorization

LEGISLATIVE ELECTION

In South Carolina and Virginia, the legislature elects judges by majority vote from among announced candidates. (In South Carolina, the candidates must first clear an election commission.) Not surprisingly, a large majority of judges selected under this plan have been former legislators (in South Carolina, the proportion once approached 100 percent).[13] In these two states, a judgeship is viewed as a highly valued reward for public service and a prestigious cap to a legislative career.

Few people other than legislators approve of legislative election. The public has no role in either choosing judges or re-electing them, so democratic accountability is minimal. The judges may be independent, but because the major criterion for selection is service as a legislator, they often lack other qualifications. Prior legislative service has little connection to the demands of a judgeship.

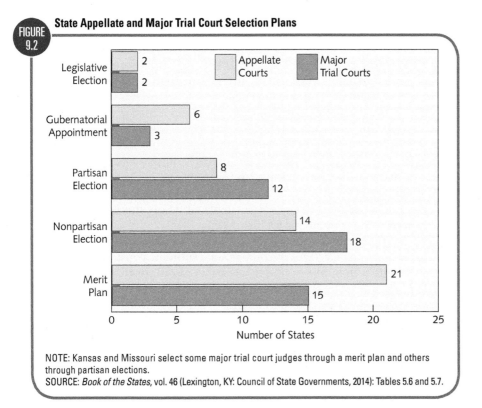

FIGURE 9.2

State Appellate and Major Trial Court Selection Plans

NOTE: Kansas and Missouri select some major trial court judges through a merit plan and others through partisan elections.
SOURCE: *Book of the States*, vol. 46 (Lexington, KY: Council of State Governments, 2014): Tables 5.6 and 5.7.

POPULAR ELECTION

Judges on one or more courts face elections in thirty-eight states. Some are listed on the ballot by party identification; others are not. In theory, elections maximize the value of judicial accountability to the people. Judges must run for office on the same ticket as candidates for other state offices. Like other candidates, they must raise and spend money for their election campaigns and deal publicly with political issues.

Partisan Popular Election This plan enjoyed widespread popularity during the Jacksonian era as a way to create a judiciary answerable to the voters. Most of the partisan election states are located in the South. In theory, partisan elections maximize the value of judicial accountability to the voters.

Nonpartisan Popular Election This plan won favor during the first half of the twentieth century, when reformers sought to eliminate party identification in the election of judges and certain other officials in state and local government. Political parties are prohibited from openly taking sides in nonpartisan judicial elections. In reality, they play a covert role in such contests. The vast majority of judges have a political party preference. Most list it in their official biographies that are available to interested voters during campaigns. A disadvantage of nonpartisan elections is that they tend to depress voter participation because incumbent judges are less likely to be challenged; another is that party identification is an important voting cue for many citizens.

The Problems with Popular Elections It is worth observing that electing judges is virtually unknown in the rest of the world, where they are appointed or selected through merit systems. Voter turnout is very low in most judicial elections, whether partisan or nonpartisan. This fact is a major criticism of both methods of electing judges: The winners may not be truly accountable to the people, which is the principal advantage commonly associated with elections. Low rates of voter interest and participation frequently combine with low-key, unexciting, and issueless campaigns to keep many incumbent judges on the bench as long as they run for re-election. One study indicates that fewer than 10 percent are defeated.[14] Still, this is comparable to state legislative races involving an incumbent.

Judicial independence is a problem. Recent research suggests that even nonpartisan judicial elections encourage state supreme court justices to align their decisions with public opinion.[15] Research also finds that a state electorate can be mobilized by engaging candidates, distressing events, controversial issues, or cases with emotional content.[16] On controversial issues, judges today seem increasingly vulnerable, particularly in partisan election states in which the voters' views on crime and punishment are harsher than those of the incumbent judge.[17] Taken together, these research findings indicate that judicial races tend to elevate judicial accountability over independence.

Two problems have become increasingly troublesome: the politicization of judicial races and the creeping realization that campaign donations influence decisions from the bench.[18] The ABA Code of Judicial Conduct forbids judicial campaigning on legal issues, but this prohibition is increasingly ignored in close contests and in elections in which crime-related concerns, such as the death penalty or an accused murderer freed on a legal technicality, claim voters' attention. Moreover, federal courts have ruled that judicial campaigning is protected speech. As in other electoral contests, negative campaigning is on the rise in judicial elections. Judicial candidates energetically sling mud at their opponents for allegedly letting drug abusers free, being corrupt, sympathizing with terrorists, and acting soft on crime. Several states have tried to restrict aggressive judicial politicking through ethics rules and other limitations. When challenged in federal or state courts, however, such restrictions are usually overturned as intrusions on the candidates' First Amendment rights to free speech.[19]

Even more serious is the problem that occurs when judges elected on a partisan ballot are accused of pandering to special interests during election campaigns and paying back campaign support through favorable court decisions. In Texas, for instance, supreme court justices deciding a $10.5 billion judgment against Texaco in favor of Pennzoil were criticized for accepting huge campaign contributions from both companies.

In some recent Ohio Supreme Court decisions, all seven judges accepted money from lawyers for the plaintiffs or defendants.[20] Nonpartisan elected judges have been open to similar charges, especially because political action committees (PACs) have boosted their contributions to candidates for state court judgeships. Research has found systematic empirical evidence that judicial decisions have followed dollars. Similar conclusions have been drawn from case study research on judicial decision making in Alabama, Ohio, West Virginia, and Georgia.[21] Elected judges themselves are troubled by the role of money in judicial elections. As an Ohio supreme court justice recently remarked, "I never felt so much like a hooker down by the bus station … as I did in a judicial race."[22]

In addition, popular elections are criticized for the growing amount of money necessary to win a state judgeship. As in other political contests, money talks: The candidate who spends the most is likely to win the election.[23] The implication is that judges have sacrificed their independence and professionalism for crass electoral politics. Following the trend set in executive and legislative contests, special interest groups spent a record $15.4 million in 2011–2012 state supreme court campaigns and political parties invested another $24.1 million. Total spending in that election cycle was an estimated $56.4 million, with the majority of it on TV advertising.[24] Seven of the top ten spenders were conservative groups, some running negative TV spots alleging candidates were "sympathetic to rapists," protective of sexual predators, and other such claims.[25]

The largest campaign contributors are usually trial lawyers, corporations, corporate attorneys, and other groups with an interest in judges' decisions, such as labor unions; business interests desiring to limit the amount of jury awards through tort reform; the U.S. Chamber of Commerce; and various professions, such as insurance or medicine.[26] In some states, attorneys complain that judges "shake them down" for campaign contributions. A supreme court incumbent was brought down in West Virginia largely through the efforts of a corporate CEO who had a lawsuit pending before the court. In "a race noted for money and malice,"[27] the CEO provided some $2.3 million to the incumbent's "friendlier" opponent. The CEO in question, Don Blankenship of Massey Energy, had shamelessly vacationed in Monte Carlo with one sitting justice whom he favored in the election while the case was under appeal.[28]

It looks as though judges running for election are forfeiting their independence in certain legal disputes while offering accountability only to the highest bidders instead of to the general public. A very high percentage (87 percent) believe that campaign dollars influence judicial decisions "a great deal," according to a recent survey.[29] If justice is indeed for sale or rent, this is highly disturbing; neither independence nor accountability is achieved, and faith in the legal system is being eroded. According to the president of the Ohio State Bar Association, "The people with money to spend who are affected by court decisions have reached the conclusion that it's a lot cheaper to buy a judge than a governor or an entire legislature, and he can probably do a lot more for you."[30] This sentiment is supported by research showing a positive correlation between campaign contributions and judges' decisions.[31]

If it is unethical for a judge to rule on a case in which he or she has accepted money from one or more of the interested parties, then it would be difficult to bring together enough judges to hear cases in some election states. Increasingly, the general sentiment is that judges should be both qualified and dignified and that elections do not further either objective. In 2011, Wisconsin joined New Mexico to launch public financing for judges' campaigns to help contain spiraling costs. Other states are imposing restrictions and penalties for false campaign advertising, but all such actions are seriously threatened by the U.S. Supreme Court's *Citizens United* decision on free speech, noted above.[32] However, the U.S. Supreme Court ruled, in an important 2009 case involving the West Virginia saga mentioned earlier, that justices must recuse or disqualify themselves from ruling on cases in which interested or involved campaign donors have spent large sums of money.[33] All too often, they do not do so.

MERIT PLAN

Dissatisfaction with other methods for selecting judges has led to the popularity of the so-called *merit plan*. Incorporating elements of gubernatorial appointment and elective systems, the merit plan attempts to provide a mechanism for appointing qualified candidates to the bench while permitting the public to evaluate a judge's performance through the ballot box.

Strongly supported today by almost the entire legal community, the merit plan has been adopted by nearly all of the states that have changed their selection systems. Missouri became the initial adopter in 1940. Another twenty states have adopted the merit plan, and others are considering it.

Three Steps Commonly referred to as the Missouri plan, the basic merit plan involves three steps:

1. A judicial nominating commission meets and recommends three or more names of prospective judges to the governor. Members of this bipartisan

commission usually include a sitting judge (often the chief justice), representatives chosen by the state bar association, and laypersons appointed by the governor. The nominating commission solicits names of candidates, investigates their records, chooses those it believes to be the best-qualified individuals, and then forwards three or more names and their files to the governor.

2. The governor appoints the preferred candidate to the vacant judgeship.
3. A retention election is held, usually after one or two years, in which the newly appointed judge's name is placed before the voters on a nonpartisan, noncompetitive ticket. The voters decide whether the judge should be retained in office. If she is rejected by a majority vote, the judicial nominating commission begins its work anew. Subsequent retention elections are held every eight or twelve years, depending on the merit plan's provision.

Various hybrids of the basic plan are also in use. For example, California's plan for choosing appellate judges begins when the governor identifies a candidate for a vacancy on the bench and sends that person's name to the Commission on Judicial Appointments. The commission, composed of two judges and the attorney general, hears testimony regarding the nominee and votes to confirm or reject. The new judge is then accepted or rejected in a retention election in the next regularly scheduled gubernatorial contest. Thus, although the governor appoints, the new judge is subject to confirmation by both the Commission on Judicial Appointments and the voters. In New Mexico's multistage merit plan, a judge is nominated by a commission and appointed by the governor. During the next general election, the judge must run in a partisan election. If he wins, he then runs unopposed in a nonpartisan retention election on the next general election ballot.

The object of the merit plan is to permit the governor some appointive discretion while removing politics from the selection of judges. If it works as intended, election or direct gubernatorial appointment is replaced with a careful appraisal of candidates' professional qualifications by an objective commission. The process is intended to ensure both the basic independence of judges and their accountability to the people.

The Politics of Merit Selection The merit plan looks great on paper, but in practice it has not fulfilled its promise. First, it has not dislodged politics from judicial selection. A judgeship is too important a political office in any state ever to be immune from politics. It is a prized job and an important point of judicial access for numerous individuals, firms, and interest groups, especially the powerful state bar association.

Politics—partisan or nonpartisan—are rampant in the judicial nominating commission's review and selection of candidates. For better or worse, the legal profession often dominates the process. Counting the judge who presides over the nominating commission, lawyers make up a majority of the commission in most of the states. Bar association lobbying is often the prime reason that merit plans are adopted in the first place. However, the legal profession is not monolithic in its politics: It is often divided into two camps—plaintiff's attorneys and defendant's attorneys.

Furthermore, the governor's influence can be exceptionally strong. The laypersons he appoints to the nominating commission are there to represent the governor's point of view and sometimes to promote specific candidates or the agenda of the governor's political party. In six states, the majority of commission members are laypersons. The member who is a judge may also respect the governor's preferences, particularly if the judge owes her appointment to that chief executive.

A second criticism of the merit plan is that the procedure intended to ensure judicial accountability to the people—the retention election—rarely generates voter interest and seldom results in the departure of an incumbent judge from office. Turnout in retention elections is normally very low and, on average, favors the incumbent by more than 70 percent.[34] Few incumbent judges have been voted out in retention elections. In most cases, merit selection means a lifetime appointment.

Voter backlashes, however, do occur against judges whose decisions are distinctly out of step with public opinion. In 1986, California Chief Justice Rose Bird and two associate justices were swept from the state supreme court by large margins in retention elections, as voters reacted negatively to a series of supreme court rulings that significantly expanded the rights of the accused and of convicted felons. Bird had voted to overturn all sixty-one capital-punishment cases brought to the court during a period when polls showed 80 percent of the public supported the death penalty in California.[35] Ten years later, Tennessee Supreme Court Justice Penny White was rejected in a retention election for failing to support the death penalty for the perpetrator of a particularly heinous crime.[36] In 2010, Iowa voters tossed out of office three supreme court justices for a ruling that a state gay marriage ban violated the state constitution's equal protection guarantee. Increasingly, campaigns to oust justices are spearheaded by Tea Party and conservative groups who pour money into attack ads against "liberal justices." But recent national efforts to remove three Tennessee supreme court judges, two judges in Kansas, and three justices in Florida failed.[37]

The final charge leveled against the merit plan is that despite reformers' claims to the contrary, it does not result in the appointment of better-qualified judges or of more women and minorities. When background, education, experience, and decision making are taken into account, judges selected through the merit plan are comparable with those selected through other plans. A large majority are white males. Most leave private practice for the bench and stay there until retirement. And a substantial majority were born, raised, and educated in the state in which they serve.

GUBERNATORIAL APPOINTMENT

All but one gubernatorial appointment states are former colonies, reflecting the early popularity of the plan. As a method per se, gubernatorial appointment rates fairly high on independence because the judge is directly appointed without an election, but it is weak on accountability because the judge is beholden to only one person for his or her job.

Although only a handful of states formally recognize it, gubernatorial appointment is in fact the most common method for selecting a majority of appellate and major trial court judges in the United States. Judges in states with popular elections or merit plans often resign or retire from office just before the end of their term.[38] Under most state legal systems, the governor has the power to make interim appointments to vacant seats until the next scheduled election or the commencement of merit-plan selection processes. The governor's temporary appointee then enjoys the tremendous advantage of running as an incumbent for the next full term. Gubernatorial appointment is also used to replace a judge who dies before the expiration of the term.

What criteria does a governor apply in making appointments to the bench? Political considerations usually come first. The governor can use the appointment to reward a faithful legislator, shore up support in certain regions of the state, satisfy the demands of party leaders and the state legal establishment, or appeal to women's groups or to minority groups.[39]

WHICH SELECTION PLAN IS BEST?

Endless debate endures over which selection plan among the five formal selection systems best achieves a healthy balance of (1) judicial independence from interest groups, attorney organizations, the next election, and other influences and (2) accountability to the people. It is unlikely ever to be settled. Legislative election and gubernatorial appointment probably maximize the value of independence, but may be the least desirable because judges selected under these systems tend to come from a rather specific political occupation (the legislature), and the general public has little opportunity to hold them accountable. Judicial accountability is maximized when judges and judicial candidates must face voters, but few incumbents are defeated in elections. (Perhaps the vast majority of sitting judges are capable and competent.) As noted above, however, significant policy issues involving the courts and aggressive campaign spending can rouse the voters to the polls in certain instances, meaning that elected judges who want to stay on the bench must pay attention to public opinion.[40]

None of the prevalent selection systems produces "better" judges, although gubernatorial appointment is more likely to benefit women than the other selection systems are.[41] And minorities have not done particularly well under any selection plan. African Americans fill about 8 percent of state court seats and Latinos 4 percent.[42] Gubernatorial appointments and nonpartisan elections apparently increase the selection opportunities for minority judges, but larger gains probably await development of a larger pool of minority attorneys.

Politics, of course, is what raises all judges to the bench, regardless of the selection method. According to research by political scientists, what matters is the path a judge takes to the bench. Those chosen through elective systems tend to view the judiciary in more political—as opposed to juridical—terms than those who reach the bench through gubernatorial or merit appointment systems. Elected judges also tend to be more activist in their decision making and more attentive to voter concerns close to election time, and they are more likely to dissent from other judges in their opinions than are appointed judges.[43] Judges who vote to overturn a popular state law are also vulnerable. Voter preferences carry extra weight in a judge's decision making when facing

LO 9.5

To perceive the tradeoffs between judicial independence and accountability

? It's Your Turn

Judges: Elected, Appointed, or Merit-Selected?

Select a state—any one except the state in which you currently reside. Determine how judges are selected for the appellate and trial courts. Based on what you have read in this chapter and other materials you can access, answer the following questions:

1. What are the pros and cons of the judicial selection process in the state you have chosen?
2. Is this the "best" or most appropriate system for this particular state? Why or why not?

competitive elections, particularly with respect to issues of criminal justice, same-sex marriage, and abortion rights.[44] Those in merit-plan states have less to fear from an angry electorate; they can be guided more by personal ideological preferences and their interpretation of the law.

In other words, judges who attain their jobs through electoral politics tend to behave similarly as other elected state officials by emphasizing political, rather than legal, factors in their decision making.[45] The irony is that voters prefer to elect their judges, but they believe that campaign spending influences what judges decide in court. The It's Your Turn feature box offers you an opportunity to weigh in on the issue of selecting judges.

REMOVAL OF JUDGES

Like anyone else, judges can and do break the law or become physically or emotionally incapable of carrying out their responsibilities. If a judge displays serious deficiencies, he must be removed from the bench. Forty-five states provide for impeachment, wherein charges are filed in the statehouse of representatives and a trial is conducted in the senate. Other traditional means for removing justices include the legislative address and popular recall. In the legislative address, both houses of the legislature, by two-thirds vote, must ask the governor to dismiss a judge. Popular recall requires a specified number of registered voters to petition for a special election to recall the judge before her term has expired. But these traditional mechanisms are cumbersome and uncertain, and hence, seldom successful.

Today, states generally use more practical methods to remove judges. Problems related to senility and old age are ameliorated in at least thirty-seven states by a mandatory retirement age (generally seventy years) or by the forfeiture of pensions for judges serving beyond the retirement age. Such measures have the added benefit of opening the courtrooms to new and younger judges, even in situations where advancing age does not impair performance.

Most states have established special entities to address behavioral problems. *Courts of the judiciary,* whose members are all judges, and *judicial discipline and removal commissions,* composed of judges, lawyers, and laypersons, are authorized to investigate complaints about judges' qualifications, conduct, or fitness. These entities may reject allegations if they are unfounded, privately warn a judge if the charges are not serious, or hold formal hearings. Hearings may result in dismissal of the charges; recommendation for early retirement; or, in some states, outright suspension or removal. Finally, in some states, chief justices or a majority vote of the supreme court can suspend a lower-court judge indefinitely for misbehavior. For example, the Pennsylvania Supreme Court suspended Justice Seamus McCaffery in 2014 for sending out hundreds of pornographic emails. McCaffery soon resigned his judgeship.

The discipline, suspension, or removal of state court judges is uncommon, but it becomes necessary in all states at one time or another. Judges have been found guilty of drunkenness and drug abuse, sexual misconduct with witnesses and defendants, soliciting and accepting bribes, using state-paid staff members to work on their campaigns, buying and selling verdicts, and just about every other kind of misconduct imaginable, including choking a fellow supreme court justice.[46]

Sometimes judicial ethics seem to be in short supply. In Rhode Island, a state seldom celebrated as a paragon of political virtue, two consecutive supreme court chief justices vacated the bench when faced with impeachment. One resigned following allegations and testimony that he associated with criminals and had adulterous relations with two women in a Mafia-linked motel, among other things. Later, another pleaded guilty to using court money to pay for personal expenses, fixing friends' and relatives' speeding tickets, and ordering his secretary to destroy financial records.[47] Alabama chief justice Roy Moore was removed by the Court of Judiciary for defying federal and state court orders to haul away a two-and-a-half-ton Ten Commandments monument he had installed in the state judicial building. Reelected as Chief Justice in 2012, Moore again fought the federal courts by refusing to honor a federal court decision allowing gay marriage in Alabama to proceed. According to Moore, the state should punish "homosexual behavior," not permit it.

Judicial Decision Making

LO 9.6

To become familiar with some of the factors that influence judicial decision making.

What factors influence the rulings of state court judges? Why are some courts widely recognized as liberal (California, Hawaii) and others as tough on crime (Arizona, Mississippi)? Why does a prosecutor "judge shop," preferring to file a case before one judge rather than another? Isn't justice supposed to be blind, like its symbol of the woman holding the scales?

Judges, alas, are mortal beings like the rest of us. The formalities and legal jargon of the courtroom tend to mask the fact that judges' decisions are no less discretionary and subjective than the decisions of a governor, legislator, or agency head. Before we examine the factors that affect judicial decision making, however, we must distinguish between the legal settings of appellate courts and trial courts.

IN AND OUT OF THE TRIAL COURT

Approximately 90 percent of all civil and criminal cases are resolved outside the courtroom or through guilty pleas. In many civil cases, the defendant never appears in court to defend himself, thereby implicitly admitting his guilt and therefore losing the case by default. Other civil cases are settled in a pretrial conference between the defendant and the plaintiff (where, for instance, payments on an overdue debt might be rescheduled) or through voluntary dispute resolution procedures such as mediation or arbitration.

The process of settling criminal cases out of court at the discretion of the prosecutor and the judge is called **plea bargaining**. Although some defendants plead guilty as originally charged, acknowledging guilt for a lesser charge is more typical in criminal proceedings. With the possible exceptions of the victim and the general citizenry, everyone benefits from plea bargaining, a fact that helps account for its extensive use. The accused gets off with lighter punishment than she would face if the case went to trial and she lost. The defense attorney frees up time to take on additional legal work. The prosecuting attorney increases his conviction rate, which looks good if he has political ambitions. The judge helps cut back the number of cases awaiting trial. Even police officers benefit by not having to spend time testifying (and waiting to testify) and by raising the department's clearance rate (the number of cases solved and disposed of).

Out-of-court settlements through plea bargaining are negotiated in an informal atmosphere in the judge's chamber, between attorneys in the halls of the court building, or over drinks in a neighboring pub. This is a disturbingly casual way to dispense justice. The process is secretive and far removed from any notion of due process. The prosecuting (district) attorney enjoys enormous discretion in making deals. Often the propensity to settle depends on the length of the prosecuting attorney's court docket or her professional relationship with the accused's attorney, not on the merits of the case. All too often an innocent person pleads guilty to a lesser offense for fear of being wrongly convicted of a more serious offense, or because he cannot post bail and doesn't want to spend any unnecessary time behind bars. Equally disturbing, particularly to a victim, is the fact that plea bargaining can soon put a guilty person back on the streets, perhaps to search for another victim.

Nonetheless, plea bargaining is widely practiced. It is almost inevitable when the prosecutor's case hinges on weak evidence, police errors, a questionable witness, or the possibility of catching a bigger fish. Negotiation of a guilty plea for a lesser offense can occur at any stage of the criminal justice process.

If the accused is unable to make a deal with the prosecuting attorney, he faces either a **bench trial** by a single judge or a **trial by jury**. Both involve a courtroom hearing with all the legal formalities. In some jurisdictions and for certain types of cases, the defendant has a choice. In other situations, state legal procedures specify which trial format will be utilized. A jury trial is always mandatory for murder cases.

In a bench trial, the judge alone hears all arguments, determines the facts, and makes rulings on questions of law. Jury trials depend on a panel of citizens who decide the facts of the case; the judge instructs the jury on the applicable law. Although judges and juries would usually reach the same decision, the uncertainty introduced by twelve laypersons is usually great enough to convince a defendant to choose a bench trial or, if offered, alternative means of resolving the dispute such as mediation. Only about 2 percent of all cases are resolved by jury trial.[48]

plea bargaining

Negotiation between a prosecutor and a criminal defendant's counsel that results in the defendant pleading guilty to a lesser charge or pleading guilty in exchange for a reduced sentence.

bench trial

Trial by a single judge, without a jury.

trial by jury

A trial in which a jury decides the facts and makes a finding of guilty or not guilty.

Controversies in States and Localities

What If the Jury Pool Becomes a Puddle?

Many courts experience problems in getting people to perform their civic duty of jury service. Jury service is required for a large cross section of the population so that trials can be scheduled in reasonable amounts of time and defendants can receive fair and considered treatment from a jury of one's peers. Moreover, research shows that serving on a jury tends to heighten levels of civic participation in other ways, including voting and other forms of engagement.[1]

Juror shortages can seriously impede the value of a speedy trial. Many individuals ignore jury summons. Some individuals shirk from jury duty to avoid the accompanying loss of income from their regular job. Some may not be able to arrange day care or elder care. Others show up, but try to avoid jury duty by exaggerating or lying about the hardships jury duty would impose on them. With increasing frequency, some people simply shrug off their responsibility to serve. Judges may respond to those who ignore their summons by sending the sheriff or bailiff to round them up and haul them before the judge. In North Dakota, New Jersey, and elsewhere, their names are published in the local newspaper. Turning to positive incentives, some states are improving the jury duty experience by installing computer workstations, snack rooms, libraries, and other amenities in the jury lounge.

What can be done to increase jury compliance rates? Among the options being tried are:

- Increase juror pay from a paltry $10 to $20 a day to a more attractive amount, such as $50–$100.
- Provide day care for children of prospective jurors who have child-care responsibilities.
- Make the juror experience more attractive by providing wireless internet, snack rooms, coffee or tea, libraries, or other amenities for use when not actively hearing a case.
- Send a court officer to the home or place of employment of jury-scofflaws and take them to court.
- Fine shirkers for noncompliance with a jury summons.

Critical Thinking Questions:

1. What actions do you think are feasible to accelerate jury participation rates? What actions would you consider to be unacceptable? Can you think of any not listed above?

2. Do you feel a personal responsibility to comply with a jury duty summons? Why or why not? Have you been summoned to jury duty? If so, what was your experience?

[1]Andrew J. Bloeser, Carl McCurley, and Jeffery J. Mondak, "Jury Service as Civic Engagement: Determinants of Jury Summons Compliance," *American Politics Research* 40 (2, 2012): 179–204.

When jury trials do occur, attorneys seek to limit the unpredictable nature of juries by extensively questioning individuals in the jury pool. Each side in the dispute has the right to strike the names of a certain number of potential jurors without giving a specific reason. Others are eliminated for cause, such as personal knowledge of the case or its principals. In high-stakes cases, the jury-selection process involves public opinion surveys, individual background investigations of potential jurors, and other costly techniques. Many courts experience problems in getting people to perform their civic duty of jury service, as the Controversies in States and Localities feature box illustrates.

INSIDE THE APPELLATE COURT

Appellate courts are substantially different from trial courts: No plaintiffs, defendants, or witnesses are present; no bargaining or pre-decision settlement is allowed. The appeal consists of a review of court records and arguments advanced by the attorneys, who frequently are not the same lawyers who originally represented the parties. Appellate court rulings are issued by a panel of at least three judges who are tasked with deciding if legal errors have occurred. Unlike decisions in most trial courts, appellate court decisions are written and published. The majority vote prevails. Judges voting in the minority have the right to make a formal, written dissent that justifies their opinion.

State supreme courts vary dramatically in ideology. Those in Hawaii, Rhode Island, and Maryland are much more liberal than those in Arizona, Mississippi, and New Hampshire. There is marked variation in the dissent rates of state appellate courts. Some courts maintain a public aura of consensus on even the most controversial matters by almost always publishing unanimous opinions. Justices may disagree, but they do not necessarily dissent formally.

Other courts are rocked by public disputes over legal questions. Personal, professional, partisan, political, and other disagreements can spill over into open hostility over casework. As an Illinois chief justice observed, "Dissents are born not of doubt but of firm convictions."[49] Supreme courts in states such as California, New York, Michigan, and Mississippi have a history of contentiousness, whereas others, like those in Rhode Island and Maryland, are havens of harmony. Dissent rates appear to be positively related to a state's socioeconomic and political complexity, such as urbanization and partisan competition. Judges with long tenure and who do not have to face the voters in elections are more likely to dissent.[50] More dissent also occurs in courts with a large number of justices and with intermediate appellate courts. The more time justices have at their disposal, the more likely they are to find reasons to disagree.

INFLUENCES OF THE LEGAL SYSTEM

In addition to the facts of the case itself, judicial decision making is influenced by factors associated with the legal system, including institutional arrangements, accepted legal procedures, caseload pressures, and the ease with which certain interested parties gain access to the legal process.

1. Institutional Arrangements The level, or tier, of court is a structural characteristic that influences decision making. Trial court judges enforce legal norms and routinely *apply* the law as it has been written and interpreted over the years. The trial court permits direct interpersonal contacts among the judge, the jury, and the parties (usually individuals and small businesses). Divorce, personal injury, traffic violations, and minor criminal violations are the types of cases that predominate in trial courts.

Appellate courts are more apt to *interpret* the law and create public policy. State constitutional issues, state-local conflicts, and challenges to government regulation of business are the kinds of issues likely to be found in appellate courts. Cases typically involve government and large corporations. A particular case in a high court sometimes has an enormous impact on public policy, particularly when judges depart from established precedent or offer new interpretations of the law. The Wisconsin Supreme Court essentially overturned a constitutional amendment guaranteeing the right to carry a concealed weapon. Nevada's highest court nullified a state constitutional provision that two-thirds of the legislature must approve tax increases. Florida's supreme court struck down an education voucher system that permitted children to attend private and religious schools at the public's expense. Washington's supreme court recently held to be unconstitutional a popular initiative that required either a public vote or a two-thirds legislative majority to enact a tax increase, and also voted to hold the state legislature in contempt for failing to obey a court order to appropriately fund public schools.

Another important institutional arrangement is the selection procedure for judges. For instance, judicial decisions may be influenced by partisan electoral competition. Especially when a judge facing re-election must vote on an issue highly salient to voters, public opinion can affect the judge's ruling.[51] Death penalty cases provide a good example of this point. A study of judicial decision making in Texas, North Carolina, Louisiana, and Kentucky found that judges seeking re-election tend to uphold death sentences. In these traditionally conservative states, a decision in support of the death penalty helps to avoid unwanted pre-election criticism from political opponents.[52]

2. Legal Procedures and Precedent On the basis of **precedent** and under the legal doctrine of *stare decisis*, the principles and procedures of law applied in one situation are applied in any similar situation. In addition, lower courts are supposed to follow the precedents established by higher courts. An individual decision may seem unimportant, but when it is made in the context of other similar cases, it helps judicial precedent evolve. Through this practice, the doctrine of equal treatment before the law is pursued. When lower-court judges refuse to follow precedent or are ignorant of it, their decisions can be overturned on appeal. Of course, several conflicting precedents may relate to a case; in such instances, a judge will choose among them in justifying his ruling. A previous decision may become obsolete, may be manifestly absurd, or may simply clash with a judge's values or point of view.

Where do judges find precedent? In previous judicial rulings, state supreme court decisions set the norms. Supreme courts themselves, however, scan the legal landscape beyond state boundaries. Decisions of the U.S. Supreme Court may influence those of the state supreme courts. Increasingly, however, state supreme courts are practicing doctrinal diversity and looking to one another for precedent. State appellate judges borrow from and cite and the decisions of other states. They especially tend to rely on the more professional, prestigious supreme courts, such as those of California, Colorado, and Washington. State courts also tend to network with courts in the same region of the country, where cultural and other environmental factors are similar.[53]

precedent
The legal principle that previous similar court decisions should be applied to future decisions.

stare decisis
The legal doctrine that precedent set in earlier cases should guide judges' rulings.

3. Caseload Pressures Caseload affects judges' decisions. The number of cases varies in accordance with crime rates, socioeconomic characteristics of the jurisdictions, state laws, the number of judges, and many other variables. It stands to reason that the quality of judicial decision making is inversely related to caseload. Judges burdened by too much litigation are hard-pressed to devote an adequate amount of time and attention to each case before them.

4. Access to the System The final legal-system characteristic affecting judicial decisions is the access of individuals, organizations, and groups to the court system. Wealthy people and corporations are better able to pay for resources (attorneys, legal research, and so on) and therefore enter the legal system with a great advantage over poorer litigants (perhaps helping account for why African Americans and Latinos tend to receive harsher sentences than white defendants). Special-interest groups also enjoy certain advantages in influencing judicial decisions. They often have specialized knowledge in areas of litigation, such as environmental or business regulation. Lobbying by interest groups is much less prominent in the judicial branch than it is in the legislative and executive branches, but groups can affect outcomes by providing financial aid to litigants in important cases and by filing *amicus curiae* (friend of the court) briefs supporting one side or the other in a dispute. Most importantly, making monetary contributions to a judge's re-election campaign can influence a judge's decision.

The states have implemented several reforms to increase access to the judicial system for those who are disadvantaged. For example, court interpreters are available in states with large Latino and Asian populations. Physical and communication barriers have been removed so that persons with disabilities can participate fully in all aspects of the legal system. Racial, ethnic, and gender biases against attorneys, plaintiffs, defendants, witnesses, and other court participants are being addressed (although women still tend to receive less severe sentences than men who commit similar crimes).[54] Night courts remain open late for people who have difficulty getting off their day jobs to appear in court. And day care is being provided for children of plaintiffs, defendants, witnesses, and jurors. Gradually, state courts are responding to changes in the nature of society.

PERSONAL VALUES, ATTITUDES, AND CHARACTERISTICS OF JUDGES

Simply put, judges do not think and act alike. Each is a product of individual background and experiences, which in turn influence decisions made in the courtroom. Studies of state court justices have found that decisions are related to the judges' party identification, political ideology, prior careers, religion, age, and gender. In other words, personal characteristics predispose a judge to decide cases in certain ways.

For example, Democratic judges tend to favor the claimant in civil rights cases, the injured party in liability (tort) cases, the government in tax disputes, the employee in worker's compensation cases, the government in business regulation cases, the defendant in criminal contests, the union in disagreements with management, and the tenant in landlord-tenant cases. Republican judges tend to support the opposite side on all these issues. Female judges, who now occupy one out of four seats on supreme courts, are more supportive of women on sex discrimination and other feminist issues; more likely to favor the accused in obscenity and death penalty cases; and, in general, are more liberal than their male colleagues.[55] And finally, the judge's race appears to have little effect on the sentences handed down to black and white defendants, although African-American judges, according to one study, tend to be tougher when sentencing all defendants than are Latino judges.[56] Obviously, these distinctions do not hold in all situations, but the point is that *justice* is an opaque concept. No wonder attorneys try to shop around for the most sympathetic judge before filing a legal action.

Judicial Federalism

LO 9.7

To understand that judicial federalism is related to increased capability and judicial activism in many state courts.

During the 1950s and 1960s, the U.S. Supreme Court was the leading judicial actor in the land. Under Chief Justice Earl Warren (1953–1969) and his liberal majority, the Court handed down a long series of rulings that overturned racial segregation, mandated legislative reapportionment, extended voting rights, and expanded the rights of accused criminals. Significant reversals of state court decisions were commonplace. "Impeach Earl Warren" billboards sprouted up across the South like kudzu.

As a growing proportion of conservative justices filled the Supreme Court, however, it changed direction. Since 1988, a conservative majority has been in control. The Court has been somewhat less intrusive in state and local affairs and has flashed a green light to state courts inclined to activism (see Chapter 2). The result is **judicial federalism**, in which state courts look first to state constitutional and statutory laws in rendering legal judgments on important state and local issues rather than to the federal courts.

JUDICIAL ACTIVISM IN THE STATES

Judicial activism is a value-laden term with ideological dimensions.[57] When associated with politically liberal court decisions, it is decried by conservatives. However, conservative judges (such as those in the majority of the U.S. Supreme Court) are also activists. Whether liberal or conservative, all tend to show strong ideological tendencies.

An objective definition of judicial activism, then, points to court-generated change in public policy that is perceived as illegitimate by opponents who favor the status quo. Judicial activism is in the eye of the beholder. All too often, an "activist" judge is one who doesn't decide a case the way one *thinks* he should.

Regardless of one's feelings on the matter, state supreme courts have clearly become *more* activist by expanding into new policy areas. They are more likely to be involved in the policy-making process by making decisions that affect policy in the executive branch, and many pre-empt the lawmaking responsibility of the legislature when, in exercising the power of judicial review, the courts invalidate a statute based on constitutional grounds.

Examples of judicial activism include the following:

judicial federalism
State constitutional and statutory laws are consulted and applied before federal law.

judicial activism
The making of judicial public policy through decisions that overturn existing law or effectively make new laws.

- California, Connecticut, and Massachusetts courts have expanded a woman's right to abortion on demand and the right to financial aid from the state for abortions. Virginia, acting to the contrary, requires parental consent before an abortion can be obtained by an underage girl.
- Although the U.S. Supreme Court has upheld state sodomy prohibitions, courts in New York, Pennsylvania, and other states have struck down

sodomy laws as violations of the right to privacy, as spelled out in the state constitution.

- Oregon's supreme court rejected a U.S. Supreme Court decision that provided guidelines for declaring certain printed and visual materials to be obscene. The Oregon court asserted that its state constitution had been authored "by rugged and robust individuals dedicated to founding a free society unfettered by the governmental imposition of some peoples' views of morality on the free expression of others." The court went on to declare, "In this state, any person can write, paint, read, say, show or sell anything to a consenting adult even though that expression may generally or universally be considered 'obscene'."[58]

How can state courts override the decisions of the highest court in the United States? The answer is that they are grounding their rulings in their own constitutions instead of basing them on the national constitution. In several decisions, the U.S. Supreme Court has upheld the right of the states to expand on the minimum rights and liberties guaranteed under the national document. Of course, when there is an irreconcilable conflict between state and federal laws, the latter prevails.

CURRENT TRENDS IN STATE COURTS

The wave of state court activism is not carrying all the states with it. Some state supreme courts remain caught in the doldrums, consistently endorsing—rather than repudiating—U.S. Supreme Court decisions. Some of them are so quiet, as one wag suggested, "that you can hear their arteries harden." But even traditionally inactive courts in states such as Wisconsin and North Carolina have been stirred into independent actions recently. State court activism seems to be contagious, as courts utilize their own information and case networks instead of those of the U.S. Supreme Court.

Of course, with rare exceptions, judges cannot seize issues as governors and legislators can; they must wait for litigants to bring them to the courthouse. And although judges can issue rulings, they must depend on the executive and legislative branches to comply with and enforce those rulings. Nonetheless, many state supreme courts are becoming more active in the policy-making process. The reluctance of the federal courts to address important and controversial issues comprehensively has resulted in more cases for state supreme courts to decide.

State court activism does have some negative points. First, courts may appear to overstep their authority and try to go too far in policy making, intruding into the proper domain of executive and legislative actors—not to mention that of the voters. For example, courts in California, New Jersey, and elsewhere issued decisions that certain state legislative budget actions violated constitutional obligations.[59] Second, judges have little knowledge or expertise in the substance of public policy or in the policy-making process. They have no specialized staff to perform in-depth policy research on particular policy issues, and they cannot realistically depend on lawyers to do policy research for them. After all, lawyers are trained and practiced in legal reasoning and process, not social or political science. Third, state courts are increasingly issuing policy decisions that have significant budgetary implications. Court rulings on school finance, prison overcrowding, and treatment of the mentally ill have severely affected state budgets. Such court actions rarely take into account their related financial effects. A fourth problem is that in the context of state constitutional rights, geography is limiting. A state-by-state approach may not be appropriate for policies in areas such as civil rights, clean air and water, and safe food, which should be provided equally to all citizens.[60] Michael Cooper, "Courts Upend Budgets as States Look for Savings," www .nytimes.com (June 6, 2011).

Administrative and Organizational Improvements in State Courts

LO 9.8

To describe efforts to reform state courts.

We have already discussed several important judicial reforms: intermediate appellate courts, court consolidation, merit-selection plans for judges, more practical means for disciplining and removing judges, and administrative and organizational improvements, including those of a financial nature. This last category deserves further consideration.

FINANCIAL IMPROVEMENTS AND FINANCIAL PRESSURES

The exorbitant costs of some trials can bankrupt local jurisdictions if state financial assistance is not forthcoming. For example, one child molestation case in Los Angeles County lasted two and a half years and carried a tab of $15 million. (Neither of the two defendants was convicted.) The price tag for a murder trial and subsequent appeals can also be counted in the millions. A high-profile multiple murder case in Georgia effectively drained the public defender system of funds and halted proceedings in seventy-two other capital cases.[61]

The national economic collapse of 2008–2011 resulted in substantial cuts to state court budgets, with serious consequences for indigent defendants and all parties interested in justice and speedy trials. In 2011, twenty-eight state judicial budgets experienced serious cuts, and more reductions have occurred since.[62] The alarming results include staff layoffs, suspensions of jury trials, restricted court operating hours, and in some cases, even permanent court closings. New Hampshire was forced to suspend jury trials for a month; Florida laid off 10 percent of its court employees. Meanwhile, caseloads for prosecutors, public defenders, and judges soared nationally with rising numbers of foreclosures, debt proceedings, civil disputes, and other filings.[63] The Massachusetts chief justice was moved to observe that state courts had reached "the tipping point of dysfunction."[64] To make matters even worse, some legislatures have been known to threaten and even implement court budget cuts because of displeasure with unpopular rulings.[65]

In response to such budget crises in the past and to even out resources throughout the court system, more than half of the states assume full financial responsibility for the operation of state and local courts. Through centralized budgeting (also referred to as *unified court budgeting*), a consolidated budget for all state and local courts is prepared by the chief administrative officer of the state court system, detailing all personnel, supplies, equipment, and other expenditures. This is intended to enhance financial management and maintain judicial independence from the executive and legislative branches.

DEALING WITH GROWING CASELOADS

Case backlogs are a commonly recognized problem, and they are getting worse with budget shortfalls. State trial courts alone entertain some 100 million new cases each year.[66] Some judges hand down more than 300 opinions annually. Delays of two years or more are not uncommon for appellate court hearings, and the unprecedented pressure is growing. Calls for **tort** reform to reduce the number of personal injury cases and the escalating size of jury awards have become increasingly insistent. (Torts account for about two-thirds of all civil trials; the average award in a tort trial, however, is only $30,000.[67])

Excessive caseloads are caused by numerous factors, including the greater propensity of losing parties to appeal lower-court decisions, the tremendous growth in litigation, heightened interest group activity, huge increases in drug-related and drunk-driving cases, and poor caseload-management procedures. Exacerbating the problem is the high demand for litigation aggravated by the prodigious quantity of lawyers in the United States, which accounts for nearly two-thirds of all the lawyers in the world. The American Bar Association counted 1,268,000 lawyers in 2012. The demographics are interesting: 92 percent are male, 88 percent white. But 47 percent of the 2012 law school enrollment was female and 24.5 percent minority. These lawyers are distributed unevenly: there are 166,000 in New York State, but only 1560 in North Dakota.[68]

The larger concern is that long delays thwart the progress of justice. The quality of evidence deteriorates as witnesses disappear or forget what they saw, and victims suffer from delays that prevent them from collecting damages for injuries incurred during a crime or an accident. Innocent defendants can be harmed by the experience of being held in jail for long periods while awaiting trial. Increasingly, criminal cases are thwarted because of witness intimidation by the accused, his friends, or others who desire to end the prosecution and free the accused.

Reducing excessive caseloads is not a simple matter. Common sense dictates establishing intermediate appellate courts and adding new judgeships. But much like a new highway draws more traffic, intermediate appellate courts, by their very existence, tend to attract more appeals. Although additional judges can speed up the trial process in lower courts, they may also add to appellate backlogs. Expanding the number of judges in an appellate court is also problematic: hearings may take longer because of more input or

tort

A civil wrong that causes harm to another person, such as an auto accident, product liability, or defamation.

factional divisions among judges. And, for better or worse, the law schools continue to spew out new lawyers, looking for something to do.

The stubborn persistence of case backlogs has led to some interesting and promising new approaches.

1. *Alternative dispute resolution.* Mediation, arbitration, or other techniques help settle litigation prior to or during formal courtroom proceedings. Mediation involves a neutral third party who tries to help the opponents reach a voluntary agreement. Arbitration consists of a binding ruling by a neutral party in favor of one party or the other. In a growing number of states, civil litigants in search of timely settlement hire private judges to arbitrate their disputes.

2. *Fines against lawyers and litigants.* Laws or court rules allow judges to levy monetary fines against lawyers and litigants guilty of delaying tactics, frivolous litigation.

3. *Case management systems.* Judges can take charge of their dockets and impose a no-nonsense case management system. Although individual systems vary widely, a typical approach is multitracking, or *differentiated case management.* It distinguishes between simple and complex cases, as well as between frivolous and potentially significant cases, and treats them differently. Complex and significant cases are waved down the traditional appellate track. Simple and frivolous cases take a shorter track, usually under the direction of staff attorneys. In Vermont, this case management system is referred to as the "rocket docket." Experiments with multitracking have been successful in reducing case delays in Arizona, Maine, New Hampshire, and other states. As previously noted, another case management innovation designed to speed the wheels of justice is problem-solving or *boutique* courts, in which environmental law disputes, drug cases, domestic violence cases, or others with special characteristics are heard by judges in specialized courts.

4. *New technology.* Technological innovations are also improving the quality and quantity of court operations. Electronic databases (e.g., LEXIS and WESTLAW) store case information and legal research and transmit information from law offices to courts. Electronic filing of court documents and online access to court information for attorneys and citizens help track child support payments, store case data for legal research, transmit data from law offices to courts, and, in general, save the courts money and staff time. Arraignment procedures, during which suspects are formally charged, are videotaped to save time or to prevent potential problems from a disruptive defendant. Video courtrooms, in which trials are filmed, create a more accurate trial record and cost much less than a written transcript by a court stenographer. Lawyers in high-tech courtrooms speed up proceedings by using PowerPoint, video clips, and Internet sources, displayed for jurors on individual monitors. Audiovisual technology permits hearings, motions, pleas, sentencing, and other proceedings to be conducted long distance between the jail and the courthouse, thereby saving money and enhancing security.

5. *Performance standards.* The National Center for State Courts has developed performance standards for state trial courts to aid self-assessment and improvement.[69] A growing number of states are not only adopting quantitative indicators of the speed with which cases are processed, but are also trying to measure broader concerns such as access to justice, fairness and integrity, public trust and confidence, and the quality of judges' decision making.

COMPENSATING THE JUDGES

At first glance, judicial salaries seem high enough. In 2013, state supreme court judges earned an average of approximately $154,000. For a general jurisdiction trial court, it was $137,151. The variation is great: California justices make $232,060, whereas their counterparts in Idaho are paid only $123,400.[70] Trial court judges are paid 10–20 percent less.

However, these amounts are substantially below what an experienced, respected attorney can expect to make. A successful lawyer who gives up private practice and perhaps a lucrative partnership for the bench must be willing to take a considerable cut in income. Unlike legislators, state judges are permitted little outside income. Therefore, it is reasonable to ask whether the best legal minds will be attracted to judgeships, given that judicial compensation is relatively low. This dilemma exists at all levels and in all branches of public service, from the municipal finance officer to the highway department director, because most state and local government compensation lags behind that for comparable professional jobs in the private sector. If we expect our judges, law enforcement officers, and other public employees to be honest, productive, and highly qualified, perhaps they should be compensated fairly.

JUDICIAL PERFORMANCE EVALUATION

Who judges the judges? In popular election and merit system states, the voters hold judges accountable. But voters have no voice in gubernatorial and legislative selection states. And even when judicial elections are held, how much do the voters really know about the candidates?

Judicial performance evaluation (JPE) offers an objective process to assess the performance of judges. Voters are educated, and judges are encouraged to use evaluation results for self-improvement. First adopted by Alaska in 1975, JPE programs are now mandated in eighteen additional states and under active consideration in several others. JPE involves confidential surveys of attorneys, court professionals, witnesses, jurors, and other court participants. Respondents are questioned about how the judge interprets the law, manages her workload, and interacts with people in the courtroom, among other factors.[71]

Research indicates that JPE can contribute to judicial self-improvement and provide valuable, job-related information on judges' performance to the voters. Used appropriately, JPE helps preserve the hallmark characteristics of independence and accountability of the judiciary.[72]

STATE COURTS TODAY

Like the other two branches of government, the state judiciary has been reformed significantly. Court systems have been modernized and simplified, intermediate appellate courts have been added, processes have been streamlined, and case delays are being addressed as resources permit. Disciplinary and removal commissions now make it easier to deal with problem judges, and JPE furnishes useful data on judicial performance. But courts are still striving for adequate funding and greater independence from political pressures and favoritism. Justice may appear at times to be an ephemeral ideal, and an expensive one at that, but it is more likely to be approximated in state judicial decisions today than ever before. The courts, like the rest of society, are participants in the technological age. New innovations and approaches will follow the recommendations of commissions in states now studying the needs of state judicial systems in the future.

Court modernization and reform have been accompanied by increased judicial activism. The newly assertive state courts have far surpassed the federal courts in public policy activism. They sometimes blatantly disagree with federal precedents and insist on decisions grounded in state constitutional law rather than in the national constitution. In short, the state courts are proactively responding to public concerns with the administration of justice, and, by inference, to the perennial issues of crime and criminal justice (see Chapter 16).

Chapter Recap

- State courts are organized into two tiers: appellate courts and trial courts.

- The five methods for selecting judges are legislative election, partisan election, nonpartisan election, merit plan, and gubernatorial appointment. Each selection plan has certain advantages and disadvantages—there is no "one best way."

- Many factors influence judicial decision making, including institutional arrangements; legal procedures; case precedent; caseload pressures; access to the legal system; and the personal values, attitudes, and characteristics of judges.

- Judicial federalism is related to increased capability and judicial activism in many state courts.

- Efforts to reform state courts include financial improvements, better caseload management, and improved compensation for judges.

KEY TERMS

civil case *(p. 227)*
criminal case *(p. 227)*
administrative case *(p. 227)*
common law *(p. 228)*
limited jurisdiction trial courts *(p. 229)*

major trial courts *(p. 229)*
supreme court *(p. 230)*
intermediate appellate court *(p. 230)*
plea bargaining *(p. 242)*
bench trial *(p. 242)*

trial by jury *(p. 242)*
stare decisis (p. 245)
precedent *(p. 245)*
judicial federalism *(p. 247)*
judicial activism *(p. 247)*
tort *(p. 250)*

INTERNET RESOURCES

The National Center for State Courts (NCSC) maintains a list of courts and their websites. NCSC's website at **www.ncsc.org** is a rich source of information on the courts, including state court decisions, caseload statistics, and court organization.

Interesting state sites include the following: California at **www.courtinfo.ca.gov/**, Florida at **www.flcourts.org**, and Alaska at **http:// courts.alaska.gov**.

The American Bar Association's website at **www.abanet.org/** provides an analysis of current controversial cases and other legal information.

The Law Forum Legal Resources site at **www .lawforum.net** has links to all online state and local courts.

For a detailed examination of all states' judicial selection systems, see **www.ajs.org/**.

To watch live performances of Indiana's court proceedings, see **www.in.gov/judiciary/ webcast**.

City Hall in Santa Monica, California
Mark & Audrey Gibson/Stock Connection Blue/Alamy

Local Government: Types and Functions

In 2015, the newly-inaugurated governor of Illinois, Bruce Rauner, created a task force with the avowed goal of streamlining local governments and making them function more efficiently. Supporters of the task force hoped that it would come up with recommendations to reduce the number of local governments . . . and potentially save millions of dollars and improve public services.[1] With nearly 7,000 units of local government of various types and sizes—far more than any other state—Illinois is ripe for a rethinking of its local government landscape.

What do citizens want from their local governments? The answer is, to be governed well. They want governmental structures that work and leaders who are effective. They want jurisdictions with adequate capacity to resolve the tough public problems of our times. But as this chapter demonstrates, "governed well" is hard to achieve. Even with improved capacity, local governments continue to confront a series of challenges, some perennial, some episodic.[2]

Orientations to Communities

Communities and their governments can be discussed in many different ways. Theoretically, at least three different orientations have some appeal. When you move from the theoretical realm to legal realities, five types of local governments can be differentiated.

THEORETICAL ORIENTATIONS

In the early days of the United States, communities were idealized as *civic republics*.[3] In a civic republic, community government is based on the principle of mutual consent. Citizens share fundamental beliefs and participate in public affairs. Their motivation for civic involvement is less materialistic self-interest than altruistic concern for community welfare. Although this idea continued to have theoretical appeal, its reality was threatened by the growing and diverse nineteenth-century populace, which preferred to maximize individual liberty and accumulation of wealth. An economically inspired conception of community, that of the *corporate enterprise*, gradually emerged. Economic growth and the ensuing competition for wealth sparked extensive conflict.[4] With the guidance of state government, local governments adopted policies and juggled the clashing interests.

These two theoretical orientations, the community as a civic republic and the community as a corporate enterprise, remain viable. An alternative orientation has emerged, however—one that portrays the community as a *consumer market*.[5] In a consumer market, citizens are consumers of public services, and governments are providers. This idea places increased emphasis on quality of life and cost-effectiveness. Individuals make choices about where they will live—in the heart of the city, a suburban jurisdiction, or a rural portion of the county. In each of these locales, the individual will encounter government or, more accurately, *governments*. The range of government services and the cost of these services vary from one place to another. Informed consumers, so the theory goes, seek communities that are in line with their preferences. You say that you want to live in the Los Angeles area? You have many jurisdictional choices: twenty-one cities share a border with the city of Los Angeles. Each one provides a different package of services, in terms of type, quality, and cost—a consumer market, indeed.

FIVE TYPES OF LOCAL GOVERNMENTS

Local government is the level of government that fights crime, extinguishes fires, paves streets, collects trash, maintains parks, provides water, and educates children. Some local governments provide all of these services; others, only some. A useful way of thinking about local governments is to distinguish between general-purpose and single-purpose local governments. **General-purpose local governments** are those that perform a wide range of governmental functions. These include three types of local governments: counties, municipalities, and towns and townships. Single-purpose local governments, as the label implies, have a specific purpose and perform one function. School districts and special districts are single-purpose governments.

LO 10.1

To classify local government into five types: counties, municipalities, towns and townships, special districts, and school districts.

---

general-purpose local government

A local government that performs a wide range of functions.

FIGURE 10.1

Cities, Townships, and School Districts in St. Joseph County, Indiana

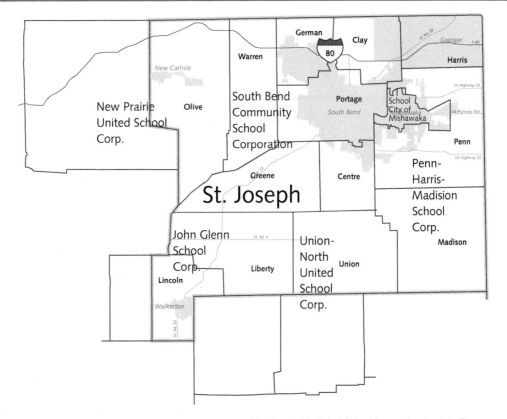

NOTE: The St. Joseph County border is indicated by the thick line. The New Prairie United School Corporation, the John Glenn School Corporation, and the Union-North Union United School Corporation extend beyond the county's borders. City names are italicized; township names are in boldface type. City land areas are shaded light blue.

SOURCE: Adapted from STATS Indiana, 2000, "Northwest Indiana Townships by County," http://www.stats.indiana.edu/maptools/maps/boundary/townships_2000/region1_townships.pdf (accessed May 23, 2012); STATS Indiana, 2006, "Northwest Indiana Unified School Districts," http://www.stats.indiana.edu/maptools/maps/boundary/school_districts/region1_unified.pdf (accessed May 23, 2012).

The boundaries of single-purpose districts may or may not coincide with the general-purpose local governments in the area. For example, the boundaries of a school district may be coterminous with the county, they may cover smaller portions of the county, or may even extend over sections of two or more counties. Figure 10.1 maps the boundaries of several cities (South Bend, for example), townships (Olive is one), and school districts (such as the John Glenn School Corporation) in, and extending beyond, St. Joseph County, Indiana. Not shown are four library districts and two other special districts within the county, over-lapping some of the other jurisdictions. The web of boundaries shown in Figure 10.1 is not unique to northern Indiana—it characterizes most places in the United States. These noncongruent, overlapping boundaries can produce significant coordination problems for local governments in an area.[6]

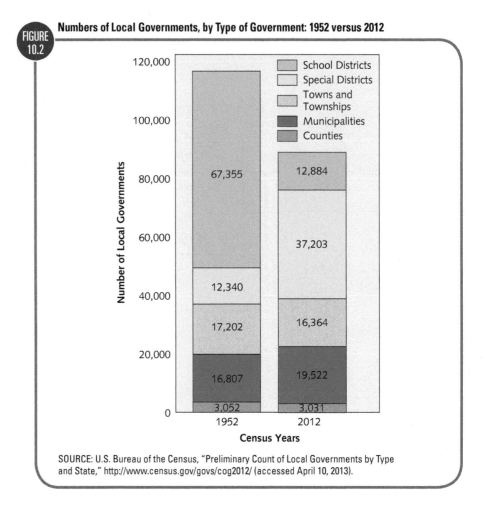

FIGURE 10.2

Numbers of Local Governments, by Type of Government: 1952 versus 2012

SOURCE: U.S. Bureau of the Census, "Preliminary Count of Local Governments by Type and State," http://www.census.gov/govs/cog2012/ (accessed April 10, 2013).

single-purpose local government

A local government, such as a school district, that performs a specific function.

metropolitan area

A central city of at least 50,000 people and its surrounding county (or counties); often called an *urban area*.

In the United States, the number of local governments exceeds 90,000. Figure 10.2 shows the number of local governments at two points in time: 1952 and 2012. Among general-purpose local governments, the number of counties and towns and townships decreased slightly over the sixty-year period as the number of municipalities increased. In terms of **single-purpose local governments**, the trends are more dramatic. From 1952 to 2012, nearly 81 percent of America's school districts were abolished or consolidated with surrounding districts; in the same period, special districts have tripled in number.

Native American reservations are not considered a formal type of local government, even though they perform many local government functions. (Chapter 2 discusses the national-tribal-state relationship in more detail.) **Metropolitan areas**, which are composed of a central city and its surrounding county (or counties), are not local governments either. The label *metropolitan statistical area* (*MSA*) is used by the federal government to designate urban areas that have reached a minimum 50,000-population threshold. As of 2014, the United States contained 381 MSAs. Another federal designation,

micropolitan statistical area, refers to places with populations between 10,000 and 49,999. The MSA and micropolitan labels are used for statistical data collection and, in some instances, in federal grant programs.

Regardless of the purpose of a local government, we must remember that it has a lifeline to state government. In short, state government gives local government its legal existence. Local citizens may instill a community with its flavor and its character, but state government makes local government official. Over time, most states have gradually relaxed their control over localities through grants of **home rule**, which give local governments more decision-making power.

American local governments were not planned according to some grand design. Rather, they grew in response to a combination of citizen demand, interest group pressure, and state government acquiescence. As a consequence, no rational system of local governments exists. What does exist is a collection of autonomous, frequently overlapping jurisdictional units. The prevalence of **jurisdictional overlap** creates layers of local governments and raises questions about their number and function. As indicated in the introduction to this chapter, the number of local governments varies from state to state. Consider the case of Pennsylvania, second only to Illinois in the number of local governments. Pennsylvania's 4,905 local jurisdictions include 66 counties, 1,015 cities, 1,546 townships, 1,764 special districts, and 514 school districts.[7] Nevada, on the other hand, has a grand total of 190 local governments.

Being so close to the people offers special challenges to local governments. Citizens are well aware when trash has not been collected or when libraries do not carry current bestsellers. They can contact local officials and attend public hearings. And they do. A recent survey asked a national sample of Americans about their interactions with government. Over 40 percent said that they had contacted an elected official or attended a community meeting.[8] The interactive nature of local government makes the questions of capacity and responsiveness all the more critical.

County Government

State governments have carved up their territory into 3,031 discrete, general-purpose subunits called counties (except in Louisiana, where counties are called *parishes*, and in Alaska, where they are called *boroughs*). Counties exist everywhere, with only a few exceptions: Connecticut and Rhode Island, where there are no functional county governments; Washington, D.C., which is a special case in itself; some municipalities in Virginia that are independent jurisdictions and are not part of the counties that surround them; and cities like Baltimore and St. Louis, which are not part of a county because of past political decisions. Also, some jurisdictions—Philadelphia and San Francisco, for example—are considered cities but they are actually consolidated city-county government structures.

NOT ALL COUNTIES ARE ALIKE

Counties can be differentiated according to their urban/rural nature. Urban, or metropolitan, counties contain one or more large cities and surrounding suburbs and serve as the employment hubs for the area. Los Angeles County,

LO 10.2

To examine the functions, organization, and performance of county government.

micropolitan statistical area

An urban cluster with a population between 10,000 to 49,999.

home rule

A broad grant of power from the state to a local government.

jurisdictional overlap

The existence of multiple local governments in the same territory.

California, with more than 10 million residents—and larger than most states—is the largest county in the United States. Even though most Americans live in metropolitan areas, most counties are actually nonmetropolitan—that is, they contain one or more small cities, with the rest of the area sparsely settled. More than three-fourths of American counties have fewer than 100,000 inhabitants. Counties that contain no incorporated places with more than 2,500 residents are the most rural of all. Loving County, Texas, with fewer than 100 people spread over its 673-square-mile territory, is an example of an extremely rural jurisdiction.

THE ROLE OF COUNTY GOVERNMENT

Counties were created by states to function as their administrative appendages. In other words, counties were expected to manage activities of statewide concern at the local level. Their basic set of functions traditionally included property tax assessment and collection, law enforcement, elections, record keeping (land transactions, births, and deaths), and road maintenance. The county courthouse was the center of government.

The twin pressures of modernization and population growth placed additional demands on county governments. As a result, their service offerings have expanded and now include health care and hospitals, pollution control, mass transit, industrial development, social services, and consumer protection. Examples of the traditional and new functions of counties appear in Table 10.1. The more new services that a county provides, the more it is delivering city-type services to its residents and businesses.[9] As a result, counties are increasingly regarded less as simple functionaries of state government and more as important policy-making units of local government. Thirty-eight states have adopted home rule provisions for at least some of their counties.[10] This has made it easier for counties to change their organizational structures and reform their practices.

Even with their gradual empowerment, counties, like other local governments, continue to chafe at the traditionally tight reins of state government control. As will be explored further in Chapter 12, counties resent state requirements that the counties themselves have to pay for. In addition, they dislike the limits that states place on their authority. The issue of empowerment is unlikely to fade anytime soon.

HOW COUNTIES ARE ORGANIZED

The traditional structure of county government is based on an elected governing body, usually called a board of commissioners or supervisors, which is the central policy-making apparatus in the county. The board enacts county ordinances, approves the county budget, and appoints other officials (such as the directors of the county public works department and the county parks department). One of the board members acts as presiding officer. Historically, this form of government has been the most popular; more than half of U.S. counties use it, although its predominance is decreasing. A typical county commission has five members and meets in regular session twice a month.

TABLE 10.1	County Government Functions		
FUNCTION		**TRADITIONAL FUNCTION**	**NEW FUNCTION**
Building and housing code enforcement			X
Disaster preparedness			X
Water supply/sewage disposal			X
Parks and recreation			X
Judicial administration		X	
County jail maintenance		X	
Planning and land-use control			X
Record keeping: land transactions, births, deaths, marriages		X	
Airports			X
Public hospitals			X
Law enforcement		X	
Local roads and bridges, construction and maintenance		X	
Consumer protection			X
Mass transit			X
Property tax assessment and collection		X	
Election administration		X	
Natural resource preservation			X
Welfare and social-service programs		X	
Libraries			X
Stadiums, convention and cultural centers			X
Pollution control			X
Public health, including clinics			X
Community development and housing			X

SOURCES: David R. Berman, *County Governments in an Era of Change* (Westport, CT: Greenwood Press, 1993); Tanis J. Salant, "Overview of County Governments," in Roger L. Kemp, ed., *Forms of Local Government* (Jefferson, NC: McFarland, 1999); J. Edwin Benton, et al., "Service Challenges and Governance Issues Confronting American Counties in the 21st Century: An Overview," *State and Local Government Review* 40 (2008): 54–68.

The board is not omnipotent, however, because several other county officials are also elected, forming a plural executive structure. In most places, these officials include the sheriff, the county prosecutor (or district attorney), the county clerk (or clerk of the court), the county treasurer (or auditor), the county tax assessor, and, in some states, even the coroner. These officials can become powerful political figures in their own right by controlling their own

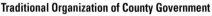

Traditional Organization of County Government
The most common form of county government lacks a central executive.

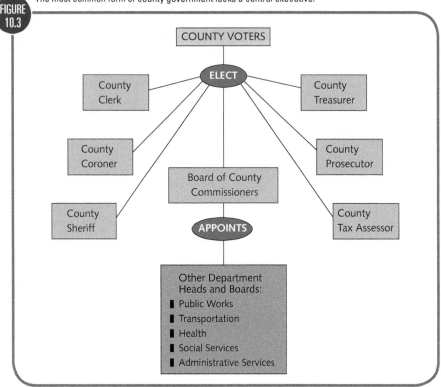

bureaucratic units. Figure 10.3 sketches the typical organizational pattern of county government.

There are two primary criticisms of this type of organizational structure. First, it has no elected central executive official, like the mayor of a city or the governor of a state. County government is run by a board. Second, it does not have a single-professional administrator to manage county government in the way a city manager does in a municipality. Elected officials are responsible for administering many major county functions.

These criticisms have led to calls for reform of the structure of county government. Two alternative county structures have grown in popularity over the past three decades. In one, called the *county council-elected executive plan*, the voters elect an executive officer in addition to the governing board. The result is a clearer separation between legislative and executive powers—in effect, a two-branch system of government. The board still has the power to set policy, adopt the budget, and audit the financial performance of the county. The executive's role is to prepare the budget, administer county operations (in other words, implement the policies of the board), and appoint department heads. More than 400 counties have adopted this arrangement; among the most recent is Cuyahoga County, Ohio, where Cleveland is located. In the other alternative structure, the *council-administrator plan*, the county board hires a professional administrator (sometimes called a "county manager") to run the government. The advantage of this form of government is that it brings to the county a highly skilled manager with a professional commitment to efficient, effective government. Approximately 1,000 counties have variations of the council-administrator structure. One of the most recent large counties to adopt such a plan is Bexar County, Texas, population 1.8 million, where San Antonio is located.

Determining the most effective structural arrangements for county government is an ongoing issue. Defections from the long-standing commission form of county government and experimentation with alternatives continue, especially in the most populous counties. Los Angeles County, which employs 100,000 people and has a budget of $20 billion, recently empowered its county administrator by giving him the power to hire and fire most department heads.[11] Does structure matter? Research has shown that there are policy consequences attributable, at least in part, to structure. For example, among fast-growing counties in Florida, the adoption of a reformed structure led to an expansion of the counties' services to its residents.[12] A national study has found a link between reformed structures and county spending on redistributive programs such as child welfare, homeless shelters, and mental health services.[13] However, other studies have raised questions about the impact of reformed structures on policy outcomes, suggesting that this question has not been answered definitively.[14] The It's Your Turn box raises a related question that several counties have confronted recently: whether to impose residency requirements on their employees.

 It's Your Turn

Should Public Employees Have to Live Where They Work?

Some counties and cities require their employees to live within their territorial boundaries. Other counties and cities that had these requirements in the past have repealed them. What do you think?

PROS	CONS
Living in the county or city gives employees a greater stake in the community.	People should be able to live where they want to, regardless of their employer.
Residents feel safer when police officers, sheriff's deputies, and firefighters, in particular, live in nearby neighborhoods.	Public employees may not be able to afford to buy or rent housing within the city or county.
Public employees are more likely to shop at local stores if they live there, thus strengthening the local economy.	Having residency requirements may discourage otherwise qualified applicants from seeking city or county employment.

THE PERFORMANCE OF COUNTY GOVERNMENT

Counties are now more prominent than they were in the old days when they were considered the shadowy backwaters of local governments. As urban populations spill beyond the suburbs into the unincorporated territory of counties, the pressure on all local governments grows. A county and the cities located within it may find themselves at odds on myriad issues. The county-state relationship can be rocky, primarily because of the spiraling costs of state-imposed mandates for programs such as indigent services and long-term health care. In addition, counties are expected to tackle tough dilemmas of affordable housing and environmental compliance at the same time that they are expanding their services to include disaster preparedness and consumer protection.

The pressures on county government are many. One novel idea for relieving the burdens on counties was suggested in California a while back, when the legislature considered a proposal to divide the state into seven regions that would be governed by thirteen-member elected boards.[15] These regional "super governments" would assume many of the development and infrastructure functions currently assigned to county governments. Although the bill did not pass, the performance of county government remains an issue in other parts of the nation. In Massachusetts, where cities and towns provide most local services, the state legislature has abolished several counties, contending that they were superfluous in the Bay State. Clearly, county governments must continue to modernize and focus on the big picture or run the risk of being bypassed. With that in mind, voters in Allegheny County, Pennsylvania (the Pittsburgh area), approved a restructuring plan in 2005 that merged several elected county positions and made some elective offices appointed.[16]

LO 10.3

To consider the forms and functions of city government, and the issues confronting municipalities around the country.

Municipal Government

Municipalities are cities; the words are synonymous and refer to a specific, populated territory, typically operating under a charter from state government. Cities differ from counties in terms of how they were created and what they do. Historically, they have been the primary units of local government in most societies—the grand enclaves of human civilization.

CREATING CITIES

incorporation

The creation of a municipality through the granting of a charter from the state.

charter

A document that sets out a city's structure, authority, and functions.

A city is a legal recognition of settlement patterns in an area. In the most common procedure, residents of an area in a county petition the state for a charter of incorporation. The area slated for **incorporation** must meet certain criteria, such as population or density minimums. In Alabama, for instance, the population threshold required for incorporation is 300 people; in Arizona, the number is 1,500. In most cases, a referendum is required. The referendum enables citizens to vote on whether they wish to become an incorporated municipality. If the incorporation measure is successful, then a **charter** is granted by the state, and the newly created city has the legal authority to elect officials, levy taxes, and provide services to its residents. Not all cities have charters, however. Most California cities, for example, operate under general state law rather than a charter.

New cities are created every year. For instance, during a single six-year period, 145 places incorporated (and 33 cities disincorporated, or ceased to exist as official locales).[17] Although most new cities tend to be small, some begin with sizable populations. For example, more than 86,000 people were living in Sandy Springs, Georgia, when the city incorporated in 2005.

Like counties, cities are general-purpose units of local government. But unlike counties, they typically have greater decision-making authority and discretion. Almost all states have enacted home rule provisions for cities, although in some states, only those cities that have attained a certain population size can exercise this option. (One of the few states without home rule for cities, New Hampshire, sought to provide it through a constitutional amendment in 2000 but the measure was defeated by voters.) In addition, cities generally offer a wider array of services to their citizenry than most counties do. Police and fire services, public works, and parks and recreation are standard features, supplemented in some cities by publicly maintained cemeteries, city-owned and operated housing, city-run docks, city-sponsored festivals, and city-constructed convention centers. Municipal government picks up garbage and trash, sweeps streets, inspects restaurants, maintains traffic signals, and plants trees.

CITY GOVERNMENTAL STRUCTURE

Nearly all city governments operate with one of three structures: a mayor-council form, a council-manager form, or a city commission form. In each structure, an elected governing body, typically called a *city council*, has policy-making authority. What differentiates the three structures is the manner in which the executive branch is organized.

Mayor-Council Form In the mayor-council form of government, executive functions such as the appointment of department heads are performed by elected officials. This form of government can be subdivided into two types, depending on the formal powers held by the mayor. In a **strong-mayor–council structure**, the mayor is the source of executive leadership. Strong mayors run city hall the way governors run the statehouse. They are responsible for daily administrative activities, the hiring and firing of top-level city officials, and budget preparation. They have a potential veto over council actions.

The strong-mayor–council structure grew out of dissatisfaction in the late nineteenth century with the **weak-mayor–council structure**. The weak-mayor–council structure, which has its roots in the colonial period of American history, limits the mayor's role to that of executive figurehead. The council (of which the mayor is a member) is the source of executive power and legislative power. The council appoints city officials and develops the budget, and the mayor has no veto power. He or she performs ceremonial tasks such as speaking for the city, chairing council meetings, and attending ribbon-cutting festivities. A structurally weak mayor can emerge as a powerful political figure in the city, but only if he or she possesses informal sources of power. Figure 10.4 highlights the structural differences between the strong- and weak-mayor–council forms of city government.

strong-mayor–council structure
The mayor is empowered to perform the executive functions of government and has a veto over city council actions.

weak-mayor–council structure
The mayor lacks formal executive power; the city council (of which the mayor is a member) is the source of executive and legislative power.

Mayor-Council Form of Government
The primary difference between these two structures concerns the power and authority possessed by the mayor. Strong mayors are more ideally situated to exert influence and control.

FIGURE 10.4

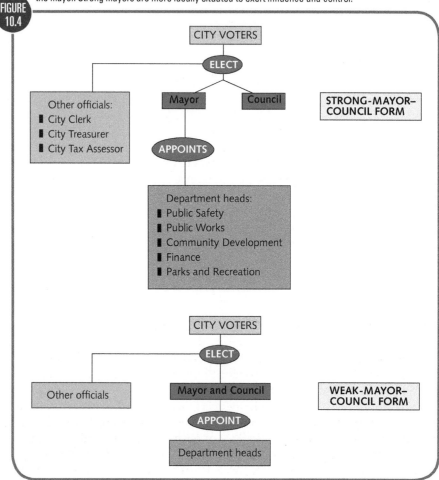

Mayor-council systems are popular both in large cities (in which populations are greater than 250,000) and in small cities (with populations under 10,000). In large cities, the clash of conflicting interests requires the leadership of an empowered politician, a strong mayor. In small communities, however, the mayor-council structure is a low-cost, part-time operation. Many large cities in which the administrative burdens of the mayor's job are especially heavy have established the position of general manager or chief administrative officer to assist the mayor.

Council-Manager Form The second city government structure, the council-manager form, emphasizes the separation of politics (the policy-making activities of the governing body) from administration (the execution of the policies enacted by the governing body). Theoretically, the city council makes policy, and administrators execute policy. Under this structure, the council hires a

Council-Manager Form of Government

The council-manager form of government places administrative responsibility in the hands of a skilled professional. The intent is to make the operation of city government less political.

FIGURE
10.5

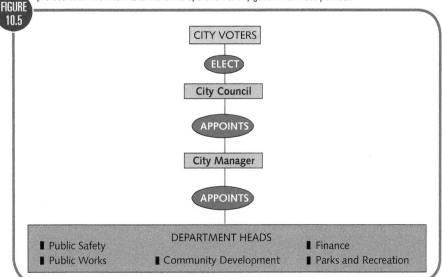

professional administrator to manage city government. Figure 10.5 illustrates this structure. (An important variation within the council-manager form is whether the mayor is directly elected by the voters [in 63 percent of council-manager cities] or selected by the council from its membership [37 percent].[18])

The administrator (usually called a **city manager**) appoints and removes department heads, oversees service delivery, develops personnel policies, and prepares budget proposals for the council. These responsibilities alone make the manager an important figure in city government. But add to them the power to make policy recommendations to the city council, and the position becomes even more powerful. In council-manager cities, the council and the manager typically have a working understanding about how far the manager can venture into the policy-making realm of city government.

More than half of U.S. cities use the council-manager form of city government. Among cities of 25,000–75,000 people, the council-manager structure predominates; it is also popular in more homogeneous suburban communities and in the newer cities of the Sunbelt region. Examples of large cities with a council-manager structure include Phoenix, San Antonio, and Dallas.

City Commission Form Under the city commission form of government, illustrated in Figure 10.6, legislative and executive functions are merged. Commissioners not only make policy as members of the city's governing body, they also head the major departments of city government. In other words, they are both policy makers and policy executors. One of the commissioners is designated as mayor simply to preside over commission meetings.

The commission form of government was created as a reaction to the mayor-council structure. Its origins can be traced back to the inability of a

city manager
A professional administrator hired by a city council to handle the day-to-day operation of the city.

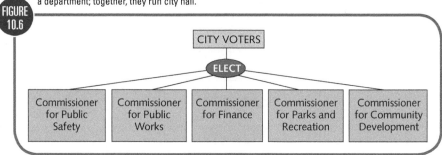

City Commission Form of Government

Executive leadership is fragmented under a commission form of government. Each commissioner heads a department; together, they run city hall.

FIGURE 10.6

CITY VOTERS

ELECT

| Commissioner for Public Safety | Commissioner for Public Works | Commissioner for Finance | Commissioner for Parks and Recreation | Commissioner for Community Development |

mayor-council government in Galveston, Texas, to respond to the chaos caused by a hurricane in 1900 that demolished the city and killed 6,000 people. Bowing to gubernatorial pressure, the Texas legislature authorized the creation of a totally new form of city government—a commission form—and by 1904, the new city government had entirely rebuilt Galveston. The success of the commission led to its adoption first by other Texas cities (Houston, Dallas, Fort Worth) and then, within a decade, by 160 other municipalities (such as Des Moines, Iowa; Pittsburgh, Pennsylvania; Buffalo, New York; Nashville, Tennessee; and Charlotte, North Carolina). Its appeal was its ostensible reduction of politics in city government.

But almost as fast as the commission form of government appeared, disillusionment set in. One problem stemmed from the predictable tendency of commissioners to act as advocates for their own departments. Each commissioner wanted a larger share of the city's budget allocated to her department. Another problem had to do with politicians acting as administrators: Elected officials do not always turn out to be good managers. The result was that public enthusiasm for the commission form declined. By 1990, when Tulsa, Oklahoma, installed a mayor-council form in place of its commission system, only a few cities continued to use a commission structure. Notable among them was Portland, Oregon, with its modified commission form of government. And Portland likes its commission form. A measure to change to a council-manager structure was handily defeated by voters in 2007. (Some council-manager cities such as Ft. Lauderdale, Florida, and Grand Rapids, Michigan, call their city council a "commission," but they do not have a formal commission structure as described here.)

WHICH FORM OF CITY GOVERNMENT IS BEST?

Experts disagree about which city government structure is best. Most would probably agree that structures lacking a strong executive officer are generally less preferable than others. By that standard, the weak-mayor–council and the commission forms are less favorable. The strong-mayor–council form of government is extolled for fixing accountability firmly in the mayor's office, and the council-manager system is credited with professionalizing city government by bringing in skilled administrators to run things. Yet strong-mayor structures are criticized for concentrating power in the mayor's office; council-manager forms are taken to task for placing too much power in the hands of an unelected city manager. A recent study adds some clarity with its finding that cities lacking a professional administrator tend to have more conflict and less cooperation in formulating public policy.[19] Ultimately, it is up to community residents to decide which form of government they want, and several have made structural changes recently.

In 2004, Richmond, Virginia, switched from a weak-mayor structure to a strong-mayor form; in 2006, San Diego replaced its city manager with a strong mayor. In Sacramento, it was the mayor himself who took up the strong-mayor cause; the city council put the question on the 2014 ballot, where it was rejected by voters. El Paso, Texas, however moved in a different direction and abandoned its strong-mayor structure and joined the ranks of council-manager cities. For some cities, a hybrid form that combines features of several structures may be the answer. For instance, both Oakland, California, and Cincinnati, Ohio, amended their council-manager form of government by adding a strong-mayor position and retaining the position of city manager. In fact, the distinction between the mayor-council form and the council-manager form may be blurring as more cities tinker with their structures, designing entities that contain elements of both.[20] A recent study of Michigan cities found just such a pattern.[21] We will return to this issue in Chapter 11 in the discussion of local leadership.

PRESSING ISSUES FOR CITIES

The pressing issues in city governments these days include planning and land use, annexation, finances, and representation. Although the issues are discussed separately in the following subsections, they are frequently intertwined. For instance, decisions about land use can affect the city's finances; the annexation of new territory may alter representation patterns.

Planning and Land Use Land is important to city governments for their economic and political well-being. City governments control land uses within their boundaries and frequently use a comprehensive plan (often called a *general* or *master plan*) to guide them. The plan divides the city into sections for commercial, industrial, and residential uses. In addition, a city might set aside areas for recreation and open space. For example, the general plan for Santa Barbara, California, designates portions of the city for parks, bikeways, and a bird refuge.

New York City enacted the first modern zoning **ordinance** in 1916; since then, cities have used *zoning* to effect land-use planning and control. Through zoning, the designations established in a city's plan are made specific. For example, land set aside for residential use may be zoned for single-family dwellings, multifamily units, or mobile homes. Commercial areas may be zoned for offices, shopping centers, or hotels. Industrial sections of the city are often separated into "light" and "heavy" zones. In addition, cities can overlay special zones onto existing ones. For instance, cities intending to restore older sections of the commercially zoned downtown area may

ordinance

Enacted by the governing body, it is the local government equivalent of a statute.

establish historic preservation zones. Once these zones are so designated, property owners are prohibited from tearing down old structures there and, instead, are encouraged to renovate them. A city eager to transform the appearance of a particular area may also create special zones so it can regulate architectural style or the height of buildings and thus achieve the right "look." Less desirable uses, such as pornographic bookstores and XXX theaters, are often clustered together in special adult entertainment zones.

Once set, zoning can be altered through applications for variances and rezoning, usually heard by a city's planning commission, and subsequently approved or denied by the city council. A variance is a waiver of a zoning requirement such as a minimum lot size or a building height limit. Rezoning involves a change in zoning designation, either to allow more intense use of the land (an upzoning) or to restrict use (downzoning). Applications for variances and rezoning are often controversial. A study of fourteen years' worth of applications to upzone parcels in Wilmington, Delaware, demonstrated that community sentiment played an important role in the outcome.[22]

Zoning is ultimately a political exercise with economic consequences. Cities use zoning to promote "good" growth such as upscale residential areas and to limit "bad" growth such as low-income housing.[23] Some cities have engaged in a practice that became known as *exclusionary zoning*. For example, a city might restrict its residential zones to 4,500-square-foot single-family dwellings on five-acre lots. The resulting high cost of housing would effectively limit the pool of potential residents to the wealthy. Recent research has documented greater segregation by income in metropolitan areas in which suburbs restrict the density of residential construction compared with places with more permissive density zoning rules.[24] Court decisions have not only found exclusionary zoning illegal, but they have also instructed local governments to provide housing opportunities for low- and moderate-income people.

Annexation **Annexation** has been a popular means by which cities can add territory, population, and tax base. In the past thirty years, many cities have found themselves squeezed by the rapid growth and incorporation of territory just outside city limits and hence beyond their control. What is worse (from a central city's perspective), some of these suburban cities have begun to threaten the central city's traditional dominance of the metropolitan area. People and jobs are finding suburban locales to their liking, and many have left the central city. To counteract this trend and to ensure adequate space for future expansion, some cities have engaged in annexation efforts. During one six-year period, U.S. cities added nearly 3.5 million acres of land via 45,000 annexations.[25]

Not all cities can annex, however. They run up against two realities: the strictures of state laws and the existence of incorporated suburbs on their borders (which means the territory cannot be annexed). State governments determine the legal procedures for the annexation process, and they can make it easy or hard.[26] Texas is a state that makes it easy for cities to annex and, not surprisingly, big Texas cities (in terms of population) have vast territories: Houston covers 600 square miles; San Antonio, 465 square miles; and Dallas, 386 square miles. Texas cities use their power of **extraterritorial jurisdiction (ETJ)** to supplement annexation. Under ETJ, they can control subdivision

annexation
The addition of unincorporated adjacent territory to a municipality.

extraterritorial jurisdiction (ETJ)
The ability of a city government to control certain practices in an adjacent, unincorporated area.

practices in unincorporated bordering territory. (The amount of territory varies from a half-mile for small cities to five miles for cities with over 250,000 people.) A Texas city can annex up to 10 percent of its territory annually without a referendum simply by providing adequate notice to the about-to-be-annexed residents.

Some states make it difficult for their cities to annex. Cities may have to wait for landowners in an adjoining area to petition to be annexed. In some instances, a city bent on annexation will put pressure on landowners outside the city who use city services such as water or sewer. Agree to be annexed, they say, or the price of the service may skyrocket or, even worse, the service might be curtailed.[27] In some states, even when a majority of the landowners request annexation, referendum elections must be held if the proportion is less than 75 percent. State law may require that the annexation be approved by referendum by both the existing city and the area to be annexed. This stipulation is known as a *dual majority*, and it complicates the annexation process.

Some of the most prominent U.S. cities have rather confined city limits. For example, of the 50 most populated cities in the country, 22 control fewer than 100 square miles of territory. The most extreme cases are Newark, New Jersey (covering 23.8 square miles); Miami, Florida (35.6); Buffalo, New York (40.6); San Francisco, California (46.4); and Boston, Massachusetts (48.4).[28] In the older, established metropolitan areas, a central city has little room to expand because it is hemmed in by incorporated suburbs. Suburban areas incorporate—that is, become legal municipal entities—for many reasons. The threat of being annexed by a neighboring city frequently stimulates the creation of new cities.

Finances City governments, like other local governments, must balance their fiscal resources against their fiscal needs. Unlike the national government, however, these governments have to operate within the constraints of a balanced budget. As a result, they have become fairly creative at finding new sources of revenue in hard times.

One standard approach to budget-balancing is to reduce the rate of growth in operational spending (expenditures related to service provision, such as city employee salaries). Another popular mechanism is to increase the level of fees and charges. For instance, a city might increase the cost of a building permit or charge more for health inspections at restaurants. It can also hike the cost of parking in a metered space or in a city-owned parking garage. (Commuting students at urban colleges with inadequate parking have probably marveled at how adept city officials are at the "make students pay" strategy.) Indeed, cities can boost revenues in several seemingly small ways. A city service that used to be free, such as a city park, may now have an admission fee. Cities can postpone or reduce their capital spending (expenditures for big-ticket items such as installation of sewer systems or the purchase of fire engines) and contract out services to private providers, for example, allowing a waste-disposal firm to collect residential garbage or a local charity to take over the operation of homeless shelters. The Controversies in States and Localities feature takes up one remedy that many cities are pursuing: the outsourcing of city services.

Controversies in States and Localities

Outsourcing City Services

When cities face budget deficits, they seek to reduce costs. For some cities and towns, outsourcing city services—contracting with nonprofit organizations, private firms, and other governments to provide the services—can be part of the solution. (This topic is discussed in Chapter 8 in the section labeled "Privatization.") In San Jose, California, in 2010, as the reality of a $118-million-dollar deficit became clear, city officials cast about for any cost-savings they could find. One solution was to hire private janitorial firms to clean both city hall and the airport, saving the city $4 million. Sandy Springs, Georgia, a newly incorporated city outside Atlanta, has gone even further by contracting out a range of services to a private firm.

For some localities, outsourcing is a way of life. Consider the city of Weston, Florida, an affluent planned community that was incorporated in 1996. The city has a population of 65,000, an annual budget of $121 million, and only nine city employees. City services ranging from park maintenance to public safety are provided through 35 contracts with private firms and with county government. A visitor to City Hall might see individuals working in various offices, but they are employees of private companies that are paid by the city. What makes Weston even more different from other outsourcing cities is that the city's charter expressly discourages hiring city employees. The only way for the city to bring a service under the purview of city government is for four of the five city council members to approve an exception.

Outsourcing offers several potential advantages to cities. The most obvious is that outsourcing usually saves cities money. If several private firms bid on a contract, the resulting cost competition works to a city's benefit. Another advantage that cities enjoy through outsourcing is flexibility: employees can be hired and laid off as demand necessitates, avoiding labor disputes with unionized city employees.

However, outsourcing is not a perfect solution. Many critics assert that outsourcing makes employees less accountable to the city and its residents. And there is always the risk that the private firm may not deliver the service as specified by the terms of the contract. Finally, negotiating contracts and monitoring compliance can be a complicated and arduous process. City governments need to exercise due diligence to make outsourcing work.

Weston, Florida, and Sandy Springs, Georgia, have moved much farther along the outsourcing path than most cities have. But it is clear that even among the most traditional city governments that have relied on city employees to provide services, the attraction of outsourcing some city services is strong.

Critical Thinking Questions:

1. Does your city government outsource the delivery of certain public services? If so, what are they?

2. From the city government's perspective, what are the differences between contracting with a private firm, a nonprofit organization, or another local government?

3. What can a city government do if contractor fails to deliver an agreed-upon public service? What are the possible consequences of the city's actions?

SOURCES: Tamara Audi, "Cities Rent Police, Janitors to Save Cash," July 19, 2010 http://online.wsj.com/article/ SB10001424052 7487043346045753391 53865582376.html (accessed May 20, 2012); Ryan Holeywell, "How Weston, Florida, a City of 65,000, Gets by on 9 Employees," May 14, 2012, www.governing.com/tmeplates/ gov_print_article?id=151147685 (accessed May 14, 2012). See also Vanessa Bouche and Craig Volden, "Privatization and the Diffusion of Innovations," *Journal of Politics* 73 (April 2011): 428–442 and Meeyoung Lamothe and Scott Lamothe, "To Trust or Not to Trust? What Matters in Local Government-Vendor Relationships?" *Journal of Public Administration Research and Theory* 22 (October 2012): 867–92.

Cities and other local governments found the financial going tough during the recessionary period late in the first decade of the twenty-first century.[29] Figure 10.7 shows how rapidly the fiscal situation deteriorated in city governments. In 2007, 70 percent of city finance officers reported that they were better able to meet their city's financial needs than in the year before. By 2009,

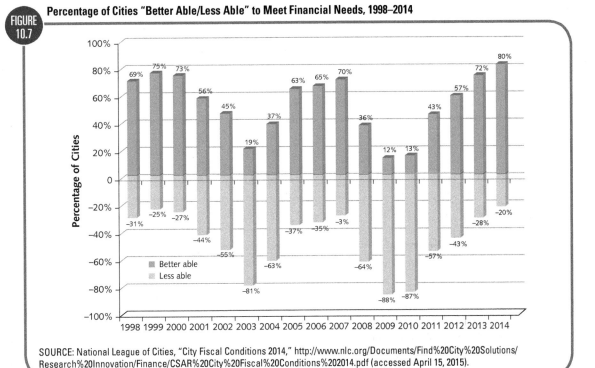

FIGURE 10.7

Percentage of Cities "Better Able/Less Able" to Meet Financial Needs, 1998–2014

SOURCE: National League of Cities, "City Fiscal Conditions 2014," http://www.nlc.org/Documents/Find%20City%20Solutions/Research%20Innovation/Finance/CSAR%20City%20Fiscal%20Conditions%202014.pdf (accessed April 15, 2015).

only 12 percent reported this to be the case, the lowest figure in decades. Fortunately, the fiscal situation has been improving, as shown by the percentages for 2011 to 2014.

Representation Representation in city government is another fundamental concern. How can citizens' preferences be represented effectively in city hall? In the colonial days of town meetings and civic republics, it was simple: a citizen showed up at the meeting hall, voiced his opinion, and the majority ruled. When this procedure proved to be unwieldy, a system of representative democracy seemed the perfect solution.

In city governments, city council members are elected in one of two ways: either at large or by districts (also called wards). In **at-large elections**, a city voter can vote in each council race. (One modification of the at-large approach requires candidates to compete for a specific seat or "place" on the council; however, the vote is citywide.) In **district (ward) elections**, a city voter can vote only in the council race in her district. From the perspective of candidates, the at-large system means that a citywide campaign must be mounted. With districts, a candidate's campaign is limited to a specific area of the city. As discussed in Chapter 11, the structural **reform movement** during the Progressive Era advocated at-large elections as a means of weakening the geographic base of political machines. Candidates running in citywide races must appeal to a broad cross section of the population to be successful.

at-large elections
Citywide (or countywide) contests to determine the members of a city council (or county commission).

district (ward) elections
Elections in which the voters in one district or ward of a jurisdiction (city, county, school district) vote for a candidate to represent that district.

reform movement

An early twentieth century effort to depoliticize local governments through nonpartisan elections, at-large representation, shorter ballots, and professional management.

The use of at-large electoral systems has significant consequences. An in-depth study of almost 1,000 city council members across the country revealed that at-large members tended to be wealthier and more highly educated than council members elected from districts.[30] At-large council members also differ from district members in terms of their relationships with constituents. Council members elected at large devote less time to answering individual complaints and direct their attention to a citywide and business constituency.

Almost half of U.S. cities with populations of 2,500 or more use an at-large method for electing their council members, but the popularity of the method decreases as the size of a city's population increases. For example, less than 15 percent of cities with populations above the half-million mark use at-large elections. This approach to city council representation is increasingly under attack for diminishing the likelihood that a member of a minority group can be elected. Research on more than 1,000 southern communities indicated that the abolition of at-large elections resulted in dramatic gains in black representation.[31] And the impact is not confined to the South. When New York City redrew city council district lines and increased the number of seats, the resulting council was composed of more African Americans and Latinos than ever before.

Although research on the topic continues, studies have shown that changing the electoral system from at large to districts has other effects such as an overall increase in citizen participation in terms of greater attendance at council meetings, higher voter turnout, and a larger number of candidates. These findings are not universal, however. For example, a recent study of 57 cities compared voter turnout in the two different electoral systems and found that turnout in at-large elections actually outpaced turnout in district elections by nearly 6 percentage points.[32] Furthermore, it is not altogether clear that changing to districts will translate into policy benefits for the previously underrepresented sectors of the city. Earlier research suggested that in terms of attitudes toward public policy, there was really no significant difference between council members elected at large and those elected from districts.[33] However, this tendency may not hold up when it comes to minority employment. Research in Texas showed that, even after accounting for other factors, school systems in which school board members were elected from wards hired more minority school administrators than at-large systems did.[34]

One alternative in jurisdictions where minority candidates have met with persistent electoral defeat is an approach called **cumulative voting**. Candidates run at large, and voters cast as many votes as there are seats to be filled. The voter may allocate these votes as she wishes, either as a bloc for one candidate or spread out among the candidates. In a community with a history of racially or ethnically polarized voting, the chance of minority-candidate success increases under a cumulative-voting arrangement. For example, when Alamogordo, New Mexico, adopted cumulative voting, a Latino candidate who would have finished fourth in a standard at-large election placed third in total votes cast.[35] Because three seats were being contested, the difference between a third- and fourth-place finish meant the difference between winning and losing. Although interest in the cumulative voting option remains

cumulative voting

Candidates compete at large and voters can cast as many votes as there are seats to be filled, either as a bloc for one candidate or spread out among several candidates.

Entryway to Oakland Park, a city in Broward County, Florida.

strong, its actual use these days is limited to a small number of jurisdictions including the city councils in Cambridge, Massachusetts, and Santa Clarita, California, and the school board in Amarillo, Texas.

Towns and Townships

The word *town* evokes an image of a small community where everyone knows everyone else, where government is informal, and where local leaders gather at the coffee shop to make important decisions. This image is both accurate and inaccurate. Towns generally are smaller, in terms of population and land area, than cities or counties. And the extent of their governmental powers depends on state government. But even where they are relatively weak, town government is increasingly becoming more formalized.

HOW DO WE KNOW A TOWN WHEN WE SEE ONE?

Towns and townships are general-purpose units of local government, distinct from county and city governments. Only 20 states, primarily in the Northeast and Midwest, have official towns or townships. In some states, these small jurisdictions have relatively broad powers; in others, they have a more circumscribed role.

In New England, towns offer the kinds of services commonly associated with cities and counties in other states. Many New England towns continue their tradition of direct democracy through a **town meeting** form of government. At a yearly town assembly, residents make decisions on policy matters confronting the community. They elect town officials, pass local ordinances, levy taxes, and adopt a budget. In other words, the people who attend the town meeting function as a legislative body. Although the mechanism of the town meeting exemplifies democracy in action, it often falls short of the ideal,

LO 10.4

To evaluate the roles and future of town and township government.

town meeting

An annual event at which a town's residents enact ordinances, elect officials, levy taxes, and adopt a budget.

primarily due to the relatively low rate of citizen participation in meetings. Often, fewer than 10 percent of a town's voters actually attend the meeting. Those who do show up tend to be older and, not surprisingly, more engaged in politics in general. Research has found that "some citizens are in fact turned off by the lack of civility of the face-to-face interactions at town meetings."[36] Larger towns in Connecticut and Massachusetts rely on representatives elected by residents to vote at the meetings.

Towns in New England, along with those in New Jersey, New York, and Pennsylvania, enjoy fairly broad powers. In large measure, they act like other general-purpose units of government. Townships in Michigan and in Wisconsin (townships are called towns in the Badger State) are similarly empowered. In the remainder of the township states (Illinois, Indiana, Kansas, Minnesota, Missouri, Nebraska, North Dakota, Ohio, and South Dakota), the nature of township government is more rural. Rural townships tend to stretch across 36 square miles of land (conforming to the surveys done by the national government before the areas were settled), and their service offerings are often limited to roads and law enforcement. In one state, Indiana, townships actually cover the entire territory and population with other jurisdictional units superimposed on them. (Revisit Figure 10.1 near the beginning of this chapter.) A part-time elected board of supervisors or trustees commonly rules the roost in townships. In addition, some of the jobs in government may be staffed by volunteers rather than salaried workers. However, the closer these rural townships are to large urban areas, the more likely they are to offer an expanded set of services to residents.

THE FUTURE OF TOWNS AND TOWNSHIPS

The demise of the township type of government has long been expected. As rural areas become more populated, they will eventually meet the population minimums necessary to become municipalities. In 2000, for instance, residents of a Minnesota township decided to incorporate as a municipality to ward off annexation by a neighboring city.[37] Even in New England, questions of town viability have arisen. For example, many Connecticut towns with populations exceeding 15,000 have found it increasingly difficult to operate effectively through town meetings.[38] Accordingly, some are adding professional managers, whereas others are considering a shift to a strong-mayor form of government.

Some other towns face a different problem. Many are experiencing substantial population exodus and, in the process, losing their reason for existence. These towns may die a natural death, with other types of government (perhaps counties or special districts) providing services to the remaining residents. The question is: Do towns and townships make sense in contemporary America? Despite dire predictions of their pending demise, towns and townships have proved to be remarkably resilient. The U.S. Census Bureau counted 16,364 towns and townships in 2012, down only 265 from the 1997 figure. Most of the decline came in Midwestern states.

Towns and townships have not sat idly by while commentators speculated on their dim future. They formed an interest group, the National Association of Towns and Townships (NATaT), to lobby on their behalf in Washington, D.C. Seven states have statewide town or township associations that offer services to member governments and promote town-related issues in the legislature. Also, many small towns have embarked on ambitious economic development strategies—industrial recruitment, tourism promotion, and amenity enhancement—in an attempt to stimulate new growth.

Special Districts

LO 10.5

To analyze the need for special districts and the concerns about them.

Special districts are established to meet certain service needs in a particular area. In other words, they do what other local governments cannot or will not do. Special districts can be formed in three different ways:

- States can create them through special enabling legislation.
- General-purpose local governments may adopt a resolution establishing a special district.
- Citizens may initiate districts by petition, which is often followed by a referendum on their creation.

Some districts have the power to levy taxes; others rely on user fees, grants, and private revenue bonds for funding. Taxing districts typically have elected governing boards; nontaxing districts—called **public authorities**—ordinarily operate with appointed boards.[39] The United States has approximately 37,000 special districts, and that number is increasing. In the fifteen-year period from 1997 to 2012, the number of special districts grew by nearly 2,500.[40] As one might expect, the pattern of special-district creation (and abolition) varies from one state to another. Colorado and Florida accounted for a large portion of the increase from 1997 to 2012 with the establishment of more than 900 and 450 special districts, respectively; Indiana however, reduced its special district count by nearly 500 during that period.

Not all special districts are organized alike. Ninety-two percent of them provide a single function, but the functions vary. Natural resource management, fire protection, housing and community development, and water and sewer service are the most common. Among the 2,309 special districts in Texas are drainage districts, utility districts, river authorities, emergency services districts, sports facility authorities, community college districts, and hospital districts. Most states have other, state-specific districts, such as Colorado's mine drainage districts and tunnel districts or Florida's beach and shore preservation districts and mobile home park recreation districts. The budget and staff size of special districts range from minuscule to mammoth. Some of the more prominent include the Port Authority of New York and New Jersey, the Chicago Transit Authority, the Washington Public Power Supply System, and the Los Angeles County Sanitation District. The states of Illinois and California have the highest number of special districts (3,232 and 2,786, respectively). Alaska and Hawaii have the fewest by far, with 15 and 17, respectively.

WHY SPECIAL DISTRICTS ARE NEEDED

Special districts overlay existing general-purpose local governments and address deficiencies in them.[41] Three general categories of "deficiencies" are worth examining: technical conditions, financial constraints, and political explanations.

public authority

A type of special district funded by nontax revenue and governed by an appointed board.

First are the technical conditions of a general-purpose local government. In some states, cities cannot extend their service districts beyond their boundaries. Moreover, the problem to be addressed may not fit neatly within a single jurisdiction. A river that runs through several counties may periodically overflow its banks in heavy spring rains—a problem affecting small portions of many jurisdictions. A flood control district covering only the affected areas may be a logical solution. Problems of scale must also be considered. A general-purpose local government simply may not be able to provide electric service to its residents as efficiently as a special utility district that covers a multitude of counties. Finally, some states prohibit the jurisdictional co-venturing that would allow localities to offer services jointly with other jurisdictions. In that case, operation of a two-county library would require the establishment of a special two-county library district.

A second set of deficiencies has to do with financial constraints. Local general-purpose governments commonly operate under debt and tax limitations. Demands for additional services that exceed a jurisdiction's revenue-raising ceiling or lead to the assumption of excessive debt cannot be accommodated. By using special districts, existing jurisdictions can circumvent the debt and tax ceilings. (A new study of Indiana's special districts found that they accounted for 8 percent of local government expenditures, but carried approximately 38 percent of total local government debt in the state.[42]) Furthermore, special districts are better suited than general-purpose governments for service-charge or user-fee financing, whereby the cost of the service can be directly apportioned to the consumer (as with water or sewer charges). Research has confirmed that the more stringent the financial limitations that a state imposes on its county governments, the greater the number of special districts in those counties.[43]

Technical and financial deficiencies of general-purpose local governments help to explain the creation of special districts, but political explanations shed even more light. Restrictive annexation laws and county governments with limited authority are political facts of life that encourage the use of special districts. For residents of an urban fringe area, a public-service district (which may provide more than one service) may be the only option. Some special districts owe their existence to a federal mandate. For example, national government policy has spurred the establishment of soil conservation and flood control districts throughout the country.

Once created, a special district may become a political power in its own right. In places where general-purpose governmental units are fully equipped legally, financially, and technically to provide a service, they may encounter resistance from special-district interests fighting to preserve an existing district.

CONCERNS ABOUT SPECIAL DISTRICTS

The arguments in favor of special districts revolve around their potential for efficient service provision and the likelihood that they will be responsive to constituents whose demands are not otherwise being met.[44] For the most part, however, scholarly observers look at special districts with a jaundiced eye.

The most frequently heard complaint is that special districts lack accountability. The public is often unaware of their existence, so they function free of much scrutiny. A study of 100 airport and seaport districts found that those with an elected governing board were no more likely to be responsive to public preferences than those with appointed boards.[45] And as research by Nancy Burns reminds us, the establishment of special districts is a costly political act.[46] Well-placed groups such as businesses, developers, and homeowners' associations are among the beneficiaries of special-district creation.

One thing is certain: the proliferation of special districts complicates the development of comprehensive solutions to public problems. It is not uncommon for cities and counties to be locked in governmental combat with the special districts in their area. All of these governmental units tend to be turf-protecting, service-providing, revenue-seeking rivals.[47] Despite the claims of district advocates, special districts may actually drive up the costs of service delivery. An analysis of 300 metropolitan areas compared services provided by special districts with those provided by general-purpose governments and found that districts actually had a higher per capita cost.[48]

Cognizant of these concerns, state governments are looking more closely at special districts and the role they play in service delivery. Several states have taken actions that give their general-purpose local governments more input into the decision to create special districts.

School Districts

School districts are a type of single-purpose local government. They are a distinct kind of special district and, as such, are considered one of the five types of local government. The trend in school districts follows the theory that fewer is better. Before World War II, more than 100,000 school districts covered the countryside. Many of these were rural, one-school operations. In many small towns, community identity was linked to the local schoolhouse. Despite serving as a source of pride, small districts were so expensive to maintain that consolidations have occurred throughout the nation, and by 2012 the number of districts was just under 13,000. Nebraska exemplifies the trend. In 1952, there were 6,392 school districts in the state; by 2012, the Cornhusker State had only 272. Now the states with the highest number of school districts by far are Texas (1,079) and California (1,025).

Consolidating schools can be a political hot potato, as the former governor of Arkansas, Mike Huckabee, learned. In 2003, Governor Huckabee proposed a consolidation plan that would eliminate school districts with fewer than 1,500 students.[49] The state supreme court had ruled that the school finance system was inequitable and that a remedy had to be designed. Since raising taxes was a political no-no, the governor offered his consolidation plan. However, the governor's plan meant eliminating two-thirds of the school districts in the state and merging them to create larger districts. Folks in the rural, small-town areas of Arkansas were displeased, to put it mildly. Governor Huckabee's plan made for a lively legislative session in 2004, as lawmakers from affected areas fought to save their school districts. Legislators eventually agreed

LO 10.6

To explore the politics and issues affecting school district government.

to allow the 57 school districts that contained fewer than 350 students each to be absorbed by larger districts or to partner with other small districts to form a new, larger entity. Kentucky and West Virginia are among other states that have wrestled recently with the issue of merging small, rural school districts.

SCHOOL POLITICS

The school board is the formal source of power and authority in the district. The board is typically composed of five to seven members, usually elected in nonpartisan, at-large elections. Their job is to make policy for the school district. One of the most important policy decisions involves the district budget—how the money will be spent.

School districts are governed by these boards and managed by trained, full-time educational administrators. Like city governments, school districts invested heavily in the reform model of governance, and the average district has become more professional in operation in the past 40 years.[50] An appointed chief administrator (a superintendent) heads the school district staff, the size of which depends on the size of the district. The staff plays an important role in making sure that new laws adopted by the state are implemented by schools in the district.

Revamping public education has been a hot topic for the past two decades. Concern over mismanagement of funds and low student achievement has led some states to shift control of schools away from the school district itself and place it in the hands of city government, typically in the mayor's office, for a period of time. New York City, Chicago, Baltimore, Cleveland, and Detroit are among the most prominent examples. At the same time, other school districts have sought to decentralize, shifting power to the individual school level. This school-based management approach has meant greater involvement of the private sector in some schools; in others it has enhanced the role of teachers and parents. Regardless, these efforts all share the same basic objective: improving the performance of public schools.

SCHOOL DISTRICT ISSUES

Among the myriad challenges faced by school districts is one persistent conundrum: how to secure sufficient funding for public education. Although the relationship is a bit more complex than the old saying "you get what you pay for," there is widespread agreement that children in well-funded school districts are better off educationally than those in poorly funded ones.

equalization formula

A means of distributing funds (primarily to school districts) to reduce financial disparities among districts.

Serious disparities in school funding, caused by wide differences in the available property taxes that provide much of the revenue for public education, have led to the increasing financial involvement of state government in local school districts. State governments use an **equalization formula** to distribute funds to school districts in an effort to reduce financial disparities. Under this formula, poorer school districts receive a proportionately larger share of state funds than wealthier districts do. Although these programs have increased the amount of funding for education, they have not eliminated the interdistrict variation. Wealthier districts simply use the state guarantee as a foundation on which to heap their own resources; poorer school districts continue to operate with less revenue. This situation prompted many state supreme courts around the country to declare their public-school finance systems unconstitutional. Legislatures struggled to design new, more equitable financial arrangements. Michigan lowered property taxes for schools and substituted sales taxes and other revenues. Other states have established lotteries and earmarked the proceeds for education. The issue of money for schools stays at the top of legislative agendas, year in and year out. This topic, along with school administration and innovations in education, is covered in more detail in Chapter 15.

Communities and Governance

Let us return to the governance issue that was raised early in this chapter and has been alluded to throughout: How do we know when a community is well governed? This chapter is full of examples of communities restructuring their governments in hopes of improving governance. Voters oust incumbents and elect new council members in a similar effort. Conflict over local government spending priorities ensues. Local jurisdictions embark on innovative efforts to respond to their citizens' concerns. And on and on. The good news is that a recent study found evidence that the policies enacted by city governments do tend to reflect the preferences of their citizens.[51] Cities with more liberal populations adopt more liberal policies; cities with conservative electorates enact more conservative policies.

On the whole, the American public seems to be reasonably satisfied with their local governments. Table 10.2 reports the results of Gallup polls

LO 10.7

To consider the issue of "good" governance at the local level.

TABLE 10.2   Public Opinion: Trust in Local Government

Poll Question: How much trust and confidence do you have in the local governments in the area where you live when it comes to handling local problems—a great deal, a fair amount, not very much, or none at all?

	GREAT DEAL (%)	FAIR AMOUNT (%)	NOT VERY MUCH (%)	NONE AT ALL (%)	NO OPINION (%)
2014	24	48	18	8	1
2013	21	50	19	9	1
2012	23	51	16	8	1
2011	19	49	21	11	1
2010	19	51	20	10	1
2009	19	50	22	8	1
2008	23	49	17	9	2
2007	22	47	19	10	2

SOURCE: Adapted from Gallup Poll, "Trust in Government." www.gallup.com/poll/5392/trust-government.aspx (accessed April 15, 2015).

conducted periodically that ask respondents about their trust and confidence in local government. Public opinion tends to be positive and stable over time with between 68 and 72 percent of respondents answering either "a great deal" or "a fair amount" of trust and confidence in localities.

Although there is no universally accepted set of criteria for evaluating the quality of governance, several researchers and organizations have come up with proxy measures.[52] For example, the National Civic League bestows its "All-America City" designation on ten jurisdictions (cities, counties, and metro areas) that successfully tackle serious community problems in a collaborative way. Winning the accolade in 2015 were these jurisdictions:

- Carson, California
- Salinas, California
- Stockton, California
- Tallahassee, Florida
- Somerville, Massachusetts
- Tupelo, Mississippi
- Geneva, New York
- Marshall, Texas
- Spokane, Washington
- Yakima, Washington[53]

The award-winning projects dealt with issues ranging from improving the lives of vulnerable young people to neighborhood revitalization, disaster recovery, and greenway development.

The governance question goes back to Plato and Aristotle, and we are unlikely to resolve it here. But the approach used in identifying All-America cities—tackling serious community problems in a collaborative way—offers some guidance for continued discussion about government structure and function.

Chapter Recap

- Theoretically, communities can be considered civic republics, corporate enterprises, or consumer markets. Legally, there are five types of local governments: counties, municipalities, towns and townships, special districts, and school districts. The United States has more than 90,000 local governments.

- Counties were created by states to serve as their local administrative extensions. Over time, they have taken on more functions and, especially in urban areas, they provide municipal-type services.

- The United States has more than 19,000 municipalities, or cities. The strong-mayor–council form of city government invests power in an elected mayor; the council-manager structure relies heavily on a professional administrator to run the city. The issue about which structure is better instigates much debate.

- Towns and townships are general-purpose local governments, like counties and cities. Twenty states, primarily in the Northeast and Midwest, have official towns or townships. Some have fairly broad powers; others, especially rural Midwestern townships, offer more limited services. Many experts have predicted that towns and townships will gradually disappear as the nation urbanizes.

- Special districts are the most prevalent and at the same time the least understood of the five types of local government. They provide a service to an area that other local governments do not provide because of technical, financial, or political considerations. Natural resource management, fire protection, housing and community development, and water and sewer service are the most common special districts. Their financing varies: some have the power to tax; others rely on user fees, grants, or bonds.

- The number of school districts has declined because of mergers and consolidations to a current level of fewer than 13,000. School districts are typically governed by elected boards and managed by trained, full-time educational administrators. School politics can create rivalries as issues such as parental choice, neighborhood schools, and effective financing are debated.

- The public wants well-governed communities. Local governments redesign their structures in the hope of improving governance. Polls show that the public's trust and confidence in local government is fairly positive and stable. Analysts continue to develop criteria such as managing for results in an effort to identify the best performing localities.

KEY TERMS

general-purpose local government *(p. 256)*
single-purpose local government *(p. 258)*
metropolitan area *(p. 258)*
micropolitan statistical area *(p. 259)*
home rule *(p. 259)*
jurisdictional overlap *(p. 259)*

incorporation *(p. 264)*
charter *(p. 264)*
strong-mayor–council structure *(p. 265)*
weak-mayor–council structure *(p. 265)*
city manager *(p. 267)*
ordinance *(p. 269)*
annexation *(p. 270)*

extraterritorial jurisdiction (*ETJ*) *(p. 270)*
at-large elections *(p. 273)*
district (ward) elections *(p. 273)*
reform movement *(p. 274)*
cumulative voting *(p. 274)*
town meeting *(p. 275)*
public authority *(p. 277)*
equalization formula *(p. 280)*

INTERNET RESOURCES

Most of the five types of government are represented by national associations, which have websites: **www.naco.org** (National Association of Counties); **www.nlc.org** (National League of Cities); **www.natat.org** (National Association of Towns and Townships); **www.nsba.org** (for school districts, the relevant website is that of the National School Boards Association).

To explore a specific school district, see **www.kcpublicschools.org** (the website of the Kansas City, Missouri, school district).

Special districts, by virtue of their specialized nature, tend to have function-specific national organizations. For example, the National Association of Conservation Districts can be found at **www.nacdnet.org**. A fifteen-county district, the Colorado River Water Conservation District, whose website can be found at **www.crwcd.org**, is an example of an individual special district. The website of one of the most famous special districts, the Port Authority of New York and New Jersey, is **www.panynj.gov**.

Cities and counties have learned that maintaining websites is a good way to connect with the public. The website for the city of Los Angeles can be found at **www.lacity.org**; the website for the county can be found at **www.lacounty.gov**. The website for the largest county in Michigan is **www.waynecounty.com;** the largest county in Nevada is at **www.clarkcountynv.gov**.

You can find information about the Big Apple at **www.nyc.gov**; for the city of New Orleans at **www.nola.gov**. The websites for the cities of Atlanta and Minneapolis are **www.atlantaga.gov** and **www.ci.minneapolis.mn.us**, respectively.

A scholarly journal that contains the latest research on local governments is *Urban Affairs Review*. Its URL is **uar.sagepub.com**.

Local Leadership and Governance: Continuity and Change

LEARNING OBJECTIVES

11.1 To critique various theories of community power.

11.2 To understand disputes over property rights as manifestations of power.

11.3 To compare different types of local executives and the challenges they face.

11.4 To appreciate the conflict inherent in local legislative bodies.

11.5 To articulate why localities need leadership.

Since 1973, there had been six proposals to replace the at-large election of city council-members in Austin, Texas, with a district election system. All of the proposals failed until 2012. That year, two options were put before the voters: the 8-2-1 plan which featured eight district seats, two at-large seats, and a mayor elected citywide and the 10-1 plan which did away with all at-large council seats in favor of electing 10 council members from districts and a mayor voted on citywide. Austinites for Geographic Representation pushed adoption of the 10-1 plan; the Austin Community for Change supported the 8-2-1 system.[1] Voters approved the 10-1 plan and in 2014, Austin elected its first council members from districts. What was the city trying to accomplish with this structural change? The intent was to produce a more diverse city council that would be responsive to the interests of the different neighborhoods in Austin. In other words, the goal was to insure that the leadership of the city reflected the city itself. Once the 10-1 plan was in place, some in Austin began to ponder another possible change with leadership consequences: adoption of a strong-mayor structure.

Leadership goes hand in hand with governance. It can make the difference between an effectively functioning government and one that lurches from one crisis to another. The local governments described in Chapter 10 require talented leaders, regardless of their structural form. The terms that conjure images of leadership in local government circles these days include *initiative, inventiveness, risk taking, high energy level, persistence, innovation*, and *vision*. These words share a common element: they denote activity and engagement. Leaders are people who make a difference. And there's an electoral payoff for doing a good job. Research findings have confirmed that higher job performance ratings translate into higher mayoral approval levels.[2] Not surprisingly, mayors with high approval are more likely to be re-elected.

One of the popular labels for contemporary leaders is *entrepreneur*. How do you know an entrepreneurial leader when you see one in local government? You can identify such leaders by their advocacy of innovative ideas. They are the people "who actively seek opportunities for dynamic changes in policy or politics."[3] Some may occupy positions of power in local government; others may emerge from the ranks of ordinary citizens. Regardless of their background, they share a commitment to new ideas and a willingness to take risks. For example, a study of Colorado communities found that entrepreneurs—experts and citizens alike—were essential in changing policy toward recreational use of various river basins in the state.[4]

The spirit of entrepreneurialism is not limited to individuals: Communities exhibit leadership too. At some point, on some issue, a jurisdiction may try something new; it may "think outside the box." For instance, in 2013, Indianapolis became the first major city to pledge to convert its entire fleet of city vehicles to alternative fuels by 2025. Replacing city-owned sedans with plug-in or hybrid vehicles is the first step followed by transitioning heavy vehicles such as garbage trucks, fire engines, and snow plows to compressed natural gas. The final piece will be converting the city's 1,900 police car fleet to alternative fuel vehicles.[5] Other cities with similar perspectives on energy security and the environment are likely to follow in Indianapolis' direction. Leading cities become models for other jurisdictions.

Community Power

LO 11.1

To understand and critique various theories of community power.

Real questions arise about who is running the show in local government. At the risk of sounding naive, we might suggest that "the people" run government; however, much of the evidence can persuade us otherwise. But we should not become too cynical, either. Citizen preferences do have an impact on public policy decisions.[6] Can we assume, therefore, that those who occupy important elected positions in government, such as the mayor and the city council, are in fact in charge? Are they the leaders of the community? These questions have interested scholars for a long time.

Two theories have been influential in sorting through the issue of who's running the show. One, **elite theory**, argues that a small group of leaders called an *elite* possesses power and rules society. Conversely, **pluralist theory** posits that power is dispersed among competing groups whose clashes produce societal rule.

THE ELITE THEORY

One of the earliest expositions of elite theory argued that any society, from underdeveloped to advanced, has two classes of people: a small set who rule and a large mass who are ruled.[7] The rulers allocate values for society and determine the rules of the game; the ruled tend to be passive and ill-informed and cannot exercise any direct influence over the rulers. This division is reflected elsewhere in society. In organizations, for example, power is inevitably concentrated in the hands of a few people. Given the pervasiveness of elite systems, should we expect decision making in communities to be any different?

A famous study of power in the community given the name of Middletown (actually Muncie, Indiana) in the 1920s and 1930s discovered an identifiable set of rulers.[8] The researchers, sociologists Robert and Helen Lynd, determined that Family X (the Ball family) was at the core of this ruling elite. Through their economic power, Family X and a small group of business leaders called the shots in Middletown. Government officials simply did the bidding of Family X and its cohorts.

Another widely read study of community power confirmed the basic tenets of elitism. Sociologist Floyd Hunter's study of Regional City (Atlanta, Georgia) in the 1950s and his follow-up research in the 1970s identified the top leadership—a 40-person economic elite—who dominated the local political system.[9] Hunter argued that an individual's power in Regional City was determined by his role in the local economy. Local elected officials merely carried out the policy decisions of the elite. To illustrate this point, Hunter compared the relatively limited power enjoyed by the mayor of Atlanta to the extensive power possessed by the president of a firm headquartered in Regional City: Coca-Cola.

Assume for a moment that elitist interpretations of community power are accurate; where do these interpretations take us? Do not be confused about the intent of an economic elite: they are not running the community out of a sense of benevolence. The following statement captures the larger meaning of elitism: "Virtually all U.S. cities are dominated by a small, parochial elite whose members have business or professional interests that are linked to local development and growth. These elites use public authority and private power as a means to stimulate economic development and thus enhance their own local business interests."[10] To most people, this conclusion is disturbing.

elite theory
A theory of government that asserts that a small group possesses power and rules society.

pluralist theory
A theory of government that asserts that multiple, open, competing groups possess power and rule society.

THE PLURALIST THEORY

The findings of the studies discussed above did not square with the prevailing orthodoxy of American political science: pluralism. Not everyone saw community power through the elitist lens, and many questioned whether the findings from Middletown and Regional City applied to other communities.

Pluralist theory views the decision-making process as one of bargaining, accommodation, and compromise. According to this view, no monolithic entity calls the shots; instead, authority is fragmented. Many leadership groups can become involved in decision making, depending on the nature and importance of the issue at hand. Granted, the size, cohesion, and wealth of these groups vary, but no group has a monopoly on resources. Pluralism sets forth a much more accessible system of community decision making than the grimly deterministic tenets of elitism do.

A study conducted by Robert Dahl in New Haven, Connecticut, challenged the sociologists' findings, particularly those of Hunter.[11] According to Dahl, decisions in New Haven in the 1950s were the product of the interactions of a system of groups with more than one center of power. Except for the mayor, no single leader was influential across a series of issue areas, and influential actors were not drawn from a single segment of the community.

Further explication of the pluralist model revealed that, although community decision making is limited to relatively few actors, the legitimacy of such a system hinges on the easily revoked consent of a much larger segment of the local population. In other words, the masses may acquiesce to the leaders, but they can also speak up when they are displeased. Success in a pluralistic environment is determined by a group's ability to form coalitions with other groups. Pluralism, then, offers a more hopeful interpretation of community power.

NEW HAVEN: IS IT ALL IN THE APPROACH?

New Haven, the setting for Dahl's affirmation of pluralist theory, has been examined and reexamined by skeptical researchers. Some of the debate between elitists and pluralists is a function of methodology—that is, the particular approach used in studying community power. Sociologists have tended to rely on what is called a **reputational approach**, whereby they go into a community and ask informants to name and rank the local leaders. Those whose names appear repeatedly are considered to be the movers and shakers. This approach is criticized on the grounds that it measures not leadership per se but the reputation for leadership. Political scientists approach the power question differently, through a **decisional method**. They focus on specific community issues and, using various sources, try to determine who is influential in the decision-making process. It is easy to see that the two different approaches can produce divergent findings.

reputational approach

A method for studying community power in which researchers ask informants to name and rank influential individuals.

decisional method

A method for studying community power in which researchers identify key issues and the individuals who are active in the decision-making process.

Users of the decisional method claim that it allows them to identify overt power rather than just power potential. In addition, it offers a realistic picture of power relationships as dynamic rather than fixed. Critics of the decisional method argue that when researchers select key issues to examine, they are being arbitrary. Also, a study of decision making may ignore the most powerful actors in a community—those who can keep issues *off* the agenda, who are influential enough to keep certain issues submerged. Table 11.1 reports the perceptions of mayors and councilmembers in eight communities in the Kansas City metropolitan area regarding the involvement of various types of groups in local politics.[12] Officials used a five-point scale ranging from 1

TABLE 11.1	Various Groups Ranked by Their Level of Activity and Influence in Local Politics	
TYPE OF GROUP	**LEVEL OF ACTIVITY**	**AMOUNT OF INFLUENCE**
Chamber of Commerce	4.51	4.01
Neighborhood groups	3.96	3.82
Developers	3.76	3.46
Task forces	3.64	3.39
Democrats	3.37	2.89
Nonprofit organizations	3.30	2.98
Historical preservationists	3.09	2.55
Churches	3.03	2.65
Republicans	2.99	2.59
Public employees	2.83	2.57
Bankers	2.73	2.58
Labor in private sector	2.51	2.26
Women's groups	2.21	1.94
Professional groups	2.14	1.93
National businesses	2.07	2.14
Clientele groups	2.04	1.96
Morality groups	1.86	1.53
Minority groups	1.82	1.66
Global businesses	1.70	1.77
Environmental groups	1.70	1.61
GLBT groups	1.42	1.23
Ethnic groups	1.27	1.18
Community action groups	0.97	0.96
Other parties	0.23	0.18
Overall Average	2.47	2.24

SOURCE: Adapted from Paul Schumaker, "Group Involvements in City Politics and Pluralist Theory," *Urban Affairs Review*, (accessed March 2013): p. 26.

(very low) to 5 (very high) to assess group activity and influence in their communities. Not surprisingly, the Chamber of Commerce and neighborhood groups were at the top of the list.

New Haven was found by Dahl to be a pluralist's delight. Convinced that the finding was affected by Dahl's methods, another researcher, G. William Domhoff, examined New Haven and emerged with a contrary view of the power structure.[13] He claimed that Dahl missed the big picture by focusing on issues that were of minor concern to the New Haven elite and that Dahl's finding of an accessible decision-making process in which many groups were involved was not an adequate test of the presence of an elite. Domhoff investigated the urban redevelopment issue and discovered that the long-time mayor, whom Dahl had seen as leading an executive-centered coalition, was in fact being actively manipulated by a cadre of local business leaders. Domhoff contended that New Haven was not quite the pluralistic paradise it was made out to be.

THE DYNAMICS OF POWER

The work of Hunter and that of Dahl remains significant, but neither elitism nor pluralism adequately explains who's running the show. Not all communities are organized alike; even within a single community, power arrangements shift as time passes and conditions change. Two examples—Miami and Chicago—offer insight into the dynamics of power. In Miami, a diverse city in which economic divisions are exacerbated by racial and ethnic tensions, an elite-dominated power structure continues to hold sway in important local decisions. According to Judith Gainsborough, who has studied the power structure in Miami, "The power to actually influence decision making is not widely dispersed."[14] Even so, the composition of the elite has changed over time, becoming more diverse itself. In Chicago, the city's political leaders joined forces with local economic leaders to create Chicago 2016, an organization devoted to bringing the Olympics to the city. Chicago 2016 formed a juggernaut, able to frame the issue and dominate debate. A fledging anti-Olympics group, No Games Chicago, pushed back, raising questions about the potential cost to the taxpayers of hosting the Games, but they were brushed aside as Chicago 2016 forged ahead.[15] In the end, the efforts of the Chicago promoters fell short as the International Olympic Committee awarded the 2016 summer games to Rio de Janeiro.

Regime Theory Is pluralism an accurate description of the power dynamics in communities across the land? Probably not. The penetration of the government's domain by private economic interests in American communities is deep. Consequently, to understand the dynamics of power in a community, one must look to the **regime**. Political scientist Clarence Stone defines regime as "the informal arrangements that surround and complement the formal workings of governmental authority."[16] Stone uses the concepts of *systemic power* and *strategic advantage* to explain why community decisions so frequently favor upper-strata interests.[17]

regime

The informal arrangements that surround and complement the formal workings of governmental authority.

The starting point of his argument is that public officials operate in a highly stratified socioeconomic system with a small upper class; a large, varied middle class; and a relatively small lower class. According to Stone, "Public officeholders are predisposed to interact with and to favor those who can reciprocate benefits."[18] Two considerations define the environment in which public officials operate: electoral accountability (keeping the majority of the public satisfied) and systemic power (the unequal distribution of economic, organizational, and social resources). Decision makers are likely to side with majority preferences on highly visible issues; but on less visible ones, the possessors of systemic power—the upper strata—will win most of the time. With their superior resources, they can set the agenda in the community and instigate (or block) change. In other words, they enjoy a strategic advantage.

An urban regime brings a certain degree of stability to a community because key leaders share a vision for the future—that is, they have an agenda that they want to implement and they interact with one another. An analysis of New Orleans found that the city's lack of a regime contributed mightily to the problems the city faced preparing for and responding to Hurricane Katrina in 2005.[19] In nonregime cities such as New Orleans, temporary coalitions spring up around various issues, but there is little shared understanding of the city's problems. Leaders do not communicate regularly, and cooperation is in short supply. The result is haphazard governance, an outcome that was on display in New Orleans in the aftermath of Katrina.

Nonprofit Organizations as Power Players **Nonprofit organizations**
have become fully integrated into the government and politics of many communities. Four types of governmentally active nonprofit organizations can be identified:

- Civic nonprofits
- Policy advocates
- Policy implementers
- Governing nonprofits[20]

The first type, civic nonprofit organizations, plays a watchdog role, monitoring government and educating the public. A local citizens' league acts in this way, attending city council meetings and publicizing council decisions. Policy advocates, the second type, move beyond the provision of information to become active supporters of particular policies or programs. For instance, if an education advocacy group endorses year-round schools, it would lobby the school board vigorously in support of such a policy change. The third type of nonprofit organization, policy implementers, actually delivers services, often through a contract with a local government. For example, homeless shelters in many communities are operated by nonprofit groups supported by city funds, federal grants, and charitable contributions. Governing nonprofits, the fourth type, are different because they may work through or with local government but they also act independently. These nonprofits are the most powerful of the four types because they offer an alternative venue for decision making.

Have nonprofit organizations upset community power structures? Policy advocates and governing nonprofits have the potential to reset agendas and effect real change. Research on the city of Detroit offers some insight into the long-term impact of nonprofit organizations. Richard Hula and Cynthia Jackson-Elmoore studied the influence of two nonprofits created in the aftermath of Detroit's civil disturbances of the late 1960s: New Detroit and Detroit Renaissance.[21] For many years, these organizations have been important players in the city's politics. Although they had a similar genesis—"both were born

nonprofit organizations
Private sector groups that carry out charitable, educational, religious, literary, service, or scientific functions.

as an elite response to and fear of civil unrest"[22]—their styles and foci have varied. New Detroit has more of a social agenda, focusing on race relations and education reform. Detroit Renaissance, a smaller organization made up of the corporate elite from the Detroit area, concentrated its energies on economic renewal. Both organizations have been active on the Detroit scene, advocating ambitious reforms and new policies over four decades. And although both organizations have enjoyed some successes, neither has been able to transform the local political agenda. Yet Hula and Jackson-Elmoore contend that the presence of New Detroit and Detroit Renaissance has had an important catalytic effect. When nonprofits join with local elected leaders, their impact increases. In other words, to become power players, nonprofit organizations must become part of the regime.

Hyperpluralism Our understanding of community power structures continues to evolve. What is certain is that some interests, especially those of the economically powerful, seem to prevail more often than others. Still, different communities have developed different arrangements for governance. In some places, weak political leadership and a dispersed business elite have resulted in a condition called **hyperpluralism**. In hyperpluralistic communities, where many interests clash, competing groups cannot form coalitions and the distribution of power tends to be unstable. Research on medium-size cities revealed at least seventeen different types of interest groups that were both active and influential on the local scene.[23] The range of interests represented by these groups is extensive, from taxes and traffic to economic development and public safety. The question of who's in charge remains an interesting one.

LO 11.2

To understand disputes over property rights as manifestations of power.

Property Rights: A Matter of Power

The issue of property rights raises interesting questions about the exercise of power. You may have heard someone say, "I own this land; therefore, I can do anything I want with it," but that would be far from accurate. Through zoning and other regulations, government can limit what you can do with your property. Moreover, government can actually take that property away from you for a public purpose. All it has to do is follow proper procedures and compensate you—that is, pay fair market value—for the **taking**. Suppose you own a half-acre vacant lot near the central business district of your city. The city may be eyeing your lot as the site for the new library it plans to construct. If you are not willing to sell the land, the city can use its power of eminent domain—that is, it can take your property. You can haggle over the value of the lot, perhaps demand an administrative hearing, and maybe even file a lawsuit to try to stop the city; but in the end, if the taking is for a public purpose, the city has the power to do so. Where the issue gets a little dicey is over the notion of "public purpose." Obviously, a library is a public purpose, but can the city use its eminent domain power to take that same lot and sell it to a developer so that he can construct an office building? The answer may surprise you.

The city council of New London, Connecticut, had voted in 2000 to take 90 acres of land for a redevelopment project. The city's development corporation

hyperpluralism

A condition characterized by a large number of groups and interests.

taking

A government action assuming ownership of real property by eminent domain.

would redevelop the area with a hotel, marina, and upscale residences that would generate much-needed jobs and tax revenue for the financially stressed city. Most of the property owners sold their land to the city, but a small group refused and, instead, filed suit claiming that the action represented an illegal taking. The plaintiffs argued that the city's plans for the land would destroy an established neighborhood to benefit private developers. In essence, they contended that the city had violated the public purpose requirement of a taking. The case, *Kelo v. City of New London*, went all the way to the U.S. Supreme Court, which, in a 5-to-4 decision in 2005, ruled in favor of the city. The reasoning went like this: New London wanted to use the land to promote economic development, which is a traditional function of government; ergo, the city's plan fulfilled a public purpose.[24]

Property rights advocates deplored the Court's decision, arguing that working-class residents and small business owners were being displaced so that the city could pursue a more productive use of the land. They had an advocate in Justice Sandra Day O'Connor, who dissented, saying, "The beneficiaries [of the Court's ruling] are likely to be those citizens with disproportionate influence and power in the political process, including large corporations and development firms."[25] Localities, not surprisingly, welcomed the decision, claiming that eminent domain was an essential tool in their efforts to regain and maintain economic vitality. They pointed to other examples of the use of eminent domain to benefit private firms, particularly a Nissan automobile facility in Canton, Mississippi, and a speedway in Kansas City, Kansas.

The court did invite states to place restrictions on localities' use of eminent domain if they so desired; and, 42 states did so, either by legislative action or by citizen initiative. Clearly, the exercise of eminent domain is costly, not only in terms of dollars but in terms of goodwill. A poll conducted in New Hampshire found that 93 percent of Granite State residents opposed governmental taking of private land for economic development. This sentiment is one of the reasons why Washington, D.C., as it acquired land for the construction of a new stadium for the Washington Nationals baseball team, explicitly refused to take property. But by the same token, New York City was not reluctant to condemn property and take it as the site for a new basketball arena for the Brooklyn Nets. The definition of *public purpose* is likely to continue to unleash a power struggle in many communities.

Local Executives

LO 11.3

To compare different types of local executives and the challenges they face.

The mantle of leadership in local government falls most often on chief executives: mayors and managers. Although it is possible for chief executives to eschew a leadership role, they rarely do.

MAYORS

Mayors tend to be the most prominent figures in city government primarily because their position automatically makes them the center of attention. Occasionally, a city council member emerges as a leader on a specific issue or stirs up some interest with verbal attacks on the mayor (which many observers interpret as jockeying for position to run against the mayor at the next election). But for the most part, attention is drawn to the mayor.

A lot is expected of the mayor. The city comptroller of New York once described the former mayor, Michael Bloomberg, positively: "He's hired a very talented group. He's run city services well. He's approached things in a balanced fashion." However, the comptroller continued, "But the mayor is not just a CEO. The mayor is an emotional leader, an inspirational leader, and in that regard I don't think he's done nearly as good a job."[26] A similar theme was echoed by Los Angeles city councilman Bernard Parks as he mulled a bid for the mayor's job. "This is a big city, a thriving city. The mayor's office doesn't make you a leader. You have to have a leader in the mayor's office."[27]

Differences between Strong and Weak Mayors Chapter 10 explained some of the differences between strong and weak mayors. It is important to note that these labels refer to the *position*, not to the person who occupies it. A structure simply creates opportunities for leadership, not the certainty of it. True leaders are those who can take what is structurally a weak-mayor position and transform it into a strong mayoralty.

A *strong-mayor* structure establishes the mayor as the sole chief executive who exercises substantive policy responsibilities. In this kind of structure, the position of city manager, someone who can expand an administrative role and become a policy rival to the mayor, does not exist. As an ideal type, a strong mayor has the following features:

- Is elected directly by the voters, not selected by the council,
- Serves a four-year, not two-year, term of office,
- Has no limitations on re-election,
- Plays a central role in budget formulation,
- Has extensive appointment and removal powers, and
- Has veto power over council-enacted ordinances.

The actual powers of a specific strong mayor may not include all these items; but the more of these powers a mayor can exercise, the stronger her position is and the easier it is for her to become a leader.

A *weak-mayor* structure does not provide these elements. Its design is such that the mayor shares policy responsibilities with the council and perhaps a manager and serves a limited amount of time in office. (In an especially weak-mayor system, the job is passed around among the council members annually, each of whom takes a turn at being mayor.) A weak-mayor structure often implies strong council involvement in budgetary and personnel matters. The variation in mayoral power is reflected in mayoral remuneration: weak mayors receive token salaries. If a mayor in a weak-mayor structure is to become a leader, he has to exceed the job description.

Mayoral leadership has been the subject of discussion in the popular press.[28] An article, "The Lure of the Strong Mayor," argued that large, diverse communities grappling with complex problems are better served by a structure that fixes leadership and accountability in the mayor's office. In response, "Beware the Lure of the 'Strong' Mayor" contended that a too powerful mayor

It's Your Turn

Should All Cities Have a Strong Mayor?

PROS	CONS
Having a strong mayor increases accountability. There's no confusion about who is in charge in city government. It's like former President Harry Truman said: "The buck stops here."	Too much power in one office introduces the possibility of abuse of power. As British Baron Acton said in the nineteenth century: "Power tends to corrupt, and absolute power corrupts absolutely."
Highly qualified candidates will seek the office of mayor if it is imbued with sufficient authority to make things happen.	Someone might be a good campaigner and win the office, but that doesn't mean that he or she will be an effective government leader. A professional city manager is trained to make city government function effectively.
The issues of the twenty-first century require smart, decisive actions. An empowered mayor will be better equipped to take those actions on behalf of the city.	Most of the issues in most city governments these days are not so complicated or contentious that they require a full-time mayor.

could run amok, building political machines based on the exchange of benefits. Structural differences can indeed have consequences. It is important to remember, however, that individuals who work within structures are the essential factor. Leaders can make structures work for them sometimes by performing minor surgery on the structure. As David Morgan and Sheilah Watson note, "Even in council-manager communities—where mayors have the fewest formal powers—by negotiating, networking, and facilitating the efforts of others, mayors clearly rise above the nominal figurehead role."[29] The It's Your Turn box invites you to consider the advantages and disadvantages of a strong mayor.

Black Mayors By 2014, African American mayors headed more than 700 cities and towns across the country. Not only can you find black mayors leading cities where the population is predominantly black, you can find them in majority-white cities, too, as the listing in Table 11.2 shows. Today's African American mayors tends to be problem solvers, not crusaders; political pragmatists, not ideologues.[30] For example, in his successful campaign for mayor of Newark, New Jersey, Cory Booker's message was about hard work . . . and hope. On his campaign website he proclaimed, "Working together we're going to make Newark's neighborhoods safe and our schools safe. . . . Bringing real change to Newark won't be easy."[31]

Increased success by blacks in mayoral elections has led some observers to talk of **deracialization**, or the de-emphasis of race as a campaign issue in

deracialization
The de-emphasis of race in politics, especially in campaigns, so that there is less racial bloc voting.

TABLE 11.2	Black Mayors in Large Cities, 2015				
CITY	STATE	MAYOR		POPULATION (2013 CENSUS ESTIMATES)	% AFRICAN AMERICAN
Philadelphia	PA	Michael A. Nutter		1,553,165	43.3%
San Antonio	TX	Ivy R. Taylor		1,409,019	6.8%
Jacksonville	FL	Alvin Brown		842,583	30.6%
Columbus	OH	Michael Coleman		822,553	27.7%
Memphis	TN	A. C. Wharton, Jr.		653,450	63.0%
Denver	CO	Michael B. Hancock		649,495	10.0%
Washington	DC	Muriel Bowser		646,449	50.1%
Baltimore	MD	Stephanie C. Rawlings-Blake		622,104	63.2%
Sacramento	CA	Kevin Johnson		479,686	13.9%
Kansas City	MO	Sly James		467,007	29.2%
Atlanta	GA	Kasim Reed		447,841	53.5%
Toledo	OH	Paula Hicks-Hudson		282,313	27.0%
Newark	NJ	Ras J. Baraka		278,427	51.7%
Plano	TX	Harry LaRosiliere		274,409	7.1%
Buffalo	NY	Byron W. Brown		258,959	37.6%
Durham	NC	William V. 'Bill' Bell		245,475	39.9%
Baton Rouge	LA	Melvin L. 'Kip' Holden		229,426	54.3%
Richmond	VA	Dwight C. Jones		214,114	49.2%
Birmingham	AL	William A. Bell, Sr.		212,113	74.1%
Rochester	NY	Lovely A. Warren		210,358	41.1%
Tacoma	WA	Marilyn Strickland		203,446	10.7%
Fontana	CA	Acquanetta Warren		203,003	9.9%
Shreveport	LA	Ollie S. Tyler		200,327	54.7%

SOURCES: U.S. Census Bureau, American Fact Finder, factfinder.census.gov/faces/nav/jsf/pages/index.xhtml (accessed February 2, 2015). U.S. Conference of Mayors, "Meet the Mayors," http://www.usmayors.org/meetmayors/mayorsatglance.asp (accessed February 2, 2015).

an effort to attract white voter support.[32] Instead of making racial appeals, candidates offer a race-neutral platform that stresses their personal qualifications and political experience.[33] In cities where the white electorate outnumbers the black electorate, such as Sacramento and Tacoma, neither Kevin Johnson nor Marilyn Strickland could have been elected without the support of white voters. Even in cities where white voters constitute a minority, they often control the electoral balance when two African American candidates square off in the mayoral race.

Deracialization works both ways. Baltimore, a majority African American city, had a black mayor from 1987 to 1999, a white mayor from 1999 to 2007, and a black mayor since then. Deracialization of local campaigns, and the manner in which a mayor elected by a multiracial coalition governs once in office, is a compelling subject for research. For example, a study of Houston found that when minority mayors run for re-election, evaluations of job performance are more important to voters than racial group affiliation is.[34]

Washington, D.C. Mayor Muriel Bowser at a press conference.

Gabriella Demczuk/Getty Images

Women Mayors More women are running for and winning local elective offices. The data from cities with populations of 30,000 or more are instructive. In 1973, fewer than 2 percent of the cities in that population range had female mayors. A quarter-century later, the number of women mayors had increased to 21 percent, a level around which it has fluctuated. (In 2015, 18 percent of cities of 30,000 or more were governed by women.) Twenty-three women were at the helm of large U.S. cities (populations of 200,000 or more) in 2015, as Table 11.3 shows, a marked increase over the numbers from just a few years earlier.

The 2015 race for mayor of one of the country's largest cities, San Antonio, took on an interesting dimension when two female candidates—one the interim mayor, Ivy Taylor, the other a former state senator Leticia Van de Putte—squared off in a runoff election. Although San Antonio city elections are nonpartisan, the results had a strong partisan cast to them.[35] Van de Putte, a Democrat, was viewed as more liberal than Taylor, who appealed to more conservative voters in the majority Hispanic city. Even though Van de Putte was the leading vote-getter among the fourteen candidates in the first election, Taylor was able to win 52 percent of the vote in the low-turnout runoff election and defeat her.

Studies of female mayoral candidates have dispelled several electoral myths.[36] For example, women do not appear to experience greater difficulty in raising money or gaining newspaper endorsements than men do. Women mayors, however, do tend to be political novices. Few female mayors in Florida, for instance, had held elective office before their mayoral election; if they had, it was usually a city council seat. Female mayors also have a policy impact: Research conducted by political scientist Mirya Holman found that cities led by women mayors allocate more funds for social welfare programs than cities with male mayors do.[37]

Visionary Mayors For mayors to become leaders, they need to have vision—that is, they need the ability to identify goals for their city and achieve

TABLE 11.3	Women Mayors in Large Cities, 2015		
CITY	**STATE**	**NAME**	**POPULATION (2013 CENSUS ESTIMATES)**
Houston	TX	Annise D. Parker	2,195,914
San Antonio	TX	Ivy R. Taylor	1,409,019
Fort Worth	TX	Betsy Price	792,727
Washington	DC	Muriel Bowser	646,449
Nashville	TN	Megan Barry	634,870
Baltimore	MD	Stephanie C. Rawlings-Blake	622,104
Las Vegas	NV	Carolyn G. Goodman	603,488
Fresno	CA	Ashley Swearengin	509,924
Omaha	NE	Jean Stothert	434,353
Raleigh	NC	Nancy McFarlane	431,746
Oakland	CA	Libby Schaaf	406,253
Minneapolis	MN	Betsy Hodges	400,070
Corpus Christi	TX	Nelda Martinez	316,381
Toledo	OH	Paula Hicks-Hudson	282,313
Greensboro	NC	Nancy Vaughan	279,639
Chula Vista	CA	Mary Casillas Salas	256,780
Reno	NV	Hillary Schieve	233,294
Irving	TX	Beth Van Duyne	228,653
Rochester	NY	Lovely A. Warren	210,358
Tacoma	WA	Marilyn Strickland	203,446
Fontana	CA	Acquanetta Warren	203,003
Columbus	GA	Teresa Pike Tomlinson	202,824
Shreveport	LA	Ollie S. Tyler	200,327

SOURCES: Center for American Women and Politics, "Women Mayors in U.S. Cities 2015," www.cawp
.rutgers.edu/fast_facts/levels_of_office/Local-WomenMayors.php (accessed January 1, 2015); U.S.
Census Bureau, American Fact Finder, factfinder.census.gov/faces/nav/jsf/pages/index.xhtml (accessed
February 2, 2015).

them, which is easier said than done. As a former Dallas mayor commented, "Mayors work in real time. You have to limit your agenda to the big stuff."[38] Three erstwhile mayors widely hailed as visionary when they were in office put their heads together to come up with a how-to list.[39] Their rules for creating and implementing successful city visions included several obvious items such as "borrow from everyone" and "build on existing strengths." But the list also instructed mayors to market their vision on a human scale so that local residents and business interests can understand its relevance to them. Getting cooperation from the community goes a long way in bolstering mayoral leadership. But the immediate tasks of keeping the city running smoothly can cause some mayors to lose sight of the vision or, at the least, put it aside as they worry about potholes, garbage collection, and budget deficits. In that vein, Los Angeles mayor Eric Garcetti, who took office in 2014, has said that his goal is to make L.A. the "best run city in America."[40]

CITY MANAGERS

City managers (as well as county administrators and appointed school superintendents) exemplify the movement toward reformed local government. Local government reform was a **Progressive Era** movement that sought to depose the corrupt and inefficient partisan political machines that controlled many American cities. To the reformers, local government had become too political; what was needed, they believed, was a government designed along the lines of a business corporation. To achieve their goals, reformers advocated fundamental structural changes in local government such as the abolition of partisan local elections, the use of at-large electoral systems, and the installation of a professionally trained city manager. Altering the structure of local government has had profound consequences for local government leadership. City managers—the professional, neutral experts whose job is to run the day-to-day affairs of the city—have become key leaders.

In the original conception, managers were to implement but not formulate policy. Administration and politics were to be kept separate. The managers' responsibility would be to administer the policies enacted by the elected officials—the city councils—by whom they were hired (and fired). In other words, they were to act as the agents of their political principals. But it is impossible to keep administration and politics completely separate. City managers are influenced not only by their training and by the councils that employ them, but also by their own political ideologies.[41] When it comes to making choices, they balance professional norms, the politics of the issue, and their own predispositions. Hence, city managers typically end up being far more influential on the local government scene than their neutral persona might suggest.

Managers as Policy Leaders According to the International City/County Management Association, the city managers' professional association, the role of the manager is to help the governing body function more effectively. "Managers—and their staffs—need to build political capacity so they can assist the elected body in framing community issues."[42] Ways in which the manager can assume a larger role in policymaking include proposing community goals and service levels; structuring the budget preparation, review, and adoption process so that it is linked to goals and service levels; and orienting new council members to organizational processes and norms. This approach has had the intended effect. James Svara, who surveyed officials in large cities, concluded that managers have become "more assertive in attempting to focus the council on long-range concerns and in shaping the tone of the policymaking process."[43]

Progressive Era

A period in the early twentieth century that focused on reforming or cleaning up government.

One indisputable role for the city manager is as an information source for the busy, part-time city council. For instance, suppose that some enterprising college students are requesting a change in a city ordinance that prohibits street vendors. The council asks the manager to study the pros and cons of street vending. At a subsequent meeting, he reports on other cities' experiences: Has it created a litter problem? Does it draw clientele away from established businesses? How much revenue can be expected from vendor licensing fees? The manager then offers alternative courses of action (allow street vending only at lunchtime, restrict pushcarts to Main Street) and evaluates their probable consequences. In some councils, the manager is asked to make a formal recommendation; in others, his recommendation is more along the lines of "Well, what do you think?" At some point, a vote is called and the council makes an official decision.

Working with Councils and Mayors City managers are not cut from one mold; they vary in terms of experience, outlook, and style. Ideally, a manager should be a near-perfect match for the community she serves. A manager who is focused on making the city function smoothly might be poorly suited for a community in need of an innovative, big-picture kind of leader. And the converse is true: a manager who wants to take on an expansive leadership role would find himself stymied in a city seeking a technical problem solver. Obviously, it is important that the city council and the city manager share similar views on the role the manager is expected to play.[44] However, a good council-manager fit can be difficult to maintain. The composition of the city council can change, new issues will emerge, and managers may shift their orientation toward the job. It is no wonder that the average tenure of a manager in a city is between six and seven years. Some are fired, of course, but some are "ladder climbers" who move on to larger cities, whereas others are "lateral movers," relocating to similar-size communities.[45] Consequently, the search for the "right" manager is nearly constant in many places.

A veteran city administrator in Missouri offered new managers this advice about dealing with elected officials:

- Don't substitute your political judgment for the judgments of the elected officials.
- Don't cut red ribbons, cut red tape . . . in other words, keep a low profile.
- Listen, count to three, and choose your words wisely.
- The council-manager relationship is not a game won on points.
- There's no great honor in being fired, but there's no shame in being fired for the right reason.[46]

As noted earlier, one new trend is the hiring of professional managers in cities that do not use the council-manager form of government. Cities are adapting their structures to employ officials with titles such as managing director or CAO.[47] These individuals have the educational credentials and professional experiences of city managers, and their role in a strong-mayor city is typically limited to administrative matters.

Local Legislatures

Local legislatures include city councils, county commissions, town boards of aldermen or selectmen, special district boards, and school boards. They are representative, deliberative policymaking bodies. In this section, we focus on city councils because that is where most of the research has taken place, but many of the points are also applicable to the other local legislative bodies such as county commissions and school boards. Although the ensuing discussion focuses on patterns across councils, it is important to remember that significant variations may exist from one city to another. For example, in some communities, council members receive high salaries, are assisted by clerical and research staff, and have no limits on the number of terms they can serve. In Chicago, for instance, city council members (called **aldermen**) earn more than $117,000 per year, have office staffs, and can serve an unlimited number of four-year terms. (To put it in perspective, the mayor of Chicago has an annual salary of $216,000.) But in Oklahoma City, a council-manager city, council members receive a yearly salary of $12,000; the mayor earns $24,000. In many smaller places, council service is considered a volunteer activity, with members receiving virtually no compensation whatsoever. The issue of elected officials' pay can be a sensitive one. An example comes from Miami-Dade County, Florida, where voters rejected a proposal in 2012 to raise county commissioners' pay from $6,000 annually to $92,000 a year. (The pay raise would have been accompanied by term limits and a ban on outside employment while serving on the commission.) This was the thirteenth time in 50 years that a proposed salary hike for commissioners had gone down to defeat.

CITY COUNCIL MEMBERS: OLD AND NEW

A former member of the city council of Concord, California, harkening back to an earlier time, commented, "When I first came on the city council, it was like a good-old-boys' club."[48] The standard description was that the city council was a part-time, low-paying haven for public-spirited white men who did not consider themselves politicians. Most councils used at-large electoral mechanisms, so individual council members had no specific, territorially based constituency. Council members considered themselves volunteers. Research on city councils in the San Francisco Bay area in the 1960s found that these volunteer members were fairly unresponsive to public pressures and tended to vote according to their own preferences.[49] In other words, there was not much representation going on.

Today, the circumstances have changed. City councils are less white, less male, and less passive than they were in the past. Now, city councilors are more engaged and active. Some of this change is due to modifications in the electoral mechanism, such as the switch from at-large or citywide elections to district (or ward) elections.[50] Table 11.4 shows the wide variation in both council size and number of members elected at large and from districts in the twenty largest American cities. Columbus, Ohio, is the only one of these large cities that continues to elect all of its council members at-large; Detroit did so

LO 11.4

To appreciate the conflict inherent in local legislative bodies.

aldermen

A label used in some communities for members of a local legislative body, such as a city council.

TABLE 11.4   City Councils of the Twenty Largest U.S. Cities

CITY	STATE	POPULATION (2013 CENSUS ESTIMATES)	COUNCIL SIZE	NUMBER ELECTED AT LARGE	NUMBER ELECTED FROM DISTRICTS
New York	NY	8,405,837	51	0	51
Los Angeles	CA	3,884,307	15	0	15
Chicago	IL	2,718,782	50	0	50
Houston	TX	2,195,914	16	5	11
Philadelphia	PA	1,553,165	17	7	10
Phoenix	AZ	1,513,367	8	0	8
San Antonio	TX	1,409,019	10	0	10
San Diego	CA	1,355,896	9	0	9
Dallas	TX	1,257,676	14	0	14
San Jose	CA	998,537	10	0	10
Austin	TX	885,400	10	0	10
Indianapolis	IN	843,393	29	4	25
Jacksonville	FL	842,583	19	5	14
San Francisco	CA	837,442	11	0	11
Columbus	OH	822,553	7	7	0
Charlotte	NC	792,862	11	4	7
Fort Worth	TX	792,727	9	1	8
Detroit	MI	688,701	9	2	7
El Paso	TX	674,433	8	0	8
Memphis	TN	653,450	13	6	7

SOURCES: U.S. Census Bureau, American Fact Finder, factfinder.census.gov/faces/nav/jsf/pages/index.xhtml (accessed February 2, 2015); Individual city websites.

until voters approved a change in the city's charter in 2009. The rest of these cities use a combination of at-large and district seats or they elect all of their council members from districts. Figure 11.1 displays the district map for Detroit, a city with a strong mayor-council structure and seven of its nine council members elected from districts.

COUNCIL DIVERSITY

Racial and ethnic minorities are making inroads into local politics in increasing numbers. One recent study found nearly 4,000 African Americans and 1,900 Hispanics serving in elected city and county offices across the country.[51] (These figures do not include service on school boards, which accounts for approximately another 1,550 African Americans and 1,650 Hispanics.) And

FIGURE 11.1

Detroit City Council District Map

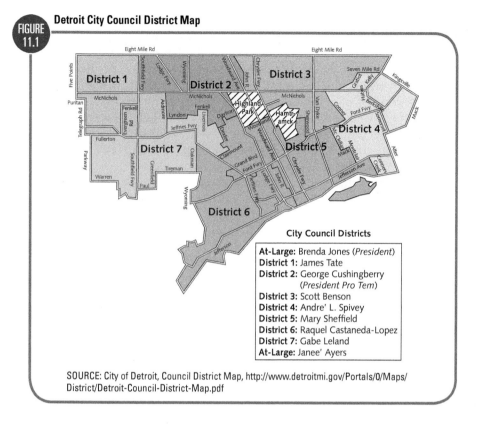

City Council Districts

At-Large: Brenda Jones (*President*)
District 1: James Tate
District 2: George Cushingberry
         (*President Pro Tem*)
District 3: Scott Benson
District 4: Andre' L. Spivey
District 5: Mary Sheffield
District 6: Raquel Castaneda-Lopez
District 7: Gabe Leland
At-Large: Janee' Ayers

SOURCE: City of Detroit, Council District Map, http://www.detroitmi.gov/Portals/0/Maps/District/Detroit-Council-District-Map.pdf

although Asian Americans accounted for just under 1 percent of locally elected officials, their numbers are also growing, especially in California localities.

Despite the rise in minority representation, the percentages remain relatively low. Much research has been done on the impact of structural considerations—for example, the at-large election format, the size of the council, and the use of nonpartisan elections—on minority representation on the council.[52] Other factors such as the size of a minority group, its geographical concentration, and its political cohesiveness affect electoral success. In general, a higher proportion of African American council members can be found in central cities that use a mayor-council structure, on larger councils, and in southern cities with large black populations. Councils with higher-than-average Latino representation tend to be found in the Southwest and Far West and in larger central cities that use council-manager structures. Thus far, Asian representation has been clustered primarily in the Pacific Coast area in larger council-manager central cities. Native American representation is highest in small communities using commission structures in the southwestern and Pacific Coast areas of the country. The increase in nonwhites on councils has policy consequences. Data from 351 city council members indicates that nonwhites tend to pursue a more liberal agenda than whites do.[53]

Given the finite number of council seats in any community and the fact that more groups are now clamoring for representation, two outcomes are possible: Minority groups may try to build coalitions, or they may opt for a more independent, competitive approach. Although temporary electoral coalitions have emerged in a few cities, it appears that interminority group competition is on the rise.[54] Research in 96 cities demonstrates, for example, that an increase in the Latino population has a negative effect on black representation on city councils.[55] Another interesting question is the extent to which the concept of deracialization can be extended to Latinos and Asian Americans in their bids for local offices. Research on the Little Saigon area of Orange County, California, showed evidence of racial bloc voting in every election for city council or school board between 1998 and 2002 in which a Vietnamese American competed against a white candidate.[56]

Nationally, women constitute approximately 28 percent of city councils, 12 percent of county governing boards and 44 percent of school boards. Alaska and Hawaii consistently report female office holding far above these national averages; Georgia and North Dakota are examples of states in which the proportion of women in local public office is substantially lower.

An early 1990s national survey of city council members showed that, compared with males, female council members were much more likely to view the representation of women, environmentalists, abortion rights activists, racial minorities, and good-government organizations as extremely important.[57] Other research of that period found that men and women on the council saw each other through different lenses. As Susan Adams Beck pointed out, "Men often express frustration that women ask too many questions, while women see themselves as well-prepared and think their male colleagues are often 'winging it.'"[58] These days, with respect to the public's perceptions of leadership, few notable gender differences exist. The public values honesty, intelligence, and decisiveness in leaders, and a recent national poll reported

MIKE KITTRELL/The Press-Register/Landov

Members of the Mobile, Alabama, city council listen to a city staffer as she discusses the city's budget

little discernible variation between men and women on these traits.[59] Seventy-five percent of those polled said that women and men make equally good political leaders, a finding that holds up across generations. However, the public did consider female leaders to be more compassionate and organized than their male counterparts and said that women were better than men at working out compromises.

Local governing boards in cities and counties are becoming more diverse in another way: The number of local elected officials (the tally includes more than city council members) who are openly gay or lesbian has risen to more than 200.[60] The Gay and Lesbian Victory Fund is a political action committee that provides technical and financial support for openly gay and lesbian candidates, many of whom are seeking local offices. Among the most prominent openly lesbian or gay local elected officials are Annise Parker, elected to three terms as mayor of Houston, Christine Quinn who until 2013 was speaker of New York City's council, and Seattle Mayor Ed Murray, elected in 2013. A study focusing on cities and counties that had anti-discrimination ordinances in place revealed several findings about the election of gays and lesbians. Based on that sample of jurisdictions, gay and lesbian electoral success was more likely in larger cities; in jurisdictions with higher numbers of nonfamily households (such as university communities); and in places with partisan, district election of council members.[61] The limited nature of the sample makes it difficult to generalize to all localities, but the research yields interesting findings about council diversity.

COUNCILS IN ACTION: INCREASING CONFLICT

In earlier times, when members of the council came from the same socioeconomic stratum (in some communities, *all* members of the at-large council came from the same neighborhood) and when they shared a common political philosophy, governing was easier. Members of the council could come together before the meeting (usually at breakfast in a restaurant near City Hall) and discuss the items on the agenda. Thus, they could arrive at an informal resolution of any particularly troubling items and thereby transform the actual council meeting into a rubber-stamp exercise. No wonder that the majority of council votes were often unanimous; members were merely ratifying what they had already settled on. Nowadays, councils appear to be less collegial. In many cities, average council tenure is relatively brief, as Figure 11.2 suggests. However, when incumbent city council members seek reelection, they have a strong advantage over their challengers.[62]

Intracouncil Conflict Council members elected by districts report more factionalism and less unanimity than do their counterparts elected at large. Recent research confirms the link between district elections and lower levels of cooperation on city councils.[63] As more cities adopt district-based electoral mechanisms, council conflict may rise in the future. However, concerns that council members elected from districts will ignore citywide interests in favor of the narrower interests of their particular district appear to be overstated, if a recent study of Los Angeles can be extended to other cities.[64]

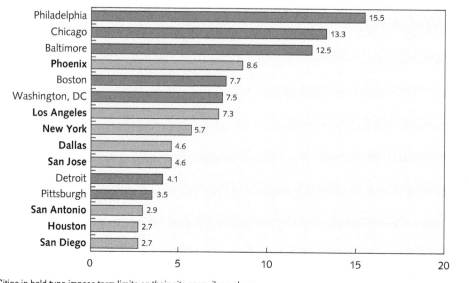

FIGURE 11.2

Average Tenure (in Years) of City Council Members in 15 Cities, as of 2010

NOTE: Cities in bold type impose term limits on their city council members.

SOURCE: Thomas Ginsberg, "City Councils in Philadelphia and Other Major Cities: Who Holds Office, How Long They Serve, and How Much It All Costs," Pew Charitable Trusts Philadelphia Research Initiative, February 2, 2011.

Battles with the Mayor Although mayors and city councils get along most of the time, relationships can become conflictive, to say the least. In fact, they can be downright hostile at times. A former mayor of Philadelphia did not pull any punches when he referred to the city council as "the worst legislative body in the free world."[65] Budget allocations and spending decisions can spark conflict. In Boston, when Mayor Martin Walsh took office in 2014, he referred to the city council as his partner in city government. That partnership frayed within months when the mayor vetoed a $20,000 salary increase (from $87,500 to $107,500) that the council had approved for itself.[66] The Controversies in States and Localities feature describes a significant tension involving the mayor and council in a Missouri city.

Council-mayor conflict is not necessarily unproductive. Conflict is expected in a political system that operates on the foundation of separation of powers. Clashes between the legislative branch and the executive branch can produce better government. But when the disagreements between the council and the mayor escalate to the point of gridlock, effective governance is stymied.

LO 11.5

To articulate why localities need leadership.

Leadership and Capacity

In the final analysis, the concept of leadership remains somewhat ephemeral. Regardless of the difficulty we might have in defining it precisely, it is a central, critical concern in local government. Much is being made of a new pragmatism among America's big-city mayors, an orientation that is independent

Controversies in States and Localities

The Mayor, the City Council, and Walmart . . . and the Community

The development of a Walmart store can be a divisive issue in a community. Opponents often cite the threat to local mom-and-pop stores, while supporters appreciate the employment opportunities and lower prices that a Walmart brings. Ellisville, Missouri, a city of almost 10,000 near St. Louis, offers an interesting example of mayor-council conflict. A developer looking to build a Walmart Supercenter in Ellisville sought a $15 million subsidy from the city to develop the property. The subsidy quickly became a hot-button issue and sparked the formation of pro-subsidy and no-subsidy groups.

Tensions escalated when the city council voted to provide a subsidy to the developer, an action that the newly-elected mayor, Adam Paul, strongly opposed. (He had campaigned on a "No Walmart" platform.) There was talk in some neighborhoods of recalling the pro-subsidy members of the council. The mayor's relationship with the council soured as he railed against their decision and it wasn't long before the council levied several charges against the mayor (giving illegal orders to employees, holding illegal meetings, among other charges) and voted to impeach him. A circuit judge reinstated Mayor Paul three months later. In the meantime, city elections had changed the composition of the council to one more favorable to the mayor's position. As numerous lawsuits were being filed by groups on both sides of the issue, the council fired the city manager who was seen by many as being supportive of the Walmart project and it denied the developer an extension of his development permit. In the fall of 2013, Walmart announced that it was dropping its plans to build in Ellisville.

So, in the end, the mayor prevailed: no subsidy was provided. Walmart does have stores in the area, but not one in Ellisville. In the aftermath, the mayor and the council sought to move forward, restoring harmonious relations in City Hall and with the citizenry . . . and to attract new, nonsubsidized retail businesses to the community.

Critical Thinking Questions:

1. If you had been on the Ellisville city council, would you have voted for or against the subsidy to develop a Walmart Supercenter?

2. As a member of the council, what types of information would you need to help you make the best decision for the community?

3. How should a council member who is elected from a specific district balance the interests of his or her constituents with the interests of the city as a whole?

4. Is the position of mayor of Ellisville strong or weak? Why?

SOURCES: KMOX, 2012, "Ellisville Approves Walmart TIF," http://stlouis.cbslocal.com/2012/05/02/ellisville-approves-walmart-tif/ (accessed May 20, 2012); Paul Hampel, "Judge Permanently Reinstates Adam Paul as Ellisville Mayor," St. Louis Post-Dispatch http://www.stltoday.com/news/local/govt-and-politics (accessed July 1, 2013); KMOX, "Ellisville Gets New Stores to Fills Its Empty Buildings," http://stlouis.cbslocal.com/2015/01/23/ellisville-get-new-stores-to-redevelop-old-best-buy-k-mart-buildings/ (accessed January 23, 2015).

of race or ethnicity. It is a back-to-basics approach to governing, one that emphasizes service delivery, balanced budgets, and working with the private sector to cure the city's ills. This new breed of mayor also seeks to build alliances with adjacent suburbs. Witness the pragmatism of Atlanta's former mayor, Bill Campbell, who wanted to greet visitors coming to his city for the 1996 Olympics with a sign reading "Welcome to Atlanta—a real city with real problems and real people working real hard every day to solve them."[67] Leave it to former New York City mayor Michael Bloomberg to put it in perspective. When asked whether he would run for higher office, he responded, "I think I have a better job than the governor and the president."[68]

At the same time, local governments are becoming more entrepreneurial. Local governments are confronting their problems and challenges by trying new ideas, exploring alternatives, and reaching out for solutions. New approaches do not necessarily work and therein lies the risk. But when they do, other places are quick to embrace them. As a result, local governments change and, one hopes, improve. Consider the case of Philadelphia. In 2007, voters elected a new mayor to take control of a city plagued by high rates of violent crime, pervasive poverty, and persistent unemployment; in addition, its school system had been taken over by state government. Not only that, a budget crisis loomed, and the contracts with public employee unions were due to be renegotiated. Despite the circumstances, the new mayor was optimistic, stating, "What I'm hoping to lead is literally the renaissance of Philadelphia."[69] Mayor Michael Nutter, reelected in 2011, would be the first to admit it has not been easy. But he—and leaders of many other local jurisdictions—remain undeterred.

Chapter Recap

- Elite theory (a small group of leaders possesses power and rules society) and pluralist theory (power is dispersed among competing groups) have dominated the study of community power. Attention has been focused more recently on regime theory and the related concepts of systemic power and strategic advantage.

- Nonprofit organizations have become increasingly important in communities.

- Mayors tend to be the central figures in city politics and government, even if they operate in formally weak-mayor structures.

- City managers have become policy leaders. Even in cities without a formal city manager structure, chief administrative officers are being hired to take on some of the management responsibilities.

- City councils have changed from the good-old-boy clubs of the past. They are more active, they are more diverse, and more conflict occurs between city council members. One of the reasons for these changes is the switch from at-large, or citywide, elections to district (or ward) election of council members.

- Leadership is the ability to realize goals. It varies from one place to another, as a function of the situation. Leadership also comes from the grassroots.

KEY TERMS

elite theory *(p. 287)*
pluralist theory *(p. 287)*
reputational approach *(p. 288)*
decisional method *(p. 288)*

regime *(p. 290)*
nonprofit organizations *(p. 291)*
hyperpluralism *(p. 292)*

taking *(p. 292)*
deracialization *(p. 295)*
Progressive Era *(p. 299)*
aldermen *(p. 301)*

INTERNET RESOURCES

The association of mayors of cities with populations of 30,000 or more, the U.S. Conference of Mayors, has a website at **www.usmayors.org**.

Mayors in a state frequently belong to a statewide organization such as **www.njcm.org** in New Jersey. In the Tar Heel State, the North Carolina Metropolitan Mayors Coalition actively represents cities' interests in state government. Its website is **http://ncmetromayors.com/**.

Specialized constituency groups often have their own organizations and websites, as does the African American Mayors Association at **our-mayors.org**.

The website for the Center for American Women and Politics at Rutgers University, **www.cawp.rutgers.edu**, contains a wealth of data on women and politics.

Information about the city and county management profession can be found at the International City/County Management Association's website, **www.icma.org**.

12

State-Local Relations: Fifty Different Systems

Protesters rally outside the Indiana State Capitol in 2015.
AP Images/Doug McSchooler

LEARNING OBJECTIVES

12.1 To grasp the fundamentals of the state-local relationship, its variations, and its changes.

12.2 To analyze the issues of urban sprawl and smart growth.

12.3 To evaluate the various forms of regionalism.

12.4 To consider the urban impacts of state policies on housing and infrastructure.

12.5 To question the future of rural America.

Several cities in Arkansas such as Little Rock, Hot Springs, and Conway passed ordinances banning discrimination in hiring based on sexual orientation or gender identity. The ordinances differed; most applied only to municipal employment, but the one in Little Rock went further by also covering businesses that have contracts with the city. When the Arkansas legislature convened in 2015, one of the first items on its agenda was consideration of a bill that would block local governments from enacting these anti-discrimination ordinances.[1] The bill passed and became law; cities with these ordinances on their books were now on a collision course with the state. Can state governments supplant local preferences? Can they limit what their localities can do? The answer is an emphatic "yes." A state can impose its will on local governments within its boundaries.

The relationship between states and their communities is often strained. On the one hand, state government gives local governments life. States create the rules for their localities. On the other hand, state governments historically have not treated their local governments well. Over time, some states have realized that mistreating their governmental offspring is counterproductive and have launched a sometimes uncoordinated process of assistance and empowerment of local government. Other states however, have not been so inclined.

Capturing this evolution is the statement of the National Conference of State Legislatures (NCSL) Task Force on State-Local Relations: "Legislators should place a higher priority on state-local issues than has been done in the past. The time has come to change their attitude toward local governments— to stop considering them as just another special interest group and to start treating them as partners in our federal system."[2] Stronger, more competent local governments are an asset to state government.

Chapter 13 will address the financial relationship between state and local governments. This chapter examines broader issues for the two entities and related trends. Let us first consider the most fundamental issue: the distribution of authority between the state and its constituent units.

The Distribution of Authority

In essence, local governments are creatures of their states. In the terminology of Chapter 2, the relationship is that of a unitary system: The state holds all legal power. Federal and state courts have consistently upheld the dependency of localities on the state since Iowa's judge John F. Dillon first laid down **Dillon's rule** in 1868. Dillon's rule established that local governments may exercise only those powers explicitly granted to them by the state, those clearly implied by the explicit powers, and those absolutely essential to the declared objectives and purposes of the local government. Any doubt regarding the legality of any specific local government power is resolved in favor of the state.[3] This perspective runs counter to the more Jeffersonian conception that local governments are imbued with inherent rights, an argument that was elaborated in a Michigan Supreme Court ruling in 1871.[4]

In the words of the U.S. Advisory Commission on Intergovernmental Relations (ACIR), "State legislatures are the trustees of the basic rules of local governance in America. The laws and constitutions of each state are the basic legal instruments of local governance."[5] The ACIR statement denotes the essence of the distribution of authority between a state and its localities. In short, it is up to the state to determine the amount and type of authority a local government may possess. As specified by Dillon's rule, localities depend on the state to give them sufficient power to operate effectively.

THE AMOUNT AND TYPE OF AUTHORITY

In general, states' regulatory reach is great. For example, states may regulate local governments':

- Finances (by establishing debt limits and requiring balanced budgets),
- Personnel (by setting qualifications for certain positions and prescribing employee pension plans),

LO 12.1

To grasp the fundamentals of the state-local relationship, its variations, and its changes.

Dillon's rule

A rule that limits the powers of local government to those expressly granted by the state or those powers closely linked to the express powers.

- Structure (by establishing forms of government and outlawing particular electoral systems),
- Processes (by requiring public hearings and open meetings and mandating financial disclosure),
- Functions (by ordering the provision of public safety functions and proscribing the pursuit of enterprise activities), and
- Service standards (by adopting solid waste guidelines and setting acceptable water-quality levels).

The preceding list makes the point: The state capitol casts a long shadow.

In actuality, the amount and type of authority that states give their local governments vary widely. Some states grant their localities wide-ranging powers to restructure themselves, impose new taxes, and take on additional functions. Others, much more conservative with their power, force local governments to turn to the legislature for approval to act. Empowerment also depends on the type of local government. As noted in Chapter 10, general-purpose governments such as counties, cities, and towns have wider latitude than special-purpose entities like school districts. Even general-purpose governments possess different degrees of authority; counties tend to be more circumscribed than cities in their ability to modify their form of government and expand their service offerings.

A look at building codes offers an illustration of the variability of state-local authority. Twenty years ago, researcher Peter May examined all fifty states to determine the amount of discretion given local governments to adopt and enforce building codes.[6] He found several different patterns. Twelve states (Kentucky and Michigan among them) played an aggressive role by imposing mandatory building codes on their local governments and overseeing local compliance. Thirteen states (including Indiana and Wyoming) had mandatory local codes but stopped short of state review or oversight. The rest of the states gave their local governments more leeway. In eight states (Iowa and Nebraska among them), local governments themselves decided whether to enforce the state building code. And seventeen states (including Delaware and Oklahoma) had no comprehensive building codes; thus, local governments were free to design and enact their own ordinances. In the years since the study was done, states have modified their building codes in numerous ways. But the fundamental point remains valid: States vary in their treatment of local government.

Many state constitutions set forth a provision for home rule (defined in Chapter 10). Although home rule falls short of actual local self-government, it is an important step in the direction of greater local decision making.[7] And local jurisdictions tend to be extremely protective of whatever power they have wrested from state government. For example, the beleaguered Baltimore school system rejected a state plan to take over the schools because, in the words of the one local official, "the solution to the problems in Baltimore city starts with Baltimore city."[8]

second-order devolution

A shift in power from state government to local government.

Devolution (the shift in power from the national government to the states) has also occurred between some states and their local governments. In the state-local case, it is called **second-order devolution**. For example, in 2011, the Alabama legislature authorized its cities and counties to create public organizations to promote tourism; in Oklahoma, municipalities were given more leeway to tear down abandoned buildings. In both cases, the state did not require local governments to act but rather gave them the authority to act if they so desired. What kinds of states tend to give their localities comparatively more power? On average, states that operate with traditional citizen-style, part-time legislative bodies are more likely to empower their local governments, as are states with slower rates of population growth and less robust economies.[9]

A STATE-LOCAL TUG OF WAR

Local governments want their states to provide them with adequate funding and ample discretion. Local officials are supremely confident of their abilities to govern, given sufficient state support. These same local officials express concern that neither their policymaking power nor their financial authority has kept pace with the increased administrative responsibilities placed on them by state government. The recognition and correction of such conditions are the state's responsibility. The state of Michigan, for example, has used its statutory authority to appoint emergency financial managers for several of its financially troubled local governments. The most famous case is the city of Detroit, which had amassed a budget deficit of more than $320 million by 2013 when a state-appointed emergency manager took control of the city's finances away from local elected officials. (Detroit eventually declared bankruptcy in 2014, allowing the city to restructure its debt, slash expenditures, and develop a plan for seeking new revenue; the state's emergency manager then returned control to local officials.) The issue of state takeovers of localities is considered in the It's Your Turn box.

It's Your Turn

Should a State Bail Out Its Financially-Stressed Local Governments?

PROS	CONS
Restoring the financial health of local governments is in the best interest of the state.	The local government got itself into the financial mess, it should figure out a solution.
A state has more resources upon which it can draw to help a troubled locality.	There is little incentive for local officials to make hard choices about expenditures and revenues if the state is going to step in and override them.
Sometimes local officials are just too close to the situation to be able to see it clearly and resolve the problems; a state official can offer fresh thinking.	It is undemocratic for appointed state officials to usurp the policymaking power of local elected officials.

States are not at all reluctant to exercise power vis-à-vis their local jurisdictions. Consider these laws passed in legislative sessions in 2011:[10]

- Utah prohibited cities from creating a local historic district or area in certain circumstances.
- Virginia established requirements for local ordinances that dealt with the siting of wind or solar energy facilities.
- Washington required counties to include an affordable housing component in their impact fee ordinances.

A persistent theme runs through the preceding list: State government can impose its will on local governments. These examples do not mean that states and localities are invariably at each other's throats. Plenty of examples of state-local partnerships exist, such as Florida's and Palm Beach County's joint effort to attract biotechnology industries. The county purchased the land to build a research facility ($200 million); the state is paying the facility's operating costs for seven years ($300 million).[11] Still, the relationship between a state and its local governments often involves conflict as each level tries to exert its will. As tensions escalate, state courts may become involved in determining whether the actions of a state or its local jurisdictions violate the provisions of the state's constitution.

The diagram presented in Figure 12.1 reflects the two fundamental ways that states can influence the authority of local governments. One way is through the vertical state-local government relationship: States can choose

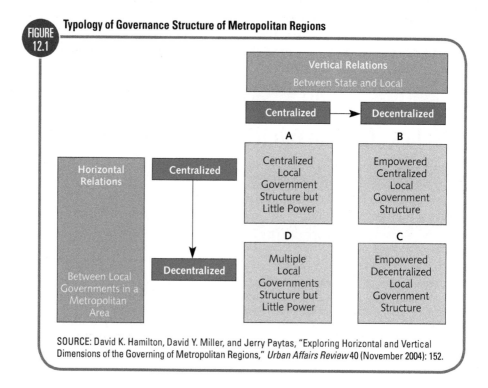

FIGURE 12.1 Typology of Governance Structure of Metropolitan Regions

Vertical Relations Between State and Local

Centralized → Decentralized

Horizontal Relations

Centralized

Decentralized

Between Local Governments in a Metropolitan Area

	A	B
Centralized	Centralized Local Government Structure but Little Power	Empowered Centralized Local Government Structure
	D	C
Decentralized	Multiple Local Governments Structure but Little Power	Empowered Decentralized Local Government Structure

SOURCE: David K. Hamilton, David Y. Miller, and Jerry Paytas, "Exploring Horizontal and Vertical Dimensions of the Governing of Metropolitan Regions," *Urban Affairs Review* 40 (November 2004): 152.

to retain power (centralize) or disperse power (decentralize). The other way is horizontal—the power relationships that local governments have with each other. Combining the two dimensions, vertical and horizontal, produces the four square-shaped boxes on the right half of the diagram.[12] Box A reflects a state that centralizes vertically and horizontally; box C is a state that decentralizes on both dimensions. In a metropolitan area in A states, there are few local governments, and they lack power. In states characterized by the pattern described in box C, many local governments exist and they enjoy substantial power. The states depicted by boxes B and D have one centralizing feature and one decentralizing feature. A state's political history, its constitution, and actions of the legislature combine to determine where a state fits in this diagram. Too, some shifts can occur over time, especially as metropolitan areas develop.

The ability of states and localities to work together effectively has been tested by the issue of homeland security. Concerned that state and local governments were ill prepared to respond to a disaster in a comprehensive and cooperative way, the federal government funded two antiterrorism exercises. One simulation, a bomb and chemical weapons attack, took place in Connecticut; the other, a bioterrorism incident, was set in New Jersey.[13] The exercises exposed weaknesses in response capability, especially communications among responders. The results of the mock disasters sent state and local officials throughout the nation back to the drawing boards to try to determine how to improve their response systems. One outcome has been the creation of "all-hazards" emergency operations plans that identify and assign responsibilities to state and local agencies—and to nonprofit organizations—in the event of a disaster. These plans are designed to improve coordination and communication not only vertically (between the state government and localities) but also horizontally (among local jurisdictions).

STATE MANDATES

Although local governments generally want increased autonomy, state governments have shared their policymaking sphere with reluctance. Rather than let subgovernments devise their own solutions to problems, states frequently prefer to tell them how to solve them. For instance, when the incidence of concussions among student-athletes became a major concern, state legislatures around the country reacted. In Connecticut, the new law enacted during the 2014 legislative session, Public Act 14-66, imposed several requirements at the local level. The law requires (1) local and regional boards of education to implement a concussion education plan, (2) schools to obtain a parent or legal guardian's signature on an informed consent form, (3) a school employee to notify an athlete's parent or legal guardian of a potential concussion, and (4) school districts to collect and report all occurrences of concussions to the state board of education.[14] These types of requirements or orders are examples of *mandates*. Unfunded mandates, especially those with a large price tag, are a persistent source of friction between state and local levels of government.

From the perspective of state government, mandates are necessary to ensure that vital activities are performed and desirable goals are achieved. State mandates promote uniformity of policy from one jurisdiction to another (for instance, regarding the length of the public school year or the operating hours of precinct polling places). In addition, they promote coordination, especially among adjacent jurisdictions that provide services jointly (as with a regional hospital or a metropolitan transportation system).

Officials at the local level tend to see state mandates as unnecessary, and often costly, intrusions into local matters. A recent nationwide survey of city managers and state legislators captured the differing perspectives of the two groups. When asked about the impact of state mandates in twelve policy areas, city managers judged them as negative across the board, while state legislators viewed nine of twelve as positive or neutral.[15]

Local officials offer several suggestions for fixing the mandate problem. Three solutions supported by more than 80 percent of officials surveyed in a Minnesota study of state mandates are as follows:

- The state should provide a clear statement of the rationale behind the mandate; in other words, the state should justify its action.
- Localities should be given greater flexibility in implementing the provisions of the mandate.
- Financial aid to local governments should be increased so that they can deal with mandates effectively.[16]

As might be expected, these solutions are substantially less popular with state officials. But certainly, more communication between state policymakers and local officials, especially at the outset, would reduce some of the friction generated by mandates. Allowing local governments more leeway in implementation, either through extension of time or variation in rules, would lessen the punch that mandates pack. Even more central to any type of mandate reform is adequate state funding of mandates. This action would go a long way toward improving state-local relationships. Recognizing that funding is one of the key considerations, many states have adopted **mandate-reimbursement requirements**. These measures require states either to reimburse local governments for the costs of state mandates or to give local governments adequate revenue-raising capacity to pay for them.

STATE-LOCAL ORGANIZATIONS

Legal, administrative, and financial ties link state and local governments. Additional interaction occurs when state governments establish organizations such as local government study commissions and advisory panels of local officials. Among the most prevalent structures are task forces, advisory commissions on intergovernmental relations, and departments of community affairs.

Task forces tend to be focused organizations set up by the governor or the state legislature in response to a perceived local-level problem. If a state wants to investigate the ramifications of changing its annexation statutes, the legislature might create a task force on annexation and boundary changes (or something similar). The task force would probably be composed of state and

mandate-reimbursement requirements

Measures that take the financial sting out of state mandates.

local officials, community leaders, and experts on the subject of annexation. First, the task force would collect information on how other states handle the annexation question; second, it would conduct a series of public hearings to get input from individuals and groups interested in the issue; finally, it would compile a report that included recommendations suitable for legislative action. Its work completed, the task force would then disband, although individual members might turn up as advocates when the task-force recommendations receive legislative attention. Task forces are quick organizational responses to local problems that have become too prominent for state government to ignore. A task force is a low-cost, concentrated reaction that undertakes specific tasks and, in some instances, actually influences legislative deliberations.

In a more comprehensive effort at state-local cooperation, twenty-five states established state-level *advisory commissions on intergovernmental relations* (*ACIRs*), modeled after the commission, now defunct, created by the U.S. Congress in 1959. State-level ACIRs are designed to promote more harmonious, workable relations between the state and its governmental subdivisions. They are intended to offer a neutral forum for discussion of long-range state-local issues—a venue in which officials can engage in focused dialogue; conduct research on local developments and new state policies; promote experimentation in intergovernmental processes, both state-local and interlocal; and propose solutions to state-local problems.

Despite their promise, many state ACIRs met their demise in the 1990s and early 2000s, among them the ACIRs in Oklahoma and Virginia, victims of state budget cuts and insufficient legislative support. (Kansas bucked the trend by creating an ACIR in 2002.) The most recent count shows that only ten state ACIRs remain viable.[17] Those that have managed to survive have been able to demonstrate their utility and steer a nonpartisan path in a partisan environment. Connecticut ACIR, for instance, has as one of its statutory responsibilities the tracking and reporting of the mandates adopted by the state's General Assembly during the legislative session.

Another way in which states can generate closer formal ties with their local governments is through specialized administrative agencies. All fifty states have created *departments of community affairs* (*DCAs*) that are involved in local activities. They have different names (Kentucky calls its DCA the Department for Local Government; Washington's is the Department of Community, Trade, and Economic Development), but their function is similar: to offer a range of programs and services to local governments. DCAs are involved in housing, urban revitalization, anti-poverty programs, and economic development; they also offer local governments services such as planning, management, and financial assistance. DCAs vary on several dimensions: their niche in state government, the sizes of their budget and staff, and whether they include an advisory board of local officials. Compared with state-level ACIRs, DCAs function much more as service deliverers and much less as policy initiators. Therefore, these two types of organizations tend to complement rather than compete with one another. Both function as advocates for local government, however, at the state level.

Metropolitics: A New Challenge for State Government

State governments often find their dealings with local governments to be confounded by the side effects of urbanization. Regardless of which state we examine, its urban areas show the effects of three waves of suburbanization. An early wave occurred during the 1920s, when automobiles facilitated the development of outlying residential areas. Although the dispersion slowed during the Great Depression and World War II, its resurgence in the 1950s triggered a second wave during which retail stores followed the population exodus, the so-called malling of America. Now a third wave of suburbanization is upon us, one fueled by what has been called America's "exit ramp economy." Office, commercial, and retail facilities are increasingly located along suburban freeways.[18] This phenomenon is occurring nearly everywhere, from New York City to San Diego, from Milwaukee to Miami. This third wave of suburbanization has caught the attention of state governments.

As a result of the transformation of American metropolitan areas, central cities have lost some of their prominence as the social, economic, and political focal points of their areas. People have moved to surrounding suburbs and beyond; businesses and firms have sprung up in the hinterlands; communities have formed their own service and taxing districts. The outward flow of people and activities has fundamentally altered metropolitan areas. As noted above, these new boom towns are not simply residential but include business, retail, and entertainment activities.

Continued outward growth beyond the central city suggests the need for changes in outmoded state government policy toward metropolitan jurisdictions. A serious concern is that rapid, unplanned growth is producing sprawl and fostering what are called shadow governments. A logical question is: What is state government doing while all of this is occurring? More than it used to, as we shall see.

URBAN SPRAWL VERSUS SMART GROWTH

Population growth is, of course, something that states and localities desire. But the consequences of rapid and unplanned population growth test the capability of governments to provide services efficiently and effectively. As growth spills beyond city limits into unincorporated areas, as **edge cities** spring up along interstate highways, the result is often traffic congestion and overcrowded schools. Far from the central city, subdivisions and strip malls sprout on land that was recently forests and farms. It costs a lot of money for government to provide infrastructure—streets, water and sewer lines, schools—to these new developments. Meanwhile, many inner cities, where the infrastructure is already in place, are plagued by empty storefronts, vacant lots, and abandoned factories. Many states and localities have struggled to balance the benefits of new growth against the attendant costs.

Sprawling Growth In many parts of the country, one of the hottest issues of the early twenty-first century is **urban sprawl**, a term that carries negative

---

LO 12.2

To analyze the issues of urban sprawl and smart growth.

edge cities

New boom towns featuring retail shops and malls, restaurants, office buildings, and housing developments, far from the central city.

urban sprawl

Development characterized by low population density, rapid land consumption, and dependence on the automobile.

connotations. It refers to development beyond the central city that is characterized by low densities, rapid land consumption, and dependence on the automobile. It is often called *leapfrog development* because it jumps over established settlements. Exit-ramp communities and edge cities are a manifestation of sprawl. Urban sprawl is resource-intensive and costly, and it is also the subject of political debate.

Until the mortgage crisis in 2008 and the subsequent recession, Las Vegas, Nevada, offered perhaps the best contemporary example of a fast-growing, sprawling city. According to the city's statistics, 200 new residents arrived in Las Vegas every day; a house was constructed every 15 minutes.[19] Traffic congestion intensified, as did concern over maintaining an adequate water supply in this desert city. As human settlement pushed ever outward to lower-cost land, local government was pressed to provide schools, parks, and roads. Growth quickly outstripped the infrastructure needed to support it. The mayor of Las Vegas proposed a $2,000-per-house **impact fee** to mitigate the effects of growth, but the city lacked the authority to levy the fee. The Nevada legislature had to approve the proposal before it could take effect.

Although the pace of growth has slowed in Las Vegas and the surrounding area, the issues related to planning and paying for new development remain. Even though revenues for local governments will increase as a result of development, costs of providing services will also rise and not necessarily commensurately. One study of Georgia counties found that for every $1.00 of revenue brought in by new housing developments, the cost of services was between $1.23 and $2.07.[20] Public education was the big-ticket item pushing up service costs. This is the primary explanation for the popularity of impact fees. Research on Florida counties found that rapid population growth stimulates the adoption of impact fees especially if nearby counties have adopted them already.[21] Only when commercial and industrial development complements subdivision growth do local governments typically enjoy a net revenue gain.

The relentless creep of urban sprawl has prompted reactions in many states and communities. In 2014, fifty-five land conservation measures appeared on ballots throughout the country; thirty-five of them passed. These measures committed more than $13 billion in new funding for land conservation. Voters in Florida approved a constitutional amendment dedicating $9 billion over twenty years for new land conservation, including major investments in the Everglades, while New Jersey voters endorsed using a portion of the state's corporate business tax revenue to protect open space.[22] One of the major defeats occurred in North Dakota where voters rejected a proposal to divert 5% of the state's oil extraction tax dollars to land conservation for the next 25 years.

Smart Growth The majority of land-use decisions occur at the local level, and many states offer guidance and provide localities with tools to manage growth. Hawaii was a pioneer in this effort with its State Land Use Law, adopted in 1961; Vermont and Oregon got on board in 1970 and 1973, respectively, with growth management acts designed to control the pace of development and protect environmentally sensitive areas. The **smart growth** movement represents the new generation in state growth management. It is an effort to

impact fee
A charge levied on new development to offset some of the costs of providing services.

smart growth
Government efforts to limit urban sprawl by managing growth.

TABLE 12.1	Ten Principles of Smart Growth
• Mix land uses.
• Take advantage of compact building design.
• Create a range of housing opportunities and choices.
• Create walkable neighborhoods.
• Foster distinctive, attractive communities with a strong sense of place.
• Preserve open space, farmland, natural beauty, and critical environmental areas.
• Strengthen and direct development towards existing communities.
• Provide a variety of transportation choices.
• Make development decisions predictable, fair, and cost-effective.
• Encourage community and stakeholder collaboration in development decisions.

SOURCE: Smart Growth Online, "Smart Growth Principles," http://smartgrowth.org/smart-growth-principles/ (accessed May 10, 2015).

reduce the amount of sprawl and minimize its impact. Communities tend to define "smart growth" in ways that fit their own particular circumstances, but the basic principles of the movement are listed in Table 12.1.

Maryland was one of the first states to take action to limit sprawl. Calling sprawl "a disease eating away at the heart of America," Governor Parris Glendening signed the Smart Growth Areas Act into law in 1997.[23] In effect, the state rewards local governments that target new growth in areas that already have infrastructure, and it denies state funding for infrastructure projects that encourage sprawl. Several other states moved quickly to follow Maryland's lead. The following year, Arizona adopted a Growing Smarter Act; by 2003, another 20 states had taken anti-sprawl actions of one sort or another.[24] A particularly ambitious plan was New Jersey's Blueprint for Intelligent Growth (BIG). Had BIG been adopted as originally drafted, huge portions of the Garden State would have been off-limits to additional development, much to the dismay of many local officials and builders.[25] Although the far-reaching anti-sprawl proposal was eventually pared down, it was clear that in New Jersey, as in many other places, state governments are reestablishing themselves as major influences in local governments' land-use decisions.

A word of caution is necessary. Not everyone thinks that sprawl is so bad. In fact, to some, sprawl is simply the consequence of the unfettered workings of a free-market system.[26] Given a choice, they contend, Americans prefer a spread-out, car-centered lifestyle. Obviously, there is some truth to that argument. Smart growth inevitably means higher density, that is, smaller lot sizes and taller buildings to accommodate more people. High-rise condominium complexes and soaring office towers appeal to some folks, but to most suburbanites, increased density is not something they want.[27]

SHADOW GOVERNMENTS

As new development pushes into the hinterlands, new forms of governance are emerging. They have become known as **shadow governments**, and although they may not be official government units, in many important ways they behave as if they were. They levy fees, regulate behavior, and provide services. Three types of shadow government exist:

- Private enterprise shadow governments, such as homeowners' associations;
- Public-private partnership shadow governments, common examples of which are development corporations and business improvement districts; and
- Subsidiaries of conventional governments with unusual powers, such as area-wide planning commissions.

Shadow governments exist within the confines of state law, but most states have not taken an active role in overseeing them.

Estimates place the number of private enterprise shadow governments at about 200,000, the majority located in suburban areas. A condominium community provides an illustration. The property owners' association makes rules for residents (from the speed limit on community streets to the color of the condo), provides services (security, maintenance, landscaping), and assesses fees (based on the size of the unit). Residents typically vote for the board of directors of the association (in some instances, developers of the project retain seats on the board), and votes tend to be weighted according to the value of the housing unit. Owners with a greater financial investment have a greater say in the governing of the community, which is a far cry from the one-person, one-vote principle.

Shadow governments, especially the first two types, raise questions about matters of power and equity (but not about their efficiency because, by most accounts, they tend to operate fairly efficiently). The power issue centers on information, influence, and accountability. Shadow governments control information, restrict influence to those who belong or can pay, and have little public accountability. They are not subject to the same legal standards as are typical governments.[28] The equity issue addresses the class discrimination inherent in these governments. A poor family out for a Sunday drive may be able to traverse public streets in their ramshackle automobile, but if they turn their car onto a private street patrolled by private police, they are likely to be followed and perhaps even stopped, questioned, and escorted out of the neighborhood.

Whatever our uneasiness over power and equity issues related to shadow governments, their number is increasing. Shadow governments are especially popular in metropolitan areas, because local government boundaries do not necessarily jibe with economic realities and development patterns. Their vaunted efficiency makes them a force to be reckoned with. Research on private enterprise shadow governments in California, Florida, and New Jersey showed each state taking vastly different approaches to their regulation.[29]

The social and economic changes in U.S. metropolitan areas have had a tremendous impact on urban governance. Urban expansion and shadow

shadow governments Entities, especially unofficial ones, that function like governments.

governments make up extended webs of interdependent jurisdictions. How can these places be governed best? Some observers have advocated a broad regionally-focused approach.

LO 12.3

To evaluate the various forms of regionalism.

REGIONAL GOVERNANCE

A typical metropolitan area in the United States is fragmented—that is, it is comprised of many local governments. One alternative to the fragmentation is the creation of a **regional government**, a larger entity to replace some of the smaller jurisdictions. State legislatures are important players in this process because, aside from the state constitution, they create the rules of the game. Their actions either facilitate or hinder local government reorganization into regional units.

City-County Consolidation In the United States, the closest thing to regional government is **city-county consolidation**, whereby area jurisdictions are absorbed into a single countywide government. In a pure form of consolidation, one police department, one fire department, and one water and sewer system exist for the area. The functions of local government—public safety, public works, health and human services, community and economic development, and recreation and arts programs—are provided by a single jurisdiction. Thirty-four consolidated city-county governments exist in the United States. Some of these consolidated jurisdictions reflect political decisions of the nineteenth century, such as the combined city-county governments of Philadelphia, San Francisco, and New Orleans. Among the most prominent mergers of the past forty years are those in Indianapolis–Marion County, Indiana; Jacksonville–Duval County, Florida; Nashville– Davidson County, Tennessee; and, Louisville–Jefferson County, Kentucky. The state of Georgia leads the nation in the number of consolidated city-county governments with seven, the most recent occurring in Macon-Bibb County in 2014.

Regional government seems so rational, yet it has proven to be quite difficult to achieve. Voters usually defeat proposals to consolidate city and county government, such as the 2012 effort in Evansville and Vandenburgh County, Indiana. At various times, voters have rejected the mergers of Des Moines and Polk County, Iowa; Spokane and Spokane County, Washington; Wilmington and New Hanover County, North Carolina; and Knoxville and Knox County, Tennessee—just to name a few. Opponents of jurisdictional consolidation often include city and county governing boards, city and county employees, and taxpayer organizations. Support for merging governments typically comes from the local chamber of commerce, real-estate developers, local newspapers, and civic organizations.[30]

To reformers, this lack of success is perplexing. The logic is straightforward: If small local governments in a metropolitan area merge to form a larger local government, two positive outcomes will occur. First, stubborn public policy problems can be tackled from an area-wide perspective. For example, the pollution generated by City A that affects City B can be handled as a regional problem rather than as a conflict between the two cities. Second, combining forces produces *economies of scale* in service delivery. Instead of

regional government

An area-wide structure for local governance, designed to replace multiple jurisdictions.

city-county consolidation

The merger of city and county governments into a single jurisdiction.

each jurisdiction constructing and operating separate jails, for example, one large regional facility can be maintained. Jail service can be provided at a lower cost to each participating jurisdiction. These anticipated outcomes are persuasive arguments in favor of consolidation.

Regional government does not always perform as expected, however. Research has shown that city-county consolidation does not necessarily reduce the costs of government, and may even increase them.[31] Another criticism of regional government is that it can be inaccessible and destructive of the hard-won political gains of minorities. Compared with a city or town government, regional government is farther away, both literally and figuratively. Residents of small towns fear the loss of identity as their community gets swept into bigger government. The effect on minority political strength is no less troublesome. Because the proportionate number of minorities may be lessened when jurisdictions are combined, their voting strength can be diluted. For instance, African Americans made up 34 percent of pre-merger Louisville but only 19.5 percent of consolidated Louisville–Jefferson Metro Government.[32]

A competing perspective on regional government comes from **public choice theory**. According to this theory, the existence of many jurisdictions in a metropolitan area gives people options, that is, they can choose to live in the central city, in nearby suburbs, or in the county. Each of these jurisdictions offers a particular mix of tax rates, policies, and public services. In deciding where to reside or open a business, individuals seek places that are in line with their own tax, policy, and service preferences.[33] To public choice theorists, consolidating cities and counties or creating regional governments robs people of important choices and creates inefficiencies. The consolidation of the city of Louisville and Jefferson County borrowed a page from public choice theory when, in a political compromise, it left eighty smaller jurisdictions in the county out of the merger. Figure 12.2 shows the boundaries of pre-consolidated Louisville and Jefferson County, as well as the other jurisdictions.

A City and Its Suburbs The former mayor of Albuquerque, New Mexico, David Rusk, after thinking long and hard about the relationship between a central city and its suburbs, jumped into the regionalism debate with this statement: "The real city is the total metropolitan area—city and suburb."[34] He uses the concept of elasticity (and inelasticity) to signify the ability of a city to expand its city boundaries (or not). In a sense, a city's elasticity is its destiny. Elastic cities have been able to capture suburban growth; by adjusting their boundaries through annexation, they can keep pace with urban sprawl. Conversely, many inelastic cities trapped in existing boundaries have suffered population loss and tax-base erosion, resulting in higher levels of racial and class segregation.

The solution offered is a familiar one: regional government. But to be effective, the regional government must include the central city and at least 60 percent of the area's population, according to Rusk. How to do this? It depends on the characteristics of the metropolitan area. In single-county metropolitan areas, empowerment of the urban county would effectively create regional government, as would city-county consolidation. And in multi-county metropolitan areas, a single regional government could be created out of existing cities and counties. Obviously, the restructuring of local governments in

public choice theory

The theory that individuals shop around to find a local government whose taxes and services are in line with their own preferences.

FIGURE 12.2   **Map of Louisville, Jefferson County, and Small Cities**

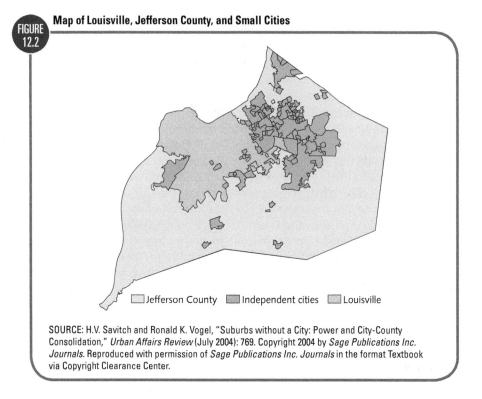

Jefferson County   Independent cities   Louisville

SOURCE: H.V. Savitch and Ronald K. Vogel, "Suburbs without a City: Power and City-County Consolidation," *Urban Affairs Review* (July 2004): 769. Copyright 2004 by *Sage Publications Inc. Journals.* Reproduced with permission of *Sage Publications Inc. Journals* in the format Textbook via Copyright Clearance Center.

these ways would engender substantial opposition; as Rusk acknowledges, however, few alternatives are available to areas with low elasticity.

The argument for a metropolitan-wide government is simple: Because economies are essentially regional in nature, governance can (and should) be, too. As discussed earlier, however, regional government has never been a popular alternative in this country. Overcoming traditional anti-regionalism sentiment will not be easy, but regional approaches may be necessary for effective competition in an increasingly global economy. And there is some evidence that thinking regionally is gaining favor. Maybe the mayor of Missoula, Montana (a college town), said it best when he commented: "It is not possible for Missoula to understand itself, or its future, except in a regional context. The city draws its strength from the region."[35]

It's Up to the States Both Portland, Oregon, and the Twin Cities area of Minnesota have embraced regionalism. In Oregon, Portland joined with its suburbs and outlying jurisdictions to develop a region-wide vision for the future. The 2040 Plan, as it is called, aims at accommodating orderly growth while maintaining a desirable quality of life in the region. The planning process involved extensive public participation, including citizen surveys and public forums. In addition, the plan's backers launched media campaigns and loaned videos to acquaint residents with the proposal. The 2040 Plan is enforced by an elected, region-wide council that works to secure the compliance of local governments.[36]

In the Minneapolis–St. Paul area of Minnesota, jurisdictions contribute 40 percent of their new commercial and industrial tax base to a regional pool. The money in this pool is redistributed to communities throughout the region on the basis of financial need, thereby reducing fiscal disparities across jurisdictions. Thus, for instance, a new industry locating in one city becomes a benefit to neighboring cities as well. With regional tax-base sharing as a start, Minnesota went even further in 1994 when the state legislature placed all regional sewer, transit, and land-use planning in the hands of a regional organization—the Metropolitan Council of the Twin Cities.[37] This significantly empowered council makes crucial decisions about growth and development in the Twin Cities area from a regional perspective.

In the final analysis, it is up to state government to provide a sufficiently supportive environment in which regionalism can take root. It was Oregon and Minnesota that created the legal environment for Portland and the Twin Cities, respectively. As political scientists Margaret Weir, Harold Wolman, and Todd Swanstrom declared in their research on city-suburban coalitions, "States are critical players; they set the terms and conditions under which regionalism occurs."[38] They have to because the natural tendency for officials in cities and their suburbs is to see each other as rivals rather than allies or partners. An extreme example of regionalism comes from California, where there was an effort to get an initiative on the 2016 ballot that would have created six regional Californias. Read about this in the Controversies in States and Localities feature.

Regional Coordination **Councils of government (COGs)** or regional planning commissions are examples of regional coordination. They do not involve a formal merger or combination of governments; instead, COGs are loose collections of local governments designed to increase communication and coordination in an area. They provide a neutral forum in which local leaders can come together to identify and discuss issues of common concern.[39] For instance, the Metropolitan Washington (D.C.) COG recently conducted a planning exercise organized around four "what-if" scenarios:

- An extended economic recession and massive government debt,
- Low oil prices that derail strong climate change policies,
- The dispersal of many federal government agencies from the region, and
- The advent of a green industrial revolution.[40]

The point of the scenario planning process was to get local leaders thinking about how large-scale events could affect the area's jurisdictions in the future.

State governments, in fact, were not active in the creation of COGs; national government programs spurred their development. For example, the federal government requires states to create metropolitan planning organizations (MPOs) to coordinate transportation programs in urban areas.[41] Nearly half of the MPOs are part of their area COG. Currently, there are more than 500 COGs active in the United States.

Although area-wide planning is the most common activity of COGs, they also perform other tasks. Member governments can turn to them for technical assistance (such as help in writing federal grant applications), professional

councils of government
Formal organizations of general-purpose governments in an area, intended to improve regional coordination.

Controversies in States and Localities

One Big California or Six Regional Californias?

California is a big state, both in terms of population and land area. Since joining the United States in 1850, many proposals to split the state in two—usually into northern and southern states—have emerged. The groups promoting a split are usually unhappy with state policy on certain issues or believe that their area is not getting its fair share of resources from the legislature.

In 2014, a California venture capitalist, Tim Draper, proposed a ballot initiative on the question of dividing the state into six separate states: Jefferson, North California, Silicon Valley, Central California, West California, and South California (see the accompanying map). Why propose such a dramatic change? In the view of Draper and his supporters, the Golden State had become ungovernable and it needed to be refreshed. The solution was to create smaller states that would be more responsive to their residents, more accountable for their actions, and more innovative in their policies.

The Six Californias proposal attracted a lot of attention and plenty of pushback. An opposition group, One California, formed, led by the Speaker of the California Assembly, Fabian Núñez, who dismissed the proposal as "a solution in search of a problem." Analyses of the proposal raised questions about the disparity in resources and revenues among the new states. For example, were the initiative to succeed, it would create both the nation's richest state (Silicon Valley) and its poorest (Central California).

Draper created a website, "Six Californias" to help publicize his idea, and hired a professional firm to handle the petition signature process. However, when the petitions were submitted to the Secretary of State's office for verification, the number of valid signatures was too low to qualify for the 2016 general election ballot. (And of course, even if the question had made it to the ballot and been approved by California voters, the split would require the approval of the U.S Congress.) With the Six Californias initiative falling short, disappointed but undaunted, Draper moved on to his next government-improvement project: The Fix California Challenge.

Critical Thinking Questions:

1. What advantages does California enjoy as the largest state in the nation? What disadvantages does it face?

2. Why are smaller states thought to be more responsive and accountable than larger states?

3. Would a layer of multi-county regional governments be a better alternative to breaking up the state?

SOURCES: Six Californias, www.sixcalifornias.com (accessed May 19, 2015); "Background," http://www.lao.ca.gov/ballot/2013/130771. aspx (accessed January 31, 2014); Jim Miller, "Six Californias Initiative Fails to Make 2016 Ballot," *Sacramento Bee*, www.sacbee. com/news/politics-government/capitol-alert/article2609555.html (accessed September 12, 2014).

services (planning, budgeting, engineering, legal advice), and information (economic data for the region).

The impact of these councils has been less significant than their creators hoped, but they have had two positive effects. First, COGs have elevated the concept of area-wide policy planning from a pipe dream to a reality. They have been heavily involved in criminal justice, water quality, housing, and especially transportation planning. Second, councils have substantially improved the operational capacity of rural local governments by providing expertise to small local jurisdictions that cannot afford to hire specialized staff.

Some localities have taken a more informal route to regional coordination through service sharing. In service sharing, jurisdictions agree to consolidate specific services, cooperate in their provision, or exchange them. For instance, recreational facilities may be provided jointly by several jurisdictions, one government may rent jail space from another, or county residents may use the city library in return for city residents' use of the county's solid waste landfill. Service-sharing arrangements are popular because they hold the promise of greater efficiency in service delivery, *and* they do not threaten the power and autonomy of existing jurisdictions the way consolidation does. Recent research suggests that local officials may be more receptive to this type of interjurisdictional cooperation than is commonly thought.[42] Still, the ability to hammer out agreements that benefit all participating governments is contingent upon numerous factors related to the problem itself and the jurisdictional context.[43] COGs and service-sharing agreements provide for a modicum of regional governance . . . without a regional government.

States and Urban Policy

LO 12.4

To consider the urban impacts of state policies on housing and infrastructure.

If you had attended an urban policy conference recently, you would have heard the phrase *state government* used repeatedly. Many states have replaced some of their policies that had a negative impact on urban areas with urban-friendly programs. Michigan was one of the leaders when, in 1998, its Urban Caucus began a process of identifying state programs that hindered investment in central cities. Since then, other states have followed suit. Three significant contemporary issues—housing, infrastructure, and new urbanism—are of particular interest in an urban environment. Let us consider each of these contemporary issues in terms of state-local interaction.

HOUSING POLICY

For middle- and upper-income city residents, the housing market can be counted on to produce affordable units, but what is affordable to these residents is out of reach for low-income households. The mechanics of market economics effectively shut them out of the system. Low-cost housing does not generate the return that higher-cost housing does. As a result, governments have intervened to create incentives for developers to produce low-income housing units and, where incentives do not work, to become providers of housing themselves. One of the aims of the federal Housing Act of 1949 was "a decent home in a suitable living environment" for all Americans.

Over time, the national government has backed away from this goal and altered its approach to housing. In 1968, it was willing to become the nation's housing provider of last resort, but by the 1980s the push was to deregulate and let market forces prevail. Modifications of national tax laws have had a negative effect on rental housing stock. Deliberate actions and inaction resulted in a decline in home ownership, an increase in the proportion of household income that is spent on housing, a decrease in the number of affordable rental units, an increase in the number of physically inadequate and abandoned structures, and an increase in the number of homeless people.[44]

In response, state governments have set up housing finance agencies, nonprofit corporations have entered the low-income housing market, and local governments have adopted regulations to preserve their affordable housing stock. New Jersey, for example, mandated that all of its 567 communities provide their fair share of affordable housing for low- and moderate-income people. In some places, housing vouchers—a form of consumer subsidy that would open currently unaffordable housing to low-income residents—have been instituted. Another approach is for local governments to require developers to include a fixed proportion of affordable units in their market-rate projects as a condition for approval of a building permit. This approach works, however, only where developers are clamoring for access.

Connecticut has been particularly innovative in addressing its affordable-housing problem. As part of its statewide plan, the state conducted a housing needs assessment. In a pilot program, Connecticut entered into mediated negotiations with local jurisdictions in a specified area to develop a fair-housing compact for the area. To encourage communities to pursue the goals of the compact, it established a housing infrastructure fund to provide state financial assistance. As a result, thousands of new affordable housing units were constructed.[45] Connecticut's effort to address the scarcity of affordable housing has been emulated by other states.

Some local jurisdictions are also playing active roles. Seattle has pioneered the resurgence of backyard cottages—small, affordable units that are constructed behind existing single-family homes. Although some homeowners use these "accessory dwelling units" to house their extended family, most rent them to tenants. Initially, the city's policy met with criticism that it would change the feel of a neighborhood, but a recent study showed this not to be the case.[46] Other cities such as Denver, Colorado, have followed Seattle's lead in adopting this affordable housing option. In some regions of the country, cities are dealing with the phenomenon of **gentrification**, in which new development occurs in underinvested and predominately poor neighborhoods. That might seem to be a positive development, but it typically leads to steep rises in housing prices that eventually displace a community's longtime residents.[47]

In states hit particularly hard by the downturn in the housing market in 2008 and 2009, problems of a different sort arose. In California, Arizona, Nevada, and Florida, plunging home values and mortgage foreclosures meant lower-property tax revenues for local jurisdictions. In addition, the number of homeless people rose in many cities, straining the capacity of shelters and leading to the creation of tent cities and encampments. By 2012, the housing market had rebounded somewhat in many areas of the country; by 2015, most areas in the United States were experiencing increased demand for housing.

gentrification

The replacement of lower-value housing and businesses with higher-value residential and commercial development. Property values increase and longtime residents are often displaced.

INFRASTRUCTURE POLICY

Infrastructure is the physical network of a community, that is, its roads and bridges, airports, water and sewer systems, and public buildings. Its importance lies in its connection to development; the simplest equation is no infrastructure = no development. Infrastructure has become an issue in many communities because of its crumbling condition and the high cost of repair or replacement. Bridges that are structurally deficient, airport runways in poor condition, drinking water facilities that are substandard, sewer pipes that overflow—all of these infrastructure problems present major challenges. One recent study estimated that nationwide, localities need between $300 billion to $450 billion in essential upgrades to their water and sewer systems.[48] The cost estimates for necessary transportation infrastructure improvements over the next decade are even higher. The federal stimulus program (formally, the American Recovery and Reinvestment Act of 2009), provided some relief with approximately $110 billion in funding for shovel-ready infrastructure projects. Clearly, substantially more money will be needed to maintain and modernize the nation's infrastructure, and all levels of government will be involved.

The stock of aging, sometimes unsafe infrastructure has prompted states and localities to cast about for solutions. In the area of transportation infrastructure, one approach receiving greater scrutiny is privatization.[49] Some states have allowed the construction of private toll roads; a few states have leased existing highways to private companies. For example, in 2006, Indiana signed a 75-year lease with a foreign firm to operate a 157-mile toll road that traverses the state. For an upfront lease payment of $3.8 billion, the investors get to keep toll road revenues during the lease period and are responsible for maintaining the roadway. Privatized highway projects are criticized on two counts. Some argue that private roadways will produce a have/have-not distinction, with the affluent traveling on pay roads and the poor being dispatched to congested freeways. Others claim that privatization offers a Band-Aid solution to the enormous transportation problems facing the nation. Despite these concerns, privatization remains an attractive option to governors and legislatures intent on holding down highway taxes.

At the local level, interest in innovative infrastructure plans has grown. Two large Midwestern cities offer illustrative examples.[50] In Indianapolis, the merger of separate utilities into a single quasi-governmental organization has resulted in cost savings, freeing up $425 million for a series of infrastructure improvements. The program, dubbed "RebuildIndy," relies heavily on the input of the public, local businesses, and experts in deciding which projects are to be prioritized. In Minneapolis, the mayor has promoted a "Development Infrastructure Fund" to be used for investment in public infrastructure that will generate private development. Small amounts of bond funds would be utilized to leverage private capital for projects that would eventually expand the city's tax base. In both Indianapolis and Minneapolis, the goal is to cement the link between infrastructure improvement and economic development.

NEW URBANISM

One of the most intriguing efforts at transforming the urban experience has its roots in architecture and urban planning. Called **new urbanism**, the approach rejects the suburban model of development in favor of a traditional small-town

new urbanism
An anti-suburban, pro–small-town version of city planning.

Donovan Reese Photography/Getty Images

The redeveloped Pearl Brewery, a 22-acre mixed-use complex in San Antonio.

style. Proponents of new urbanism, especially Miami-based architects Andres Duany and Elizabeth Plater-Zyberk, have advocated what is essentially a high-density, pedestrian-friendly, environmentally sensitive design for communities.[51] In theory, residents of these new urban places will acquire a sense of community and become engaged in civic life. One of the first experiments with new urbanism was the development of Seaside, Florida. (Movie buffs will remember it as the town where *The Truman Show* was filmed.) Another, called Celebration, has been created by the Walt Disney Company on 5,000 acres on the fringe of Orlando, Florida. It is a corporate-planned town with a private government.

The real test for new urbanism will be in an existing city, not in a geographically separate enclave. Can new urbanism work in a place plagued by social disorder and disinvestment? The answer to that question will not be known for years, and many observers are skeptical. But the Congress for the New Urbanism (CNU), a nonprofit organization committed to promoting the concept, is forging ahead. Annually CNU selects exemplary projects, both in the United States and abroad, that embrace new urbanism principles. Table 12.2 lists four of the projects that won the 2015 award.

TABLE 12.2	Award Winning Projects, Congress of New Urbanism, 2015	
CITYWIDE SCALE:		
El Paso, Texas	Implementation of Smart Growth principles in an eight-square mile section as a starting point in re-orienting and densifying the sprawling city.	
NEIGHBORHOOD SCALE:		
New Orleans, Louisiana	Iberville Offsites: An affordable housing development of 46 homes emphasizing both historic preservation and innovative green technology.	
San Antonio, Texas	Pearl Brewery Redevelopment Master Plan: Conversion of abandoned industrial structures into a mixed-use commercial area.	
Wyandanch, New York	Creation of a transit-oriented neighborhood with new infrastructure, public space, and mixed residential-commercial development.	

SOURCE: Congress for the New Urbanism, "2015 Charter Awards," https://www.cnu.org/sites/www.cnu.org/files/cnu_2015_charter_awards-lores.pdf (accessed May 6, 2015). Reprinted by permission.

So far, states have not taken new urbanism to heart. But as states seek ways to revitalize declining central cities, new urbanism may be seen as a promising approach.

States and Their Rural Communities

LO 12.5

To question the future of rural America.

When the local Dairy Queen closes its doors, a small town in rural America knows that it is in trouble. The Dairy Queen, like the coffee shop on Main Street, serves as a gathering place for community residents. Its demise symbolizes the tough times that a lot of rural communities face. In fact, some analysts argue that the major distinctions in regional economics are no longer between Sunbelt and Frostbelt, or East Coast and West Coast, but between metropolitan America and the countryside.[52] People are leaving many rural areas, with the most relentless decline occurring in a broad swath stretching northward from west Texas through North Dakota.[53] By 2012, only about 19 percent of the population called rural America home, with about 17.2 percent of these rural residents living in poverty.[54]

The decline of rural America has provoked a question: What can state governments do to encourage the right kind of growth in rural areas? Short of pumping enormous amounts of money into the local economy, they can encourage the expansion of local intergovernmental cooperation, whereby small rural governments join together to increase their administrative capacity to deliver services and achieve economies of scale. Two state actions facilitate such cooperation. One is the reforming of state tax codes so that jurisdictions can share locally generated tax revenues, similar to the Twin Cities model discussed earlier. Rather than competing with one another for a new manufacturing plant or a shopping mall, local governments can cooperate to bring the new facility to the area; regardless of where this facility is located, all jurisdictions can receive a portion of the tax revenue. A second useful state action is

A rural area that has been bypassed by the interstate highway system

Photos by Andy/Shutterstock.com

the promotion of statewide land-use planning. As one observer has noted, "Currently too many rural local governments engage in wasteful inter-community competition, mutually antagonistic zoning, and contradictory development plans."[55]

Twelve small towns in Kansas have embraced a new strategy to reverse population loss: offering free land to relocating families. By 2009, Marquette, a central Kansas town of 500 people a few years ago, had given away 40 free residential lots and had seen its population reach 682.[56] Others of these proverbial one-stoplight towns offer additional inducements to new residents: free water and sewer hookups, no-cost building permits, and memberships at nearby golf courses.

In an effort to find new ways to compete, rural places are getting entrepreneurial. For instance, an action that may bear fruit is the attempt to foster business by installing high-speed Internet connections to isolated rural areas. Indiana created its I-Light program to bring broadband to its farming communities; Alabama and Alaska give tax credits to broadband firms committed to investing in rural areas.[57] Also, the abundance of wind in the Great Plains region has spurred talk of the possibilities of developing large-scale wind farms to provide an alternative energy source to other parts of the country. And music festivals—Wakarusa in the Arkansas hills; Dfest, Rocklahoma, and Country Fever in rural Oklahoma; and Bonnaroo in south central Tennessee—provide a significant shot in the arm to rural economies.

Still, the future of rural America continues to be debated, as large cities get larger and many rural areas experience population decline. It is no wonder that the Public Broadcasting Service featured a segment titled, "Is Rural America a Thing of the Past?" on its NewsHour program in 2014.[58] But one characteristic of rural Americans is resiliency, so the search for innovative economic development strategies continues.

The Interaction of State and Local Governments

Constitutionally, state governments are supreme in their dealings with local governments. New York City, Los Angeles, and Chicago are large, world-class cities, but even they have to follow the dictates of their respective state governments. For example, when the mayors of these cities sought to increase their control over local public schools, it took action by their respective state legislatures to make it happen. Even so, power does not flow in only one direction. The political realities are such that these cities and their smaller counterparts influence what happens in their state capitols. Suffice it to say, the state-local relationship is subject to constant adjustment. A Governor's Task Force to Renew Montana Government, for instance, adopted several provisions aimed at diminishing the influence of the state in what are considered purely local issues. But in a different vein, when Philadelphia's mayor proposed closing some fire stations to cut costs, state legislators intervened, passing a bill to prevent the city from doing so.[59] (The governor of Pennsylvania at the time, himself a former mayor of Philadelphia, vetoed the bill, saying it infringed on the city's home rule power.)

Some issues or problems require a statewide, uniform response, whereas others are the particular concern of a single local jurisdiction. Consider the problem of drought, a condition that has affected most of the western states since 2000. Some areas of Colorado, such as Denver, have been especially hard hit. A local agency, Denver Water, is responsible for water management in the city; a state agency, the Colorado Water Conservation Board, has statewide authority. To address the drought problem, both agencies had to work together. The comments of a hydrologist capture the situation, "There needs to be a state coordinating mechanism, but it needs to be sensitive to the local context."[60] Thus, even with the constitutional superiority of the state, the state-local relationship is much more nuanced.

When he was elected governor of New York, George Pataki said that, "as a former mayor, I know firsthand the importance of freeing our cities, towns, and counties from the heavy hand of state government."[61] But as Governor Pataki quickly learned, a governor has to engage in big-picture, statewide thinking, and it is awfully tempting to impose the state's will on those same localities. To make sure their voice is heard, many local governments do what those in California do: hire lobbyists to represent their interests in the state legislature. Localities in the Golden State spent nearly $40 million lobbying lawmakers during one year.[62] Even so, cities and counties found themselves on the losing side of several key measures, including one that diverted funds for local transportation projects to the state. The state-local relationship can be rocky indeed.

Chapter Recap

- States vary in the amount and type of authority they give their local governments. The general trend has been toward increased state assistance and empowerment of localities, but some states continue to keep their local governments on a short leash.

- The issue of mandates is a particularly contentious state-local matter.

- Three types of state-local organizations are common: task forces, advisory commissions on intergovernmental relations, and departments of community affairs.

- Urban sprawl has become a major issue in state-local relations. States have begun to adopt smart-growth laws that are designed to help localities manage growth.

- Regionalism continues to be advocated as a solution to many local problems. More jurisdictions are creating regional organizations to link their local governments.

- States are looking for innovative solutions to challenging housing and infrastructure problems.

- New urbanism promotes a back-to-the-future community that appeals to a particular segment of the market.

- With many rural communities in decline, states are seeking ways of revitalizing them.

- Even as the interaction of states and localities becomes more positive, the tug of war between the two levels continues.

KEY TERMS

Dillon's rule *(p. 311)*
second-order devolution
(p. 312)
mandate-reimbursement
requirements *(p. 316)*
edge cities *(p. 318)*

urban sprawl *(p. 318)*
impact fee *(p. 319)*
smart growth *(p. 319)*
shadow governments
(p. 321)
regional government *(p. 322)*

city-county consolidation
(p. 322)
public choice theory *(p. 323)*
councils of government *(p. 325)*
gentrification *(p. 328)*
new urbanism *(p. 329)*

INTERNET RESOURCES

The National Association of Regional Councils maintains a website at **www.narc.org/**. It shows the differences and similarities of regional councils across the country.

The Association of Bay Area Governments' award-winning site can be found at **www.abag .ca.gov**.

The website for the regional planning agency that deals with 189 cities and six counties in Southern California is **www.scag.ca.gov**.

For information on the activities of a state-level ACIR, see the Tennessee ACIR at **www.tn.gov/ tacir**. Utah replaced its ACIR with the Utah Intergovernmental Roundtable at **www.cppa .utah.edu/uir/**.

The Urban Institute's site for research on economic and social policy can be found at **www .urban.org**. It is a useful source of information on states and localities.

To learn more about new urbanism, **see www .cnu.org**, the website for the Congress for the New Urbanism.

The Kansas Free Land program is described at **www.kansasfreeland.com/**.

Georgia's rural development council maintains an informative website at **www.ruralgeorgia .org**. Other states with rural development councils have similar websites.

A vacant house in Detroit shows signs of fire.
TennesseePhotographer/iStockphoto.com

13

Taxing and Spending: Where the Money Comes from and Where It Goes

Detroit, Michigan became the largest U.S. city ever to file for Chapter 9 bankruptcy on July 18, 2013. Once, Detroit was an industrial dynamo of 1.8 million people. Virtually all American automobiles were manufactured there. But Motor City melted down to only 700,000 residents, surrounded by tens of thousands of abandoned buildings and houses. Public services were cut to the bone and debts rose to an estimated $18–20 billion—about $27,000 per person.

What brought Detroit to this sorry state? Auto manufacturing moved overseas and to the Southern states in pursuit of cheaper labor; jobs fled with the auto industry. Employee pension and health care liabilities mounted to unsustainable levels. Taxes were raised to fund growing operating deficits. And as employment opportunities and quality of life declined, people moved to suburban municipalities, leaving Detroit with a shrunken tax base to maintain a huge, 139-square mile municipal jurisdiction.[1]

The state assumed financial control of the city. Michigan Governor Rick Snyder appointed an emergency manager to guide the city back to solvency, granting him the powers to diminish labor contracts, reduce pensions and health care payouts, eliminate city departments, and even sell city assets. Sixteen months later, a federal judge approved a plan for Detroit to exit bankruptcy. Perhaps realizing the enormity of the challenges before them, interested parties, including the largest creditors, worked together to forge a recovery plan that lopped off $7 billion in liabilities and debts. The court permitted the city to invest $1.7 billion to purchase new fire trucks, ambulances, and other outdated equipment, remove blighted buildings and houses, and to take other actions to help move Motown to a measure of financial stability.[2] Elected officials were restored to power in city hall.

This chapter deals with state and local finance: the politics and policies of taxing and spending. Finance is a topic of continuing, visceral interest in state and local jurisdictions, and it is an activity characterized by much change and experimentation. From taxpayer revolts to spending mandates, the fiscal landscape has changed profoundly. More change is certain as state and local governments strive to meet taxpayer service demands economically and creatively.

The Principles of Finance

A major purpose of government is to provide services to citizens. But this costs money: Equipment must be purchased and employees must be paid. Governments raise needed funds through taxes, fees, and borrowing. In a democracy, the voters decide what range and quality of services they desire, and they register their decisions through elected representatives. Sometimes, when elected officials don't listen, voters revolt and take matters directly into their own hands.

Two basic principles describe state and local financial systems: *interdependence* and *diversity*. State and local fiscal systems are closely interlinked and heavily influenced by national financial activities. Intergovernmental sharing of revenues is a pronounced feature of our interdependent federal fiscal system. Yet our state financial structures and processes are also highly diverse. Though affected by national activities, their own economic health, and competitive pressures from one another, the states enjoy substantial autonomy in designing individual revenue systems in response to citizens' policy preferences.

own-source revenue

Monies derived by a government from its own taxable resources.

intergovernmental transfers

The movement of money or other resources from one level of government to another.

INTERDEPENDENCE

U.S. governments raise huge amounts of money. The states and localities collected about $2 trillion in taxes in 2012. Total **own-source revenue** was over 3 trillion when charges and fees applied to people, services, and products within the jurisdiction of each level of government were counted. State and local governments also benefit from **intergovernmental transfers**. The national government contributes about one-quarter of all state and local revenues; however, more than 60 percent of this federal money is "passed through" to *individual* recipients such as those receiving Medicaid. For their part, states pass on some $470 billion to their cities, counties, and special-purpose governments.[3] Some states are economic powerhouses. California's economy exceeds $2 trillion, making it the eighth largest in the world.

Local governments rely heavily on the states and, to a lesser degree, on the national government for financial authority and assistance. *Only the states* can authorize localities to levy taxes and fees, incur debt, and spend money. State constitutions and laws place many conditions on local government taxing and spending. In return, states provide monetary support of local governments through state grants-in-aid and revenue sharing; they also assume financial responsibility for activities carried out by localities—in particular, education and social welfare costs. Most local governments are fine with this arrangement. But the role of the states as senior financial partners in state-local finance is criticized in some quarters as being both inadequate and unduly restrictive of local financial flexibility.

State-local finances are linked closely to activities of the national government. For instance, when the federal government changes the tax code, it can wreak havoc on those thirty-five states that base their own income taxes on the federal tax code. Congress's phase-out of the estate tax in 2014 was expected to cost the states billions of dollars a year. The 2013 federal budget "sequester," totaling $1 trillion in cuts, also cost the states billions in support for education, law enforcement, and other programs.

When the national economy falls into a recession, state and local governments suffer most. They cannot, after all, print money or run an operating budget deficit into the future. This fact is sometimes recognized by Congress, which lent substantial amounts of **countercyclical aid** to the states and localities to help them recover from the ravages of the Great Recession. Special aid is targeted to states suffering natural disasters such as hurricanes, floods, and fires. Federal largess can also salvage budgets during recessions, as did the massive 2008–2011 federal stimulus package that helped alleviate about 40 percent of the massive state budget deficits.

DIVERSITY

The second basic principle of state and local finance systems is diversity of revenue sources. Each level of government depends on one type of revenue device more than others. For the national government, it is the income tax; for the states, the sales tax; and for local governments, the property tax. But diversity triumphs among the states. Differences in **tax capacity** (wealth), **tax effort** (burden), and tax choices are obvious even to the casual traveler. Most states tax personal income and merchandise sales, but a handful does not. Several states garner substantial revenues from severance taxes on oil, gas, and minerals.

Some states, such as New Jersey and New York, tax with a heavy hand. Others, including Nevada and Alaska, are relative tax havens. Most fall somewhere

countercyclical aid

A transfer of federal dollars to states and localities to counteract a downturn in the economic cycle.

tax capacity

The taxable resources of a government jurisdiction.

tax effort

The extent to which a jurisdiction exploits its taxable resources.

in the middle. If the basic objective of taxing is to pluck the maximum number of feathers from the goose with the minimum amount of hissing, the wealthy states hold a great advantage. They can reap high-tax revenues with much less effort than can poor states, which must tax at high rates just to pull in enough money to pay for the basics. Per capita state and local tax revenues vary from $11,869 in energy-dependent Alaska to $2,951 in poverty-stricken Alabama. The U.S. average is $4,423.[4]

There is a close relationship between state wealth (as measured by personal income) and tax burden. Table 13.1 shows how the states compare in state and local tax burdens (taxes, controlling for personal income). Tax levels

TABLE 13.1 State/Local and Total Taxes by State, as a Percentage of Personal Income and Per Capita

STATE	STATE/LOCAL TAXES AS A % OF INCOME	STATE/LOCAL TAX COLLECTION PER CAPITA
U.S. Average	9.8	4,423
New York	12.6	7,751
New Jersey	12.3	6,073
Connecticut	11.9	6,950
California	11.4	4,833
Wisconsin	11.0	4,629
Minnesota	10.7	5,226
Maryland	10.6	5,133
Rhode Island	10.5	4,978
Vermont	10.5	5,137
Pennsylvania	10.3	4,468
Massachusetts	10.3	5,574
Arkansas	10.3	3,523
Illinois	10.2	5,166
Maine	10.2	4,620
Delaware	10.1	4,575
Oregon	10.1	3,789
North Carolina	9.8	3,534
Ohio	9.7	4,053
West Virginia	9.7	3,803
Hawaii	9.6	5,331

(*continued*)

TABLE 13.1	State/Local and Total Taxes by State, as a Percentage of Personal Income and Per Capita (*continued*)	
STATE	**STATE/LOCAL TAXES AS A % OF INCOME**	**STATE/LOCAL TAX COLLECTION PER CAPITA**
Michigan	9.6	3,666
Indiana	9.5	3,750
Kentucky	9.5	3,432
Idaho	9.5	3,043
Nebraska	9.4	4,379
Kansas	9.4	4,335
Washington	9.4	4,269
Utah	9.4	3,347
Iowa	9.3	4,411
Virginia	9.2	4,053
Florida	9.2	3,344
Colorado	9.0	4,083
Missouri	9.0	3,388
Arizona	8.9	3,388
Georgia	8.8	3,258
North Dakota	8.8	9,449
New Mexico	8.6	3,625
Montana	8.6	3,602
Oklahoma	8.5	3,480
Mississippi	8.4	3,252
Alabama	8.3	2,951
South Carolina	8.3	3,020
Nevada	8.1	3,856
New Hampshire	8.0	3,988
Tennessee	7.6	3,095
Louisiana	7.6	3,684
Texas	7.5	3,750
South Dakota	7.1	3,471
Alaska	7.0	11,869
Wyoming	6.9	6,669

SOURCE: www.taxfoundation.org, http://taxpolicycenter.org/taxfacts/displayafact.cfm?Docid=513

also reflect factors such as citizen preferences, population characteristics and trends, business climate, limitations on tax increases and/or expenditures, and the quality, as well as quantity, of government services. And taxing is only one means of plucking the public goose. State and local governments increasingly rely on fees and charges for services rendered. Examples include entrance fees for parks and recreation facilities, sewer and garbage fees, and motor vehicle fees.

Revenues

Although the state and local finance systems have their own strengths, weaknesses, and peculiarities, certain trends can be found in all of them. The property tax is always unpopular. It is no longer a significant source of state revenue; its contribution to total own-source local coffers, though, is remains strong. User fees and other miscellaneous charges are gradually growing. States continue to depend heavily on the sales tax, but alternatives are being used more widely. Intergovernmental revenues from the federal government make up nearly one-quarter of the total. In fact, tax diversification is an important trend in all state and local tax systems (see Figure 13.1).

LO 13.2

To understand criteria for evaluating taxes.

CRITERIA FOR EVALUATING TAXES

Numerous criteria can be used to evaluate taxes. What one person or interest group likes about a tax may be what another dislikes. Nevertheless, political scientists and economists generally agree that among the most important criteria are equity, efficiency, yield, political accountability, and acceptability.

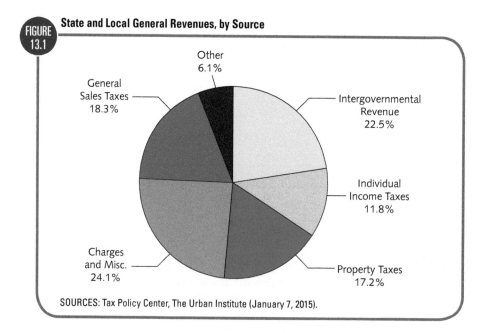

FIGURE 13.1

State and Local General Revenues, by Source

- Other 6.1%
- General Sales Taxes 18.3%
- Intergovernmental Revenue 22.5%
- Individual Income Taxes 11.8%
- Charges and Misc. 24.1%
- Property Taxes 17.2%

SOURCES: Tax Policy Center, The Urban Institute (January 7, 2015).

Equity If citizens or firms are expected to pay a tax, they should view it as fair. In the context of taxation, *equity* usually refers to distributing the burden of the tax in accordance with ability to pay: High income means greater ability to pay and therefore a larger tax burden. Equity includes other dimensions as well, such as the relative tax burden on individuals versus firms and the impact of various types of taxes on income, age, and social class. It is interesting to observe that despite the constant complaints about taxes, the typical American pays much less in total taxes today (as a percentage of income) than he or she did 30 years ago.[5]

Taxes may be regressive, progressive, or proportional. A **regressive tax** places a greater burden on low-income citizens than on high-income citizens. Thus, the ability-to-pay principle is violated, with the result that upper-income groups contribute a smaller portion of their incomes than do lower-income groups. Most state and local levies, including property and sales taxes, are considered regressive. For example, both low-income and high-income people would pay, say, a 7 percent sales tax. The latter will likely make more purchases and contribute more total dollars in sales tax, but at a lower percentage of their total income, than the low-income individuals.

A **progressive tax** increases as a percentage of a person's income as that income rises. The more you make, the greater proportion of your income is extracted by the progressive tax. Thus, those better able to pay carry a heavier tax burden than do the poor. California's personal income tax is the most progressive, varying from 1.4 to 13.3 percent of taxable income. The more you earn, the higher your *income tax bracket.*

A **proportional tax**, sometimes called a **flat tax**, burdens everyone equally, at least in theory. For instance, a tax on income of, say, 10 percent that is applied across the board is a proportional tax. Whether you earn $100,000 or $10,000, you pay a flat 10 percent of the total in taxes. Of course, a low-income person is more burdened by a proportional income tax than is a high-income person (as in the case of the sales tax).

In place of ability to pay, some people advocate the **benefit principle**. Under this principle, those who reap more benefits from government services should shoulder more of the tax burden than people who do not avail themselves of service opportunities to the same degree. As a hypothetical example, it might be argued that parents whose children attend public schools should pay higher taxes for education than should senior citizens, childless couples, or single people without children. The benefit principle is the theoretical underpinning for user fees, which charge a taxpayer directly for services received. The unfortunate downside is that it disadvantages those who have the least ability to pay.

Efficiency This refers to the amount of money a tax contributes to government coffers compared to the effort and expense it takes to administer and collect it. Taxes that return substantial sums of money at minimal collection costs to the government are preferred to taxes that require large outlays for moderate revenues. Income and sales taxes have high yields because they raise large sums of money at low expense. They are simple to understand and fairly easy to collect. Property taxes, however, have lower yields because they are

regressive tax
A tax in which the rate falls as the base or taxable income rises, advantaging those with higher income.

progressive tax
A tax in which the rate rises as the base or taxable income rises, advantaging those with lower income.

proportional (flat) tax
A tax in which people pay an identical rate regardless of income or economic transaction.

benefit principle
The principle that taxes should be levied on those who benefit directly from a government service.

more expensive to assess and collect. Property values must be regularly appraised, which involves a certain degree of subjectivity.

Yield Yield depends on base and rate: The broader the tax base and the higher the rate, the higher the yield. As a simple example, a sales tax applied to all purchases yields much more than a sales tax on cigarette purchases, and a $1.00-per-pack tax produces more money than a 25¢ tax.

Political Accountability Tax increases should not be hidden. Instead, state and local legislative bodies should have to approve them deliberately—and publicly. Citizens should know how much they owe and when it must be paid. For example, some state income taxes are silently hiked as wages rise in response to cost-of-living increases. After inflation is accounted for, taxpayers make the same real income as they did before, but they are driven into a higher-income bracket for tax purposes. This phenomenon, known as *bracket creep,* can be eliminated by **indexing** income tax brackets to changes in the cost of living.

Tax expenditures, also known as tax breaks, or more cynically as corporate welfare, depress political accountability. These are tax preferences that benefit certain taxpayers through credits, exemptions, deductions, and other favorable treatment. For example, specified manufacturing companies may pay a lower sales tax on new equipment than other companies, or receive payments for each new job created. Tax expenditures have little or no visibility to the voting public.

Acceptability The type and mix of taxes imposed should be congruent with citizen preferences. No tax commands wild enthusiasm, and a portion of the citizenry will *always* be opposed to *any* tax, but some are less disagreeable than others. Tax acceptability varies, depending on numerous factors, including equity implications and the perceived pain of paying. Large, one-time payments, such as the annual property tax, inflict greater pain than small, frequently paid sales taxes. And a tax on someone else is always preferable. As Senator Russell Long of Louisiana put it many years ago, "Don't tax me, don't tax thee; tax that man behind the tree."

LO 13.3

To describe where state and local governments get revenue, and how they spend it.

MAJOR STATE AND LOCAL TAXES

The principal types of taxes are those on property, sales, and income. Various miscellaneous taxes and fees also provide revenue for state and local governments.

indexing

A system in which tax brackets are automatically adjusted to account for inflation.

Property Tax Taxes on personal and corporate property account for about one-third of state and local tax revenue. States hardly utilize the property tax at all today (it represents less than 2 percent of their total revenues), but local governments continue to depend on this fiscal workhorse for three-quarters of all their own-source revenues. Other revenue sources have augmented the property tax so its proportionate contribution has diminished. As always, there is considerable state-by-state variation, but more than three out of every four dollars in local revenues come from the property tax.

Property taxes are widely reviled. Assessments of value may seem to change suddenly or appear to stack up unfavorably against similar properties, and to appeal assessments involves a frustrating process. Acceptability, efficiency, and accountability rank low in relation to other taxes. The best feature of the property tax is that it is certain: Owners of property must pay it or the government may seize and sell their land, buildings, or other taxable possessions. But it tends to be regressive and sometimes must be paid in a large lump sum.

On first thought, it seems that property taxes cannot be truly regressive because only those people who own property pay taxes on it directly; however, renters pay property taxes indirectly through their monthly rent checks to the landlord. When property tax assessments climb, so do rental charges. Property taxes can also violate the ability-to-pay principle when housing values spiral upward. Retirees and other homeowners on fixed incomes may discover with alarm that their annual property tax bills are doubling or tripling as housing prices escalate. Alternatively, as property values plummet as they did during the Great Recession of 2008–2011, tax values remain the same until the next scheduled reassessment.

Just this sort of situation helped precipitate California's Proposition 13, which was credited with kicking off a taxpayer revolt across the United States. In the Los Angeles and San Francisco Bay areas during the 1970s, property taxes doubled and then tripled in only a few years. Some senior citizens were forced to sell their homes to pay their property tax. Proposition 13 reduced property tax bills by approximately $7 billion in the first year, and it imposed strict limitations on the ability of local governments to raise property and other taxes in the future. California dropped from the eighth-highest property tax state to the twenty-eighth. This example illustrates the importance of political accountability.

Property taxes are difficult to administer and somewhat arbitrary. The process of levying an annual fee on "real property" (land and buildings) begins with an assessor making a formal appraisal of the market value of the land and the buildings on it. Then property values are "equalized" so that similarly valued real estate is taxed at the same level. Time is set aside to make corrections and to review appeals on appraisals that the owner believes are too high. Next, an assessment ratio is applied to the property. For instance, houses might be assessed for tax purposes at 80 percent of market value. A rate is placed on the assessed value to calculate the annual tax amount. (Assessed at a market price of $100,000, taxed at a ratio of 0.80 and a rate of $3 per $100 [30 mils], a house would produce a tax due of $2,400). Determining market value may seem fairly straightforward, but ultimately the appraised market value depends on the findings of the assessor, who may or may not be unbiased, properly trained for the job, or fully aware of conditions in the local housing market (statistical models remove some of the guesswork). Property can thus be underappraised or overappraised. For the sake of equity, property should be appraised regularly (e.g., every two or three years). Otherwise, property that does not change ownership becomes increasingly undervalued or overvalued, depending on the local real estate market.

Property tax systems are further criticized for exempting certain types of real estate and buildings. Government buildings such as hospitals and state and federal offices are not taxed, even though they utilize police and fire protection, trash collection, and other local government services. Churches, synagogues, mosques, and related property used for religious purposes are also partly or wholly exempted in the vast majority of jurisdictions, as is property owned by charitable and nonprofit organizations.

The amount of tax-exempt property in most populous cities has been growing as more land and buildings are acquired by nonprofit organizations, particularly those in education and health care. Thirty percent of Baltimore's entire tax base escapes property taxation.[6] A relatively small portion of this "lost" revenue is captured through payments in lieu of taxes (PILOTs), which are agreements negotiated by state and local governments and the nonprofit owner. In addition, some state and local governments are sharpening the definition of which organizations qualify for tax exempt status.

In an effort to make property taxation more equitable and more in keeping with ability to pay, most states have enacted some form of **circuit breaker**. For instance, the property of low-income individuals is excluded from taxation in some states; others assign lower-assessment ratios to the homes of senior citizens or set a top limit on the tax according to the owner's income (e.g., 4 percent of net income). Many states have "truth-in-taxation" laws that roll back property tax rates as appraised values rise rapidly. Most also offer homestead exemptions, in which owner-occupied homes are taxed at lower rates or assessed at lower values than are rental homes or business property. Massachusetts municipalities permit seniors to earn credits against their tax bills through public service activities.

Despite such attempts to make the property tax fairer, differences in property values among cities, counties, and school districts still have important implications for the quality and distribution of services. Jurisdictions with many wealthy families, capital-intensive industries, or rapid construction growth can provide high levels of services with low-tax rates, whereas areas with weak property tax bases must tax at high rates merely to yield enough revenue to maintain minimal services. Residential property tax rates vary widely from city to city. Altering the unequal distribution of property values is essentially beyond the control of local governments. As a result, "wealthy suburbs remain wealthy, poor communities remain poor, and services remain unequal."[7] As discussed in Chapter 15, inequity in school funding has been the target of litigation in nearly every state.

Sales Tax States currently collect more of their revenues from the general sales and gross receipts tax than from any other source. It accounts for almost one-half of total state general revenues. Only five states do not levy a general sales tax: Alaska, Delaware, Montana, New Hampshire, and Oregon. State sales tax rates vary from 7.5 percent in California to 2.9 percent in Colorado. Some states, particularly those that do not have personal income taxes, are exceptionally dependent on the sales tax: Louisiana, South Dakota, Arkansas, Tennessee, and Washington derive more than half of their own-source revenues from the sales tax.

The sales tax has remained in favor for two major reasons. First, citizen surveys have consistently shown that when a tax must be raised, voters

circuit breaker

A limit on taxes applied to certain categories of people, such as the poor or elderly.

reluctantly prefer the sales tax. Although the reasons are not entirely clear, this tax is perceived to be fairer than other forms of taxation. Second, there is an abiding belief that high state income taxes depress economic development, and the property tax is widely detested.

Thirty-eight states authorize at least some of their municipalities and counties to levy local sales taxes. When state and local sales taxes are combined, the total tax bite can be painful. In Tennessee cities, the purchase of a $1.00 item requires up to 9.45¢ in sales tax. Sales taxes are usually optional for the local jurisdiction, but may require state legislative approval in some cases. Typically, states impose ceilings on how many pennies the localities can attach to the state sales tax; states also specify which sizes and types of local governments are permitted to exercise this option.

When applied to all merchandise, the sales tax is clearly regressive. Poor folks must spend a larger portion of their incomes than rich people spend on basics, such as food and clothing. Therefore, the sales tax places a much heavier burden on low-income people. Most of the 45 states with a sales tax alleviate its regressive nature by excluding certain "necessities." Thirty-one states do not tax food purchased from the grocery store; only a handful taxes prescription drugs; most exempt consumer electric and gas utilities; and five exclude clothing.[8] New Jersey excludes paper products. When the sales tax was extended to paper products in 1990, enraged Jerseyites mailed wads of toilet paper—some of it used—to horrified legislators, who quickly rescinded the tax. Sixteen states hold "sales tax holidays" in which specified merchandise, such as hurricane supplies and clothing, are exempt from the sales tax for a weekend or longer.[9]

States can improve the yield of the sales tax by broadening the base to include services. In this way, more of the burden is passed on to upper-income individuals, who are heavier users of services. Approximately half of the states tax services such as household, automobile, and appliance repairs; barber and beauty shop treatments; printing; rentals; dry cleaning; and interior decorating. Hawaii, Texas, and South Dakota tax almost all professional and personal services. New Jersey taxes hair transplants and tummy tucks, and Arkansas taps into tattoos and nose rings. Colorado, Washington, Hawaii, and Alaska tax recreational marijuana sales. Maryland residents must pay a "flush tax" of $30.00 on their sewer bills to help clean up polluted Chesapeake Bay. However, states can move too far and too fast with taxes on services. Florida, Massachusetts, and Michigan broadened the base of their sales tax to services, only to have it repealed shortly afterward through lobbying efforts by the business community. Sweeping proposals to tax services are typically defeated by vested interests. These setbacks may be temporary. Services are the largest and fastest growing segment of the U.S. economy. Eighty-five percent of new jobs are in services. As one political commentator asked, "How can one rationalize taxing autos, videocassettes, and toothpaste, but not piped-in music, cable TV, parking lot services, or $100 beauty salon treatments?"[10] Pet grooming services, legal and financial services, and many others from landscaping to vehicle repairs have lost their tax-favored status as states extend sales taxes to services incrementally, fighting industry and lobbyists one at a time.

Whatever form the sales tax takes, elasticity is not a strong point, although its productivity falls when consumer purchases slow and rises as consumers boost their spending. Broadening the base helps. States sometimes attempt to make the sales tax more responsive to short-term economic conditions by increasing it on a temporary basis, to make up for lower-than-anticipated revenues, and then reducing it when needed monies are collected. A problem with these tactics, however, is that consumers tend to postpone major purchases until the tax rate falls.

The sales tax is relatively simple for governments to administer. Sellers of merchandise and services are required to collect it and remit it to the state on a regular basis. Political accountability is also an advantage because legislative bodies must enact laws or ordinances to increase the sales tax rate. And, as we have observed, the sales tax is the least unpopular of the major taxes.

However, a vibrant market has developed in cigarettes smuggled from low tobacco-tax to high tobacco-tax states. It has been estimated that more than 50 percent of the cigarettes smoked in New York and Arizona are contraband.[11] An estimated $7–10 billion in state tax revenue is lost annually to smuggled smokes. For the black market operators, profits run up to half a million dollars for one large shipment from South Carolina to New York.[12]

A big fight has erupted over state and local governments' right to tax an enormously promising revenue stream—electronic commerce on the Internet. Twenty-one states were levying taxes or fees on Internet access, data downloads, or goods purchased on the Internet. Then pressures from Internet interests, including servers (e.g., Google, Yahoo), media companies, and retail businesses, led Congress to pass the Internet Tax Freedom Act, which imposed a moratorium on taxing Internet access and online sales. State and local officials strongly opposed such limitations, citing estimates that it costs them more than $23 billion in annual revenues because more and more goods are purchased on the Internet or otherwise from out-of-state. Already states estimate that they forfeit another $5 billion a year in uncollected taxes from interstate catalog sales. Only Internet and catalog sales to citizens living in the same state in which the vendor company has a physical presence in the state are taxed. And many states require citizens to declare and pay such sales taxes in their annual state income tax returns, but usually to little avail because of the difficulty of enforcement.

Taxation of Internet sales is both complicated and controversial, and it has become a compelling issue for the states. A 1992 U.S. Supreme Court ruling blocked taxation of catalog sales on the grounds of violating the Interstate Commerce Clause, a ruling that has obvious applicability to taxing Internet commerce today.[13] Yet the Court seemed to reverse itself in a 2013 decision.[14] Predictably, Congress has been tied in knots on the issue, but no less than the fiscal integrity of state revenue systems is at stake. If states continue to lose billions of dollars to a tax-free Internet, how will the gaping budget holes be filled? What about Main Street brick-and-mortar retailers whose prices are made less competitive by the amount of the sales tax? Contrary to protestations by Internet vendors that compliance with state and local sales taxes as set by 7,600 taxing jurisdictions is a heavy burden, available software programs can calculate amounts due each jurisdiction relatively easily.

A compromise is the streamlined sales tax (SST), wherein states collapse all their local sales tax rates into one (or just a few) statewide rates, resulting in a manageable number of Internet tax jurisdictions.[15] This approach has the added advantage of laying the foundation for taxing mail-order catalog sales.

As of 2014, twenty-four states had passed the SST model legislation. Sixteen additional states have adopted a sales tax on online purchases of music, games, ring tones, and other video entertainment. Vendors are required to apply the state sales tax when a product is sold and remit it to the state. Hope for a national solution to taxing Internet sales rests on a reluctant and recalcitrant Congress that, nonetheless, came very close to passing the Marketplace Fairness Act in 2013. Meanwhile, states have been independently fighting retailers such as giant Amazon.com, arguing that distribution centers and other facilities for Internet sales constitute a "physical presence." Amazon proved to be a particularly fierce political infighter, spending millions of dollars to lobby and influence Congress and state legislatures and cutting off several states' "affiliate" sellers of online merchandise via Amazon. However, the retailing behemoth has recently cut individual deals with sixteen states, with more surely to follow. (The "Amazon tax" brought in an estimated $107 million in California in 2012.) Skeptics believe that Amazon is cutting individual state deals to ward off Congressional action.

Income Tax Most states tax personal and corporate income. Wisconsin was the first, in 1911, two years before the national government enacted its own personal income tax. Forty-one states have broad-based taxes on personal income; two states (Tennessee and New Hampshire) limit theirs to capital gains, interest, and dividends. Only Alaska, Texas, South Dakota, Florida, Nevada, Washington, and Wyoming leave all personal income untaxed. Nevada, Texas, Washington, and Wyoming also abstain from taxing corporate income. Personal income taxes garner 28 percent of all state own-source taxes, and the corporate tax brings in about 4 percent. Fifteen states permit designated cities, counties, or school districts to levy taxes on personal income.[16]

State and local income taxes are equitable when they are progressive. Progressivity normally entails a sliding scale, so that high-income filers pay a greater percentage of their income in taxes than do low-income filers. California has the steepest scale, ranging from 1.0 to 13.3 percent of taxable income. Most states do not levy a personal income tax on people whose earnings fall below a certain floor—say, $10,000. Overall, state personal income taxes are moderately progressive. Eight states, however, tax income at a flat rate varying from 3.07 percent in Pennsylvania to 7 percent in Tennessee.

Personal and corporate income taxes are superior to other taxes on the criteria of yield and elasticity. By tapping almost all sources of income, they draw in large sums of money and respond fairly well to short-term economic conditions (though the income tax has become more volatile, particularly during periods of boom and bust).[17]

Through payroll withholding, income taxes are fairly simple to collect. Also, many states periodically adjust income tax rates in response to annual revenue needs. As mentioned earlier, political accountability can be problematic with respect to income taxes during periods of rising prices. Unless income tax rates are indexed to inflation, as they are in seventeen states, cost-of-living increases push salaries and corporate earnings into higher-tax brackets.

Miscellaneous Taxes A wide variety of miscellaneous taxes are assessed by state and local governments. "Sin taxes" raise a small—but growing—percentage of all state revenues. All states tax cigarettes and many have boosted this tax during the past few years. New York's $4.35 tax boosts the average price per pack to $9.20. Some cities levy additional taxes on smokes; the price per pack in New York City is now $11. Yet Missouri charges only 17 cents per pack. This startling disparity in prices has led to a flourishing trade in cigarette smuggling from low- to high-tax states, as noted above.

In 1998, the states experienced the equivalent of winning the lottery. A court settlement with tobacco companies is sending as much as $206 billion into state coffers over a period of 25 years. Ideally, the funds would be used for public health and smoking prevention programs. But few strings are attached, and states have spent the windfall on economic development initiatives, balancing the budget, new government office buildings, and even golf courses.[18] Nine states took the fiscally unsound step of selling bonds to be paid off with future projected tobacco settlement money, thus mortgaging the future for dollars today. Ironically, the amount of tobacco settlement dollars pledged to the states is based on the number of packs of cigarettes sold. But all states are experiencing shrinking sales as smokers beat the habit or take advantage of Indian reservations, Internet sales, and black market cigarettes. In an effort to recapture lost tobacco tax revenues states are now moving to tax electronic cigarette cigarettes and vapor devices at regular cigarette rates.

So far, taxes on recreational marijuana sales in the states permitting them have come in slightly above or below expectations. Taxes on medical marijuana in twenty-three states produce relatively insignificant revenues. The It's Your Turn feature raises questions on when and how marijuana should be taxed.

Alcoholic beverages are taxed in all fifty states, although rates vary according to classification: beer, wine, or spirits. Beer guzzlers should steer clear of Tennessee, where the tax per gallon of beer is $1.17; frequent imbibers are invited to visit Wyoming, where the tax is only 2¢ per gallon. Excise taxes on a gallon of wine range from $3.16 in bourbon-swilling Kentucky to 10¢ in Louisiana. Though not a "sin," gasoline falls under taxation's shadow as well. The highest state tax on gasoline in 2015 was in New York (69.6¢ per gallon). The lowest was in Alaska (26.40¢). Alas, the gas tax is running toward empty as motorists reduce the number of miles they drive in response to high gas prices and as vehicles are becoming more fuel efficient. The surprising collapse in the price of gasoline at the pump in 2015 further reduced gas tax revenues in some states. The result is depletion of road construction and maintenance funds for which gasoline taxes are earmarked.

Most states tax death in one form or another. Estate taxes must be paid on the financial assets and property of a deceased person in fourteen states before the remainder is disbursed to the survivors. Inheritance taxes are imposed in six states on non-spouses who inherit substantial assets (typically valued at more than $1 million). Rates are generally staggered according to the value of the estate and the survivors' relationship to the deceased. A reduction of the federal estate tax has resulted in a decline for such state taxes as well, unless the states amend their estate tax laws.

Should Medical Marijuana Be Taxed?

Put simply, a sales tax is exacted on the buyer of a good; it is applied to a retail transaction on purchases, such as clothing or groceries. An excise tax is imposed on a particular product, such as gasoline or tobacco. Both increase the buyer's cost. For recreational marijuana sales, Colorado levies an excise tax of 15 percent and a retail sales tax of 10 percent. Washington State's excise and sales taxes are both 25 percent on weed-for-fun.

But what about medical marijuana? Should states apply both excise and sales taxes, one of them, or neither? How about infused medical marijuana products such as cookies or candies?

PROS	CONS
State and local governments should apply both sales and excise taxes to all medical marijuana products at relatively high levels because they raise needed revenues.	Medical marijuana should not be taxed at all; it should be treated like prescription medications, which most states do not tax.
High marijuana taxes will discourage abuse or overuse of the drug.	Medical marijuana should not be taxed, or only taxed minimally, because it is for an approved medical condition (that currently is not covered by health insurance).
Buyers should be willing to pay taxes because they no longer have to worry about arrest for possession and use of illegal marijuana.	If medical marijuana is taxed too heavily, users will purchase the herb on the black market instead of approved dispensaries.

Other miscellaneous sources of revenue include hunting and fishing licenses, business licenses, auto license fees, parking tickets, traffic violation fines, and telecommunications fees. Utah imposes a 10 percent "pole tax" on strip clubs and on escort services. Another interesting instrument is the "jock tax." Twenty states and several cities require professional athletes to pay a prorated income tax for games played in their jurisdiction. For example, L.A. Laker Kobe Bryant, today's highest paid NBA player at $23.5 million a year, receives a jock tax bill of $5,863 for each game he plays in Ohio.[19] For highly paid baseball, basketball, and football players, the jock tax is a minor itch. But for the lower-paid athletes, the jock tax burns. Some professional athletes must file tax returns in as many as twenty different states, depending on which states tax their team's visit.

USER FEES

Setting specific prices on goods and services provided by state and local governments is one method that clearly pursues the *benefit principle*: Only those who use the goods and services should pay. User fees have been in existence for many years. Examples include college tuition, water and sewer charges, and trash collection assessments. Toll roads and bridges are coming back in fashion as well.

Building and inspection fees, food truck licenses, and even fire service charges are assessed in some local jurisdictions. Today, user fees are being applied broadly as state and especially local officials attempt to tie services to their true costs. Such fees are increasingly being levied on "nonessential" local government services, such as parks and recreation, libraries, and airports. User fees make up approximately a significant proportion of local governments' own-source revenues.

User fees offer several advantages. If priced accurately, they are perfectly fair under the benefit principle, and they enjoy a relatively high level of political acceptability. But those people who do not have enough money to purchase the goods and services may have to do without—a circumstance that violates the ability-to-pay principle. A good case in point is higher education, which is shifting increasingly from state funding to tuition and fee-based funding. (Rebates, scholarships, fee waivers, and reduced-fee schedules help mitigate ability-to-pay difficulties among low-income residents.)

User fees are structured to yield whatever is needed to finance a particular service. An added benefit is that service users who do not live in the taxing jurisdiction must also pay the price, say, for a day at the state zoo. Yield may be achieved if the amount of the charge is varied so that it always covers service costs. In many instances, user fees can be levied without specific permission from the state.

Because service users must be identified and charged, some user fees can be difficult to administer. Political accountability is low because the charges can be increased without legislative action. However, a special advantage of user fees is that they can be employed to ration certain goods or services. For instance, entrance charges can be increased to reduce attendance at an overcrowded public facility or varied according to the day of the week to encourage more efficient utilization. If the city museum has few visitors on Mondays, it can cut the entrance fee on that day of the week by one-half.

An increasingly popular and specialized form of user charge is the local impact fee, or exaction, requiring private land developers to contribute roads, sewers, and other infrastructure as the price for local regulatory approval for development projects such as subdivisions or retail facilities. The cost of infrastructure is thus shifted to firms and, ultimately, to those who purchase or use their buildings or facilities. A related concept is applied through a special sales tax on travel and tourism-related services. Here, taxes on lodging, rental cars, and other services paid largely by out-of-towners are imposed at rates averaging 12 percent.

Table 13.2 rates various taxes and fees based on the five criteria discussed at the beginning of this section.

SEVERANCE TAX

States blessed with petroleum, coal, natural gas, and minerals tax these natural resources as they are taken from the land and sold. A fortunate few (Alaska, North Dakota, and Wyoming among the most fortunate) are able to "export" a substantial portion of their tax bite to people living in other states. In-staters, however, must pay the same tax rate as out-of-staters.

A large majority of states (thirty-eight) place a severance tax on some form of natural resources, but just ten states collect 90 percent of all severance

TABLE 13.2	Rating State and Local Taxes According to Five Criteria				
TAX	**EQUITY**	**YIELD**	**POLITICAL ACCOUNTABILITY**	**ACCEPTABILITY**	**EFFICIENCY**
Property	C	C	D	D	D
Sales	D	B	A	B	A
Personal and corporate income	B	A	C	C	B
User fees	C	B	C	B	A

NOTE: A = excellent, B = good, C = fair, D = poor.

SOURCE: NASBO (www.nasbo.org [accessed March 5,2012]).

tax revenues. Taxes on oil and natural gas account for billions of dollars in state revenues in Alaska, North Dakota, and Wyoming. These three states bring in about half of their revenues from severance taxes on coal, oil, and gas (which may explain why these states are able to forgo personal income taxes). Several states are rather creative in applying the severance tax. Washington levies the tax on oysters, salmon, and other food fish; and Louisiana, on freshwater mussels.[20]

Severance taxes are popular in states rich in natural resources because they help keep income, property, and sales taxes relatively low. Severance tax revenues also help to pay for environmental damage resulting from resource extraction operations, such as strip mining and fracking. The major disadvantage is that a state economy too dependent on severance taxes can be damaged badly when the price or supply of its natural resources declines, as severance-tax-dependent states experienced when oil and natural gas priced tumbled in 2014–2015. Even so, natural resources have been individually enriching for Alaskans. For more than twenty years, every man, woman, and child resident of Alaska has received a rebate from the state's Permanent Fund. Checks totaled $3,269 in 2008, but the amount fell to only $900 in 2013 (it rose to $1884 in 2014). Established primarily with severance taxes on petroleum, the Permanent Fund's $51 billion in reserves are diversified through investments in office buildings, industrial complexes, stocks, and bonds.[21]

GAMBLING: LOTTERIES AND CASINOS

The lottery is an old American tradition; initially established in the 1600s, it was popular from the colonial days until the late 1800s. Lotteries flourished throughout the country as a means of raising money for good causes such as new schools, highways, canals, and bridges. But scandals and mismanagement led every state and the national government to ban "looteries." From 1895 to 1963, no legal lotteries operated. Then New Hampshire established a new one, followed in 1967 by New York. Forty-three more states operate lotteries today.

Several factors account for the rebirth of "bettor government." First, lotteries can bring in meaningful sums of money—some $20 billion in "profits" in 2013.[22]

Second, they are popular and entertaining. And they are voluntary—you do not have to participate. In addition, lotteries help relieve pressure on major taxes. In some states, net lottery earnings take the place of a 1¢ increase in the sales tax.

But lotteries also have disadvantages. They are costly to administer and have low yields. Prize awards must be great enough to encourage future ticket sales—the higher the payout, the more people play. New games must be created to retain enthusiasm. Ticket vendors must be paid commissions. And tight (as well as expensive) security precautions are required to guarantee the game's integrity. As a result, lotteries generate only a small percentage of most states' total revenues. The average yield for players is low: About 60 percent of the total revenue is returned to players in prize money, far below the returns of other games of chance, such as slot machines, roulette, or craps. Although many states earmark lottery proceeds for popular programs, especially education, the result is often a shell game. For instance, Florida's lottery officially benefits schools and colleges; but in reality, lottery money simply replaces general-fund revenues rather than actually enhancing education funding.

Lotteries can also be attacked on the grounds of equity. Although the purchase of a ticket is voluntary and thus seemingly fair, studies indicate that low-income individuals are more likely to play. Participation is also higher among African Americans, Latinos, males, seniors, and those with low levels of education. The lottery, then, is a regressive way to raise money.[23] Furthermore, lotteries also tend to encourage compulsive gambling (one could further assert that states themselves become addicted to gambling revenues). In recognition of this problem, some states earmark a portion of lottery proceeds for treatment programs. As interstate lottery competition has saturated markets and depressed profits, states have adopted other forms of legalized gambling, including pari-mutuel betting on horse and dog races, "racinos," with slot machines at the tracks, as well as gaming on river boats, Indian reservations, and at Old West historical sites. Once restricted to Atlantic City and Las Vegas, casino gambling and slot parlors are now offered in forty states, including operations on about 440 Native American reservations. Gambling establishments virtually blanket Minnesota and Mississippi. Touted as producers of jobs, tourist attractions, and generators of higher revenues, casinos and slot parlors share many of the same disadvantages as lotteries, including diminishing returns as new casinos open monthly across the country. Yet they do rake in a significant sum of revenues. Now, get ready for legal Internet gambling. Previously forbidden by the federal government under the 1961 Federal Wire Act, Internet gambling (other than sports wagering) was approved in a U.S. Justice Department ruling in 2011. Nevada was the first to proceed with "ultimate poker," soon followed by Delaware and New Jersey. Although Congress will probably need to regulate Internet gaming, the potential take for the states is substantial, estimated to be $2–4 billion in tax revenues.[24]

LO 13.4

To evaluate the political economy of taxation.

The Political Economy of Taxation

Decisions to raise or lower taxes and fees are inherently political. There are winners and losers, payers and receivers, both in the taxing and in the spending that follows.

SPENDING

Taxes fuel government spending. The principle of diversity in state and local finance is evident, given what state and local governments choose to do with their revenues. First, these governments spend a great deal of money. State and local spending has ascended much faster than the gross national product and the level of inflation. The functional distribution of spending varies from state to state. As indicated in Figure 13.2, education consumes the largest total portion of state and local spending, followed by Medicaid.

Within each of these functional categories lies a wide range of financial commitments. For instance, higher-education expenditures in a recent year ran from 25.0 percent of total state spending in Iowa to only 1.5 percent in Oregon. North Dakota dedicated 16.7 percent to transportation, whereas Georgia set aside just 4.9 percent for the same purpose.[25] Such differences represent historical trends, local economic circumstances, and citizens' willingness to incur debt to pay for services. Demographic factors also play a role. For instance, states with high populations of children invest more money in schools than do states with large proportions of senior citizens. State population growth drives up expenditures for such services as water and sewer systems, street maintenance, and law enforcement. The largest expenditure gains in recent years have been registered in Medicaid, as populations of the medically indigent have swelled.

FIGURE 13.2

Total State Government Spending by Service Delivered

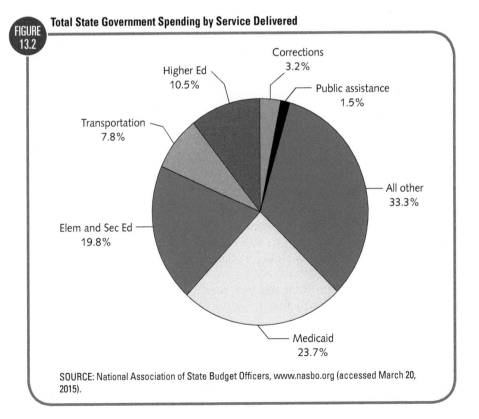

Corrections 3.2%
Higher Ed 10.5%
Public assistance 1.5%
Transportation 7.8%
All other 33.3%
Elem and Sec Ed 19.8%
Medicaid 23.7%

SOURCE: National Association of State Budget Officers, www.nasbo.org (accessed March 20, 2015).

One of the most difficult decisions for an elected official is to go on record in favor of raising taxes (lowering taxes is always popular). The political heat can scorch even the coolest incumbent. But when revenues do not equal service costs and citizens do not want to cut services, raising taxes may be the only answer. However, most people do not want higher taxes. This dilemma is the familiar **tax–service paradox**: People demand new, improved, or at least the same level of government services, but do not want to pay for them through taxes. For instance, the people of Washington State, in their collective wisdom, voted in a 1999 constitutional initiative to slice taxes. But the very next year, they passed another initiative to reduce class sizes and boost teacher pay—without, of course, providing any new money. Voters in a dozen other states have taken similar action. As a former legislator put it, "I wouldn't say voters are stupid. But the same voter who wants unlimited services also does not want to pay for it. There is a disconnect."[26] Is it any wonder that user charges have become a popular option?

The tax–service paradox reflects a certain alienation between government and its citizens. The widespread belief that government at all levels has become too big and wasteful undoubtedly has some basis in fact. The size and responsibilities of state and local governments have grown dramatically, and waste and inefficiency have sometimes accompanied this growth. But the unwillingness of citizens to accept the inevitable reductions in services that follow tax cuts borders on mass schizophrenia.

Helping promote the tax–service paradox are the news media, which enthusiastically belabor alleged government waste and incompetence. Prime-time television news capsules on "how government wastes your money" and typical reporting on actions of states and localities search for and emphasize the negative while ignoring the positive. Government bashing is a popular conservative talk-radio sport. Meanwhile, state and local government functions have become much more complex and technical, tending to make government more difficult to understand, interact with, and communicate with.

State and local governments are responding with outreach efforts designed to educate citizens about what their governments are doing for them and where their tax dollars are going. Local governments send notices showing taxpayers what their money goes to pay for. In several recent cases, most notably in California, state voters have repealed or loosened up restrictions on taxing and spending, indicating, perhaps, the ability of state leaders to get their "dollars and sense" messages across to voters. Thus, the **political economy**—the set of political choices that frames economic policy—has become enormously perplexing for state and local officials. Several features of contemporary state and local economies merit additional discussion: the tax revolt, fiscal stress, limited discretion in raising new revenues, and underfunded retiree pensions and health care benefits.

tax–service paradox

Situation in which people demand more government services but do not want to pay for them through higher taxes.

political economy

Political choices that have economic outcomes.

TAX REVOLT

Taxpayer resentment of property taxes and changes in assessment practices and the general perception that government is too big, too costly, and too wasteful, first took on a tangible form in 1978 with the passage of Proposition 13 in California. Its most Draconian embodiment was adopted by Colorado voters in 1992 as the Taxpayer's Bill of Rights, known as TABOR.[27] (Some of TABOR's severity was lessened in a subsequent referendum adopted in 2005.) Today, nearly every state has enacted statutory or constitutional limitations on taxing and spending by restricting personal or corporate income tax increases, indexing their income taxes to the cost of living, limiting expenditures to increases in cost of living, and other measures. In most instances, citizens have taken tax matters into their own hands through the initiative process. In other cases, state legislators jumped in front of the parade and cut taxes and spending themselves.

Taxpayer revolts come and go today. Their legacy, however, remains enormously important. Watchdog organizations such as the Americans for Tax Reform, led by famous taxophobe Grover Norquist, insist that candidates for elective office sign a "no-tax" pledge. Public officials must work hard to justify tax increases; otherwise, they risk a voter uprising and perhaps political death. Indeed, the stirrings of new tax revolts are constantly in evidence. Oklahomans approved a 2012 ballot measure that limited property tax increases to 3 percent a year, and four other states endorsed their own property tax limitations.

Taxation and expenditure limitations (TELs), then, are restrictions on government taxing and spending, such as Oklahoma's. Forty-six states have some sort of property tax restrictions in effect, and many place limitations on other forms of taxation as well. Raising taxes now requires a constitutional amendment, voter approval, or an extraordinary legislative majority in quite a few states. States and localities usually resist reducing service levels, opting instead to shift tax burdens or find new sources of revenues, such as user charges.[28]

Political and economic consequences of the tax revolt have been much studied. In many cases, TELs have made state and local finance an extraordinarily difficult undertaking: Voters insist on passing spending mandates for education, law enforcement, or other popular programs while at the same time tying the hands of legislatures with restrictions on new revenue-raising, spawning political and bureaucratic legerdemain and new fees to gather sufficient funds to pay for essential services. So far, TELs have not significantly reduced the size and cost of government, or exerted positive effects on employment or per capita income, as had been advertised.[29] However, TELs have led local governments to depend more on the states and to greater recognition by public officials of the continuing need to measure the taxpaying public's pulse on tax issues.[30]

FISCAL STRESS

During national and regional economic downturns, many state and local jurisdictions experience severe **fiscal stress**: They struggle to pay for programs and provide services that citizens want and need without taxing the citizens at unacceptably high levels. Many factors contribute to fiscal stress. Typically, adverse social and economic conditions, mostly beyond state and local government control, establish an environment conducive to financial problems.

taxation and expenditure limitations (TELs)
Restrictions on state and/or local government taxing and spending.

fiscal stress
Financial pressure on a government from factors such as revenue shortfalls and taxing and spending limitations.

The unwinding of the national economy during the Great Recession in 2008–2011 was due largely to the deregulation of the financial industry, personal and corporate greed, the housing and mortgage loan meltdowns, and other macroeconomic factors (though some jurisdictions incurred unrealistic long-term spending obligations even as taxes were lessened). Yet state and local governments paid the greatest financial price.

Older industrial cities are particularly vulnerable. Many jobs and manufacturing industries have been lost because of the gradual but inexorable shift to a service- and information-based economy and company relocation to the Sunbelt and foreign sites. In cities such as Detroit and Philadelphia, the exodus of jobs and firms has eroded the value of taxable resources (mostly property), yet citizens left behind have growing service demands. In New Orleans and other Gulf Coast communities, the local tax base was essentially wiped out by Hurricane Katrina in 2005, and, after modest recovery, was badly damaged again as a result of the 2010 BP oil spill.

Concentration of the poor and minorities in deteriorating housing, the shortage of jobs, high levels of crime, the illegal drug trade, homelessness, large expanses of blighted property, and related factors have produced crisis-level situations. Declining infrastructure also plagues older cities: Water and sewer lines, treatment plants, streets, sidewalks, and other components of the urban physical landscape are in dire need of restoration or replacement. The American Society for Civil Engineers estimates that $3.6 trillion in infrastructure spending is needed by 2020.[31] The estimated amount needed to replace New York City's crumbling and leaking natural gas lines alone is a shocking $10 billion over seven years. Most of these problems, it should be noted, will require tax or fee increases and national government attention if they are to be addressed effectively.

SCOTT COHEN/Reuters/Landov.

A collapsed Minnesota bridge visually illustrates the problems of aging infrastructure.

Political contributions to fiscal stress typically compound the economic problems of cities. Mismanagement of resources and inefficient procedures and activities are common complaints. Pressures from city workers and their unions have also driven up service-provision costs in some localities. Thus, service demands and the costs of providing services grow while taxes and intergovernmental revenues decline. This is a well-tested recipe for fiscal stress that evokes fears of bond defaults and even bankruptcy. Recessions come and go, but many states and localities face chronic fiscal shortfalls because of structural problems deeply embedded in their revenue systems. Structural imbalances result from out-of-date tax systems developed for radically different state economies of fifty years past, as well as from unwise financial management practices.

LIMITED DISCRETION

TELs have placed ceilings on the rates and amounts of taxation and spending, thus limiting the discretion of the nonnational governments. Other constraining factors, too, keep state and local governments from falling prey to the temptation of taxing and spending orgies. One important factor is interstate competition for jobs and economic development. High-tax states run a risk of having jobs, firms, and investments "stolen" by low-tax states.

Earmarking taxes for popular programs also limits state and local taxing and spending discretion. Earmarking is well established: Fuel taxes have been set aside for road and highway programs since automobiles first left ruts in muddy cow pastures. Approximately 25 percent of state tax revenues are earmarked. What differs today is the levels of specificity and creativity in earmarking. Surpluses may accumulate in some dedicated funds, such as highways, whereas other important needs such as education or law enforcement are not sufficiently met. The hands of government officials are tied, however, because they cannot move the funds around. Typical state earmarks fund local drainage, water, or sewer projects; enhance fisheries or environmental cleanups; or pay for municipal or county building improvements. Cigarette buyers in Washington cough up millions of dollars each year to help clean up Puget Sound. Several states earmark a penny of the sales tax for public education.

Financial discretion is partly determined by one's position on the fiscal food chain. The national government can essentially tax and spend as it wishes, subject only to its highly underdeveloped capacity for self-discipline. States must meet federal spending mandates for Medicaid, education, and other services while somehow balancing their budgets each year. Local governments, in addition to suffering reductions in state aid during tough times in this seemingly eternal game of "shift and shaft federalism," must comply with an increasing number of state spending mandates, even as their legal authority to raise revenues remains severely circumscribed in most states. In some ways, local governments are not masters of their own fiscal fate.[32]

Pensions and Health Care When the U.S. General Accounting Standards Board (GASB) issued standards requiring state and local governments to publicly report the funding status of employee pension and health care benefits, most jurisdictions were caught with their financial pants down. As noted above, for many years most states and many localities have been underfunding the future liabilities of employee retirement benefits The estimated gap between what states have promised their retirees for pension benefits and what they have available to pay for them was estimated to be $2.0 trillion in 2013. Chicago's unfunded pension liability is estimated to be $7.1 billion.[33]

Equally serious are the unfunded billions in future liabilities of health care for retirees and their families. California is in the red for $65 billion, New Jersey for $64 billion, and New York for $67 billion. The larger the state employment numbers, the higher the future debt in most cases. But on a per capita basis, states such as Connecticut and Hawaii are particularly hard hit.[34] Connecticut is underfunded by more than $5,500 per state resident, and Hawaii for nearly $7,640 per resident.[35] Cities are overstretched as well, falling some $100 billion short of full health care funding. Chicago is again the poster child for poor financial management, with more than $19 billion of unfunded health care liabilities.[36]

There are several reasons for these huge pension and retiree health care debts. The baby boom bulge in the government workforce has now reached retirement age. Unwise state borrowing from pension funds during difficult economic times is a major cause in some jurisdictions. Overly optimistic assumptions about health care inflation have been common. And, of course, legislators have a tendency to spend today and worry about the future tomorrow (or let the next generation of lawmakers worry about it).

Addressing the problem will require innovative thinking, as well as aggressive pre-funding of future liabilities. The good thing about the GASB standards is that states and localities are required to publicly account for future liabilities. The bad thing is that in some cases tax increases and reductions in promised benefits for government employees will have to be implemented to bring pension and health care liabilities to sustainable levels.

Managing Money

LO 13.5

To discuss how state and local governments manage money.

Every state except Vermont is constitutionally or statutorily required to balance their *operating budgets* each fiscal year. In turn, the states require that local governments balance *their* budgets. However, these requirements apply only to operating budgets, which are used for daily financial receipts and disbursements. *Capital budgets*, used for big purchases that must be paid for over time (for instance, a new bridge or school building), typically run substantial deficits. Operating budgets may also run in the red during the fiscal year, so long as expenditures equal revenues at the end of the year. Consequently, the reliability of revenue estimates is a vital consideration.

ESTIMATING REVENUES

Not so long ago, state and local governments estimated their annual revenues simply by extrapolating from past trends. This approach was simple, inexpensive, and worked well during periods of steady economic growth, but it failed miserably during years of boom or bust. The finance officers of states and most larger cities and counties are much more sophisticated today. Using computer software, they employ econometric modeling to derive mathematical estimates of future revenues. Economic forecasting firms and/or academics assist or provide independent projections.

Econometric modeling places key variables in equations to predict the fiscal-year yield of each major tax. A wide variety of variables are used, including employment levels, food prices, housing costs, oil and gas prices, consumer savings levels, interest rates, intergovernmental aid projections, and state and local debt obligations. Because state and local economies are increasingly linked to national and international factors, estimates often include measures for the value of the dollar, international trade and investment, and national fiscal policy. Despite sophisticated econometric models and financial software, predictions can be wildly off the mark. State revenue estimates fell short by an average of more than 10 percent in 2009 as the Great Recession wreaked havoc.[37]

Two critical factors determine the accuracy of revenue estimates: the quality of the data and the validity of the economic assumptions. Indeed, econometric modeling of state and local economies can be a voyage into the unknown. Data problems include difficulty in measuring key variables; periodic revisions of historical economic data, which require new calculations; and modifications in tax laws or fee schedules. But the major sources of error are the economic assumptions built into the models. Examples are legion: The national economy may not perform as expected; federal financial policy can change to either benefit or harm state and local revenues; federal government shutdowns and sequesters, as occurred in 2013–2014, ripple through the state and local economies; energy prices may plummet or soar; natural or human disasters may disrupt state or local economic growth. Recessions are particularly damaging to fiscal stability because state and local sales and income taxes are highly sensitive to economic downturns.

RAINY DAY FUNDS

Because a balanced budget is mandatory but estimation errors are inevitable, forty-eight states and many localities have established contingency, "budget stabilization," or reserve funds. Popularly known as *rainy day funds*, these savings accounts help insulate budgets from fiscal distortions caused by inaccurate data or faulty economic assumptions; they are also available to alleviate revenue shortfalls. In years of economic health, the funds accumulate principal and interest. When the economy falters, governments can tap into their savings accounts to balance the budget and avoid imposing tax and fee increases.

During sunny days, the states typically fill up their contingency funds to as much as 10 percent of total spending. Amidst the recessionary storms of 2008–2011, states were forced to dig deeply, simply to retain essential services. Many states completely drained their rainy day funds.[38] The task of balancing the budget is especially daunting to local governments, given their lack of economic diversity, dependency on state taxes and financial aid, and sensitivity to economic dislocations. The departure of a single large employer can disrupt a local economy for years. So can weather: The epic winter of 2014–2015 in the Northeast overwhelmed snow removal efforts and closed businesses. The prodigious potholes that appeared with the spring daffodils placed extra stress on local budgets. So the potential advantages of rainy day funds are numerous in the fragile fiscal context of cities and counties.

OTHER FINANCIAL MANAGEMENT PRACTICES

State and local governments, of necessity, are becoming more knowledgeable about how to manage cash and investments. Cash reserves that once sat idly in non-interest-bearing accounts or a desk drawer are now invested in short-term notes, money market accounts, U.S. Treasury bills, certificates of deposit, and other financial instruments so that governments can maximize interest earnings. Most states have local government investment pools that manage billions of dollars in short-term assets. The process of spending and collecting monies is also manipulated to advantage. For example, large checks are deposited in interest-bearing accounts on the day they are received; conversely, payable checks are drawn on the latest date possible. In general, state and local financial management today resembles that of a large corporation instead of the mom-and-pop approach of years ago. After all, the nonnational governments spend and invest some $3.0 trillion annually.

The most important state or local investment is usually the public-employee pension fund. In the past, these funds were conservatively managed and politically untouchable. Today, however, they tend to be invested in more aggressive instruments such as corporate stock. They also represent a tempting honey pot for financially strapped states, whose governors have dipped their hands in the funds and pulled out billions to balance the budget. As described above, many state retirement plans have very large unfunded liabilities. State and local investments must not be managed too aggressively nor too recklessly, as the case of Orange County, California, illustrates. One of the nation's biggest and wealthiest counties, Orange County became the largest in history to file for federal bankruptcy in 1994. The county's financial nightmare commenced when its investment pool manager, Robert L. Citron, placed millions of dollars in financial instruments called derivatives. These instruments "derive" their value from underlying assets such as stocks, bonds, or mortgages. The derivatives' value changes when the price of the underlying assets changes. Orange County lost $1.5 billion when its derivatives, which were tied to interest rates, declined precipitously in value. In effect, Citron was borrowing money from stocks, bonds, and other assets to bet on the direction of interest rates. He lost, and so did Orange County's taxpayers.[39]

Long-Term Borrowing Like corporations, state and local governments issue long-term debt obligations, typically for five to twenty-five years. Bonds are the most common form of long-term borrowing. Because of federal and state tax breaks for investors, the state and local governments are able to finance bonded indebtedness at significantly lower rates than corporations.

Controversies in States and Localities

The State's Responsibility in Local Bankruptcy Events

Harrisburg, Pennsylvania, won the dubious award for first state capital to file for bankruptcy on October 12, 2011, attributing the action to a failed plan to finance and construct an incinerator and to "cash flow problems." On November 9, 2011, Jefferson County, Alabama, surpassed Orange County as the largest county government bankruptcy declaration in history, seeking relief from a debt of more than $4 billion. Jefferson County, home of Birmingham, ran up its huge debt thanks to political corruption, a bad investment in a sewer system, and dumb spending decisions. And as stated in the introduction to this chapter, Detroit recently became the largest municipality to file for bankruptcy.

For these and a handful of other local governments that declared bankruptcy during and after the Great Recession, the decisions were not made without deliberation (and desperation). The consequences of bankruptcy are dire. Businesses may flee, as well as residents concerned about property values. Services, even police and fire, are drastically reduced or eliminated altogether. And the reputation of the city or county is seriously damaged.

The process of filing for bankruptcy is challenging. Only local governments—not states—may do so under federal law, and they must have state approval. To be eligible, the local government must demonstrate insolvency and that it has made a good-faith effort to settle with creditors. Once declared, the bankruptcy proceedings move into the state courts to help chart a path toward financial relief. Though painful, bankruptcy does have the advantages of providing legal protection from

creditors and additional time for the local government to get its financial house in order.[1] It may take years to emerge from bankruptcy with a balanced budget and stable finances. But the city or county may prefer the bankruptcy option, which does permit a good deal of local decision making space, to a state takeover of the locality, its finances, and even its government. Nineteen states have adopted laws enabling them to intervene in local government financial crises, and other states can do so with special legislation.[2]

Critical Thinking Questions:

1. When a city or county goes under water financially, what should the state do? Let the local jurisdiction find its own way back financially? Help it out with loans, grants, or other financial assistance? Take over the jurisdiction and turn over its budget and operations to an external emergency manager?

2. What conditions (e.g., mismanagement, corruption, a declining tax base, etc.) should guide state action?

[1]Campbell Robertson, Mary Williams Walsh, and Michael Cooper, "Bankruptcy Rarely Offers Easy Answer for Counties," *nytimes .com* (November 10, 2011); John Gramlich, "Municipal Bankruptcy Explained: What It Means to File for Chapter 9," www.stateline.org (November 22, 2011); Ryan Holeywell, "How Bad Is It?" *Governing* (May 2011): 26–30.

[2]Elaine S. Povich, "States Intervene in City Fiscal Crises," www .stateline.org (July 1, 2014); Liz Farmer, "The 'B' Word: Is the Stigma of Municipal Bankruptcy Going Away?" *Governing* (March 2013): 36–41; Liz Farmer, "Exiting the Penalty Box," *Governing* (December 2014): 54–6.

There are three conventional types of bonds: general obligation bonds, revenue bonds, and industrial development bonds.

The principal and interest payments on **general obligation bonds** are secured by the "full faith, credit, and taxing power" of the state or local jurisdiction issuing them. General-obligation bonds are used to finance public projects such as highways, schools, and hospitals. Lenders are guaranteed repayment as long as the bond-issuing government is solvent; defaults are nearly nonexistent, but downgrades of cities' credit worthiness occur from time to time.

general obligation bond

A debt instrument supported by the full financial resources of the issuing jurisdiction.

Revenue bonds are backed by expected income from a specific project or service; examples include a toll bridge, a municipal sewer system, or sports complex. Revenue bonds are payable only from the revenues derived from the specified source, not from general tax revenues. Because they typically represent a riskier investment than general-obligation bonds, they command a higher rate of interest.

The **industrial development bond (IDB)** is a type of revenue bond issued by a local government on behalf of a private company to further economic development, such as a new manufacturing facility. The payment of principal and interest on IDBs depends solely on the ability of the industry using the facilities financed by the bond to meet its financial obligation. If the user fails to make payments, creditors can seize and sell any real or personal property associated with the facility. Private interests, such as developers and retailers, are the primary beneficiaries of IDBs. Conventionally, these private-purpose bonds are issued by local governments to attract economic activity and investments; in fact, they are frequently used to furnish loans at highly favorable interest rates to small- or medium-size firms.

The **qualified private activity bond** is a municipal security that enables a firm to finance certain projects with bonds exempt from federal taxes. These financial instruments have been criticized for favoring select businesses with government subsidies. Among the questionable uses have been for a Pakistani company's fertilizer plant in Indiana whose chemicals appeared in improvised explosive devices in Afghanistan, and financial offices for large and wealthy firms such as Goldman Sachs Group and Bank of America.[40] Any "public purpose" for such private activity bonds is hard to discern.

Short-term borrowing is available to state and local governments that need temporary funds just to help tide them over or to meet unexpected circumstances. To borrow money on a short-term loan (e.g., one to six months), governments may access capital markets or even secure a loan from a bank or credit union.

Limits on Borrowing Almost all states place constitutional or statutory restrictions on their own and local government borrowing. Some have set maximum levels of indebtedness; others require popular referenda to create debt or to exceed specified debt limits. They tightly restrict local government debt, especially general-obligation bonds. (State-imposed constraints normally do not apply to revenue bonds.)

The bond market places its own informal limitations on debt by assessing the quality of bonds, notes, and other debt instruments. Investors in government bonds rely on Moody's Investors Service, Standard and Poor's Corporation, Fitch Ratings, and other investment services for ratings of a jurisdiction's capacity to repay its obligations. Criteria taken into consideration in bond ratings include existing debt levels, rainy day funds, market value of real estate, population growth, per capita income, employment levels, and other measures of overall financial health and solvency. Highly rated bond issues receive ratings of *aaa*, *aa*, and *a*. Variations of *b* indicate medium to high risk. A rating of *c* is reserved for bonds in immediate danger of default. The average interest rate on low-rated bonds usually exceeds that of top-rated ones by 1½ to 2 percentage points, which translates into a considerable difference in interest payments.

revenue bond
A bond paid off from income derived from the facility built with the bond proceeds.

industrial development bond (IDB)
A type of revenue bond issued to fund the construction of a facility to be used by a private firm.

qualified private activity bond
A tax-exempt state or municipal security issued to a private firm to finance a project or facility.

Bond ratings tend to rise during periods of economic growth but can fall rapidly during recessions, driving up borrowing costs. Downgrades in general obligation bond ratings cost states or localities millions of dollars. States recently suffering rating declines include Kansas, Illinois, and New Jersey.

Current Issues in State and Local Finance

Dollars define state and local relations. Local governments today recognize that their financial future depends more on the states than on Washington, D.C.

LO 13.6

To be able to discuss current issues in state and local political economy.

THE UNPLEASANT REALITY

Rapid and severe deterioration in revenues slammed state and local governments during the Great Recession and posed a monumental challenge to balancing budgets. Jurisdictions took a variety of actions, both large and small. Across-the-board cuts, hiring freezes, employee furloughs, and layoffs were common. A total of 535,000 layoffs of public workers were recorded over a three-year period.[41] California cut 17,500 state jobs and hacked K-12 and higher education budgets. Colorado and Virginia closed highway rest stops. Michigan canceled the state fair. Minnesota effectively shut down state government over a lack of a balanced budget, laying off 22,000 employees. And, as noted above, local government bankruptcy filings increased.

State and local governments are experiencing significant long-term problems in political economy. Tax systems designed for a primitive industrial age are badly out of step with today's service- and information-based global economy. Beset with its own chronic, self-inflicted financial travails and a record high budget deficit from wars and overspending, the budget-impaired federal government is not a consistently reliable fiscal partner. Indeed, the federal government threatened to revoke the tax exempt status of municipal bonds during the 2013 sequestration .

The spiraling costs of health care, Medicaid, corrections, and public education cannot be shouldered by a single level of government. Mandates without money are certainly no help. When mandates and program responsibilities are pushed to a different rung of the government ladder, funds should follow. Local governments in particular require more revenue-raising authority and broader tax bases to pay for the services they deliver. Most states have been receptive to these principles, but during the Great Recession many states cut funding to local governments, pulled back local governments share of sales and other tax revenues, while foisting even more service delivery responsibilities on them.

The need to increase state and local capability and responsiveness by reinventing and reinvigorating government has perhaps never been greater. The financial structures and processes of state and local governments must be made more appropriate to the social and economic environment in which they operate, which includes a service-based economy; global markets; aging baby boomers; and the changing gender, racial, and ethnic composition of the labor force. These challenges to state and local governments are not being met sufficiently by present revenue systems. The longer they remain unmet, the more severe the problems and the actions that will have to be taken to rectify them.

Education is also needed for taxpayers, who do not always grasp the relationship between taxes paid and services rendered. Resistance to new or existing taxes is to be expected, but campaigns can educate citizens that the result of reducing or eliminating taxes will be fewer or lower-quality services.

Chapter Recap

- The two basic principles of state and local financial systems are the interdependence of the three levels of government and the diversity of revenue sources.

- Among the criteria for evaluating taxes are equity, yield political accountability, acceptability, and efficiency.

- The major state and local taxes are those assessed on property, sales, and income. Other taxes and fees are also imposed.

- Legalized gambling and gaming also raise money.

- Taxpayer resistance has produced tax and expenditure limitations in many states, increased sensitivity of state and local officials to taxpayer preferences, and in some cases fiscal stress for governments.

- State and local governments estimate annual revenues and set aside money in rainy day funds for emergencies and contingencies.

- State and local financial relationships are characterized by sharing and cooperation but also by conflict over mandates and limited local discretion.

KEY TERMS

own-source revenue (p. 336)
intergovernmental transfers (p. 336)
countercyclical aid (p. 337)
tax capacity (p. 337)
tax effort (p. 337)
regressive tax (p. 341)
progressive tax (p. 341)

proportional (flat) tax (p. 341)
benefit principle (p. 341)
indexing (p. 342)
circuit breaker (p. 344)
tax–service paradox (p. 354)
political economy (p. 354)
taxation and expenditure limitations (TELs) (p. 355)

fiscal stress (p. 355)
general-obligation bond (p. 361)
revenue bond (p. 362)
industrial development bond (IDB) (p. 362)
qualified private activity bond (p. 362)

INTERNET RESOURCES

The National Conference of State Legislatures' Principles of a High Quality Tax System are available for viewing at **www.ncsl.org**.

One of the best individual sites on state tax and budget information is "where the money goes" at the Texas State Comptroller at **www.window .state.tx.us**.

For current reports in developments, trends, and policy changes in state government finances, see the website of the Center for the Study of the

States at SUNY–Albany, **www.stateandlocal-gateway.rockinst.org**.

Comparative state and local revenue, tax, and expenditure data may be found at the U.S. Census Bureau's website (**www.census.gov**) and at the Tax Foundation's website (**www. tax-foundation.org**).

See **www.taxsites.com** for general tax resources and official state tax sites.

States compete for new investment such as the Volvo manufacturing facility being constructed in South Carolina.
AP Images/Jeffrey Collins

Economic Development: Competing for Growth

14

S outh Carolina won a big economic plum in 2015 when it was selected by Swedish car maker Volvo as the site of its new $500 million factory. Initially, three other states were in the running—Georgia, Kentucky, and North Carolina—with Georgia and South Carolina eventually emerging as the two finalists. Each of the competing states set about identifying possible sites and assembling incentive packages in an effort to win over Volvo. Several factors worked in the Palmetto State's favor, including the proximity to seaports, the presence of a skilled workforce, and the state's business-friendly climate.[1] The value of the incentives—tax breaks, job training, land purchases, and infrastructure development—offered by the state to Volvo totaled $200 million over a multi-year period. Why was the state willing to provide these sweeteners? There are several reasons. First, the Volvo plant would have an estimated economic impact of $4.8 billion per year and it would add between 2,000 and 4,000 new jobs to the area. Second, the state was already home to BMW; adding Volvo would help cement its reputation as a location for high-end automobile production. And last but not least, South Carolina was compelled to offer a generous incentive package because the other competing states were. As an official once said about state competition for industry, "If you're going to play in the big leagues, you have to come to the field with more than your glove."[2]

Attracting new investment like the Volvo facility is what **economic development** is all about these days. Capital investment, employment rates, income levels, tax base, and public services—all are linked to economic development. And it is a competitive process often pitting one state against another. Reflect on the salvo fired in 2010 by Texas Governor Rick Perry. He sent letters to 90 top businesses in Washington saying, "As the State of Washington considers a multibillion dollar tax increase for citizens and businesses, I invite you to consider your future in America's new land of opportunity: the State of Texas."[3] Not surprisingly, Washington Governor Chris Gregoire unleashed a counterstrike claiming that the Evergreen State had for several years ranked ahead of Texas in its business-friendliness. (Washingtonians voted down the proposed tax increase, perhaps coincidentally.) As the Texas vs. Washington dust-up suggests, resurgent state and local governments are pursuing economic development with a vengeance.

LO 14.1

To understand regional differences in economic prosperity.

Regional Differences in Economic Prosperity

The United States continues to be a nation of diverse regional economies. When the headline in *USA Today* trumpets "Nation's economy improves," be assured that not all places are experiencing the same level of improvement. As economist Mark Crain notes, during the last three decades of the twentieth century, living standards (measured by real income per capita) in the United States increased by 50 percent.[4] However, this average figure masks a considerable range in the data: from a low of 28 percent in Alaska to a high of 64 percent in North Carolina. Even within regions, economies can vary. Detroit and Columbus are both located in the Midwest, but the largest city in Michigan and the largest city in Ohio are worlds apart economically.[5] Different economic mixes of manufacturing, services, and retail employment mean different economic conditions. The effects of global economic restructuring coupled with a prolonged national recession hit states and communities hard in the early twenty-first century. Some places have done better than others in adjusting to the new economic realities.

The business network CNBC evaluates the states annually on 56 different measures related to business competitiveness.[6] The individual measures—tax burden, job training programs, wage rates, regulatory environment, venture

economic development

A process by which a community, state, or nation increases its level of per capita income, high-quality jobs, and capital investment.

State Business Competitiveness

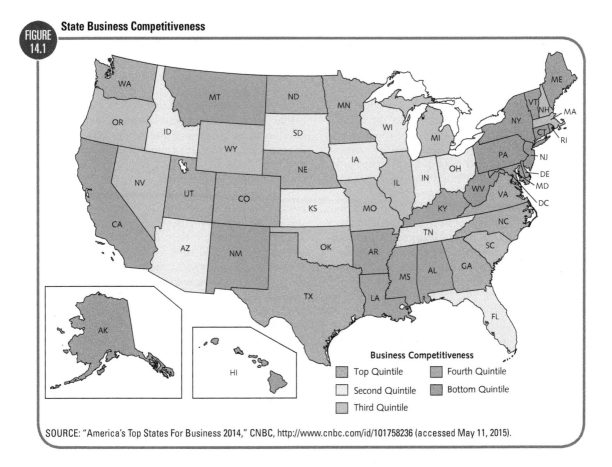

Business Competitiveness

- Top Quintile
- Second Quintile
- Third Quintile
- Fourth Quintile
- Bottom Quintile

SOURCE: "America's Top States For Business 2014," CNBC, http://www.cnbc.com/id/101758236 (accessed May 11, 2015).

capital, and quality of life, among others—are weighted and aggregated to produce scores and rankings. Figure 14.1 organizes the states into quintiles based on these rankings. Georgia and Texas were the top two scoring states in CNBC's 2014 analysis; Rhode Island edged out Hawaii for the lowest score.

Remember that economies are dynamic—that is, economic momentum can slow down and speed up. The personal income growth in a state, the change in unemployment rates, and the level of population change are three indicators that can be combined into a useful index of economic momentum, or change. The figures for 2012 showed North Dakota, Texas, and Oklahoma at the top of the list, with Mississippi and Alabama at the bottom.[7] The index for the same period in 2006 found Nevada, Arizona, and Utah leading the way, with Louisiana and Washington at the end.

Local economies are also dynamic. Some cities that were once the economic engines of the country—Cleveland, Detroit, St. Louis—have been replaced by others—Austin, Raleigh, San Jose. As some cities decline, others surge. The Controversies in States and Localities feature discusses cities that have become magnets for what has been called the "creative class."

Controversies in States and Localities

The Creative Class and Cool Cities

What's the hottest thing for cities these days? Well, to be cool. Metropolitan areas across the country are in a race for the informal title of the coolest city in America. They want to be considered hip, trendy, and sophisticated. This is because the cool cities attract well-educated, talented young professionals to their environs. They are magnets for the creative class, people whose work involves producing new ideas, new technology, or new creative content. It is this demographic of innovators that is, some contend, the driving force for economic development. And with a recent study showing that two-thirds of college graduates will choose where to live before looking for employment, this gives states and localities considerable leverage in attracting the urban crowd.

Cool cities possess what Richard Florida calls in his book *The Rise of the Creative Class* the three T's: technology, tolerance, and talent. Their economies are knowledge based, their policies promote social tolerance, and their communities nurture the arts and culture. Jobs are plentiful, gays and lesbians are welcomed, and the nightlife is lively. Cities that embrace such a culture experience an influx of entrepreneurial, ambitious, and creative young people. And this trend has a snowball effect, attracting a continual stream of well-educated, mobile fun-seekers to cool cities. Consequently, cities lacking in some or all of the three T's fall more and more behind, out of step with the cool places.

This three T's framework has proven so insightful that many state and local governments are implementing its precepts. Florida's consulting agency has helped begin thirty-three initiatives across seven cities, all with the end goal of developing a local "cool" culture. There are initiatives that promote the work of local artists, such as the creation of a sculpture garden in El Paso, Texas, which features exclusive work from the area's most talented sculptors. Promoting local events and workshops is another popular initiative, such as Tacoma's "Love Tacoma" social networking program, which sponsors cultural activities like glass blowing, boutique tours, and farmers' markets. Environmental awareness and initiatives that cater to the eco-friendly crowd are gaining a lot of momentum. Pedestrian-friendly downtowns, public transit systems, trails, bike paths, and local parks are all selling points to the creative class.

So, based on the above criteria of what defines cool, which cities top the list? According to one study, the top five cities for young singles are Boulder, Colorado; San Francisco, California; Washington, D.C.; Madison, Wisconsin; and Boston, Massachusetts. Their colorful social events and local flair give them a unique cultural personality tailored just for the creative class. Another study selected Washington, D.C., Seattle, Austin, Houston, and San Francisco as the five coolest cities in the country. Meanwhile, many other cities are implementing their own "cool" initiatives that could rival the current leaders.

Critical Thinking Questions:

1. Has your city tried to cultivate a "cool" image? If so, what indicators can be used to determine how successful it has been?

2. All cities have a unique culture. What culture could your area leverage to develop a more hip or unique image?

3. Should cities expend resources trying to create a cool image, or is this a distraction from other ways to develop the economy?

SOURCES: Anne Markusen, "Creative Cities: A 10-Year Research Agenda," *Journal of Urban Affairs* 36 (August 2014): 587–89; Erin Carlyle, "Washington, D.C., Tops Forbes 2014 List of America's Coolest Cities, *Forbes*, http://www.forbes.com/sites/erincarlyle/2014/08/06/washington-d-c-tops-our-list-of-americas-coolest-cities/ (August 6, 2014).
Carl Grodach, "Before and After the Creative City: The Politics of Urban Cultural Policy in Austin, Texas," *Journal of Urban Affairs* 34(1, 2011): 81–97; "Best Cities for Gen Ys," *Business Week,* http://images.businessweek.com/ss/09/06/0609_top_gen_y_cities/1.htm (July 26, 2009); Richard Florida, *The Rise of the Creative Class* (New York: Basic Books, 2002).

Approaches to Economic Development

LO 14.2

To differentiate the four waves of economic development policy.

Governments devise elaborate strategies *and spend a lot of money* to promote economic development within their boundaries. The approaches they use have evolved over time, but even some of the oldest tools remain viable today.

EARLY APPROACHES: FIRST AND SECOND WAVES

Community efforts to spur economic development have a long history, but the first statewide program of industrial recruitment was created during the Great Depression. Mississippi, with its Balance Agriculture with Industry plan, made it possible for local governments to issue bonds to finance the construction or purchase of facilities for relocating industry. Other southern states followed suit, luring businesses from elsewhere with tax breaks, public **subsidies**, and low wages. Called *smokestack chasing*, aggressive industrial recruitment had spread beyond the South by the 1970s. By the end of that decade, as states raided other states for industry, statistics showed that between 80 and 90 percent of new jobs came from existing firm expansions and start-up businesses, not from relocating businesses. About the same time, pressure from foreign competition intensified. Policy makers feverishly cast about for strategies that would spawn new businesses and keep state economies strong. These efforts began a new era, or second wave, in economic development. States established **venture capital pools**, created **small-business incubators**, and initiated workforce training programs in an attempt to support home-grown enterprise. Even with these new initiatives in place, many states continued to chase out-of-state industry.

subsidy

Financial assistance given by a government to a firm or enterprise.

venture capital pools

Special funds earmarked for new, innovative businesses that cannot get conventional financing.

small-business incubators

Facilities that provide services aimed at nurturing start-up businesses.

NEWER APPROACHES: THIRD AND FOURTH WAVES

The 1990s saw a third wave gather strength. This wave represented a rethinking of the role of government in promoting economic growth. Second-wave programs, well-intentioned perhaps, simply did not have sufficient scale or focus to transform state economies. An **enterprise zone**, for example, may revitalize a neighborhood, but unless an extensive network of such zones exists throughout the state, the overall impact is marginal. Third-wave efforts sought to correct some of the deficiencies of second-wave programs. One of the keys to the third wave was moving economic development programs out of state agencies and into private organizations. Rather than directly supplying the program or the service, as it had done in the first and second waves, government would provide direction and seed capital.

The latest ripple flowing from the third wave is called **clusters**. It reconfigures the economy as clusters of firms that compete and trade with one another and have common needs. By focusing on interconnections and working relationships among businesses, nonprofit organizations, and government, a state gets a better sense of its economic foundations.[8] Arizona pioneered the concept in its Strategic Plan for Economic Development. The state identified ten clusters ranging from food, fiber, and natural products to environmental technologies,

enterprise zone

Areas of a community that offer special government incentives aimed at stimulating investment. Also called an *empowerment zone*.

clusters

Geographically concentrated firms that compete and trade with each other and have similar needs.

to mining and minerals.[9] Each cluster has spawned an organization in which ideas can be shared, common strategies developed, and joint ventures negotiated. In Connecticut, the clusters are tourism, aerospace, and bioscience. To nurture and support its clusters, the Connecticut legislature redesigned the state's research and development tax credits. High technology remains an important cluster in many places around the country despite the slowdown the industry experienced in the early 2000s.[10]

Third-wave thinking continues to influence states and localities, but a fourth wave has already developed. Political scientist Susan Clarke and geographer Gary Gaile contend that a distinctively different set of strategies is needed.[11] This new set, or fourth wave, is more attuned to global markets, especially localities' use of trade and telecommunications to their economic advantage. The fourth wave is also more focused on human capital—that is, on educating and training its work force. Even as states and localities turn to these third- and fourth-wave approaches, however, they continue to use strategies from the first and second waves. How to pursue economic development remains a hotly debated subject.

A leading figure who has headed economic revitalization efforts in three states points to five key trends that states must understand as they design their economic development policies:

- The economic playing field is the world, not the neighboring county or state.
- The new infrastructure is technology and telecommunications.
- Regionalism provides an opportunity for states and others to work together. Boundaries are falling.
- Sustainable development strategies that recognize the interdependence of the economy and the environment are necessary.
- Successful economic development efforts are built on a high-quality work force.[12]

THE FOURTH WAVE AND THE "NEW ECONOMY"

The fourth wave in economic development approaches is linked to what some are calling the "**new economy**." The list of trends at the end of the preceding section identifies fundamental changes in the U.S. economy. According to adherents of the new economy, states that fail to adapt their development strategies to these new circumstances will be left behind. A public policy think tank, the Information Technology and Innovation Foundation (ITIF), lays it out: "The New Economy is a global, entrepreneurial, and knowledge-based economy in which the keys to success lie in the extent to which knowledge, technology, and innovation are embedded in products and services."[13] ITIF recently evaluated the states according to how close each one is to achieving a new economy. A total of twenty-five indicators was used; among them were items such as state export capacity, in-migration of knowledge workers, number of fast-growing companies, residential use of broadband technology, and industry investment in research and development. Weighting each of the twenty-five indicators according to its importance, ITIF calculated scores for

new economy

An economy based in global technology and knowledge, as opposed to the old economy based in national manufacturing.

FIGURE 14.2

State Scores on the "New Economy"

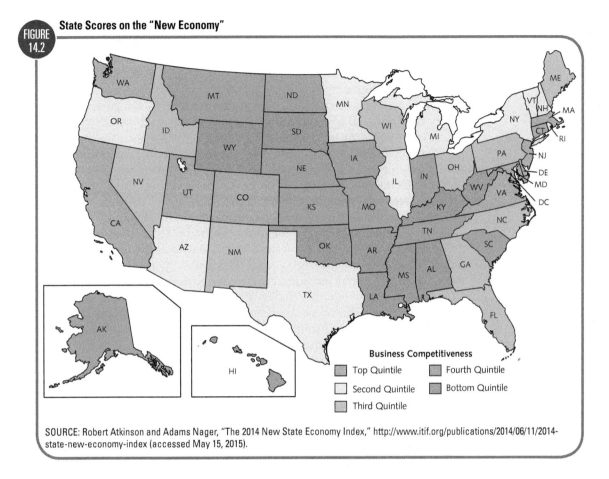

Business Competitiveness
- Top Quintile
- Second Quintile
- Third Quintile
- Fourth Quintile
- Bottom Quintile

SOURCE: Robert Atkinson and Adams Nager, "The 2014 New State Economy Index," http://www.itif.org/publications/2014/06/11/2014-state-new-economy-index (accessed May 15, 2015).

each state. The map in Figure 14.2 groups the states into quintiles based on the aggregate scores. Leading new economy states are Massachusetts, Delaware, and California; at the other end of the score sheet are Oklahoma, West Virginia, and Mississippi.

The Politics of Economic Growth

Economic development occupies a central role in campaigns for state and local elective office. Like reducing crime and improving education, it is a consensus issue: Everybody is in favor of it. Thus, each candidate tries to convince the voters that his or her approach to economic development will be the most effective. At both the state and local levels, candidates' campaign rhetoric typically emphasizes jobs and employment, and candidates talk in terms of "sustaining and expanding economic growth."

Most states have created several mechanisms to implement economic development strategies.[14] Ideally, a state government should be internally united for its economic development effort, but several natural cleavages—

LO 14.3

To appreciate the politics inherent in economic development.

partisan politics, legislative-executive disputes, and agency turf battles—make cohesion difficult. Because economic development is a central issue, it inspires a lot of political posturing. In the end, a state government with a unified, cohesive approach to economic development is likely to be more successful than a state without one.

As a state's top elected official and chief executive, the governor commonly takes the lead in economic development. For example, when he took office, Utah governor Jon Huntsman reorganized state agencies to create a new Governor's Office of Economic Development (GOED), declaring, "Economic development is the cornerstone of my administration."[15] Organizations like GOED try to come up with fresh ideas and new tactics, maximizing the state's strengths and minimizing its weaknesses. And states are more than willing to borrow ideas that have been successful in other states.

Once an economic development strategy is in place, the next challenge is implementation. During what we earlier referred to as the first wave of economic development strategies, the responsibility for implementation belonged to state agencies. Adherents to the third wave argue, however, that state agencies have not responded creatively and effectively to the challenges confronting them. Third-wave advocates want government agencies out of the economic development business, with more flexible, public-private hybrids or private-sector organizations as their replacements. Florida was the first state to replace its Department of Commerce with a public-private organization, which it named Enterprise Florida (or eFlorida). Arizona was one of the most recent converts to the public-private approach when it abolished its Department of Commerce to create the Arizona Commerce Authority.

Greater involvement by nongovernment organizations in providing economic development programs and services is risky. State governments have always had a complex relationship with the private sector. They must contend with demands from various interests, of which business is only one (albeit a powerful one). Nevertheless, state policy makers have generally tried to accommodate the demands of the business community. In fact, one persistent criticism of state legislatures is that they have been *too* receptive to the entreaties of business. Business leaders believe that because their success is central to a state's economy, they ought to be treated as a public-interest rather than as a special-interest group. A state may thus feel that it is less a partner than a prisoner. In response to the question "Who runs Massachusetts?" one state legislator responded, "The businesses that threaten to move out of the state. They have a chokehold on us."[16] This statement may be extreme in tone, but it conveys the frustration that some state officials feel about their government's relationship with business. It also highlights the skepticism with which many state policy makers greet calls for less government involvement in economic development.

A successful partnership that has emerged in some states is the one between industries and universities. The Committee for Economic Development, a national group of prominent business executives and educators, identifies five ways in which states can facilitate these partnerships: through state-established centers, state grants to university research centers, research incubators, small-business development centers, and research parks.[17]

A potentially fertile area for industry-university collaboration is bioscience, especially stem-cell research. Minnesota was one of the first states to take action when it established a Stem Cell Institute at the University of Minnesota and set up tax-free zones for bioscience companies; Wisconsin, another pioneer, has its nonprofit WiCell Research Institute. New Jersey passed legislation in 2004 that legalized stem-cell research in the Garden State and promptly budgeted $6.5 million a year through 2010 in support of it. California, where many biotech companies are located, approved a massive spending initiative on its 2004 ballot. The California Stem Cell Research and Cures Initiative allocated a whopping $300 million a year for ten years. The California Institute for Regenerative Medicine was created; it in turn has funded 12 stem cell research facilities and distributed millions of dollars in grants. Stem-cell research could lead to significant advances in health, but for states, the economic development benefits are just as—and maybe more— appealing. Accordingly, when President Barack Obama lifted the federal ban on funding stem-cell research in 2009, the promise of new federal grants had many states paying attention. In the words of former Missouri governor Bob Holden, "Whether it's pharmaceuticals, biotechnology, or medical research—life sciences technologies will create the jobs of tomorrow."[18]

Current Approaches

LO 14.4

To explain strategic planning and four economic development approaches popular with states and localities.

State governments, aware that their economic development activities have appeared incoherent and even counterproductive to the outside world, have attempted to clarify their role. In doing so, many states have engaged in strategic planning. Economic sectors commonly targeted by states include travel and tourism, the arts, sports, and international trade.

STRATEGIC PLANNING

Strategic planning can be useful for several reasons. First, it produces an understanding of the state's economic bedrock. Second, it provides a venue in which public- and private-sector leaders can exchange perspectives and develop a consensus about the state's economic future. In addition, strategic planning moves the economic development issue from goal setting to implementation. Finally, it provides a mechanism for adjusting and correcting the state's actions to match emerging economic trends.

Wisconsin was one of the first states to engage in strategic planning for economic development. A twenty-three–member strategic development commission was established by the governor during a time of economic turmoil growing out of the loss of industrial jobs. The commission's assignment was to analyze the Wisconsin economy and identify avenues for government action. Eighteen months and half a million dollars later, it produced its strategic plan. The focus was on preserving the existing job base, fostering new jobs, and adopting the ethos that "Wisconsin is first in quality."[19] More than 100 specific recommendations were included in the plan.

strategic planning
An approach to economic development that emphasizes adaptation to changing conditions and anticipation of future events.

Since then, most states have undertaken strategic planning exercises. Missouri's 2011 "Strategic Initiative for Economic Growth" is typical. With the goal of transforming the Show Me State's economy within five years, the plan identified eight strategies:

- Attract, retain, and develop a workforce with the education and skills to succeed in the twenty-first–century economy.
- Support local developers in the retention and expansion of existing businesses and employers.
- Optimize state tax, incentive, and regulatory policies to best support the growth of high-value target sectors.
- Invest in technology and innovation to attract, launch, and sustain the growth companies of the future.
- Aggressively market the state to select domestic and international audiences.
- Develop a best-in-class foreign trade initiative.
- Develop a culture that encourages small and minority business development and entrepreneurism.
- Provide the infrastructure necessary for companies and communities to be successful.[20]

Missouri's plan sets out a series of tactics within each of the strategies, as well as seven clusters the state will be targeting. As with any plan, the biggest hurdle is translating the rhetoric into reality.

Strategic planning is an important first step. The actual programs and tools that state and local governments employ to accomplish their economic development objectives are many and varied. Four that have maintained their popularity are travel and tourism, the arts, sports, and international trade.

Michigan has launched a major promotional effort to attract tourists to the state.

TRAVEL AND TOURISM

Travel and tourism are big business. According to the U.S. Travel Association, direct spending by travelers reached $928 billion in 2014, generating 8 million jobs and contributing $141 billion in tax revenue.[21] To attract big-spending tourists, states spend big—and some states spend really big. Michigan spends about $25 million annually on its "Pure Michigan" marketing effort; Connecticut's "Still Revolutionary" promotion carried a two-year price tag of $27 million.[22] At the local level, convention and visitors' bureaus, which are frequently the joint ventures of the chamber of commerce and city government, have been created to promote individual communities and their assets.

States are actively marketing the virtues of their coasts, mountains, Civil War battlefields, national parks, regional cuisine, casinos—whatever might attract a tourist dollar. States develop advertising campaigns around a catchy slogan: The South with a Twist (Georgia), Come See for Yourself (New Jersey), Restart Your Engines (Indiana), Possibilities . . . Endless (Nebraska). As Iowa's tourism director noted, "We're looking for a type of kick-butt theme that gets on people's minds."[23] Major cities do the same thing. "That's So LA" and "Second to None" are the marketing slogans of Los Angeles and Chicago, respectively.

Appealing images abound on state travel and tourism websites. For example, read how Oregon's coast is described on the state's official tourism website:

> All 363 miles of the Oregon Coast are free and open to all of us. Which means how you choose to explore it is entirely up to you. You can sandboard or dune buggy the sand dunes down south, or hit your way out of a sand trap inside the best public golf resort in America. You can investigate its tide pools, hike up its cliffs or down through ancient old-growth forests to discover its hidden surf spots. You can hunt for agates, or beach-comb, or build forts from washed-up driftwood.[24]

On its tourism website, Idaho focuses on its rivers, promising "Endless miles of smiles;" Kansas, in a tribute to *The Wizard of Oz*, has identified a series of "yellow brick road trips" throughout the state.

Travel and tourism are especially appealing because of the tax yield. Most states levy an **accommodations tax** (commonly referred to as a bed tax), and the money spent by travelers and tourists is also subject to state as well as local sales taxes. All in all, nonresidents contribute a significant sum to the tax base of tourism-rich locales. However, the fiscal stress of the Great Recession led many states to cut their advertising and tourism-promotion budgets, some rather substantially. For instance, Arizona's Office of Tourism had a $19 million budget in 2009, but only $8.6 million in 2012 and $12.9 million in 2013.[25] As a result, the Office targeted its advertising to markets like Chicago and Los Angeles, which were expected to yield more visitors than other markets would. Washington went so far as to shut down its tourism promotion office, prompting several tourism-related businesses to create an alliance to advertise the state.[26] In the meantime, the state of Montana rented several billboards in the Seattle area advertising the beauty of Big Sky Country. No doubt about it: Tourism is a competitive activity for states and localities. Many

accommodations tax
A tax on hotel-or motel-room occupancy, with the revenues usually earmarked for tourism-related uses.

observers contend that budget-slashing actions are shortsighted, arguing that the cost savings will result in fewer visitors and, therefore, less tax revenue generated by nonresidents.

THE ARTS

Throughout the country, in medium-size to large cities, performing arts lovers (patrons of dance, opera, theater, and orchestra) are joining with business leaders to forge a coalition. Their intent is to use the arts as a development strategy. Promoting the arts as a development tool may not be as far-fetched as one might initially think.[27] Cities hope that, by sponsoring world-class concerts in acoustically perfect arenas, they can bring audiences of white- collar workers back to the city's center. Such events would also generate secondary spending by the audience (and participants) at restaurants, retail shops, parking garages, and hotels. And just as important, a new sense of liveliness and vitality would infuse the nightlife. In fact, the accessibility of community **amenities** such as the arts is a factor that frequently contributes to business-relocation decisions. Members of arts coalitions argue that company officials might look more favorably on their city if it regularly attracts Broadway shows and the Bolshoi Ballet. They point out that a successful performing arts center could stimulate additional physical development in the downtown area. Indeed, a community might invest in an arts strategy for many reasons.

Aware that the arts can provide a valuable boost, several cities have cast an envious eye at Chicago's Millennium Park, a sculpture garden that opened to rave reviews (and a lot of visitors) in 2004. St. Louis took a page from the same book and created Citygarden in 2009, a three-acre sculpture park on downtown land that was previously vacant. Both San Francisco and Minneapolis invested in massive overhauls of their art museums, and Louisville built a brand-new performing arts and educational center. Denver sports a new opera house, and Atlanta advertises the Georgia Aquarium, billed as the largest indoor fish tank in the world.[28]

But the arts need not be high-brow to affect development. Popular culture—be it multiplex theaters, theme restaurants, sports arenas, or entertainment-oriented stores—is turning around many central cities. Street art, especially sculptural displays, is another popular art form that many places have embraced. Chicago kicked it off with that city's colorful and clever Cows on Parade: 320 life-size fiberglass bovines. Cultural leaders in other cities took the idea and ran with it. There were pigs in Cincinnati, Ohio; horses in Lexington, Kentucky; geckos in Orlando, Florida; and cornstalks in Bloomington, Illinois. Clearly, the arts have become an important economic development tool.

SPORTS

amenities

Comfort and conveniences that contribute to quality of life.

Professional sports and big-league cities go hand in hand. Hosting a professional sports franchise is evidence that a city has arrived—that it is not simply a large city but a major-league city. Only sixty cities in the country host a top-level professional baseball, basketball, football, or hockey team. Smaller cities eagerly court minor-league teams to enhance the quality of life in the community.

The Minnesota Vikings will kick off their 2016 NFL season in a new stadium built in part with public money.

Acquiring or retaining professional sports teams has become an important element in local economic development plans. Cities want professional sports franchises, but they don't come easily. In fact, ownership groups have to bid for franchises, typically with some sort of public subsidy. This subsidy usually comes in the form of below-market-rate leases and tax breaks for the stadium (depending on whether the facility is publicly or privately owned). City leaders defend these subsidies, arguing that the return, both economically and symbolically, is worth it. But the public is increasingly skeptical. Even in football-friendly Texas, some residents of Arlington, the home of the Dallas Cowboys' new $1.12 billion mega-stadium, balked at the use of local tax revenue ($325 million) and the city's **eminent domain** power in support of the stadium.[29]

When public financial support is not forthcoming, team owners frequently threaten to relocate. The threat can be a potent one, as Seattle found out when the Supersonics basketball team left town to become the Oklahoma City Thunder. But owners are beginning to find their relocation options narrowing. Few politicians want a treasured professional team to relocate. Thus, the governor of Minnesota, an opponent of stadium bills when he was a state legislator, proposed the construction of new stadiums for the Twins (baseball) and the Vikings (football). Governor Tim Pawlenty explained his flip-flop this way: "Bottom line: I don't want to lose the Twins or the Vikings on my watch."[30] (The Twins got their new stadium in downtown Minneapolis in 2010; the Vikings were scheduled to move into their new digs in 2016). Table 14.1 shows the wide range in the percentage of public money in recent stadium construction.

A study on the impact of sports stadiums on local economies found that the stadiums had negligible effects on jobs and development; instead, they diverted economic development from manufacturing to the service sector.[31]

eminent domain
The right of a government to seize private property for public use, in exchange for payment of fair market value.

TABLE 14.1   Public Financial Support of Sports Stadiums

MLB			NFL		
TEAM	YEAR	PUBLIC FUNDS (%)	TEAM	YEAR	PUBLIC FUNDS (%)
Cincinnati Reds	2003	96	Arizona Cardinals	2006	76
Detroit Tigers	2000	38	Cincinnati Bengals	2000	89
Houston Astros	2000	68	Dallas Cowboys	2009	30
Miami Marlins	2012	76	Denver Broncos	2001	73
Milwaukee Brewers	2001	71	Detroit Lions	2002	36
Minnesota Twins	2010	72	Houston Texans	2002	73
New York Mets	2009	19	Indianapolis Colts	2008	50
New York Yankees	2009	32	Minnesota Vikings	2016	51
Philadelphia Phillies	2004	50	New England Patriots	2002	0
Pittsburgh Pirates	2001	85	New York Giants/Jets	2010	0
San Diego Padres	2004	66	Philadelphia Eagles	2003	39
San Francisco Giants	2000	0	Pittsburgh Steelers	2001	69
St. Louis Cardinals	2006	12	San Francisco 49ers	2014	12
Washington Nationals	2008	100	Seattle Seahawks	2002	83

NBA			MLS		
TEAM	YEAR	PUBLIC FUNDS (%)	TEAM	YEAR	PUBLIC FUNDS (%)
Brooklyn Nets	2012	0	Chicago Fire	2006	100
Charlotte Bobcats	2005	100	Chivas USA/LA Galaxy	2003	0
Dallas Mavericks	2001	30	Colorado Rapids	2007	50
Houston Rockets	2003	100	FC Dallas	2005	85
Memphis Grizzlies	2004	83	Houston Dynamo	2012	32
Oklahoma City Thunder	2002	100	New York Red Bulls	2010	0
Orlando Magic	2010	87.5	Philadelphia Union	2010	65
San Antonio Spurs	2002	84	Real Salt Lake	2008	41
			Seattle Sounders FC	2002	66
			Sporting Kansas City	2011	0
			Toronto FC	2007	55

SOURCE: *Sports Facility Reports*, 2011, National Sports Law Institute, Marquette University, https://law.marquette.edu/national-sportslaw-institute/sports-facility-reports-volume-12-summer-2011; updated http://law.marquette.edu/national-sports-law-institute/sports-facility-reports-volume-15-2014 (accessed May 19, 2015).

And a cost-benefit analysis of minor-league stadiums turned up negative.[32] But economic analyses of hosting the Olympics are more positive. The 1996 Summer Olympics in Atlanta produced an estimated $5.1 billion for Georgia's economy. And the tax revenues were put at $165 million. Called by some the "world's largest economic development opportunity," the Olympic Games are the ultimate sports prize. This is why Chicago launched an ambitious but ultimately unsuccessful effort to beat out Madrid, Tokyo, and Rio de Janeiro (the eventual winner) to host the 2016 Summer Olympic Games. Those kinds of numbers help in creating a broad base of community support for the Olympics. The United States did not submit a bid to host the 2020 Summer Olympic Games, but selected Los Angeles as the nation's entry for the 2024 event.

When opposition to an Olympics bid does arise, it tends to be piecemeal and sporadic, aimed at diverting development from a specific location or mitigating negative consequences.[33] Environmental activists, neighborhood groups, taxpayer organizations, and citizen advocacy groups fought against certain aspects of the 2002 Salt Lake City Winter Olympics and even enjoyed occasional successes in having venues relocated. But there was no anti-Olympic coalition intent upon stopping the games. The very successful Winter Games brought international media attention to Salt Lake City (and to Utah) and long-lasting economic benefits.

INTERNATIONAL TRADE

States are no longer content to concentrate on domestic markets for the goods and services produced in their jurisdictions—they are venturing abroad. States pursue international trade for two reasons. First, foreign markets can be important consumers of state goods. Second, foreign investors may have capital to commit to projects in a state. Thus, the promotion of international trade is a two-way street: State products are exported and investment capital is imported.

One highly visible means by which state governments pursue international markets and investments is through trade missions in which the governor, top business leaders, and economic development agency officials make formal visits, most often to Europe and Asia. The state delegation exchanges information with representatives of the country's public and private sectors and establishes ties that delegation members hope will lead to exports and investments.

State governments perform three important roles in export promotion:

- Brokering information,
- Offering technical support, and
- Providing export financing.[34]

As information brokers, states conduct seminars and conferences, sponsor trade shows, provide market research, publish export handbooks, and offer individual counseling to American businesses. Oklahoma, for instance, has set up an international division in its commerce department to encourage export activity. One of its key functions is to identify export opportunities for Oklahoma's business firms. Once an opportunity has been identified, the division provides technical support to help the relevant firm become more knowledgeable about the exporting process.

Technical support is critical because U.S. firms may not be aware of the details involved in exporting: working with international banks, complying with another country's laws and regulations, securing the necessary licensing agreements, designing appropriate packaging for products, and the like. Thus, states conduct seminars to inform businesses of the details. Export finance is also important because without it, a state's information brokerage and technical support functions are weakened. The first state to tackle the export finance issue was Minnesota; it provides a firm with operating capital for the period between the signing of a sales agreement and the delivery of a product. In addition to working capital, some states offer insurance and export credit. The availability of financing converts the fantasy of exporting into reality. Texas and California, not surprisingly, led the other states in terms of the value of exports, with 14.8 and 13.4 percent of the U.S. total, respectively.[35]

State government is also involved in promoting the state as a place for foreign investment. According to the U.S. Bureau of the Census, more than 5.5 million jobs are a direct result of foreign investment. (More than 10 percent of them are in California.)[36] Delaware leads all states with 7.3 percent of its workforce in foreign-owned businesses, followed by South Carolina (6.9 percent), Connecticut (6.6 percent), and New Hampshire (6.6 percent).

The enactment of foreign trade agreements such as the North American Free Trade Agreement (NAFTA) and the decrees of the World Trade Organization (WTO) add another dimension to the globalization of trade for states and localities. NAFTA gradually eliminates trade barriers and investment restrictions among the United States, Canada, and Mexico. NAFTA opens new markets to a state's industries, but it also puts pressure on those industries to remain competitive. In addition, the agreement imposes new limitations and duties on state governments. Under NAFTA, for example, states may no longer discriminate in favor of homegrown service providing firms, nor can they restrict foreign ownership of land, unless these policies are specifically grandfathered into the agreement.

The WTO picks up where NAFTA leaves off by, in effect, knocking down protectionism and opening borders throughout the world. California got schooled on the ins and outs of NAFTA and WTO when it adopted a new law that would recycle old tires into paving materials for use in highway construction projects. At issue was whether the requirement that the recycled tires be of U.S. origin violated NAFTA by discriminating against Canadian and Mexican tire manufacturers.[37] After multiple interpretations and reinterpretations of the new law and the treaty, the Golden State's law was allowed to stand. But in 2015, meat producing states lost when the WTO refused to reconsider its decision outlawing the country-of-origin labeling (COOL) law enacted by the United States.

Persistent Questions

LO 14.5

To debate both sides of the three persistent questions about government's role in the economy.

A robust economy provides jobs for residents and revenues for governments. Therefore, economic health is a central public policy concern. Government actions intended to spark economic development are typically considered to be in the public interest. Still, three questions in particular are associated with government involvement in the economy, and they pertain to the impact, the extent, and the fairness of government action.

DO STATE AND LOCAL GOVERNMENT EFFORTS MAKE MUCH DIFFERENCE?

Views about the impact of government actions on the economy diverge widely. Some studies suggest that many of the important factors that affect an economy are beyond the control of state and local governments, whereas others contend that government action can greatly influence the fate of a local economy.[38] Both views contain a kernel of truth. One widely cited study of the location decisions of large firms found that a favorable labor climate and proximity to suppliers and consumers were important criteria to most firms.[39] Governments can affect the first factor but not the second. Also, states vary in the degree to which their economies are influenced by external forces.

Questions about impact and return on investment continue to haunt state and local development officials. Can the actions of states and localities affect employment levels, income, and investment? Statistical tests suggest that the outcomes are both mixed and marginal. Research has shown that, in some places, at some times, some economic development tools produce the intended outcomes.[40] A study of 40 government-assisted development projects in 10 medium-size cities reached similar conclusions.[41] Regardless of the modest results, however, governments continue to intervene in their economies. This behavior may rest in the political benefits of successful development projects to elected officials. Or it may be an outgrowth of business influence in public policy making. Whatever the explanation, the behavior continues.

An example illustrates the dilemma that states face. After the South Carolina General Assembly voted down a proposal in 2011 to give sales tax incentives to an Amazon distribution center, the company immediately ceased construction of the facility. On the heels of Amazon's decision, two other manufacturing firms dropped their plans to build major plants nearby, citing an uncertain political climate. Moreover, one of the Palmetto State's largest homebuilders shelved plans to construct hundreds of new houses in the area.[42] A political firestorm ensued and supporters of the tax breaks—or more likely, the 2,000 jobs that Amazon had projected—prevailed upon the legislature to reconsider its decision. It did so, approving the tax break late in the legislative session, and Amazon's distribution center began operations in 2012. Would the company have built the facility eventually without the tax breaks? South Carolina and plenty of other states do not appear willing to take the risk.

If the fourth wave in economic development is upon us, then perhaps states should heed the words of a former Maryland governor: "We are all having to learn new rules for the new economy. Under the old rules, states attracted businesses based on tax structures or incentive packages. But the high-tech companies that are the driving engines in this new economy can locate anywhere. They are motivated by the quality of the work force and the quality of life that is offered."[43] Initial research findings suggest that grants and loans in support of technology development can increase an area's share of high-technology employment.[44] Other fourth-wave approaches such as increased local-global links and investment in human capital have been shown to contribute to state economic growth.[45]

DOES GOVERNMENT SPEND TOO MUCH?

Some observers claim that government gives away too much in its pursuit of economic health. This concern develops out of the fundamental relationship between a federal system of government and a capitalistic economic system. Governmental jurisdictions cover specific territories, but capital is mobile, so business firms can move from one location to another. Because these firms are so important to a local economy, governments offer incentives to influence their location decisions. As noted, the impact of these incentives on firms' decisions is not clear, but most jurisdictions believe that they cannot afford *not* to offer them. Concern is increasing, however, that competition among jurisdictions to attract business may be counterproductive and too costly to government. As a consequence, citizens are beginning to look more closely at the **incentive packages**—tax breaks, low interest loans, and infrastructure development—that their governments offer to business.

Examples of government concessions to the automobile industry abound—the Toyota truck facility in Texas, the Kia plant in Georgia, the Hyundai facility in Alabama. The fundamental question is, how extensive should incentives be? The answer typically involves calculation of the return on the state's investment. In the late 1980s, Kentucky put together one of the first big automotive deals when it attracted a new Toyota assembly plant to the community of Georgetown. Twenty-five years later, the investment seems to have paid off—the facility employs 6,300 full-time workers and is credited with spurring the creation of an additional 25,000 jobs in the Bluegrass State.[46]

Jurisdictions compete for major investments such as automobile manufacturing facilities, and that competition has the effect of ratcheting up the value of incentive packages. When German automaker Mercedes-Benz announced that it was seeking a location for its first U.S. facility, more than thirty-five states expressed interest. Five states—Alabama, Iowa, Nebraska, North Carolina, and South Carolina—survived the winnowing process. Each state tried to outdo the others by offering generous packages of tax breaks and low-cost land. In the end, Mercedes selected Vance, Alabama, as the site of the $300 million facility. But the price that Alabama paid was a dear one. The state provided $92.2 million in land and facility construction costs, $77.5 million in infrastructure development, $60 million in training, and a twenty-five–year tax abatement. Estimates put the state costs at approximately $179,000 per job. The extravagant bidding for the Mercedes plant raised some eyebrows; but in the words of one Alabama economist, "The symbolism [of winning the Mercedes facility] may be as important as the direct economic impact."[47]

Concern about government overspending lingers, and it extends beyond the automobile industry. For instance, Wisconsin found that its efforts to attract the film industry bore fruit, but at a high price. An analysis of one big-budget film showed that two-thirds of the money filmmakers spent went out of state; moreover, Wisconsin's incentives package meant that the state refunded 90 percent of what filmmakers spent in the state.[48] The It's Your Turn box takes up the issue of incentives for the film industry.

incentive packages

The enticements that state and local governments offer to retain or attract business and industry.

It's Your Turn

Should a State Government Provide Tax Incentives to the Film Industry to Make Movies There?

In 2000, four states offered tax incentives to the film industry; by 2010, that number had risen to 43 states. But now states are rethinking their generosity and wondering whether it is worthwhile. What do you think: Should states offer tax incentives to moviemakers?

PROS	CONS
Movies can be made anywhere; a state has to offer incentives to attract the industry, especially if other states are doing so.	Offering tax breaks to one industry has the effect of increasing the tax burden on other industries.
Subsidies to moviemakers may be costly, but there are substantial indirect economic benefits to the state from being the site for a film.	It's a competition in which states try to emulate and outdo one another. It becomes an escalating "arms race" of incentives that is ultimately inefficient.
Serving as the setting for a major film can generate a positive buzz about a state in the media. In other words, it is another way to advertise the state to a wide audience.	Film production does not create permanent jobs and many of the temporary jobs go to out-of-state workers.

A recent study by the Pew Center on the States found that only one-quarter of states have undertaken comprehensive reviews to assess the economic impact of their incentive programs.[49] To gauge whether economic development subsidies are working as anticipated, states are encouraged to:

- Build evaluation of incentives into policy and budget debates,
- Develop a schedule to review incentives,
- Use solid data and analysis to measure the economic impact of incentives, and
- Clarify the goals of incentives, then evaluate incentives against those goals.[50]

Figure 14.3 displays the states that are leading the way in these evaluations, those that are lagging, and those that are somewhere in between. One example of a leading state is Oregon, where a new law sets expiration dates for most tax credits for economic development. This means that the legislature will reexamine each subsidy to determine if it is performing as expected, and if not, abolish or redesign it.

Clearly, as state governments continue to offer these packages, many are becoming more savvy about the potential risks. Concern that a government-supported development project might turn sour has led to the imposition of **clawbacks**. Clawbacks require a subsidized firm that fails to deliver on its

clawbacks

Requirements that subsidized firms repay some or all of the subsidy if they fail to deliver on their promises.

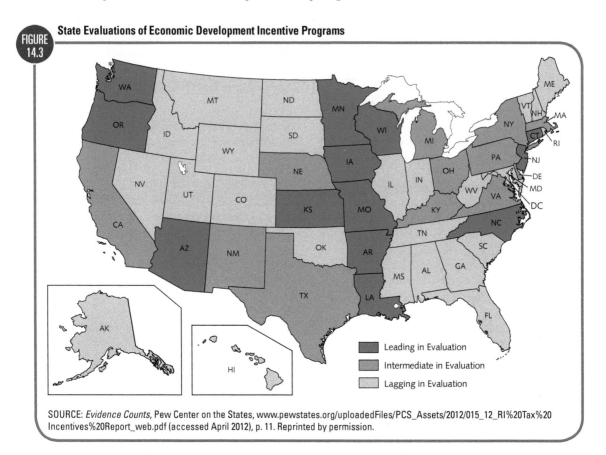

FIGURE 14.3

State Evaluations of Economic Development Incentive Programs

Leading in Evaluation
Intermediate in Evaluation
Lagging in Evaluation

SOURCE: *Evidence Counts*, Pew Center on the States, www.pewstates.org/uploadedFiles/PCS_Assets/2012/015_12_RI%20Tax%20 Incentives%20Report_web.pdf (accessed April 2012), p. 11. Reprinted by permission.

promises (regarding number of jobs, say, or amount of investment) to repay some or all of its subsidy. In this way, generous states and localities are not left holding the bag. Consider the case of United Airlines and its new maintenance facility in Indianapolis. To attract United to Indiana, the state offered the company a deal that contained $300 million in assorted tax breaks but with several clawback provisions. When it failed to create the number of jobs the agreement called for, United Airlines had to return more than $30 million to the Hoosier State.[51]

DOES GOVERNMENT SPEND FAIRLY?

Traditionally, government involvement in economic development has taken the form of efforts to reduce costs to business. According to economic development professionals, the central business district, local developers, the local labor force, and existing business firms derive the greatest benefit from city-sponsored economic development activity.[52] As citizens began to ask *who* benefits, however, some state governments refocused their efforts toward direct investments in human resources. Based on research on minority entrepreneurs, this approach should pay dividends: investment in human capital and access to financial resources can lead to the creation of new firms.[53]

Local governments have been especially active in expanding the concept of economic development beyond a narrow concern with business investment. Led by the pioneering efforts of San Francisco and Boston, some U.S. cities are tying economic development initiatives to the achievement of social objectives, an approach called **linkaging**. For instance, local governments have linked large-scale commercial development (office and retail buildings and hotels) to concerns such as housing and employment. This movement grew out of frustration over the disappearance of older low-income neighborhoods from revitalized, commercially oriented downtown areas.[54] The upscaling of formerly low-income neighborhoods—a process known as gentrification—displaces existing residents. With linkaging, developers are required to provide low- or moderate-income housing or employment to targeted groups or to contribute funding to programs that support these objectives. In return for the opportunity to enter a lucrative local market, a developer pays a price. This process has been called "the cities' attempt to share the profits of their prospering sectors with their poor."[55]

Linkaging works best in cities with booming economies. But even in cities with more stable economies, local government can negotiate with developers for social concessions. In Richmond, Virginia, for example, city officials convinced developers to provide substantial minority participation in a major retail project in the downtown area. In return for city approval of a massive redevelopment project in Jersey City, New Jersey, developers agreed to reserve a certain percentage of dwelling units for low- and moderate-income individuals.

Twenty-nine states and the District of Columbia have taken a different direction in addressing the fairness issue: They have adopted legislation that increases the minimum wage paid to hourly workers in their jurisdictions beyond the level set by the federal government. As of 2015, the hourly minimum wage in Washington was $9.47; in Oregon, it was $9.25; and in Connecticut and Vermont, it was $9.15. (The federal minimum wage was $7.25 an hour.) Some cities with relatively high costs of living, such as San Francisco, have raised the wage in their communities even higher ($12.25 as of 2015, increasing to $15.00 in 2018). Other cities have followed suit, Seattle and Los Angeles among them, with cities such as New York and Washington, D.C. poised to do the same. Although these actions are popular with workers, owners of small businesses such as restaurants are decidedly less enthusiastic. But supporters contend that without such increases, many people cannot afford to live in the city.

The Implications of Economic Development Policy

A healthy economy is central to the functioning of government. State and local officials know this and act accordingly. The slogan for Rhode Island's economic development campaign several years ago sums up the attitude: "Every state says they'll move mountains to get your business. We're moving rivers."[56] The ad did not exaggerate: Rhode Island redirected two rivers as part of a $200 million redevelopment project in its capital city of Providence.

linkaging

A method by which local governments use large-scale commercial development projects to accomplish social objectives.

Yet when an observer steps back and ponders such strategies and deals, a degree of skepticism is inevitable. Could New York City have better spent the millions it committed to Chase Manhattan Bank to keep the financial institution from moving 4,600 office workers to New Jersey? The deal involved $235 million worth of tax abatements, discounted utilities, site improvements, and job-training tax credits over the next 20 years.[57] And which state really won when a division of Eastman Kodak turned down Maryland's $4.5 million package of subsidized land, tax breaks, and employee training in favor of Pennsylvania's $14 million deal? Some might conclude that corporations are staging raids on public treasuries. But many state and local government officials would argue that concessions for business serve an important function by creating jobs and generating economic activity, thus improving the local tax base, which in turn funds public services. Maybe the third and fourth waves of economic development will be characterized by more creative and productive efforts at achieving this outcome.

Local economies are evaluated, compared, and ranked on the basis of numerous indicators. Most common among the indicators are quality of life, the number of start-up businesses, the growth in population, and the level of employment. Table 14.2 compares the ten large metropolitan areas that in 2014 were considered by many to be the most favorable places for small businesses.[58] Of interest is the variation in both the average unemployment rate and the change in housing prices across the ten areas.

As one might expect, states and localities scoring high on these rankings place far more value on them than their low-scoring counterparts do—at least

TABLE 14.2   Top 10 U.S. Metropolitan Areas for Small Businesses 2014

CITY	AVERAGE 2014 UNEMPLOYMENT	5-YEAR CHANGE IN HOUSING PRICES, 2010–2014
Austin, TX	4.2%	27.4%
Miami-Fort Lauderdale, FL	6.3%	21.9%
Provo, UT	3.5%	12.3%
San Jose, CA	5.3%	37.3%
Houston, TX	4.9%	23.2%
Bradenton-Sarasota, FL	5.8%	16.5%
Oklahoma City, OK	4.0%	10.2%
Orlando, FL	5.9%	5.8%
Denver, CO	4.8%	24.7%
Raleigh, NC	4.9%	4.4%

SOURCES: G. Scott Thomas, "Best (and Worst) Metro Areas for Small Business: Exclusive Rankings," http://www.bizjournals.com/bizjournals/on-numbers/scott-thomas/2014/04/best-and-worst-metro-areas-for-small-business.html#g3; Bureau of Labor Statistics, "Unemployment Rates for Metropolitan Areas," http://www.bls.gov/lau/lamtrk14.htm; Federal Housing Finance Agency http://www.fhfa.gov/AboutUs/ReportDocuments/2014Q4_HPI.pdf (accessed May 26, 2015).

publicly. But allowing for the inherent biases in the rankings, they certainly suggest that some communities are faring quite well in the economic development wars.

Critics claim that competition for economic development is nothing more than the relocation of a given amount of economic activity from one community to another, with no overall increase in national productivity. Mercedes-Benz was going to open a U.S. manufacturing facility anyway; the question was simply, where? By playing states against one another, Mercedes-Benz was able to exact a subsidy of unheard-of proportions from Alabama.[59] Many critics call for increased cooperation among jurisdictions in their quest for economic development. However, this objective has been elusive at both the state and local levels, and jurisdictions continue to use financial carrots to gain an edge in the competition. A case in point: the new headquarters for the Boeing Company. Three areas—Denver, Dallas-Ft. Worth, and Chicago—were in the running for the facility. Denver and Dallas-Ft. Worth developed cooperative regional efforts to try to land Boeing; Chicago did not, but offered an incentive package worth up to $51 million.[60] Which jurisdiction did Boeing select? Chicago.

Thus far, the courts have not been receptive to legal challenges seeking to outlaw the use of corporate tax incentives. The U.S. Supreme Court rejected the arguments of a group of Ohio taxpayers who sought to undo a $281 million package of tax breaks given to Daimler Chrysler for a Jeep plant in Toledo.[61] Even when jurisdictions agree not to raid companies from each other, the agreements can unravel. Within months after signing a cooperative no-poaching pact, Miami-Dade, Broward, and Palm Beach counties in south Florida reverted to their old competitive behaviors.[62] Economic development continues to be a singular proposition, with each jurisdiction pursuing its own destiny.

Chapter Recap

- The economic performance of the states varies. Even in an individual state, its economic health changes over time. The same is true for localities: Their economies are dynamic.

- Economic development has had four waves of different approaches or strategies. The first wave was characterized by smokestack chasing. The latest, or fourth, wave emphasizes globalization and human capital. Even now, states continue to use approaches from the earlier waves.

- The relationship between state government and the private sector can be complicated. Some states have begun to use public-private hybrid organizations in economic development functions.

- States have offered huge incentives to attract automobile manufacturers. But with trends showing a decline in manufacturing as a proportion of the job base, the emphasis is shifting toward research and technology. Many states have begun to invest in bioscience research.

- States have taken on many different economic development initiatives, including strategic planning, travel and tourism, the arts, sports, and international trade.

- Three major questions continue to surface with regard to government involvement in the economy: Do state and local government efforts make much difference? Does government spend too much to attract and grow new business and to retain old business? Does government spend fairly; that is, does reducing costs for business come at a cost to other groups?

- Many organizations rank states and localities on aspects of economic development. In evaluating these rankings, it is important to consider the criteria used in their compilation.

- Economic development is a competitive activity, pitting one jurisdiction against others. Efforts are underway to foster more cooperative behavior among jurisdictions.

KEY TERMS

economic development *(p. 366)*
subsidy *(p. 369)*
venture capital pools *(p. 369)*
small-business incubators
(p. 369)

enterprise zone *(p. 369)*
clusters *(p. 369)*
new economy *(p. 370)*
strategic planning *(p. 373)*
accommodations tax *(p. 375)*

amenities *(p. 376)*
eminent domain *(p. 377)*
incentive packages *(p. 382)*
clawbacks *(p. 383)*
linkaging *(p. 385)*

INTERNET RESOURCES

Two economic development organizations, one with a national focus, the other with an international emphasis, maintain useful websites. These are the Corporation for Enterprise Development (CFED) at **www.cfed.org** and the International Economic Development Council at **www.iedconline.org**.

All states have a web presence in economic development, typically through a state agency. The comprehensive website of the Arizona Commerce Authority can be found at **www.azcommerce.com**.

Explore a more targeted approach to economic development at **commerce.idaho.gov**, which is a part of Idaho's Department of Commerce website.

Other examples of states with less traditional economic development websites are the state of Kentucky's new economy website at **http://kyinnovation.com** and Enterprise Florida at **www.enterpriseflorida**.

A statewide organization devoted to local economic development is the California Association for Local Economic Development, **www.caled.org**.

www.nycedc.com is the website for the New York City Economic Development Corporation.

For economic development from a private sector perspective, check out the website of *Site Selection* magazine at **www.siteselection.com**. It tracks new business activity around the nation.

Enthusiastic students in a public school. Fuses /Getty Images

Education Policy: Reading, Writing, and Reform

Can you interpret a bus schedule? Follow a map? Balance a checkbook? Fill out a job application? Were you able to follow the last chapter? If not, you are functionally illiterate, like one in four of your fellow adult Americans. Convincing evidence reports that too many students cannot read, write, and do math at grade level. And a substantial proportion of U.S. teenagers are shockingly ignorant of history and government. This is not breaking news. In a much-cited 1983 report *A Nation at Risk*, the National Commission on Excellence in Education lamented the erosion of the educational foundations of society "by a rising tide of mediocrity that threatens our very future."[1]

Disturbing studies document the persistent underperformance of U.S. students in comparison with students in other developed countries. Despite much higher per-pupil spending on schools, scores in mathematics, science, and reading earned by U.S. 15-year-olds—even those from well-to-do and educated families—consistently rank poorly, behind such countries as Poland, China, and Vietnam.[2] U.S. firms corroborate these concerns with stories about their frustration in finding new employees who can read, write, and perform basic math functions. But the other

389

side of the coin is that many public school systems are doing an outstanding job of preparing youngsters for college and the work world, especially those in middle-class and upper-middle-class communities where funding is adequate and education is considered important. An important portion of the perceived crisis in public education is a product of demographics—poverty, homelessness, culture, dysfunctional or unsupportive families, and poor health and nutrition. The majority of our public school students come from low-income families, and most of them begin first grade already behind their more privileged peers.[3] These societal problems are factors that cannot be corrected by teachers or principals.

In the opinion of many Americans, education is the most important function performed by state and local governments. The facts support this point of view. Education consumes more of state and local budgets than any other service. More than $850 billion is spent on public elementary and secondary schooling by the states and localities. That translates to around $11,735 per pupil.[4] The importance of education is also demonstrated by the sheer number of people involved in it as students, parents, teachers, administrators, and staff. Citizens have high expectations for their schools, assuming that they will teach everything from the basics to good citizenship. To a great extent, the future of this country and its economy is linked to the quality of public education.

But which level of government is—or should be—responsible for ensuring that American children receive a public education commensurate with this nation's economic and military power? Governmental role confusion prevails. Once overwhelmingly a local government responsibility, public education has evolved into a shared responsibility of the national, state, and local governments. Business and nonprofit organizations are increasingly engaged as well. This chapter maps the education landscape along with its dead ends, pitfalls, and promising paths.

Is There a Crisis in Education?

LO 15.1

To understand the perceived crisis in education.

Education policy is controversial and frequently proclaimed to be in crisis. Policy makers, parents, teachers, and others have long debated how schools should be organized and financed, and what should be taught. If there is an education crisis, it is a perennial and permanent condition. There are, however, significant shortcomings of our current education efforts and outcomes, and the public is intensely aware of them. Despite billions of dollars in federal, state, and local government spending, along with a spate of institutional and classroom reforms, these shortcomings are not easily resolved.

One seemingly straightforward sign of problems in the quality of schooling makes headlines in newspapers throughout the country each year: student performance on standardized college entrance exams. Scholastic Aptitude

Average SAT Verbal and Mathematics Scores, 1963–2014

Average SAT verbal and math scores began a prolonged period of decline in the early 1960s but turned upward in 1982. The current trend is moderately to the downside.

FIGURE 15.1

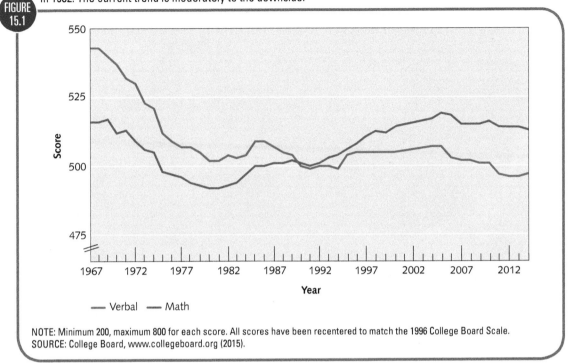

NOTE: Minimum 200, maximum 800 for each score. All scores have been recentered to match the 1996 College Board Scale.
SOURCE: College Board, www.collegeboard.org (2015).

Test (SAT) and American College Test (ACT) scores on verbal and math sections dropped almost annually from 1963 to 1982, to levels below those existing at the time of the last declared crisis in education (see Figure 15.1). Following a brief rally during the mid-1980s, scores again began eroding slowly, but then stabilized. The recent scores for both SAT and ACT tests have been basically holding steady.

Striking differences in SAT scores among the states reflect population characteristics such as race and ethnicity, immigration, poverty levels, and urban-suburban-rural population. But the greatest variation is accounted for by the percentage of high school students taking the SAT. Generally, the higher the percentage of high-schoolers who take the test is, the lower the state scores will be. A more comprehensive assessment of the quality of education in the states is found in Figure 15.2, which grades them using composite scores calculated from three different measures not related to the SAT.

Is the U.S. education system failing? Or is perception more pessimistic than reality? Public opinion surveys reveal that Americans are mostly satisfied with their own public schools but generally critical of everyone else's. The media bombardment about failing public schools notwithstanding, many school systems are academically strong and most others have shown recent improvements. State scores on the National Assessment of Educational Progress (NAEP), given to fourth, eighth, and twelfth-graders, have also shown

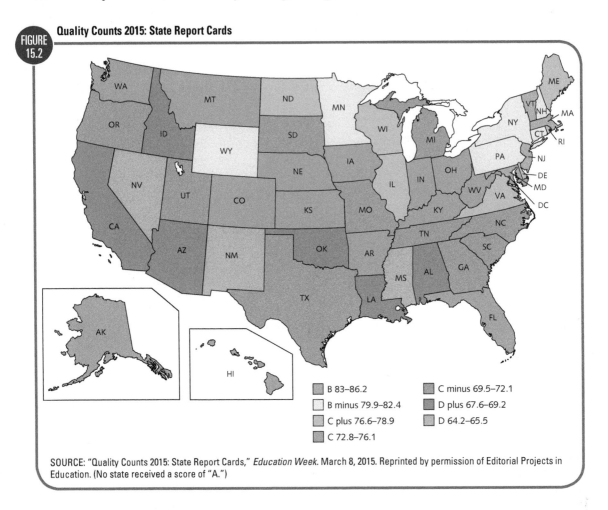

FIGURE 15.2

Quality Counts 2015: State Report Cards

Legend:
- B 83–86.2
- B minus 79.9–82.4
- C plus 76.6–78.9
- C 72.8–76.1
- C minus 69.5–72.1
- D plus 67.6–69.2
- D 64.2–65.5

SOURCE: "Quality Counts 2015: State Report Cards," *Education Week*. March 8, 2015. Reprinted by permission of Editorial Projects in Education. (No state received a score of "A.")

gains since 1992 in reading and math, but little or no improvement in the scores of twelfth-grade students.[5] Dropout rates dropped to a record low in 2014, as students are staying in school longer. But few would dispute that the U.S. education system suffers serious problems and needs improvement. The most widely recognized policy problems can be reduced to four major variables: standards, students, teachers, and the education bureaucracy.

STANDARDS

Schools have suffered from a malady that might be called *curriculum drift*. Courses designed to teach basic reading comprehension, writing, and mathematics are sometimes de-emphasized as nonessential topics become popular. State legislatures and school boards have mandated courses and topics on slavery, the Holocaust, genocide, "green literacy," gay and lesbian contributions (California), climate change denial (Texas, Louisiana), and the Irish potato famine—worthy topics, perhaps, but no substitute for the basics. To many critics, education sometimes seems to neglect instruction in basic skills and the ability to think analytically. Business, military, and university leaders complain about having to invest millions of dollars in remedial education before ill-prepared high school graduates are ready to work, serve in the armed forces, or succeed in college. They further lament the prevalence of social promotions and a basic ignorance of history, culture, and government. Many students graduate from high school prepared for neither college nor the job market. The argument that the native intelligence of U.S. youth has declined has no basis, so considerable blame has been placed on weak and vacillating educational standards for curricula and courses.

STUDENTS

Students themselves have not escaped criticism. Some choose to soften their curriculum with easy nonacademic courses rather than English, math, science, social studies, and foreign languages. Today's students are said to be poorly motivated and lazy in comparison with their predecessors. They are faulted for seeking instant gratification through television, video games, the Internet, drugs, alcohol, and sex instead of seriously applying themselves to coursework. In a typical year and depending on the school, anywhere from 1 to 40 percent of students give up high school altogether by dropping out. The national high school dropout rate was 7 percent in 2014. Hispanic (14 percent) and African American (8 percent) rates have been declining, while white (5 percent) and Asian (4 percent) rates remain stable.[6]

Clearly, however, the legal and moral responsibility for providing direction to a young person's life rests with his or her parents; school readiness starts at home. This responsibility includes encouraging the child to complete homework assignments and regulating extracurricular activities, television, video game, cell phone, and Internet access. Researchers have found that U.S. children start the first grade with fewer academic skills than their Asian counterparts, whose parents give them a head start by regularly working with them at home before they enter school. Coaching after school helps children in several Asian countries maintain their early advantage. But U.S. parents tend to abdicate to the schools the responsibility for educating their children. Often parents have little choice; as a result of the high percentage of single-parent and two-worker households, many parents have little time, and less energy, to spend helping their children. The shortage and expense of professional day care and after-school learning opportunities compound the problem.

TEACHERS

Teachers are the linchpins between students and the learning process and the single most important factor in student success. Effective teaching can bestow lifelong learning skills, whereas poor teaching can result in academic indifference among good students and dropping out for marginal students. One problem with teaching is that, for many years, the quality of individuals who choose to enter the teaching profession has declined. The gradual decline in the quality of teachers is partly due to changes in the nature of the workforce and the elevated expectations and demands placed on teachers. (However,

FIGURE 15.3   Thou Shalt Not

THOU SHALT NOT

1922 Contract, Salisbury, N.C.

Miss _____ agrees:

1. Not to get married. This contract becomes null and void immediately if the teacher marries.
2. Not to have company with men.
3. To be at home between the hours of 8:00 pm and 6:00 am unless in attendance at a school function.
4. Not to loiter downtown in ice cream stores.
5. Not to leave town at any time without the permission of the Chairman of the Trustees.
6. Not to smoke cigarettes. This contract becomes null and void immediately if the teacher is found smoking.
7. Not to drink beer, wine, or whiskey. This contract becomes null and void immediately if the teacher is found drinking beer, wine, or whiskey.
8. Not to ride in a carriage or automobile with any man except her brother or father.
9. Not to dress in bright colors.
10. Not to dye her hair.
11. To wear at least two petticoats.
12. Not to wear dresses more than two inches above the ankles.
13. To keep the classroom clean:
    (a) to sweep the classroom floor at least once daily.
    (b) to scrub the classroom floor at least once weekly with soap and hot water.
    (c) to clean the blackboard at least once daily.
    (d) to start the fire at 7:00 am so that the room will be warm at 8:00 am when the children arrive.
14. Not to wear face powder, mascara, or to paint the lips.

From "North Carolina Women: Making History" by Margaret Supplee Smith and Emily Herring Wilson.

behavioral expectations have certainly changed for the better, as shown by the socially repressive teacher contract from 1922 reproduced in Figure 15.3.)

Many top-notch young men and women enter the noble profession of teaching. But academically gifted women who once would have chosen the teaching profession are now more likely to seek out higher-paying, more prestigious positions in government; the legal, medical, and other professions; and the private sector. In their place, less able college graduates elect to become teachers, resulting in a severe shortage of qualified teachers in some states. In 2014, verbal and math SAT scores for education majors averaged 964 versus 1,010 for other subject majors.[7] Also reflecting the drop in quality of the teaching labor pool is that many of those hired to teach each year lack the proper qualifications and preparation for the courses they teach.

Part of the blame must also be placed on universities, whose teacher programs continue to emphasize educational methodology courses, which teach prospective instructors how to teach rather than giving them substantive knowledge of their subject matter. Another reason it has been difficult to find good teachers is that, in some states, teaching remains a low-wage occupation, with the starting salary comparing unfavorably with starting salaries in other professional fields.

In an effort to help improve pay and working conditions, most teachers join unions such as the American Federation of Teachers (AFT) and the National Education Association (NEA). According to some critics, these unions have become part of the problem with public education because they further teachers' narrow self-interest and protect incompetents from being fired. (See the Controversies in States and Localities feature.)

Meanwhile, many of those who do become teachers quickly exit the profession. About 15 percent of all teachers call it quits each year. Teacher drop-out rates are particularly high at high-poverty schools, making the teacher dropout rate exceed that of students![8] Many discouraged teachers feel that they are not valued or respected by students, the public, and state legislators, and even scorned by some of them. Excessive testing inhibits their ability to teach—other than to tests. Seemingly endless busy-work, including detailed lesson plans and reports, suck up teaching time. The frustrations of teaching also come from lack of parental interest and support, and students' absence of discipline and use of drugs. Noisy, disruptive behavior by a handful of students spoils the learning environment for all. Teachers are assaulted in the classroom, and violent crimes occur on or near school grounds. Empty gestures by elected officials such as mandating posting of the Ten Commandments (Jackson County, Kentucky) on classroom walls, requiring uniforms (Memphis, New York City), or requiring students to address teachers as *ma'am* and *sir* (Louisiana) do not help. Teacher stress is augmented, especially in poor schools, by crumbling buildings, chronic supply and equipment shortages, overcrowded classrooms, crushing paperwork burdens, and the threat of being fired or laid off.Further, problems with the supply of teachers are being worsened by the retirement of baby boomers. Because of this demographic fact and the dissatisfactions noted above, severe shortages of qualified teachers have developed, especially in the fields of mathematics, science, foreign languages, and special education. Shortages are most severe in the Sunbelt, where student populations are growing. Acute teacher shortfalls force too many school districts to hire unqualified, ill-prepared people simply to put a warm adult body in the classroom.

THE EDUCATION BUREAUCRACY

Bureaucracy is publicly vilified everywhere, and the schools are no exception. A strong case can be made that the United States has too many school administrators, rules, reports, and restrictions and too few teachers. The ratio is as high as one nonteaching employee for every eight teachers in some districts. Critics say that school districts and their bureaucracies act like classic monopolies. They are guaranteed customers (students) and income (tax revenues), yet they face little or no competition because parents have limited choice about where to send their children to school. The results of these monopolistic school bureaucracies allegedly include a lack of accountability to parents and the community (and ultimately to students and teachers), unnecessary rules and red tape, inefficient use of human resources, and time constraints and odious mounds of paperwork for teachers. Like most bureaucracies, those in the education establishment are reactive and resistant to innovation and change and therefore viewed as recalcitrant enemies of reform.

Research is inconclusive on the bureaucracy issue. Some research finds that large, centralized bureaucracies with restrictive rules and red tape tend to reduce school effectiveness.[9] Findings of other scholars show no significant effects of bureaucracy and that school bureaucracies tend to grow larger when schools perform poorly because administrators take actions to improve performance. In other words, bureaucracy does not harm school performance; rather, it is a rational response intended to arrest decline and boost performance by developing and putting into place new policies, programs, and oversight.[10]

Before reviewing the responses of the national, state, and local governments to these critical problems in public education, we will look at how the complex intergovernmental relationships in education have evolved.

Intergovernmental Roles in Education

LO 15.2

To be able to explain intergovernmental roles in education.

The responsibility for establishing, supporting, and overseeing public schools is reserved to the states under the Tenth Amendment and expressly provided for in the state constitutions. Day-to-day operating authority is delegated to local governments by all states except Hawaii, which has a unitary, state-run system, and Oregon, which centralizes control over the public school system in the governor's office. A large majority of U.S. primary and secondary school systems are operated by independent school districts, but cities, counties, towns, or townships run the schools in some states. Although local control is the tradition, the states are the dominant policy makers, deciding important issues such as the duration of the school year, curriculum requirements, textbook selection, teacher certification and compensation, minimum graduation requirements, and pupil-teacher ratios. But the national government's role in education has become more prominent in recent years, heavily influencing what states and local school districts decide to do or not to do. The selection and dismissal of teachers, certain budget decisions, and management and operating details are typically carried out locally.

State involvement has also intensified, largely because of recognized inequalities among schools and school districts, the accountability demands of federal education policy, and forceful actions by governors and legislatures to address the perceived education crisis. Centralization of state authority in education policy is greatest in the South, where poverty and race relations have called for high levels of state intervention. Conversely, the tradition of local education autonomy is strongest in New England. But in the final analysis, it is difficult to identify a single important school policy issue today that is not subject to state or federal, rather than local, determination.

Another reason more state and federal involvement in the public schools has occurred is because of financial difficulties and the fact that some citizens and policy makers have lost confidence in the schools' ability to provide a quality education. In several instances, local school systems have essentially lost their independence as the states and some municipalities have assumed full operational responsibilities—an especially likely outcome when the local school districts are unable to respond adequately to political and financial pressures. States and some cities have imposed the ultimate sanction on failing schools by shutting them down entirely. Chicago recently closed 50 schools; Michigan Governor Rick Snyder placed 34 failing Detroit schools into a statewide district under state control.

THE NATIONAL GOVERNMENT PRESENCE IN EDUCATION

The federal government traditionally played a minimal role in primary and secondary education, especially when compared with the governments of most other countries, where public education is treated as a national responsibility. The first grant of money for education came only in 1917, when the Smith-Hughes Act financed vocational education in secondary schools. Much later, the National Defense Education Act provided funds to improve math, science, and foreign-language education.

The national role was substantially enlarged during the 1960s and 1970s, primarily through the Elementary and Secondary Education Act (ESEA) of 1965. The ESEA established a direct national subsidy for education, providing funds to almost every school district in the United States. Amounts were allocated for library acquisitions, audiovisual materials, teachers' aides, and compensatory programs for children of poor families and for the mentally and physically handicapped. Parochial (religious) schools also benefit from ESEA funding, although no funds are provided for religious materials, courses, or teacher salaries. With each reauthorization of ESEA, Congress has taken the opportunity to pile on all manner of mandates about how the money must be spent.

During the 1960s and 1970s, the federal government exercised targeted policy leadership in education. The Head Start program helped prepare poor children for school and provided many of them with their first medical, dental, and nutritional care. Matching grants encouraged states and localities to experiment with other programs, and research findings, statistics, and new policy information were disseminated by the National Institute of Education and the National Center for Education Statistics. The national commitment to public schools received an important symbolic boost in 1979 with the creation of the U.S. Department of Education.

These new commitments brought the national share of total school expenditures from 4.4 percent in 1960 to 9 percent in 1980. The federal government's proportion of education expenditures today is about 10 percent. Head Start—demonstrated to be successful in several evaluations—was reauthorized and expanded to Early Head Start: all-day, all-year programs for low-income, at-risk infants and toddlers. The Community and National Service Act established scholarships and tuition reimbursements for community service. New federal monies were also provided for school modernization and construction, to improve technological literacy of teachers and students, and to promote charter schools.

The most recent reauthorization of ESEA in 2002, No Child Left Behind, insinuated the federal government in the schools debate as the "national schoolmarm, hovering over state school reform efforts and whacking those states that fail to record satisfactory and timely progress toward federal education goals with financial penalties and mandatory corrective actions."[11] NCLB was viewed as particularly onerous in its testing and performance mandates. The law significantly increased federal financial support for the schools, but it also required substantial new state and local education spending.

The $12 billion No Child Left Behind law promised to transform public education, but saddled the states and their schools with significant new (and mostly unfunded) mandates, including mandatory and frequent testing and a stipulation that failing schools not making sufficient progress in any one of numerous student demographic categories would have to restructure, offer students a transfer or private tuition, or even close down entirely.

The broad goals of NCLB were admirable and widely accepted: No child would be neglected and left behind in school, and all would have an equal chance to succeed. But the devil was in the details of implementation. Teachers, principals, chief state school officers (CSSOs), governors, and state legislators soon howled like scalded hounds as they became aware of their predicament. The costs of annual testing amounted to millions of dollars more than what Congress provided. Established, and demonstrably effective, state standards and testing programs were threatened with replacement by cumbersome federal mandates. Local control of public education appeared to be the victim of a "regime change" replete with federal mandates and regulations.

Implementation of NCLB did not go smoothly as intergovernmental conflict immediately erupted. Michigan, Texas, Vermont, and the NEA filed suit against the federal government on the grounds that NCLB illegally imposed unfunded mandates on the states. Other states also litigated or threatened to refuse to comply with NCLB. Gradually, accommodations to state and local concerns were made by the U.S. Department of Education through waivers of certain requirements.

The state and school district issues with NCLB are many. To take one example, when schools and districts fail to meet their goals for a certain period of time, the U.S. Department of Education can declare them "failed," leading to closure or a state takeover. In 2012, an estimated 49 percent of the nation's schools had been officially declared to be "failing, though very few were shut down and most escaped the "failing" category the next year through federal waivers of accountability requirements."[12] NCLB has been up for reauthorization by Congress since 2007, but state and local objections and partisan gridlock pushed Congress into a deadlock that persists. To relieve pressure on the states while Congress dithered, the Obama administration approved waiver requests from forty-four states to relieve them of some of NCLB's most vexing requirements. A 2009 federal initiative designed to help states cope with the ravages of the Great Recession, labeled Race to the Top, required states to compete for competitive, discretionary grants, with priority given to those that adopted federal standards-based priorities. The stakes were high: More than $4 billion was divvied out to winning (and compliant) states.

Without question, the requirements of NCLB have caused an education regime change and interjected a loud federal voice in the education debate.

No matter how strenuously state and local school districts may object, the federal role in public education is now substantial. For the foreseeable future, federal education assistance will flow based on demonstrated improvements in teacher quality, academic standards, and performance, with testing as the principal means of data collection.

The Political and Financial Pressures on Public Schools Political pressures constantly roil the waters of public education as teacher organizations, nonprofit foundations, minority groups, business, conservative and religious organizations, and parents make new demands on their schools. Teachers and their unions want more control over what goes on in the classroom. Minority groups are concerned with inequities and poor performance of heavily minority schools. Bilingual education is an issue in states with large Hispanic or other non-English–language populations. And religious groups fight to keep prayer, abstinence education, antidrug programs such as DARE, and "intelligent design" in the classroom and Charles Darwin, "safe sex," and secular values out. If local school boards wilt under the crescendo of demands, then parties interested in education policy take their demands to higher political levels—the governor, the state legislature, the courts, and the state board of education, none of which may be in agreement on what to do about any given issue. In this way, school politics, once the province of local school boards and professional educators, has evolved into highly contentious interest group politics.

Financial Pressures Increased financial pressure on the schools is a second factor producing education policy centralization. Historically, schools have been funded mostly through revenues derived from the property tax. A school district can assess taxes only on property within its local boundaries, so wealthy districts with much highly valued residential and/or commercial property can afford to finance public schools at generous levels, whereas poor districts (even though they often tax their property at much higher rates than wealthy districts) tend to raise fewer dollars because of their lower property values. The consequence of such financial inequities is that some children receive a more expensive, and probably higher-quality, education than other children do, even though the parents of the advantaged group of children may contribute fewer tax dollars. Predictably, it is the children of the poor and minorities who fare the worst.

The states' assumption of primary financial responsibility for public schools has important constitutional components. In the landmark case of *Serrano v. Priest* (1971), the California Supreme Court declared that inequalities in school-district spending resulting from variations in taxable wealth were unconstitutional. The court observed that local control is a "cruel illusion;" poor districts simply cannot achieve excellence in education because of a low tax base, no matter at how high a rate property is taxed.[13] Therefore, education must be considered a fundamental interest of the state; in other words, the state must ensure that expenditures on education are not determined primarily by the taxable wealth of the school district.

Following *Serrano*, lawsuits were filed in other states by plaintiffs who sought to have their own property tax-based systems declared unconstitutional.

One of these cases, *San Antonio Independent School District v. Rodriguez* (1973), made its way to the U.S. Supreme Court. A federal district court had found the Texas school finance system to be unconstitutional under the equal protection clause of the Fourteenth Amendment. However, the Supreme Court reversed the lower court, holding that education is not a fundamental right under the U.S. Constitution (in which it is not even mentioned).[14] The issue was thus placed exclusively in the constitutional domain of the states, in which plaintiffs would have to rely on their own constitutions—and courts—to prevent arbitrary circumstances from predetermining the quality of a child's education.

All but a handful of state supreme courts have heard cases on educational financing; litigation is ongoing in approximately half of the states. Some thirty states have determined that existing funding schemes were unconstitutional because they did not provide an adequate education for all children, or give them reasonable opportunity to attain state education goals, and have ordered equal funding for poor districts. Kansas, New York, Texas, California, and Washington are currently involved in such litigation.

All states have made efforts to equalize funding among school districts, usually by applying distribution formulas (the equalization formulas noted in Chapter 11) for state aid that take into account property values and property-tax effort in individual districts. Most increased state support has been targeted to districts with low property values through **foundation programs**, which ensure that all school districts receive a minimum level of funding per pupil. State education allocations also take into account the characteristics of students. For instance, a New Jersey formula distributes state aid based on enrollment, with additional funds designated for districts with high concentrations of students who are poor, have special needs, or have limited English-language abilities.[15] The tendency over time is for states to "level up" so that aid to poor districts does not come at the expense of more affluent districts.[16]

Figure 15.4 displays the intergovernmental revenue contributions for public schools over time. Note that the federal portion, averaging only about 9.0 percent since 1970, grew to more than 12 percent in 2012 before declining slightly.

A disturbing legacy of the Great Recession is that many school districts have been rapidly escalating the amount of fees imposed on students for particular courses, extracurricular activities such as sports, and even for riding the bus. The principle of a free public education is becoming an historical artifact of the twentieth century.

The Impact of Property-Tax Cuts

Additional impetus to the state assumption of school costs may be attributed to state legacies of the taxpayer revolt. Statutory and constitutional limitations on taxing were typically aimed at the unpopular property tax. If public schools were to avoid such draconian measures as closing their doors, the states had to increase their education contributions.

One state, Michigan, completely tossed away its property tax-based school-financing system. Prompted by numerous voter defeats of proposed property-tax increases to fund public schools, the Michigan legislature repealed all

foundation program

A means of state education funding that allocates a basic level of funding to all districts.

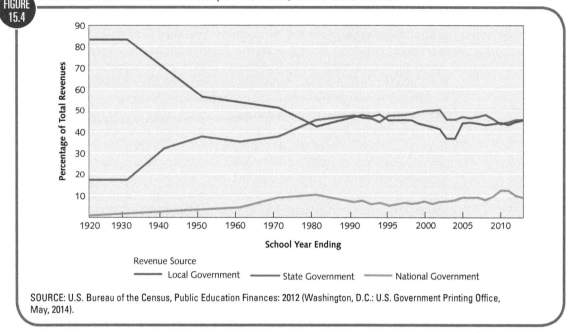

Trends in Revenue Sources for Public Elementary and Secondary Education
Elementary and secondary education receives the greatest portion of revenues from state and local government. The national contribution rose to 12.4 percent in 2011, but has since declined.

FIGURE 15.4

SOURCE: U.S. Bureau of the Census, Public Education Finances: 2012 (Washington, D.C.: U.S. Government Printing Office, May, 2014).

property taxes supporting the public schools. The legislature then gave voters a choice: increase the state sales tax from 4 to 6 percent and triple the cigarette tax, or raise the state income tax. In a statewide constitutional referendum, voters picked the first option.

An important principle of education policy today is that state political power and control follow financial responsibility (see Figure 15.4 again for the intergovernmental distribution of financial resources for education over time). A long tradition of local control of schools has been displaced in Michigan, Minnesota, New Mexico, Oregon, Vermont, and elsewhere because state and federal governments have become the prime education policy decision makers. Local school districts in some states have become weak administrative appendages of the states.

School Equity and Adequacy Although centralization of state control of education and efforts to equalize funding for poor districts have helped, inequities continue to exist. Anyone who compares a school in a wealthy suburb with one in a poor rural district or urban center cannot fail to be impressed by the differences in facilities and resources. Simply put, wealthy states can afford to allocate more money to schools than poor states can. This invidious geography of inequality is an advantage to those who live in a wealthy school district in a prosperous state.[17]

Common sense tells us that money surely contributes to the quality of schooling. Modern, well-designed buildings, up-to-date technology, the latest learning materials, low pupil-teacher ratios, and well-paid teachers should enhance student achievement, as should a rich offering of honors and advanced placement (AP) courses. But research has revealed an astonishing paradox: There is no consistent, significant statistical relationship between school spending and student performance.[18] Table 15.1 ranks the states on average expenditures per pupil, teacher salaries, high school graduation rates, and composite Quality Counts scores to illustrate the differential state monetary investments in public education as compared to two outcomes.

The first research to reach this conclusion was the so-called Coleman Report in 1966.[19] Sociologist James S. Coleman examined thousands of school situations and discovered that curricula, facilities, class size, expenditures, and other resource factors were not associated with achievement. He *did* find that the family and socioeconomic backgrounds of students influenced performance, with children of well-off, well-educated parents outperforming those brought up in less-advantageous surroundings, a finding supported in more recent research.[20] Also, black students performed better in predominantly white schools than in predominantly black schools—a finding that later served as the grounds for implementing busing to put an end to school segregation. Coleman's staggering conclusions were re-examined in an

TABLE 15.1   Average Teacher Salaries and Expenditures per Pupil, Graduation Rates, and Quality Counts Ranks 2014

STATE	EXPENDITURE RANK	TEACHER SALARY RANK	GRADUATION RATE RANK	QUALITY COUNTS RANK
Alabama	40	35	32	44
Alaska	4	6	34	26
Arizona	50	45	22	46
Arkansas	33	40	17	36
California	26	3	28	41
Colorado	21	28	31	21
Connecticut	6	4	10	6
Delaware	10	11	23	15
Florida	36	41	33	28
Georgia	35	22	35	31
Hawaii	17	19	19	23
Idaho	42	47	38	45
Illinois	14	12	39	17
Indiana	47	27	1	25
Iowa	27	25	4	24
Kansas	31	38	11	20
Kentucky	32	26	40	29

(*continued*)

TABLE 15.1	Average Teacher Salaries and Expenditures per Pupil, Graduation Rates, and Quality Counts Ranks 2014 (*Continued*)			
STATE	**EXPENDITURE RANK**	**TEACHER SALARY RANK**	**GRADUATION RATE RANK**	**QUALITY COUNTS RANK**
Louisiana	23	24	45	43
Maine	38	33	41	14
Maryland	13	7	42	3
Massachusetts	9	2	43	1
Michigan	12	10	44	32
Minnesota	16	16	26	10
Mississippi	45	49	30	50
Missouri	25	37	18	33
Montana	22	30	15	30
Nebraska	30	31	5	22
Nevada	43	17	37	49
New Hampshire	7	18	6	5
New Jersey	3	5	12	2
New Mexico	28	44	36	48
New York	2	1	27	9
North Carolina	46	42	24	34
North Dakota	41	39	7	16
Ohio	19	15	20	18
Oklahoma	48	48	46	47
Oregon	24	13	50	40
Pennsylvania	11	9	13	8
Rhode Island	5	8	47	13
South Carolina	34	34	49	42
South Dakota	37	50	14	39
Tennessee	40	36	8	37
Texas	44	32	9	38
Utah	49	43	48	35
Vermont	1	21	2	4
Virginia	20	29	16	12
Washington D.C.	29	23	29	19
West Virginia	15	44	25	27
Wisconsin	18	20	3	11
Wyoming	8	14	21	7

SOURCE: Compiled by the authors from various data sources.

extensive review of 120 studies; only eighteen found a statistically significant positive relationship between school expenditures and student performance. The overall conclusion is that no strong or systematic relationship exists between them.[21] However, the research consistently finds that minority students perform at lower levels than white students,[22] and the black-white, Hispanic-white performance gaps worsen with grade level.[23]

The Minority Achievement Gap The performance distance between minorities and whites is a stubborn and troubling issue. According to research in psychology, there is no quantifiable difference between black and white infants.[24] The gap, then, is caused by what happens later. The problem is complicated by the fact that the achievement gap for African Americans who are early high achievers grows faster across the grades than it does for initially low-performing children.[25] And overall, the minority achievement gap expands as all African American and Latino students move through the grade levels. These disparities are as resistant to a cure as the common cold. Desegregation of the schools has not been the answer, and a recent U.S. Supreme Court decision, along with persistent segregated housing patterns, dilutes school diversity efforts.[26] Money has not helped, either.[27] But some important research findings have been reported that could help narrow the achievement gap. For example, it appears that the achievement gap might widen because white children have more extensive summer learning opportunities than children of color.[28] Other intriguing findings are that some high-achieving African American students experience negative peer pressure for "acting white,"[29] and that white students have greater access to high-performing teachers.[30]

The Education Policy Actors

The proliferation of independent school districts in the latter part of the nineteenth century was accompanied by intensive politicization. School districts in big cities and rural areas alike were as inclined to hire teachers and principals on the basis of patronage as on the basis of professional competence. Reformers (mostly professional educators) struggled to remove partisan politics from the public schools by electing school boards on a nonpartisan, at-large basis and by giving the professionals the primary responsibility for running school systems. These efforts were successful, but a new type of politics arose as teachers, school administrators, and state-level education actors began to dominate policy decisions as the "education establishment."

LO 15.3

To analyze the education establishment policy actors and their roles.

THE EDUCATION ESTABLISHMENT

In the past, the members of the education establishment, popularly referred to as the "education bureaucracy," tried to dominate school policy making by resolving issues among themselves and then presenting a united front before legislative bodies and the governor. They constituted a powerful political coalition that managed to win substantial financial commitments to the schools. Because of the political and financial pressures already mentioned, however, the education establishment is fractured today.

Teachers As noted, teachers had little power or influence outside the classroom until they began to organize into professional associations and unions. Once, teacher organizations, particularly the NEA, focused their primary attention on school improvement rather than on the economic well-being of teachers themselves, and teachers and administrators maintained a common front before the state legislature. Gradually, however, a newer teacher organization challenged the dominance and docility of the NEA, especially in large cities. This rival organization, the AFT, openly referred to itself as a labor union and struggled to win collective bargaining rights for teachers. With the election of the AFT as the bargaining agent for teachers, the teachers began carving a home for themselves outside the cozy family of the education establishment. As both the AFT and then later the NEA lobbied for state legislation permitting collective bargaining and concentrated their efforts on winning better pay and working conditions for teachers. Today, approximately three-fourths of the nation's schoolteachers belong to one of these groups. However, many NEA locals, primarily in the southern and western states, do not engage in collective bargaining, either because they choose not to or because their state does not permit it.

Teacher militancy accompanied unionization. Strikes and other job actions disrupted many local school districts as teachers battled for higher pay, fewer nonteaching duties, and other demands. The rise of teachers' unions forever fragmented the education lobby in most states as teachers sought to look out primarily for their own interests rather than the interests of school administrators. Teachers remain perhaps the most powerful of education interest groups at the state level, although lately they have drawn heavy fire from conservative politicians, dissatisfied citizens, and other education stakeholders. (Former U.S. secretary of education Rod Paige famously referred to the NEA as a "terrorist organization.") Each year, the opening day of school is delayed in some districts because teachers go out on strike over concerns such as pay and benefits, working conditions, and education quality issues. Chicago teachers walked off the job in 2012 over pay, teacher evaluations, and other issues, halting classes for seven days.

Local School Boards Another member of the education establishment, the local school board, is a legislative body responsible for governing and administering public education at the local level. About 14,000 of these local bodies exist. Local school boards are made up of laypeople, not representatives of the professional education community. Board members are elected by voters in independent school districts in most states.

The original American ideal of local control of public schools lodged its faith in local school boards, which were popularly elected and therefore responsive to citizens' opinions and points of view. In fact, their true authority has never equaled the myth of local control. The status and influence of local boards have diminished, except perhaps for those boards that have the authority to adjust property tax rates. Some school boards have contracted with private entities to run their schools. Others, rife with politics, patronage practices, and scandals, have been pushed aside and effectively replaced by city governments (e.g., Boston, Chicago, Detroit, New York City, and Philadelphia). One critic called local school boards "the worst kind of anachronism . . . ripe for corruption, as a springboard for aspiring politicians, and a venue for disgruntled former school employees to air their dirty laundry."[31]

School boards still commonly do financial planning and oversight, and as noted above, some set school taxes on property in the district. They also hire district superintendents of education and school administrators, approve teacher appointments and school assignment policies, determine building and facility needs, and debate program needs. In fact, some local boards are criticized for trying to micromanage the daily minutiae of school operations instead of properly focusing on broad policy issues. Policy issues, however, are increasingly settled by state and federal standards and regulations, collective bargaining contracts, and court decisions.

Many local school boards suffer from yawning public apathy, extremely low turnouts for board elections, and widespread ignorance of what such boards are supposed to be doing. Others teem with partisan politics. About the only events that focus citizen attention on local boards are the occasional bond or tax referendum that proposes to raise property taxes in the school district, or vitriolic debates over conflicting goals and values such as school redistricting, funding equity, sex education, and the respective places of Darwin and Jesus in the classroom.

Other Policy Actors Also known as the state education agency, the *state board of education* (SBE) exercises general supervision over all primary and secondary schools. The SBE members are appointed by the governor or legislature, elected, or selected through some combination of processes. Like local boards, state boards sometimes become consumed by politics. The Texas and Kansas state boards of education have been arguing for years about the proper roles of science, creationism, and global climate change in the classroom and in school texts. Most SBEs make policy and budget recommendations to the governor and legislature. With few exceptions, however, they are not significant policy actors. They tend to lack political clout, policy expertise, and public visibility.

Like local school boards, state boards of education defer to the authority and expertise of another policy actor—in this case, the *chief state school officer* (CSSO). This CSSO, also known as the state superintendent of schools or the commissioner of education, establishes and enforces standards and accountability for local school curricula, teacher certification, standardized student testing, and certain other matters and provides technical and other assistance to the schools. She may be appointed by the SBE, popularly elected on a statewide ballot, or appointed by the governor. Although the formal relationship between the CSSO and the SBE varies, nearly all CSSOs serve as executive officers and professional advisers to their state boards of education. As governors and state legislatures have increasingly provided policy leadership for the schools, the influence of CSSOs has declined.

Yet another administrative creature, *the state department of education* (SDE), is responsible for rulemaking and for furnishing administrative and technical support to the CSSO and the SBE. It also administers national and state-aid programs for public schools. The state department of education is almost exclusively the habitat of education professionals. State departments have grown in size, competency, and power. They have taken on the difficult job of monitoring state education reforms, and they have significantly increased their capacities for research, program evaluation, performance measurement, and testing.

THE STATE EDUCATION POLICY LEADERS

LO 15.4

To analyze the new education policy actors and their roles.

As the coalition of actors described above has fragmented and lost influence, state-level education actors and community and business organizations have increased their interest in school issues and their capacity to respond to them, and governors and legislatures have added staff and augmented their ability to collect data and conduct research. Education policy making today orbits around state and federal governments rather than local education professionals, although the demand for, and tradition of, local control remains important.

Governors State chief executives are deeply involved in all major aspects of education policy making. Education issues often receive passionate attention during campaigns and in State of the State addresses. Occasionally, education clearly dominates governors' policy agendas. Education policy is the most important perennial issue in most states, and a significant concern of voters.

In formulating, lobbying for, and implementing education policy, the governors rely heavily on their staff. Many governors have special divisions of education. Staff members facilitate the flow of information to and from the governor's office and the desks of other key education policy makers. They analyze information from all levels of government, in and out of state, and from national organizations such as the National Governors' Association and the Education Commission of the States. They also draft bills, lobby legislators and education and business groups, and attempt to influence public opinion on education issues. Recently, Republican governors in Michigan, North Carolina, Wisconsin, New Jersey, and other states have orchestrated policies that deprivilege teachers and their unions while enhancing charter schools and voucher programs. The most successful governors have managed to weave delicate advocacy coalitions among all significant education policy actors to increase their chances of winning significant reform programs.

State Legislatures Legislatures have always had the final responsibility for enacting broad education policy and for determining state funding of public schools. They were the leading state policy actors until governors upstaged them, but the critical policy battles are still fought on legislative turf.

Lobbyists for the education establishment are quite busy in the statehouse, but their influence has diminished because issue conflicts have precluded a united front. Numerous other interests, including business, minority groups, the disabled, community organizations, the economically disadvantaged, and those promoting school choice also receive a hearing from legislators.

Like governors, legislatures have expanded their capabilities. They have added their own education staff specialists, enhanced their research capabilities, and extended efforts to oversee and even overturn the actions of governors and education agencies.

Courts Federal and state courts, especially the U.S. Supreme Court, are important factors in public education. They have issued rulings on several issues affecting students, such as censorship of school newspapers, personal dress and grooming standards, female participation in sports programs, student discipline, student drug testing, and school prayer. Federal courts imposed desegregation policies on public schools through a series of decisions beginning with *Brown v. Board of Education of Topeka* (1954), which declared that racial segregation violated the Fourteenth Amendment's equal protection clause.[32] Court-ordered busing to achieve school desegregation was mandated in *Swann v. Charlotte-Mecklenburg County Schools* (in North Carolina) in 1971 and in other decisions involving districts that had practiced government-approved racial segregation.[33] These decisions, and the subsequent busing, were highly controversial and contributed to white flight to the suburbs in many places. In some cities, such as Boston, Massachusetts, court-ordered busing led to violent protests.

Racial segregation of the schools remains a serious and intractable problem. Clearly, aggressive busing has not worked: Research confirms that more school segregation of blacks and Latinos exists now than it did 25 years ago.[34] Racial and social disparities from housing segregation have created "islands of immunity" to school integration.[35] It appears that a tipping point is reached when nonwhite enrollment surpasses 25 percent, triggering white flight to different school districts or private schools. Remaining behind are the children of poverty and color.[36] African Americans in particular continue to live in segregated housing and attend segregated schools. Yet with the endorsement of a conservative majority of the U.S. Supreme Court, many school districts, including Charlotte–Mecklenburg and Boston, have dismantled desegregation plans in favor of combining neighborhood schools with various "choice" options such as charter, magnet, and private schools.

State courts, too, have ordered changes in education policy. As we have noted, many state supreme courts have mandated school-finance reform to attain greater equity in the funding of public education. State courts are also asked to resolve various legal disagreements spawned by education reforms. Individuals and groups representing minority positions can often capture the attention of top policy makers only through the legal system.

The Corporate Community Because many high school graduates lack the basic skills and knowledge to succeed in the workplace, of necessity, businesses are involved in the public schools. Consequently, some firms have developed their own training and education programs, often incorporating fundamental reading and writing skills.

To members of the education establishment, business leaders are partly to blame for the sad state of the schools. Some industries based primarily on low-wage labor and unsophisticated skills historically opposed education reform as an unnecessary expense. Firms are also criticized for negotiating local property-tax breaks that deprive school districts of much-needed revenues, then complaining about the poor quality of education in those very districts they are starving financially. Today, however, due to the changing nature of work, most corporate leaders are vocal proponents of education improvement at all levels, from preschool to college. They differ significantly, however, on how to attain it.

Corporate involvement encompasses a broad range of activities, including purchasing technology and supplies for local school, sponsoring opportunities in which students may concentrate on a specially designed curriculum in areas such as finance, IT, or biotechnology, and offering work in paid summer internships. Overall, the role of business varies from state to state, but in most locations its contribution is largely rhetorical and episodic. Commercialization of the classroom is a growing problem. Product advertisements, exclusive lunchroom franchises for soft-drink bottler and fast-food chains, and even advertising on school buses raise questions about the true interests of business in the schools.

Recently, large private foundations such as the Gates, Kellogg, and Annie E. Casey foundations, have taken on a more active role in public education by advocating for school and teacher improvement policies, common core standards, and other issues.[37] Moreover, they are strategically ponying up millions of dollars in support of their ideas.

Private Schools The widespread presence of private schools, most of them church sponsored, makes them influential policy actors. They enroll approximately 10 percent of K-12 students nationwide. To their supporters, the superiority of private schools in providing quality education is taken on faith. Private schools do provide a superior education in some instances, but in others, private schools are academically inferior, or they are little more than devices used by parents to keep their children in a religious environment or predominantly white classrooms.

Educational Innovation in the States

LO 15.5

To describe educational innovation in the states.

In the time since *A Nation at Risk* called national attention to the acute need for educational reforms, the states have responded on a large scale. Hundreds of task forces have thoroughly studied school problems and issued recommendations for resolving them. Many of these recommendations have been enacted into law as innovative programs to improve the quality of public education. The federal NCLB incorporated many principles and innovations first adopted by the states.

A broad and powerful coalition of state and local elected officials, professional educators, community organizations, parents, and business interests has been instrumental in the drive to improve public education. Democrats, Republicans, and independents alike generally agree that the economic future of the United States depends on the quality of schooling. What they do not agree on is how to best obtain improved outcomes.

The states have been busily innovating in the four critical areas of standards, students, teachers, and the education bureaucracy. Every state has recorded remarkable program achievements in at least one of these categories, and, in some instances prodded by NCLB and its progeny, a majority have implemented reforms in all four. But incremental reforms have not been sufficient to reverse the strong tide of school mediocrity and even failure in many troubled settings, opening up a growing demand for more far-reaching restructuring of public education.

STANDARDS

Standards and levels of assessment have been raised in almost every state. Curriculum and graduation requirements have been strengthened, instructional time has been increased, steps have been taken to minimize overcrowding, and technology has been ushered into the classroom. Special programs have been developed to encourage gifted students and to assist developmentally challenged students.

Competency testing for basic skills and subject matter has been another widely adopted reform. All states now test students at several grade levels to monitor progress in the basics, and most require students to pass a competency test (or exit exam) before graduating from high school. All states require school "report cards" to hold schools accountable for student performance. Successful schools and their teachers may receive financial rewards. Low-performing schools may be overhauled, receive special assistance, or, if hopeless, even be taken over or closed.

Yet many teachers, parents, and students openly wonder if, prodded by the federal government and the states, schools have gone overboard with frequent—and often intrusive—testing. The stress associated with over-testing affects not only teachers, but also students and parents. In some states, required testing (and test preparation) consumes up to one-third of the school year.[38] Research indicates that many states have actually lowered their testing standards to comply with NCLB requirements that all schools be proficient in math and reading.[39] "Teaching to the Test" has become endemic in many schools. And disturbing evidence of teachers and administrators tampering with tests has appeared in Texas, Georgia, Massachusetts, Virginia, and elsewhere.[40] In April 2015, eleven Atlanta teachers and administrators were convicted of racketeering for altering test answer sheets. Other Atlanta educators received lesser punishments.[41]

The National Governors Association and the Council of Chief State School Officers launched the Common Core Standards Initiative in 2009. All but five states adopted the standards for English and Math, and the first exams were administered in 2014–2015.[42] The common or national exams are intended to replace previous state tests in English language and math. The common core standards became a political football in 2015 as conservative and other concerned groups attacked it as unwanted federal intrusion into the schools (even though the governors and state school administrators developed the program). The It's Your Turn box solicits your views on Common Core.

Another effort to raise standards is year-round schooling, now required for millions of students in public schools. Three-month summer breaks—the legacy of an agrarian economy in which children were needed to plant and bring in the crops—are being replaced with multi-tracking arrangements in which students and teachers are divided into several groups, or tracks.

It's Your Turn

Should States Implement Common Core Standards?

Originally conceived and enthusiastically adopted by the states, common core standards have become a political football, with supporters asserting that the idea is sound and badly needed, while opponents decry national government intrusion into a traditional state and local education policy arena.

Where does your state stand on CCS? Has opposition arisen? If so, from what quarters? What are your thoughts on the desirability of national CCS implemented by the states? Is CCS a good idea?

PROS	CONS
Common core standards were not in fact mandated by the federal government. Rather, they were conceived, developed, and coordinated by the governors and chief state school officers.	Critics assert that the CCS reflects national (Obama administration) priorities and amounts to federal overreach, not state and local priorities.
CCS offer an accurate means of measuring and comparing student achievement across the states.	Public education is a state and local—not national—responsibility, and must be treated as such.
The standards identify and test for the knowledge and skills U.S. children need to compete globally.	States should be free to set their own standards and develop their own testing systems.
The federal government offers grant funds to states willing to implement CCS.	Some CCS are actually set below those standards previously existing in some states.
The federal government has granted waivers to nearly all the states to provide flexibility in establishing their own accountability systems.	CCS impose more testing requirements on already over-tested students, who should spend more time learning and less in preparing for tests.
	Opposition to CCS is broad, incorporating Tea Party zealots, liberal-minded teachers and their organizations, and parents.

They attend classes for forty-five, sixty, or ninety days, and then go on break for a two- or three-week intersession.

Although the research remains inconclusive, year-round schooling may improve learning by ensuring that children keep their mental sharpness and do not forget much of what they have learned over the summer. It also saves money by maximizing the use of school buildings and resources. Certain problems arise, however. For example, it is difficult to schedule maintenance on buildings and equipment, and extended schooling can interfere with sports and other extracurricular activities and disrupt family vacations and day-care arrangements. A more effective approach may be to increase the length of the school day or academic year to pack in more time for teaching and learning.

STUDENTS

Of course, students are the intended beneficiaries of the improvements and strengthening of standards. In general, expectations for student academic performance and classroom behavior have been raised. However, based on SAT and ACT scores and results of the National Assessment of Educational Programs tests, there are, at best, only modest indications of improvement. Great disparities remain among states, suburban and urban districts, minority groups, and family-income categories.

One commonsense approach is to better prepare students to begin school in the first place. The federal Head Start program is one such program, and states are also helping to build first-graders' learning foundations through highly structured and innovative preschool programs. Kindergarten is one step removed from first grade and can be very helpful in preparing kids for school. But the trend is pre-kindergarten initiatives that can involve children as young as three years. Early childhood programs boost reading and math skills for entering kindergarteners by four to six months ahead of those who remain at home[43] and help to identify medical and social service needs. Importantly, they also involve parents in the learning process. Approximately 28 percent of four-year-olds are enrolled in state-funded preschool programs. Head Start enrollment brings the national total to 40 percent.[44]

Virtually all states have raised course requirements for students to graduate from high school. Students are required to take more upper-level math and science courses and more foreign-language classes, and a larger proportion of students are enrolling in honors and AP courses than ever before.

The national education paradigm today is known as **outcomes-based or performance-based education**. National standards, such as a common core curriculum and achievement tests on the basics, are said to enhance school accountability by helping to determine and test for levels of student knowledge, skills, and abilities, as well as for curriculum and teacher development needs. Although almost everyone agrees that standards must be raised and many think that national testing is a good idea, moving beyond broad goals and relatively painless incremental changes is proving to be difficult. Many Americans support national standards, but they distrust the national government and fear federal intrusion into the schools and what they teach. However, outcomes-based education appears to be here to stay. With federal government encouragement, mandates, and monetary incentives, states are developing or revising curricula to emphasize what children should know and be able to do regarding key subjects and testing them on that knowledge.

Student classroom behavior has been a target of reformers in many states. Strict discipline codes are being enforced, as are stronger attendance policies. In especially difficult school settings, police officers, closed-circuit television monitors, metal detectors, airport-style screeners, and other devices help maintain order. Most states have adopted anti-bullying laws. More stringent discipline policies have made it easier for teachers to remove troublemakers from the classroom. Many school districts are using zero-tolerance policies to expel violent students. Other violence prevention programs teach conflict-resolution and anger-management skills to reduce fighting and discourage

outcomes-based or performance based education

A reform that strives to hold schools, teachers, and administrators accountable for student performance, primarily based on standardized test scores.

gang membership. Ironically, corporal punishment (paddling, usually) remains legal in nineteen states and is still used (mostly in the Bible Belt states) to discipline unruly students.[45]

Student drug testing is an active issue in some districts. The U.S. Supreme Court has ruled that schools may perform drug tests on students participating in sports and other extracurricular activities. (Before that ruling, public-school students were presumed to be excluded from drug testing by the Fourteenth Amendment's protection against illegal search and seizure.) Presumably, drug (urine) testing would identify trouble-prone students and send a discouraging message to those contemplating smoking weed, consuming alcohol, or getting involved with more serious substances. Professional educators and health groups oppose drug testing, arguing that students engaging in extracurricular activities are less likely to use drugs, and that requiring screening as a condition of participation in sports, band, clubs, and other activities would deter students from participating. At a more fundamental level remains the matter of overcoming *state* constitutional provisions regarding privacy and illegal search and seizure.

Hungry children cannot learn. Free school lunch and breakfast programs help ensure low-income students have full bellies on school days. To help avoid unnecessary distractions during class time, about 850 public schools segregate classrooms by gender. Another positive incentive to stay in school (and, therefore, stay out of prison and off public assistance), students who graduate from high school with a B or better average in New York, Georgia, and several other states are guaranteed state payment of full tuition at a state college or university, as long as they maintain a B average or better. Such scholarship programs have the added benefit of helping stem the brain drain of top students who attend college out of state and never move back. Houston, New York City, Atlanta, Memphis, Baltimore, and other cities are also paying kids for performance. Incentives for regular, punctual attendance are being offered in some locales, including guarantees of admission to college to all graduating seniors with a minimum grade point average and having regular attendance. Some states permit tenth graders who pass certain exams to receive their diplomas two years early and enroll directly in community college.[46] Other states allow high-performing high school students to take community college courses for dual high school and college credit.

Some offer cash for high attendance or for passing AP exams.[47] Taking a punitive tack, North Carolina and other states revoke the driver's license of any high school student who drops out or fails to pass 70 percent of his or her courses. Naugatuck, Connecticut, fines truant students or their parents $20.00 a day, and also prohibits withdrawal from school before the age of 17. The goal, of course, is to keep in school some of the hundreds of thousands of students who drop out each year, at a huge cost in lost tax revenues and increased expenditures associated with welfare, unemployment, and crime.

TEACHERS

Of the many factors influencing student learning, the quality of the teacher in the classroom usually makes the greatest difference. Good teachers not only help raise their students' test scores, but they also contribute to lower rates of teen pregnancy, higher college attendance, and higher lifetime earnings, according to one study.[48] Teachers have been the beneficiaries (or victims, depending on one's standpoint) of the most extensive and far-reaching educational reforms. They welcome higher pay, improved fringe benefits, and more opportunities for professional improvement. Smaller class sizes are particularly desirable, giving teachers more time to interact with each student. Teachers have been much less pleased with paperwork and accountability requirements, performance appraisals, testing of teachers, and teacher merit-pay schemes.

The national average of teacher salaries has basically tracked increases in the cost of living over the past ten years. But variations among the states continue to be rather pronounced, in response to differences in local cost of living, labor market conditions, and other factors. In 2014, teachers in New York earned an average salary of $75,379; those in South Dakota averaged only $39,008.

Teacher Shortages Because of retirements, attrition, and a spurt in public-school enrollment, critical shortages of qualified teachers, particularly for math and science courses, continue to exist in many states. Baby boomer retirements are depleting America's classrooms of experienced teachers. Projections of new classroom teacher needs indicate even worse problems to come.

The states are experimenting with several strategies to relieve teacher shortfalls. Most are taking steps to entice former teachers and education majors who are working in other fields back into the classroom, and nearly all have relaxed or set up streamlined teacher certification requirements. One particularly rich pool for new teachers consists of people who have departed from military service, business, or government. Such nontraditional recruiting not only helps alleviate the teacher-supply problem, but also has the added benefit of elevating the quality and diversity of the teaching pool. Approximately one-third of new teachers are such mid-career entrants.[49] Another valuable pipeline is the Teach for America program, which recruits high-performing college graduates to teach in high-need schools in low-income communities. Many states offer special scholarships, signing bonuses, or loans to attract college students into the teaching profession.

Research finds that many education problems stem from the failure to recruit, train, and retain good teachers. Some schools serve as retirement homes for the inept. Some teachers' colleges do an inadequate job of preparing teachers for the classroom. Some schools require teachers to teach out of their field of expertise and training. And once in the classroom, many teachers, especially in urban and low-income schools, soon lose their enthusiasm and confidence in their own abilities when faced with at-risk children.

States are taking steps to solve these and related problems. A majority of states have recently bulked up teacher preparation policies, setting higher academic proficiency requirements for teacher education programs and testing for content-specific knowledge. Teacher-licensing and classroom certification requirements are being tightened up to include longer classroom internships, mastery of subject matter material, and comprehensive classroom readiness assessment including lesson plans, homework assignments, and videotaped teaching sessions. Schools are adopting programs to mentor new teachers with experienced teachers. State education statutes and collective bargaining contracts are being modified to make it easier to end teacher tenure and dismiss teachers who should no longer be in the classroom.

Merit-pay plans that seek to reward high-performing teachers with special pay increases are popular. (See the Controversies in States and Localities feature.) Career ladders, which promote outstanding teachers up several levels to higher job classifications, have also been tried.

For various reasons—including budget cuts, teacher dissatisfaction with the plans, and fierce union opposition—these initiatives generally have not been successful. Teacher shortages in math, science, special education, and bilingual education continue to plague many districts. And enrollment in teacher education programs has dropped substantially.

BUREAUCRACY AND SCHOOL CHOICE

A single, boilerplate plan does not exist for improving the schools, but most strategies hold one factor in common: **school choice**. Its most essential elements include a market-based, decentralized approach that permits individual selection of the school that the child will attend, while providing tax dollars to accompany the student to the chosen school. The expectation is that, in the scramble to attract tuition dollars, heretofore fossilized schools will try new ideas, offer new or specialized curricula, and take other steps to reinvigorate public education, and new schools will be established. Schools unable or unwilling to adapt to and compete within the education marketplace will be forced to consolidate with more successful schools or close their doors altogether.

Magnet Schools A common school-choice program, found in nearly all large urban school districts, is the **magnet school**. A form of public school and under school district control, the magnet school offers specialized curricula to attract students from various backgrounds who share a common interest in areas such as the performing arts, science and technology, engineering, or international studies. Originally conceived as an alternative to busing, successful magnet schools help attract affluent children to the inner city and poor children to the suburbs. An estimated 2.8 million students attend magnet schools.

Related to magnet schools are **open enrollment programs** that permit students either to select schools only inside the existing school district or to choose any public school in the state. Within-district choice keeps resources and tax dollars in the same local jurisdiction. Between-district enrollment allows children to attend a school in a different district, perhaps many miles away. Open enrollment plans are intended to increase educational opportunities for students regardless of minority or socioeconomic status. They are available in twenty-two states.

Open enrollment is not without its problems, however. An important shortcoming is that white and middle-class children tend to "choose" to flee low-performing schools for those that are better-performing. Such an

school choice
A market-based approach to education improvement that permits parents and students to choose which school the child will attend. Examples include charter schools and voucher programs.

magnet school
A public school whose curriculum emphasizes a specialized area, such as science or performing arts, and that is intended to attract a diverse set of students.

open enrollment program
An option that permits students to attend a public school of their choice within a designated jurisdictional area. The intent is to increase educational options for all children.

Controversies in States and Localities

Should Teachers Have Tenure?

All of us have experienced good teachers and bad teachers. Shouldn't the good ones be encouraged to stay and the bad ones sacked? Union contracts build in strong protections for teachers in collective bargaining states. Even in non-union settings, it is difficult to dismiss an underperforming or badly behaving teacher. Typically, the inadequate teacher remains in the classroom, to the disadvantage of the students, or is simply transferred to a different school. The difficulty in firing incompetent teachers is a common complaint of school administrators, parents, and education reformers alike.

Teacher tenure, a long-standing job protection right, is the politically charged focal point. Teachers are awarded tenure after three to five years of acceptable performance. Tenure helps keep experienced teachers in the profession. But what happens if a tenured teacher stops trying, becomes emotionally unstable, or commits a felony? To revoke tenure and dismiss a teacher usually requires proof of felonious acts or serious misconduct. Tenure rights are so strong that seldom is simple incompetence or consistently poor performance sufficient to push a teacher out of the classroom without years of charges and appeals. The poster child for the problem is New York City's "rubber rooms," in which hundreds of teachers accused of wrongdoing or incompetence were banned to trailers or unused classrooms to while away their time doing nothing while enjoying full pay for years until the cases were resolved. At one point, $30 million a year was being paid in salaries to teachers in legal limbo. Another egregious example is the case of an eighth-grade science teacher in Ohio, whose dismissal for branding crosses on the arms of public school students took two years and $900,000.

Three potential solutions are being tested in the states. The first is simply to terminate tenure and replace it with annual contracts. A poorly performing teacher would not have her contract renewed. South Dakota, Idaho, Florida, and North Carolina have ended tenure altogether. The second is to make it easier to fire teachers who have tenure but receive poor performance reviews. Arizona, Rhode Island, Colorado, and Nevada diluted tenure protections by making the process of dismissing teachers easier and faster to dismiss bad teachers.

The third solution involves identifying struggling teachers and either helping them improve sufficiently, convincing them to find a different profession, or firing them. The best example of this strategy is found in Toledo, Ohio. Toledo's Peer Assistance Review (PAR) assigns skilled veteran teachers to troubled teachers. The "consulting teachers" must be pulled from their classrooms to perform their mentoring duties, which is certainly a disadvantage of PAR, but recent research finds that significant cost savings are realized when novice teachers are transformed into accomplished performers and the hopeless are weeded out. For example, to fire a tenured teacher averages a cost of $128,941 in legal and other expenses, compared with only about $8,000 to counsel someone out of the profession.

Despite the widely recognized need to usher poor teachers out the door, there is much controversy over how it should be done: the "big stick" approach of the tenure bashers, the "tough love" tactic of Toledo, or something in between. And decisions must be guided by teacher assessments.

Critical Thinking Questions

1. Should teachers have tenure? Why or why not?
2. On what basis should teachers be evaluated? Student test scores? Student progress? Or other factors?

SOURCES: Adrienne Lu, "Teacher Tenure and Dismissal on Trial," www.pewstates.org (accessed April 1, 2014); Sharon Otterman, "New York Teachers Still in Legal Limbo," nytimes.com (December 7, 2010); Trip Gabriel, "Plan Offered to Overhaul Discipline of Teachers," nytimes.com (January 19, 2011); Jonathan Walters, "Tough Love for Teachers," *Governing* (March 2011): 40–43.

outcome has obvious implications for minority and social-class balance in the schools. School-choice proponents claim that children of poor parents can also transfer to more desirable schools, but without special assistance, many poor children cannot afford transportation to outlying districts. This problem has been at least partially addressed in states that furnish or help pay transportation costs for low-income children. However, students still face the additional hurdle of gaining admission to their school of choice, which might be fully enrolled.

Charter Schools Unlike open enrollment programs, which provide greater choice among existing schools, charter schools expand the total number of school possibilities for parents to choose from. **Charter schools** are independent entities operating within the public-school system under charters, or contracts that specify operating procedures and performance indicators. The charters are negotiated between their organizers and a sponsoring organization. The sponsor may be a local school board, teachers, parents, private business, or other entity.

Charter schools promise to deliver results in exchange for being unleashed from the bureaucratic chains of the education establishment. Flexibility and innovation are their strong suits. Most design their own curricula, hire and fire teachers, and generally run their own show. Some feature a back-to-basics curriculum; others target math and science geeks. In actuality, however, their degree of autonomy varies widely depending on state authorizing legislation. Using public (mostly state) tax dollars to compete with private and traditional public schools, charter schools are intended to improve responsiveness to parents and enhance the quality of education throughout the jurisdiction. Some public schools have adopted charter school features such as longer school days and one-on-one tutoring.[50]

Charter school laws have been adopted in forty-two states. They are particularly popular in Texas, California, Louisiana, and Florida. There are about 2.9 million students enrolled in more than 6,700 nationwide. Charter schools are resisted by teachers unions, and some school boards are also skeptical of charter-reform efforts. Across the United States, charter schools have been closed for various reasons, typically from poor student performance and financial problems. Reliable evaluative research is only now appearing on how well they measure up, and the results are mixed for charter schools.[51] Some boost student achievement, but others do no better—or worse—than standard public schools.[52]

Voucher Plans In a system using a **voucher plan**, parents receive a certificate from the state or from their local school district that may be used to subsidize the tuition for a public, private, or religious school of their choice. The concept is quite similar to that of the G.I. bill and Pell grants for federal reimbursements to colleges and universities. Voucher programs are operating in about half the states, nearly all governed by Republican majorities. Despite displays of public enthusiasm for voucher programs, they have gone down to defeat in several state initiative and referendum votes. Several state courts have also proven to be less than friendly to voucher plans, having blocked them from operating in Arizona, Florida, Maine, and Vermont, among other states.

The *federal* constitutional legitimacy of spending public money on religious schools was established by the U.S. Supreme Court in 2002 in *Zelman v. Simmons-Harris et al.*, a decision heralded as an important ruling on religion and the schools.[53] The Court's 5–4 majority concluded that Cleveland, Ohio's

charter school

An alternative public school established by contract with a sponsoring agency, school district, business, or other organization.

voucher plan

An arrangement in which the state or school district subsidizes tuition for students to enroll in a school of student/parent choice.

plan offered "a genuine choice between religious and nonreligious schools," despite the enrollment of 96 percent of voucher recipients in religious schools.[54] Left undetermined was the constitutionality of such vouchers according to the *state* courts.

The Florida program, enacted by the legislature in 1999, offered "opportunity scholarships" to students in chronically low-performing schools, permitting them to transfer to a better-performing public school or to any private school. The Florida voucher program was struck down as unconstitutional by the state supreme court in 2006, on the grounds that public money cannot be used to finance private schools.[55] Taking a different tack, Florida then adopted a tax credit for private school tuition, effectively achieving the ends sought by the legislature. Such a tax-credit approach has been adopted by several other states to avoid constitutional issues.

The largest and most-examined voucher experiment began in 1999 in Milwaukee. The Milwaukee school-choice program provides low-income parents with vouchers to send their children to private schools. It is used by about 27,000 low-income students, who receive about $7,210 each. The majority are enrolled in religious (mostly Catholic and Lutheran) schools.[56] Unlike in Florida, the Wisconsin state supreme court permitted vouchers to be applied to parochial schools. The court's reasoning was that the voucher money was going to parents, not to schools.

Nevada recently became the bellwether for voucher-related programs by providing an Education Savings Account to all public school students. The ESA offers 100 percent of what the state pays for public school students, currently $5,700 a year, to disabled students and those from poor families, and 90 percent to all others. Dollars may be spent for public, private, or religious schooling, textbooks, and even dual-enrollment college credits.[57]

Overall, it does appear that voucher programs have encouraged parents to participate more in their children's education and that parental satisfaction with schools has increased. There is no shortage of voucher champions, chiefly among political conservatives and religious supporters.[58] But there is only very modest evidence for vouchers improving student achievement. In Milwaukee and Cleveland, the most thorough analyses to date indicate that school-choice students have not performed any better than similar non-choice students.[59] Also undetermined is the effect of shifting public tax dollars from public schools to private ones on the quality of public schools. Will public schools improve so that they can compete with private schools, or will they become education hovels for the remaining poor children? Will vouchers truly benefit children of low-income families who, even with a voucher, still must come up with thousands of dollars annually to pay private-school tuition? Or will vouchers disproportionately help upper- and middle-income families? What will be the impact on minority and social-class segregation?

PRIVATIZATION

Perhaps the most radical restructuring plan of all involves turning over management and operation of the public schools to a private firm. K-12 Inc, Connections Education, and other companies operate for-profit standard and charter schools in twenty-three states. One of the most interesting privatization experiments is in Philadelphia. Following a state takeover of Philadelphia's troubled school system in 2002, thirty-eight failing public schools were transferred to seven outside administrators, including Edison, Temple University, and the University of Pennsylvania.[60] Results from the City of Brotherly Love have been mixed. Six of the schools were retaken by the Philadelphia School District in 2008 because of poor performance and financial issues, and several others were placed on notice that they faced the same fate unless improvements were made.[61] Meanwhile, scores of standard Philadelphia schools have been closed because of city budget shortfalls.

Noteworthy failures of schools-for-profit have also occurred in Hartford, Connecticut, Dallas, Texas, and other cities because of high financial costs and disappointing student performance. In an early analysis by the Rand Corporation, comparing student test scores in public schools with privately run schools in six cities, results again were mixed. Students in traditional schools did better on standardized reading and science tests in Cleveland and St. Paul but did worse than test takers in privately managed schools in Denver and San Francisco.[62] Early schools-for-profit providers, Edison and EAI, have left the marketplace or declared bankruptcy, but other firms have stepped in with privately-run charter schools.

HOMESCHOOLING

In addition to the large number of children enrolled in private schools (approximately 10 percent of the student population), it is estimated that up to 1.8 million school-age children are taught at home by their parents.[63] Many homeschoolers are from religious families uncomfortable with the public school's environment, performance, or secular values. The homeschool curriculum, testing, and other factors are regulated by most—but not all—states. Some states accommodate homeschooling by permitting selected public-school activities. For instance, Idaho public schools must allow homeschooled children in their districts to participate in any school activity, including sports. Studies of homeschooled children generally show positive results, with stay-at-home kids outperforming their public-school counterparts on standardized achievement tests.[64] However, home schoolers may be ill-prepared for college if they have not mastered advanced mathematics and science.

VIRTUAL SCHOOLS

Widely available technology makes it possible for students to learn at home from long-distance teachers. The Florida Virtual School serves more than 60,000 full-time students and 375,000 part-time across the state in Internet-based instruction. Almost all states offer online courses to at least some students, and most permit certain students to attend virtual schools full time. Idaho requires all high school students to take some online classes.

The virtual school can be particularly appropriate for rural states with great distances between schools, such as Alaska and Wyoming. During influenza or other epidemics, virtual education is a means to ensure that teaching and learning continue while kids are isolated at home to avoid spreading the virus. It has also attracted attention from charter schools.

Issues with virtual schooling include test security, student performance assessment, parental involvement, unmotivated students, and the potentially negative effects of education without interpersonal interaction. Research has raised questions about the quality of online high school education.[65] There is also research showing that some privately run virtual schools take state and local funds for students who never even log in.[66]

THE REPORT CARD ON SCHOOL CHOICE

Will the school-choice movement save the public schools or destroy them? Is the most salient objective improvement of the quality of public education, or is it something different? The fight over school reform is currently being won by those groups favoring the market-oriented approaches of school choice through vouchers, charter schools, and private schools.[67] The education establishment that dominated school policy for decades has lost ground to a new alignment of interests populated by conservative advocacy groups, foundations, and those seeking reform through standards and accountability approaches. But the education establishment is fighting back by challenging market-based reforms, asserting that the real problems with under-performing schools are poverty, racial segregation, poor parenting, and a lack of resources.[68]

Are parents truly capable and do they have sufficient information to make the best educational choices for their children? Arguments are proffered from various perspectives. So far, relatively small numbers of students participate in school-choice programs, though their numbers are rapidly rising. Still, evaluative data are limited, precluding comprehensive assessment of student performance or possible unintended consequences of school-choice programs.

One thing is certain: School choice is highly controversial and, except for the magnet-school option, is perceived as a threat by almost the entire education establishment, particularly teachers and school board members, who fear losing funding from reduced enrollment and being saddled with the most difficult, at-risk children. When school-choice proposals involve public tax dollars for parochial schools, they are especially controversial.

LO 15.6

To discuss the continuing challenges of public education.

The Continuing Challenges of Public Education

The states, as well as the national government, are serious about excellence in education and providing direction and leadership to attain it. The vitality, innovation, and capability of the states are prominent in education policy, but the federal government is an increasingly influential partner.

A troubling gap separates policy goals and enactment from policy implementation. More time must pass before we can accurately gauge the consequences of many state and federal initiatives. It will take a tremendous act of political will and much hard work to bring to fruition the state and national educational improvement goals and to reinstate the United States as a world leader in K-12 performance.

The continuing problems in public education are manifold and daunting, and reform is extremely controversial, complex, and elusive. As education reform seemingly plods along, many frustrated parents opt for alternative arrangements. The number of private schools and the number of children instructed at home have grown significantly. Meanwhile, during this prolonged period of debate about the future of the public schools, many thorny dilemmas persist. Students and teachers must learn how to utilize information technology productively, billions must be invested in much-needed building repairs and new construction, and the special problems of at-risk and immigrant children must be addressed more effectively.

Putting effective state education reforms into practice requires the cooperation of many fragmented interests, including teachers, school administrators, superintendents, students, parents, conservative groups, foundations, and levels of government, each group with their own interests and turf to defend. Triumph over this fractured and increasingly ideologically-driven policy subsystem will come only through civic action that mobilizes a vast array of public, private, and nonprofit actors and interests into a united front committed to reform over the long term—decades or more.

The unfinished portrait for educational excellence has been sketched by governors, legislatures, the state education community, and the national government. States must encourage innovation and creative thinking at the local level while maintaining needed standards and accountability. Constitutionally, and in practice, education remains primarily a state and local responsibility. This truth was recognized in the Obama administration through liberal granting of NCLB waivers to states dissatisfied with provisions of the federal law.

The national government has an important and legitimate role. But NCLB, though its premises are laudable, has been perceived as unduly intrusive and costly. It certainly provides no final answer to the persistent problems of public education. State and local reform efforts are hobbled by childhood poverty, broken families, and other social problems that the national government could help address. And by funding and disseminating the results of research and experimental projects, the national government can elevate capacity and stimulate state and local innovation by state and local school districts If the current education reforms fail to move us toward providing quality education for our children, radical rethinking and restructuring of American public education may well be needed.

Chapter Recap

- Education is the single most important—and most costly—function in state and local governments.

- There is a perceived crisis in the public schools; criticism involves standards, student performance, teachers, excessive testing, and the education bureaucracy.

- The activities of state, local, national, and private actors and the education establishment largely determine policy development and outcomes.

- The role of the national government in education policy has become more important with No Child Left Behind and subsequent programs.

- The education establishment has fragmented; the new key policy actors are governors, legislatures, courts, private schools, the corporate community, conservative groups, and the national government.

- A wave of education innovations in the states has raised standards, attempted to improve student retention and performance, and attempted to address a critical shortage of classroom teachers.

- The most controversial innovations have involved various school-choice programs, including magnet and charter schools, vouchers, and private schools.

- The problems of reforming public education are multifaceted and complex, requiring the continual attention of government at all levels.

KEY TERMS

foundation program *(p. 400)*
outcomes-based or performance-based education *(p. 412)*

school choice *(p. 415)*
magnet school *(p. 415)*
open enrollment program *(p. 415)*

charter school *(p. 417)*
voucher plan *(p. 417)*

INTERNET RESOURCES

For the National Report Card on state school systems, see **www.edweek.org**. This site, which may require payment for access, can also be used to find informative articles on school reform.

School finance data are available from the National Center for Education Statistics at **www.nces.ed.gov** and on the U.S. Department of Education's website at **www.ed.gov**.

State education agencies may be explored at **www.ccsso.org**, home for the Council of Chief State School Officers.

One of the best places to go for education policy information and trends is the website of the Education Commission of the States at **www.ecs.org**.

Teacher salary data and education policy analysis may be found on the American Federation of Teachers' website at **www.aft.org** and at **www.nea.org**, the website of the National Education Association.

Criminal Justice: Cops and Corrections

16

There is often a fine line between assertive policing and the civil rights of people apprehended and arrested. National headline news in 2014–2015 featured incidents of unnecessary and deadly police violence. Ferguson, Missouri exploded into violence following a white police officer's shooting and killing of an unarmed black teenager who was being arrested for a theft of cigarillos from a nearby store. A twelve-year-old African-American boy armed with a toy gun was shot and killed on a Cleveland, Ohio playground by a white police officer. In Baltimore, a young black man died from a severed spine while in police custody. Today, more than two dozen local law enforcement agencies are under federal investigation for excessive use of force, including in Albuquerque, New Mexico, where police shot and killed thirty-seven individuals over a four-year period.

Police across the country are being accused of regularly abusing suspects with beatings, tasers, and other actions. In addition, police departments have been over-arming themselves with

LEARNING OBJECTIVES

16.1 To explain how much crime there actually is, and how it is measured.

16.2 To understand the ongoing challenge of crime fighting.

16.3 To understand intergovernmental roles in criminal justice.

16.4 To identify the actors in criminal justice policy, and their respective roles.

16.5 To explain how policy participants interact.

16.6 To assess the benefits and problems of capital punishment.

16.7 To understand and evaluate state correctional policy.

16.8 To discuss correctional policy alternatives for states and localities.

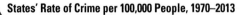

FIGURE
16.1

States' Rate of Crime per 100,000 People, 1970–2013

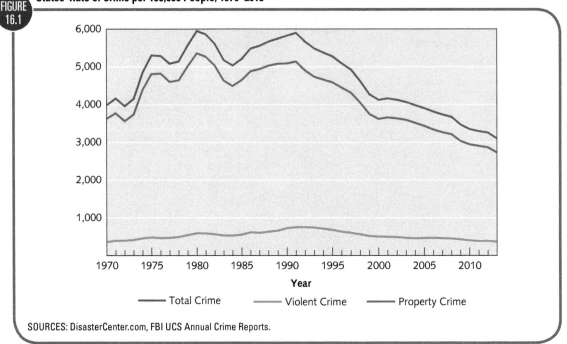

SOURCES: DisasterCenter.com, FBI UCS Annual Crime Reports.

machine guns, night vision equipment, and armored vehicles. Has crime become serious and dangerous enough to warrant such an aggressive approach to enforcing the law?

According to crime statistics, the answer would appear to be no. Both violent and property crime rates have dropped dramatically over the past twenty-five years, as shown in Figure 16.1. Why? The answers are complex and multifaceted—and sometimes contradictory. More police officers on the beat, aggressive community policing programs, and high-tech policing are some of the reasons for the decline in criminal activity. But there are other factors that may be pushing the crime rate down as well, such as an aging population.

LO 16.1

To explain how much crime there actually is, and how it is measured.

How Much Crime Is There?

Crime data are available from three major sources: the Federal Bureau of Investigation's (FBI's) *Uniform Crime Reports,* its victimization surveys, and self-report surveys. The FBI's annual crime index, drawn from state and local law enforcement agencies nationwide, covers four kinds of violent crime (assault, murder, rape, robbery) and four categories of property crime (arson, burglary, larceny, motor vehicle theft). It tracked a sharp increase in criminal behavior between 1960 and 1980, during which time the rate of violent crime tripled and that of property crime more than doubled. But recently, the rates of both types of crime have dropped (see Figure 16.1). It is a paradox that fear of crime persists even in the face of declining crime rates.

The FBI's statistics are suspect, however—for three reasons. First, they reflect only those crimes reported to local police departments. It is estimated that only about half of total crimes committed are reported to the police. Second, some types of crime are more likely to be reported than others. Police themselves have an incentive to underreport crime to make jurisdictions appear safer than they are. Murders, auto thefts, robberies, and aggravated assaults are usually reported, whereas larceny and rape victims, whether out of embarrassment, fear, or other reasons, may remain silent. Third, the FBI's crime data include only eight types of criminal behavior. Most white-collar crimes and drug crimes are excluded, despite their high numbers. Thus, the index provides only a partial picture of actual criminal activity.

Because of these disadvantages, a second, more accurate approach to measuring crime is used. *Victimization surveys* scientifically survey approximately 160,000 people in jurisdictions in some 90,000 households across the country twice a year, asking them whether they or members of their households have been victims of personal or property crime during the past six months. Also utilized by large metropolitan areas and some states, victimization surveys have been conducted on a nationwide basis by the U.S. Bureau of the Census since 1973. Victimization statistics show identifiable patterns. Men, African Americans, Latinos, young people, and urban dwellers are more likely to be crime victims than others are. According to the National Crime Survey, the true rate of crime is nearly two-and-one-half times greater than that reported by the *Uniform Crime Reports.* Yet even with this measure, the rates of nearly all types of crime have declined markedly.

A third, unofficial source of criminal activity is *self-report surveys,* in which criminologists survey people—and especially juveniles—on their own law-breaking behavior during the prior year. Remarkably, as much as 85 to 90 percent of respondents have reported having committed criminal acts.[1] More than 40 percent of today's age-23-and-under population has been arrested for a crime.[2]

Prediction is problematic because we do not really know what *causes* crime. We can state, however, that it is associated with certain factors. From a broad perspective, criminal activity is normally associated with economic recessions, joblessness, and opportunity, though the significant decline in crime during the most recent recessions would appear to contradict these associations. Crime is most likely to be committed by young males, many of them from impoverished and/or broken families. Crime rates are higher in densely populated cities and states than in rural areas. Urban areas present more targets of opportunity, various sociocultural problems that promote criminal behavior, a better chance of escape for criminals, and a haven for gangs. Crime also appears to be related to poverty, unemployment, low levels of education, marital instability, drug abuse, and race.[3] A recipe for crime and incarceration is to take a male, unemployed, African American high school dropout from a low-income, unstable family background and place him in an urban setting. Approximately one-third of such individuals have served time by their mid-thirties.[4]

But crime is complex. Businesspeople engage in insider trading, fraud, solicit and pay kickbacks, launch Ponzi schemes, and commit other white-collar crimes that cost their victims millions of dollars. Some contractors rig bids on government construction projects and Pentagon defense contracts; some bankers embezzle money; some judges accept bribes; the occasional priest or minister sodomizes a child. The underlying causes of these and other sad cases cannot be attributed to economic deprivation, age, neighborhood, race, or the entertainment industry. Greed certainly contributes to many crimes, as does opportunity; the origins of others remain unknown.

Although reasonable people disagree about the causes of crime, most agree that law enforcement is not as effective as it should be in apprehending and deterring criminals. Fewer than 20 percent of all property crimes reported to the police are "cleared" by an arrest. For violent crimes, the record is better: approximately 48 percent.[5] Probably two-thirds of the arrests, however, do not result in a conviction or in any sort of punishment for the offender. Extrapolation from these somewhat rough estimates indicates that a criminal has only a slight chance—maybe one in a hundred—of being both arrested *and* convicted of a crime.

Fighting Crime

Throwing money at the problem does not seem to be the final answer; research has been unable to find a strong link between higher police expenditures on personnel and materials and a subsequent reduction in crime. Obviously, *how* the money is spent makes a difference. Most criminal activities cannot be prevented by law enforcement officials, and unreported crimes are very difficult to investigate. More prisons and longer sentences have some effect on crime rates. Other factors that appear to be associated with higher arrest rates, and lower crime rates as well, are related to the behavior, tactical deployment, and tools of police officers. Aggressive and active police work in responding to calls from citizens and technology-enhanced prediction and investigation of criminal events seem to help, as does the use of more officers on the streets.

Community policing is the popular terminology for a hands-on law enforcement approach. Typically, officers are assigned specific territorial areas of responsibility and encouraged to use their imagination, experience, and personal touch in fighting crime. Police work directly with citizens and with relevant government and nonprofit organizations to identify problems and solve them creatively. If drug houses, junkies, and prostitutes infest a community, the citizens and community police officer find a way to run them out. They converse with children and adults, aiming to foster trust. Minor troublemakers are identified and counseled before they become big-time offenders. To be effective, officers must add community engagement and social work to their law enforcement duties to make their assigned neighborhood one in which they would themselves be willing to live.[6]

Political scientist James Q. Wilson developed the "Broken Window" approach to fighting crime in a 1982 article he wrote with George L. Kelling. In the authors' words, "If a window in a building is broken and is left unrepaired, all the rest of the windows will soon be broken."[7] The message of a broken window is that no one cares. Of course, the metaphor doesn't apply only to broken windows but extends to all manifestations of neighborhood decay, including dilapidated buildings, public consumption of alcohol and drugs, drug dealing, hookers on street corners, aggressive panhandlers, graffiti, and gang activity. Visual deterioration of a neighborhood leads to social degeneration and makes the area more vulnerable to crime. By preventing or correcting visible manifestations of neighborhood decline, or by "repairing" the "broken windows," neighborhoods will host fewer criminal activities, and positive forces can take root and flourish. Community policing and attention to "broken windows" are said to be at least partly responsible for the dramatic decline in violent crime in large cities since the 1990s, though research findings are mixed.[8]

More controversial, but also believed to be effective, is "stop and frisk," a straightforward approach to reducing violent crime by removing guns from the street. In New York City, Cleveland, Philadelphia, and other cities, officers are trained to profile individuals on the street for the likelihood of packing a weapon or toting illegal drugs. Constantly hitching one's trousers, tightening one's belt, patting an inside pocket, and wearing a heavy coat in warm weather are all indicators of a weapon. Hundreds of handguns and pounds of drugs have been seized in high-crime neighborhoods using stop and frisk tactics. The tactic won approval by the U.S. Supreme Court,[9] but it is very controversial in minority neighborhoods and opposed by civil rights groups. In New York, for example, perceived excess in arrests of young black and Latino males for possession of small amounts of marijuana (50,684 arrests in 2011 alone) convinced Governor Andrew Cuomo to call for decriminalization of possession of small amounts of weed. As community groups organized against seemingly random and heavy-handed street stops and a state judge ruled such practices illegal, the number of stop-and-frisk occurrences has dropped sharply in New York City and elsewhere.[10]

Other crime-fighting approaches are increasingly in use, and they, too, are raising concerns. Video surveillance systems are being widely adopted by cities to keep an eye on crime-ridden areas. The cameras produce a constant stream of intelligence data and appear to reduce the crime rates, while offsetting the need for more uniformed officers. Of course, the cameras must be strategically deployed and actively monitored. Another video application that helps document traffic stops, arrests, and other officer-citizen encounters is the body-mounted camera. Attached to the officer's chest or patrol car, the devices provide visual evidence that can be used in the courtroom. An added bonus is that allegations of police misconduct are caught on film, as are violent encounters with suspects.

Using another sense—that of hearing—gunshot tracking systems help police respond almost immediately to shootings, assist victims, and nab suspects. Sensors placed in troubled areas transmit a gunshot's distance and direction from the sensor directly to police headquarters. When combined with video surveillance, gunshot tracking can be a powerful law enforcement tool.

Other forms of high-tech, data-driven policing include integrating criminal activity data with day, location, season, and previous crime patterns.

It's Your Turn

Should Potentially Invasive Data-Driven Policing Technology be Restricted or Prohibited?

The National Security Agency (NSA) is well known for using invasive techniques to track telephone and Internet-based communications under the guise of fighting terrorism. But a growing number of state and local governments are learning fast, and accessing new technology that raises important questions about the long arm of the law. At least twenty-six states permit federal, state, or local law enforcement agencies to search photo databases, including drivers' licenses, to identify people. Accessing facial recognition technology, Ohio and other states are using facial features from drivers' license photos to help identify criminals from video and other sources. Pinellas County, Florida can search more than 120 million individuals in photo databases in Florida and elsewhere.

Facial recognition systems are biometric tools that can be deployed remotely from police laptops, just as license plates scans have for years. Still-emerging biometrics permit individuals to be identified through their irises, vein prints, palm prints, skin tone, and gait.[+]

Data can come not only from drivers' licenses but also from video cameras and other means of surveillance. Facebook and other social media networks? They, too, are fair game for data gathering and facial recognition technology.[++] What's next—drones that spy on us? Actually, yes. A growing number of law enforcement agencies are employing an eye in the sky to keep watch on protests, suspected gang activity, and the whereabouts of suspects.[+++]

Should state and local governments start restricting such invasive actions to protect our liberties and freedom?

[+]Craig Timberg and Ellen Nakashima, "State Photo-ID Databases Become Troves for Police," www.washingtonpost.com (June 16, 2013).

[++]John Buntin, "Social Science: Facebook and Other Social Media Networks are Up-Ending the Way Chicago Fights Gag Violence," *Governing* (October 2013): 27–33.

[+++]Eli Richman, "Rise of the Machines," *Governing* (December 2012): 55–57.

PROS	CONS
What one does, so long as it does not involve breaking the law, is one's own business—not the government's.	These law enforcement technologies protect citizens and governments from criminals and terrorists and help police identify suspects and make arrests.
These are tools for routine, suspicion-less surveillance of vehicles and individuals; as such, they intrude on our freedom and right to privacy.	These are tools to advance law enforcement; they are used cautiously so that privacy rights are not violated.
Facial searches and other biometric techniques ignore the boundaries between criminal and non-criminal databases by placing innocent people's images in what amounts to perpetual digital lineups.	Advanced technology is a weapon in the war on terrorism.
These technologies are first steps towards developing a national ID system through drivers' licenses.	If you are not doing anything wrong, you have nothing to worry about.
	Any restrictions should be the responsibility of the national government—not the states or localities.

GIS technology can map crime and cross reference related variables in a massive database on criminals and criminal activity, helping predict when and where the next incident is likely to occur. This "evidence-based policing" involves targeting, testing, and tracking people and places to better utilize police resources.[11] A growing number of some departments are sharing some of the data online so residents can be informed about criminal activity in their neighborhood.[12]

Through such creative adaptation of emerging technology, law enforcement attempts to stay one step ahead of criminals and better protect people and property. A certain balance, however, must be sought between surveillance technology and citizens' right to privacy. It's Your Turn presents more on some disturbing developments.

The Ongoing Challenge of Crime Fighting

LO 16.2

To understand the ongoing challenge of crime fighting.

The vast proportion of dollars spent on law enforcement comes from states and localities. Congress and the president provide plenty of rhetoric but relatively little material assistance. In the majority of jurisdictions, crime is under control and citizens feel relatively safe. But many jurisdictions, particularly in urban poverty areas, are victims of demographics. High poverty rates, dysfunctional families, free-flowing illegal drug markets, and violent gangs are all factors invariably associated with high crime rates. The hard-pressed police often find themselves simply trying to contend with the worst crimes. As for politicians, it is easy for them to talk "tough on crime" but then offer little extra financial assistance for fighting crime. For the cop on the street, tough and immediate judgment calls must often be made: arrest or mediate in a domestic dispute? Call for backup now or deal with the situation first? Does this berserk halfwit have a gun? Should I draw and fire now?

Community policing, the broken windows approach, stop-and-frisk, and high-tech policing all are being tried across jurisdictions in the United States. Nonetheless, much of the effectiveness of law enforcement depends on the officers themselves, who work in a most dangerous and stressful occupation.

Intergovernmental Roles in Criminal Justice

LO 16.3

To understand intergovernmental roles in criminal justice.

Problems with the U.S. system of criminal justice cannot be attributed to a lack of human and material resources. About 1.1 million employees work full-time in state and local police agencies. Total state and local payroll exceeds $7.7 billion.[13]

The states and localities exercise jurisdiction over more than 95 percent of all crime that occurs in the United States. Municipal and county police and sheriff's departments bear much of the burden of law enforcement, employing a large majority of all sworn police employees; the state law enforcement organizations (highway patrol and special agencies) employ many fewer.[14]

These state and local entities enforce state laws and local ordinances. Federal crimes such as treason, kidnapping, and counterfeiting are dealt with by the FBI and processed through the federal courts and correctional system. The two systems are separate, but some cooperation occurs. For instance, the FBI and state law enforcement agencies exchange information such as fingerprints, mug shots, data, and details on the movements of fugitives, suspected terrorists, and drug smugglers; they sometimes work together in criminal investigations, as they have in numerous drug busts and anti-terrorist activities.

Nine out of every ten dollars spent on police protection and corrections come from the coffers of state and local governments—an illustration of the decentralized nature of criminal justice spending in the United States. The national government's resources are concentrated on homeland security and federal corrections agencies. However, Washington provides certain forms of direct financial assistance to the states and localities, totaling more than $1 billion, to hire more police and adopt crime-fighting strategies.

Greater national involvement in state and local law enforcement is being called for, given the rise in sophisticated cybercrime; the growing economic, political, and global dimensions of organized crime; human trafficking; drug trafficking; the ever-present threat of terrorist acts; and the fact that criminal activities do not respect jurisdictional boundaries. States and localities can do only so much to combat the poverty, poor housing, inadequate education, and other social and economic conditions that are conducive to crime.

LO 16.4

To identify the actors in criminal justice policy and their respective roles.

Actors in Criminal Justice Policy

There is a large cast of characters in state and local criminal justice systems. State policy leadership is exercised by the governor, who sets the tone for the pursuit of law and order through State of the State addresses, proposed legislation, and public presentations. It is the rare governor who does not announce a new law enforcement program of some type.

Legislative bodies decide what a crime is and prohibit it through laws, establish the structure of the legal system, and determine sentencing parameters including the option of capital punishment. Legislatures tend to be responsive to citizen pressures on law enforcement issues, as demonstrated by lawmakers' activity in areas such as gun control, the death penalty, and sentencing reform.

LAW ENFORCEMENT OFFICIALS

The state attorney general formally heads the law enforcement function in most states; county and city attorneys and district attorneys typically follow the attorney general's lead. These positions call for a great deal of discretion in deciding whom to prosecute for which alleged crimes or civil violations. The prosecution of offenses is a politically charged endeavor, particularly when it is within the authority of people who aspire to higher political office. On the other side of the courtroom are public defenders and private defense attorneys, who try to negotiate dropped charges, a favorable plea bargain, or get their clients declared innocent.

The highway patrol (state troopers), special state law enforcement divisions modeled on the FBI, county sheriffs, police chiefs, local line and staff officers, and civilian employees are also important. They are responsible for implementing the policies decided on by elected officials and for carrying out the basic day-to-day activities connected with enforcing the law. But it is the highway patrol, the county sheriff, and the cops on the street who are the frontline law enforcers. Dangerous and stressful, policing is a profession in high demand.

THE COURTS

State and local courts decide the innocence or guilt of defendants brought before them, based on the evidence submitted (see Chapter 9). In the great majority of cases, however, plea bargaining prevails and the case never goes to trial. Courts can also influence criminal justice through rulings that specify correct police procedures in criminal cases. U.S. Supreme Court decisions, in particular, have shaped the criminal justice process. The federal courts have the final word on cases in which the defendants claim that their federal rights have been violated by state or local law enforcement personnel. (State courts handle alleged violations of state constitutional rights.)

Critics have asserted that the Supreme Court has made it more difficult to convict criminals through decisions that have expanded the rights of the accused. The most controversial and oft-criticized case is *Miranda v. Arizona* (1966)[15]; this decision expanded the rights of the accused by requiring police officers to inform anyone suspected of a crime of the right to remain silent; the fact that anything said can and will be used against him or her in a court of law; and the right to be represented by counsel, paid for by the state if necessary. Evidence obtained when the accused has not clearly indicated his understanding of these *Miranda* warnings or explicitly waived his rights is not legally admissible in the courtroom because it is considered a violation of the Fifth Amendment right not to incriminate oneself.

The U.S. Supreme Court also influenced state and local criminal procedures in the case of *Mapp v. Ohio* (1961). Basing its decision on the due process clause of the Fourteenth Amendment, the Court ruled that evidence obtained illegally by the police cannot be introduced in court.[16] This "exclusionary rule" extended the Fourth Amendment's protection from illegal search and seizure. The police must have a search warrant specifying which person or place will be searched and what will be seized. Over time, these and other early decisions favoring the accused have been relaxed by a conservative Supreme Court.

THE PUBLIC'S INVOLVEMENT

The voting public also participates in justice policy. Citizens make demands on officials (the governor, legislators, judges, police, and so on) to conform to public opinion on crimes and criminals. Generally, the pressure is on for more law and order, and it results in strict criminal codes and correctional policies. Citizens also participate directly in the criminal justice system by serving on juries. Most citizens consider it their public duty to serve on a jury from time to time, and such service does tend to be an interesting (if not always edifying) experience. Trials usually last fewer than four days, and many prospective jurors are never called into the courtroom. But occasionally, a jury trial will drag out over a lengthy period; one of the longest was concluded in Belleville, Illinois, after a 44-month marathon concerning liability for a toxic chemical spill. Attorneys for the losing party then announced that they would appeal.[17]

Citizens also participate in criminal justice by sitting on grand juries. A **grand jury** (which is typically composed of 12 members) serves as a check on the power of the state or local prosecutor by considering evidence in a case and then deciding whether to indict the accused. Twenty states require a grand jury **indictment** for serious crimes. In other states, it is optional, or a preliminary hearing of charges and evidence before a judge is used instead. In practice, grand juries are inclined to rubber-stamp whatever course of action is recommended by the prosecutor. Rarely does one question the professional legal opinion of the district attorney or attorney general.

An additional function of the grand jury is to act as an investigatory body for certain types of crimes, particularly vice, political and corporate corruption, and organized crime. In this capacity, it is empowered to issue subpoenas for evidence and suspects whom it wishes to examine. A statewide grand jury is most appropriate for criminal investigations because it can deal with activities that cross county or district boundaries. Among the states that provide for statewide grand juries are Arizona, Colorado, Florida, New Jersey, South Carolina, and Virginia.

Finally, the public may become involved in the criminal justice process by tackling crime on its own. Telephone and web-based crime report lines; neighborhood crime watches and patrols; neighborhood complaints of prostitution, drug dealing, or gang activity; and similar actions to report "broken windows" help take a bite out of crime.

THE VICTIM

An often ignored influence on criminal justice policy is the victim. Many victims are left psychologically, physically, and/or financially damaged after a crime. States have responded to this sad fact by developing victim compensation programs. These programs are typically administered by a board, which assesses the validity of victims' claims and decides on a monetary award to help compensate for hospital and doctor bills, loss of property, and other financial needs resulting from the crime. Maximum state benefits, supplemented by the federal Victims of Violent Crime Act (VOCA), usually vary from $10,000 to $25,000, depending on the state (60 percent of the money comes from the federal government). Rarely is a victim made whole by these limited payments, but at least some assistance is provided to help the person deal with the various traumas of the crime.[18]

States permit use of victim-impact statements in court before sentencing a convicted criminal. The statements may include victims' and family members' views on how the crime has affected them, and their feelings about the

grand jury

A group of citizens appointed to determine if there is enough evidence to bring a person to trial.

indictment

A formal, written accusation submitted to a court by a grand jury, alleging a specified crime.

crime and the accused. Most states and many counties now provide victim notification systems so that crime victims are made aware of their assailants' subsequent prison release. The federal Megan's Law requires notification of a community when a convicted sex offender moves into the neighborhood. (Megan was a seven-year-old girl who was sexually assaulted and murdered by a neighbor who had recently been released from prison after serving time as a sex offender.)[19] States post their sex offender registry on the web, listing the names and whereabouts of offenders.

How Policy Participants Interact: Two Policy Areas

LO 16.5

To explain how policy participants interact.

All states do not define or treat crimes in the same manner. The states' handling of criminal justice in two policy areas—victimless crimes and capital punishment—illuminates this point.

VICTIMLESS CRIME

Prostitution, pornography, illegal drug use, music and movie pirating, and flouting mandatory seatbelt and motorcycle helmet laws are all examples of victimless crimes. Statutes enacted by legislative bodies define what constitutes criminal behavior, and public opinion usually influences what activities the legislatures treat as criminal. **Victimless crimes** are voluntary acts that violate the law but no one's individual rights. Some such acts are perceived to present little or no threat to individuals or society. Yet up to 50 percent of all arrests in urban areas is estimated to be on charges of victimless crimes.

One may argue that such crimes should be wiped off the books because those who engage in these activities suffer willingly (if at all). A strong case can be made for legalizing, regulating, and taxing prostitution and recreational drugs. People will pursue these activities anyway, the argument goes, so why criminalize and incarcerate a large portion of the population unnecessarily? Instead, why not get a little piece of the action for the public purse? State regulation of gambling helps diminish the role of organized crime, and regulation of prostitution can help prevent the spread of sexually transmitted diseases by requiring regular medical checkups for prostitutes. Though "massage parlors" and "escort services" exist in all major cities, only Nevada has legalized and regulated prostitution.

Finally, legalizing "recreational" drugs promises to take the profits out of the drug trade and to reduce drug-related crime and corruption. An estimated one-third of all new state prisoners have been convicted of drug-related crimes. The tens of billions of dollars spent annually by the United States on the "war on drugs" have resulted in a pathetic failure, leaving us today with just as many addicts, swelling prison populations containing some half a million (mostly nonviolent) drug offenders, an enormously profitable, gang-driven importation and distribution system that lures young people and even grade-school children into the trade, and a great deal of drug-related violence.[20] By shifting drug enforcement money and efforts to medical and psychiatric treatment of addicts

victimless crimes
Illegal acts that, in theory, do no one any harm.

and users, perhaps legalization would even lead to less addiction, while padding the public purse. As discussed in Chapter 3, many states have decided to legalize and tax medical and/or recreational marijuana.

In states where legislative bodies define the scope of criminal behavior broadly to include victimless crimes, an extra burden is placed on other actors in the criminal justice system. Prosecutors and law enforcement authorities find much of their time consumed by these relatively minor and nonthreatening activities when they could be concentrating on more serious crimes, such as murder, rape, and robbery. The courts must also spend a great deal of time processing these cases. The legalization of certain victimless crimes would immediately shorten the dockets of prosecutors, police, and judges; render the process more manageable; and reduce the burgeoning prison and jail population. A less radical strategy is *decriminalization*—the prescribing of a minor penalty (usually a small fine) for specified crimes. For example, many states and localities have decriminalized possession of small amounts of marijuana.

Opponents claim that *victimless* is the wrong word to describe these actions. For example, with the selling of sex, prostitutes and their clients can become infected with the HIV virus and other communicable diseases. It is not uncommon for prostitutes to endure serious emotional and physical costs. Legalization of drugs such as methamphetamines, heroin, or crack cocaine might lead to a significant rise in addiction rates and require higher spending for treatment and health care. And if legalization were selective (say, only marijuana, cocaine, and ecstasy were made available legally), then new, more powerful designer drugs would likely continue to debut on the market.

In practice, hard-pressed prosecutors often drop charges against perpetrators of victimless crimes, judges dismiss the least offensive cases or administer a small fine or a suspended sentence, and law enforcement personnel tend to look the other way when passing near a prostitute or a smoker of weed. De facto decriminalization is the norm for many victimless crimes in much of the United States, especially in the case of legally prohibited sexual behavior between consenting adults, including sodomy, adultery, and the ever-popular fornication.

LO 16.6

CAPITAL PUNISHMENT

To assess the benefits and problems of capital punishment.

Capital punishment offers a second example of how states vary in their approach to criminal justice. In this area, the interactions among individuals and institutions are critically important. Public opinion helps determine a legislature's propensity to enact and courts to carry out a death penalty statute. Prosecutors must decide under which circumstances to seek the death penalty. Only juries can find a defendant guilty or innocent in a capital case. Judges apply the penalty of death, subject to lengthy appellate review. Governors have the power to commute a sentence of execution. And the federal courts have played an important role in determining the conditions under which a state can legally put a person to death for a crime.

Criminal executions were once commonplace in the United States. In colonial days, public hangings were considered appropriate for adulterers, religious heretics, blasphemers, and thieves. A total of 717 people were legally executed during the 1950s. But public opinion slowly began to turn against capital punishment and so did the U.S. Supreme Court. In the 1972 case of *Furman v. Georgia*, a 5-to-4 majority held that the death penalty had been applied in a cruel, arbitrary, and racist manner by the states.[21] The Supreme Court expressly declared unconstitutional the capital punishment statutes in Louisiana and North Carolina and implicitly invalidated similar laws in many other states. It held that death penalty laws could be valid only if used in accordance with correct procedures and standards and could be invoked solely for lethal crimes.

The Supreme Court later ruled that the use of the death penalty for those who committed crimes while juveniles is unconstitutional.[22] But in one seemingly bizarre 2003 case, the Court let stand lower court rulings that Arkansas could forcibly administer drugs to an insane murderer to render him sane enough to be executed.[23] However, the Court did prevent the execution of a retarded murderer in 2002 and of a man who raped, but did not kill, his eight-year-old stepdaughter in a 2008 decision.[24]

Several states voluntarily abolished capital punishment in the 1960s and 1970s. The majority, however, rewrote their statutes to conform to the Supreme Court's guidelines (see Figure 16.2). In 2008, the U.S. Supreme Court held in

States With and Without the Death Penalty, and Post-1976 Executions, May 2015
Most states permit capital punishment, although some have not actually carried out the death penalty for many years. The map shows the number executed since 1976 or the year the death penalty was abolished.

FIGURE 16.2

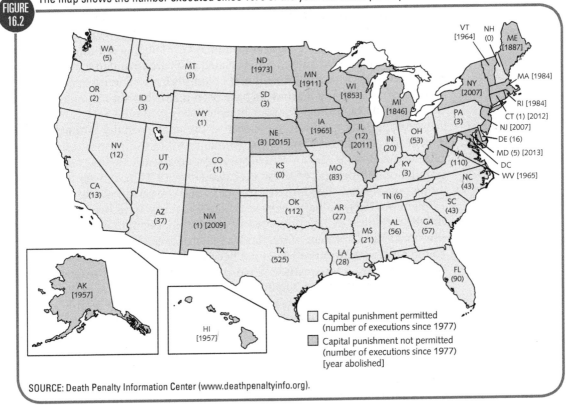

SOURCE: Death Penalty Information Center (www.deathpenaltyinfo.org).

Baze v. Rees that the three-drug cocktail used to lethally inject the accused in Kentucky (and by implication in many other states) was constitutionally valid; executions then recommenced in several states following an unofficial six-month moratorium while the case was under review.[25]

A total of thirty-two states permit executions today. The most commonly used technique is lethal injection. Several states permit the condemned to choose the method of execution, adding to lethal injection the possibilities of lethal gas (five states), electrocution (eight states), hanging (three states), or firing squad (only Utah and Oklahoma permit this method). Those states supportive of the death penalty tend to have both a politically conservative population and a high murder rate. Some 3,019 inmates were languishing on death row in state penitentiaries in early 2015. While statutes were being rewritten and clarified between 1968 and 1976, no executions were carried out. Since January 1977, however, 1,408 people have made the long walk from death row to the death chamber, more than 80 percent of them in the South. Texas is the leading executioner; the state used lethal injection to execute 525 felons between 1976 and May 2015.[26]

Recent public opinion polls indicate that 56 percent of the American people favor capital punishment, a figure that has been declining. But when presented with the alternative of life without parole, the "in favor" group drops to below 50 percent.[27] Execution remains a rather tedious and enormously expensive endeavor. The prisoners executed today have spent, on average, around eleven years on death row. The appeals process presents numerous opportunities for delay, and it is not unusual for an inmate, after languishing for a decade or more on death row, to escape the death penalty through the legal process. The price tag on death is shocking, averaging millions of dollars per execution when court and other related costs are considered; the price in Maryland recently was estimated at $186 million for five executions since 1976. Not surprisingly, arguments have been made that abolishing the death penalty would be positive for state budgets.

An especially troublesome aspect of the death penalty is that African Americans receive this form of punishment well out of proportion to their numbers. Although African Americans make up about 13 percent of the U.S. population, 35 percent of those executed since 1977 have been black, and 42 percent of death-row inmates are black. Blacks who kill whites are significantly more likely to be sentenced to death. Latinos have been executed in rough proportion to their presence in the overall population—8 percent—and they make up 13 percent of death-row inmates. Less than 2 percent of those condemned to death since 1977 have been women, and very few women have been executed.[28] A recent study in North Carolina indicates that female murderers tend to have fewer aggravating factors in their offense, and they also tend to have more mitigating factors, such as no prior record or only indirect participation in the murder.[29]

Under various U.S. Supreme Court rulings, application of the death sentence must not be idiosyncratic or capricious. Critics of the death penalty claim, however, that it is applied capriciously, from the decision of a prosecutor to ask the jury to determine that a given crime is a capital offense to the requisite review of a jury's death sentence by the state supreme court.

The offender's race is definitely a consideration, as noted earlier. And those who murder police officers, women, the elderly, or multiple victims are more likely to be sentenced to death, as are those who kill after a sexual assault or robbery.[30] Aggravating factors such as rape typically weigh heavily in jury decisions to invoke the death penalty.

Obviously, a great deal of controversy surrounds the issue of executing criminals. Researchers generally agree that if punishment is to discourage future criminal behavior, it must be swift and certain. Neither of these conditions is met by the death penalty in the United States. And few reasonable and informed people today argue that capital punishment acts as a deterrent, except in the specific case of the guilty individual who is executed. Studies comparing homicide rates in states with and without death penalties either find no significant differences in homicide rates or find that states with capital punishment actually have higher rates of homicide.

Also disturbing is the fact that the personal characteristics of judges influence their decisions. Republicans are much more likely to vote for the death penalty, as are older judges and those with previous experience as a prosecutor.[31] In this sense, the death penalty resembles a judicial lottery. Application of the death penalty can also be cruel and unusual punishment in more ways than one. In one case, Florida's "Old Sparky" overheated, causing flames and smoke to erupt from a leather mask worn by the unfortunate murderer, Pedro Medina. (This gruesome scene helped to convince Florida officials to replace the electric chair with lethal injection.) As noted above, even lethal injection has come under fire as a cruel and unusual cause of death. Efforts to locate a suitable vein in a former junkie can take hours. Recently, an Arizona prisoner took two hours to die, struggling for breath. Execution of an Oklahoma inmate was stopped after he grimaced and struggled after his three-drug cocktail, only to die of a heart attack shortly thereafter. Prison officials had searched for a usable vein for nearly an hour before finally inserting the needle into his groin.

Typically, three chemicals are injected into the prisoner: a barbiturate, a paralytic, and then a heart-stopping substance. If the first chemical is improperly administered and therefore ineffective, the other two can cause extreme agony. A U.S. shortage of one of the three drugs began in 2011, and along with resistance of other countries to exporting it to these shores, resulted in introduction of a new death drug, pentobarbital. (It is commonly used to euthanize pets). New drug combinations are being tried in what one critic called "human science experiments."

The public has become increasingly ambivalent about the death penalty because of growing evidence of serious problems in the justice system, and a growing citizen concern for possible innocence.[32] Studies have found that two of every three death sentences are eventually overturned, usually due to errors by incompetent defense attorneys or evidence withheld by prosecutors and police officers.

Calls for an end to executions have grown louder, and some states have heeded them. Illinois' legislature wrote the epitaph of the death penalty in 2011, Maryland repealed it in 2013, and high courts in Kansas, Nebraska, and New York ruled executions to be unconstitutional. A number of states in which the death penalty is legally condoned have not put anyone to death for years.

Concern is growing that innocent people are being put to death. The arbitrary nature of the death penalty and other public concerns are registered in statistics. From a post-1977 peak of ninety-eight executions in 1999, the number plummeted to only thirty-five in 2014. Similarly, the number of death sentences had declined from 315 in 1996 to just seventy-two in 2014.[33] DNA testing makes identification of a killer a statistical certainty when such evidence is available, and more states are demanding that DNA evidence be submitted before extinguishing a person's life and that inmates proven to be innocent are freed. It is estimated that more than 130 men and women have been exonerated since 1973, many of them as a result of negative DNA tests, and others because of incompetent defense attorneys or prosecutorial or police misconduct.[34] Two mentally deficient North Carolina brothers sentenced to death in 1984 were freed thirty years later when evidence was uncovered that crime scene DNA implicated a different man, since deceased.

On the side of those favoring the death penalty is the argument for the legitimacy of *lex talionis*, the principle that the punishment should fit the crime. According to this view, some crimes are so heinous that only the death of the perpetrator can balance the scales of justice and relieve the moral outrage of society. This argument for justice as retribution cannot be validated on empirical grounds; it is an ethical question that each state must legislatively resolve.

LO 16.7

To understand and evaluate state correctional policy.

Correctional Policy

A person convicted of a crime in a court of law becomes the object of correctional policy, which, as its name implies, aims to correct behavior that society finds unacceptable. In theory, an offender should first be punished, both for retribution and to serve as a lesson for other potential criminals. Second, convicted lawbreakers should be rehabilitated so they can become productive law-abiding citizens after fulfilling the terms of their punishment. Third, criminals who represent a danger to society should be physically separated from the general public.

If correcting criminal behavior is the overarching goal of correctional policy in the states, we have a terrible policy failure on our hands. As already noted, most crimes do not result in an arrest. Even when an offender is detained by the police, she stands a good chance of avoiding conviction or incarceration. Thus, deterrence is a dubious proposition at best. Remember that the best way to prevent undesirable behavior is through swift and certain punishment. Those of us who quizzically stuck a foreign object into an electrical outlet in childhood received the shock of swift punishment. If we were foolish enough to try it a second time, we discovered that the punishment was certain. Only the imbecilic or masochistic among us would subject themselves to such abuse a third time. That is how our correctional policy would have to work if deterrence is to be achieved. But for various reasons, swift and certain punishment is unlikely.

The U.S. Department of Justice estimates that over 40 percent of former inmates released from state prisons commit another serious offense or violate the terms of parole or probation within three years and return to prison because of it. It appears that prisons actually increase the likelihood that an individual will commit additional crimes when he is freed. Our state prisons have been called breeding pens for criminals. Instead of being rehabilitated, the first-time offender is likely to receive expert schooling in various criminal professions. Overcrowding, understaffing, physical and sexual brutality, gangs, and rampant drug abuse do not help an offender become a law-abiding citizen. Many approaches have been tried—counseling, vocational training, basic education, and others—but none has consistently been able to overcome the criminalizing environment of state prison systems.

Without doubt, most incarcerated offenders see deprivation of their freedom as punishment, and so retribution does occur. For the average felon, "going to jail sucks."[35] Just as surely, prison effectively removes some undesirable characters from our midst. These two objectives of correctional policy are achieved to some degree, although cynics point out that sentencing tends to be rather inconsistent and a significant proportion of criminals are released before serving out their sentences. Most important, and contrary to the conventional wisdom, research consistently shows that state imprisonment rates are not significantly related to crime rates. In fact, supporting the notion that prisons are colleges for criminals, incarceration might actually boost crime.[36]

SENTENCING

Sentencing reform has recently received a great deal of attention in the states. The inconsistency of criminal sentencing is obvious if we examine incarceration rates. About one of every thirty-five U.S. adults is in prison or jail, with state figures varying from one in thirteen in Georgia to one in eighty-eight in New Hampshire[37] (see Figure 16.3). Southern states tend to be toughest on crime: they are more than twice as likely as other states to convict people arrested on felony charges, and their sentences are more severe than those in other regions. As observed above, however, crime rates and incarceration rates are not closely related. Some states with relatively high rates of crime lock up fewer people than do other states with lower crime rates.

One striking inconsistency is the extremely high lockup rate of African Americans in state and federal prisons: Black men are six times as likely as white men to be locked up: they comprise about 40 percent of the male prison population, according to federal statistics. This imbalance has been attributed to poverty, poor education, and other demographics of criminal activity, which drive up the black crime rate, as well as law enforcement's focus on crack cocaine, which is found predominantly in the inner-city black communities.[38] Possession of crack is punished more severely in the courts than offenses involving other illegal drugs. The political climate also matters: States dominated by conservative Republicans tend to imprison disproportionate rates of blacks.[39] Similarly, Latino defendants tend to receive harsher sentences than whites.[40] It should not come as a surprise that blacks and Latinos are much more suspicious of police and distrustful of criminal justice systems than are whites. With some 2.3 million prisoners, the United States has the second highest incarceration rate in the world, trailing only the island nation of Seychelles. With only 5 percent of the earth's people, the United States has about one-quarter of the world's prisoners.

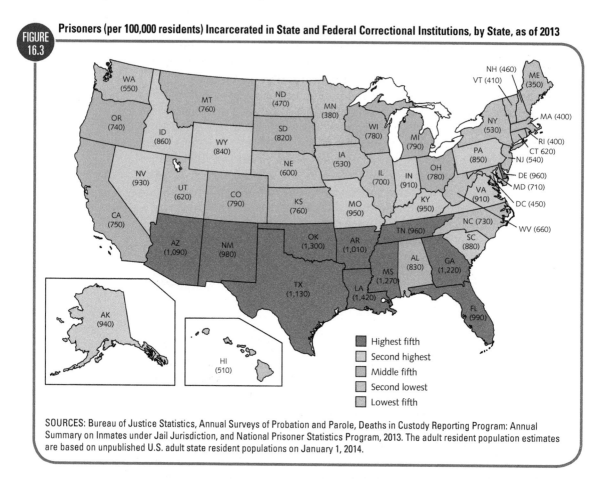

FIGURE 16.3

Prisoners (per 100,000 residents) Incarcerated in State and Federal Correctional Institutions, by State, as of 2013

Legend:
- Highest fifth
- Second highest
- Middle fifth
- Second lowest
- Lowest fifth

SOURCES: Bureau of Justice Statistics, Annual Surveys of Probation and Parole, Deaths in Custody Reporting Program: Annual Summary on Inmates under Jail Jurisdiction, and National Prisoner Statistics Program, 2013. The adult resident population estimates are based on unpublished U.S. adult state resident populations on January 1, 2014.

indeterminate sentencing

Sentencing in which a judge exercises discretion when deciding on the number of years for the sentence.

determinate sentencing

Mandatory sentencing that is determined by law, not a judge's discretion.

Why is our incarceration rate so high? First, prison sentences are harsh compared with those in other countries. Historically, state courts applied **indeterminate sentencing**, whereby judges have great discretion in deciding the number of years for which an offender should be sentenced to prison. The offender then becomes eligible for parole after a minimum period is served, based on good behavior and meeting prison goals. For instance, a ten- to twenty-year sentence for armed robbery might require the inmate to serve at least five years. After that time, he becomes eligible for parole, subject to the judgment of a parole board, which reviews the case and the prisoner's behavior in prison.

But the trend has been **determinate sentencing**, in which offenders are given mandatory terms that they must serve without the possibility of parole. Under so-called truth-in-sentencing laws, about half the states require violent offenders to serve at least 85 percent of their sentences, or even "life without possibility of parole." Determinate sentencing is designed to reduce the sentencing disparity among judges. It also eliminates the need for parole. Naturally, determinate sentencing keeps prisoners incarcerated for longer periods than indeterminate sentencing does.

A second explanation is public opinion, which tilts toward a punitive approach for criminals. Opportunistic politicians tend to assume a "law and order" posture and attempt to validate it by enacting strict sentencing laws.[41] This punitive attitude that the public has taken toward criminals has helped stiffen not only the sentences awarded by judges, but also the judgments of parole boards.

The "lock-'em up" syndrome is perhaps best shown by the "three-strikes-and-you're-out" legislation that has been enacted in twenty-eight states. Such laws mandate tough sanctions for habitual felons who are convicted of a third violent or serious crime. In some three-strikes states, even a *minor* conviction can invoke a twenty-five-year-to-life sentence, for stealing golf clubs, possessing only a dusting of cocaine, or serving as middleman in a $10 sale of marijuana. The price tag for "three strikes" has been projected at billions of dollars annually for new prisons and their operating costs. Additional judges have to be hired and more courtrooms operated to hear the increased number of jury trials. As a consequence, three-strikes laws are rarely applied in most states. In California, where the three-strikes law had imprisoned more than 400 offenders for life for committing non-violent (mostly drug-related) crimes, voters passed a 2012 initiative that permits nonviolent "strikers" to apply for shorter terms. A subsequent study found that the early release prisoners had lower rates of recidivism than other paroled prisoners.[42]

A third contributing factor to high imprisonment rates is drug enforcement penalties. Most drug-related offenses do not involve violence and are "victimless," yet they have been severely punished as part of the failed war on drugs. As mentioned earlier, we "lost" the war on drugs many years ago. Drug supplies are ample and cheap, yet large proportions of our jails and prisons are populated with nonviolent drug offenders.

States are rethinking mandatory minimum sentences for drug offenders. Arkansas, Louisiana, New York, Texas, and other states have rolled them back, favoring community-based drug treatment programs instead. California voters passed an initiative that mandates treatment rather than prison for first and second drug offenses. By diverting and treating drug offenders, such policy changes have significantly reduced prison populations in some states.[43]

But most criminals *are* doing more time, and prisons are increasingly serving as expensive geriatric hospitals for relatively harmless criminals who are senior citizens. Prisoners aged fifty-five or older account for about 8 percent of state prisoners, a figure that is expected to rise sharply. Already, states are grouping aging inmates within assisted living correctional facilities and nursing homes for their special health care needs, as well as to protect them from younger, more violent inmates.[44] The average yearly cost of housing a sickly, geriatric prisoner, who may have ailments ranging from HIV/AIDS, liver or kidney disease, to mental illness or dementia, can run three times the amount for a younger, healthy inmate. Yet "criminal menopause" apparently afflicts felons in their twilight years, making them unlikely to commit a new crime if released.

PRISON CONDITIONS

As noted above, 2.3 million people are confined to state prisons and local jails in the United States. The number of prisoners was growing by about 4 percent annually until 2010, when lower crime rates and state sentencing reforms helped reverse the trend. Prisons continue to operate beyond official capacity in many states, despite the construction of numerous new facilities to reduce the problems of prison overcrowding and its accompanying conditions of poor sanitation, inadequate health care, and high levels of violence. Traditionally, courts assumed a hands-off policy toward offenders once they were behind prison walls. The administration of state correctional systems was the sole responsibility of corrections officials. But in a series of decisions, the federal courts applied the Eighth Amendment prohibition on cruel and unusual punishment and the Fourteenth Amendment provision for due process and equal protection of the laws to prison inmates. In addition, the Supreme Court permitted inmates of state and local facilities to bypass less sympathetic state courts and file suits alleging violations of their civil rights in federal courts. Such federal court rulings have altered the nature of correctional policy and changed it greatly.

Much of the litigation has concerned overcrowding. As more and more people were sentenced to prison, corrections officials responded by doubling, tripling, and even quadrupling cell arrangements. It was not unusual for inmates to be crowded together at the rate of one per ten square feet of floor space. Drastic improvements were long overdue in Arkansas and Alabama, for instance. At Arkansas's dreaded maximum-security institution, Cumming Farms, inmates were worked in the fields like slaves, ten hours a day, six days a week, in all types of weather. At night they slept in 100-man barracks. Rapes and other forms of physical violence occurred regularly. A federal lawsuit led to the finding that Arkansas's entire penal system was in violation of the Eighth Amendment.

The adult prison systems of several states are presently being run under federal court orders. A 2009 federal intervention was in California, when a panel of federal judges ordered state officials to reduce the state prison population by 40,591 inmates, to a total of 110,000, within two years. By operating prisons at 190 percent of capacity, California was found to be in violation of the Eight Amendment's prohibition of cruel and unusual punishment, particularly for sick and mentally ill inmates.[45] An average of one death per week was being registered as inmates suffered from medical malpractice and inattention.[46] State officials facing decisions on how to comply with the court order transferred certain categories of prisoners to county jails, and provided funds to assist the counties in constructing new jails and other expenses. Early release was ordered for thousands of inmates to further reduce crowding.

The intrusion of the federal courts into state correctional policy is quite controversial, particularly when they have taken over full operating responsibility or ordered increased state and local expenditures for prisons or mass inmate releases. Important questions concerning the proper division of power between the national government and the states have been raised, as have questions about the competence of federal court officials to run state prison systems. However these important issues in federalism are ultimately resolved, the immediate problem for many states is providing adequate space for their prison populations and finding the money to pay for it.

Prisons have become financial albatrosses. On average, corrections spending trails only education and Medicaid in state budget allocations. State and local spending on prisons and jails, currently estimated at over $47 billion a year, rose at startling rate of 674 percent from 1985 to 2010.[47] Room, board, and care for one state prison inmate averages about $30,000 per year, but can reach up to $60,000 for maximum security prisons. Prison and jail guards must be paid; prisoners fed and tended to. And each new prison bed space for growing ranks of confined criminals can cost up to $100,000. Prison costs are also escalating as a result of health care inflation. Prisoners are a particularly unhealthy subset of the population: Most smoke, many are drug abusers, some have acute mental problems, a troubling proportion is HIV positive, and a growing number are seniors. There seems to be no easy end in sight for prison spending, because of "Murphy's Law of Incarceration": The number of inmates expands to fill all available space, or "if you build them, you'll fill them." However, the prison-building boom is tapering off for three reasons: Many new prisons have already come on line, states are adopting alternatives to incarceration, and state budget problems have resulted in significant cuts to corrections budgets.

Policy Alternatives for States and Localities

LO 16.8

To discuss correctional policy alternatives for states and localities.

In addition to the immediate responses made necessary by federal court actions and budget shortfalls, states and localities are attempting to devise a more comprehensive approach to coping with the problem of prison overcrowding. Whatever their past failings, and primarily for reasons of budget rather than conscience, they are demonstrating today an increasing propensity for experimentation and innovation. Three basic strategies are being employed to bring and keep inmate populations in line with institutional capacity: back-door strategies, front-door strategies, and capacity enhancement.

BACK-DOOR STRATEGIES

Back-door strategies include several methods for releasing offenders from prisons on probation or parole before they have served their full sentences. This strategy is the most conventional of the three, but some interesting innovations are being tested.

One of the less imaginative but nonetheless quite effective ways to deal with prison overcrowding is to grant early release. Most states have early-release programs in place, but the method of implementation varies. In some states, the governor or parole board simply pares off the last few months or weeks of sentences that are nearly completed, until the necessary number of inmates have left the prison. Other states apply a risk analysis approach that predicts the likelihood that certain inmates, if released, will not commit another serious offense. For example, nonviolent offenders are freed before violent offenders, larcenists before burglars, marijuana users before heroin dealers, and so on. An inmate's personal characteristics, prison behavior, and work history may also be taken into consideration. Early release reduces inmate populations quickly, but public outcries are certain to follow when an offender released before expiration of his or her sentence commits a highly publicized violent crime. Ex-cons discharged without oversight and assistance are not likely to become model citizens overnight. Old habits and felonious friends tend to return, and most employers hesitate to hire a convicted felon. Today, felons incarcerated during the lock-'em-up mentality of the 1990s and early 2000s are returning home in record numbers. Past patterns indicate that many will become repeat offenders within three years, a "revolving door" problem that states and localities ignore at their own peril.

Reinventing Parole Many states are taking a close look at new civilian reentry approaches for convicts to boost their chances for successful transition from behind prison walls to the streets. Job-related skills training, placement services, and alcohol and drug counseling (80 percent of ex-cons are released with substance abuse problems) are typical. New, more comprehensive programs are also receiving experimentation. Maryland's Reentry Partnership develops collaborative transition plans for inmates. The state corrections and parole division, local police and health departments, and community organizations work together to determine (with the prisoner's input) individual needs, including counseling, transportation, and housing. Caseworkers and a prisoner's advocate coordinate the services. Hawaii's Opportunity Probation with Enforcement (HOPE) program has reduced recidivism by half through imposing correctional "time outs" for backsliding offenders. Anyone violating the terms of parole or probation is sent immediately back to jail for a few days, then given another opportunity.[48] Programs such as these are much cheaper than what it takes to keep an inmate locked up—a daily cost of less than $10 for probationers and parolees, versus up to $100 to keep an offender behind bars.[49]

Conventional **parole** or **probation** has not been particularly effective, although these programs account for three out of four individuals in the corrections population. In most states that utilize this technique, the parole and probation officers (whose duty it is to keep up with the progress of the released offender) are terribly overworked. An estimated 4.8 million adults are under parole supervision.[50] It is not unknown for one parole officer to be responsible for 200 offenders—a nearly impossible task. (The average is about 60 parolees per case officer and about 100 probationers.)[51] Most probationers and parolees are supposed to receive substance abuse counseling, pay restitution to their victims, or comply with other terms of their release, but many do not. About 9 percent soon end up back behind bars.

Innovations in probation and parole can save serious money. Texas expanded drug treatment programs, reformed parole practices, and established drug courts. As a result, it has saved nearly $1 billion in new prison costs.[52]

Electronic House Detention An approach to parole that takes advantage of technology to monitor parolees' whereabouts is called *electronic house detention*. This technique requires released nonviolent inmates to wear a GPS transmitter (usually on the ankle) that steadily emits signals to a receiver in their home. Failure to detect a signal causes the receiver to contact a central computer automatically. The computer is programmed to know when the inmate is permitted to be away from home (usually during work hours). If an unusual

parole
Program in which offenders are released from prison to serve the remainder of their sentence under community supervision.

probation
Instead of incarceration, this program permits minor offenders to remain in the community under supervision, or to serve brief sentences followed by probation.

signal appears, the computer notifies law enforcement officers. Removal of the transmitter also triggers an alarm at the central computer.

Electronic monitoring is a popular way to cope with prison overcrowding. It is much cheaper than jail or prison (the cost is about $5,500 a year in Florida), and it enables a working prisoner to pay his or her own share of the program and, in some cases, to repay the victim of the crime as well. But it has not been found to significantly reduce new offenses, escapes, or recidivism, though the evidence is mixed.[53] But it is not appropriate for an escape-minded individual, who can cut off the anklet and walk away, perhaps to commit more crimes.

Vocational Programs Another back-door strategy reduces the sentences of prisoners who participate in educational and vocational programs. These programs are intended to teach convicts skills that can help them obtain jobs once they are out of prison, and they have the added benefits of keeping inmates involved in productive, rather than destructive, activities while behind prison walls, and saving the state money. Education and vocational training both reduce recidivism and improve job prospects when prisoners are released.[54] This would seem to be a good investment, since 95 percent of prisoners are eventually released back into the community.

The idea of profiting from prison work has considerable appeal. In addition to using their time productively and learning marketable skills, inmates earn wages that can help defray the cost of their room and board, provide monetary restitution to victims, fund savings accounts for the inmates to use after their release, and even earn early release. Several programs have had encouraging results, including the making of stained-glass windows and restoring of classic cars by Nevada prisoners, training and socializing rescued dogs for adoption in Oklahoma and Kansas, fighting forest fires in Oregon and Georgia, saddle-making and tilapia raising and packaging in Colorado, and the sewing of everything from bed covers to Victoria's Secret lingerie in South Carolina. Prison industries may include more conventional activities like printing, metalworking, textiles, signs and license plates, and basic manufacturing.

FRONT-DOOR STRATEGIES

The second basic strategy used to balance the number of prisoners with the supply of beds is the front-door approach, which aims to keep minor offenders out of prison in the first place by directing them into alternative programs.

Creative Sentencing One front-door strategy is to grant judges more flexibility in determining sentences. **Creative sentencing**, also known as evidence-based sentencing, permits judges or community boards to match the punishment with the crime while keeping the nonviolent offender in society. A common option is community service—sentencing the offender to put in a specified number of hours cleaning up parks or streets; working in a public hospital; painting public buildings; or performing specialized tasks related to the person's professional expertise, such as dentistry or accounting.

creative sentencing

Sentencing in which the punishment matches the crime and the characteristics of the convicted person.

Another option is to link the sentence to available prison space. This about-face from determinate sentencing is applied in an elaborate grid in North Carolina that helps judges balance the seriousness of a crime and the perpetrator's past criminal record with the number of beds available in the prison system. In determining the length of the sentence, the judge refers to the grid for minimum and maximum terms. Offenders must serve at least the minimum term without the possibility of parole. Nonviolent offenders such as petty thieves, embezzlers, and minor drug offenders are assigned to halfway houses, drug treatment, or other programs.

Yet another strategy is for judges to assess fines in lieu of prison for relatively serious nonviolent crimes. A substantial fine, some argue, is just as strong a deterrent as a short stay in jail. So is the loss of a valued personal belonging. A Texas judge ordered a father who physically abused his son to spend the next thirty nights sleeping in the family doghouse (no explanation is offered of where the dog slept).

Those convicted of the offense of child molestation in California, Florida, Louisiana, and six other states can be chemically castrated. The hormone-therapy process requires regular injections of a female contraceptive that reportedly shrinks and disables the male sex organs for as long as the drug is taken.[55] Texas law permits surgical castration of the offender's male equipment permanently.

Regional Restitution Centers Another front-door strategy used in Florida, Texas, Georgia, and other states is the *regional restitution center* (also known as *diversion centers*), a variation on the standard work-release center. Nonviolent offenders are housed in restitution centers near their homes and work in the community during the day; they receive regular supervision. Their paychecks are turned over to center staff members, who subtract expenses for food and housing and distribute the remainder to the offenders' victims as restitution, to the court for payment of fines, and to the offenders' spouses and children for support. Anything left over belongs to the inmates.

Diversion of the Mentally Ill from Jail or Emergency Room A surprisingly large amount of police time is given to dealing with the mentally ill who may present a threat to others or to themselves. Usually, police apprehend such a person and take him directly to jail or an emergency room. Neither place is equipped to handle mental illnesses adequately. But San Antonio, Texas and other cities are trying something different called "smart justice." In San Antonio, police officers take a required forty-hour course learning how to handle mental health crises. Instead of jail or the hospital, the Restoration Center, with a psych unit and medical assistance, is available for the troubled individual.[56]

Intensive Probation Supervision A third front-door strategy is *intensive probation supervision (IPS)*. IPS is somewhat like house arrest because it is designed to keep first-time offenders guilty of a serious but usually nonviolent crime (e.g., drunk driving, drug possession or distribution) out of state institutions. Those who qualify for the program face intense, highly intrusive supervision and surveillance for a prescribed period. Among other things, IPS requires face-to-face contacts between offenders and the IPS staff each week in the office, on the job, or in the home; random alcohol and drug testing and mandatory counseling for abusers; weekly employment verification; and an early nightly curfew (usually 8:00 p.m.). The program is basically self-supporting because probationers pay money into the program, in addition to any restitution they provide to their victims. Prisons get much-needed breathing space and save a substantial sum of money for each offender diverted from prison.

A front-door approach to easing prison overcrowding now losing favor is boot camps, or *shock incarceration.* Young (17- to 25-year-old) first-time felony offenders are given the option of serving their prison term or spending several months in a **shock incarceration** center, which resembles boot camp in the U.S. Marine Corps. In fact, former Marine drill instructors are often in charge. Those inmates who successfully complete the three- to six-month program earn early release. Those who fall short are assigned to the regular prison population.

Shock incarceration is aimed at more than just relief of prison overcrowding. It is also intended to teach self-control and self-discipline to young people who come from dysfunctional homes or from selfish, undisciplined personal backgrounds. If shock incarceration had the long-term impact its advocates claim, it should keep thousands of young offenders from becoming recidivists; however, boot-camp dropout rates are high, and in most states the recidivism rate for graduates is similar to that for the regular prison population. Of course, dropouts and recidivists end up in prison, canceling any savings generated from boot camp. Savings are also lost when judges assign youths to boot camp instead of probation. Disappointing results have led several states, including Arizona, New York, and California, to close their camps.

CAPACITY ENHANCEMENT

Capacity enhancement is the third major strategy for matching available prison beds with the number of inmates. Usually it entails construction of new prison facilities, which is very costly, and operating them is even more so. Some states, most recently Virginia, completed new facilities, but were not been able to afford to staff and run them. Many taxpayers resent spending so much money on the care and feeding of criminals—although, ironically, they want criminals to be locked up. Others oppose having a new prison located in their community. But poor, rural areas often perceive prisons to be a desirable form of economic development. A new prison typically brings 300 institutional jobs with 1,000 inmates. Prisons are supply-driven, and the flow of criminals is dependable. Prisons also purchase local goods and services. They pay sales taxes, water and sewer fees, and landfill charges. Also, because inmates are considered residents of local jurisdictions, their presence means more federal and state funding.

The prison construction boom seems to have hit pause for now, primarily for financial reasons, a falling crime rate, early release policies, and alternatives to incarceration.

Private Prisons A popular capacity enhancement innovation is private prisons, or prisons for profit, an idea spawned from the near-hopelessness of

shock incarceration

Prison boot camps provide this option for young offenders, who receive paramilitary and physical training intended to "shock" the offender into staying out of trouble and learning self discipline.

A group of arraigned men awaits trial in a crowded holding cell, Maricopa County Jail, AZ.

many overcrowded state correctional systems. The private sector has long provided certain services and programs to prisons, including health care, food services, and alcohol and drug treatment. Privately operated prisons existed more than 100 years ago in Louisiana, New York, and a handful of other states, but they were closed down amid revelations of prisoner abuse.

About 8 percent of incarcerated adults and juveniles are held in privately run correction institutions today. These institutions include medium-security prisons in Virginia, Texas, Oklahoma, and Tennessee. The two largest prison management firms, Corrections Corporation of America and Geo Group,[57] control 75 percent of the private corrections market (see the Controversies in States and Localities feature).

Does Prison Pay? The construction and operation of prisons has been the fastest-growing budget item in many states, even faster than the growth of Medicaid. Yet every dollar sunk into correctional facilities is one less to pay for highways, social services, education, and the needs of children. Our priorities seem skewed indeed when we invest only $4,000–$8,000 per year for a child's education, whereas a prisoner costs up to ten times that amount to keep incarcerated.

Does prison pay by keeping repeat offenders out of action? Benefit–cost analyses comparing the costs of incarceration with estimated savings to society from foregone burglaries, larcenies, murders, and rapes do indicate some net benefit to society. One study found that "prison pays for most state prisoners," especially those who are either repeat or violent offenders who pose an immediate danger if released.[58]

Prison does not pay, however, for drug offenders, most of whom could be placed under supervision or substance abuse counseling and treatment, or released altogether. And it doesn't pay for older offenders who are no longer

Controversies in States and Localities

Are Private Prisons a Good Idea?

Despite its rapid growth to 8 percent of the total prison population, prison privatization is controversial. Those who support it claim that prisons built and operated by the private sector save the taxpayers money. Because of less red tape, facilities can be constructed and operated more economically. Most important, advocates point out, private prisons reduce overcrowding.

Opponents of privatization, however, question whether firms can in fact build and operate correctional facilities significantly less expensively than state or local governments can. They believe that the profit motive is misplaced in a prison setting, where firms may skimp on nutritious food, health care, or skilled personnel to cut operating costs. A "prison-industrial complex," whose businesses profit from constructing and filling up cell space, lobbies and contributes campaign dollars to legislators in the interest of stricter sentencing requirements and additional private prisons. CCA and other private prison firms actually require occupancy of 80–100 percent to be guaranteed in their contracts.

Lately, evidence on the economics of prison privatization urges caution. Most of the private facilities house juveniles, illegal aliens, and minimum- and medium-security offenders. The majority of studies and several states' experiences indicate that operating cost savings have been marginal or much less than promised. An Arizona study found that operating private prisons actually cost $1,600 more per year than state prisons, even though the firms "cherry pick" healthy, low-maintenance inmates. Several states have taken over privately-run prisons because of understaffing, safety issues, contract non-compliance, and other concerns.

Who should be responsible for prisons? Economic considerations are obviously important, but constitutional and legal issues challenge prisons for profit. A basic question is whether the delegation of the corrections function to a private firm is constitutionally permissible. So far, no major court has ruled to the contrary. However, the Supreme Court spoke on one related issue by declaring that private prison guards who violate inmates' rights are not entitled to qualified immunity—unlike public-sector guards.

Another set of considerations concerns practical accountability for the day-to-day operation of jails and prisons. Who is responsible for developing operational rules, procedures, and standards and for ensuring that they are carried out? What happens if prison employees strike? (Strikes by state correctional employees are illegal, but those by their private-sector counterparts are not.) What if the corporation hikes its fees substantially? Or shuts its doors because of an unprofitable shortage of inmates, as happened Texas in 2011? Or declares bankruptcy because of financial mismanagement or a liability suit? Who is liable if prisoners are abused and have their civil rights violated by a firm's guards, as happened with Missouri felons doing time in a Texas prison run by a Mississippi company? Consider this case: In Texas, two men escaped from a private prison near Houston. They nearly made it to Dallas before they were caught. But Texas authorities couldn't prosecute because by breaking out of a private facility, the men had not committed an offense under Texas law. The men, who had been sent to the private facility from Oregon, could not be prosecuted for escape in Oregon because the event happened in Texas.

Economic and legal issues aside, perhaps the most important question is, who *should* operate our jails and prisons? Legal scholar Ira Robbins suggests that we should remember the words of the novelist Fyodor Dostoevsky: "The degree of civilization in a society can be judged by entering its prisons." The state, after all, administers justice in the courtroom. Shouldn't it also be responsible for carrying out justice in the correctional facilities? Should profits be derived from depriving human beings of their freedom? Or does saving taxpayer dollars deserve consideration, too?

Critical Thinking Questions:

1. Are private prisons a good idea? Explain your answer.

2. What are the proper roles of private sector entities in corrections? Are there any lines that should not be crossed?

Credit: B. E. Price, Merchandizing Prisoners: Who Really Pays for Prison Privatization (Westport, CT: Praeger, 2006); Anne Morrison Piehl and John J. Dilulio, Jr., "Does Prison Pay?" The Brookings Review (Winter 1995): 21–25; Richard A. Oppel, Jr., "Private Prisons Found to Offer Little in Savings," nytimes.com (May 18, 2011); Richardson v. McKnight 138 L.Ed. 2d 540 (1997).

high-risk individuals. And as noted earlier, incarceration appears to have no measurable effect on the crime rate. States with the highest incarceration rates also have among the highest crime rates.

The Current Challenge in Crime and Corrections

The idea of placing people in prisons to punish them with deprivation of their freedom was devised only 200 years ago. Until fairly recently, brutality was the operating norm. Deliberately painful executions, maiming, flogging, branding, and other harsh punishments were applied to both serious and minor offenders. Misbehavior in prison was likely to be met with beatings or with more elaborate tortures such as stretching from ropes attached to a pulley in the ceiling or long confinement in an unventilated sweat box. By contrast, prison conditions in the states today seem almost luxurious. Inmates typically enjoy recreational activities; training and educational opportunities; the use of televisions and other entertainment devices in their cells; and other amenities. Rules enforcement is also much more civilized and respectful of inmates' human rights. But a backlash is evident in some states. Surveys show that most citizens don't want criminals coddled. They agree with former Massachusetts governor William Weld that prisons should offer "a tour through the circles of hell"—not the easy life. Today, shackled work crews can still be seen along the highways of Alabama, Arizona, and Wisconsin.

But state budget problems have forced a reality check. To cut corrections costs, states continue to shift money into community programs and treatment programs—both saving money compared to prison or jail. Several states, including Kansas and Michigan, have recently closed correctional facilities, generating savings from payroll and operating expenses. Recidivism continues to haunt state corrections systems, and early release could produce more criminal activities. The result could be renewed citizen pressures to "lock-'em up."

Crime and corrections present major challenges to state and local governments. Certainly any long-term success will have to come from the recognition that all major components of the criminal justice system are interrelated to some extent. Thus, a broad approach to courts, crime, and corrections is called for. That means beginning with the identification of at-risk children, creating an educational and social welfare support system for them, providing alcohol and drug abuse rehabilitation for prisoners and minor offenders, and helping to repair families and communities that are lacking in resources. It means addressing homelessness, poverty, and gangs. Some policies do seem to be driving down the crime rate. The aging of the U.S. population is an important factor, but so are technology enhancements and community-based activities such as community policing, drug treatment, and citywide crackdowns on gang leaders and serial offenders. Before the states can fully cope with the challenges described in this chapter, we must understand such complex relationships more fully and attack the causes of crime, as well as its effects.

Chapter Recap

- Crime data are collected through the FBI's *Uniform Crime Reports* and victimization surveys. Both sources show a reduction in crime.

- Criminal justice is overwhelmingly a state and local government responsibility, with modest federal involvement.

- Key actors in criminal justice policy are law enforcement officials, the courts, the public, victims, and the accused.

- Victimless crimes and capital punishment are two policy issues that illustrate the variation in state approaches to criminal justice policy.

- Corrections policy deprives some criminals of their freedom, but little rehabilitation occurs.

- Policy alternatives for addressing prison capacity problems include back-door and front-door strategies and making additional prison cells available. Prison privatization is one controversial approach.

- Crime and corrections have become perennial challenges for state and local governments.

KEY TERMS

grand jury *(p. 432)*
indictment *(p. 432)*
victimless crimes *(p. 433)*

indeterminate sentencing *(p. 440)*
determinate sentencing *(p. 440)*

parole *(p. 444)*
probation *(p. 444)*
creative sentencing *(p. 445)*
shock incarceration *(p. 447)*

INTERNET RESOURCES

Law enforcement and corrections-related sites proliferate on the web. A few of the more interesting include the Federal Bureau of Investigation (FBI) homepage at **www.fbi.gov** and the Police Guide at **www.policeguide.com**.

For community policing, see the Office of Community Oriented Policing (COPS) at **www.cops.usdoj.gov**.

Chilling yet fascinating collections of "last words" from Texas' busy death chamber may be read at **www.goodbyewarden.com** or **www.tdcj.state.tx.us**.

Links to most major criminal justice policy issues are available at **www.corrections.com**.

www.sentencingproject.org is a nonprofit organization that promotes alternatives to prison.

For corrections and sentencing data, and other valuable information, see **www.ojp.usdoj.gov/bjs/** and **www.ncjrs.org**. Another general source is the web address of the National Archive of Criminal Justice Data at **www.icpsr.umich.edu/NACJD**.

The Death Penalty Information Center (**www.deathpenaltyinfo.org**) provides a wealth of statistics and reports on capital punishment.

Social Welfare and Health Care Policy: Addressing Poverty and Sickness

A family with two children begs for money at a gas station.
Tony Freeman/PhotoEdit

Brandi Harris, a 35-year-old mother of two young children, is in desperate straits. Her live-in boyfriend left her 18 months ago with nothing but a rented trailer and a 15-year-old Dodge. Unable to arrange daycare, find work, and with the car broken down, Brandi sells everything of value she has. Following numerous eviction notices for unpaid rent, she now lives in the car and on the streets with her kids. The youngest child, a girl 6 years old, is ready to join her 8-year-old sister in school—but to which school district do they belong? The local homeless shelter looks to be unsafe for the children, and they cannot stay there for more than a few weeks anyway. Where should they go? What should they do? What resources are offered by the city, community organizations, state, or federal offices to help them in this time of need?

State and local governments must interact with people and situations such as these every day. There will always be people who, for various reasons, need help coping with poverty, unemployment, physical disabilities, drug or alcohol addiction, mental illness, or other burdens that afflict them either temporarily or permanently. Most of those who need assistance actively seek it out through federal, state, local, and nonprofit social welfare and health care programs. Some do not receive welfare benefits but choose to fight their battles themselves or perhaps with family assistance; some need temporary help until they get back on their feet again; and some will be dependent on government assistance for the rest of their lives. Many of the poor work full-time jobs at low wages; others have never drawn a paycheck.

Welfare and health care policy is an abiding concern in the states. With Congress bogged down in a swamp of rhetoric and partisan mudslinging, the states have embarked on a path of unprecedented health and welfare innovations. The growth in the states' capacity to design, develop, and administer such programs is remarkable. It is confirmation of their responsiveness to problems besetting their citizens and capability to address some of the most difficult and persistent problems of our time both creatively and effectively.

Thinking About—and Measuring— Poverty

LO 17.1

To explain the meaning of poverty and how it is measured.

There are very few cases of absolute deprivation in this country. The necessities of life—food, clothing, housing—are available to all through government programs and nonprofit organizations (the homeless represent a perplexing and painful exception). The extreme, life-threatening poverty found in Sudan or Haiti simply does not occur here. (The World Bank defines absolute poverty as $1.25 a day or less to live on.) Instead, poverty in the United States consists of relative deprivation: People are poor when they have substantially less wealth and income than most others; and despite their best efforts, they have grave difficulty making ends meet. Within this wealthy nation, relative differences in wealth and income equality are profound, and worsening. The United States has the highest degree of economic inequality among all advanced nations and one of the highest in the entire world.

The federal government uses a statistic called the *poverty threshold* to define poverty in quantitative terms. The amount has been set at three times the amount of income necessary to purchase essential food. The official poverty threshold changes each year as the cost of food rises (or, very rarely, falls). In 2013, it was pegged at $23,624 for a family of four and at $11,888 for an individual.[1] The poverty figure is important because it helps determine who qualifies for various forms of public assistance. More than 45 million "officially" poor people lived in the United States in 2013, or around 14.5 percent of the population. In New Mexico, 21.4 percent of the state's population is officially poor; in New Hampshire, only 9.6 percent of the population is. In race and ethnicity comparisons, poverty rates ranged from 27.2 percent for African Americans and 23.5 percent for Latinos, to 9.6 percent for whites and 10.5 percent for Asians and Pacific Islanders.[2]

Measuring poverty is far from an exact science. Government statistics fail to account for regional cost-of-living differences; variations in states' ability and willingness to fund welfare programs; a decline in the inflation-adjusted value of the minimum wage; changes in consumption patterns; the cost of housing, energy, child care, and health care; in-kind assistance such as food stamps; the earned income tax credit; and the value of off-the-books income and barter income earned by individuals. And the poverty threshold is based on outdated assumptions about relative food costs and preferences taken from the year 1963! It is widely acknowledged that the official poverty numbers are inexact. Some economists say the figures significantly understate the actual degree of poverty, but others believe the opposite is true.[3]

Poverty in the United States was once associated largely with old age, but this view is no longer true. As the population has grown older, senior citizens have organized as a formidable interest group. Social Security benefits, federal programs such as Medicare, and age-based preferences in local property and state income taxes have eased elderly people's financial burdens. Today, only 9.5 percent of those aged 65 and older are considered poor. The most alarming poverty victims are children: Some 20 percent live in poverty, including a shocking 40 percent of African-American children from birth to age 18.[4] In the context of limited government resources, a generational reckoning is inevitable; society will have to decide how to allocate its resources between the old and the young. Social Security and Medicare outlays to seniors are growing rapidly as a proportion of federal spending, while children's poverty statistics and youth unemployment remain disturbingly high.

Social Welfare and Ideology

LO 17.2

To analyze social welfare and ideology.

Intense debates over political ideology and values have always stormed across the social welfare policy landscape, resulting in confused policy goals and a faulty, confusing patchwork of programs. Conservatives and liberals have propounded starkly opposing points of view on the causes of poverty and the appropriate government response.

Conservatives (usually Republications, Libertarians, or Tea Partiers), who generally believe in a restricted role for government, have tended to accept a modern version of the nineteenth-century view that "the giving of relief is a violation of natural law."[5] According to this viewpoint, the poor are victims of their own deficiencies. If they are to rise above poverty, they must hoist themselves up by their own bootstraps. In other words, they must work hard and live prudently. From this perspective, the poor get what they deserve. Conservatives attack the social welfare system for interfering with "the free market," discouraging more productive allocations of public funds, undermining the work ethic, encouraging immoral behavior, and creating a permanent "underclass" of dependent welfare recipients. Conservatives favor policies that encourage marriage; discourage illegitimacy, unmarried sex, and teen pregnancy; promote individual responsibility; and cut welfare spending and dependency on public support.[6]

For liberals (usually Democrats, or progressives), who generally believe in a broad and active role for government, poverty is a structural problem. People fall into poverty largely because of factors essentially beyond their control, such as inadequate schooling, poor and/or dysfunctional parents, divorce, lack of jobs, various forms of discrimination, and the up-and-down cycles of a capitalistic economy. According to this view, most people cannot help being poor; and so it becomes the responsibility of government not only to relieve their poverty through public assistance programs, but also to provide the poor with the appropriate skills and physical environment to enable them to become self-sufficient.

What does the typical American think about welfare? Contrary to conventional wisdom, most Americans favor government efforts to help the poor and are willing to pay taxes to assist them. But people do tend to make a distinction between the "deserving" poor and those who are not willing to work and be personally responsible for their behavior. Media reports, conservative talk shows, and racial stereotyping contribute to the widespread—but erroneous—belief that most welfare recipients are African Americans who lack a work ethic and behave irresponsibly.[7]

THE ORIGINS OF SOCIAL WELFARE POLICY

Social welfare programs developed later in the United States than in Western European nations. The U.S. programs in place today are also much less uniform and generous than those in Western Europe. These differences have been attributed to the federal system and especially to the competition among states for economic development. States attempt to create an attractive business climate characterized by low taxes and limited social program expenditures. This means less money for social services.

Our fragmented social welfare policy is a reflection of shifting conservative and liberal control of Congress and the presidency, and the inherently controversial nature of redistributive policies—those that result in taking from one group of people to give to another.

Although its roots may be traced back to pensions for Revolutionary War veterans and their widows, the basic foundations of the welfare system were laid by the liberal Democratic administration of Franklin D. Roosevelt in response to the Great Depression of the 1930s. Private charity and state and local relief programs were completely inadequate for combating a 25 percent unemployment rate and a collapsed national economy. The federal government responded with massive programs designed to provide temporary relief through public assistance payments, job creation, and Social Security. Since the 1930s, competing political parties and ideologies have sewn together a patchwork of programs to help the poor and unfortunate. The most far-reaching effort was President Lyndon B. Johnson's "War on Poverty" in the 1960s, which included VISTA, the Job Corps, food stamps, and the Elementary and Secondary Education Act, among many other programs. It is estimated that today there are more than 170 separate federal anti-poverty programs, and many more at the state and local levels.

A SOCIAL WELFARE CONSENSUS

A social welfare consensus emerged among conservatives and liberals and led to a coalition for reform in the late 1980s. Conservatives admitted government's responsibility to help the truly needy and economically vulnerable, and liberals saw the need to attach certain obligations to welfare and to address the behavioral dependency of the underclass. Behavioral dependency means that poor people become dependent on government for their economic well-being by reason of their own choices, and it is a serious problem for this country's underclass, which is disproportionately young, male, minority, and urban. Many of these people are school and societal dropouts—borderline illiterates with no job skills. A disproportionate number become involved in drugs and crime. Agreement existed that welfare dependency must be reduced so that people can get off the dole and on the job. For those involved in crime and illegal drug activity, aggressive law enforcement, incarceration, substance abuse counseling and treatment, or social work were called for.

The social welfare consensus was broad enough to enable congressional passage of the Family Support Act of 1988. This law incorporated conservative principles of personal responsibility with liberal principles of poverty relief. Then, in 1996, President Clinton made good on his promise to end welfare as we know it by signing a law that eliminated the nation's largest welfare program, Aid to Families with Dependent Children (AFDC). Eligibility for federal welfare benefits was limited to no more than five years. With this law, an enormous challenge was thrown down to state and local governments to assume the lead in helping the poor exchange welfare checks for paychecks.

This consensus reflected a somewhat common, mainstream view of poverty, but disagreement about how to solve the problem persists. The consensus began unraveling in the early 2000s. Most agree that different types of poverty should be treated distinctively. For example, children, seniors, the disabled, single parents, working adults, and nonworking adults all have different needs. Many also agree that government should help those who can climb out of poverty through job training and other programs and that able-bodied welfare recipients have an obligation to seek and secure a job or perform public work. Beyond these basic elements, the consensus tends to unravel. Conservatives seek better behavior from the poor, admonishing them to complete high school, find jobs (even at low wages), and either get married and stay married or not have babies at all and get off welfare. Liberals are more willing to utilize social programs to transfer government resources to the poor, with fewer conditions.

It's simple to say that public assistance recipients should just "get a job." But with unemployment soaring to more than 10 percent during the trough of the Great Recession (the highest rate since 1940), jobs were very hard to find. There is a significant proportion of the population who dwell in "deep poverty," without work *or* welfare, struggling to get by from one day to the next.[8] The plight of the poor remains complex and multifaceted. There may be very little absolute poverty in the United States, but relative poverty—referred to today as inequality—has risen at a shocking rate. The top 1 percent of households receive nearly 23 percent of all income today, while the income share of the bottom 10 percent has fallen deeply.[9]

Current Social Welfare Policy

During and after the Great Depression, social welfare policy became primarily the responsibility of the federal government, with limited roles reserved to the states and localities. The states brought the various federal programs into action, administered them, and drew up rules to determine who was eligible for benefits. But with the 1996 welfare reform bill, entitled the Personal Responsibility and Work Opportunity Reconciliation Act (PRWORA), the federal government ceded a large portion of the policy field to the states and localities. Replacing AFDC was a new program, **Temporary Assistance for Needy Families (TANF)**, which emphasized maximum state discretion. As a consequence, state and local governments are in the vanguard of innovation and program experimentation, perhaps even more so than in other public policy fields.

Dramatic variations among the states exist in levels of social welfare spending. Massachusetts, New York, and Alaska generally spend more per person on public assistance than Mississippi, Alabama, and South Carolina. Some states pay relatively high benefits for one program, such as Medicaid, but relatively low benefits for another, such as TANF—the result of battles among various constituencies over a limited social welfare pie. States controlled by the Democratic Party tend to be more generous than Republican-dominated states, and strong party competition within a state drives up benefit levels. Race is important: Eligibility policies are stricter and benefits are lower in states with high African American caseloads.[10] Political beliefs have an impact as well. The relationship between a dominant liberal or conservative ideology and state welfare spending levels should be obvious.

Types of Social Welfare Programs

Together, social welfare programs provide a safety net for those less fortunate and those who have fallen on hard times. They may be sorted into two basic categories: public assistance and social insurance. Public assistance programs, such as Medicaid and TANF, involve government payments of money or in-kind benefits to disadvantaged people who meet various qualifying criteria. Social insurance programs, such as Social Security, include recipient contributions (e.g., the Social Security payroll tax), as well as government payments. Our concern in this chapter is primarily with public assistance programs.

To convey a basic understanding of the complex intergovernmental web of social welfare policies, we examine the most significant ones individually. For purposes of discussion, we divide public assistance policies into two types: direct cash transfers and in-kind benefits. Social insurance programs also receive attention (see Table 17.1). Most social welfare programs are so-called "entitlement programs," meaning that these are government spending programs with eligibility criteria. If a recipient meets the criteria (age, income, and so on), he or she is entitled to the benefit.

LO 17.3
To understand current social welfare policy.

Temporary Assistance for Needy Families (TANF)
A provision of the Personal Responsibility and Work Opportunity Reconciliation Act (PRWORA) of 1996, which replaced AFDC with a flexible program that allows states to set their own conditions and benefit levels for welfare recipients to help them secure and maintain employment.

LO 17.4
To define the types of social welfare programs.

TABLE 17.1	Major Social Welfare and Social Insurance Programs			
PROGRAM CATEGORY AND NAME	NUMBER OF RECIPIENTS (IN MILLIONS)	WHO FUNDS	WHO ADMINISTERS	TOTAL EXPENDITURES (IN BILLIONS OF DOLLARS)
DIRECT CASH TRANSFER				
TANF	3	National	State	14
SSI	8	National	National, state	50
Earned Income Tax Credit	27.4	National	National	54
IN-KIND PROGRAM				
Supplemental Nutrition Assistance Program (formerly Food Stamps)	46	National	State, local	74
Medicaid	62	National, state	State, local	383 (national $)
Child Nutrition	30	National	State, local	18
State Children's Health Insurance Program (S-CHIP)	70	National, state	State	13
SOCIAL INSURANCE				
Social Security (OASDI)	59	National	National	710
Medicare	54	National, state	National, state	492
Unemployment compensation	10	State, private	State	3
Worker's compensation	No data	State, private	State	No data

SOURCE: U.S. Bureau of the Census, *Statistical Abstract of the United States*, 2014 (Washington, D.C.: U.S. Government Printing Office, 2014); www.census.gov; Medicare and Social Security Administration reports; and data from the Rockefeller Institute of Government and the Kaiser Foundation. Various years (most recent data available) are reported above.

DIRECT CASH TRANSFERS

direct cash transfer

The transfer of cash, such as in the form of a disability check, from one level of government to an individual citizen beneficiary.

Direct cash transfers are welfare programs that directly convey money, in the form of government checks, to qualified recipients. Administrative arrangements vary by type of program. *Aid to Families with Dependent Children* was included in the Social Security Act of 1935 to furnish financial aid to poor children whose fathers had died. By 1996, however, AFDC payments went almost entirely (90 percent) to single-parent families in which the living father was absent.

AFDC was the most costly and most controversial social welfare program in the United States. Critics claimed that it caused marriages to break up or to be consciously avoided; encouraged young, nonworking, unwed women to have babies; promoted migration of the poor to states paying higher AFDC benefits; and perpetuated dependency into future generations. No one professed fondness for AFDC, not even the recipients.

As noted earlier, AFDC was abandoned in 1996 with passage of the new welfare reform act, PRWORA, which replaced AFDC grants to individuals with block grants to the states. The states in turn designed programs for promoting work and individual responsibility. The states received vast new authority and flexibility for reinventing welfare, subject to certain federal requirements. States submit TANF plans outlining how the state will assist needy families with children and help prepare parents to become self-sufficient. The law stipulates that adults have up to two years to find a job without losing benefits and a lifetime limit of five years to receive benefits. Up to 20 percent of the state's welfare population may receive hardship exemptions for circumstances such as mental or physical disabilities. This "tough love" approach to getting people off public support also has a financial stick to move any recalcitrant states ahead. States must demonstrate that at least 50 percent of TANF recipients are engaged in work or work-related activities for 20 to 30 hours per week, depending on the age of children; two-parent families must record a total of 35 to 55 hours per week.

The states combined TANF requirements with previously existing state welfare-to-work programs to drop welfare caseloads dramatically (by 50–90 percent in the states and by three-quarters nationwide). Many diverse approaches are being pursued by the states, including family caps that limit or eliminate additional payments for children born after a mother begins receiving benefits; transferring impaired clients to disability programs; and individual development accounts, which permit recipients to establish savings accounts to pay for items such as college or technical education, a new home, or the start of a business. Most states provide some form of child-care assistance, job training, and transportation aid (so that workers can have a dependable way to get to and from their jobs). Some states use TANF funds to provide post-employment services to help clients keep their jobs and even win promotions. States also vary in their approach to the controversial question of how to treat immigrants and citizens moving from other states.

Following the initial years of success, the states now find themselves hard-pressed to locate jobs for the least able of the welfare population, who experience serious, and often multiple, barriers to employment, even while the federal government has tightened up its demands that they do so. Many—if not most—of the available jobs pay minimum wage, which, by itself, is not nearly sufficient to raise a person out of poverty or even provide for basic needs. Moreover, high unemployment levels during and since the Great Recession are indicative of serious labor market problems. The states believe that they are much better suited than the national government to handle welfare-to-work programs. Yet substantial cuts to TANF benefits occurred in 2008–2012 as states struggled through their financial difficulties. As states tightened up restrictions to qualify for TANF during the Great Recession, welfare rolls declined even as the number of poor escalated.[11]

Supplemental Security Income (SSI) is financed and operated by the national government, except that state officials determine who is eligible for the program and have the option of enhancing SSI payments. Created in 1974, SSI combines three programs: Old Age Assistance, Aid to the Blind, and Aid to the Disabled. Its recipients are people who are unable to work because of old age or physical or mental disabilities and increasingly, children with behavioral or learning disabilities. Average monthly payments are about $540.

The *Earned Income Tax Credit* provides cash assistance to low-income working individuals and families through a refundable federal income tax credit. It was created in 1975 to offset the burden of Social Security taxes and to encourage work. Many states offer a state EITC match for state taxes, averaging 3.5 percent in Louisiana up to 32 percent in Vermont.

General Assistance is a state and local program intended to help poor people who do not qualify for other direct cash or in-kind transfer programs, such as the nonworking but physically able poor. State benefit levels vary greatly. Twenty-one states do not offer the program at all, and many of the others reduced benefits during the recent economic difficulties.[12]

IN-KIND PROGRAMS

In-kind programs provide benefits in goods or services, rather than in cash, as a way to address specific problems of poverty, hunger, illness, and joblessness.

The Supplemental Nutrition Assistance Program (SNAP), formerly known as the Food Stamp Program, provides low-income individuals and families with financial aid for purchasing food. The program was established in 1964, and benefit levels are uniform throughout the United States. Both the working and nonworking poor are eligible if their income falls sufficiently close to the poverty level. More than 20 million new SNAP recipients were added to the rolls during the Great Recession.

Medicaid is a health care assistance program for the poor (SSI recipients automatically qualify). It is jointly funded by the national (57 percent) and state (43 percent) governments (the match varies, based on state per-capita income), and it is enormously expensive (more than $383 billion in 2014 federal funding, constituting more than 24 percent of state budgets. The Medicaid program provides free health care services to uninsured poor people and is the principal source of assistance for long-term institutional care for the physically and mentally disabled and the elderly. It must be distinguished from Medicare, which is an entitlement program that grants health care assistance to those aged 65 or older.

Since the inception of Medicaid in 1965, it has been wracked with scandals: Doctors, pharmacists, dentists, and other professionals have been charged with everything from performing unnecessary surgery and inflating fees to filing reimbursements for imaginary patients. Fueled by expansions of the program and rising health care costs, Medicaid has also placed an increasingly onerous burden on state budgets. In a desperate search for Medicaid savings, states are cutting payments to service providers, cracking down on fraud and waste, reducing benefits, improving care management for the chronically ill, and reforming health care delivery systems to enhance the quality and efficiency of patient treatment and care.

The Patient Protection and Affordable Care Act (ACA or "Obamacare") of 2010 added an estimated 3 million new recipients to Medicaid rolls by 2014. States have the option to accept to accept these Medicaid funds or not; about half of them have decided to accept. Those that choose not to take the

in-kind program

The payment of a noncash social welfare benefit, such as food stamps or clothing, to an individual recipient.

federal money generally have Republican-dominated legislatures and governors' offices,[13] whose office holders have shown themselves to be averse to almost any policy associated with President Obama, and who say they are concerned about the federal government honoring its promise to pay 90 percent of future Medicaid costs.

State Children's Health Insurance Program (S-CHIP) is jointly funded by the federal and state governments to provide health insurance to children in families who cannot afford private insurance but who earn too much income to qualify for Medicaid. Under S-CHIP, the states enjoy great flexibility in designing and implementing their own plans. The ACA maintained S-CHIP and boosted the federal matching rate to 93 percent.

Housing programs exist in several forms today. The federal housing program helps pay for public housing or provides rent subsidies directly to the poor, who apply them to private rental units. States administer a portion of approximately 1.2 million subsidized apartment units; the U.S. Department of Housing and Urban Development administers the rest. As homelessness rates soared across the country in 2008–2011, emergency shelters were overwhelmed. Tent cities arose in Phoenix, Arizona; Reno, Nevada; Sacramento, California; and many other cities. A majority of the homeless are families with children. States have responded with expanded shelters, new subsidized housing, and other attempts to relieve the problem until the economy—and its innocent victims—recover. The Controversies feature elaborates on the homeless problem and state-local efforts to combat it.

Other in-kind programs include numerous types of public assistance, such as the *Child Nutrition*, or school lunch, program, Head Start, energy assistance for low-income families, legal services, family planning, foster care, and services for the physically and mentally disabled. National, state, and local

A woman at a homeless encampment packs up her few belongings.

Justin Sullivan/Getty Images

Controversies in State and Local Government

Combatting Homelessness

Data indicate that the size of America's adult homeless population is more than 610,000. The Great Recession took the number of homeless to an all-time high of around 750,000. If one loses his or her job, cannot find another one, goes belly up on the mortgage and has the house foreclosed, can't make car payments and sees that car repossessed, despair may set in. When no friends or relatives are available to help, that leaves the local homeless shelter or the streets. Homeless encampments dot the landscapes of our cities. Many of the victims are children: an estimated 2.5 million are homeless (though not accounted for in official figures), crashing on friends' couches, in all-night cafes, or motels. Some are with one or both parents, others are on the streets or otherwise on their own. These children are highly vulnerable to sex trafficking and other forms of abuse.[14]

Homelessness is a complex problem that often involves more than the loss of income and housing. Minimum wage earners cannot afford apartments at market rates. Mental health problems, substance abuse issues, and post-traumatic stress disorder (PTSD) can also drive individuals to the streets, under bridges, or to wooded areas in a city. And truly, we don't really have a solid grip on the extent of the homeless problem, as the population is notoriously difficult to count. Homelessness puts the police in a bind: Do you arrest and risk packing the jails with the homeless (some of whom prefer a bunk in the county jail—with a meal or two—to a park bench) or let them be, despite citizen complaints? Ship them out of town on a bus? Should more shelters be constructed? If so, where should they be located? Who should pay for treatment, shelter and food expenses, or hospitalization?

Those who study and attempt to resolve homelessness understand that each case is different.

The war veteran with PTSD has different issues (and treatment opportunities) than the mother with children or the elderly alcoholic. Multiple interventions are called for in some cases, including substance abuse treatment, medication for emotional disorders, housing, and food. A network approach is often recommended, with state and local agencies, faith-based organizations, nonprofit service providers, and others offering a range of services.

The Obama administration stepped up the battle against homelessness in 2010, and pledged to end veterans' homelessness by 2015. Federal agencies provide rental-assistance housing vouchers, along with health care services and counseling for veterans. The federal government learned lessons from local governments such as Lee County, Florida, Trenton, New Jersey, and Salt Lake City, Utah. These local governments are combatting homelessness with "rapid rehousing," a strategy that provides housing and stability while the recipient accesses counseling, job planning, and other services until they can get work that pays enough for them to eventually pull their own weight.[15]

Critical Thinking Questions:

1. What should the respective responsibilities of federal, state, and local governments be with respect to homelessness? What should be the role, if any, of the nonprofit and private sectors?

2. What is the homelessness situation in your state's largest city? How is it being addressed?

Credit: Bill Kaczor, "Fla. Welfare Applicants Less Likely to Use Drugs," Associated Press (September 28, 2011); Pamela Prah, "More States Pass Drug Testing for Welfare Recipients," Pew Center on the States (May 17, 2012); Lizette Alvarez, "No Savings Are Found from Welfare Drug Tests," nytimes.com (April 17, 2012).

participation depends on the specific program in question. Under TANF, states have flexibility in offering in-kind aid to help move welfare recipients into jobs and keep them working. Examples include child-care services, job training, transportation, technical and college education, workshops on how to find and keep a job, and even state-subsidized salaries until the worker earns full-time employment. The diversity of in-kind programs is compelling evidence of the complexity of the poverty problem.

SOCIAL INSURANCE

Social insurance is distinguished from public assistance programs by the fact that recipients (or their relatives or employers) contribute financially through the Social Insurance and Medicare trust funds, established by federal law. In effect, participants pay in advance for their future well-being through payroll deductions. Although not considered to be a public assistance program, social insurance helps greatly in the broad effort to relieve poverty. Contributions to social insurance come from Social Security payments by individual workers and by their employers.

Social Security (officially known as Old Age, Survivors, Disability, and Health Insurance) is run entirely by the national government and is paid for through a payroll tax on employers and employees. Monthly checks are sent electronically to retired people; to the disabled; and to the spouses and dependent children of workers who retire, die, or become disabled.

Medicare provides federal health care, hospital, and prescription drug benefits for people over the age of 65 in exchange for a monthly premium and co-payments. It was created in 1965 through an amendment to the Social Security Act. Medicare costs have escalated rapidly as a result of the growing number of senior citizens and ballooning health care bills and prescription drug prices.

Unemployment compensation was mandated by the Social Security Act of 1935. It requires employers and employees to contribute to a trust fund administered by the states. Those who lose their jobs through layoffs or dismissals can draw combined state and federal unemployment benefits. States vary in their unemployment compensation time limits.

Worker's compensation is also part of the Social Security Act. Financed by employers and administered by the states, it establishes insurance for workers and their dependents to cover job-related accidents or illnesses that result in death or disability. Its cost, which is closely associated with the price of health care, has escalated.

Social welfare policy clearly demonstrates the interdependent nature of the federal system. The national government pays for and operates some programs on its own; Social Security is one example. State and local governments take care of others. The states and localities perform key administrative roles in most social welfare efforts and serve as incubators for new ideas and programs, many of which have later been incorporated into national policy. The private and nonprofit sectors contribute through charities such as United Way agencies and institutions such as hospitals, clinics, nursing homes, and myriad community-based organizations. Contracting by all levels of government with nonprofit service providers has made hidden partners of these organizations, which attend to Americans' problems from cradle to grave.

social insurance
A jointly funded benefit program made available by a government to its citizens as a right of its citizens.

State Innovations in Social Welfare

Public assistance policy today has two critical goals. One pertains to the well-being of children and the family. The other goal is to end welfare dependency where possible. The respective roles and contributions of national, state, and local governments in these two policy goals are continually being sorted out.

LO 17.5

To discuss state innovations in social welfare.

A perplexing array of welfare traps snares even the most carefully devised policy proposals (see Figure 17.1). Undeniably, however, the states and localities are important innovators in social welfare policy and the governments closest to the needs of the poor and disadvantaged.

In addressing the problems and causes of poverty, the states are a beehive of experimentation and creative activity, but they have learned that a great chasm exists between establishing a new program and making it work effectively. Policy implementation is hindered by the complexities of our federal system, the waxing and waning of elected officials' attention, partisan, ideological, and interest group politics, and the enormity of our social welfare problems.[16] Government programs, no matter how well intended, sometimes cannot cause desired behavioral changes in target populations. The ravages of drugs, crime, and poverty, the lack of parenting skills, and other issues place many Americans at risk of long-term welfare dependency.

SAVING THE CHILDREN

Several important reasons explain the plight of children. Many children live with a single parent because of high divorce rates (almost half of all children experience life with a divorced parent during childhood), births to unwed mothers (some 40 percent of all infants, or some four million a year), and irresponsible fathers who refuse to support or even recognize their offspring.

Even if single mothers have the necessary education or skills to secure employment, their children often must be placed in the care of older siblings or left on their own if family or friends cannot care for them. Some are at risk of abuse. Opportunities for affordable, subsidized, or free day care are generally limited to Head Start and oversubscribed state-run and charitable programs. Finally, too many children are born not only into poverty but also into sickness. Because of inadequate diets, lack of health insurance, ignorance about prenatal care, drug abuse, and the spread of sexually transmitted diseases such as acquired immune deficiency syndrome (AIDS), many mothers give birth to premature, underweight, and sickly children. Some infants do not survive.

Children's issues have risen near to the top of national and state policy agendas. Historically, the national government has addressed these problems, and it continues to do so today through programs such as Head Start, which provides preschool education and medical, dental, and social services for approximately 967,275 children up to 5 years of age. Head Start is a popular program that also promotes parental self-sufficiency. In addition, the states and some local governments have their own approaches. Successful programs that assist children now will eventually help reduce welfare expenditures for future adults and the elderly.

To deal with the growing problem of absentee fathers (97 percent of non-paying parents are male), the states withhold court-ordered child support payments from the wages of absent parents, even if the parent has not fallen behind in payments. States are also required to establish paternity, through blood tests and DNA techniques, for children born out of wedlock. The result is that more fathers are being held financially responsible for their offspring.

FIGURE 17.1

Ten Welfare Traps

The policy objective seems simple: Make welfare a reciprocal arrangement in which the poor must look for and accept a job in exchange for government assistance in preparing for work. If recipients refuse, they should lose their benefits. Welfare should offer a helping hand, not a lifetime handout. But many traps make achieving this seemingly simple objective both complex and elusive, and they present significant roadblocks to state policy innovation.

Trap 1: Some people *cannot* work. A large number of welfare recipients are simply incapable of holding down a job. Whether because of substance abuse, emotional problems, physical or learning disabilities, or other conditions, these people need long-term support for themselves and their children. It is not always easy to distinguish members of this group from the able-bodied.

Trap 2: Providing financial and other support may actually reduce the potential rewards of working. Taking even a low-wage job forces people to forgo the safety net of Medicaid, food stamps, and other programs.

Trap 3: The creation of community service or make work jobs for the poor is opposed by labor unions and other groups that fear welfare recipients will displace workers in low-wage, low-skilled jobs, sending *them* onto the welfare rolls.

Trap 4: Unless the government separates children from their parents and places them in foster homes, or other care facilities, help for poor children also means help for their parents. If welfare recipients are denied benefits for not working, their children may suffer hardships. The denial of additional assistance for the single welfare mother's second or third child unfairly punishes the innocent child.

Trap 5: "Deadbeat Dads" who do not pay court-ordered child support present a conundrum. If jailed, they cannot work to pay the support. If laboring in a low-wage job, they cannot afford to shelter and feed themselves plus turn over hundreds of dollars a month to the mother.

Trap 6: To get people off welfare and thus save money in the long term means spending money today. Most welfare reform proposals require spending for education, job training, child care, and related services. Failure to invest sufficiently can result in public assistance programs that are underfunded and doomed to fail. It is cheaper in the short run to send the poor their welfare checks. The long-run solution requires a large financial investment.

Trap 7: Bureaucracy can get in the way of compassion and good sense. The average length of a federal food-stamps form—which is designed by individual states—is twelve pages. Some run more than thirty pages. Confusing legalese and intrusive questions inhibit applications. Some states ask applicants to list the value of a burial plot, or what a child earns from cutting grass. Maryland requires applicants to list "deemor expenses" (a phrase not in the working vocabulary of most Americans).

Trap 8: Welfare policy sets a double standard: It pushes the poor mother to exercise "parental responsibility" by leaving her children for a job to support them, yet the middle-class woman is praised for staying home to raise her children.

Trap 9: The typical job-training program requires that participants be job-ready, have a high school diploma, read at the eighth-grade level or higher, and provide their own day care and transportation. But the typical unemployed person has little or no work experience, has a tenth-grade education, reads at the sixth-grade level, has limited access to day care, and has no personal transportation. As a result, job training may not help.

Trap 10: If most new jobs are found in the suburbs, but the majority of the poor live in central cities, access to reliable transportation to their place of work is unlikely. The same is true if the poor live in declining suburbs but the jobs are mostly in the central city.

SOURCES: The authors; also Kent Weaver, "Old Traps, New Twists," *Brookings Review* (Summer 1994): 14–21; Clare Nolan, "States Use Red Tape to Shrink Food Stamp Program," www.stateline.org (accessed August 14, 2000): 1–2.

The states have additional authority to speed up judicial and administrative procedures for obtaining paternal support, to establish guidelines for judges to determine the appropriate size of child support awards, and to monitor support payments. Many states use a "deadbeat dad" approach to publicize and prosecute delinquent fathers. A national database has been established, consisting of each person newly hired by every U.S. employer. States can plug into the database to track down deadbeat parents across state lines and hold them accountable.

Despite these efforts, about one-quarter of women owed child support never receive a dollar, and others receive only a portion of that which is owed. If the father is incarcerated for failure to make his payments or for unrelated reasons, payments halt.

DAY CARE

The issue of day care for children of working and single parents has received a great deal of attention from the state and local governments, while the national government has struggled in vain to produce child-care legislation. Hundreds of thousands of youngsters are home alone each day from the time they return from school until a parent or relative arrives. State and local governments are subsidizing day-care programs through tax breaks and are offering various child-care arrangements under TANF. Nearly all states partly or fully fund child-care expenses for TANF recipients. States are also taking the lead in improving prenatal care, gradually reducing the nation's shameful infant mortality rate, which exceeds the rate of most other industrialized nations. Certainly it is less costly to invest at the front end of a person's life than to try correcting medical and other ailments later.

TEENAGE MOTHERS

Teenagers are highly likely to produce at-risk children (children more likely to experience school failure than other children). The rate of births to teen mothers accelerated during the 1970s and 1980s, then leveled off, but has since dropped to an historic low of 26.5 births per 1,000 teens, and by some 60 percent over the past 25 years.[17] Most births to teens are out of wedlock, and most of these children and their mothers live in poverty. The annual taxpayer bill for aiding these almost certainly dysfunctional families is staggering.

Reduction in the high teen birthrate is attributed to greater use of effective birth control methods, reality TV horror stories, and peer pressure.[18] Federal law prohibits using federal Medicaid funds for abortions for poor girls and women unless their pregnancies are the result of incest or rape. Abortion is an extremely controversial "hot stove" issue in the states. State-paid abortions for poor women would undoubtedly reduce the number of unplanned births further and provide a family-planning option that is widely available to middle- and upper-income women. It would also save taxpayers the expense of supporting a substantial number of children born into poverty, perhaps with serious and costly health problems. But abortion is highly distasteful to many and sinful to pro-life advocates. To its most rabid opponents, it is grounds for assassinating physicians who perform abortions. To conservative legislators, abortion is an act to be severely restricted or banned altogether.

State programs to reduce teen pregnancy take several directions. Minnesota integrates teen pregnancy prevention with human immunodeficiency virus (HIV) and sexually transmitted disease (STD) awareness and prevention. North Carolina targets middle-school adolescents and teens who are at risk of sexual activity. Catawba County's Teen Up program, for example, provides classes in sexual abuse, sexuality, drug abuse, handling peer pressure for sex, managing emotions and conflict, and other topics for students identified by school counselors.

California, Delaware, Florida, and many other states attack teen pregnancy by strengthening enforcement of long-neglected statutory rape laws. The goal is to discourage "sexual predators"—older males who prey on girls under the legal age of consent (14 in Hawaii, 18 in California and a dozen others, and 16 in most states).

Despite the reduction in teen births, the problem remains serious and perplexing. Teen pregnancy is an unmarried mother's recipe for a lifetime of poverty. It encourages dependency and greatly reduces career and life choices for the mother. Teen pregnancies cost taxpayers billions of dollars for social welfare and health care support for the child and the mother, most of whom receive no assistance from the father. A large majority of teen mothers never complete high school.

Turning Welfare Checks into Paychecks

LO 17.6

To explain how welfare checks can be turned into paychecks.

Before the 1996 Welfare Reform Act and TANF, checks were handed over to AFDC recipients, and little was required of them in return. The driving idea now is to help people find jobs and become independent. Jobs should produce more household income, along with improved self-image and self-reliance for recipients, and financial savings for taxpayers.

The states have taken two different approaches to moving clients from welfare to work. With an eye to meeting required federal work-participation rates, many states have "work-first" strategies that stress immediate job searches. Others, more concerned about the long-term reduction of poverty, focus on helping recipients develop necessary job skills through education, training, and other pre-employment preparation. TANF has evolved into additional efforts to help recipients retain jobs, and earn promotions and pay increases. Examples of work-first approaches are the widely praised Greater Avenues for Independence (GAIN) program in Riverside County, California, and Wisconsin Works. Another is Georgia Works!, which provides minimum wage to pick up trash in downtown Atlanta for forty hard-to-employ felons and homeless people. Recipients must remain drug free and save 20 percent of their program income, and pay $100 weekly for room and board. Graduates are highly likely to stay employed and out of trouble.[19]

In a different direction, several states have privatized all or most major components of public assistance programs. Private firms or nonprofit organizations were given contracts to process forms and applications in Arizona and elsewhere. Some county job centers in Wisconsin are run by private companies and nonprofits. Indiana contracted out management of its entire TANF program, as well as the food-stamps program, but terminated the $1.16 billion privatization contract because of excruciatingly long client waiting periods for food-stamps processing.[20] Privatization has not proven to be a panacea. Texas' ambitious effort to privatize public assistance program client intake and screening "turned into a dark comedy of bungled work and unanswered and dropped phone calls; applications lost, ignored, and misdirected."[21]

Many additional state and local efforts are under way. A growing number of states and cities have set minimum wages substantially above the $7.25 per hour the federal government imposed in 2009. As of 2015, twenty-nine states had adopted such laws, averaging $8.42 per hour. Massachusetts hiked its minimum wage in stages to $11 an hour by 2017.

As indicated by the welfare traps discussed in Figure 17.1, however, divine intervention to settle the welfare conundrum would not be unwelcome. State and local efforts to significantly reform welfare—courageous and well intentioned as they may be—encounter enormous difficulties. Complicating factors abound. For example, what should be done about welfare recipients who truly want but cannot find a job? And what about the high proportion of TANF recipients who have physical or mental impairments? Make-work or community service sounds promising, until one examines the costs of arranging, monitoring, and paying for it. What if a recipient is addicted to drugs or alcohol and cannot hold a job? Detoxification and counseling are not cheap, but kicking the recipient off assistance could well result in a new enlistee in the ranks of criminals, the incarcerated, or the homeless. Most states deny TANF benefits to convicted drug felons, and several jurisdictions have required their general assistance recipients to undergo mandatory drug tests. Those testing positive must submit to treatment or forgo their assistance. The It's Your Turn feature considers the pros and cons of recipient drug testing.

After six decades of public assistance as an entitlement under AFDC, a regime grounded in work and self-sufficiency is firmly in place. Rapidly declining welfare caseloads in nearly every state elated supporters of TANF and state and local innovators. But the early job placements essentially removed the better-educated and job-ready people from the welfare rolls. Those who simply do not want to work also dropped off public assistance. Those still seeking a declining number of low-skill jobs in a national economy characterized by growing inequality and stagnant economic and social mobility are increasingly hard-pressed to make do, let alone achieve "the American Dream." Welfare rolls have been cut, but many—particularly single moms and their kids—live in precarious circumstances.

Fears of a race to the bottom, in which states seek to drive out the poor by cutting welfare benefits to the bare bone, and a "magnet hypothesis," which predicted that poor people would move to states with relatively generous welfare benefits, have not been realized, though research indicates that interstate competition tends to reduce the generosity of state welfare programs.[22] Much is at stake, and state and local governments are engaging the issues as best they can.

It's Your Turn

Should Welfare Recipients be Drug Tested?

At least eight states have required that TANF applicants be tested for illegal drug use before they can acquire public assistance. The most onerous requirements were adopted by Florida, which not only mandates the urine test but also makes the person being tested pay for it (refundable if the test is passed). Those in favor of drug testing tend to be, predictably, political conservatives who subscribe to the belief that welfare clients are lazy, drug-abusing individuals whose sorry plight is their own fault. Opponents of client testing are generally those who believe that the downtrodden and unemployed are largely victims of circumstances beyond their control and that mandatory drug testing is unnecessarily punitive, perpetuates negative stereotypes, and "blames the victim."

The American Civil Liberties Union filed a legal action and won a temporary injunction in federal court alleging that testing was an "unreasonable search." A federal district judge upheld that decision in 2014, confirming that the law was an unconstitutional violation of the 4th Amendment. Florida appealed. As the case continues to work its way through the courts, research has revealed that drug testing saved Florida no money, and indeed was cost-negative. Few users were identified; only 2.6 percent of tests had positive results, and another 2 percent refused to be tested. Nine months of testing 5,550 public assistance recipients in Mississippi produced only eight failed tests. At an average price of $30, the tests cost the states quite a lot of money to identify so few users, the vast majority of whom test positive for marijuana. It appears, then, that welfare applicants are no more likely to use drugs than the general population. Humorist Carl Hiaasen concluded that Florida state legislators themselves should submit to a "patriotic whiz-fest" to determine how many of "them" are drug users.

PROS	CONS
By screening out drug users, the taxpayers will save money on welfare costs and ensure that TANF funds go toward helping recipients secure jobs and get off the dole, rather than to support a drug habit. The Florida and Mississippi research is flawed and unpersuasive.	Opponents cite federal appellate court decisions finding that mandatory testing violates the Fourth Amendment to the U.S. Constitution, which prohibits illegal search and seizure.
Welfare drug testing has been upheld by courts in Texas, Indiana, and New Jersey.	Warrantless, suspicionless testing is coercive and unfairly stigmatizes welfare recipients.
Testing may deter drug use.	Few drug users are identified; the primary beneficiaries of drug testing are the companies that do the testing and reap profits.
Illegal drug use is harmful to a child in the family of the abuser. Drug testing protects these children, who deserve drug-free homes.	
Recipients are unlikely to become self-sufficient if they are using illegal drugs.	

LO 17.7

To understand and analyze federal and state health care policy.

Affordable Care Act (ACA)

Also known as Obamacare, this 2010 congressional act requires states to establish Health Benefits Exchanges, or to rely on the federal exchange, and gives them the option of accepting a generous federal subsidy to expand state Medicaid rolls, among other provisions.

Health Care

A national debate has raged over health care reform for more than a quarter century, with politicians and interest groups' hysteria and hand-wringing over each new proposal. Americans have learned a lot about the problems and politics of health care, along with a new vocabulary of health care terms (see Table 17.2). Then finally, in 2010, Congress enacted President Obama's Patient Protection and **Affordable Care Act (ACA)**. Under the ACA, the states are developing innovative policies of their own.

THE PROBLEM

Nearly everyone agrees that, although the quality of health care technology in the United States is unsurpassed, the U.S. health care system is far too expensive and dysfunctional. Costs have been soaring for three decades. The nation's total annual health care bill is about $3 trillion, or 18 percent of the economy—by far the highest in the world.[23] Medicare alone pays medical bills for more than 54 million aging citizens. Medicaid costs have soared and now gobble up the single largest proportion of state budgets. These costs include millions of elderly people in nursing homes, children in low-income families, physically disabled individuals who require daily living assistance, and the mentally disabled. The Great Recession of 2008–2011 pushed large numbers of new enrollees into Medicaid as people lost their houses, cars, and jobs.

TABLE 17.2   An Essential Dictionary of Health Care Terms

MANAGED CARE ORGANIZATIONS: Involves several types of health plans that seek to contain costs by restricting the physicians and services that patients can access, promoting preventive health care, and capping hospital and physician payments. Managed care is available through private insurance firms and nonprofits, consisting of gatekeeper physicians who direct patients to approved hospitals and other providers, and *preferred provider organizations* (PPOs), which are networks of approved doctors and hospitals. Managed care organizations typically receive a fixed sum per patient from the state to manage the patient's care.

ACCOUNTABLE CARE ORGANIZATIONS: Groups of doctors, hospitals, and other health care providers who voluntarily cooperate to provide coordinated care to Medicaid patients. The goals are to avoid duplication of services while delivering high-quality care, all within a set budget.

MANAGED COMPETITION: Market-driven insurance plans that create incentives for competing insurance companies to provide health care services at low prices through negotiated fees.

PORTABILITY: The ability of individuals to take health care coverage with them wherever they work or live.

SINGLE PAYER: A government agency administrating a health care system financed through taxes. Called "socialized medicine" by its critics, this system is prevalent in Great Britain, Canada, and several European countries. An example in the United States is the federal Medicare program.

FEE-FOR-SERVICE: The traditional means of paying for health care in which providers charge for specific patient services. This approach is known for being unnecessarily expensive and incentivizing unnecessary tests and procedures.

Inflating health care costs are the aging U.S. population, which means more people with illnesses directly associated with old age; the obesity epidemic; and increased use of expensive medical technology such as MRI. Expansions of eligibility for health care entitlement programs drive up costs. So do fraud and abuse. For example, some physicians sell prescriptions for narcotics. Some nursing homes charge for services not provided, and some home health care companies' bill for nursing visits never made. (In some Florida nursing homes, patients in comas were billed for speech therapy.)[24] In pill mills, a conspiracy of doctors, clinic owners, and pharmacists prescribe drugs and obtain government reimbursements, yet no drugs actually change hands. All told, Medicare overpayments ran as high as $65 billion in 2013 due to errors, waste, and fraud.

Prior to passage of the ACA, even though per-capita U.S. health care spending far exceeded that of other countries, a large portion of the population (estimated to be one in four people under age 65) did not have health insurance. Consequently, the U.S. health care system was inferior to those of most other advanced nations in terms of access, mortality rates, patient safety, efficiency, equity, and many other measures.[25] Uninsured Americans have had to spend their personal resources to the point of bankruptcy before they could qualify for government aid through Medicaid. A layoff or job change could result in the loss of insurance coverage, meaning entire families courted financial disaster. When uninsured, sick, or injured people take advantage of free government health care programs, usually in hospital emergency rooms or free clinics, individuals with health care insurance are the ones who pay. Doctors, hospitals, and others simply garner revenue lost from the uninsured through higher fees charged to those who can pay. The result was a fragmented, profit-driven, two-tiered system in which the insured received state-of-the-art health care and the uninsured experienced health care services that were surpassed by those of some Third World countries.

Medical malpractice suits complicate the financial issues of health care policy. Physicians and other health care providers bemoan astoundingly high jury awards for pain and suffering, and soaring insurance premiums. Some doctors in New Jersey, Florida, and West Virginia have literally walked off the job in protest. Trial lawyers fight caps on jury awards and defend victims' rights to seek fair and just compensation for preventable medical mistakes. With no action forthcoming from Congress, states are left to grapple with the issue, and a large majority have set limits on jury awards for "pain and suffering" and other noneconomic claims.[26]

THE AFFORDABLE CARE ACT OF 2010

It would be a challenge to explain the confusion and political furor over the ACA. The Act requires citizens and residents of the U.S. to have health insurance or pay a fine. States were to create Health Benefits Exchanges through which coverage may be purchased. If they choose not to create their own state-run exchange, state residents will be covered by a federal health exchange. Employers are required to either provide health insurance to their workers or pay a penalty for not doing so. Federal subsidies are available to assist

FIGURE 17.2

Status of State Action on the Medicaid Expansion Decision, May 2015

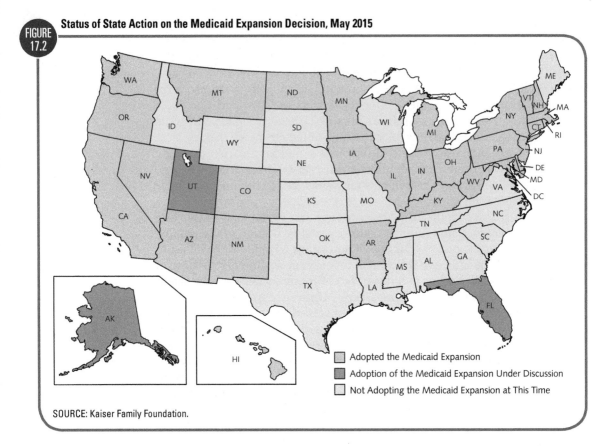

Adopted the Medicaid Expansion

Adoption of the Medicaid Expansion Under Discussion

Not Adopting the Medicaid Expansion at This Time

SOURCE: Kaiser Family Foundation.

uninsured low-income individuals. States were originally mandated to extend Medicaid coverage to residents with incomes of less than 133 percent of the federal poverty level, but this mandate was declared invalid by the U.S. Supreme Court in a 2012 decision, *National Federation of Independent Businesses et al v. Sebelius.*[27]

Confusion reigned when the federal government failed miserably in the disastrous launch of its website, www.healthcare.gov. The site was plagued by serious software problems, including sudden crashes and lengthy user delays. The technical problems were corrected and the federal site now works fine, but the political rancor and fierce opposition of Republicans, Tea Partiers, and other conservatives continue unabated.[28] The Act was back before the U.S. Supreme Court in 2015 and at risk of being gutted, but a 6-3 majority of the Court upheld the essential constitutionality of the Act.[29]

While noncooperating states sued in federal courts and their legislatures proposed—and some passed—a raft of anti-ACA bills, other states have taken advantage of the ACA by creating and operating their own health care exchanges and expanding Medicaid coverage. It is likely that some of the states that did develop their own health care exchanges will soon move to the federal exchange.

Of course, health care problems endure and—for better or for worse—will be revisited by Congress. Meanwhile, managed care and managed competition are resulting in mergers and consolidation in the health care industry and monetary efficiencies as doctor, hospital, and pharmaceutical fees and prices are squeezed. But most of the juice is out of the orange, and future state Medicaid costs are expected to grow at an average annual rate of about 6 percent.[30]

STATE AND LOCAL HEALTH CARE INNOVATION

Prior to Congress acting on national health care, the states were busily engaged in reforming health care themselves. Innovations tested by states served as models for major provisions of the ACA. Indeed, Massachusetts' "Commonwealth Care" program served as a model for the ACA. Each state has its own perspective on what is wrong with health care and its own approach to fixing it. State actions are also guided by economics and special circumstances.

The Act provides generous financial support to cooperating states seeking to improve the quality and cost of health care. Several states took early advantage and successfully launched early state health care exchanges. Relatively flawless launchings took place in Kentucky, Connecticut, Washington, and California. Other states learned important lessons from these early innovators, as they did from other states whose exchanges encountered difficulties. Among the lessons learned were: (1) To extensively beta-test the software and website; (2) to forgo fancy bells and whistles for a simple, straightforward website; (3) to enable users to browse the website without first logging in and setting up an account with personal data;[31] and (4) to hire a proven firm to oversee health exchange development and integrate it with Medicaid enrollment systems.[32]

A major concern, of course, is holding down Medicaid costs. Below are a few examples of specific approaches by state and local governments to rein in health care costs while providing quality services:

- Minnesota is a leader in Accountable Care Organizations (ACOs) (see Table 17.2). A network of physicians and health care facilities receive a fixed budget in return for accepting responsibility for providing care for a specified group of patients. If the goal of supplying coordinated, quality services for less cost is achieved, the ACO and the state share in the savings.[33] Primary, preventive care is emphasized to help avoid more expensive services—such as emergency room visits—down the road.
- Arkansas received federal permission under an ACA waiver to privatize its Medicaid program, paying health care insurance companies and other providers based on quality of care instead of services rendered. The state has established standards for pricing specified services, from heart attacks to pregnancies, based on the total costs, from initial consultation and facility admission to discharge from the hospital or clinic. Each provider is evaluated annually with respect to its average costs; it may then receive a bonus, or it may have to return money to the state.[34]
- Several states, including California, Florida, and New Jersey, are focusing on Medicaid fraud prevention. California searches for unusual payments

suggesting waste or fraud. Florida officials conduct unannounced visits to providers to audit payments and services; New Jersey uses federal and state databases to identify repeated fraudulent practices by individuals.[35]

- Massachusetts, California, and other states have taken steps to mesh Medicaid with Medicare. Older (Medicare) and poor (Medicaid) people have been treated as two separate populations, with the result being duplication of services and wasted funds. Now, "dual eligible" (both age 65 or older *and* poor) carry a single benefits card and receive a unified plan under a case manager. Significant cost savings will be realized if the programs are successful: dual eligible account for 15 percent of all Medicaid enrollees but consume almost 40 percent of costs.[36]

- Hennepin County, Minnesota is experimenting with a holistic care program for chronic users of costly emergency services. A coordinator is assigned to such individuals to assist with ongoing, consistent health care attention and guidance, and with other related problems such as homelessness or alcoholism.[37]

STATE HEALTH CARE REFORM IS NEVER-ENDING

Huge variations exist in state health care spending. The southeastern states present special health care problems because of the high prevalence of obesity, diabetes, and stroke. In the West and Southwest, especially Utah, teetotaling, nonsmoking Mormons enjoy good health and help keep costs down. Florida's large senior population is a heavy consumer of nursing homes and other health care facilities, driving these costs up. Figure 17.3 shows state health rankings. States that spend relatively high amounts per capita do not necessarily rank high on state health indicators.

State and local governments have always been concerned with the health of their citizens and indeed are delegated this responsibility in the U.S. Constitution. Colonial towns assumed responsibility for impoverished sick people in the 1600s, providing almshouses and primitive medical treatments involving leeches and native herbs. Cities and counties, along with private charities, built and operated public hospitals for the poor in the 1800s. Today, the states are hard at work dealing with the complexities of the ACA, including the decision of whether to keep or establish health benefits exchanges or to depend on the federal exchange.

Medicaid will continue to burden the states financially. This entitlement program, growing substantially as a result of the ACA, already comprises the largest portion of state expenditures. It will be interesting to see if the states whose political leaders are adamantly opposed to expanding Medicaid rolls as a condition of accepting the federal Medicaid subsidy will eventually bow to federal pressure and the lobbying of the health insurance and hospital industries and comply with the ACA's terms.

Medicaid costs are not the only serious problem. Prescription drug prices are escalating. A disturbing and deleterious nurse shortage threatens the quality of medical care. The nursing-home industry is riddled with problems, as is care for the mentally disabled.

State Health Rankings, 2014
These rankings, from most healthy to least healthy, are based on various health indicators, including
unemployment, poverty, smoking, availability of health services, obesity, and death rates. Low scores
indicate the most healthy states, high scores the least healthy.

FIGURE 17.3

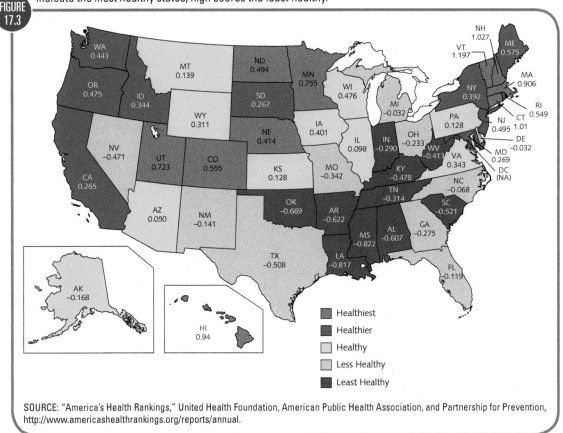

SOURCE: "America's Health Rankings," United Health Foundation, American Public Health Association, and Partnership for Prevention,
http://www.americashealthrankings.org/reports/annual.

A national approach to health care has been a long time coming, but
states—and their highly disparate preferences—will not be ignored. They will
continue to act as service integrators, implementers, and innovators in their
classic "middleman" role in U.S. federalism. Moreover, they continue clearing
new trails that will inform and influence future federal policy making.

Chapter Recap

- Social welfare and health care are major en-
trees on the federal-state policy menu. The
national government may own the restaurant, but the cooks who turn out the policy
dishes are the state and local governments.

- Poverty in the United States is measured,
somewhat inaccurately, using a statistic
called the poverty level. This statistic is,
nonetheless, an important indicator of
citizen well-being.

- The Affordable Care Act now serves as national health care policy, but the state and local governments are fully engaged in program design, experimentation, and administration.

- Programs to help poor children and to move adults from welfare rolls to payrolls have received special attention through state innovations.

KEY TERMS

Temporary Assistance for Needy Families (TANF) *(p. 457)*

direct cash transfer *(p. 458)*

in-kind program *(p. 460)*

social insurance *(p. 463)*

Affordable Care Act *(p. 470)*

INTERNET RESOURCES

An excellent source of information on health care issues is the Kaiser Family Foundation at **http://www.kff.org/**.

For information on federal and state health care, see the Centers for Medicaid and Medicare Services at **www.cms.hhs.gov**. The Administration for Children and Families (ACF), within the U.S. Department of Health and Human Services (DHHS), is responsible for federal programs that promote economic and social well-being. Information about their programs can be obtained from their website at **www.acf.hhs.gov**.

Families USA is a nonprofit organization that works at the national, state, and local levels to achieve high-quality, affordable health care and long-term care for all Americans. Their website, **www.familiesusa.org**, serves as a clearinghouse for information about the health care system.

For information on children's issues, see the Children's Defense Fund at **www.childrensdefense.org**.

For general information and links on welfare programs and initiatives, see **www.welfareinfo.org**.

A sign at a Seattle lake warns of potential pollution after heavy rainfalls. Jimmy Anderson/Getty Images

Environmental Policy: Regulation and Innovation

18

For two days in August 2014, thousands of people in Toledo, Ohio, lined up to get containers of drinking water after the city's water source, Lake Erie, turned green. The lake changed colors due to growth of potentially dangerous algae blooms, which can develop when nutrients such as phosphorus from farm fertilizers, livestock manure, and sewage overflows accumulate in the water, especially when the weather is warm. Algae blooms contain the toxin microcystin, which can produce headaches or vomiting when swallowed; longer exposure can lead to organ damage. One problem for Toledo and other affected areas was that no national standard had been set for allowable levels of microcystin in drinking water. Moreover, water system operators were not required to test for it when performing regular water analyses. However, in the absence of federal government action, a few states had already taken steps to address the issue. Minnesota, for instance, had adopted a standard that set the allowable microcystin level at 0.45 parts per billion (ppb). Even after the algae blooms were removed from Lake Erie and the water returned to its normal condition, the public clamored for governments at all levels to "do something" to keep them safe. In May 2015, the U.S. Environmental Protection Agency (EPA) issued guidelines for microcystin, setting the safe level at 0.3 ppb for children younger than school age and 1.6 ppb for everyone else. However, these federal guidelines were advisory, not binding on local water systems, so states can continue to adopt their own standards and regulations.[1]

Environmental protection policy in the United States is characterized by three features: its intergovernmental nature, its regulatory focus, and lately, its innovative design. The federal government is extensively involved in environmental policy, as are states and localities. These governments play different roles depending on the environmental problem and the era. The activity of government tends to be regulatory, that is, making rules and setting standards that affect the private sector, monitoring compliance, and imposing penalties. Finally, solutions to environmental problems are moving beyond the more traditional approaches and are becoming increasingly innovative and fresh. As will be evident in this chapter, environmental policy tests the capacity of states and localities to make smart choices for the future.

LO 18.1

To articulate the relationship between environmental protection and economic growth.

The Political Economy of Environmental Protection

Environmental policy choices are made especially difficult by their economic implications. Controlling pollution is a significant economic cost for many firms today. In the essentially nonregulatory era prior to the 1960s, this expense was either quite low or nonexistent. Increasing government regulatory intervention in industrial processes and outputs reflects the indisputable fact that market forces by themselves will not guarantee the protection of our health and the environment. Clean air and clean water are public goods that should be available to all of us, but polluters often have little economic incentive to stop polluting.

When left unregulated, most firms tend to maximize profits by minimizing costs—including the costs of environmental protection. Determining exactly what constitutes pollution or environmental degradation and deciding how stringently to regulate polluting activities have tremendous economic implications for firms and governments. Too much regulation could depress economic growth at national, state, and local levels; reduce employment; and even force some companies into bankruptcy. These concerns are not simply conjecture. To some degree, states that imposed costlier regulatory burdens on the private sector experienced lower rates of new capital investment.[2] Obviously, the trade-offs between economic growth and environmental protection can spawn conflict.

PUBLIC OPINION

Research tells us that Americans generally support the goals of environmental protection. Public opinion polls indicate that most people are in favor of increased government spending for environmental protection and oppose efforts to weaken environmental standards.[3] This resounding endorsement lessens, however, when environmental protection is pitted against goals such as economic growth and adequate energy. When members of the environmental group Earth First! square off against loggers in the forests of the Pacific Northwest, environmentalism becomes more than an abstraction. Environmental protection does not occur in a vacuum; achievement of its goals comes at a cost to other valued objectives.

Although support among the public for protecting the environment was strong in the early part of the century, it eventually began to lose ground as the priority accorded economic growth increased. Figure 18.1 shows the fluctuation in national public opinion from 2000 to 2014, as reported by the Gallup Poll. The polling question requires the respondent to weigh environmental protection against economic development and was worded in this manner:

> With which one of these statements about the environment and the economy do you most agree—protection of the environment should be given priority, even at the risk of curbing economic growth (or) economic growth should be given priority, even if the environment suffers to some extent?[4]

As Figure 18.1 shows, the gap between the two priorities narrowed over time; and by 2009, the public preferred economic growth to environmental protection. The increased importance of economic growth can be attributed in part to the downturn in the nation's economy during the period. By 2014, with the economy back on track, support for environmental protection (50 percent) once again took precedence over economic growth (41 percent). Even when the economy is a greater priority, environmental protection continues to be

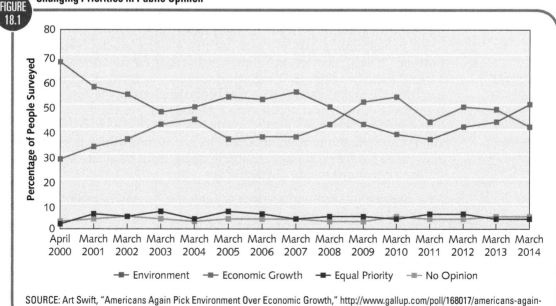

FIGURE 18.1

Changing Priorities in Public Opinion

SOURCE: Art Swift, "Americans Again Pick Environment Over Economic Growth," http://www.gallup.com/poll/168017/americans-again-pick-environment-economic-growth.aspx (accessed June 5, 2015).

valued because all of us are potential or actual victims of environmental problems. Polluted air, water, and land offend us aesthetically but, more important, they threaten the health and safety of ourselves, our children, and our grandchildren. People who drink contaminated water and breathe polluted air experience the costs directly.

From a different perspective, all citizens must help pay the price of a safe and clean environment. We pay for a clean environment through the portion of our taxes that goes to government pollution-control efforts and through the prices we pay for goods, which include the cost of pollution control. The costs to consumers are especially heavy where the products of chemical companies, the auto industry, and coal-burning power plants are concerned. These industries have lobbied vigorously against what they perceive to be excessive regulation. One policy that is intended to improve relations between business and regulators is the **environmental self-audit**, which allows firms to self-report violations. If the firm then corrects the problem voluntarily, the penalty levied by government is less than it would have been otherwise. Although proponents of this approach tout its promise, a recent study found that the environmental performance of firms participating in these self-monitoring programs actually lags that of firms subject to traditional regulation.[5]

LO 18.2

To discuss the concept of sustainability.

NEW APPROACHES: MOVING TOWARD SUSTAINABILITY

Government's role is to balance economic growth with environmental protection by regulating polluters. The political economy of environmental protection argues strongly for national domination of policymaking. Because states and local governments compete for industry (as discussed in Chapter 14), some jurisdictions might be tempted to relax environmental protection standards and thus influence a firm's decision about where to construct or expand a new manufacturing facility, a behavior that is often called a "**race to the bottom**." Indeed, new research indicates that state environmental agencies are influenced by other states' regulatory actions.[6] Moreover, state regulators pay attention to the effects of their regulatory decisions on industries' investment decisions. National policies and standards can prevent the sacrifice of environmental quality in jurisdictions that seek growth and development at almost any cost. But concern about the high costs of traditional regulatory approaches has spawned some creative thinking about alternatives. This new thinking has moved in four directions:

environmental self-audit

A form of self-policing in which the regulated firm conducts its own review of its performance and voluntarily reports violations.

race to the bottom

Occurs when states alter their behaviors—relaxing regulations, lowering taxes, or reducing benefits—to gain an advantage over competing states.

- Changing production processes to limit the amount of pollution produced in the first place,
- Reducing exposure to pollutants rather than trying to eliminate pollution altogether,
- Exploring the trade-offs between regulatory costs and environmental benefits to determine when an unacceptable imbalance exists, and
- Replacing traditional administrative procedures with economic incentives and other market strategies with the hope of achieving both environmental protection and economic efficiency.[7]

It is not clear whether these new approaches will achieve what some of their proponents intend, that is, the marrying of environmental protection and economic development. The word often used to describe this marriage is **sustainability**, that is, an approach to economic growth that prevents harm to the environment. Numerous studies have shown that as a nation's economy prospers, the public's concern over environmental quality increases.[8] These intertwined goals present continued challenges for policy makers.

Clean Air, Clean Water, and Politics

In the early days of the United States, government involvement in environmental protection was minimal at best. Natural resources were abundant, the country was developing, and the future seemed limitless. The first government forays into the now-tangled jungle of environmental protection policy began in the early 1800s with local ordinances aimed at garbage; human and animal waste; contaminated drinking water; and other unsanitary, health-endangering conditions in American cities. Local failures to contain and control such problems were punctuated by cholera and typhoid epidemics throughout the nineteenth century and into the early twentieth century. In 1878, a yellow fever epidemic caused 5,000 deaths and the exodus of another 25,000 fearful residents from Memphis, Tennessee. Such episodes prompted the states to begin regulating conditions causing waterborne diseases, thereby redefining what had been a private problem into a problem for state government. By 1948, states had taken over responsibility for water pollution control. Their early regulatory efforts were rather weak, however.

LO 18.3

To understand the intergovernmental relationships that define environmental policy.

A waterfall at Chewacia State Park near Auburn, Alabama.

Rob Hainer/Shutterstock.com

sustainability

The simultaneous achievement of economic development and environmental protection.

THE CENTRALIZATION OF ENVIRONMENTAL POLICY

The issue of water pollution control shows the evolving centralization of federal government authority in environmental decision making. Although the federal government acted to protect natural resources by setting aside land for national parks in the late nineteenth century, it paid little attention to environmental problems until after World War II. At that point, the forces of urbanization and industrial production began to draw attention to the national dimensions of environmental dangers. The initial federal statutory step into the policy field was the Water Pollution Control Act of 1948. Under the original version of this act, the national government assumed limited enforcement authority for water pollution. Since then, seven other major federal statutes or amendments have been enacted to address the problem. Using this overall statutory framework, the federal government pre-empted existing state and local water quality standards and substituted national standards.

The reasons for this pre-emption are not difficult to understand. We have already noted that as states compete for economic development, they may be tempted to lower environmental standards to gain an edge over other states. In addition, because pollution problems are often cross-boundary (i.e., they extend beyond a single jurisdiction), solutions can be difficult to design. Toxins dumped into a river upstream have deleterious consequences for jurisdictions located downstream. The failure of states to work together to solve shared environmental problems led to more involvement by the federal government.

Increasingly strong federal statutes also addressed the problems of air pollution, pesticides, and hazardous waste. For example, the first national legislation on air quality, the Air Pollution Control Act of 1955, made funding available for research on the health effects of bad air. It was superseded by the Clean Air Act of 1963, which encouraged the development of emissions standards. The Clean Air Act of 1970, a massive overhaul of its predecessor, set air quality standards and strictly regulated emissions from factories and motor vehicles. By the late 1970s, the federal government had extended its authority to endangered species, strip mining, coastal zones, toxic substances, and many other areas. Thus, environmental protection was redefined as a national problem requiring national solutions. Since then, studies have found that the public prefers the federal government to take the lead on non-local pollution matters.[9] The federal government does not operate alone, however; state and local governments play a significant role in implementing federal legislation.

States and localities speak with an important policy voice even in environmental fields that appear to be outside their sphere of influence. For example, one group of northeastern and mid-Atlantic states took on the issue of greenhouse gas emissions in a creative way by developing a regional cap-and-trade program. The Regional Greenhouse Gas Initiative (RGGI) sets an emissions cap for utilities and then auctions off emissions permits. The funds raised through the auctions are reinvested in programs related to energy efficiency, renewable energy, and other measures that help lower consumer electricity bills. RGGI has been quite successful. Even as the regional economy grew, by 2013, RGGI states experienced a 40 percent reduction in power-sector carbon dioxide pollution.[10]

TABLE 18.1	Federal Land Ownership in the States				
STATES WITH MOST FEDERAL LAND (AS % OF STATE LAND AREA)	FEDERAL ACREAGE (IN THOUSANDS OF ACRES)	PERCENTAGE OF THE STATE	STATES WITH LEAST FEDERAL LAND (AS % OF STATE LAND AREA)	FEDERAL ACREAGE (IN THOUSANDS OF ACRES	PERCENTAGE OF THE STATE
Nevada	56,962	81.1	Connecticut	9	0.3
Utah	35,034	66.5	Iowa	123	0.3
Alaska	225,848	61.8	Kansas	301	0.6
Idaho	32,636	61.7	New York	211	0.7
Oregon	32,665	53.0	Rhode Island	5	0.8

NOTE: The figures include the lands of the four major federal land management agencies (U.S. Forest Service, National Park Service, Fish and Wildlife Service, and Bureau of Land Management) and the Department of Defense but exclude lands administered by other federal agencies such as the Agricultural Research Service, the Department of Energy, and NASA. Therefore the percentages may be understated.

SOURCE: Ross Gorte, et al., "Federal Land Ownership: Overview and Data," Congressional Research Service, 7-5700, http://www.fas.org/sgp/crs/misc/R42346.pdf (accessed February 8, 2012).

Another example is public lands. Governed by Congress and managed by eight federal agencies, including the Bureau of Land Management, the U.S. Forest Service, and the National Park Service, the nation's 700 million acres of public lands make up almost one-third of the continental United States and more than 60 percent of the land area of four western states: Alaska, Idaho, Nevada, and Utah. (Table 18.1 displays federal land ownership figures for ten states.)

These lands contain vast timber, petroleum, coal, and mineral resources. The states have an enormous economic stake in the way these resources and their environmental implications are managed. In 2012, two Western state legislatures passed bills demanding that the federal government relinquish ownership of much of the land and if it fails to comply, giving states the right to seize the disputed land. In Utah, the governor signed the bill into law; in Arizona, the governor vetoed a similar bill. The primary complaint of the aggrieved state leaders is that federal policies toward the land are overly restrictive, making too much land off-limits to commercial activities, especially energy development.[11] The issue continues to percolate: In 2015, bills laying the groundwork for land transfers were introduced in the legislatures of seven western states—Alaska, Arizona, Colorado, Montana, New Mexico, Washington, and Wyoming. Several Republican members of Congress from western states have been receptive to the idea of large-scale land transfers; however, the full Congress is decidedly less enthusiastic.

NATIONAL POLITICS AND THE ENVIRONMENT

The lead agency in national environmental policy is the U.S. Environmental Protection Agency (EPA), which was created in 1970 as an independent regulatory body for pollution control. With its director appointed by the president, the EPA is faced with the task of coordinating and enforcing the broad array of environmental protection programs established by Congress. To help with this task, the agency has decentralized much of its operation to ten regional offices located in major cities throughout the country. The scope of the EPA's responsibility can be overwhelming, involving regular interaction and conflict with other federal agencies, powerful private interests, and state and local governments. Its job is complicated by the tendency of Congress to pass environmental legislation that sets unattainable program goals and unrealistic implementation dates. Many deadlines for compliance with federal laws have been missed by the EPA, which lends ammunition to its critics on all sides. Litigation brought by regulated industries and environmental groups has further ensnarled the agency, and a shortage of money and staff has plagued the EPA since the administration of President Reagan.

An example of the scope of the EPA's responsibilities is water pollution control. Every private and public facility that discharges wastes directly into water must obtain a permit from the EPA or, in some instances, from its state counterpart. The national government, through the EPA, establishes specific discharge standards. Day-to-day oversight and implementation, however, are performed by the states. In effect, the national government makes the rules and lets the states enforce them according to their own circumstances (a process known as **partial pre-emption**). The national government also disburses grants to state and local governments for the treatment and monitoring of water resources. Billions of federal dollars have been spent for the construction of wastewater treatment plants; millions more have gone for technical assistance and research and development.

One interesting attempt to build a more cooperative relationship between the EPA and state-level environmental protection agencies is the performance partnership agreement (PPA) that was promoted by the Clinton administration. PPAs allow a state to combine its EPA funding into block grants that can be used for comprehensive statewide environmental problems.[12] Basically, PPAs give states more power to set their own spending priorities. The idea was pilot-tested in North Dakota, New Hampshire, and Massachusetts with sufficient success to warrant its extension to other interested states, and now nearly all states are engaged in PPAs.

During the presidency of George W. Bush, several states challenged the federal government, arguing that EPA should regulate greenhouse gases as pollutants under the Clean Air Act (CAA). In 2007, a U.S. Supreme Court ruling instructed the agency to study the issue and in 2009, after thorough scientific analysis, the EPA declared greenhouse gases pollutants that threaten public health. In 2014, the Court upheld the agency's plans to regulate greenhouse gas emissions from power plants and factories using the CAA. Besides the emissions rules, other areas of emphasis for the Obama administration have been the promotion of green jobs and the development of new fuel efficiency standards for motor vehicles.

The Greening of States and Localities

State and local governments have taken on greater responsibility for financing and operating environmental protection programs and have become policy initiators. For example, Congress was gridlocked on acid rain legislation for

partial pre-emption
An approach common to federal environmental laws that requires states to apply federal standards.

years, but some states took unilateral actions to cut sulfur dioxide emissions within their borders (New Hampshire and New York were the first). Several states, including New Jersey and Ohio, passed legislation requiring firms to clean up hazardous wastes from industrial property before selling the property. Such legislation helps prevent companies from abandoning polluted sites that present health risks and leaving them for the states to clean up. California's far-reaching policies to improve the nation's worst air quality have become a model for other states and the national government. The Golden State also has led the way in its efforts to conserve water through, among other things, a statute requiring the use of water-efficient washing machines.

Today, states have ventured forth on several environmental fronts, notably climate change. More than half of the states have set goals for increased reliance on renewable energy sources for at least some of their utilities' power generation. For example, the state of Washington has created a series of financial incentives to spur the use of renewable energy sources. The state gives homeowners and small businesses with solar power and wind power systems a credit on their electric bills. Consumers get an even bigger break for using systems whose components were manufactured in Washington.[13] The bottom line is that states have become central actors in environmental protection through their innovative ideas.

As indicated in the preceding section, states operate many of their pollution-control programs under the auspices of federal legislation and the EPA. They must develop and implement plans and standards under a host of federal laws. The Safe Drinking Water Act, for instance, requires local water systems to meet national standards for acceptable levels of contaminants such as coliform (a type of bacteria), asbestos, copper, and lead in their water supply. The Clean Air Act mandates the creation of vehicle inspection and maintenance programs for smog-stricken jurisdictions. States and localities are closer to pollution problems and hence are best situated to address them on a day-to-day basis. The problem with this approach, according to states and localities, is that they have to pay a large portion of the costs themselves. Approximately 77 percent of the money in state environmental budgets comes from state revenues. Even the EPA acknowledged that the cost of federally imposed environmental mandates on state and local governments could bust their budgets, requiring millions of dollars of new spending.

STATE COMMITMENT TO ENVIRONMENTAL PROTECTION

LO 18.4

To differentiate among states and localities as to their eco-friendliness.

During the Great Recession, environmental protection took a hit, with many states eliminating or cutting back programs and staff. Examples of programs affected by cutbacks included air quality inspections, water monitoring, environmental education, and recycling. Most reductions in environmental protection agency staff were accomplished through attrition, although furloughs and terminations did occur in some states. Even as the economy improved, states were slow to return to pre-recession spending levels.

State environmental protection agencies and natural resource departments vary in their structure and responsibilities. An example of the more comprehensive, single-agency structure is found in Delaware's Department of Natural

Controversies in States and Localities

The Challenges of Regulating Polluters

When coal is burned to generate electricity, it creates a waste byproduct called coal ash. In 2014, Duke Energy, the nation's largest utility, spilled 39,000 tons of coal ash into the Dan River in North Carolina, coating 70 miles of river bottom with a gray sludge containing toxic metals that threatened drinking water and aquatic life. Many environmentalists blamed not only Duke Energy but also the state's Department of Environment and Natural Resources (DENR) for failing to enforce federal and state regulations. The agency defended itself by noting that its budget for water pollution programs had been cut by 10 percent, and furthermore, that the North Carolina governor had conveyed a preference for a more relaxed stance on regulatory enforcement. The head of DENR said that the governor had told him that "I want you to protect the environment and I want you to help us grow this economy." When Duke Energy fought demands from environmental groups that the utility relocate coal ash from unlined ponds to lined pits away from drinking water sources, the agency sided with the utility. However, the spill caused a critical reexamination of DENR's relationship with Duke Energy. Both the agency and the utility vowed to work together to establish an effective regulatory balance. In the meantime, the utility pleaded guilty to violating the Clean Water Act and negotiated an agreement with federal prosecutors to pay $102 million in fines and restitution.

Critical Thinking Questions:

1. Some people view environmental regulations as a yoke on the neck of industry, and regulatory agencies as roadblocks to economic progress. Others see environmental regulations as a necessary protection of the health and quality of life for people in a given area and regulatory agencies as the authority that ensures public and environmental health and safety. Which of these philosophies more closely reflects your personal views? Why?

2. Regulatory agencies can either be preventive by insuring that industries adhere to rules and regulations or reactive by fining companies after an event requiring cleanup. Preventive measures are often seen as "red tape" that makes doing business more difficult. However, reactive measures take place after the environmental damage has already been done. How can regulatory agencies find a happy medium between these two perspectives?

3. A state environmental protection agency ends up working closely with the industries it regulates. What are some of the consequences of working closely together?

SOURCE: Trip Gabriel, "Ash Spill shows How Watchdog Was Defanged," *New York Times*, www.nytimes.com/2014/03/01/us/coal-ash-spill (accessed May 27, 2015); "Duke Energy Fined $102 Million in Coal Ash Spill," CBS News, www.cbsnews.com/news/duke-energy-fined-102-million-in-coal-ash-spill/ (accessed May 14, 2015).

Resources and Environmental Control, composed of five divisions: Air and Waste Management, Fish and Wildlife, Parks and Recreation, Soil and Water Conservation, and Water Resources. Arizona separates functions across a Department of Environmental Quality, a Game and Fish Department, and a Natural Resources Division within the State Land Department. Different still are states such as South Carolina, which combine environmental protection and public health in the same department. Clearly, there is no "one best way" to organize. In 2011, Connecticut merged its departments of Environmental Protection and Public Utility Control to form a Department of Energy and Environmental Protection. The same year, Michigan split its Department of Natural Resources and Environment into two separate agencies just 18 months after its creation.[14] The Controversies in States and Localities considers the relationship of state environmental protection agencies to powerful utility companies.

As noted earlier, states often face pressure from economic interests to weaken environmental regulations. Despite this pressure, at least some states have exceeded the guidelines set by the EPA to ensure better air quality. A survey of states found that nearly 30 percent had ambient air standards that went beyond the requirements of federal law.[15] What causes states to adopt more stringent regulations than the EPA requires? The answer seems to lie in the strength of green interest groups, supportive public opinion, and the ability to convert this pro-environment political climate into legislative action.

States are often ranked on their environmental conditions, policies, and programs. One recent rating by the financial products information website, wallethub.com used fourteen key indicators of environmental quality and eco-friendly behaviors to evaluate the states. The criteria included air, water, and soil quality, carbon dioxide emissions, number of green-certified buildings, energy efficiency actions, green transportation, and recycling rates, among others. The analysis utilized data from independent scientific organizations and government sources, and it controlled for population differences among states. In 2015, the five greenest states were Vermont, Oregon, New York, Minnesota, and Massachusetts; at the bottom of the list was Louisiana. Figure 18.2 categorizes

FIGURE 18.2

How Green Are the States?

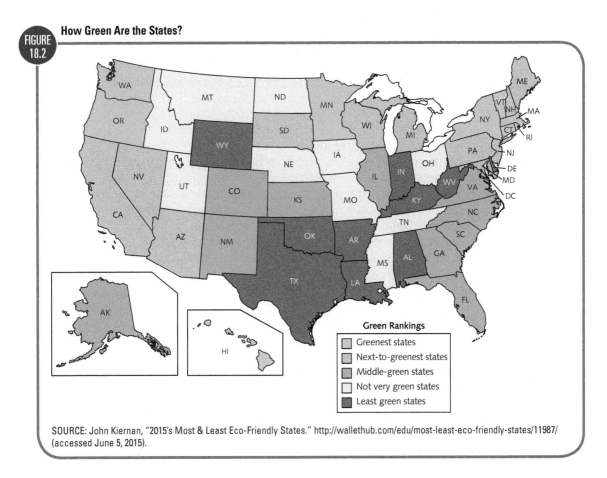

Green Rankings
- Greenest states
- Next-to-greenest states
- Middle-green states
- Not very green states
- Least green states

SOURCE: John Kiernan, "2015's Most & Least Eco-Friendly States." http://wallethub.com/edu/most-least-eco-friendly-states/11987/ (accessed June 5, 2015).

the states into five groups, based on the wallethub.com ratings. One notable pattern is the absence of southern states from the top two groupings. In general, research has shown that support for environmental protection tends to be strong among Democrats, liberals, the affluent, and the educated.[16]

GREEN LOCALITIES

Local governments regularly take action to protect the environment and conserve natural resources. For instance, Atlanta has sponsored a tree-planting project for National Arbor Day; Kansas City, Missouri, promoted its Keep Kansas City Beautiful anti-litter campaign; the green power program in Riverside, California, offered classes on recycling and composting; Spokane, Washington, adopted a special tax in support of open-space conservation. Meanwhile, New York City added 300 Toyota Prius vehicles—with a fuel efficiency rating of 50 miles per gallon—to its municipal fleet. More than 1,000 cities joined the Cities for Climate Protection campaign to reduce the emissions of greenhouse gases. Others have adopted green building codes to spur the construction of buildings that are substantially more energy efficient and less resource intensive than regular buildings.

But even as cities and counties make decisions and allocate funds to protect the environment, they take plenty of actions that contribute to environmental degradation and natural resource loss. Think about the negative environmental consequences of a city government's approval of a developer's request to construct a new shopping mall at the city's edge. Natural resources are lost as the land is cleared of trees and vegetation, and wildlife habitat is destroyed. Once the mall opens, traffic congestion leads to polluted air; storm-water runoff from parking lots results in polluted rivers. As a city grows and develops, it produces a large **ecological footprint** in terms of its impact on the earth and its resources.

Many cities have taken steps to become more green, that is, to soften the impact of their ecological footprint. Seattle is one such city, beginning with its 1994 comprehensive plan, Toward a Sustainable Seattle. In functions such as land use, transportation, and housing, among others, the city set goals and adopted policies designed to make it more environmentally friendly. City departments were required to assess the environmental impact of their operations and devise ways of lessening that impact. Political scientist Kent Portney's research compared cities' commitment to sustainability, and found Portland, Oregon, San Francisco, and Seattle tied for the top spot, followed by Denver.[17] Table 18.2 displays the sustainability rankings and scores for the 55 largest cities in the United States.

The approach taken by San Francisco is especially interesting: The city's sustainability plan identified several areas of concern such as air quality, biodiversity, climate change, and open spaces. For these areas of concern, specific indicators were developed to gauge the progress that the city has or has not made. For instance, the number of native plant species in parks is one indicator of biodiversity, as is the number of different bird species sighted. Given the city's propensity, it was not a surprise when, in 2007, it became the first jurisdiction in the country to ban the use of plastic checkout bags at supermarkets.

ecological footprint

The size of the environmental impact imposed on the earth and its resources.

TABLE 18.2 Fifty-Five Largest U.S. Cities and Their Sustainability Scores

RANK	CITY	SUSTAINABILITY SCORE
1	Portland, OR	35
1	San Francisco, CA	35
1	Seattle, WA	35
4	Denver, CO	33
5	Albuquerque, NM	32
5	Oakland, CA	32
7	Chicago, IL	31
7	Columbus, OH	31
7	Minneapolis, MN	31
7	Philadelphia, PA	31
7	Phoenix, AZ	31
7	Sacramento, CA	31
13	New York, NY	30
13	San Diego, CA	30
13	San Jose, CA	30
16	Austin, TX	29
16	Charlotte, NC	29
16	Nashville-Davidson, TN	29
16	Tucson, AZ	29
16	Washington, DC	29
21	Boston, MA	28
21	Los Angeles, CA	28
21	Kansas City, MO	28
24	Dallas, TX	27
24	Indianapolis, IN	27
26	Fresno, CA	26
26	Miami, FL	26
26	Las Vegas, NV	26
26	Raleigh, NC	26
26	San Antonio, TX	26
31	Baltimore, MD	25
31	Louisville Metro, KY	25

(continued)

TABLE 18.2   Fifty-Five Largest U.S. Cities and Their Sustainability Scores (*continued*)

RANK	CITY	SUSTAINABILITY SCORE
33	Cleveland, OH	24
33	Fort Worth, TX	24
33	Milwaukee, WI	24
36	El Paso, TX	23
36	Jacksonville, FL	23
39	Honolulu, HI	22
39	Houston, TX	22
39	Long Beach, CA	22
39	Mesa, AZ	22
43	Arlington, TX	20
43	Memphis, TN	20
43	Tampa, FL	20
46	Omaha. NE	19
46	St. Louis, MO	19
48	Oklahoma City, OK	18
48	Tulsa, OK	18
50	Detroit, MI	17
50	Virginia Beach, VA	17
52	Pittsburgh, PA	16
52	Santa Ana, CA	16
54	Colorado Springs, CO	15
54	Wichita, KS	7

SOURCE: Kent E. Portney, 2011, *Taking Sustainable Cities Seriously,* 2nd ed. (Cambridge, MA: MIT Press), pp. 80–81.

And then in 2009, San Francisco began requiring households and businesses to compost food scraps; those who do not comply can be fined. The city's goal is zero waste by 2020, meaning that it intends to reduce, reuse, and recycle such that the city sends no waste to landfills or incinerators.

LO 18.5

To summarize the issues related to waste management.

Dealing with Waste

One of the by-products of modern life is waste of all varieties. Households, schools, hospitals, businesses, and factories produce massive quantities of waste daily. When garbage collectors in New York City went on strike several years ago, the towers of smelly refuse that piled up on city streets reminded

New Yorkers how important this particular city service was. More threatening to public health and the environment are the toxic wastes generated by certain industrial processes and the wastes associated with nuclear power. One of the challenges for government is finding better ways to manage all this waste.

RECYCLING SOLID WASTE

Vast quantities of household and commercial refuse are generated daily in the United States. Americans produce about 251 million tons of trash annually, or 4.38 pounds per person per day.[18] In general, states with more commercial and industrial activity tend to generate more solid waste than those with a more agricultural economy. Of the solid waste generated in a year, 12 percent is combusted in waste-to-energy plants and another 34 percent is recycled or composted, leaving about 54 percent destined for landfills. Thousands of landfills were in operation in the 1980s; today there are about 1,900. Many of them are so-called super dumps, where more than 500 tons of waste is disposed of daily.

Like nuclear and hazardous waste, solid waste often brings out the not-in-my-backyard (**NIMBY**) syndrome. Everyone generates garbage, and lots of it, but no one wants to have it smelling over the back fence or threatening the well water. (There are some exceptions, of course, which have given rise to the term **PIMBY**, or put-in-my-backyard.) The shortage of disposal sites has naturally driven up the price of land disposal in the dumps that still operate, and disposal fees have tripled in many localities during the past few years. Many cities must ship their waste hundreds of miles and across state lines to find an open dump site. For example, household garbage from suburban New York City communities may be transported to a dump in central Illinois or rural Virginia. One-quarter of the trash dumped in Michigan's landfills comes from other states or from Canada.[19] Burning trash in waste-to-energy plants once seemed the perfect solution: disposing of solid waste and creating electrical power. But the high cost of building and operating these incinerators, especially as air-quality standards increased, has lessened their promise.

Recycling is a waste management solution that makes good sense. Approximately 27 percent of municipal solid waste is paper, another 14 percent is yard trimmings, and nearly all of these waste streams could be recycled.[20] Packaging and containers, often made of plastic, comprise a significant portion of municipal solid waste, and at least some of this waste could be recycled. Figure 18.3 shows the types of materials that make up municipal solid waste. Many states have aggressively tackled the mounting garbage problem by adopting statewide recycling laws, and a growing number of cities and counties have begun their own recycling efforts. There are an estimated 9,000 curbside recycling programs in the United States. On average, we recycle or compost approximately 1.5 pounds of the waste we generate daily for a recycling rate of about 34.5 percent.

Recycling is not a panacea for the solid waste problem, however. It requires citizen cooperation if it is to be affordable, and some people simply will not cooperate. Recycling rates for aluminum cans and plastic soft drink bottles peaked a few years ago at 63 percent and 41 percent, respectively. But

NIMBY

Not in my backyard; the public desire to keep an unwanted facility out of a neighborhood.

PIMBY

Put in my backyard; a willingness to accept what others do not want, usually because of the economic benefit.

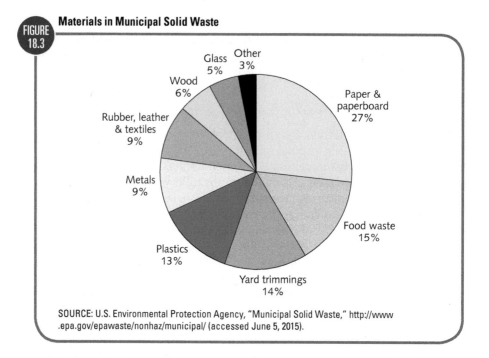

FIGURE 18.3

Materials in Municipal Solid Waste

- Other 3%
- Glass 5%
- Wood 6%
- Rubber, leather & textiles 9%
- Metals 9%
- Plastics 13%
- Yard trimmings 14%
- Paper & paperboard 27%
- Food waste 15%

SOURCE: U.S. Environmental Protection Agency, "Municipal Solid Waste," http://www .epa.gov/epawaste/nonhaz/municipal/ (accessed June 5, 2015).

a city cannot refuse to collect nonparticipants' garbage without creating a public health problem. Another dilemma is the shortage of markets for recycled paper, aluminum cans, plastics, and other materials.

For some states, glutted markets and low prices for recyclables make it difficult to reach their recycling goals. During the recent recession, the demand for recycled materials such as cardboard, newspaper, plastic, and metals dropped dramatically. Many states had enacted laws and adopted policies aimed at stimulating demand for recycled goods including sanctions (such as taxes on manufacturers based on their use of virgin materials), incentives (such as the provision of rebates to manufacturers using recovered materials), and exhortations (such as buy-recycled programs). And most state governments have adopted rules requiring or encouraging their agencies to purchase recycled paper products. But even with these market-priming mechanisms in place, when the economy slowed, many localities that once made money selling recyclables were forced to pay waste haulers to take the bottles, cans, and newspapers off their hands.[21]

As noted, approximately one-third of the nation's solid waste is recycled, but the figures are substantially higher in some jurisdictions than in others. The explanation for why some states recycle at a greater rate than others is fairly straightforward: access and economics. In other words, recycling rates are higher in states that offer comprehensive curbside recycling programs and impose unit charges for refuse disposal. Making recycling convenient for consumers and creating an economic disincentive not to recycle stimulates behavior. For instance, Michigan, which has a bottle deposit law for certain beverage

? It's Your Turn

Should Cities Enact Plastic Bag Bans?

Several major cities—San Francisco, Los Angeles, Chicago, and Seattle among them—have banned the use of plastic bags in supermarkets and stores; other cities such as Washington, D.C. and Boulder, Colorado, require stores to charge fees (usually five or ten cents) to consumers who opt for plastic bags at checkout. (Dallas repealed its plastic bag fee in June 2015; it had raised $500,000 in the five months it was in effect.) What do you think: Should the use of plastic bags by grocery stores and other retail outlets be banned by cities?

PROS	CONS
Most plastic bags do not biodegrade; discarded plastic bags harm wildlife on land and in the water for years to come.	Plastic bags are reusable and recyclable. Rather than banning bags, cities should educate consumers about reuse and recycling.
Many plastic bags end up as litter, an eyesore that can have negative effects on city tourism and require cities to conduct cleanups.	Letting cities ban bags means that in a single state, there will be different ordinances in different cities. This lack of uniformity across a state will create confusion.
Most plastic bags are manufactured from petroleum products and natural gas, thereby depleting natural resources.	Bag bans are an example of overzealous regulation, limiting the choices of retailers and consumers.

containers, can boast that 97 percent of those beverage bottles and cans are returned.[22] Managing the vast quantity of solid waste generated in our mass consumption, throwaway society is not easy. Recycling is an appealing option, but we cannot recycle everything. Some of the garbage must therefore be incinerated or deposited in a landfill. Every new waste technology has its own difficult issues, and the states and localities, with limited assistance from the federal government, are striving to deal effectively with the huge task of managing the country's garbage. The It's Your Turn box considers one way some cities have tried to address the waste issue.

MANAGING HAZARDOUS WASTE

The image of garbage mountains rising above the horizon is disconcerting, to say the least. But solid waste is just one of several contributors to environmental destruction. Another insidious public health threat comes from hazardous waste—the poisonous by-products of industrial processes. If these by-products are toxic, corrosive, flammable, or reactive, they are considered hazardous. The industries that generate 90 percent of the hazardous waste in the United States are chemical and allied products, primary metals, petroleum and coal

TABLE 18.3 State Leaders in Toxic Releases, 2013	
STATES LEADING IN TOTAL ON-AND-OFF SITE RELEASES (ALL INDUSTRIES, ALL CHEMICALS)	**AMOUNT (IN THOUSANDS OF POUNDS)**
Alaska	970,610
Utah	525,434
Nevada	369,702
Texas	223,822
Indiana	153,537

SOURCE: United States Environmental Protection Agency. TRI Explorer, 2013 Dataset (released March 2015) http://www.epa.gov/triexplorer (accessed June 2, 2015).

products, fabricated metal products, and rubber and plastic products. Table 18.3 lists the five states where the largest amounts of toxic chemicals were released into the air, water, and ground in 2013. In Alaska, which leads the list, toxic releases typically end up in the ground, on-site.

Hazardous waste is more ubiquitous than most people realize. Pesticide residues, used motor oil, discarded cadmium batteries, used refrigerants, and paint sludge are hazardous leftovers that are frequently found in households and in so-called nonpolluting industries. It is no exaggeration to say that hazardous waste is all around us.

The primary dilemma concerning hazardous waste is what to do with it. The discovery that wastes were not being properly or safely disposed of triggered government involvement; when hazardous liquids began seeping into people's basements from long-buried barrels, children playing in fields uncovered rotting drums of toxic waste, and motorists developed unusual skin rashes from pesticides sprayed along the roadway, government was called in. Some states feared that imposing tough new hazardous waste regulations would make them less attractive to industry. Others were concerned that tightening the laws for waste disposal would have the perverse effect of increasing the incidence of illegal dumping. A national policy initiative seemed preferable to state attempts at solving the problems.

The national government responded to the mounting crisis with two pieces of legislation: the Resource Conservation and Recovery Act (RCRA) of 1976 and the Comprehensive Environmental Response, Compensation, and Liability Act of 1980 (also known as Superfund). RCRA provides for cradle-to-grave tracking of waste and establishes standards for its treatment, storage, and disposal. Any firm that generates 220 pounds of hazardous waste per month (an amount that typically fills a 55-gallon barrel about halfway) is covered by the law. RCRA is considered partially pre-emptive because states have a degree of discretion and flexibility in implementation. Once the EPA is satisfied that a state program meets its standards and possesses adequate enforcement mechanisms, the agency authorizes the state to operate its own hazardous waste management program. Under RCRA, states can impose fines and hold individuals criminally liable for violating its provisions.

Superfund was passed in recognition of the fact that no matter how comprehensive and cautious hazardous waste management will be in the future, the pollution of the past remains with us. Under Superfund, the national government can intervene to clean up a dangerous hazardous waste site and later seek reimbursement from responsible parties. Originally, the law contained a provision dubbed "polluter pays," which created a cleanup fund from fees levied on chemical manufacturers and the petroleum industry. These fees, which generated between $1 and $2 billion annually, allowed government to step in and begin the cleanup before all the complex legal issues were resolved. The cleanup fund provision expired in 1995 however, and affected industries have been successful in blocking its renewal. Thus, Superfund has become a program funded by taxpayers.[23] In fact, federal stimulus money was used in 2010 to help accelerate the cleanup of fifty Superfund sites in 28 states.[24]

One of the first actions taken under Superfund was the identification of particularly troublesome sites in need of immediate cleanup, the National Priorities List (NPL). New Jersey was the state with the most sites on the list; Nevada had the fewest. One factor confounding the Superfund program is determining which parties—waste generators, waste transporters, site owners—are responsible for paying for the cleanup. Some of the firms that dumped toxic waste at these sites have gone out of business, and the hope of recovering any of the cleanup costs is remote. As time passed, frustration grew over the slow pace of remediation. Subsequent amendments to the law increased funding levels for the program (although Superfund expenditures peaked in 2001) and expanded the role for state governments in selecting cleanup remedies. In addition, the EPA launched a new initiative to clean up and redevelop contaminated industrial sites, or **brownfields**. Many states have adopted their own mini-Superfund statutes that authorize them to conduct site assessments and initiate remedial cleanup actions or force a responsible party to do so. Some states have also passed laws making it easier to redevelop brownfields, adopted community right-to-know (about hazardous wastes in the area) statutes, and conducted household hazardous waste collection drives.

An issue that has bedeviled the states is disposing of hazardous waste. Disposal sites are locally unwanted land uses (**LULUs**). When efforts to find new disposal facilities are thwarted, states look beyond their borders for solutions. Some states and tribal governments have been willing to accept other states' hazardous waste for disposal—the PIMBY phenomenon— seeing it as a way to generate revenue. But even waste-importing states have their limits. At one point, Alabama banned hazardous waste importation from twenty-two states, an action that was struck down eventually by the federal courts. Alabama lawmakers responded with a fee schedule that taxed out-of-state waste at three times the rate of in-state-generated waste. The effect was dramatic: The quantity of out-of-state waste dropped by one-half, but the business still generated $30 million for the state treasury. Unfortunately for Alabama, the U.S. Supreme Court ruled that the surcharge on out-of-state waste violated the

brownfields

Abandoned industrial sites with real or perceived environmental contamination.

LULU

Locally unwanted land use; a broad category of undesirable facilities such as landfills and prisons.

interstate commerce clause. Regardless, efforts to block out-of-state waste will continue until solutions to the hazardous waste disposal problem are found. One eminently plausible, if partial, solution to waste-disposal dilemmas is to reduce the amount of waste generated in the first place. Less waste produced means less waste to dispose of.

STORING NUCLEAR WASTE

Nuclear power is thought by some to be a solution to the nation's energy problems, but it carries a heavy price: deadly, radioactive waste. Until 2009, the federal government had planned to bury high-level nuclear waste, which retains its toxicity for hundreds of thousands of years, at Yucca Mountain, an isolated spot 100 miles northwest of Las Vegas. This plan generated a firestorm of protest from environmentalists and Nevada officials and became an issue in the 2008 presidential election. One concern was the rate of corrosion for the canisters in which the waste would be stored; another was the possibility of earthquakes in the area, and still another was the safety of shipping the waste to the site. In 2009, President Obama, making good on a campaign promise, terminated the Yucca Mountain waste disposal project and, with the support of Congress, allocated funds to convene a blue-ribbon commission to come up with an alternative plan.[25]

Low-level radioactive wastes (LLWs) are much less toxic in a relative sense because they break down to safe levels of radioactivity in anywhere from a few weeks or months to 300 years. LLWs are produced by commercial nuclear power installations (46 percent), nuclear-related industries (39 percent), and medical and research institutions (15 percent). The waste, much of it stored in 55-gallon steel drums, includes items such as contaminated laboratory clothes, tools, equipment, and leftover bomb materials, as well as bulk wastes.

The Low-Level Radioactive Waste Policy Act of 1980 made each state responsible for the disposal of the waste generated within its borders. States have the choice of managing LLWs within their own jurisdictions (i.e., developing their own disposal sites) or entering into an interstate compact for out-of-state disposal. As expected, a few states have opted to handle the problem alone, but most have joined with their neighbors to forge a regional answer to the disposal question.

The use of **interstate compacts** to address the LLW problem was particularly inventive because nuclear waste disposal has historically been considered a federal responsibility. When interstate compacts are successful, they are a shining example of what the states can accomplish when left to their own devices.[26] Potential member states have to negotiate a draft compact that must be ratified by their legislatures and by Congress. Negotiations often break down as each state tries to get the best deal for itself, precisely the goal of each of the other participating states. As of 2015, ten interstate LLW compacts had been formed; eight states remained unaligned, preferring to go it alone. As shown in Figure 18.4, several of the compacts are decidedly nonregional in their composition. For example, the two Dakotas joined Arizona and California to form the Southwestern Compact; Texas teamed up with Vermont to create the Texas Compact.

interstate compacts

Formal agreements among a subset of states, usually to solve a problem that affects each of the member states.

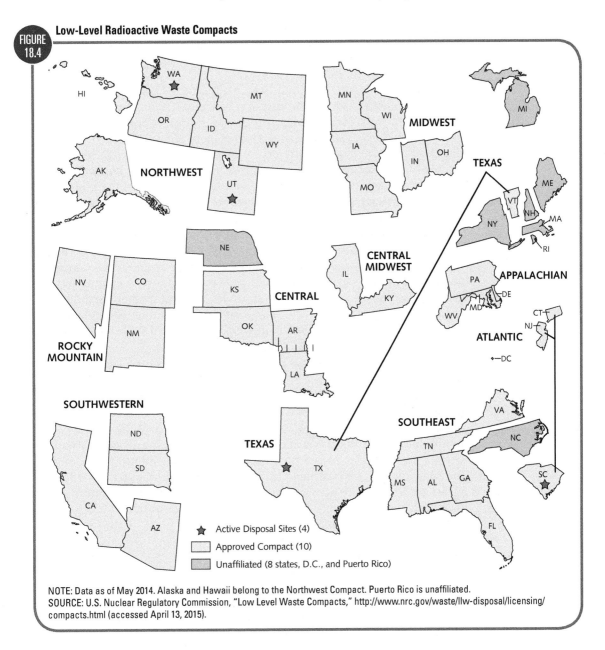

FIGURE 18.4

Low-Level Radioactive Waste Compacts

★ Active Disposal Sites (4)
☐ Approved Compact (10)
▨ Unaffiliated (8 states, D.C., and Puerto Rico)

NOTE: Data as of May 2014. Alaska and Hawaii belong to the Northwest Compact. Puerto Rico is unaffiliated.
SOURCE: U.S. Nuclear Regulatory Commission, "Low Level Waste Compacts," http://www.nrc.gov/waste/llw-disposal/licensing/compacts.html (accessed April 13, 2015).

The case of the Midwest Compact demonstrates the hard decisions faced by all the compacts. The Midwest Compact was one of the first to win congressional consent. Seven states were members; each agreed that it would take its turn to host a disposal facility for the entire compact. Weighing three factors for each state—the volume of LLW produced, the radioactivity of that waste, and transportation modes and routes—compact members selected Michigan as the first host state. Michigan spent several years evaluating the suitability of three possible disposal locations only to reject all of them. The compact was no closer to a regional disposal site than it had been at the outset. In reaction, the other states booted Michigan out of the Midwest Compact (Michigan is currently unaligned). Ohio, the runner-up to Michigan in the earlier state-selection process, became the host state.

With compacts in place and host states selected, the next challenge is the actual construction of new disposal facilities. This step can be difficult because of the **NIMTOO** (not in my term of office) phenomenon. But time is of the essence because existing sites have begun to restrict access. For example, the Hanford, Washington, site accepts waste only from members of the Northwest and Rocky Mountain Compacts and, in 2008, the Barnwell, South Carolina, site began excluding waste from outside the Atlantic Compact. In the meantime, generators are being told to store their waste on site or contract with private vendors for safe storage.

The lack of guarantees about the future consequences of nuclear waste disposal makes it a prospect both fascinating and frightening. Some observers predict that if California's power shortages of the early 2000s occur again—and spread to other states—the demand for nuclear power will grow.[27] However, the earthquake and tsunami in Japan in 2011 and resultant meltdown at the Fukushima nuclear facility dampened public enthusiasm for nuclear power. The debate over disposal issues will likely intensify.

LO 18.6

To assess the various environmental challenges facing states and localities.

Two Challenges for Policy Makers

Several challenges loom for those who are tangled up in the thicket of environmental protection policymaking. The growing influence of economic logic on environmental decisions is one; the widespread but shifting public support for environmentalism is another. A problem that is only going to intensify is water shortages, a dilemma that already strains interstate relations in the West and, in 2015, caused California to enact strict water conservation measures. The two challenges discussed below, environmental justice and hydraulic fracturing, will force policymakers to confront some disturbing realities of environmental policy.

ENVIRONMENTAL JUSTICE

In the early 1980s, protesters who fought vigorously against the dumping of polychlorinated biphenyl (PCB)-contaminated soil in a rural North Carolina county spawned a new movement: environmental justice. In general, the argument is that poor and minority communities suffer disproportionate exposure to environmental health risks. An example of environmental injustice is the area referred to as "Cancer Alley," an 85-mile strip along the Mississippi River in Louisiana that is home to more than 100 chemical, petrochemical, refining, and industrial plants. The households located within harm's way of these plants are disproportionately minority and low-income.[28] Two law school professors put the matter this way:

NIMTOO

Not in my term of office; the desire by elected officials to avoid accepting LULUs while they are in office.

> People of color throughout the United States are receiving more than their fair share of the poisonous fruits of industrial production. They live cheek by jowl with waste dumps, incinerators, landfills, smelters, factories, chemical

plants, and oil refineries whose operations make them sick and kill them young. They are poisoned by the air they breathe, the water they drink, the fish they catch, the vegetables they grow, and in the case of children, the very ground they play on.[29]

Research has found inequities in environmental policy. For instance, one study of the relationship between race and the enforcement of environmental laws by the EPA showed that white communities received faster action and more satisfactory results than did minority communities; other research uncovered race-based disparities in state inspections of hazardous waste generating facilities.[30] One of the distinctive differences between areas that contain commercial hazardous waste facilities and those that do not is the proportion of minority residents.[31] Communities with these facilities tend to have double the proportion of minority residents than those without them. Another study found that single-mother families are overrepresented in environmentally hazardous areas.[32] Other research, however, takes issue with contentions of environmental inequities. Statewide studies of Superfund site locations in New Jersey and hazardous waste facilities in South Carolina did not find statistically significant links to race or ethnicity.[33] Why are polluting facilities located where they are? The answer is multifaceted:

- Scientific rationality (e.g., the geologic characteristics of the site);
- Market factors (e.g., land prices, available labor pool);
- Neighborhood transition (e.g., changing demographics in the area over time);
- Political power (e.g., whether the residents in the area are politically active); and
- Intentional discrimination (e.g., targeting poor and minority neighborhoods).[34]

Concern over environmental justice has led more than thirty states to take some sort of policy action. For example, Arkansas passed legislation that discourages the location of high-impact solid waste management facilities within twelve miles of each other. Exemptions may be granted if specific benefits are provided to the host community in the form of jobs, fees, and improvements to infrastructure. In Louisiana, the Department of Environmental Quality was instructed to hold public hearings and make policy recommendations on environmental equity issues. Pennsylvania added an Environmental Justice Advisory Board to its environmental protection agency. The federal government and EPA took up the issue as well, establishing a National Environmental Justice Advisory Council charged with ensuring that environmental justice be addressed in the agency's policies, programs, and activities. Clearly, environmental justice will continue to be a salient topic for policy makers well into the future.[35]

HYDRAULIC FRACTURING

The nation has long sought a clean domestic energy source, one that is in plentiful supply and will reduce the country's dependence on foreign sources of energy. Natural gas has been touted by many as the answer. There are vast

Anti-fracking protestors gather in New York City to express their views on the state's fracking ban.

deposits of natural gas in the United States; and as an energy source, natural gas produces fewer greenhouse gases than conventional sources such as petroleum or coal.

At issue is hydraulic fracturing, or "fracking," a process in which a mixture of water, sand, and chemicals is injected at high pressure into the ground to break up dense rock and release the gas. Technological advances have led to horizontal fracking, thereby allowing drillers to reach more distant rock formations that previously had been considered impractical and uneconomical to pursue. Now that these extensive natural gas deposits are more accessible, more drilling is occurring in more places. According to the U.S. Department of Energy, by 2013, there were more than 487,000 producing gas wells operating in thirty-two states.[36]

Enthusiasm for fracking is far from universal, however. Fracking comes with questions about the degree to which the process pollutes ground and surface waters. In 2005 Congress, relying on a 2004 study by the U.S. Environmental Protection Agency that concluded that fracking posed a minimal threat to drinking water, exempted fracking from regulation under the federal Safe Drinking Water Act (SDWA). The study's conclusion was criticized by many environmentalists because the research involved no direct monitoring of water wells but instead relied on scientific literature and interviews with industry and state and local government officials.[37]

States with natural gas resources have found themselves caught in the crossfire between the industry seeking permits to drill and environmentalists seeking bans on drilling. At the community level, disputes between neighbors have arisen with some landowners wanting to lease their land for drilling while others want nothing to do with it.[38] Public awareness of the fracking issue increased with the release of a 2010 documentary film, *Gasland* and the follow-up documentary in 2014, *Gasland II*. The films offered a very critical look at fracking and were denounced by many in the oil and gas industry. One of the most riveting scenes in *Gasland* was one in which a man lit water from his faucet on fire, claiming that natural gas drilling was responsible for the situation. Although most experts were skeptical of that particular scene, in 2011, EPA announced that compounds likely associated with fracking chemicals had been detected in the groundwater beneath a central Wyoming town where residents had complained their well water reeked of chemicals. This announcement put more pressure on states to take action.

Maryland and New York were among the states that placed a moratorium on fracking, awaiting further study and scientific review of the issue; in 2015 both states decided to let the fracking bans stay in place. Vermont, in 2012, was the first state to ban the practice of fracking altogether; that same year, the New Jersey legislature enacted a new law banning the disposal of fracking wastewater in the Garden State. The North Carolina legislature lifted its moratorium on fracking in 2012; but the governor vetoed the bill stating, "Our drinking water and the health and safety of North Carolina's families are too important. We can't put them in jeopardy by rushing to allow fracking without proper safeguards."[39] The North Carolina legislature later overrode her veto and by 2015, the state had rules in place to allow fracking. Texas, a state in which the oil and gas industry is a powerful player, surprised many when it enacted a law requiring drillers to publicly disclose the chemicals they use in the fracking process. However, when the voters in the Texas city of Denton approved a ban on fracking within the city's limits, the Texas legislature responded by overturning the ban.

Meanwhile, back in the nation's capital, bills to make fracking subject to the dictates of the SDWA and to require drillers to disclose the chemicals they use in their injection process have not been acted upon in Congress. In 2010, Congress did, however, request EPA to conduct a multi-year, comprehensive study to better understand any potential impacts of hydraulic fracturing on drinking water and ground water. In the meantime, the agency developed rules intended to reduce air pollution, primarily volatile organic compounds and air toxics, by requiring drillers to capture natural gas that escapes into the air.[40] The EPA report that Congress requested was released in 2015 and caused a furor with its finding that no conclusive evidence existed linking fracking to widespread, systemic pollution of drinking water.[41] The report did raise concerns about the amount of water used in fracking and the potential for poorly designed injection wells that store fracking fluids to leak into groundwater. It seems reasonable to conclude that fracking will remain on the governmental agenda for some time to come.

Chapter Recap

- Public opinion shows support for environmental protection and economic growth; however, achieving one goal often comes at the expense of the other. After several years of preferring economic growth, public opinion has recently shifted in favor of environmental protection. Government's role is to balance the two objectives.

- The national government has been an important force in environmental protection. Performance partnership agreements and grants give states more power to set their own spending priorities.

- Environmental conditions and state programs vary from one state to another. A recent study found Vermont and Oregon to be the greenest states, and Louisiana to be the least green.

- Many cities, such as Portland, Oregon, San Francisco, and Seattle have embraced sustainability and have adopted green policies.

- A tremendous amount of solid waste is generated daily in the United States. Although most of it is disposed of in landfills, recycling continues to be a promising approach.

- Two major federal programs, RCRA and Superfund, have set the hazardous waste management agenda. States play a major part in implementing RCRA, and they partner with the federal government in Superfund cleanups.

- Interstate compacts (there are ten) are used for the disposal of low-level radioactive waste.

- Two challenges facing contemporary policy makers are environmental justice and hydraulic fracturing.

KEY TERMS

environmental self-audit *(p. 480)*
race to the bottom *(p. 480)*
sustainability *(p. 481)*

partial pre-emption *(p. 484)*
ecological footprint *(p. 488)*
NIMBY *(p. 491)*
PIMBY *(p. 491)*

brownfields *(p. 495)*
LULU *(p. 495)*
interstate compacts *(p. 496)*
NIMTOO *(p. 498)*

INTERNET RESOURCES

The official website of the Environmental Protection Agency (EPA) is **www.epa.gov**. It is packed with information about the EPA's programs and initiatives.

The official website of the Department of the Interior is **www.doi.gov**. It contains a wealth of information about the various activities of the agency.

All states have agencies devoted to environmental protection and natural resource conservation. See, for example, Oregon at **www .oregon.gov/deq/** and Ohio at **www.dnr .state.oh.us**.

A good place to track environmental protection policies, laws, and regulations is at **enviro .blr.com**. This site is maintained by Business and Legal Reports, a firm that advertises itself as "making state environmental compliance easier."

Greenopia bills itself as "experts on green living," and rates products and corporations as to their eco-friendliness at **www.greenopia.com/**.

For more information about environmental issues, contact the Sierra Club at **www.sierraclub .org**, the National Wildlife Federation at **www .nwf.org**, the Nature Conservancy at **www.nature .org**, and the Grassroots Recycling Network at **www.grrn.org**.

To learn about the impact of pollution on the public, explore the website of the Environmental Justice Foundation at **www.ejfoundation .org**.

References

CHAPTER 1 STATE AND LOCAL GOVERNMENTS: NEW DIRECTIONS

1. Governor Steve Bullock, "The State of Our State," http://governor.mt.gov/Portals/16/docs/012815StateoftheState_Final.pdf (January 28, 2015).
2. Bruce Wallin, "State and Local Governments Are American, Too," *Political Science Teacher* 1 (Fall 1988): 1–3.
3. Mike Sullivan, quoted in "Wyoming's Governor Signs Law to Restructure State Government," *Denver Post* (March 5, 1989), p. 8B.
4. Mark Murphy, "Elimination and Consolidation of State Entities," National Conference of State Legislatures, http://www.ncsl.org/documents/fiscal/eliminations2011.pdf (August 1, 2011).
5. Council of State Governments, "Capitol Ideas," www.csg.org/pubs/capitolideas/index.aspx (April 4, 2015).
6. Beth Walter Honadle, "Defining and Doing Capacity Building: Perspective and Experiences," in Beth Walter Honadle and Arnold M. Howitt, eds., *Perspectives on Management Capacity Building* (Albany, NY: SUNY Press, 1986), pp. 9–23.
7. Katherine Barrett and Richard Greene, "Grading the States '08," *Governing* 21 (March 2008): 24–95.
8. Julie Bund and Gene M. Lutz, "Connecting State Government Reform with Public Priorities: The Iowa Test Case," *State and Local Government Review* 31 (Spring 1999): 73–90.
9. David M. Hedge, *Governance and the Changing American States* (Boulder, CO: Westview Press, 1998).
10. "No Child Left Behind Act to Be Waived in 10 States, Official Says," *Politico.* http://www.politico.com/news/stories/0212/72672.html (February 9, 2012).
11. Terry Sanford, *The Storm Over the States* (New York: McGraw-Hill, 1967), p. 21.
12. Quoted in Sanford, *The Storm Over the States.*
13. John Herbers, "The New Federalism: Unplanned, Innovative, and Here to Stay," *Governing* 1 (October 1987): 28.
14. Sheryl Gay Stolberg, "As Congress Stalls, States Pursue Cloning Debate," *The New York Times*, www.nytimes.com (May 26, 2002).
15. Ann O'M. Bowman and Richard C. Kearney, *The Resurgence of the States* (Englewood Cliffs, NJ: Prentice-Hall, 1986).
16. Sanford, *The Storm Over the States.*
17. Ann O'M. Bowman and Richard C. Kearney, "Dimensions of State Government Capability," *Western Political Quarterly* 41 (June 1988): 341–62; David R. Morgan and Kenneth Kickham, "Modernization Among the U.S. States: Change and Continuity from 1960 to 1990," *Publius* 27 (Summer 1997): 23–39.
18. Andrew Karch, *Democratic Laboratories: Policy Diffusion Among the American States* (Ann Arbor: University of Michigan Press, 2010).
19. Craig Savoye, "States Spare Residents from Telemarketers," *Christian Science Monitor* (December 22, 2000), p. 8.
20. M. Alex Johnson, "Smokers Burned Up over 'Fire-Safe' Cigarettes," www.msnbc.msn.com/id/28796322/ns/health-addictions/t/smokers-burned-over-fire-safe-cigarettes/#.T0Gy1EcRr_k (January 27, 2009).
21. U.S. Conference of Mayors Climate Protection Center, "Mayors Leading the Way on Climate Protection," www.usmayors.org/climateprotection/revised/ (July 1, 2010).
22. Lawrence J. Grossback, Sean Nicholson-Crotty, and David A. M. Peterson, "Ideology and Learning in Policy Diffusion," *American Politics Research* 32 (September 2004): 521–45; David M. Glick and Zoe Friedland, "How Often Do States Study Each Other? Evidence of Policy Knowledge Diffusion," *American Politics Research* 42 (November 2014): 956–85.
23. David W. Winder and James T. LaPlant, "State Lawsuits Against Big Tobacco: A Test of Diffusion Theory," *State and Local Government Review* 32 (Spring 2000): 132–41.
24. Keith Loria, "Thirty-Three States Settle Computer Chip Suit," Legal Newsline, www.legalnewsline.com (June 25, 2010). See also Colin Provost, "An Integrated Model of U.S. State Attorney General Behavior in Multi-State Litigation," *State Politics and Policy Quarterly* 10 (Spring 2010): 1–24.
25. Ann O'M. Bowman, "Horizontal Federalism: Exploring Interstate Interactions," *Journal of Public Administration Research and Theory* 14 (October 2004): 535–46.
26. Governor George Voinovich, quoted in "Reassessing Mandates," *State Policy Reports* 11 (October 1993): 16.
27. Brad Knickerbocker, "States Take Clean Air Measures into Their Own Hands," *Christian Science Monitor* (April 19, 2005), pp. 1, 12; N.C. Aizenman, "Opponents Present Case Against Obama's Health-Care Law in 20-State Lawsuit," *Washington Post*, www.washingtonpost.com (September 14, 2010).
28. Jeffrey M. Jones, "Illinois Residents Least Trusting of their State Government," http://www.gallup.com/

poll/168251/illinois-residents-least-trusting-state-government.aspx (March 3, 2015).

29. As quoted in "It's Scary: State of the States 2009," *State News* 52 (May 2009): 9.

30. National Conference of State Legislatures. 2011. *State Budget Update: Summer 2011*. Denver, CO: NCSL.

31. Pamela M. Prah, "Reports: State Income Levels Plunge," www.stateline.org (June 19, 2009).

32. Rudolph Bush, "Dallas City Council Knows 'Brutal' Budget Cuts Coming," *Dallas Morning News*, www.dallasnews.com (June 18, 2009).

33. Lawrence L. Martin, Richard Levey, and Jenna Cawley, "The 'New Normal' for Local Government," *State and Local Government Review* 44 (August 2012): 17S–28S.

34. Ralph Vartebedian, "The Race to Steal Bases Heats Up," *Los Angeles Times*, www.latimes.com (November 29, 2004).

35. Michael Johnston, "Right and Wrong in American Politics: Popular Conceptions of Corruption," in Arnold J. Heidenheimer and Michael Johnston, eds., *Political Corruption: Concepts and Contexts* (New Brunswick, NJ: Transaction, 2002), pp. 173–91; see also Richard T. Boylan and Cheryl X. Long, "Measuring Public Corruption in the American States," *State Politics and Policy Quarterly* (Winter 2003): 420–38.

36. Steven P. Lanza, *The Economics of Ethics: The Cost of Political Corruption* (Storrs, CT: Connecticut Center for Economic Analysis, 2004).

37. Boylan and Long, "Measuring Public Corruption in the American States."

38. Dick Simpson, et al. "Chicago and Illinois, Leading the Pack in Corruption," Chicago: University of Illinois at Chicago (February 15, 2012).

39. U.S. Census Bureau, "Overview of Race and Hispanic Origin: 2010," www.census.gov/prod/cen2010/briefs/c2010br-02.pdf (accessed February 20, 2012).

40. U.S. Census Bureau, "Foreign-Born Population—Selected Characteristics by Region of Origin: 2010," www.census.gov/compendia/statab/2012/tables/12s0041.pdf (accessed February 20, 2012).

41. Michael Hoefer, Nancy Rytina, and Bryan Baker, "Estimates of the Unauthorized Immigrant Population Residing in the United States: January 2011," www.dhs.gov/xlibrary/assets/statistics/publications/ois_ill_pe_2011.pdf (accessed March 16, 2015).

42. Rodney E. Hero and Caroline J. Tolbert, "A Racial/Ethnic Diversity Interpretation of Politics and Policy in the States of the U.S.," *American Journal of Political Science* 40 (August 1996): 851–71; Rodney E. Hero, *Faces of Inequality: Social Diversity in American Politics* (New York: Oxford University Press, 2000).

43. U.S. Census Bureau, "The Next Four Decades: The Older Population in the United States: 2010 to 2050," www.census.gov/prod/2010pubs/p25-1138.pdf (accessed February 22, 2012).

44. U.S. Census Bureau, "Annual Estimates of the Resident Population: April 1, 2010 to July 1, 2014,"

http://factfinder.census.gov/faces/tableservices/jsf/pages/productview.xhtml?pid=PEP_2014_PEPANNRES&src=pt (accessed April 2, 2015).

45. U.S. Census Bureau, "Table 27. Incorporated Places with 175,000 or More Inhabitants in 2010-Population," *Statistical Abstract of the United States: 2012* (Washington, D.C.: U.S. Census Bureau, 2012).

46. Aaron Blake, "Census 2010 Shows Red States Gaining Congressional Seats," *Washington Post*, http://voices.washingtonpost.com/thefix/redistricting/red-states-gain-as-new-congress.html (December 21, 2010).

47. Daniel J. Elazar, *American Federalism: A View from the States*, 3rd ed. (New York: Harper & Row, 1984).

48. Jody L. Fitzpatrick and Rodney E. Hero, "Political Culture and Political Characteristics of the American States: A Consideration of Some Old and New Questions," *Western Political Quarterly* 41 (March 1988): 145–53.

49. Keith Boeckelman, "Political Culture and State Development Policy," *Publius* 21 (Spring 1991): 49–92; Russell L. Hanson, "Political Culture Variations in State Economic Development Policy," *Publius* 21 (Spring 1991): 63–81.

50. James P. Lester, "A New Federalism: Environmental Policy in the States," in Norman Vig and Michael Kraft, eds., *Environmental Policy in the 1990s* (Washington, D.C.: Congressional Quarterly Press, 1994), pp. 51–68; Lawrence M. Mead, "State Political Culture and Welfare Reform," *Policy Studies Journal* 32 (May 2004): 271–96.

51. Joel Lieske, "Regional Subcultures of the United States," *Journal of Politics* 55 (November 1993): 888–913; Joel Lieske, "The Changing Regional Subcultures of the American States and the Utility of a New Cultural Measure," *Political Research Quarterly* 63 (September 2010): 538–52.

52. Emily Van Dunk, "Public Opinion, Gender and Handgun Safety Policy Across the States," paper presented at the annual meeting of the Midwest Political Science Association, Chicago, April 2000.

53. Elaine B. Sharp, "Introduction," in Elaine B. Sharp, ed., *Culture Wars and Local Politics* (Lawrence, KS: University Press of Kansas, 1999), pp. 1–20.

54. William G. Jacoby, "Is There a Culture War? Conflicting Value Structures in American Public Opinion," *American Political Science Review* 108 (November 2014): 754–71.

55. Shanna Rose and Cynthia Bowling, "The State of American Federalism 2014–15," *Publius: The Journal of Federalism*," 45 (Summer 2015): 351–79.

56. John Shannon, "The Return to Fend-for-Yourself Federalism: The Reagan Mark," *Intergovernmental Perspective* 13 (Summer/Fall 1987): 34–37.

57. Alan Ehrenhalt, "The Increasing Irrelevance of Congress," *Governing* 11 (January 1998): 6–7; see also J. Mitchell Pickerill and Cynthia Bowling, "The State of American Federalism 2013–2014, *Publius: The Journal of Federalism* 44 (Summer 2014): 369–98.

CHAPTER 2 FEDERALISM AND THE STATES: SORTING OUT ROLES AND RESPONSIBILITIES

1. Richard Cowan, "Wave of Migrant Children Threatens to Swamp U.S. Immigration Courts," www.Reuters.com, (July 22, 2014).
2. Jake Grovum, "Reciprocity: The New Front in the Gay Marriage Debate," www.stateline.org (June 28, 2013); Grovum, "States Fill Federal Vacuum on Immigrants," www.stateline.org (August 22, 2014).
3. Quoted in Richard Hofstadter, *The American Political Tradition* (New York: Vintage Books, 1948), p. 5.
4. Ibid., pp. 9–10.
5. Richard H. Leach, *American Federalism* (New York: W. W. Norton, 1970), p. 1.
6. David C. Hendrickson, *Peace Pact: The Lost World of the American Founding* (Lawrence, KS: University Press of Kansas, 2003).
7. Charles S. McCoy, "Federalism: The Lost Tradition?" *Publius* 31 (Spring 2001): 1–14.
8. Walter Berns, "The Meaning of the Tenth Amendment," in Robert A. Goldwin, ed., *A Nation of States* (Chicago, IL: Rand McNally, 1961), p. 130.
9. Forrest McDonald, *States' Rights and the Union: Imperium in Imperio* (Lawrence, KS: University Press of Kansas, 2000); David B. Walker, *The Rebirth of Federalism*, 2nd ed. (New York: Chatham House, 2000), Chapter 2.
10. Hofstadter, *The American Political Tradition*, p. 72.
11. *McCulloch v. Maryland*, 4 Wheaton 316 (1819).
12. *Gibbons v. Ogden*, 9 Wheaton 316 (1819).
13. Eric Kelderman, "Real ID Showdown Averted," stateline.org (April 4, 2008).
14. Daniel C. Vock, "Feds Push Gently on 'Real ID'," www.stateline.org (January 22, 2014).
15. *National League of Cities v. Usery*, 426 U.S. 833 (1976).
16. *Garcia v. San Antonio Metropolitan Transit Authority*, 105 S.Ct. 1007, 1011 (1985).
17. Ibid. (O'Connor, dissenting).
18. John C. Pittenger, "Garcia and the Political Safeguards of Federalism: Is There a Better Solution to the Conundrum of the Tenth Amendment?" *Publius* 22 (Winter 1992).
19. *U.S. v. Lopez*, 115 S.Ct. 1424 (1995). See Kenneth T. Palmer and Edward B. Laverty, "The Impact of *U.S. v. Lopez* on Intergovernmental Relations," *Publius* 26 (Summer 1996): 109–26.
20. *Kansas v. Hendricks*, 117 S.Ct. 2072 (1997).
21. *Printz v. U.S.*, 521 S.Ct. 98 (1997).
22. *Kelo v. New London* (2005). 545 U.S. 469 (2005).
23. *Cuno v. Daimler-Chrysler.* 547 U.S. 332 (2006).
24. *Seminole Tribe of Florida v. Florida*, 116 S.Ct. 1114 (1996).
25. *Nevada Department of Human Resources v. Hibbs*, S.Ct. 01-1368 (2003).
26. *Federal Maritime Commission v. South Carolina Ports Authority*, No. 01-46 (2002).
27. *Nevada Department of Human Resources v. Hibbs*, S.Ct.149 (1999).
28. *Lorillard Tobacco v. Reilly*, No. 00-596 (2000).
29. J. Mitchell Pickerill and Cynthia J. Bowling, "Polarized Parties, Politics, and Policies: Fragmented Federalism in 2013–2014," *Publius* (44, 3, 2014): 369–98.
30. *American Electric Power Co. v. U.S.* S.Ct. 10-174 (2011).
31. Christopher Shortell, "The End of the Federalism Five? Statutory Interpretation and the Roberts Court," *Publius* (42, 3, 2012): 516–537.
32. Grovum (6/13) John Kincaid, "State-Federal Relations: Civil War Redux?" *Book of the States*, vol. 43 (2011: 21–28).
33. *Citizens United v. Federal Election Commission* 558 U.S. S.Ct. 130 (2010); the Montana case is *American Tradition Partnership v. Attorney General for the State of Montana*, 11A762.
34. Martha Derthick, "American Federalism: Half-Full or Half-Empty?" *Brookings Review* (Winter 2000): 24.
35. Jake Gruvum, "States Air Their Differences at Supreme Court," www.stateline.org (January 15, 2014).
36. William H. Stewart, "Metaphors, Models and the Development of Federal Theory," *Publius* 12 (Spring 1982): 5–24.
37. Deil S. Wright, *Understanding Intergovernmental Relations*, 3rd ed. (Pacific Grove, CA: Brooks/Cole, 1988), pp. 40–42.
38. Walker, *The Rebirth of Federalism*, Chapter 4.
39. Timothy J. Conlan, "Federalism and Competing Values in the Reagan Administration," *Publius* 16 (Winter 1986): 29–47.
40. Jennifer Wolak and Christine Kelleher Palus, "The Dynamics of Public Confidence in U.S. State and Local Government," *State Politics and Policy Quarterly* (December 2010): 421–45.
41. John Kincaid and Richard L. Cole, "Changing Public Attitudes on Power and Taxation in the American Federal System," *Publius* 31 (Summer 2001): 205–14.
42. Alan Greenblatt, "The Washington Offensive," *Governing* (January 2005): 26–29.
43. (Lexington, KY: Council of State Governments, 2011):21–28; Peter Harkness, " 'Shift-and-Shaft' Federalism," Governing.com (March 9, 2008).
44. Peter A. Harkness, "What Brand of Federalism Is Next?" *Governing* (January 2012): 16–17.
45. Timothy J. Conlan and Paul L. Posner, "Inflection Point? Federalism and the Obama Administration," *Publius* 41 (3, 2011): 421–46.
46. Pickerill and Bowling, 2014.
47. W. Dale Mason, *Indian Gaming: Tribal Sovereignty and American Politics* (Norman, OK: University of Oklahoma Press, 2000).
48. Erich Steinman, "American Federalism and Intergovernmental Innovation in State-Tribal Relations," *Publius* 34 (Spring 2004): 95–115.
49. Laura E. Evans, *Power from Powerlessness: Tribal Governments, Institutional Niches, and American Federalism*, (New York: Oxford University Press, 2011); Laura E. Evans, "Expertise and Scale of Conflict: Governments as Advocates in American Indian Politics," *American Political Science Review* 105 (November 2011): 663–682.

50. Joseph F. Zimmerman, *Horizontal Federalism: Interstate Relations*, (Albany: State University of New York Press, 2011); Ann O'M. Bowman and Neal D. Woods, "Strength in Numbers: Why States Join Interstate Compacts," *State Politics and Policy Quarterly* 7 (Winter 2007): 347–68.

51. Zimmerman, *Horizontal Federalism*, 2011.

52. Edella Schlager, Tanya Heikkila, and Carl Case, "The Costs of Compliance with Interstate Compacts: Lessons from Water Compacts in the Western United States," *Publius* (42, 3, 2012): 494–515.

53. Ibid., Schlager, 2012.

54. Jake Grovum, "Supreme Court Rejects Texas' Claim to Oklahoma Water," www.stateline.org (June 13, 2013); Jim Malewitz, "Red River Showdown: Texas-Oklahoma Water War Could Reverberate Across US," www.stateline.org (April 24, 2013).

55. Marsha Mercer, "Interstate Egg Fight Erupts Over Cramped Hen Cages," www.stateline.org (November 4, 2014).

56. www.whitehouse.gov (November 20, 2014).

57. Sean Nicholson-Crotty, "Leaving Money on the Table: Learning from Recent Refusals of Federal Grants in the American States," *Publius* (42, 3, 2012): 449–66.

58. National Conference of State Legislatures, "Mandate Monitor" (2011); http://www.ncsl.org/standcomm/scbudg/manmon.htm

59. Ibid. www.cbo.gov (November 12, 2014).

60. U.S. G.A.O., "Unfunded Mandates: Views Vary about Reform Act's Strengths, Weaknesses, and Options for Improvement," GAO-05-454 (March 31, 2005).

61. Dylan Scott, "The Untied States of America," *Governing* (June 2013): 42–47.

62. Martha Derthick, "American Federalism: Half-Full or Half-Empty?" Brookings Review (Winter 2000): 24.

63. J.B. Wogan, "States and Localities Are Losing their Influence in Washington," governing.com (June 2014).

64. Alan Greenblatt, "Recipe for Respect," *Governing* (February 2008): 22–26.

65. Samuel H. Beer, "The Future of the States in the Federal System," in Peter Woll, ed., *American Government: Readings and Cases* (Boston, MA: Little, Brown, 1981), p. 92.

66. Richard P. Nathan, "Updating Theories of American Federalism," Paper presented at the annual meeting of the American Political Science Association, Philadelphia, PA, September 2, 2006.

CHAPTER 3 STATE CONSTITUTIONS: THE FUNDAMENTAL RULES OF STATE GOVERNMENT

1. G. Alan Tarr, *Understanding State Constitutions* (Princeton, NJ: Princeton University Press, 1999).

2. U.S. Advisory Commission on Intergovernmental Relations (ACIR), *State Constitutions in the Federal System*, A-113 (Washington, D.C.: ACIR, 1989), p. 2.

3. Donald S. Lutz, "The United States Constitution as an Incomplete Text," *Annals of the American Academy of Political and Social Science* 496 (March 1989): 23–32.

4. Quoting James Quayle Dealey, *Growth of American State Constitutions* (1915) in Robert F. Williams, *The Law of American State Constitutions* (New York: Oxford University Press, 2009); G. Alan Tarr, "Constitutional Theory and State Constitutional Interpretation," *Rutgers Law Journal* 22: 841, 848–56 (1991)

5. Donald S. Lutz, "Toward a Theory of Constitutional Amendment," *American Political Science Review* 88 (June 1994): 356; G. Alan Tarr, *Constitutional Politics in the States* (Westport, CT: Greenwood Press, 1996), p. xv.

6. Donald S. Lutz, "The Iroquois Confederation Constitution: An Analysis," *Publius* 22 (Spring 1998): 99–127.

7. Daniel J. Elazar, "The Principles and Traditions Underlying State Constitutions," *Publius* 12 (Winter 1982): 11.

8. Quoted in Perry Gilbert Miller, "Thomas Hooker and the Democracy of Early Connecticut," *New England Quarterly* 4 (1931): 695.

9. Bruce Fraser, *The Land of Steady Habits: A Brief History of Connecticut* (Hartford, CT: Connecticut Historical Commission, 1986), p. 10.

10. Willi Paul Adams, *The First American Constitutions* (Lanham, MD: Madison House, 2000), p. 61.

11. John Estill Reeves, *Kentucky Government* (Lexington, KY: University of Kentucky, 1966), p. 7. As quoted in Penny M. Miller, *Kentucky Government and Politics* (Lincoln: University of Nebraska Press, 1994), p. 82.

12. Albert L. Sturm, "The Development of American State Constitutions," *Publius* 12 (Winter 1982): 61.

13. Ibid., pp. 62–63.

14. Paul G. Reardon, "The Massachusetts Constitution Makes a Milestone," *Publius* 12 (Winter 1982): 45–55.

15. David McCullough, *John Adams* (New York: Touchstone Books, 2001).

16. Quoted in James Bryce, "Nature of the American State," in Bruce Stinebrickner, ed., *State and Local Government*, 3rd ed. (Guilford, CT: Dushkin, 1987), pp. 20–23.

17. Quoted in Thomas Parrish, "Kentucky's Fourth Constitution Is a Product of Its 1980 Times," in Thad L. Beyle, ed., *State Government: CQ's Guide to Current Issues and Activities 1991–92* (Washington, D.C.: Congressional Quarterly Press, 1991), p. 46.

18. Pamela M. Prah, "Alabama's Past, Future on Ballot," www.pewstates.org (August 13, 2012).

19. David Fellman, "What Should a State Constitution Contain?" in W. Brooke Graves, ed., *Major Problems in State Constitutional Revision* (Chicago, IL: Public Administration Service, 1960), p. 146.

20. Sturm, "The Development of American State Constitutions," p. 64; see Christopher W. Hammons, "Was James Madison Wrong? Rethinking the American Preference for Short, Framework-Oriented Constitutions," *American Political Science Review* 93 (December 1999): 837–49.

21. Josh Goodman, "Seizing the Initiative," *Governing* (October 2008), p. 32.

22. David C. Nice, "Interest Groups and State Constitutions: Another Look," *State and Local Government Review* 20 (Winter 1988): 22.

23. Donald S. Lutz, "Patterns in the Amending of American State Constitutions," in G. Alan Tarr, ed., *Constitutional Politics in the States* (Westport, CT: Greenwood Press, 1996), pp. 24–27.

24. U.S. Advisory Commission on Intergovernmental Relations (ACIR), *A Report to the President for Transmittal to the Congress* (Washington, D.C.: U.S. Government Printing Office, 1955).

25. National Municipal League, *Model State Constitution*, 6th ed., rev. (New York: National Municipal League, 1968).

26. John J. Carroll and Arthur English, "Traditions of State Constitution Making," *State and Local Government Review* 23 (Fall 1991): 103–109.

27. *Gitlow v. New York* 268 U.S. 652 (1925).

28. Thomas C. Marks, Jr., and John F. Cooper, *State Constitutional Law* (St. Paul, MN: West, 1988), p. 38.

29. Ibid., pp. 38–42.

30. Thomas Jefferson to James Madison, "Popular Basis of Political Authority" in Philip B. Kurland and Ralph Lerner, eds., *The Founders' Constitution* Web Edition, http://press-pubs.uchicago.edu/founders, 1987.

31. Michael Besso, "Constitutional Amendment Procedures and the Informal Political Construction of Constitutions," *The Journal of Politics* 67 (February 2005): 6987.

32. Marks and Cooper, *State Constitutional Law*, p. 47.

33. Tarr and Porter, "Introduction," p. 9.

34. Stanley H. Friedelbaum, "The Complementary Role of Federal and State Courts," *Publius* 17 (Winter 1987): 48.

35. As quoted in Aaron Deslatte, "Critics Call Failed Constitutional Amendments Too Conservative, Too Controversial," www.orlandosentinel.com (November 12, 2012).

36. Goodman, "Seizing the Initiative," 2008.

37. Vladimir Kogan, "Lessons from Recent State Constitutional Conventions," *California Journal of Politics and Policy* 2 (2010): 1–24.

38. Janice C. May, "State Constitutions and Constitutional Revision: 1988–89 and the 1980s," *The Book of the States 1990–91* (Washington, D.C.: Council of State Governments, 1991): 25.

39. Quoted in U.S. Advisory Commission on Intergovernmental Relations, *State Constitutions in the Federal System* (Washington, D.C.: ACIR, 1989), p. 37.

40. Albert L. Sturm, "The Development of American State Constitutions," *Publius* 12 (Winter 1982): p.104.

41. W. Brooke Graves, "State Constitutional Law: A Twenty-five Year Summary," *William and Mary Law Review* 8 (Fall 1966): 12.

42. ACIR, *The Question of State Government Capability*, p. 60.

43. Richard H. Leach, "A Quiet Revolution: 1933–1976," in *The Book of the States 1975–76* (Lexington, KY: Council of State Governments, 1976), p. 25.

44. Terry Sanford, *Storm Over the States* (New York: McGraw-Hill, 1967), p. 1983.

CHAPTER 4 CITIZEN PARTICIPATION AND ELECTIONS: ENGAGING THE PUBLIC IN GOVERNMENT

1. Lindsay A. Powers, "Takoma Park Grants 16-Year Olds Right to Vote," Washington Post, http://www.washingtonpost.com/local (May 14, 2013).

2. Robert D. Putnam, *Bowling Alone: The Collapse and Revival of American Community* (New York: Simon & Schuster, 2000); see also Nojin Kwak, Dhavan V. Shah, and R. Lance Holbrook, "Connecting, Trusting, and Participating: The Direct and Interactive Effects of Social Associations," *Political Research Quarterly* 57 (December 2004): 643–52.

3. John D. Griffin and Brian Newman, "Are Voters Better Represented?" *Journal of Politics* 67 (November 2005): 1206–27.

4. Jennifer Oser, Jan E. Leighley, and Kenneth M. Winneg, "Participation, Online and Otherwise: What's the Difference for Policy Preferences?" *Social Science Quarterly* 95 (December 2014): 1259–77.

5. William E. Lyons, David Lowery, and Ruth Hoogland De Hoog, *The Politics of Dissatisfaction* (Armonk, NY: M. E. Sharpe, 1992); Albert O. Hirschman, *Exit, Voice and Loyalty: Responses to Decline in Firms, Organizations, and States* (Cambridge, MA: Harvard University Press, 1972).

6. Nicholas A. Valentino, et al., "Election Night's Alright for Fighting: The Role of Emotions in Political Participation," *Journal of Politics* 73 (January 2011): 156–70.

7. Zoltan Hajnal and Jessica Trounstine, "Identifying and Understanding Perceived Inequities in Local Politics," *Political Research Quarterly* 67 (2013): 56–70.

8. Lapo Salucci and Kenneth Bickers, "Exit, Voice, and Electoral Turnover," *Urban Affairs Review* 47 (March 2011): 155–82.

9. Henry E. Brady, Sidney Verba, and Kay Lehman Schlozman, "Beyond SES: A Resource Model of Political Participation," *American Political Science Review* 89 (June 1995): 271–94; see also Jennifer Jerit, Jason Barabas, and Toby Bolsen, "Citizens, Knowledge, and the Information Environment," *American Journal of Political Science* 50 (April 2006): 266–82.

10. Richard Murray and Arnold Vedlitz, "Race, Socioeconomic Status, and Voting Participation in Large Southern Cities," *Journal of Politics* 39 (November 1977): 1064–72; Fredrick C. Harris, Valeria Sinclair-Chapman, and Brian D. McKenzie, "Macrodynamics of Black Political Participation in the Post-Civil Rights Era," *Journal of Politics* 67 (November 2005): 1143–63.

11. Virginia Sapiro, *The Political Integration of Women* (Urbana, IL: University of Illinois Press, 1983).

12. Amy Linimon and Mark R. Joslyn, "Trickle Up Political Socialization: The Impact of Kids Voting USA on Voter Turnout in Kansas," *State Politics and Policy Quarterly* 2 (Spring 2002): 24–36.

13. J. Eric Oliver, "City Size and Civic Involvement in Metropolitan America," *American Political Science Review* 94 (June 2000): 361–73.

14. Anthony Downs, *An Economic Theory of Democracy* (New York: Harper & Row, 1957). See also Moshe Haspel and H. Gibbs Knotts, "Location, Location, Location: Precinct Placement and the Costs of Voting," *Journal of Politics* 67 (May 2005): 560–73.

15. Jan E. Leighley and Arnold Vedlitz, "Race, Ethnicity, and Political Participation," *Journal of Politics* 61 (November 1999): 1092–1114; Debra Horner, "Critiquing Measures of Political Interest," Paper presented at the annual meeting of the Midwest Political Science Association, Chicago, IL, 2000.

16. Kim Quaile Hill and Jan E. Leighley, "Party Ideology, Organization, and Competitiveness as Mobilizing Forces in Gubernatorial Elections," *American Journal of Political Science* 37 (November 1993): 1158–78.

17. Alan S. Gerber and Todd Rogers, "Descriptive Social Norms and Motivation to Vote: Everybody's Voting and So Should You," *Journal of Politics* 71 (January 2009): 178–91.

18. Peter L. Francia and Paul S. Herrnson, "The Synergistic Effect of Campaign Effort and Election Reform on Voter Turnout in State Legislative Elections," *State Politics and Policy Quarterly* 4 (Spring 2004): 74–93.

19. "Voter Registration Information," Council of State Governments, knowledgecenter.csg.org/drupal/system/files/6.6.xls (March 15, 2010).

20. Barry C. Burden, et al., "Election Laws, Mobilization, and Turnout: The Unanticipated Consequences of Election Reform," *American Journal of Political Science* 58 (January 2014): 95–109.

21. Michael McDonald, "2014 November General Election Turnout Rates," United States Election Project, www.electproject.org/2014g (February 15, 2015).

22. Andrea McAtee and Jennifer Wolak, "Why People Decide to Participate in State Politics," *Political Research Quarterly* 64 (March 2011): 45–58.

23. Neil Malhotra, et al., "Text Messages as Mobilization Tools: The Conditional Effect of Habitual Voting and Election Salience," *American Politics Research* 39 (July 2011): 664–81.

24. Henry E. Brady and John E. McNulty, "Turning Out to Vote: The Costs of Finding and Getting to the Polling Place," *American Political Science Review* 105 (February 2011): 115–34.

25. Michael Cooper, "New State Laws Raising Hurdles at Voting Booth," *The New York Times*, www.nytimes.com (October 3, 2011).

26. "Absentee and Early Voting," National Conference on State Legislatures, http://www.ncsl.org/research/elections-and-campaigns/absentee-and-early-voting.aspx (February 11, 2015).

27. Robert M. Stein and Greg Vonnahme, "Engaging the Unengaged Voter: Vote Centers and Voter Turnout," *Journal of Politics* 70 (April 2008): 487–97.

28. Priscilla L. Southwell, "Voting Behavior in Vote-by-Mail Elections," *Analyses of Social Issues and Public Policy* 10 (December 2010): 106–15. See also Cynthia Rugeley and Robert A. Jackson, "Getting on the Rolls: Analyzing the Effects of Lowered Barriers on Voter Registration," *State Politics and Policy Quarterly* 9 (Spring 2009): 56–78.

29. Michael J. Hanmer, et al., "Losing Fewer Votes: The Impact of Changing Voting Systems on Residual Votes," *Political Research Quarterly* 63 (March 2010): 129–42.

30. "Methods of Nominating Candidates for State Offices," in *The Book of the States 2014* http://knowledgecenter.csg.org/kc/system/files/6.3%202014.pdf (February 22, 2015).

31. "State Primary Elections Types," National Conference of State Legislatures, http://www.ncsl.org/legislatures-elections/elections/state-primary-election-systems.aspx (September 28, 2011).

32. Charles S. Bullock, III, Ronald Keith Gaddie, and Anders Ferrington, "System Structure, Campaign Stimuli, and Voter Falloff in Runoff Primaries," *Journal of Politics* 64 (November 2002): 1210–24.

33. Kentucky Legislative Research Commission, "Election Filing Dates and Runoff Primary," www.lrc.ky.gov/record/08RS/SB3/SCS1LM.doc (July 1, 2009).

34. Randall W. Partin, "Economic Conditions and Gubernatorial Elections," *American Politics Quarterly* 23 (January 1995): 81–95.

35. "Vermont Governor Re-elected After Failing to Win Majority," *New York Times* http://www.nytimes.com/aponline/2015/01/08/us/ap-us-vermont-governor.html?_r=0 (February 2, 2015).

36. StateVote 2014: Election Results, National Conference of State Legislatures, http://www.ncsl.org/research/elections-and-campaigns/statevote-2014-post-election-analysis635508614.aspx (November 19, 2014).

37. Kimberly L. Nelson, *Elected Municipal Councils: Special Data Issue* (Washington, D.C.: International City/County Management Association, 2002).

38. Brian F. Schaffner, Gerald Wright, and Matthew Streb, "Teams Without Uniforms: The Nonpartisan Ballot in State and Local Elections," *Political Research Quarterly* 54 (March 2001): 7–30.

39. Zoltan Hajnal and Jessica Trounstine, "Where Turnout Matters: The Consequences of Uneven Turnout in City Elections," *Journal of Politics* 67 (May 2005): 515–36.

40. Arnold Fleischmann and Lana Stein, "Campaign Contributions in Local Elections," *Political Research Quarterly* 51 (September 1998): 673–89.

41. Luis Ricardo Fraga, "Domination through Democratic Means: Nonpartisan Slating Groups in City Electoral Politics," *Urban Affairs Quarterly* 23 (June 1988): 528–55; Christopher A. Cooper and Anthony J. Nownes, "Citizen Groups in Big City Politics," *State and Local Government Review* 35 (Spring 2003): 102–11.

42. Elizabeth R. Gerber, ed., *Stealing the Initiative* (Upper Saddle River, NJ: Prentice-Hall, 2001).

43. "Election Results 2014: Yes on Marijuana and Minimum Wage, No on Taxes," Ballotwatch http://www.iandrinstitute.org/BW%202014-2%20Election%20results%20%28v2%29%202014-11-21.pdf (November 21, 2014).

44. Jeff Hastings and Damon Cann, "Ballot Titles and Voter Decision Making on Ballot Questions, *State and Local Government Review* 46 (June 2014): 118–27.

45. Mark A Smith, "The Contingent Effects of Ballot Initiatives and Candidate Races on Turnout," *American Journal of Political Science* 45 (July 2001): 700–706; Caroline J. Tolbert, Ramona S. McNeal, and Daniel A. Smith, "Enhancing Civic Engagement: The Effect of Direct Democracy on Political Participation and Knowledge," *State Politics and Policy Quarterly* 3 (Spring 2003): 23–41; John A. Grummel, "Morality Politics, Direct Democracy, and Turnout," *State Politics and Policy Quarterly* 8 (Fall 2008): 282–92; Frederick J. Boehmke and R. Michael Alvarez, "The Influence of Initiative Signature-Gathering Campaigns on Political Participation," *Social Science Quarterly* 95 (March 2014): 165–83.

46. Joshua J. Dyck, "Initiated Distrust: Direct Democracy and Trust in Government," *American Politics Research* 37 (July 2009): 539–68. See also Justin H. Phillips, "Does the Citizen Initiative Weaken Party Government in the U.S. States?" *State Politics and Policy Quarterly* 8 (Summer 2008): 127–49.

47. John Myers, "New Law Brings Big Changes to California's Initiative Process," KQED, http://ww2.kqed.org/news/2014/09/27/big-changes-to-california-initiative-process-signed-by-jerry-brown/ (September 27, 2014).

48. Alana S. Jeydel and Brent S. Steel, "Public Attitudes Toward the Initiative Process in Oregon," *State and Local Government Review* 34 (Fall 2002): 173–82.

49. Elisabeth R. Gerber, Arthur Lupia, and Mathew D. McCubbins, "When Does Government Limit the Impact of Voter Initiatives? The Politics of Implementation and Enforcement," *Journal of Politics* 66 (February 2004): 43–68.

50. Valentina A. Bali, "Implementing Popular Initiatives: What Matters for Compliance?" *Journal of Politics* 65 (November 2003): 1130–46.

51. "Scott Walker Recall Elections Cost Taxpayers $13.5 Million," TwinCities.com, www.twincities.com/ci_21545007/scott-walker-recall-elections-cost-13-5-million (August 14, 2012)

52. Nathan Dickerson, "Electronic Communications and Public Records," Council of State Governments (February 2012): 3.

53. "New Report Ranks All Fifty States on Government Spending Transparency," U.S. PIRG http://www.uspirg.org/news/usp/new-report-ranks-all-fifty-states-government-spending-transparency (March 18, 2015).

54. Neal D. Woods, "Promoting Participation: An Examination of Rulemaking Notification and Access Procedures," *Public Administration Review* 69 (May/June 2009): 518–30.

55. Jonathan Walters, "Polling the Populace," *Governing* 20 (April 2007): 66–68.

56. Stephen Knack, "Social Capital and the Quality of Government: Evidence from the States," *American Journal of Political Science* 46 (October 2002): 772–85.

57. Ericka Harney, "State of Volunteers," *State News* 52 (May 2009): 16–18.

58. Markus Prior, "News vs. Entertainment: How Increasing Media Choice Widens Gap in Political Knowledge and Turnout," *American Journal of Political Science* 49 (July 2005): 577–92.

59. Evan J. Ringquist et al., "Lower-Class Mobilization and Policy Linkage in the U.S. States: A Correction," *American Journal of Political Science* 41 (January 1997): 339–44.

60. Coffee with Council 2015, https://www.youtube.com/watch?v=imv3sRxL4eE (March 3, 2015).

CHAPTER 5 POLITICAL PARTIES, INTEREST GROUPS, AND CAMPAIGNS: INFLUENCING PUBLIC POLICY

1. Reid Wilson, "Where Your Ideology Says You Should Live," Washington Post, www.washingtonpost.com/blogs/govbeat/wp/2014/06/17/where-your-ideology-says-you-should-live (June 17, 2014); "What Towns Matches Your Politics?" http://www.claritycampaigns.com/townrank (March 31, 2015).

2. David Doherty and E. Scott Adler, "The Persuasive Effects of Partisan Campaign Mailers," *Political Research Quarterly* 67 (September 2014): 562–73.3.

3. Gallup, "Record-High 42% of Americans Identify as Independents," www.gallup.com/poll/166763/record-high-americans-identify-independents.aspx (January 8, 2014).

4. Marjorie Randon Hershey, *Party Politics in America*, 11th ed. (New York: Pearson Longman, 2005).

5. Gallup, "Party Affiliation," www.gallup.com/poll/15370/party-affiliation.aspx (March 16, 2015).

6. David Von Drehle, "Culture Clash: Geography, Technology, and Strategy Have Nurtured a Political Split," *Washington Post National Weekly Edition* (May 24–30, 2004), pp. 6–7.

7. James G. Gimpel and Jason E. Schuknecht, "Reconsidering Political Regionalism in the American States," *State Politics and Policy Quarterly* 2 (Winter 2002): 325–52.

8. Hershey, *Party Politics in America*.

9. Malcolm E. Jewell and Sarah M. Morehouse, *Political Parties and Elections in American States*, 4th ed. (Washington, D.C.: Congressional Quarterly Press, 2001).

10. John H. Aldrich, "Southern Parties in State and Nation," *Journal of Politics* 62 (August 2000): 643–70.

11. Robert E. Hogan, "Candidate Perceptions of Political Party Campaign Activity in State Legislative Elections," *State Politics and Policy Quarterly* 2 (Spring 2002): 66–85.

12. Ibid.

13. Shanna Pearson-Merkowitz and John Michael McTigue, "Partisan Mountains and Molehills: The Geography of U.S. State Intraparty Factionalism," *State Politics and Policy Quarterly* 8 (Spring 2008): 7–31.

14. Louis Jacobson, "In 2014 Governors Races, Where's the Tea Party?" Governing, www.governing.com/

topics/elections/gov-tea-party-missing-governors-races.html (March 17, 2015).

15. "The Legislators: Numbers, Terms, and Party Affiliations: 2011," *The Book of the States 2011* (Lexington, KY: Council of State Governments, 2011).

16. Richard L. Berke, "U.S. Voters Focus on Selves, Poll Says," *The New York Times* (September 21, 1994), p. A12; Todd Donovan, Janine A. Parry, and Shaun Bowler, "O Other, Where Art Thou? Support for Multiparty Politics in the United States," *Social Science Quarterly* 86 (March 2005): 147–59.

17. "Elected Officials," www.lp.org/candidates/elected-officials; "Green Officeholders," www.gp.org/green-officeholders (March 17, 2015).

18. Charles Barrilleaux, "A Test of the Independent Influence of Electoral Competition and Party Strength in a Model of State Policymaking," *American Journal of Political Science* 41 (October 1997): 1462–66.

19. Thomas M. Holbrook and Raymond J. La Raja, "Parties and Elections," in Virginia Gray, Russell L. Hanson, and Thad Kousser, eds., *Politics in the American States: A Comparative Analysis*, 10th ed. (Washington, D.C.: Congressional Quarterly Press, 2013), pp. 63–104.

20. Everett Ehrlich, "Virtual Political Reality," *Washington Post National Weekly Edition* (December 22, 2003–January 4, 2004), p. 22.

21. Michael Slackman, "Voters Choosing None of the Above, and Parties Scramble," *The New York Times*, www.nytimes.com (April 13, 2004).

22. Justin H. Phillips, "Does the Citizen Initiative Weaken Party Government in the U.S. States?" *State Politics and Policy Quarterly* 8 (Summer 2008): 127–49.

23. J. P. Monroe, *The Political Party Matrix: The Persistence of Organization* (Albany, NY: SUNY Press, 2001).

24. Sarah M. Morehouse, "Interest Groups, Parties, and Policies in the American States," Paper presented at the annual meeting of the American Political Science Association, Washington, D.C., 1997.

25. Virginia Gray and David Lowery, *The Population Ecology of Interest Representation: Lobbying Communities in the American States* (Ann Arbor, MI: University of Michigan Press, 1996).

26. Virginia Gray and David Lowery, "A Niche Theory of Interest Representation," *Journal of Politics* 58 (February 1996): 91–111; Michael T. Heaney, "Issue Networks, Information, and Interest Group Alliances, The Case of Wisconsin Welfare Politics, 1993–99," *State Politics and Policy Quarterly* 4 (Fall 2004): 237–70.

27. Donald P. Haider-Markel, "Interest Group Survival: Shared Interests versus Competition for Resources," *Journal of Politics* 59 (August 1997): 903–12.

28. Clive S. Thomas, Ronald J. Hrebenar, and Anthony J. Nownes, "Interest Group Politics in the States," in *The Book of the States 2008* (Lexington, KY: Council of State Governments, 2008), p. 327.

29. National Institute on Money in State Politics, "Total Lobbyist Clients for 2011," www.followthemoney. org/database/graphs/lobbyistlink/lobbymap. phtml?p=1&y=2011&I=0 (May 1, 2013).

30. Peter L. Francia, "Interest Groups and their Influence," in Richard G. Niemi and Joshua J. Dyck, eds., *State Politics and Policy* (Washington, DC: CQ Press, 2014).

31. Alan Rosenthal, *The Third House* (Washington, D.C. Congressional Quarterly Press, 1993).

32. Chris Joyner, "Lobbyist Spending Jumps while Lawmakers Dine," *Atlanta Journal Constitution*, www .ajc.com (February 8, 2012).

33. Anthony J. Nownes and Krissy Walker DeAlejandro, "Lobbying in the New Millennium: Evidence of Continuity and Change in Three States," *State Politics and Policy Quarterly* 9 (Winter 2009): 429–55.

34. Anthony J. Nownes and Patricia Freeman, "Interest Group Activity in the States," *Journal of Politics* 60 (February 1998): 86–112.

35. Daniel E. Bergan, "Does Grassroots Lobbying Work?" *American Politics Research* 37 (March 2009): 327–52.

36. National Conference of State Legislatures, "Ethics: Legislator Gift Restrictions Overview," www.ncsl. org/legislatures-elections/ethicshome/50-state-table-gift-laws.aspx#ia (February 2012).

37. Joshua Ozymy, "Assessing the Impact of Legislative Lobbying Regulations on Interest Group Influence in U.S. State Legislatures," *State Politics and Policy Quarterly* 10 (Winter 2010): 397–420; Joshua Ozymy, "Keepin' on the Sunny Side: Scandals, Organized Interests, and the Passage of Legislative Lobbying Laws in the American States," *American Politics Review* 41 (January 2013): 3–23.

38. Patrick Flavin, "Lobbying Regulations and Political Equality in the American States," *American Politics Research* 43 (March): 304–26.

40. William P. Browne and Delbert J. Ringquist, "Michigan Interests: The Politics of Diversification," Paper presented at the annual meeting of the Midwest Political Science Association, Chicago, IL, 1987, p. 24.

41. Fred Monardi and Stanton A. Glantz, "Tobacco Industry Campaign Contributions and Legislative Behavior at the State Level," Paper presented at the annual meeting of the American Political Science Association, San Francisco, CA, 1996, p. 8.

42. Louay M. Constant, "When Money Matters: Campaign Contributions, Roll Call Votes, and School Choice in Florida," *State Politics and Policy Quarterly* 6 (Summer 2006): 195–219.

43. National Conference of State Legislatures, "State Limits on Contributions to Candidates," www .ncsl.org/Portals/1/documents/legismgt/Limits_to_ Candidates_2011–2012.pdf (September 30, 2011).

44. Zach Patton, "Chasing the Shadow," *Governing* 19 (June 2006): 43–5.

45. Center for Responsive Politics, "527s, Advocacy Group Spending 2012," www.opensecrets.org/527s/ index.php (April 30, 2013).

46. David H. Folz and P. Edward French, *Managing America's Small Communities* (Lanham, MD: Rowman & Littlefield, 2005).

47. Christopher A. Cooper and Anthony J. Nownes, "Perceptions of Power: Interest Groups in Local Politics," *State and Local Government Review* 37 (2005): 206–16; Paul Schumaker, "Group Involvements in City Politics and Pluralist Theory," *Urban Affairs Review* 49 (March 2013): 254–81.

48. Brian E. Adams, *Citizen Lobbyists: Local Efforts to Influence Public Policy* (Philadelphia, PA: Temple University Press, 2007).

49. Juliet Musso, Christopher Weare, and Kyu-Nahm Jun, "Democracy by Design: The Institutionalization of Community Participation Networks in Los Angeles," Paper presented at the Tenth National Public Management Research Conference, Columbus, OH, 2009.

50. Christopher A. Cooper and Anthony J. Nownes, "Citizen Groups in Big City Politics," *State and Local Government Review* 35 (Spring 2003): 102–11.

51. Daniel M. Shea and Michael John Burton, *Campaign Craft: The Strategies, Tactics, and Art of Political Campaign Management* (Westport, CT: Praeger, 2001), pp. 75–98.

52. R. Michael Alvarez, Asa Hopkins, and Betsy Sinclair, "Mobilizing Pasadena Democrats: Measuring the Effects of Partisan Campaign Contacts," *Journal of Politics* 72 (January 2010): 31–44.

53. Jerry Hagstrom and Robert Guskind, "Selling the Candidate," *National Journal* 18 (November 1, 1986): 2619–26.

54. Alan S. Gerber, et al., "How Large and Long-lasting Are the Persuasive Effects of Televised Campaign Ads? Results from a Randomized Field Experiment," *American Political Science Review* 105 (February 2011): 135–50.

55. Laura Packard, "Making Your Campaign Site Work for Mobile," *Campaigns & Elections,* www.campaignsandelections.com/campaign-insider/2429/making-your-campaign-site-work-for-mobile (April 9, 2015).

56. Patrick McGreevy, "New California Rules Aim for Transparency in Online Campaign Material," Los Angeles Times, http://articles.latimes.com/2013/sep/19/local/la-me-web-campaigns-20130920 (September 19, 2013).

57. Cleveland Ferguson, III, "The Politics of Ethics and Elections," *Florida State University Law Review* 25 (Fall 1997): 463–503.

58. Ted Braden, "Striking a Responsive Chord: How Political Ads Motivate and Persuade Voters by Appealing to Emotions," *American Journal of Political Science* 49 (April 2005): 388–405.

59. L. Marvin Overby and Jay Barth, "Radio Advertising in American Political Campaigns," *American Politics Research* 34 (July 2006): 451–78.

60. Owen G. Abbe and Paul S. Herrnson, "Campaign Professionalism in State Legislative Elections," *State Politics and Policy Quarterly* (Fall 2003): 223–45.

61. Ibid.

62. Donald A. Gross and Robert K. Goidel, "The Impact of State Campaign Finance Laws," *State Politics and Policy Quarterly* 1 (Summer 2001): 180–95. See also Nicholas R. Seabrook, "Money and State Legislative Elections: The Conditional Impact of Political Context," *American Politics Research* 38 (May 2010): 399–424.

63. Robert E. Hogan, "Campaign and Contextual Influences on Voter Participation in State Legislative Elections," *American Politics Quarterly* 27 (October 1999): 403–33; Robert E. Hogan, "Campaign Spending and Voter Participation in State Legislative Elections," *Social Science Quarterly* 94 (September 2013): 840–64.

64. Eric Kelderman, "Small Donors Equal Big Bucks for State Party Coffers," www.stateline.org (July 3, 2004).

65. National Conference of State Legislatures, "State Limits on Contributions to Candidates."

66. National Conference of State Legislatures, "Public Financing of Campaigns: An Overview," www.ncsl.org/legislatures-elections/elections/public-financing-of-campaigns-overview.aspx (January 6, 2010).

67. Neil Malhotra, "The Impact of Public Financing on Electoral Competition: Evidence from Arizona and Maine," *State Politics and Policy Quarterly* 8 (Fall 2008): 263–81.

68. Kedron Bardwell, "Campaign Finance Laws and the Competition for Spending in Gubernatorial Elections," *Social Science Quarterly* 84 (December 2003): 811–25.

69. General Assembly of North Carolina, ssl.csg.org/dockets/29cycle/29B/2009bdocketbills/1629b01nc.pdf (July 16, 2009).

CHAPTER 6 STATE LEGISLATURES: THE PEOPLE'S REPRESENTATIVES

1. Saira Blair, as quoted in Alan Greenblatt, "Financial Pressures May Table Republicans' Bold Initiatives," governing.com (January 2015).

2. Karl T. Kurtz et al., "Full-Time, Part-Time, and Real Time: Explaining State Legislators' Perceptions of Time on the Job," *State Politics and Policy Quarterly* 6 (Fall 2006): 322–38.

3. Ellen Perlman, "The 'Gold-plated' Legislature," *Governing* 11 (February 1998): 36–40.

4. Justin H. Kirkland, "Chamber Size Effects on the Collaborative Structure of Legislatures," *Legislative Studies Quarterly* 39 (May 2014): 169–98.

5. David E. Broockman, "Distorted Communication, Unequal Representation: Constituents Communicate Less to Representatives Not of Their Race," *American Journal of Political Science* 58 (April 2014): 307–21.

6. National Conference of State Legislatures, "Legislator Demographics: State-by-State," www.ncsl.org/legislatures-elections/legisdata/legislator-demographic-map.aspx (accessed April 2, 2012).

7. Lilliard E. Richardson, Jr., Brian E. Russell, and Christopher A. Cooper, "Legislative Representation in Single-Member versus Multiple-Member District System: The Arizona State Legislature," *Political Research Quarterly* 57 (June 2004): 337–44.

8. *Reynolds v. Sims*, 84 S.Ct. 1362 (1964).

9. Michael P. McDonald, "A Comparative Analysis of Redistricting Institutions in the U.S.," *State Politics and Policy Quarterly* 4 (Winter 2004): 371–95; see also "Redistricting Commissions: Legislative Plans," www.ncsl.org/legislatures-elections/redist/2009-redistricting-commissions-table.aspx (accessed April 15, 2012).

10. Andrew Karch, Corrine M. McConnaughy, and Sean M. Theriault, "The Legislative Politics of Congressional Redistricting Commission Proposals," *American Politics Research* 35 (November 2007): 808–25.

11. Michael A. Smith, "One Piece at a Time: The Role of Timing and Sequencing in Pivotal Politics," *Perspectives on Politics* 2 (March 2004): 85–89. See also Todd Makse, "Strategic Constituency Manipulation in State Legislative Redistricting," *Legislative Studies Quarterly* 37 (May 2012): 225–50.

12. William March, "Black Voters Win, Lose with Districting," *Tampa Tribune* (April 6, 1998), pp. B-1, B-5; see also Michael C. Herron and Alan E. Wiseman, "Gerrymanders and Theories of Law Making: A Study of Legislative Redistricting in Illinois," *Journal of Politics* 70 (January 2008): 151–67.

13. Ronald E. Weber, "Emerging Trends in State Legislative Redistricting," *Spectrum* 75 (Winter 2002): 13.

14. "2014 State Legislator Compensation /Living Expense Allowances During Session," National Conference of State Legislatures, www.ncsl.org/research/about-state-legislatures/2014-ncsl-legislator-salary-and-per-diem-table.aspx (accessed April 10, 2015).

15. Peverill Squire and Gary Moncrief, *State Legislatures Today: Politics under the Domes* (Boston: Longman, 2010).

16. Nancy Martorono, "Distributing Power: Exploring the Relative Powers of Presiding Officers and Committees in the State Legislative Process," Paper presented at the annual meeting of the American Political Science Association, Chicago, 2004; see also Peverill Squire, "Member Career Opportunities and the Internal Organization of Legislatures," *Journal of Politics* 50 (August 1988): 726–44.

17. "Women in State Legislative Leadership Positions 2010," Center for American Women and Politics, www.cawp.rutgers.edu/fast_facts/levels_of_office/documents/leglead.pdf (accessed April 5, 2012).

18. Josh Goodman, "Contention and Compromise in Virginia, Oregon Tied Chambers," www.stateline.org/live/printable/story?contentID=643855 (accessed April 6, 2012).

19. Henry A. Kim and Justin H. Phillips, "Dividing the Spoils of Power: How Are the Benefits of Majority Party Status Distributed in U.S. State Legislatures?" *State Politics and Policy Quarterly* 9 (Summer 2009): 125–50. See also Kristin Kanthak, "U.S. State Legislative Committee Assignments and Encouragement of Party Loyalty: An Exploratory Analysis," *State Politics and Policy Quarterly* 9 (Fall 2009): 284–303.

20. Keith E. Hamm, Ronald D. Hedlund, and Stephanie S. Post, "Committee Specialization in State Legislatures During the Twentieth Century: Do Legislatures Tap the Talents of Their Members?" *State Politics and Policy Quarterly* 11 (September 2011): 299–325.

21. Ralph G. Wright, *Inside the Statehouse: Lessons from the Speaker* (Washington, D.C.: Congressional Quarterly Press, 2005).

22. L. Marvin Overby, Thomas A. Kazee, and David W. Prince, "Committee Outliers in State Legislatures," *Legislative Studies Quarterly* 29 (February 2004): 81–107; David W. Prince and L. Marvin Overby, "Legislative Organization Theory and Committee Preference Outliers in State Senates," *State Politics and Policy Quarterly* 5 (Spring 2005): 68–87.

23. Molly Jackman, "Parties, Median Legislators, and Agenda Setting: How Legislative Institutions Matter," *Journal of Politics* 76 (January 2014): 259–72.

24. Allen Ehrenhalt, "Putting Practice into Theory," *Governing* 14 (November 2000): 6, 8.

25. Roy Brasfield Herron, "Diary of a Legislator," *Southern Magazine* 2 (May 1988).

26. Christopher A. Cooper and Lilliard E. Richardson, Jr., "Institutions and Representational Roles in American State Legislatures," *State Politics and Policy Quarterly* 6 (Summer 2006): 174–94. See also Shannon Jenkins, "The Impact of Party and Ideology on Roll-Call Voting in State Legislatures," *Legislative Studies Quarterly* 31 (May 2006): 205–34.

27. Eric M. Uslaner and Ronald E. Weber, "U.S. State Legislators' Opinions and Perceptions of Constituency Attitudes," *Legislative Studies Quarterly* 4 (November 1979): 582.

28. "Table 3.19 Bill and Resolution Introductions and Enactments, 2013 Regular Sessions," *The Book of the States 2014* http://knowledgecenter.csg.org/kc/content/book-states-2014-chapter-3-state-legislative-branch (accessed April 15, 2015).

29. Smith, "One Piece at a Time."

30. Alan Rosenthal, "The Legislature as Sausage Factory," *State Legislatures* 27 (September 2001): 12–15.

31. Tom Loftus, *The Art of Legislative Politics* (Washington, D.C.: Congressional Quarterly Press, 1994), p. 76.

32. Ibid., p. 77.

33. David C. Saffell, "School Funding in Ohio: Courts, Politicians, and Newspapers," *Comparative State Politics* 18 (October 1997): 9–25.

34. Citizens' Conference on State Legislatures, *The Sometimes Governments: A Critical Study of the 50 American Legislatures,* 2nd ed. (Kansas City, MO: CCSL, 1973), pp. 41–42.

35. Karl Kurtz and Brian Weberg, "What Legislatures Need Now," *State Legislatures* 36 (July/August 2010): 47–50.

36. Alan Rosenthal, "The New Legislature: Better or Worse and for Whom?" *State Legislatures* 12 (July 1986): 5.

37. Charles W. Wiggins, as quoted in Andrea Patterson, "Is the Citizen Legislator Becoming Extinct?" *State Legislatures* 12 (July 1986): 24.

38. Representative Vic Krouse, as quoted in Patterson, "Is the Citizen Legislator Becoming Extinct?" p. 24.

39. Peverill Squire, *The Evolution of American Legislatures: Colonies, Territories, and States, 1619–2009.* (Ann Arbor: University of Michigan Press, 2012). See also Daniel C. Bowen and Zachary Greene, "Should We Measure Professionalism with an Index? A Note on Theory and Practice in State Legislative Professionalism Research," *State Politics and Policy Quarterly* 14 (September 2014): 277–96.

40. Alan Rosenthal, "The State Legislature," Paper presented at the Vanderbilt Institute for Public Policy Studies, November 1987; James D. King, "Changes in Professionalism in U.S. State Legislatures," *Legislative Studies Quarterly* 25 (May 2000): 327–43.

41. National Conference of State Legislatures, "Full and Part-Time Legislatures," www.ncsl.org/research/about-state-legislatures/full-and-part-time-legislatures.aspx (June 1, 2014).

42. Richard Nathan, as cited in Kathe Callahan and Marc Holzer, "Rethinking Governmental Change," *Public Productivity Management & Review* 17 (Spring 1994): 202.

43. Brad Bumsted, "Rendell Jumps on Reform Bandwagon," *Pittsburgh Tribune-Review*, www.pittsburghlive.com (accessed March 22, 2007).

44. Stuart Rothenberg, "How Term Limits Became a National Phenomenon," *State Legislatures* 18 (January 1992): 35–39.

45. Joel A. Thompson and Gary F. Moncrief, "The Implications of Term Limits for Women and Minorities: Some Evidence from the States," *Social Science Quarterly* 74 (June 1993): 300–309.

46. Karen Hansen, "The Third Revolution," *State Legislatures* 23 (September 1997): 20–26; Thad Kousser, "The Limited Impact of Term Limits Contingent Effects on the Complexity and Breadth of Laws," *State Politics and Policy Quarterly* 6 (Winter 2006): 10–29.

47. Gary Moncrief and Joel A. Thompson, "On the Outside Looking In: Lobbyists' Perspectives on the Effects of State Legislative Term Limits," *State and Local Government Review* 1 (Winter 2001): 394–411; Joel Thompson and Gary Moncrief, "Lobbying Under Limits: Interest Group Perspectives on the Effects of Term Limits in State Legislatures," in Farmer, Rausch, and Green, eds., *The Test of Time: Coping with Legislative Term Limits,* pp. 211–24; Thad Kousser, *Term Limits and the Dismantling of State Legislative Professionalism* (New York: Cambridge University Press, 2005).

48. Robert A. Bernstein and Anita Chadha, "The Effects of Term Limits on Representation: Why So Few Women?" in Rick Farmer, John David Rausch, Jr., and John C. Green, eds., *The Test of Time: Coping with Legislative Term Limits* (Lanham, MD: Lexington Books, 2003), pp. 147–58; Stanley M. Caress et al., "Effect of Term Limits on the Election of Minority State Legislators," *State and Local Government Review* 35 (Fall 2003): 183–95.

49. John M. Carey, Richard G. Niemi, Lynda W. Powell, and Gary F. Moncrief, "The Effects of Term Limits on State Legislatures: A New Survey of the 50 States," *Legislative Studies Quarterly* 31 (February 2006): 105–34; Susan A. Miller, Jill Nicholson-Crotty, and Sean Nicholson-Crotty, "Reexamining the Institutional Effects of Term Limits in U.S. State Legislatures," *Legislative Studies Quarterly* 36 (February 2011): 71–97.

50. Daniel C. Lewis, "Legislative Term Limits and Fiscal Policy Performance," *Legislative Studies Quarterly* 37 (August 2012): 305–28. For a different view, see Luke Keele, Neil Malhotra, and Colin H. McCubbins, "Do Term Limits Restrain State Fis-cal Policy?" *Legislative Studies Quarterly* 38 (August 2013): 291–26.

51. Andrew B. Hall, "Partisan Effects of Legislative Term Limits," *Legislative Studies Quarterly* 39 (August 2014): 407–29.

52. Carol S. Weissert and Karen Halperin, "The Paradox of Term Limit Support: To Know Them Is Not to Love Them," *Political Research Quarterly* 60 (September 2007): 516–30.

53. Daniel A. Smith, "Overturning Term Limits: The Legislature's Own Private Idaho?" *PS: Political Science and Politics* 36 (April 2003): 215–20.

54. Governor Haley Barbour, State of the State Address, January 26, 2004.

55. Madeleine Kunin, as quoted in Sharon Randall, "From Big Shot to Boss," *State Legislatures* 14 (June 1988): 348.

56. Travis J. Baker and David M. Hedge, "Term Limits and Legislative Executive-Conflict in the American States," *Legislative Studies Quarterly* 38 (May 2013): 237–58.

57. Thad Kousser and Justin H. Phillips, "Who Blinks First? Legislative Patience and Bargaining with Governors," *Legislative Studies Quarterly* 34 (February 2009): 55–86.

58. Brian J. Gerber, Cherie Maestas, and Nelson C. Dometrius, "State Legislative Influence over Agency Rulemaking," *State Politics and Policy Quarterly* 5 (Spring 2005): 24–46.

59. Jerry Brekke, "Supreme Court of Missouri Rules Legislative Veto Unconstitutional," *Comparative State Politics* 19 (February 1997): 32–34.

60. "Summary of Sunset Legislation," *The Book of the States 2006* (Lexington, KY: Council of State Governments, 2006), pp. 132–34.

61. William M. Pearson and Van A. Wigginton, "Effectiveness of Administrative Controls: Some Perceptions of State Legislators," *Public Administration Review* 46 (July/August 1986): 328–31.

62. Alan Rosenthal, *Heavy Lifting: The Job of the American Legislature* (Washington, D.C.: Congressional Quarterly Press, 2004), p. 85. See also Alan Rosenthal, *Engines of Democracy: Politics and Policymaking in State Legislatures* (Washington, D.C.: Congressional Quarterly Press, 2009).

63. Lilliard E. Richardson, Jr., David M. Konisky, and Jeffrey Milyo, "Public Approval of U.S. State Legislatures," *Legislative Studies Quarterly* 37 (February 2012): 99–116.

64. Kurtz and Weberg, "What Legislatures Need Now," p. 47.

CHAPTER 7 GOVERNORS: POWER, POLITICS, AND EXECUTIVE LEADERSHIP

1. Thad Beyle, "The Governors," in Virginia Gray and Russell L. Hanson, eds., *Politics in the American States: A Comparative Analysis*, 8th ed. (Washington, D.C.: Congressional Quarterly Press, 2004), pp. 194–231.
2. Larry Sabato, *Goodbye to Goodtime Charles: The American Governorship Transformed* (Lexington, MA: Lexington Books, 1978), p. 13.
3. Alan Rosenthal, *The Best Job in State Politics* (Washington, D.C., CQ Press, 2012).
4. www.jonathanforgovernor.us (accessed May 15, 2006; no longer active in October 2006).
5. Dylan Otto Krider, "Georgia Candidate for Governor Says Sex with Mules, Watermelon Behind Him," http://www.examiner.com/ (April 28, 2009).
6. Audrey Wall, "Gubernatorial Elections, Campaigns, and Winning Governors," (Lexington, KY: Council of State Governments, 2014), Table C.
7. Randall W. Partin, "Assessing the Impact of Campaign Spending in Governors' Races," *Political Research Quarterly* 55 (March, 2002): 213–24.
8. John R. Wright, "Unemployment and the Democratic Electoral Advantage," *American Political Science Review* 106 (4, 2012): 685–702; Thad L. Beyle, "The Governors," *The Book of the States 2005* (Lexington, KY: Council of State Governments), p. 180.
9. Peveril Squire, "Challenger Profile and Gubernatorial Elections," *Western Politics Quarterly* 45 (1992): 125–42.
10. Thad L. Beyle, "Being Governor," in Carl E. Van Horn, ed., *The State of the States*, 3rd ed. (Washington, D.C.: Congressional Quarterly Press, 1996), p. 88.
11. Sharon Sherman, "Powersplit: When Legislatures and Governors Are of Opposing Parties," *State Legislatures* 10 (May/June 1984): 9–12.
12. Sander M. Polster, "Maine's King Makes Independence a Virtue," www.stateline.org (November 30, 1999).
13. *New York Daily News* as reported by www.governing.com (September 11, 2008).
14. Josh Goodman, "The Christie Way," *Governing* (August 2010): 29–32.
15. Michael Dukakis, as quoted in Thad L. Beyle and Lynn Muchmore, *Reflections on Being Governor* (Washington, D.C.: National Governors Association, 1978), p. 45
16. Council of State Governments, *Book of the States* (Washington, DC: CSG, 2014): Table A.
17. Jason Hancock, "Gov. Jay Nixon's Vetoes of Tax Cut and Gun Bills Stand on Missouri," http://www.kansascity.com (September 11, 2013).
18. Josh Goodman, "Politics, Kentucky Style," *Governing* (December 2009): 15.
19. Laura Vozzella, "At Executive Mansion, McAuliffe Puts Out the Welcome Mat," www.washingtonpost.com/local/virginia-politics.
20. Lizette Alvarez, "Facing Flurry of Lawsuits, a Governor Loses a Round," www.nytimes.com (August 17, 2011).
21. John Gramlich, "How a Court Ruling Ended Nevada Budget Fight," www.stateline.org (June 8, 2011).
22. Jennifer Burnett, "Governors' Salaries 2014," *Book of the States*, 2014 (Washington, D.C.: Council of State Governments, 2014). Table 4.3.
23. "Grading Mr. Fix-it," www.national journal.com (June 20, 2013).
24. Beyle and Muchmore, "The Governor and the Public," p. 24.
25. Ibid.
26. J.B. Wogan, "Losing their Voice," *Governing* (June 2014): 52–5.
27. Adam R. Brown, "Are Governors Responsible for the State Economy? Partisanship, Blame, and Divided Federalism," *The Journal of Politics* 72 (July, 2010): 605–615; Jeffrey E. Cohen and James D. King, "Relative Unemployment and Gubernatorial Popularity," *Journal of Politics* 66 (November 2004): 1267–82.
28. This exchange is cited in Rosenthal, *Governors and Legislators*, p. 18.
29. Thad L. Beyle and Lynn R. Muchmore, "The Governor as Party Leader," in Beyle and Muchmore, eds., *Being Governor*, pp. 44–51; Morehouse, *Governor as Party Leader*, pp. 45–51.
30. Alfred E. Smith, as quoted in George Weeks, "Statehouse Hall of Fame, Ten Outstanding Governors of the 20th Century," paper presented at the annual meeting of the Southern Political Science Association, Memphis, Tennessee, November 1981.
31. John Wagner, "Hunt," *The News and Observer* (April 1, 2001): 1A, 18A.
32. Diane Kincaid Blair, "The Gubernatorial Appointment Power: Too Much of a Good Thing?" in Beyle and Muchmore, eds., *Being Governor*, p. 117.
33. Thad Beyle, "The Governors," in Virginia Gray and Russell Hanson, eds., *Politics in the American States* (Washington, D.C.: Congressional Quarterly Press, 2004), p. 216.
34. Alan Ehrenhalt, "The Veto Gambit," *Governing* (August 2006): 11–12.
35. John Buntin, "Dr. Yes," *Governing* (December 2013): 29.
36. Matthew Yi, "Governor Sets Record for Vetoing Bills," *San Francisco Chronicle*, www.sfgate.com (October 2, 2008).
37. Nelson C. Dometrius and Deil S. Wright, "Governors, Legislatures, and State Budgets across Time," *Political Research Quarterly* 63 (4, 2010): 783–95.
38. Charles Barrilleaux and Michael Berkman, "Do Governors Matter? Budgeting Rules and the Politics of State Policymaking," *Political Research Quarterly* 56 (December 2003): 409–17.
39. Dan Durning, "Governors and Administrative Reform in the 1990s," *State and Local Government Review* 27 (Winter 1995): 36–54.
40. James K. Conant, "State Reorganization: A New Model?" *State Government* 58 (April 1985): 130–38.

41. Robert F. Bennett, as quoted in H. Edward Flentje, "The Political Nature of the Governor as Manager," p. 70, in Beyle and Muchmore, 1983. For a description of failure in reorganization in Florida, see also Less Garner, "Managing Change through Organization Structure," *State Government* 60 (July/August 1987): 191–95.

42. Michael Berkman and Christopher Reenock, "Incremental Consolidation and Comprehensive Reorganization of American State Executive Branches," *American Journal of Political Science* 48 (October 2004): 796–812.

43. *Book of the States*, 2014, Table 4.3

44. Barry L. Van Lare, "The Many Roles of the Governors' Chiefs of Staff," *Book of the States*, vol. 40, 174–79.

45. Thomas M. Holbrook, "Institutional Strength and Gubernatorial Elections: An Exploratory Analysis," *American Politics Quarterly* 21 (July, 1993): 261–71.

46. Tom Ferrick, Jr., "Alienating a State from East to West" www.nyti.ms/1onKbCO (October 20, 2014).

47. Colin Woodard, "Maine's Governor is in Trouble Again," www.governing.com (July 8, 2014).

48. Beyle, "The Governors," p. 206.

49. Alan Greenblat, "The Job of a Lifetime," *Governing* (June 2009), 24–30.

50. Rob Gurwitt, "The Ordeal of David Paterson," *Governing* (March 2009): 26–33.

51. See Thad L. Beyle, "Enhancing Executive Leadership in the States," *State and Local Government Review* 27 (Winter 1995): 18–35.

52. Ibid.

53. See Paul West, "They're Everywhere! For Today's Governors, Life Is a Never-Ending Campaign," *Governing* 3 (March 1990): 51–55.

54. A. G. Sulzberger, "Jokes and Secret Hopes for Lieutenant Governors," www.nytimes.com (December 3, 2010).

55. Josh Goodman, "The Second Best Job in the State," www.*governing.com* (April 2009).

56. *The Book of the States*, (2014): Table 4.14.

57. Eric Lipton, "Energy Firms in Secretive Alliance with Attorneys General," www.nytimes.com (December 6, 2014); Lipton, "Lobbyists, Bearing Gifts, Pursue Attorneys General," www.nytimes.com (October 28, 2014).

58. Rob Moritz, "Update: Feds Allege Shoffner Received Kickbacks for Targeted Transactions," www.Arkansasnews.com (May 21, 2013).

59. Kay Stimson, "Secretaries of State Confront the Growing Problem of Business Identity Theft," *The Book of the States*, vol. 43 (2011): 167–69.

CHAPTER 8 PUBLIC ADMINISTRATION: BUDGETING AND SERVICE DELIVERY

1. H. George Frederickson, "Can Bureaucracy Be Beautiful?" *Public Administration Review* 60 (January/February 2000): 47–53.

2. Judith Rayner, et al., "Public Service Ethos: Developing a Generic Measure," *J Public Adm Res Theory* (2011) 21 (1): 27–51; Ari Salminem and Venya Mantysalo, "Exploring the Public Service Ethos," *Public Integrity* 15 (April, 2013):167–86).

3. See, for example, Theodore H. Poister, and Gary T. Henry, "Citizen Ratings of Public and Private Service Quality: A Comparative Perspective," *Public Administration Review* 54 (March/April 1994): 155–59.

4. Mary E. Guy, Meredity A. Newman, and Sharon H. Mastracci, *Emotional Labor: Putting the Service in Public Service* (Armonk, NY: M. E. Sharpe, 2008).

5. Robert Jesse Willhide, *Annual Survey of Public Employment and Payroll Summary Report: 2013*. www.census.gov (December 19, 2014).

6. Steven Maynard-Moody and Michael Musheno, *Cops, Teachers, Counselors: Stories from the Front Lines of Public Service* (Ann Arbor, MI: University of Michigan Press, 2003).

7. Harold D. Laswell, *Politics: Who Gets What, When, Where, How?* (Cleveland, OH: World, 1958).

8. Ellen Perlman, "Stat Fever," *Governing* (January 2007): 48–49.

9. Katherine Barrett and Richard Greene, "The Big Picture on Budgeting," *Governing* (November 2010): 60–62; Zach Patton, "Culture Change," *Governing* (January 2008): 68–69.

10. Aaron Wildavsky, "Toward a Radical Incrementalism," in Alfred De Grazia, ed., *Congress: The First Branch of Government* (Washington, D.C.: American Enterprise Institute, 1966).

11. Nelson C. Dometrius and Deil S Wright, "Governors, Legislatures, and State Budgets across Time," *Political Research Quarterly* 63 (4, 2010): 783–95; Christian Breunig and Chris Koski, "Punctuated Budgets and Governors' Institutional Powers," *American Politics Research* 37 (6, 2009): 1116–38.

12. Dave McKinney, "Court Strikes Down State's $31 Billion Capital Program," www.suntimes.com (January 27, 2011).

13. Johm M. Kamensky, "When Citizens Decide How Public Money is Spent," www.governing.com (September 15, 2014).

14. Charles E. Lindblom, "The Science of Muddling Through," *Public Administrative Review* 19 (Spring 1959): 79–88.

15. Elaine S. Povitch, "State Budgeting with an Eye on Results," www.stateline.org (August 28, 2014); Janet M. Kelly and William C. Rivenbark, *Performance Budgeting for State and Local Government* (Armonk, NY: M. E. Sharpe, 2003).

16. Laurie Cohen, "City Hiring to Remain under Court Scrutiny," www.chicagotribune.com (March 21, 2009).

17. David K. Hamilton, "The Staffing Function in Illinois State Government after Rutan," *Public Administration Review* 53 (July/August 1993): 381–86.

18. H. George Frederickson, "The Airport that Reforms Forgot," *PA Times* (January 2000): 11.

19. J. Edward Kellough and Sally Coleman Selden, "The Reinvention of Public Personnel Administration: An Analysis of the Diffusion of Personnel Management Reforms in the States," *Public Administration Review* 63 (November/December 2003): 165–76.

20. Jerrell D. Coggburn, "Deregulating the Public Personnel Function," in Steven W. Hays and Richard C. Kearney, eds., *Public Personnel Administration: Problems and Prospects*, 4th ed. (Upper Saddle River, NJ: Prentice-Hall, 2003), pp. 75–79.

21. Robert J. McGrath, The Rise and Fall of Radical Civil Service Reform in the States, *"Public Administration Review* 73 (July/August, 2013): 638–49.

22. Lael R. Keiser, et al., "Lipstick and Logarithms: Gender, Institutional Context, and Representative Bureaucracy," *American Political Science Review* 96(3) (2002): 553–64; Vicky M. Wilkins and Lael R. Keiser, "Linking Passive and Active Representation by Gender: The Case of Child Support Agencies," *Journal of Public Administration Research and Theory* 16 (Winter 2005): 87–102; Vicky M. Wilkins "Exploring the Causal Story: Gender, Active Representation, and Bureaucratic Priorities," *Journal of Public Administration Research and Theory* 17 (Winter 2006): 77–94.

23. Vicky Wilkins, "Exploring the Causal Story: Gender, Active Representation, and Bureaucratic Priorities," *Journal of Public Administration Research and Theory* 17 (2006): 77–94.

24. David E. Brockman, "Black Politicians are Intrinsically Motivated to Advance Blacks' Interests: A Field Experiment Manipulating Political Incentives," *American Journal of Political Science* 57 (July, 2013): 521–36.

25. Nick A. Theobald and Donald P. Haider-Markel, "Race, Bureaucracy, and Symbolic Representation: Interactions between Citizens and Police," *Journal of Public Administration Research and Theory* 19(2) (2008): 409–26.

26. Nick A. Theobald and Donald P. Haider-Markel, "Race, Bureaucracy, and Symbolic Representation: Interactions between Citizens and Police," *Journal of Public Administration Research and Theory* 19(2) (2008): 409–26.

27. Mark D. Bradbury and J. Edward Kellough, "Representative Bureaucracy: Exploring the Potential for Active Representation in Local Government," *Journal of Public Administration Research and Theory* 18 (2011, 697–714).

28. See *Ricci v. DeStefano* (No. 07-1428, 2009); J. Edward Kellough, "Affirmative Action and Diversity in the Public Sector," in Steven W. Hays, Richard C. Kearney, and Jerrell D. Coggburn, *Public Human Resource Management: Problems and Prospects*, 5th ed. (New York: Pearson Education, 2009), pp. 219–35.

29. *Schuette v Coalition to Defend Affirmative Action*, No. 12-682 (April 22, 2014).

30. *Gretz v Bollinger*, No. 02-241 F.3d732 (June 23, 2003).

31. *Fisher v. University of Texas* 11–345 (June 24, 2013).

32. Jared J. Llorens, Jeffrey B. Wenger, and J. Edward Kellough, "Choosing Public Sector Employment: The Impact of Wages on the Representation of Women and Minorities in State Bureaucracies," *Journal of Public Administration Research and Theory* 18(3) (2008): 397–413.

33. Mary E. Guy, "The Difference that Gender Makes," in Hays and Kearney (2003), pp. 256–70; Norma M. Riccucci, *Managing Diversity in Public Sector Workforces* (Boulder, CO: Westview Press, 2002).

34. Mary E. Guy, "Three Steps Forward, Two Steps Backward: The Status of Women's Integration into Public Management," *Public Administration Review* 53 (July/August 1993): 285–91.

35. M. G. Alkadry and L. E. Tower, *Women in Public Service: Barriers, Challenges, and Opportunities* (Armonk, NY: M. E. Sharpe, 2009); Heidi Voorhees and Rachel Lange-Skaggs, "Women Leading Government," www.icma.org/en/press/pm_magazine/article/105323.

36. Cynthia J. Bowling, et al., "Cracked Ceilings, Firmer Floors, and Weakening Walls: Trends and Patterns in Gender Representation among Executives Leading American State Agencies, 1970–2000," *Public Administration Review* 66 (November/December 2006): 823–36.

37. J. Edward Kellough, *Understanding Affirmative Action* (Washington, D.C.: Georgetown University Press, 2006); Daniel N. Lipson, "Where's the Justice? Affirmative Action's Severed Roots in the Age of Diversity," *Perspectives on Politics* 6 (December 2008): 691–705.

38. Sonia Ospina and James F. O'Sullivan, "Working Together: Meeting the Challenge of Workplace Diversity," in Hays and Kearney (2003), pp. 238–55; Riccucci, *Managing Diversity in Public Sector Workforces*, 2002.

39. *Meritor Savings Bank v. Vinson*, 1986, 477 U.S. 57; *Teresa Haris v. Forklift Systems, Inc.*, U.S. Supreme Court, 92–1168 (November 9, 1993).

40. Steve Miletich, "County to Pay $1 Million to 3 Detectives in Sex-Harassment Case," www.seattletimes.com (December 18, 2013).

41. www.bls.gov/news.release/pdf/union2.nr0.htm (accessed February 14, 2015).

42. Richard C. Kearney and Patrice M. Mareschal, *Labor Relations in the Public Sector*, 5th ed. (New York: CRC Press, 2014).

43. Kearney and Mareschal, 2014: Chapter 6.

44. Kearney and Mareschal, *Labor Relations in the Public Sector*, 5th ed. (New York: CRC Press, 2009): 194–6.

45. Eric M. Patashnik, *Reforms at Risk: What Happens after Major Policy Changes Are Enacted* (Princeton, N.J. Princeton University Press, 2008), p. 161.

46. Michael Lipsky, *Street-Level Bureaucrats: The Dilemmas of the Individual in Public Service* (New York: Sage, 1980).

47. *The Book of the States*, 2014 (Lexington, KY: Council of State Governments, 2014).

48. David Osborne and Ted Gaebler, *Reinventing Government* (New York: Penguin Books, 1993).

49. John M. Bryson, Barbara C. Crosby, and Laura Bloomberg, "Public Value Governance: Moving Beyond Traditional Public Administration and the New Public Management," *Public Administration Review* 74 (4, 2014): 445–56.

50. Robert Mohr and Steven C. Deller, "Alternative Methods of Service Delivery in Small and Rural Municipalities," *Public Administration Review* (November/December 2010): 894–904.

51. "Intergovernmental Cooperation: The Growing Reform," in ICMA, The Municipal Year Book, 2014 (Washington, D.C.: ICMA Press, 2014).

52. Morten Jakobsen and Simon Calmar Andersen, "Coproduction and Equity in Public Service Delivery," *Public Administration Review* 73 (5, 2013): 704–13.

53. David Segal, "A Georgia Town Takes the People's Business Private," www.nytimes.com (August 23, 2012).

54. Stephen C. Fehr, "Study: Why Pa. Turnpike Plan Failed," www.stateline.org (March 24, 2009).

55. Ryan Holeywell, "Public-Private Practical?" *Governing* (November 2013): 34–41; Gerald T. Gabris and Douglas M. Ihrke, "Unanticipated Failures of Well-Intentional Reforms: Some Lessons Learned from Federal and Local Governments," *International Journal of Organization Theory and Behavior* 6 (February 2003): 195–225.

56. Tony Cook, "Indiana Gov. Mitch Daniels' Legacy: Privatization," www.indystar.com (January 1, 2013).

57. M. Ernita Joaquin and Thomas J. Greitens, "Contract Management Capacity Breakdown? An Analysis of U.S. Local Governments," *Public Administration Review* 72 (6, 2012): 807–16.

58. Lawrence L. Martin, "Public–Private Competition: A Public Employee Alternative to Privatization," *Review of Public Personnel Administration* 19 (Winter 1999): 59–70.

59. Melissa Maynard, "Why States Need Social Media Policies," www.stateline.org (October 29, 2013); "IBM Survey: Too Much Data in Public Sector Stymies Effective Analysis," www.govtech.com (May 16, 2011); Sharon S. Dawes, "The Evolution and Continuing Challenges of E-Governance," *Public Administration Review* 68 (December 2008): S86–S102.

CHAPTER 9 THE JUDICIARY: INDEPENDENCE VS ACCOUNTABILITY

1. Aaron Marshall, "Ohio House Makes 'Don't Touch' the Rule in Strip Clubs," www.Cleveland.com (accessed September 22, 2007).

2. Associated Press, "Judge: No More Nudity in Mo. Clubs," www.newstribune.com (August 27, 2010); W. John Moore, "In Whose Court?" *National Journal* (October 15, 1991): 2396.

3. Terri Langford, "Controller to Strip Clubs: Pay Up," www.texastribune.org (May 6, 2014).

4. Henry Robert Glick and Kenneth N. Vines, *State Court Systems* (Englewood Cliffs, NJ: Prentice-Hall, 1973), p. 19.

5. Ibid., p. 21.

6. Caroline Cournoyer, " 'Neighborhood Courts' to Reduce Crowding, Cut Costs," www.governing.com (May 2, 2011).

7. *Goodridge v. Department of Public Health et al.*, 440 Mass 309 (2003).

8. Caroline Cournoyer, ""Neighborhood" Courts to Reduce Crowding, Cut Costs," www.governing.com (May 2, 2011).

9. Charles H. Sheldon and Linda S. Maule, *Choosing Justices: The Recruitment of State and Federal Judges* (Pullman: Washington State University Press, 1997).

10. G. Alan Tarr, *Without Fear or Favor: Judicial Independence and Judicial Accountability in the States* (Stanford: Stanford University Press, 2012).

11. Lawrence Baum, "State Courts in Their Political Environments," in Carol E. Van Horn, ed., *The State of the States*, 4th ed. (Washington, D.C.: Congressional Quarterly Press, 2006), pp. 91–92.

12. Adam Liptak and Janet Roberts, "Campaign Cash Mirrors a High Courts' Rulings," *The New York Times* (October 1, 2006): 1–10.

13. Richard P. Caldarone, Brandice Canes-Wrone, and Tom S. Clark, "Partisan Labels and Democratic Accountability: An Analysis of State Supreme Court Abortion Decisions," *The Journal of Politics* 71 (April 2009), 560–73.

14. Melinda Gann Hall and Chris W. Bonneau, "Mobilizing Interest: The Effects of Money on Citizen Participation in State Supreme Court Elections," *American Journal of Political Science* 52(3) (2008): 457–70.

15. Brandice Canes-Wrones, Tom S. Clark, and Jason P. Kelly, "Judicial Selection and Death Penalty Decisions," *American Political Science Review* 108 (February, 2014): 23–39; Paul Brace and Brent D. Boyea, "State Public Opinion, the Death Penalty, and the Practice of Electing Judges," *American Journal of Political Science* 52(2) (April 2008): 360–72.15; *Republican Party of Minnesota v. White*, No. 01–521 (2000).

16. James P. Gibson and Gregory A. Caldeira, "Campaign Support, Conflicts of Interest, and Judicial Impartiality: Can Recusals Rescue the Legitimacy of Courts?" *The Journal of Politics* 74 (January 2012): 18–34.

17. *Republican Party of Minnesota v. White*, 536 US 765 - 2002 - Supreme Court (2002); *Citizens United v. Federal Election Commission*, No. 08-205 U.S. Supreme Court (January 21, 2010).

18. www.brennancenter.org, (October 23, 2013).

19. Liptak and Roberts, 2006.

20. Gibson and Caldeira, 2012; Stephen Ware, "Money, Politics, and Judicial Decisions: A Case Study of Arbitration Law in Alabama," *Journal of Law and Politics* 15 (Fall 1999): 645–86; Madhavi McCall, "The Politics of Judicial Elections: The Influence of Campaign Contributions on the Voting Patterns of Texas Supreme Court Justices," *Politics and Policy* 31 (June 2003): 314–33.

21. Maggie Clark, "Do Campaign Donations in Judicial Races Influence Court Decisions?" www.pewstates.org (June 11, 2013).

22. Liptak and Roberts, 2006; "The Best Judges Business Can Buy," *The New York Times* editorial, www.nytimes.com (accessed June 18, 2007).

23. www.brennancenter.org "The New Politics of Judicial Elections, Online," (February 27, 2015).

24. See Carrie Johnson, "Report: Too Much Money Going to State Court Races," www.npr.org (August 16, 2010); David B. Rottman and Roy A. Schotland, "2004 Judicial Elections," in *The Book of the States 2005* (Lexington, KY: Council of State Governments, 2005), pp. 305–308.

25. Kathleen Hunter, "Money Mattering More in Judicial Elections," www.lawforum.net (May 12, 2004): 1–3.

26. Adam Liptak, "Justices Tell Judges Not to Rule on Major Backers," www.nyt.com (June 9, 2009); Len Boselovic, "W. Va. Chief Justice Accused of Bias," www.post-gazette.com (January 15, 2008).

27. www.brennancenter.org, "The New Politics of Judicial Elections, Online," (accessed February 27, 2015).

28. As quoted in Sheila Kaplan, "Justice for Sale," *State Government: CQ's Guide to Current Issues and Activities, 1986–87* (Washington, D.C.: Congressional Quarterly Press, 1987), pp. 51–57.

29. Damon M. Cann, "Justice for Sale? Campaign Contributions and Judicial Decisionmaking," *State Politics and Policy Quarterly* 7 (Fall 2007): 281–97; Chris W. Bonneau, "Campaign Fundraising in State Supreme Court Elections."

30. William Glaberson, "States Take Steps to Rein in Excesses of Judicial Politicking," *The New York Times* (June 15, 2001): 1–4.

31. *Caperton v. A.T. Massey Coal Co.*, No. 08–22, U.S. Supreme Court, 2009.

32. Melinda Gann Hall, "State Supreme Courts in American Democracy: Probing the Myths of Judicial Reform," *American Political Science Review* 95 (June 2001): 315–30.

33. John Culver, "California Supreme Court Election: 'Rose Bird and the Supremes,'" *Comparative State Politics Newsletter* (February 1987): 13.

34. Steven D. Williams, "The 1996 Retention Election of Justice White," *Comparative State Politics* 17 (October 1996): 28–30.

35. Jan Biles, "State Supreme Court Justices Stave Off Ousting Campaign," cjonline.com (November 10, 2014); Mary Ellen Klas, "Fla. Supreme Court Justices Fight Back to Retain Seats, www.miamiherald.com (October 6, 2012).

36. Melinda Gann Hall, "Electoral Politics and Strategic Voting in State Supreme Courts," *Journal of Politics* 54 (1992): 427–46.

37. Hall, "State Supreme Courts in American Democracy," p. 319.

38. Melinda Gann Hall and Chris W. Bonneau, "Attack Advertising, the *White* Decision, and Voter Participation in State Supreme Court Elections," *Political Research Quarterly* 66 (1, 2013): 115–26.

39. Kathleen Bratton and Rorie Spill, "Existing Diversity and Judicial Selection: The Role of Appointment Method in Establishing Gender Diversity in State Supreme Courts," *Social Science Quarterly* 83 (June 2002): 504–18.

40. American Bar Association, *National Database on Judicial Diversity in State Courts,* www.abanet.org (accessed February 27, 2015).

41. Melinda Gann Hall, "Representation in State Supreme Courts: Evidence from the Terminal Term," *Political Research Quarterly* 67 (2, 2014): 335–46; Melinda Gann Hall, "Electoral Politics and Strategic Voting in State Supreme Courts," *Journal of Politics* 54 (1992): 427–46; Melinda Gann Hall, "Toward an Integrated Model of Judicial Voting Behavior," *American Politics Quarterly* 20 (1992): 147–68.

42. Hall, "State Judicial Politics," p. 136.

43. James P. Wenzel, Shaun Bowler, and David J. Lanoue, "Legislating from the State Bench: A Comparative Analysis of Judicial Activism," *American Politics Quarterly* 25 (July 1997): 363–79.

44. Todd Justice, "Supreme Court Flap Between Justice Ann Bradley and Justice David Prosser Leads to Investigation," www.postcrescent.com (June 28, 2011).

45. "New Questions about Rhode Island Chief Justice," *The New York Times* (October 3, 1993), section 1,

p. 22; "Ex-Top Judge Ends Rhode Island Appeal with a Guilty Plea," *The New York Times* (April 30, 1994), section 1, p. 12; "Justice in Impeachment Inquiry Quits in Rhode Island," *The New York Times* (May 29, 1986), p. A14.

46. Walter Schaefer, "Precedent and Policy: Judicial Opinions and Decision Making," in David M. O'Brien, ed., *Judges on Judging: Views from the Bench* (Washington, D.C.: Congressional Quarterly Press, 2004), p. 108.

47. Brent D. Boyea, "Does Seniority Matter? The Conditional Influences of State Methods of Judicial Retention," *Social Science Quarterly* 91 (1) (2010):209–27.

48. Hall, "Electoral Politics and Strategic Voting."

49. Melinda Gann Hall, "Justices as Representatives: Elections and Judicial Politics in the American States," *American Politics Quarterly* 23 (October 1995).

50. Jake Dear and Edward W. Jessen, "Followed Rates and Leading State Cases, 1940–2005," *Davis Law Review* 41 (2007): 683.

51. S. Fernando Rodriguez, Theodore R. Curry, and Gand Lee, "Gender Differences in Criminal Sentencing: Do Effects Vary across Violent, Property, and Drug Offenses?" *Social Science Quarterly* 87 (June 2006): 318–39.

52. Gerald S. Gryski, Eleanor C. Main, and William J. Dixon, "Models of State High Court Decision Making in Sex Discrimination Cases," *Journal of Politics* 48 (February 1986): 143–55; Donald R. Songer and Kelley A. Crews-Meyer, "Does Judge Gender Matter? Decision Making in State Supreme Courts," *Social Science Quarterly* 81 (September 2000): 750–62.

53. Chris W. Bonneau and Heather Marie Rice, "Impartial Judges? Institutional Context and U.S. State Supreme Courts," *State Politics and Policy Quarterly* 9 (4) (2009): 381–403; Rodriguez, Curry, and Lee, "Gender Differences in Criminal Sentencing."

54. Stephanie A. Lindquist and Frank B. Cross, *Measuring Judicial Activism* (New York: Oxford University Press, 2010); John J. Scheb, III, Terry Bowen, and Gary Anderson, "Ideology, Role Orientations, and Behavior in the State Courts of Last Resort," *American Politics Quarterly* 19 (July 1991): 324–35.

55. Ibid.

56. Laura Langer and Paul Brace, "The Preemptive Power of State Supreme Courts: Adoption of Abortion and Death Penalty Legislation," *Policy Studies Journal* 33 (2005): 317–39.

57. Michael Cooper, "Courts Upend Budgets as States Look for Savings," www.nytimes.com (June 6, 2011).

58. See Adam Skaggs and Maria da Silva, "America's Judiciary: Courting Disaster," www.latimes.com (July 8, 2011), citing study by the National Center for State Courts.

59. Ibid.

60. John Gramlich, "Court Cuts Trigger Blunt Warnings," www.stateline.org (February 18, 2009).

61. David Rothman and Jesse Rutledge, "Facing Down a Budget Crisis," p. 283.

62. National Center for State Courts, *Examining the Work of State Courts: An Analysis of 2009 State Caseload Statistics*, www.courtstatistics.org (accessed April 17, 2012); Melinda Gann Hall, "State Courts: Politics and the Judicial Process," pp. 229–255, in Virginia Gray, Russell L. Hanson, and Thad Kousser, eds., *Politics in the American States*, 10th ed. (Thousand Oaks, CA: CQ Press, 2013).

63. Ibid.

64. www.ncsc.org/Topics/Court-Management/ Performance-Measurement/Resource-Guide.aspx (accessed April 17, 2012).

65. Sharon Paynter and Richard C. Kearney, "Who Watches the Watchmen? Evaluating Judicial Performance in the States," *Administration and Society* (1 (January) 2010).

66. Ibid.

CHAPTER 10 LOCAL GOVERNMENT: TYPES AND FUNCTIONS

1. Illinois Government News Network, "Governor Names Members of Local Government and Unfunded Mandates Task Force," www3. illinois.gov/PressReleases/ShowPressRelease. cfm?SubjectID=1&RecNum=12991 (March 13, 2015).

2. John Nalbandian, et al., "Contemporary Challenges in Local Government," *Public Administration Review* 73 (July/August 2013): 567–74.

3. John Kincaid, "Municipal Perspectives on Federalism," unpublished manuscript, 1987.

4. Dennis Hale, "The City as Polity and Economy," *Polity* 17 (Winter 1984): 205–24.

5. Kincaid, "Municipal Perspectives," p. 56.

6. Justin M. Ross, Joshua C. Hall, and William G. Resh, "Frictions in Polycentric Administration with Noncongruent Borders: Evidence from Ohio School District Class Sizes," *Journal of Public Administration Research and Theory* 24 (July 2014): 623–49.

7. "Local Governments and Public School Systems by Type and State: 2007," *2007 Census of Governments*, www.census.gov/govs/cog/GovOrgTab03ss.html (August 9, 2009).

8. Council for Excellence in Government 2000, www .excelgov.org (July 9, 2003).

9. Christopher Hoene, Mark Baldassare, and Michael Shires, "The Development of Counties as Municipal Governments," *Urban Affairs Review* 37 (March 2002): 575–91.

10. Dale Krane, Platon N. Rigos, and Melvin B. Hill Jr., *Home Rule in America: A Fifty State Handbook* (Washington, D.C.: Congressional Quarterly Press, 2001).

11. Alan Greenblatt, "New Clout in a Big County," *Governing* 20 (May 2007): 22–23.

12. J. Edwin Benton, "The Impact of Structural Reform on County Government Service Provision," *Social Science Quarterly* 84 (December 2003): 858–74.

13. Jayce Farmer, "County Government Choices for Redistributive Services," *Urban Affairs Review* 47 (January 2011): 60–83.

14. Chris Tausanovitch and Christopher Warshaw, "Representation in Municipal Government," *American Political Science Review* 108 (August 2014): 605–41.

15. "Counties Out of Date," *State Legislatures* 17 (March 1991): 17.

16. Jerome Sherman, "6 Elected Row Officers Become 3 Appointed," *Pittsburgh Post–Gazette*, www.post-gazette.com (May 18, 2005).

17. See Olesya Tkacheva, "New Cities, Local Officials, and Municipal Incorporation Laws: A Supply-Side Model of City Formation," *Journal of Urban Affairs*. 30 (2008): 155–74.

18. Kimberly L. Nelson and James H. Svara, "Adaptation of Models versus Variations in Form: Classifying Structures of City Government," *Urban Affairs Review* 45 (March 2010): 544–62.

19. Kimberly L. Nelson and Karl Nollenberger, "Conflict and Cooperation in Municipalities: Do Variations in Form of Government Have an Effect?" *Urban Affairs Review* 47 (September 2011): 696–720

20. Victor S. DeSantis and Tari Renner, "City Government Structures: An Attempt at Clarification," *State and Local Government Review* 34 (Spring 2002): 95–104; H. George Frederickson, Gary A. Johnson, and Curtis H. Wood, *The Adapted City: Institutional Dynamics and Structural Change* (Armonk. NY: M. E. Sharpe, 2004); Megan Mullin, Gillian Peele, and Bruce E. Cain, "City Caesars? Institutional Structure and Mayoral Success in Three California Cities," *Urban Affairs Review* 40 (September 2004): 19–43; Cheon Geun Choi, Richard C. Feiock, and Jungah Bae, "The Adoption and Abandonment of Council-Manager Government," *Public Administration Review* (September/October 2013): 727–36.

21. Jered Carr and Shanthi Karuppusamy, "Beyond Ideal Types of Municipal Structure," *American Review of Public Administration*, 39 (2009): 304–21.

22. Brian M. Green and Yda Schreuder, "Growth, Zoning and Neighborhood Organizations," *Journal of Urban Affairs* 13, no. 1 (1991): 97–110.

23. Arnold Fleischmann and Carol A. Pierannunzi, "Citizens, Development Interests, and Local Land-Use Regulation," *Journal of Politics* 52 (August 1990): 838–53; Abigail York, et al., "Zoning and Land Use: A Tale of Incompatibility and Environmental Injustice in Early Phoenix," *Journal of Urban Affairs* 36 (December 2014): 833–53

24. Jonathan T. Rothwell and Douglas A. Massey, "Density Zoning and Class Segregation in U.S. Metropolitan Areas," *Social Science Quarterly* 91 (December 2010): 1123–43.

25. Mary Edwards, "Annexation: A Winner-Take-All Process?" *State and Local Government Review* 31 (Fall 1999): 221–31; Bev Wilson and Mary M. Edwards, "Annexation and Ethnicity in the American Midwest," *Urban Affairs Review* 50 (May 2014): 417–47

26. Rex L. Facer II, "Annexation Activity and State Law in the United States," *Urban Affairs Review* 41 (May 2006): 697–709. See also David Rusk, "Annexation and the Fiscal Fate of Cities," *Brookings Institution Survey Series* (August 2006).

27. Rob Gurwitt, "Not-So-Smart Growth," *Governing* 14 (October 2000): 34–38.

28. "Cities with 100,000 or More Population in 2000 Ranked by Land Area," *County and City Data Book 2000*, www.census.gov/statab/ccdb/cityrank.htm (January 17, 2006).

29. Christopher W. Hoene and Michael A. Pagano. *City Fiscal Conditions in 2009* (Washington, D.C.: National League of Cities, 2009).

30. Susan Welch and Timothy Bledsoe, *Urban Reform and Its Consequences: A Study in Representation* (Chicago: University of Chicago Press, 1988).

31. Chandler Davidson and Bernard Grofman, "The Effect of Municipal Election Structure on Black Representation in Eight Southern States," in Davidson and Grofman, eds., *Quiet Revolution in the South* (Princeton, NJ: Princeton University Press, 1994), pp. 301–21.

32. Curtis Wood, "Voter Turnout in City Elections," *Urban Affairs Review* 39 (November 2002): 209–31.

33. Welch and Bledsoe, *Urban Reform and Its Consequences*; Jeffrey D. Greene, "Reformism and Public Policies in American Cities Revisited," paper presented at the annual meeting of the Southern Political Science Association, Atlanta, Georgia, 2000.

34. Kenneth J. Meier et al., "Structural Choices and Representational Biases: The Post-Election Color of Representation," *American Journal of Political Science* 49 (October 2005): 758–68.

35. Richard L. Cole and Delbert A. Taebel, "Cumulative Voting in Local Elections: Lessons from the Alamogordo Experience," *Social Science Quarterly* 73 (March 1992): 194–201.

36. Victor S. DeSantis and David Hill, "Citizen Participation in Local Politics: Evidence from New England Town Meetings," *State and Local Government Review* 36 (Fall 2004): 172.

37. Melissa Conradi, "But Definitely Not St. Ventura," *Governing* 14 (January 2001): 16.

38. Dave Drury, "Town Meetings: An Enduring Image Changes," *Hartford Courant* (September 22, 1991), pp. A1, A10–A11. See also David K. Hamilton. "Township Government: A Tale of One State," *National Civic Review* (2008): 37–49.

39. Kathryn A. Foster, *The Political Economy of Special Purpose Government* (Washington, D.C.: Georgetown University Press, 1997).

40. U.S. Bureau of the Census, "Number of Special Districts," www.census.gov/govs/go/number_of_special_districts_by_county.html (Accessed May 5, 2015).

41. John C. Bollens, *Special District Governments in the United States* (Berkeley: University of California Press, 1957).

42. Larita Killian and Dagney Faulk, "Policy Brief: Special Districts and Local Government Reform," Center for Business and Economic Research, Ball State University (March 2012).

43. Jered B. Carr and Jayce Farmer, "Contingent Effects of Municipal and County TELs on Special District Usage in the United States," *Publius: The Journal of Federalism* 41 (Fall 2011): 709–33.

44. Barbara Coyle McCabe, "Special District Formation among the States," *State and Local Government Review* 32 (Spring 2000): 121–31.

45. Michael A. Molloy, "Local Special Districts and Public Accountability," paper presented at the annual meeting of the Midwest Political Science Association, Chicago, Illinois, 2000. See also Nicholas Bauroth, "The Effect of Limiting Participation in Special District Elections to Property Owners: A Research Note," *Public Budgeting & Finance* 27 (2007): 71–88.

46. Nancy Burns, *The Formation of American Local Governments* (New York: Oxford University Press, 1994).

47. Christopher R. Berry, *Imperfect Union: Representation and Taxation in Multilevel Governments* (New York: Cambridge, 2009).

48. Foster, *The Political Economy of Special Purpose Government.*

49. Alan Ehrenhalt, "The Consolidation Divide," *Governing* 16 (March 2003): 6.

50. Jason A. Grissom and James R. Harrington, "Local Legislative Professionalism," *American Politics Research* 41 (January 2013): 76–98.

51. Tausanovitch and Warshaw, "Representation in Municipal Government."

52. Frank Hendriks, "Understanding Good Urban Governance: Essentials, Shifts, and Values," *Urban Affairs Review* 50 (July 2014): 553–76.

53. "Announcing the 2014 All-American City Award Winners," http://ncdd.org/15300 (accessed March 31, 2015).

CHAPTER 11 LOCAL LEADERSHIP AND GOVERNANCE: CONTINUITY AND CHANGE

1. Mike Kanin, "What's Left," *The Texas Observer*, http://www.texasobserver.org/whats-left/ (December 2, 2013); "Districts Would Better Serve Austin's Diverse Voices," *Austin American Statesman*, www.statesman.com/news/news/opinion/districts-would-better-serve-austins-diverse-voice/nSwCg/ (November 3, 2012).

2. Susan E. Howell and William P. McLean, "Performance and Race in Evaluating Minority Mayors," *Public Opinion Quarterly* 65 (2001): 321–43.

3. Mark Schneider, "Public Entrepreneurs as Agents of Change in American Government," *Urban News* 9 (Spring 1995): 1.

4. Deserai Anderson Crow, "Local Media and Experts: Sources of Environmental Policy Initiation?" *Policy Studies Journal* 38 (February 2010): 143–64.

5. Ryan Holeywell, "Indy's Clean and Green Fleet," *Governing* (March 2013), p. 19.

6. Chris Tausanovitch and Christopher Warshaw, "Representation in Municipal Government," *American Political Science Review* 108 (August 2014): 605–41.

7. Gaetano Mosca, *The Ruling Class* (New York: McGraw-Hill, 1939).

8. Robert S. Lynd and Helen M. Lynd, *Middletown* (New York: Harcourt Brace and World, 1929); Robert S. Lynd and Helen M. Lynd, *Middletown in Transition* (New York: Harcourt Brace and World, 1937).

9. Floyd Hunter, *Community Power Structure* (Chapel Hill, NC: University of North Carolina Press, 1953); Floyd Hunter, *Community Power Succession* (Chapel Hill, NC: University of North Carolina Press, 1980).

10. Harvey Molotch, "Strategies and Constraints of Growth Elites," in Scott Cummings, ed., *Business Elites and Urban Development* (Albany, NY: SUNY Press, 1988), pp. 25–47.

11. Robert Dahl, *Who Governs?* (New Haven, CT: Yale University Press, 1961).

12. Paul Schumaker, "Group Involvements in City Politics and Pluralist Theory," *Urban Affairs Review* 49 (March 2013): 254–81. See also Eric Heberlig, Suzanne Leland, and Dustin Read, "Local Politics, Organized Interests, and Land-Use Policy," *Urban Affairs Review* 50 (November 2014): 890–903.

13. G. William Domhoff, *Who Really Rules?* (Santa Monica, CA: Goodyear, 1978). For a different perspective, see Douglas W. Rae, *City: Urbanism and Its End* (New Haven, CT: Yale University Press, 2003).

14. Juliet Gainsborough, "A Tale of Two Cities: Civic Culture and Public Policy in Miami," *Journal of Urban Affairs* 30 (2008): 431.

15. Monica Davey, "Recession Shadowing Chicago Bid for Games," *The New York Times*, www.nytimes.com (July 26, 2009).

16. Clarence N. Stone, *Regime Politics: Governing Atlanta, 1948–1988* (Lawrence: University Press of Kansas, 1989), p. 3.

17. Clarence N. Stone, "Systemic Power in Community Decision Making," *American Political Science Review* 74 (December 1980): 978–90.

18. Ibid., p. 989.

19. Peter Burns and Matthew O. Thomas, "The Failure of the Nonregime: How Katrina Exposed New Orleans as a Regimeless City," *Urban Affairs Review* 41 (March 2006): 517–27.

20. J. M. Ferris, "The Role of the Nonprofit Sector in a Self-Governing Society," *Voluntas* 9 (1998): 137–51.

21. Richard C. Hula and Cynthia Jackson-Elmoore, "Governing Nonprofits and Local Political Processes," *Urban Affairs Review* 36 (January 2001): 324–58.

22. Ibid., p. 326. See also Kelly LeRoux, "Nonprofits as Civic Intermediaries," *Urban Affairs Review* 42 (January 2007): 410–22.

23. Christopher A. Cooper, Anthony J. Nownes, and Steven Roberts, "Perceptions of Power: Interest Groups in Local Politics," *State and Local Government Review* 37, no. 3 (2005): 206–16.

24. William Yardley, "After Eminent Domain Victory, Dispute Project Goes Nowhere," *The New York Times*, www.nytimes.com (November 21, 2005).

25. Sandra Day O'Connor, dissenting, *Kelo et al. v. City of New London et al.*, No. 04-108, www.laws.findlaw.com/us/000/04-108.html (June 23, 2005).

26. Elizabeth Kolbert, "The Un-Communicator," *The New Yorker* (March 1, 2004): 38–42.

27. Jessica Garrison and Patrick McGreevy, "Parks to File for Mayoral Race," *Los Angeles Times*, www.latimes.com (April 7, 2004).

28. Rob Gurwitt, "The Lure of the Strong Mayor," *Governing* 6 (July 1993): 36–41; Terrell Blodgett, "Beware the Lure of the 'Strong' Mayor," *Public Management* 76 (January 1994): 6–11. See also Tod Newcombe, "The Rise of Cities and the Strong Mayors Who Run Them," *Governing* (September 2013), p. 23.

29. David R. Morgan and Sheilah S. Watson, "The Effects of Mayoral Power on Urban Fiscal Policy," paper presented at the annual meeting of the American Political Science Association, New York City, 1994. See also, R. Douglas Arnold and Nicholas Carnes, "Holding Mayors Accountable: New York's Executives from Koch to Bloomberg," *American Journal of Political Science* 56 (October 2012): 949–63.

30. W. John Moore, "From Dreamers to Doers," *National Journal* (February 13, 1988): 372–77; Daniel J. Hopkins and Katherine T. McCabe, "After It's Too Later: Estimating the Policy Impacts of Black Mayoralties in U.S. Cities," *American Politics Research* 40 (July 2012): 665–700.

31. Cory Booker, "Fighting for Newark's Future" (audio), www.corybooker.com/main/cfm (July 5, 2006).

32. Huey L. Perry, "Deracialization as an Analytical Construct in American Urban Politics," *Urban Affairs Quarterly* 27 (December 1991): 181–91; Nicholas O. Alonzie, "The Promise of Urban Democracy: Big City Black Mayoral Service in the Early 1990s," *Urban Affairs Review* 35 (January 2000): 422–34.

33. Mary E. Summers and Philip A. Klinkner, "The Daniels Election in New Haven and the Failure of the Deracialization Hypothesis," *Urban Affairs Quarterly* 27 (December 1991): 202–15.

34. Robert M. Stein, Stacy G. Ulbig, and Stephanie Shirley Post, "Voting for Minority Candidates in Multiracial/Multiethnic Communities," *Urban Affairs Review* 41 (November 2005): 157–81.

35. John Tedesco, "In Mayoral Election, San Antonio Was a City Divided," *San Antonio Express-News*, www.expressnews.com/news/local/article/In-mayoral-election-San-Antonio-was-a-city-6256780.php (May 12, 2015).

36. Several of these studies are summarized in Susan A. MacManus and Charles S. Bullock III, "Women and Racial/Ethnic Minorities in Mayoral and Council Positions," *The Municipal Year Book 1993* (Washington, D.C.: ICMA, 1993), pp. 70–84.

37. Mirya R. Holman, "Sex and the City: Female Leaders and Spending on Social Welfare Programs in U.S. Municipalities," *Journal of Urban Affairs* 36 (October 2014): 701–15.

38. "What Makes a Great Mayor?" *Talk of the Nation*, www.npr.org (December 10, 2003).

39. "From Vision to Reality: How City Administrations Succeed in the Long Haul," www.civic-strategies.com (September 30, 2003).

40. John Buntin, "Does Eric Garcetti Have a Big Enough Vision for L.A.?" *Governing* www.governing.com/topics/mgmt/gov-eric-garcetti-los-angeles-mayor.html (August 2014).

41. Clifford J. Wirth and Michael L. Vasu, "Ideology and Decision Making for American City Managers," *Urban Affairs Quarterly* 22 (March 1987): 454–74.

42. Martin Vanacour, "Promoting the Community's Future," in Charldean Newell, ed., *The Effective Local Government Manager*, 3rd ed. (Washington, D.C.: International City/County Management Association, 2004), pp. 84–85. See also Timothy

B. Krebs and John P. Pelissero, "Urban Managers and Public Policy: Do Institutional Arrangements Influence Decisions to Initiate Policy?" *Urban Affairs Review* 45 (January 2010): 391–411.

43. James H. Svara, "Conflict and Cooperation in Elected-Administrative Relations in Large Council-Manager Cities," *State and Local Government Review* 31 (Fall 1999): 173–89. See also James H. Svara, "Exploring Structures and Institutions in City Government," *Public Administration Review* 65 (2005): 500–506.

44. Tansu Demir and Christopher G. Reddick, "Understanding Shared Roles in Policy and Administration: An Empirical Study of Council-Manager Relations," *Public Administration Review* 72 (July/August 2012): 526–36.

45. Douglas J. Watson and Wendy L. Hassett, "Career Paths of City Managers in America's Largest Council-Manager Cities," *Public Administration Review* 64 (March 2004): 192–99.

46. Mark M. Levin, "How to Work with Elected Officials," *Public Management* (December 2008): 4–5.

47. H. George Frederickson, Gary A. Johnson, and Curtis H. Wood, *The Adapted City: Institutional Dynamics and Structural Change* (Armonk, NY: M. E. Sharpe, 2004). See also Alan Ehrenhalt, "The Mayor-Manager Merger," *Governing* 20 (October 2006): 9–10.

48. Larry Azevedo, as quoted in Alan Ehrenhalt, "How a Liberal Government Came to Power in a Conservative Suburb," *Governing* 1 (March 1988): 51–56.

49. Kenneth Prewitt, *The Recruitment of Political Leaders: A Study of Citizen-Politicians* (Indianapolis, IN: Bobbs-Merrill, 1970).

50. Melissa Marschall, Anirudh V. Ruhil, and Paru Shah, "The New Racial Calculus: Electoral Institutions and Black Representation in Local Legislatures," *American Journal of Political Science* 54 (January 2010): 107–124.

51. "State and Local Officials of Color," *Gender and Multicultural Leadership Project*, www.gmcl.org/maps/national/state.htm (August 10, 2009).

52. Joshua G. Behr, *Race, Ethnicity and the Politics of Redistricting* (Albany, NY: SUNY Press, 2004); Jessica Trounstine and Melody D. Valdini, "The Context Matters: The Effects of Single-Member versus At-Large Districts on City Council Diversity," *American Journal of Political Science*, 52 (July 2008): 554–69; Melissa J. Marschall, Anirudh V.S. Ruhil, and Paru R. Shah, "The New Racial Calculus: Electoral Institutions and Black Representation in Local Legislatures," *American Journal of Political Science* 54 (January 2010): 107–24.

53. Bari Anhalt, "Minority Representation and the Substantive Representation of Interests," paper presented at the annual meeting of the American Political Science Association, San Francisco, California, 1996; James H. Svara, "Two Decades of Continuity and Change in American City Councils," (National League of Cities, 2003).

54. Manning Marable, "Building Coalitions among Communities of Color," in James Jennings, ed., *Blacks, Latinos, and Asians in Urban America* (Westport, CT: Praeger, 1994), pp. 29–43.

55. Paula D. McClain and Steven C. Tauber, "Racial Minority Group Relations in a Multiracial Society," in Michael Jones-Correa, ed., *Governing American Cities: Immigrants and Inter-Ethnic Coalitions, Competition, and Conflict* (New York: Russell Sage Foundation, 2001).

56. Christian Collett, "Bloc Voting, Polarization, and the Panethnic Hypothesis: The Case of Little Saigon," *Political Research Quarterly* 67 (August 2005): 907–33.

57. James Svara, "Council Profile: More Diversity, Demands, Frustration," *Nation's Cities Weekly* 14 (November 18, 1991).

58. Susan Adams Beck, "Rethinking Municipal Governance: *Gender Distinctions on Local Councils*," in Debra L. Dodson, ed., *Gender and Policymaking: Studies of Women in Office* (New Brunswick, NJ: Center for the American Woman and Politics, 1991), p. 103.

59. "Women and Leadership," Pew Research Center, www.pewsocialtrends.org/2015/01/14/women-and-leadership/ (January 14, 2015).

60. "Openly LGBT Appointed and Elected Officials," *Gay and Lesbian Partnership Institute*, www.glli.org/out_officials/officials_map (August 13, 2009).

61. James W. Button, Kenneth D. Wald, and Barbara A. Rienzo, "The Election of Openly Gay Public Officials in American Communities," *Urban Affairs Review* 35 (November 1999): 188–209.

62. Jessica Trounstine, "Evidence of a Local Incumbency Advantage," *Legislative Studies Quarterly* 36 (May 2011): 255–80.

63. Kimberly L. Nelson and Karl Nollenberger, "Conflict and Cooperation in Municipalities: Do Variations in Form of Government Have an Effect?" *Urban Affairs Review* 47 (September 2011): 696–720. See also Brianne Heidbreder, et al., "Determinants of Policy Conflict in Michigan Municipalities," *State and Local Government Review* 43 (April 2011): 32–45.

64. Craig M. Burnett and Vladimir Kogan, "Local Logrolling? Assessing the Impact of Legislative Districting in Los Angeles," *Urban Affairs Review* 50 (September 2014): 648–71.

65. Rob Gurwitt, "Are City Councils a Relic of the Past?" *Governing* 16 (April 2003): 20–24.

66. Meghan E. Irons, "Honeymoon Over for Walsh, Council," *Boston Globe* www.bostonglobe.com/metro/2014/11/09/clashes-highlight-tensions-between-mayor-walsh-and-council/NO3ff9DEKNkvb9VoDFWQ2N/story.html (November 9, 2014).

67. Jack E. White, "Bright City Lights," *Time* (November 1, 1993): p. 32.

68. Michael Bloomberg, as quoted in "Observer," *Governing* 19 (July 2006), p. 18.

69. Josh Goodman, "Out of the Blue," *Governing* 20 (October 2007): 40.

CHAPTER 12 STATE-LOCAL RELATIONS: FIFTY DIFFERENT SYSTEMS

1. Alan Greenblatt, "Discrimination Law," *Governing*, www.governing.com/topics/politics/gov-arkansas-discrimination-gay.html (May 13, 2015).

2. Steven D. Gold, "NCSL State-Local Task Force: The First Year," *Intergovernmental Perspective* 13 (Winter 1987): 11.

3. *Merriam v. Moody's Executors*, 25 Iowa 163, 170 (1868). Dillon's rule was first written in the case of *City of Clinton v. Cedar Rapids and Missouri Railroad Co.* (1868).

4. Jeffrey I. Chapman, "Local Government Autonomy and Fiscal Stress: The Case of California Counties," *State and Local Government Review* 35 (Winter 2003): 15–25.

5. U.S. Advisory Commission on Intergovernmental Relations, *The Organization of Local Public Economies* (Washington, D.C.: ACIR, December 1987), p. 54. See also Jesse J. Richardson, Jr., "Dillon's Rule Is from Mars, Home Rule Is from Venus: Local Government Autonomy and the Rules of Statutory Construction," *Publius: The Journal of Federalism* 41 (Fall 2011): 662–85.

6. Peter J. May, "State Regulatory Roles: Choices in the Regulation of Building Safety," *State and Local Government Review* 29 (Spring 1997): 70–80.

7. Dale Krane, Platon N. Rigos, and Melvin B. Hill, Jr., *Home Rule in America: A Fifty-State Handbook* (Washington, D.C.: Congressional Quarterly Press, 2001).

8. As quoted in Laura Vozzella and David Nitkin, "City Rejects State Plan, Offers Own School Loan," *Baltimore Sun* (March 9, 2004): 1.

9. Ann O'M. Bowman and Richard C. Kearney, "Second Order Devolution: Who's Got the Power," paper presented at the annual meeting of the Midwest Political Science Association, Chicago, 2010.

10. Ann O'M. Bowman and Richard C. Kearney, "Easy Pickings: State Legislatures Look to Their Local Governments," paper presented at the 12th Annual State Politics and Policy Conference, Houston, 2012.

11. Christopher Swope, "States Go for the Biotech Gold," *Governing* 17 (March 2004): 46.

12. David K. Hamilton, David Y. Miller, and Jerry Paytas, "Exploring Horizontal and Vertical Dimensions of the Governing of Metropolitan Regions," *Urban Affairs Review* 40 (November 2004): 147–82.

13. David Kocieniewski and Eric Lipton, "Two States Get High Marks for Five-Day Antiterrorism Exercise," *The New York Times*, www.nytimes.com (April 9, 2005).

14. "State Mandates on Municipalities: Actions in 2014," www.ct.gov/opm/lib/opm/2014_ACIR_Mandates_Report.pdf (accessed May 5, 2015).

15. Ann O'M. Bowman and Richard C. Kearney, "Second-Order Devolution: Data and Doubt," *Publius: The Journal of Federalism* 41 (Fall 2011): 563–85.

16. Lawrence J. Grossback, "The Problem of State-Imposed Mandates: Lessons from Minnesota's Local Governments," *State and Local Government Review* 34 (Fall 2002): 191.

17. Richard L. Cole, "The Current Status and Roles of State Advisory Commissions on Intergovernmental Relations in the U.S. Federal System," *Public Administration Review* 71 (Mar/Apr 2011): 190–95.

18. Bruce Katz, *Smart Growth: The Future of the American Metropolis?* (Washington, D.C.: The Brookings Institution, 2002), p. 2.

19. William Fulton and Paul Shigley, "Operation Desert Sprawl," *Governing* 12 (August 1999): 16.

20. Christina McCarroll, "Measuring the Cost of Growth," *Christian Science Monitor* (February 6, 2002): 13.

21. Moon-Gi Jeong, "Local Choices for Development Impact Fees," *Urban Affairs Review* 41 (2006): 338–57.

22. "3 Big States Lead Record Vote for Land Conservation," The Trust for Public Land, www.tpl.org/media-room/3-big-states-lead-record-vote-land-conservation (November 5, 2014).

23. Jayson T. Blair, "Maryland Draws Line against Sprawl," *Boston Globe* (December 7, 1997): A26.

24. Christopher Swope, "McGreevey's Magic Map," *Governing* 16 (May 2003): 45–48.

25. Iver Peterson, "War on Sprawl in New Jersey Hits a Wall," *The New York Times* (October 21, 2003): A15.

26. Christopher R. Conte, "The Boys of Sprawl," *Governing* 13 (May 2000): 28–33. See also Christopher Hawkins, "Electoral Support for Community Growth Management Policy," *Social Science Quarterly* 92 (March 2011): 268–84.

27. Alan Ehrenhalt, "Breaking the Density Deadlock," *Governing* 20 (March 2007): 11–12.

28. Robert Jay Dilger, "Residential Community Associations: Issues, Impacts, and Relevance for Local Government," *State and Local Government Review* 23 (Winter 1991): 17–23; Barbara Coyle McCabe, "Homeowners Associations as Private Governments: What We Know, What We Don't Know, and Why It Matters," *Public Administration Review* 71 (August 2011): 535–42; Jill L. Tao and Barbara C. McCabe, "Where a Hollow State Casts No Shadow: Homeowner Associations in Local Governments," *American Review of Public Administration* 42 (November 2012): 678–94.

29. Evan McKenzie, *Privatopia: Homeowners' Associations and the Rise of Residential Private Government* (New Haven, CT: Yale University Press, 1996).

30. Jered B. Carr and Richard C. Feiock, "Who Becomes Involved in City-County Consolidation?" *State and Local Government Review* 34 (Spring 2002): 78–94.

31. H. V. Savitch and Ronald K. Vogel, "Suburbs without a City: Power and City-County Consolidation," *Urban Affairs Review* 39 (July 2004): 758–90; Benedict Jimenez and Rebecca Hendrick, "Is Government Consolidation the Answer?" *State and Local Government Review* 42 (December 2010): 258–70.

32. Alan Greenblatt, "Anatomy of a Merger," *Governing* 16 (December 2002): 20–25.

33. Ronald J. Oakerson, *Governing Local Political Economies: Creating the Civic Metropolis* (Oakland, CA: Institute for Contemporary Studies, 1999).

34. David Rusk, *Cities without Suburbs* (Washington, D.C.: Woodrow Wilson Center Press, 1993), p. 5.

35. Daniel Kemmis, as quoted in Neal R. Peirce, "Missoula's 'Citistate' Claim Marks a New Way to Define Regions," *The News & Observer* (July 1, 1993): 14A

36. Randolph P. Smith, "Region Idea Works, Oregon City Says," *Richmond Times-Dispatch* (October 30, 1994): A1, A18.

37. Myron Orfield, *American Metropolitics: The New Suburban Reality* (Washington, D.C.: The Brookings Institution, 2002).

38. Margaret Weir, Harold Wolman, and Todd Swanstrom, "The Calculus of Coalitions: Cities,

Suburbs, and the Metropolitan Agenda," *Urban Affairs Review* 40 (July 2005): 730–60.

39. James F. Wolf and Tara Kolar Bryan, "Identifying the Capacities of Regional Councils of Government," *State and Local Government Review* 41 (2009): 61–68.

40. Arnab Chakraborty, "Scenario Planning for Effective Regional Governance: Promises and Limitations," *State and Local Government Review* 42 (August 2010): 156–67.

41. James F. Wolf and Margaret Fenwick, "How Metropolitan Planning Organizations Incorporate Land Use Issues in Regional Transportation Planning," *State and Local Government Review* 35 (Spring 2003): 123–31. See also Alan Ehrenhalt, "Ready-To-Go Regionalism," *Governing* 22 (May 2009): 11–12.

42. David S. T. Matkin and George Frederickson, "Metropolitan Governance: Institutional Roles and Interjurisdictional Cooperation," *Journal of Urban Affairs* 31 (2009): 45–66.

43. Richard Feiock, "Metropolitan Governance and Institutional Collective Action," *Urban Affairs Review* 44 (2009): 338–57.

44. Mara S. Sidney, *Unfair Housing: How National Policy Shapes Community Action* (Lawrence: University Press of Kansas, 2003).

45. *Beyond Shelter: Building Communities of Opportunity* (Washington, D.C.: U.S. Department of Housing and Urban Development, 1996).

46. Zach Patton, "Thinking Small," *Governing* (May 2011): 36–41.

47. Mike Maciag, "Gentrification in America Report," *Governing*, www.governing.com/gov-data/census/gentrification-in-cities-governing-report.html (February 2015).

48. "Municipalities Need $300B in Sewer, Water Work," *Governing* www.governing.com/news/local (February 9, 2012).

49. Liz Farmer, "Obama Proposed P3 Tool to Help States Finance Infrastructure," *Governing*, www.governing.com/topics/transportation-infrastructure/gov-obama-sotu-financial-tool.html (January 21, 2015).

50. Stephen Goldsmith, "Creative Mayors and the Infrastructure Puzzle," *Governing* www.governing.com/templates (October 9, 2011).

51. Hugh Bartling, "Private Governance and Public Opinion in a Company Town: The Case of Celebration, Florida," paper presented at the annual meeting of the Midwest Political Science Association, Chicago, Illinois, 2000. See also Bruce Podobnik, "Assessing the Social and Environmental Achievements of New Urbanism: Evidence from Portland, Oregon," *Journal of Urbanism* 4 (July 2011): 105–26.

52. Peter T. Kilborn, "Boom in Economy Skips Towns on the Plains," *The New York Times* (July 2, 2000): A12.

53. "The Great Plains Drain," *The Economist* (January 19, 2007): 35.

54. Gillian B. White, "Rural America's Silent Housing Crisis," *The Atlantic*, www.theatlantic.com/business/archive/2015/01/rural-americas-silent-housing-crisis/384885/ (January 28, 2015).

55. Jim Seroka, "Community Growth and Administrative Capacity," *National Civic Review* 77 (January/February 1988): 45.

56. Steve Piper, Marquette Development Company, Inc., interview (August 14, 2009).

57. Patrik Jonsson, "North Carolina's Gambit to Bring Internet Age to Rural Areas," *Christian Science Monitor* (July 1, 2004).

58. Kristin Miller, "Is Rural America a Thing of the Past?" PBS NewsHour, www.pbs.org/newshour/updates/rural-america-thing-past/ (March 23, 2014).

59. Arthur Holst, "Review of Local Government and the States: Autonomy, Politics, and Policy," *Publius* 35 (Fall 2005): 644–45.

60. Christopher Conte, "Dry Spell," *Governing* 16 (March 2003): 20–24.

61. George Pataki, "Governor Pataki Offers $1 Billion Plan to Help Local Governments," Press Release, January 10, 1997.

62. Patrick McGreevy, "Cities, Counties Pay Price for Capital Clout," *Los Angeles Times,* www.latimes.com/news/local (September 12, 2007).

CHAPTER 13 TAXING AND SPENDING: WHERE THE MONEY COMES FROM AND WHERE IT GOES

1. Monica Davey and Mary Williams Walsh, "Billions in Debt, Detroit Tumbles into Insolvency," www.nytimes.com (July 18, 2013)

2. Monica Davey and Mary Williams Walsh, "Plan to exit Bankruptcy is Approved for Detroit," www.nytimes.com (November 7, 2014).

3. U.S. Bureau of the Census, www.census.gov (accessed March 19, 2015).

4. www.taxfoundation.org, *Facts and Figures: How Does Your state Compare?* 2015.

5. Binyamin Applebaum and Robert Gebeloff, "Tax Burden for Most Americans is Lower than in the 1980s," nytimes.com (November 29, 2012).

6. Mike Machiag, "Tax Exempt Properties Rise as Cities Cope With Shrinking Tax Bases," *Governing* (November 2012): 54–8.

7. Mark Schneider, "Local Budgets and the Maximization of Local Property Wealth in the System of Suburban Government," *Journal of Politics* 49 (November 1987): 11–14.

8. *The Book of the States* 444 (Lexington, KY: Council of State Governments, 2013), p. 284.

9. "Sales Tax Holidays: Politically Expedient but Poor Tax Policy, 2014," www.taxfoundation.org (July 31, 2014).

10. Neal R. Peirce, "Service Tax May Rise Again," *Public Administration Times* 11 (August 12, 1996): 2.

11. Elaine S. Povich, "Cigarette Smuggling Cuts States' Per-Pack Tax Revenues," www.pewstates.org (May 31, 2013).

12. Mark Niquette and Esmé E. Deprez, "Cigarette Smuggling Increase Prompts Crackdown by States," www.bloomberg.com (May 24, 2014).

13. *Quill v. North Dakota* 504 U.S. 298 (1992).

14. "U.S. Supreme Court's Refusal to Rule on Online Taxes Leaves It Up to States," www.governing.com (December 3, 2013).

15. Penelope Lemov, "States Look to Collect Internet Sales Taxes," www.governing.com (May 18, 2011); David C. Powell, "Internet Taxation and U.S. Intergovernmental Relations: From Quill to the Present," *Publius* 30 (Winter 2000): 39–51.

16. Council of State Governments, *Book of the States, 2014* (Lexington, KY): Table 7.21.

17. Elaine S. Povich, "Volatile Income Tax Revenue Stumps States," www.stateline.org (October 13, 2014).

18. Jim Estes, "How the Big Tobacco Deal Went Bad," www.nytimes.com (October 6, 2014).

19. Elaine S. Povich, "Superstar Athletes Pay Big Jock Taxes," www.stateline.org (October 23, 2013).

20. *The Book of the States*, Table 7.15 (2011).

21. Alaska Permanent Fund, www.apfc.org (accessed March 22, 2015).

22. www.factfinder.census.gov (accessed March 3, 2015).

23. Elizabeth A. Freund and Irwin L. Morris, "The Lottery and Income Inequality in the States," *Social Science Quarterly* 86 (2005): 996–1012; Patrick A. Pierce and Donald E. Miller, *Gambling Politics* (Washington, D.C.: Congressional Quarterly Press, 2004).

24. Pamela M. Prah, "Nevada Has Head Start as States React to Federal Gambling Decision," www.stateline.org (January 6, 2012).

25. www.nasbo.org (accessed March 20, 2015).

26. Center on Budget and Policy Priorities, www.cbpp.org (accessed July 15, 2009).

27. Christine R. Martell and Paul Teske, "Fiscal Management Implications of the TABOR Bind," *Public Administration Review* (July/August, 2007): 673–86.

28. Changhoon Jung and Suho Bae, "Changing Revenue and Expenditure Structure and the Reliance on User Charges and Fees in American Counties, 1972–2002," *American Review of Public Administration* (Spring 2010): 1–19.

29. Thad Kousser, Matthew D. McCubbins, and Ellen Moule, "For Whom the TEL Tolls: Can State Tax and Expenditure Limits Effectively Reduce Spending?" *State Politics and Policy Quarterly* 8 (Winter 2008): 331–61.

30. Suho Bae, Seong-gin Moon, and Changhoon Jung, "Economic Effects of State-Level Tax and Expenditure Limitations," *Public Administration Review* 72 (5, 2012): 649–58.

31. http://www.infrastructurereportcard.org www.infrastructurereportcard.org (accessed March 17, 2015).

32. Michael A. Pagano and Jocelyn M. Johnston, "Life at the Bottom of the Fiscal Food Chain: Examining City and Council Revenue Decisions," *Publius* 30 (Winter 2000): 159–70.

33. Alex Brown and Josh Franzel, Retirement and Health Care Benefits for State and Local Employees in 2014, www.cslge.org (December 2014); see "The Widening Gap," www.pewstates.org (April, 2011); Richard C. Kearney, Robert Clark, and Jerrell Coggburn, *At a Crossroads: The Financing and Future of Health Benefits for State and Local Government Retirees* (Washington, D.C.: Center for State and Local Government Excellence, 2009): Table 2.6.

34. Pew Center on the States, *The Trillion Dollar Gap: Unfunded State Retirement Systems and the Roads to Reform* (Washington, D.C.: Pew Center on the States, February 2010).

35. Brown and Franzel, 2014.

36. Brian Chappatta, "Largest Public Pensions Face $2 Trillion Hole, Moody's Says," www.bloomberg.com (September 25, 2014).

37. Stephen C. Fehr, "States Get Off Revenue Roller Coaster," www.stateline.org (March 1, 2011).

38. John Gramlich, "As State Budgets, Payroll Shrink, so Do Ambitions," www.stateline.org (January 10, 2011).

39. Sallie Hofmeister, "Fund Head Resigns in California" and "Many Questions, but Too Late," *The New York Times* (December 6, 1994): D1, D2;

40. Mary Williams Walsh and Louise Story, "A Stealth Tax Subsidy for Business Faces New Scrutiny," (March 4, 2013).

41. Peter Harkness, "States, Localities Face a 'Lost Decade'," www.governing.com (March 9, 2010); Peter Harkness, "Harsh Realities," *Governing* (September 2011): 16–18.

CHAPTER 14 ECONOMIC DEVELOPMENT: COMPETING FOR GROWTH

1. Aaron M. Kessler, "Volvo Selects South Carolina for Its $500 Million Assembly Plant," *New York Times*, www.nytimes.com/2015/05/12/automobiles/volvo-selects-south-carolina-for-500-million-assembly-plant.html?_r=0 (May 11, 2015); "Volvo Rates a Grand Welcome," *The Post and Courier*, www.postandcourier.com/article/20150512/PC1002/150519833/1506/volvo-rates-a-grand-welcome (May 12, 2015).

2. Jack Lyne, "Virginia Readies for Rolls," *Site Selection*, www.siteselection.com/ssinsider/bbdeal/bd071206.htm (December 3, 2007).

3. As quoted in "Washington State Gov. Chris Gregoire Says That Washington Has Consistently Ranked in the Top Five of Forbes' Best States for Business, Ahead of Texas," www.polifact.com (November 5, 2010).

4. W. Mark Crain, *Volatile States: Institutions, Policy, and the Performance of American State Economies* (Ann Arbor, MI: University of Michigan Press, 2003).

5. Yolanda K. Kodrzycki and Ana Patricia Muñoz "Economic Distress and Resurgence in U.S. Central Cities: Concepts, Causes, and Policy Levers," *Economic Development Quarterly* 29 (May 2015): 113–34.

6. "America's Top States for Business 2014," CNBC, www.cnbc.com/id/101758236 (accessed May 11, 2015).

7. Jonathan Tilove, "Louisiana Ranks High on Index of State Economic Momentum," *The Times-Picayune*, www.nola.com/politics/index.ssf/2012/05/louisiana_ranks_9th_on_state_r.html (May 4, 2012).

8. Maryann P. Feldman and Johanna L. Francis, "Homegrown Solutions: Fostering Cluster Formation," *Economic Development Quarterly* 18 (May 2004): 127–37; Harold (Hal) Wolman and Diana Hincapie, "Clusters and Cluster-Based Development Policy," *Economic Development Quarterly* 29 (May 2015): 135–49.

9. Mary Jo Waits, "Building an Economic Future," *State Government News* 38 (September 1995): 6–10.

10. Ross Gittell, Jeffrey Sohl, and Edinaldo Tebaldi, "Do Entrepreneurship and High-Tech Concentration Create Jobs? Exploring the Growth in Employment in U.S. Metropolitan Areas From 1991 to 2007," *Economic Development Quarterly* 28 (August 2014): 244–53.

11. Susan E. Clarke and Gary L. Gaile, *The Work of Cities* (Minneapolis, MN: University of Minnesota Press, 1998).

12. J. Mac Holladay, "Trends That Strengthen Economies," *State Government News* 40 (August 1997): 6–7; see also Edwin Melendez, et al., "The Restructured Landscape of Economic Development: Challenges and Opportunities for Regional Workforce Development Collaborations," *Economic Development Quarterly* 29 (May 2015): 150–66.

13. Robert D. Atkinson and Scott Andes, "The 2010 State New Economy Index," http://www.itif.org/publications/2010-state-new-economy-index (accessed June 15, 2012).

14. Caroline Hanley and Michael T. Douglass, "High Road, Low Road, or Off Road? Economic Development Strategies in the American States," *Economic Development Quarterly* 28 (August 2014): 220–29.

15. Governor's Office of Economic Development, www.goed.utah.gov (July 5, 2006).

16. As quoted in Richard Reeves, *American Journey* (New York: Simon & Schuster, 1982), p. 46.

17. Committee for Economic Development, *Leadership for Dynamic State Economies* (Washington, D.C.: Committee for Economic Development, 1986), pp. 73–77. See also Maryann P. Feldman, Lauren Lanahan, and Iryna V. Lendel, "Experiments in the Laboratories of Democracy: State Scientific Capacity Building," *Economic Development Quarterly* 28 (May 2014): 107–31.

18. As quoted in Laurie Clewett, "State of the States," *State Government News* (March 2004): 20.

19. National Association of State Development Agencies, *The NASDA Newsletter* (January 21, 1987), p. 5.

20. Missouri Department of Economic Development, "Executive Summary: Missouri Strategic Initiative for Economic Growth," http://ded.mo.gov/Content/Executive%20Summary-Final%20Report%20of%20Strategic%20Initiative.pdf (April 11, 2011).

21. U.S. Travel Association, "Travel Answer Sheet," https://www.ustravel.org/news/press-kit/travel-facts-and-statistics (accessed May 25, 2015).

22. Ken Braun, "Pure Spending—GOP Finds More for Tourism Subsidies," Michigan Capitol Confidential, www.mackinac.org/14703; Mara Lee, "'Still Revolutionary:' $27 Million State Tourism Campaign Launched," *Hartford Courant*, http://articles.courant.com (May 14, 2012).

23. David Reynolds, as quoted in Charles Mahtesian, "How States Get People to (Love) Them," *Governing* 7 (January 1994): 47.

24. "Travel Oregon," http://traveloregon.com/ (accessed May 25, 2015).

25. Roger Yu, "States Cut Back on Efforts to Draw Tourists," *USA Today*, http://travel.usatoday.com (August 1, 2011).

26. William Yardley, "A Tourism Office Falls Victim to Hard Times," *The New York Times* www.nytimes.com (July 11, 2011).

27. J. Allen Whitt, "The Arts Coalition in Strategies of Urban Development," in Clarence N. Stone and Heywood T. Sanders, eds., *The Politics of Urban Development* (Lawrence: University Press of Kansas, 1987), pp. 144–56.

28. "If You Build It," *Governing* 19 (January 2006): 18.

29. Richard Sandomir, "A Texas-Size Stadium," *The New York Times*, www.nytimes.com/2009/07/17/sports/football/17cowboys.html?scp=1&sq=a+texas+size+stadium&st=nyt (July 17, 2009).

30. Conrad Defiebre and Jay Weiner, "Pawlenty Unveils Plans for Stadiums," *Minneapolis Star Tribune*, www.startribune.com/viewers/story (March 16, 2004).

31. Rodd Zolkos, "Cities Blast Stadium Study," *City & State* 4 (April 1987): 3, 53. See also Kevin G. Quinn, Christopher P. Borick, and Paul B. Bursick, "The Stadium Game: An Empirical Analysis," paper presented at the annual meeting of the Midwest Political Science Association, Chicago, Illinois, 2000.

32. Gary Enos and Rodd Zolkos, "Stadiums Ding Home Runs," *City & State* 8 (September 23–October 6, 1991): 1, 24.

33. Matthew J. Burbank, Charles H. Heying, and Greg Andranovich, "Antigrowth Politics or Piecemeal Resistance?" *Urban Affairs Review* 35 (January 2000): 334–57.

34. John Larkin, "States Spark Foreign Relations of Their Own," *PA Times* (June 1, 1992): 1, 20. See also Jeffrey A. Finkle, "State Economic Development Strategies: Trends and Issues," in *The Book of the States 2006* (Lexington, KY: Council of State Governments, 2006), pp. 511–14.

35. "Trade Statistics," Statemaster.com, www.statemaster.com/graph/tra_exp_tot_ove_val-trade-export-totals-overall-value (accessed June 20, 2012).

36. U.S. Census Bureau, "Foreign Commerce and Aid," *Statistical Abstract of the United States: 2011*, www.census.gov/prod/2011pubs/11statab/foreign.pdf.

37. Mark K. Matthews, "States Chart Their Own Foreign Policy," stateline.org, http://www.stateline.org/live/ViewPage.action?siteNodeId=136&languageId=1&contentId=103597 (April 12, 2006).

38. Richard S. Krannich and Craig R. Humphrey, "Local Mobilization and Community Growth: Toward an Assessment of the 'Growth Machine' Hypothesis," *Rural Sociology* 48 (Spring 1983): 60–81; John M. Levy, *Urban and Metropolitan Economics* (New York: McGraw-Hill, 1985); G. Jason Jolley, Mandee Foushee Lancaster, and Jiang Gao, "Tax Incentives and Business Climate: Executive Perceptions From Incented and Nonincented Firms," *Economic Development Quarterly* 29 (May 2015): 180–84.

39. Roger Schmenner, "Location Decisions of Large Firms: Implications for Public Policy," *Commentary* 5 (January 1981): 307.

40. Paul Brace, *State Government and Economic Performance* (Baltimore, MD: Johns Hopkins University Press, 1993); Laura A. Reese, "The Alchemy of Local Economic Development," *Economic Development Quarterly* 28 (August 2014): 206–19.

41. Michael A. Pagano and Ann O'M. Bowman, *Cityscapes and Capital* (Baltimore, MD: Johns Hopkins University Press, 1995).

42. Tim Flach, "Amazon Furor Already Taking Economic Toll," *The State*, www.thestate.com (April 30, 2011).

43. Parris Glendening, "Smart Growth Tops Governors' Agenda," *Washington Post* (July 12, 2000): A14.

44. Craig Jenkins, Kevin T. Leicht, and Arthur Jaynes, "Creating High-Technology Growth: High-Tech Employment Growth in U.S. Metropolitan Areas, 1988–1998," *Social Science Quarterly* 89, no. 2 (2009): 456–81.

45. J. Norman Baldwin, Stephen A. Borrelli, and Michael J. New, "State Educational Investments and Economic Growth in the United States: A Path Analysis," *Social Science Quarterly* 92 (March 2011): 226–45.

46. Jay S. Baron, "At 25, Toyota Plan Still Lean, Flexible, World-Famous," www.kentucky.com (November 13, 2011).

47. Mac R. Holmes, as quoted in Peter Applebome, "States Raise Stakes in Fight for Jobs," *The New York Times* (October 4, 1993): A10.

48. Jim Malewitz, "Report: Few States Study Impact of Costly Tax Breaks," www.stateline.org (April 12, 2012).

49. *Evidence Counts*, Pew Center on the States, www.pewstates.org/uploadedFiles/PCS_Assets/2012/015_12_RI%20Tax%20Incentives%20Report_web.pdf (April 2012).

50. Susan K. Urahn, "Showing the Way on Tax Incentives," *Governing*, www.governing.com (June 13, 2012).

51. William Fulton, "The Clawback Clause," *Governing* 16 (October 2002): 72.

52. Ann O'M. Bowman, *The Visible Hand: Major Issues in City Economic Policy* (Washington, D.C.: National League of Cities, 1987).

53. Darrene Hackler and Heike Mayer, "Diversity, Entrepreneurship, and the Urban Environment," *Journal of Urban Affairs* 30 (2008): 273–307.

54. Peter Waldman, "Cities Are Pressured to Make Developers Share Their Wealth," *The Wall Street Journal* (March 10, 1987): 1.

55. Carol Steinbach, "Tapping Private Resources," *National Journal* (April 26, 1986): 993.

56. "Taking Care of Business," *The Economist* (February 18, 1989): 28.

57. Neal Peirce, "Cities Must Learn When to Say No," *Houston Chronicle* (February 13, 1989): A12.

58. G. Scott Thomas, "Austin Is Best U.S. City for Small Businesses," *Austin Business Journal*, www.bizjournals.com (April 13, 2012).

59. Charles J. Spindler, "Winners and Losers in Industrial Recruitment: Mercedes-Benz and Alabama," *State and Local Government Review* 26 (Fall 1994): 192–204.

60. Joel Rast and Virginia Carlson, "When Boeing Landed in Chicago: Lessons for Regional Economic Development," *State and Local Government Review* 38 (Winter 2006): 1–11.

61. Daniel C. Vock, "Court Allows Smokestack Chasing—For Now," www.stateline.org (May 16, 2006).

62. Charles Mahtesian, "A Non-Poaching Peace Pact Is Under Fire in Florida," *Governing* 13 (May 2000): 88; see also Christopher W. Hawkins, "Competition and Cooperation: Local Government Joint Ventures for Economic Development," *Journal of Urban Affairs* 32 (2, 2010): 253–75.

CHAPTER 15 EDUCATION POLICY: READING, WRITING, AND REFORM

1. National Commission on Excellence in Education, *A Nation at Risk: The Imperative for Educational Reform* (Washington, D.C.: U.S. Government Printing Office, 1983), p. 1

2. /nces.ed.gov/surveys/pisa/pisa2012 (accessed April 16, 2015); Amanda Ripley, "Your Child," *The Atlantic* (December 2010): 94–98.

3. Lyndsey Layton, "Majority of U.S. Public School Students in Poverty," www.washingtonpost.com (January 15, 2015).

4. www.edweek.org (accessed April 4, 2015).

5. www.nces.gov "National Assessment of Educational Progress (accessed April 8, 2015).

6. Pew Research Center (www.pewresearch.org), October 2, 2014; National Center for Education Statistics, *Digest of Education Statistics, 2014*.

7. College Board, *Total Group Profile Report*, www.collegeboard.com (accessed April 16, 2015).

8. *The Condition of Education*, U.S. Department of Education; www.nces.ed.gov (accessed April 7, 2015).

9. John Bohte, "School Bureaucracy and Student Performance at the Local Level," *Public Administration Review* 61 (January/February 2001): 92–99; John E. Chubb and Terry Moe, *Politics, Markets, and America's Schools* (Washington, D.C.: The Brookings Institution, 1990).

10. Kevin B. Smith and Christopher W. Larimer, "A Mixed Relationship: Bureaucracy and School Performance," *Public Administration Review* 64 (November/December 2004): 728–36; Kevin B. Smith and Kenneth J. Meier, *The Case Against School Choice: Politics, Markets, and Fools* (Armonk, NY: M. E. Sharpe, 1995); Kevin B. Smith and Christopher W. Larimer, "A Mixed Relationship: Bureaucracy and School Performance," *Public Administration Review* 64 (November/December 2004): 728–36; see also Robert Maranto, Scott Milliman, and Scott Stevens, "Does Private School Competition Harm Public Schools?" *Political Research Quarterly* 53 (March 2000): 177–92.

11. Patrick McGuinn, "The National Schoolmarm: No Child Left Behind and the New Educational Federalism," *Publius* 35 (Winter 2005): 41–69.

12. Wayne Riddle, *Major Accountability Themes of Second-Round State Applications for NCLB Waivers*, (Washington, D.C.: Center on Education Policy, May 2012).

13. *Serrano v. Priest,* 5 Cal.3d 584 (1971).

14. *San Antonio Independent School District v. Rodriguez,* 411 U.S. 1 (1973).

15. Kristen Alloway and Jeanette Rundquist, "Court Shifts on School Aid," *The Star-Ledger,* www.nj.com (May 29, 2009).

16. Wong, "The Politics of Education."

17. Douglas S. Reed, *On Equal Terms: The Constitutional Politics of Educational Opportunity* (Princeton, NJ: Princeton University Press, 2001).

18. See Eric A. Hanushek and Alfred A. Lindseth, *Schoolhouses, Courthouses, and Statehouses: Solving the Funding-Achievement Puzzle in America's Public Schools* (Princeton: Princeton University Press, 2009).

19. James S. Coleman, *Equality of Educational Opportunity* (Washington, D.C.: U.S. Government Printing Office, 1966).

20. Michael A. Gottfried, "Peer Effects in Urban Schools: Assessing the Impact of Classroom Composition on Student Achievement," *Educational Policy* 28 (5), 2014: 607–47; Eric A. Hanushek, John F. Kain, Jacob M. Markman, and Steven G. Rivkin, "Does Peer Ability Affect Student Achievement?" *Journal of Applied Econometrics* 18 (September/October 2003): 527–44; available at www.edpro.stanford.edueahpaperspeersaug01.pdf/.

21. Eric A. Hanushek, "The Economics of Schooling: Production and Efficiency in Public Schools," *Journal of Economic Literature* 24 (September 1986): 1141–77.

22. Michael T. Hartney and Patrick Flavin, "The Political Foundations of the Black-White Achievement Gap," *American Politics Research* 42 (1, 2014): 3–33; Nathan Glazer, *We Are All Multiculturalists Now* (Cambridge, MA: Harvard University Press, 1997).

23. R. L. Linn and K. G. Welner, eds., *Race-Conscious Policies for Assigning Students to Schools: Social Science Research and the Court Cases* (Washington, D.C.: National Academy of Education, 2007).

24. Roland G. Fryer, Jr., and Steven D. Levitt, "Testing for Racial Differences in the Mental Ability of Young Children," *American Economic Review* 103 (2, 2013): 981–1005.

25. Eric A. Hanushek and Steven G. Rivkin, "Harming the Best: How Schools Affect the Black-White Achievement Gap," *Journal of Policy Analysis and Management* 28, no. 3 (2009): 366–93.

26. *Meredith v. Jefferson County Board of Education,* U.S. Sup Ct No. 05-915 (2007).

27. Hanushek and Rifkin, "Harming the Best;" Hanushek and Lindseth, *Schoolhouses.*

28. Karl L. Alexander, Doris R. Entwisle, and Linda Steffel Olson, "Lasting Consequences of the Summer Learning Gap," *American Sociological Review* 72 (April 2007): 167–80.

29. See, for example, Fryer G. Roland, " 'Acting White': The Social Price Paid by the Best and Brightest Minority Students," *Education Next* 6 (1) 2006: 52–59.

30. Hartney and Flavin, 2014.

31. Michael B. Berkman and Eric Plutzner, *Ten Thousand Democracies: Politics and Public Opinion in America's School Districts* (Washington, D.C.: Georgetown University Press, 2005).

32. *Brown v. Board of Education of Topeka,* 347 I.S. 483 (1954).

33. *Swann v. Charlotte-Mecklenberg County Schools,* 402 U.S. 1 (1971).

34. Gary Orfield and Erica Frenkenberg, "Brown at 60: Great Progress, a Long Retreat, and an Uncertain Future," Civil Rights Project (www.ucla.edu, May 25, 2014); Amanda Paulson, "Resegregation of U.S. Schools Deepening," *Christian Science Monitor* (January 25, 2008); Gary Orfield and John Yun, *Resegregation in American Schools,* (Cambridge: Harvard University Press, 1999); Wong, "The Politics of Education," p. 362.

35. Reed, *On Equal Terms.*

36. Charles T. Clotfelter, "Public School Segregation in Metropolitan Areas," *Land Economics* 75 (December 1999): 487–504.

37. Sarah Reckhow, *Follow the Money: How Foundation Dollars Change Public School Politics* (New York: Oxford University Press, 2013); Also see Alan Greenblatt, "Billionaires in the Classroom," *Governing* (October 2011): 27–35.

38. Lisette Alvarez, "States Listen as Parents Give Rampant Testing an F," www.nytimes.com (November 9, 2014).

39. Sam Dillon, "Federal Researchers Find Lower Standards in Schools," www.nytimes.com (October 30, 2009).

40. Heather Vogell, John Pery, Alan Judd, and M.B. Pell, "Cheating Our Children: Suspicious School Test Scores across the Nation," www.ajc.com (January 26, 2012); Trip Gabriel, "Under Pressure, Teachers Tamper with Test Scores," www.nytimes.com (June 10, 2010).

41. Alan Blinder, "Educators Convicted in School Cheating Scandal," www.nytimes.com (April 1, 2015).

42. Dylan Scott, "States Begin Implementing Common Core Standards," www.governing.com (February 7, 2012).

43. David L. Kirp, *The Sandbox Investment: The Preschool Movement and Kids-First Politics* (Cambridge, MA: Harvard University Press, 2007).

44. "The State of Preschool 2013," www.nieer.org (accessed April 16, 2015).

45. Center for Effective Discipline, www.gundersonhealth.org (accessed April 14, 2015).

46. Sam Dillon, "High Schools to Offer Plan to Graduate 2 Years Early," www.nytimes.com (February 18, 2010).

47. Jay Matthews, "Maybe Paying for Good Grades is Not So Bad," www.washingtonpost.com (March 30, 2014).

48. Raj Chetty, John N. Friedman, and Jonah E. Rockoff, "The Long-Term Impacts of Teachers: Teacher Value-Added and Student Outcomes in Adulthood," (Washington, D.C.: National Bureau of Economic Research Paper No. 17699, December 2011).

49. William H. Marinell and Susan Moore Johnson, "Midcareer Entrants to Teaching: Who They Are and How They May, or May Not, Change Teaching," *Educational Policy* 28 (6, 2014): 743–79.

50. Dan Wieder, "Charter-School Debate Takes Different Turns in Georgia, New Jersey," governing.

com (March 29, 2012); Diana Jean Schemo, "Study of Test Scores Finds Charter Schools Lagging," *The New York Times* (August 23, 2006): 1–3 (citing a federal study).

51. Rand Corporation, *How Charter Schools Affect Student Outcomes*, (Santa Monica, CA: Rand Corporation, 2009); Center for Policy Alternatives, *Education: School Vouchers* (Washington, D.C.: Policy Alternatives, 2005), p. 85.

52. Pricilla Wohlsteter, Joanna Smith, and Caitlin C. Farrell, *Choices and Challenges: Charter School Performance in Perspective* (Cambridge, MA: Harvard University Press, 2013).

53. *Zelman et al. v. Simmons-Harris et al.* (No. 001751, June 27, 2002).

54. Sam Dillon, "Florida Court Strikes Down School Voucher Program," *The New York Times* (January 5, 2006).

55. Erin Richards, "Wisconsin Voucher Programs March Toward 30,000 Student Threshold," *The Journal Sentinel* (December 8, 2014); www.edchoice.org (accessed June 14, 2015).

56. Stacy Teicher Khadaroo, "Nevada's Groundbreaking School Choice Law: Help or Hindrance to Public System? www.csmonitor.com (June 3, 2015).

57. Lauren McDonald, "Think Tanks and the Media: How the Conservative Movement Gained Entry Into the Education Policy Arena," *Educational Policy* 28 (6, 2013): 845–80; Associated Press, "School Vouchers Spark Legal and Political Fights," www.governing.com (April 9, 2012).

58. Patrick Wolf, "The Comparative Longitudinal Evaluation of the Milwaukee Parental Choice Program: Summary of Final Reports," SCDP Milwaukee Evaluation, Report No. 36, www.uaedreform.org (February 2012); Borsh and Wolf; "Study Finds Academic Gains Not Superior among Students Enrolled in Privately-Run Schools," www.rand.org (February 1, 2007).

59. Jacques Steinberg, "At 42 Newly Privatized Philadelphia Schools, Uncertainty Abounds," *The New York Times* (April 19, 2002): 1–3.

60. Kristen A. Graham, "Philadelphia Taking Back 6 Privatized Schools," www.philly.com (June 19, 2008).

61. Brian Gill, Michael Timpane, and Dominic Brewer, *Rhetoric versus Reality: What We Know and What We Need to Know about School Vouchers and Charter Schools* (Santa Monica, CA: Rand Corporation, 2001).

62. www.nces.gov (accessed April 14, 2015).

63. Brian D. Ray, "Home Education: Reason and Results," www.nheri.org (accessed April 16, 2015); Brian D. Ray and Bruce K. Eagleson. "State Regulation of Homeschooling and Home-schoolers' SAT Scores," *Academic Leadership*, www.academicleadership.org (August 2008).

64. Lyndsey Layton, "Study Raises Questions about Virtual Schools," www.washingtonpost.com (October 24, 2011).

65. Saul, "Profits and Questions . . ."

66. McDonald, 2013.

67. Diane Ravitch, *Reign of Error: The Hoax of the Privatization Movement and the Danger to America's Public Schools* (New York: Random House, 2014).

68. Bryan Shelley, *Money, Mandates, and Control in American Public Education* (Ann Arbor: University of Michigan Press, 2011).

CHAPTER 16 CRIMINAL JUSTICE: COPS AND CORRECTIONS

1. *Criminal Justice 2000*, vol. 4, National Criminal Justice Reference Series (www.ncjrs.gov), accessed December 7, 2011.

2. Reported in Erica Goode, "Many in U.S. Are Arrested by Age 23, Study Finds," www.nytimes.com (December 19, 2011); see also Robert Brame, Michael G. Turner, Raymond Paternoster, and Shawn D. Bushway, "Cumulative Prevalence of Arrest From Ages 8 to 23 in a National Sample," Pediatrics 132 (2012): 21–27.

3. William J. Wilem, *When Work Disappears: The World of the New Urban Poor* (New York: Alfred A. Knopf, 1996); Alex Piquero, John MacDonald, and Karen F. Parker, "Race, Local Life Circumstances, and Criminal Activity," *Social Science Quarterly* 83 (September 2002): 654–70.

4. "Chart of the Week: the Black-White Gap in Incarceration Rates," www.pewresearch.org (July 18, 2014); Bruce Western, *Punishment and Inequality in America* (New York: Russell Sage Press, 2006).

5. Federal Bureau of Investigation, "Crime in the United States, 2013," www.fbi.gov/ucr (2014) (accessed May 12, 2015).

6. Gary Cordner, "Community Policing," in Michael D. Reisig and Robert J. Kane, eds., *The Oxford Handbook of Police and Policing* (New York: Oxford University Press, 2014): 148–71; Mark A. Glaser and Janet Denhardt, "Community Policing and Community Building: A Case of Officer Perception," *American Review of Public Administration* 40 (3), 2009: 309–25.

7. James Q. Wilson and George L. Kelling, "Broken Windows: The Police and Neighborhood Safety," *Atlantic Monthly* (March 1982): 29–38. See also Rob Gurwitt, "Not by Cops Alone," *Governing* 8 (May 1995): 16–26.

8. Joshua C. Hinkle, "The Relationship between Disorder, Perceived Risk, and Collective Efficacy: A Look into the Indirect Pathways of the Broken Windows Thesis," *Criminal Justice Studies* 26 (4, 2013): 408–32.

9. *Terry v. Ohio*, 392 U.S. 1 (1968).

10. Joseph Goldstein, "Safer Era Tests the Wisdom of "Broken Windows" Focus on Minor Crime," www.nytimes.com (July 24, 2014).

11. Lawrence W. Sherman, "The Rise of Evidence-Based Policing: Targeting, Testing, and Tracking," *Crime and Justice* 42(1): 377–451.

12. Jenni Bergal, "Touting Prevention, Police Put Crime Info Online," www.pertrusts.org (January 20, 2015).

13. www.census.gov/govs/apes/10 stus.txt (December 7, 2011).

14. Federal Bureau of Investigation, *Crime in the United States* (Washington, D.C.: U.S. Department of Justice, 2011).

15. *Miranda v. Arizona*, 384 U.S. 486 (1966).

16. *Mapp v. Ohio*, 307 U.S. 643 (1961).
17. "Free at Last, Free at Last," *Time* (November 2, 1987): 55.
18. National Association of Crime Victims Compensation Board, www.nacvb.org (accessed May 14, 2015).
19. http://klaaskids.org/pg-legmeg2.htm.
20. Renee Scherlen, "The Never-Ending Drug War: Obstacles to Drug War Policy Termination," *PS* (January 2012): 67–74.
21. *Furman v. Georgia*, 408 U.S. 239 (1972).
22. *Roper v. Simmons* (2005).
23. *Singleton v. Norris*, 02–10605 (2003).
24. *Kennedy v. Louisiana* (2008) U.S. Sup. Ct. No. 07–343.
25. *Baze v. Rees* (2008) U.S. Sup. Ct No. 07–5439.
26. Death Penalty Information Center, 2015.
27. www.gallup.com/poll/1606/death-penalty.aspx (accessed May 16, 2015).
28. Death Penalty Information Center, www.deathpenaltyinfo.com (accessed May 16, 2015).
29. Tara N. Richards, et al. (4 others), "An Examination of Capital Sentencing: A Propensity Score Matching Approach," *American Journal of Criminal Justice* 39 (2014): 681–97.
30. Death Penalty Information Center, www.deathpenaltyinfo.org (2015).
31. Melinda Gann Hall and Paul Brace, "The Vicissitudes of Death by Decree: Forces Influencing Capital Punishment Decision Making in State Supreme Courts," *Social Science Quarterly* 75 (March 1999): 1368.
32. Frank Baumgartner, Suzanne L. DeBoef, and Amber E. Boydstun, *The Decline of the Death Penalty: The Discovery of Innocence* (Cambridge University Press, 2008).
33. "The Death Penalty in 2014: Year End Report," www.deathpenaltyinfo.org (accessed May 16, 2015).
34. Samuel R. Gross, Barbara O'Brien, Chen Hu, and Edward H. Kennedy, "Rate of False Conviction of Criminal Defendants Who Are Sentenced to Death," *Procedings of the National Academy of Science* 111 (20, 2014) 7230–35; see also Gramlich, "No End in Sight to Death Penalty Wrangling."
35. David C. May, Brandon K. Applegate, Rick Ruddell, and Peter B. Wood, "Going to Jail Sucks (And It Really Doesn't Matter Who You Ask," *American Journal of Criminal Justice* 39 (2014): 250–66.
36. See Oliver Roeder, Lauren Brooke-Eisen, and Julia Bowling, "What Caused the Crime Decline?", Report of Brennan Center for Law and Justice, 2015.
37. Pew Charitable Trusts, "One in 31," (Washington, D.C.: Pew Charitable Trusts, March 2009).
38. Jeff Yates and Richard Fording, "Politics and State Punitiveness in Black and White," *Journal of Politics* 67 (November 2005): 1118.
39. Jon Hurwitz and Mark Peffley, "Explaining the Great Racial Divide: Perceptions of Fairness in the U.S. Criminal Justice System," *Journal of Politics* 67 (August 2005): 762–83.
40. Stephen Demuth and Darrell Steffensmeier, "Ethnicity Effects on Sentence Outcomes in Large Urban Courts: Comparisons among White, Black, and Hispanic Defendants," *Social Science Quarterly* 85 (December 2004): 994–1011.
41. Marie Gottschalk, *The Prison and the Gallows: The Politics of Mass Incarceration in America* (New York: Cambridge University Press, 2006).
42. Erik Eckholm, "California Convicts Are out of Prison after Third Strike, and Staying Out," www.nytimes.com (February 26, 2015).
43. Erica Goode, "U.S. Prison Populations Decline, Reflecting New Approach to Crime," www.nytimes.com (July 25, 2013); John Buntin, "Game Changers," *Governing* (February 2012): 35–38.
44. Christine Vestal, "For Aging Inmates, Care Outside Prison Walls," www.pewtrusts.org (August 12, 2014); David Levine, "Jailhouse Shock," *Governing* (March 2012): 18.
45. D. Walsh, "Judges Order California to Cut Prison Population by 40,591," *Sacramento Bee* (August 5, 2009).
46. Ryan Holeywell, "Crowded Out," *Governing* (February 2014): 31–35.
47. VERA Institute of Justice, *The Continuing Fiscal Crisis in Corrections* (Washington, D.C.: VERA): 2010.
48. Pew Center on the States, *One in 31: The Long Reach of American Corrections* (Washington, D.C.: Pew Center on the States, 2009), p. 12.
49. Ibid, p. 13.
50. Erinn J. Herberman and Thomas P. Bonczar, "Probation and Parole in the United States," www.bjs.gov (January 21, 2015).
51. Buntin, "Game Changers" Keith B. Richburg, "States Seek Less Costly Substitutes for Prison," *The Washington Post* (July 13, 2009).
52. Pew Center on the States, *One in 31*, p. 80.
53. Avdi S. Avdija and JiHee Lee, "Does Electronic Detention Home Detention Program Work? Evaluating Program Suitability Based on Offenders' Post-Program Recidivism Status," *Justice Policy Journal* 11 (Fall, 2014):1–15.
54. Rand Corporation, "Education and Vocational Training in Prison Reduces Recidivism, Improves Job Outlook," www.rand.org (August 22, 2013).
55. Candace Rondeaux, "Can Chemical Castration Be a Solution for Sex Offenders?" *Washington Post* (July 5, 2006): B 01.
56. Jenny Gold, "A National Model for Decrowding Jails and Helping the Mentally Ill," www.governing.com (August 20, 2014).
57. See Justice Policy Institute, www.justicepolicy.org (accessed July 12, 2012).
58. Rebecca Boone, "Otter: State to Take Over Privately Run Prison," www.idahostatesman.com (January 4, 2014).

CHAPTER 17 SOCIAL WELFARE AND HEALTH CARE POLICY: ADDRESSING POVERTY AND SICKNESS

1. http://www.census.gov/hhes/www/poverty/ (accessed July 11, 2012).
2. Ibid.
3. Thomas B. Edsall, "How Poor Are the Poor?," www.nytimes.com (March 25, 2015).
4. www.census.gov (accessed March 4, 2015).

5. Fred Block, Richard A. Cloward, Barbara Ehrenreich, and Francis Fox Piven, *The Mean Season: The Attack on the Welfare State* (New York: Pantheon Books, 1987), p. 92.

6. See Charles Murray, *Coming Apart: The State of White America, 1960–2010* (New York: Crown Forum, 2012); and *In Our Hands: A Plan to Replace the Welfare State* (Washington, D.C.: American Enterprise Institute, 2006).

7. Martin Gilens, *Why Americans Hate Welfare: Race, Media, and the Politics of Antipoverty Policy* (Chicago, IL: University of Chicago Press, 1999).

8. Jake Grovum, "In Some States, Low Poverty Rate Obscures Deeper Despair," www.stateline.org (September 24, 2014).

9. www.inequality.org (accessed May 30, 2015).

10. Matthew C. Fellowes and Gretchen Rowe, "Politics and the New American Welfare States," *American Journal of Political Science* 48 (April 2004): 362–73.

11. Pamela M. Prah, "Why Are Welfare Rolls Flat, While the Food Stamp Program Grows Rapidly?" www.stateline.org (accessed July 1, 2012); Jason DeParle, "Welfare Limits Left Poor Adrift as Recession Hit," nytimes.com (April 7, 2012).

12. Romy Varghese, "Pennsylvania Joins States Yanking Safety Net for Disabled," www.Bloomberg.com (July 3, 2012).

13. Robert Pear, "Data on Health Law Shows Largest Drop in Uninsured in 4 Decades, the U.S. Says," www.nytimes.com (March 17, 2015).

14. Teresa Wilitz, "'Invisible' Homeless Kids Challenge States," www.pewtrusts.org (December 3, 2014).

15. Tim Henderson, "Attacking Homelessness with "Rapid Rehousing,'" www.pewtrusts.org (April 21, 2015).

16. Juliet F. Gainsborough, *Scandalous Politics: Child Welfare Policy in the States* (Washington, D.C.: Georgetown University Press, 2010).

17. Centers for Disease Control and Prevention, www.cdc.gov (accessed June 1, 2015).

18. www.pewtrusts.org (March 3, 2015).

19. www.georgiaworks.net (accessed June 1, 2015).

20. Francesca Jaroz, et al., "Rollout of Indiana Welfare Changes Halted," www.INDYSTAR.com, www.indystar.com (July 31, 2008).

21. Jonathan Walters, "Is Welfare Working?" *Governing* (February 2008): 28–34.

22. Mark Carl Rom, "State Health and Welfare Programs," in Virginia Gray, Russell L. Hanson, and Thad Kousser, eds., *Politics in the American States*, 10th ed. (Los Angeles: Sage/CQ Press, 2013): 347.

23. Kaiser Family Foundation, www.kff.org (accessed June 2, 2015).

24. Marilyn Werber Serafini, "Medicare Crooks," *National Journal* 29 (July 19, 1997): 1458–60; Malcolm Sparran, *License to Steal: Why Fraud Plagues America's Health Care System* (Boulder, CO: Westview Press, 1996).

25. United Health Foundation, *America's Health Rankings: A Call to Action for Individuals and Their Communities* (United Health Foundation, 2008).

26. American Medical Association, www.ama-assn.org (accessed July 11, 2012).

27. *National Federation Of Independent Business et al v. Sebelius et al.* No. 11–393. June 28, 2012.

28. Timothy Callaghan and Lawrence R. Jacobs, "Process Learning and the Implementation of Medicaid Reform," *Publius: The Journal of Federalism* 44 (4, 2014): 541–63; Simon F. Haeder and David L. Weimer, "You Can't Make Me Do it: State Implementation of Insurance Exchanges under the Affordable Care Act," *Public Administration Review* 73 (September/October, 2013): 534–47; Frank J. Thompson, *Medicaid Politics: Federalism, Policy Durability, and Health Reform* (Washington, D.C.: Georgetown University Press, 2012).

29. *King v. Burwell* 576 U.S. _____ (2015)

30. Center for Medicaid and Medicare Services, www.cms.gov (accessed July 12, 2012).

31. Sarah Kliff, "Healthcare. Gov is Busted: These Four State Exchanges Aren't," www.washingtonpost.com (October 25, 2013).

32. Christine Vestal, "Why Some State-Run Health Exchanges Worked," www.pewstates.org (December 10, 2013).

33. Chris Kardish, "By Changing How They Pay for Them," *Governing* (September, 2014): 47–49.

34. Dylan Scott, "Could Arkansas Crack the Cost-Containment Code?," *Governing* (August 2013): 11.

35. David Levine, "Fraud Prevention's ROI,"*Governing* (May 2013): 22.

36. Christine Vestal, "States Meld Medicare and Medicaid," www/pewstates.org (February 12, 2014).

37. Chris Kardish, "Creating Connections," *Governing* (February, 2014): 48–51.

CHAPTER 18 ENVIRONMENTAL POLICY: REGULATION AND INNOVATION

1. Tom Henry, "EPA Issues Recommendation on Microcystin in Tap Water," *Toledo Blade*, http://www.toledoblade.com/Medical/2015/05/06/EPA-issues-recommendation-on-microcystin-in-tap-water.html (accessed June 6, 2015).

2. Richard C. Feiock and Christopher Stream, "Environmental Protection versus Economic Development: A False Trade-Off?" *Public Administration Review* 61 (May/June 2001): 313–21.

3. Deborah Lynn Guber, *The Grassroots of a Green Revolution* (Cambridge, MA: MIT Press, 2003).

4. Art Swift, "Americans Again Pick Environment over Economic Growth," http://www.gallup.com/poll/168017/americans-again-pick-environment-economic-growth.aspx (accessed June 5, 2015); see also Steven E. Barkan, "Explaining Public Support for the Environmental Movement: A Civic Voluntarism Model," *Social Science Quarterly* 85 (December 2004): 913–37.

5. Nicole Darnall and Stephen Sides, "Assessing the Performance of Voluntary Environmental Programs: Does Certification Matter?" *Policy Studies Journal* 36 (2008): 95–117.

6. David M. Konisky, "Regulator Attitudes and the Environmental Race to the Bottom Argument," *Journal of Public Administration Research and Theory* 18 (2008): 321–44.

7. Walter A. Rosenbaum, *Environmental Politics and Policy*, 5th ed. (Washington, D.C.: Congressional Quarterly Press, 2002), pp. 12–13.

8. Lawrence S. Rothenberg, *Environmental Choices: Policy Responses to Green Demands* (Washington, D.C.: Congressional Quarterly Press, 2002); Matthew Kahn, *Green Cities: Urban Growth and the Environment* (Washington, DC: Brookings Institution Press, 2006).

9. David M. Konisky, "Public Preferences for Environmental Policy Responsibility," *Publius: The Journal of Federalism* 41 (Winter 2011):76–100.

10. Regional Greenhouse Gas Initiative, "Investment of RGGI Proceeds through 2013," http://www.rggi.org/docs/ProceedsReport/Investment-RGGI-Proceeds-Through-2013.pdf (accessed June 5, 2015).

11. John M. Glionna, "Western Land War: 5 States Fight D.C. for Control of Federal Areas," *Los Angeles Times*, http://articles.latimes.com (April 26, 2012); Brian Calvert, "Western States Eye Federal Lands—Again," *High Country News* www.hcn.org/issues/ (October 27, 2014).

12. "Performance Partnership Agreements," www.epa.gov/ocir/nepps/pp_agreements.htm (July 24, 2006).

13. "National Model for Renewable Energy," *State Legislatures* (February 2006), p. 9.

14. Elizabeth Daigneau, "Consolidating 'Green' Departments," *Governing*, www.governing.com (accessed June 26, 2012).

15. Matthew Potoski, "Clean Air Federalism: Do States Race to the Bottom?" *Public Administration Review* 61 (May/June 2001): 335–42.

16. Travis Coan and Mirya R. Holman, "Voting Green," *Social Science Quarterly* 89 (2008): 1121–35; David M. Konisky, Jeffrey Milyo, and Lilliard E. Richardson, "Environmental Policy Attitudes: Issues, Geographical Scale, and Political Trust," *Social Science Quarterly* 89 (2008): 1066–85.

17. Kent E. Portney, 2011, *Taking Sustainable Cities Seriously*, 2nd ed. (Cambridge, MA: MIT Press).

18. "Municipal Solid Waste Generation, Recycling, and Disposal in the United States: Facts and Figures for 2012," U.S. Environmental Protection Agency www.epa.gov/osw/nonhaz/municipal/pubs/msw_fs.pdf (accessed June 5, 2015).

19. Hugh McDiarmid, Jr., "Michigan's Trash Heap Grows Larger," *Detroit Free Press,* www.freep.com (February 3, 2004).

20. "Municipal Solid Waste Generation, Recycling, and Disposal in the United States," p. 4.

21. Christopher Swope and Brendan Schlauch, "Recycling Recession," *Governing* (June 2009): 20.

22. "Recycling: For Economy and Environment, We Must Improve Dismal Rate," *Lansing State Journal,* www.lsj.com (April 23, 2012).

23. Katherine N. Probst and David M. Konisky, *Superfund's Future: What Will It Cost?* (Washington, D.C.: Resources for the Future, 2001).

24. John M. Broder, "Without Superfund Tax, Stimulus Aids Cleanups," *The New York Times,* www.nytimes.com (April 26, 2009).

25. "Yucca Mountain Nuclear Waste Dump Dead," *Environment News Service,* www.ens-newswire.com/ens/jul2009/2009-07-30-01.asp (July 30, 2009).

26. Anthony L. Dodson, "Interstate Compacts to Bury Radioactive Waste: A Useful Tool for Environmental Policy?" *State and Local Government Review* 30 (Spring 1998): 118–28.

27. Josh Goodman, "The Nuclear Option," *Governing* 20 (November 2006): 43–45.

28. Abigail D. Blodgett, "An Analysis of Pollution and Community Advocacy in 'Cancer Alley': Setting an Example for the Environmental Justice Movement in St James Parish, Louisiana," *Local Environment* 11 (2006): 647–61.

29. Regina Austin and Michael Schill, "Black, Brown, Red, and Poisoned," in Robert D. Bullard, ed., *Unequal Protection* (San Francisco, CA: Sierra Club Books, 1994), p. 53.

30. Deb Starkey, "Environmental Justice: Win, Lose, or Draw?" *State Legislatures* 20 (March 1994): 28; Francesca Spina, "Environmental Justice and Patterns of State Inspections," *Social Science Quarterly* 96 (June 2015): 417–29.

31. United Church of Christ Commission for Racial Justice, *Toxic Waste and Race* (New York: United Church of Christ, 1987).

32. Liam Downey and Brian Hawkins, "Single-Mother Families and Air Pollution: A National Study," *Social Science Quarterly* 89 (2008): 523–36.

33. Susan Cutter, "Race, Class, and Environmental Justice," *Progress in Human Geography* 19 (March 1995): 111–22.

34. Evan J. Ringquist, "Environmental Justice: Normative Concerns, Empirical Evidence, and Government Action," in Norman J. Vig and Michael E. Kraft, eds., *Environmental Policy: New Directions for the Twenty-First Century* (Washington, D.C.: Congressional Quarterly Press, 2006).

35. Evan J. Ringquist and David H. Clark, "Issue Definition and the Politics of State Environmental Justice Policy Adoption," *International Journal of Public Administration* 25 (February/March 2002): 351–89.

36. U.S. Department of Energy, "Number of Producing Gas Wells," http://www.eia.gov/dnav/ng/ng_prod_wells_s1_a.htm (June 29, 2012).

37. John Manuel, "Mining: EPA Tackles Fracking," *Environmental Health Perspectives* www.ncbi.nlm.nih.gov/pmc/articles/PMC2866701/?tool=pmcentrez (May 2010).

38. See, for example, Tanya Heikkila et al., "Understanding a Period of Policy Change: The Case of Hydraulic Fracturing Disclosure Policy in Colorado," *Review of Policy Research* 31 (March 2014): 65–87.

39. Wade Rawlins, "North Carolina Governor Rejects Fracking Law," www.Reuters.com (July 1, 2012).

40. U.S. Environmental Protection Agency, U.S. Environmental Protection Agency, "EPA Issues Final Air Rules for the Oil and Natural Gas Industry," www.epa.gov/airquality/oilandgas/actions.html (April 17, 2012).

41. U.S. Environmental Protection Agency, "Assessment of the Potential Impacts of Hydraulic Fracturing for Oil and Gas on Drinking Water Resources (External Review Draft)," http://cfpub.epa.gov/ncea/hfstudy/recordisplay.cfm?deid=244651 (June 4, 2015).

Index

STATE	CAPITAL	OFFICIAL NICKNAME	YEAR ENTERED UNION
Alabama	Montgomery	Yellowhammer State	1819
Alaska	Juneau	The Last Frontier	1959
Arizona	Phoenix	Grand Canyon State	1912
Arkansas	Little Rock	Natural State	1836
California	Sacramento	Golden State	1850
Colorado	Denver	Centennial State	1876
Connecticut	Hartford	Constitution State	1788
Delaware	Dover	First State	1787
Florida	Tallahassee	Sunshine State	1845
Georgia	Atlanta	Peach State	1788
Hawaii	Honolulu	Aloha State	1959
Idaho	Boise	Gem State	1890
Illinois	Springfield	Prairie State	1818
Indiana	Indianapolis	Hoosier State	1816
Iowa	Des Moines	Hawkeye State	1846
Kansas	Topeka	Sunflower State	1861
Kentucky	Frankfort	Bluegrass State	1792
Louisiana	Baton Rouge	Pelican State	1812
Maine	Augusta	Pine Tree State	1820
Maryland	Annapolis	Old Line State	1788
Massachusetts	Boston	Bay State	1788
Michigan	Lansing	Great Lakes State	1837
Minnesota	St. Paul	North Star State	1858
Mississippi	Jackson	Magnolia State	1817
Missouri	Jefferson City	Show Me State	1821